International Law

Written by one of the world's leading international lawyers, this is the new and updated edition of Professor Klabbers' landmark textbook. International law can be defined as 'the rules governing the legal relationship between nations and states', but, in reality, it is much more complex, with political, diplomatic, and socio-economic factors shaping the law and its application. This refreshingly clear, concise textbook encourages students to view international law as a dynamic system of organizing the world. Bringing international law back to its first principles, the book is organized around four questions: where does it come from? To whom does it apply? How does it resolve conflict? What does it say? Building on these questions with both academic rigour and clarity of expression, Professor Klabbers breathes life and energy into the subject. Footnotes point students to the wider academic debate, while chapter introductions and final remarks reinforce learning. The second edition has been updated throughout, with particular attention to recent judicial decisions, and features new sections on sovereign debt relief, the prompt release of vessels, and the Antarctic.

JAN KLABBERS is currently Academy Professor (Martti Ahtisaari Chair) at the University of Helsinki, on leave from his position as Professor of International Law at the University of Helsinki. He has held visiting professorships in New York, Geneva, and Paris, and is currently Visiting Research Professor at the Erasmus School of Law, Rotterdam. He was one of the Inaugural Fellows at the Straus Institute for the Advanced Study of International Law and Justice at New York University (2009–10), and has served as Director of the Academy of Finland Centre of Excellence in Global Governance Research (2006–11).

International Law

Jan Klabbers

Second Edition

CAMBRIDGE
UNIVERSITY PRESS

CAMBRIDGE
UNIVERSITY PRESS

University Printing House, Cambridge CB2 8BS, United Kingdom

One Liberty Plaza, 20th Floor, New York, NY 10006, USA

477 Williamstown Road, Port Melbourne, VIC 3207, Australia

314-321, 3rd Floor, Plot 3, Splendor Forum, Jasola District Centre, New Delhi - 110025, India

79 Anson Road, #06-04/06, Singapore 079906

Cambridge University Press is part of the University of Cambridge.

It furthers the university's mission by disseminating knowledge in the pursuit of education, learning, and research at the highest international levels of excellence.

www.cambridge.org
Information on this title: www.cambridge.org/9781107141551
DOI: 10.1017/9781316493717

First published 2017
5th printing 2018

Printed in the United Kingdom by TJ International Ltd. Padstow Cornwall

A catalogue record for this publication is available from the British Library.

ISBN 978-1-107-14155-1 Hardback
ISBN 978-1-316-50660-8 Paperback

Contents

PART I THE STRUCTURE OF INTERNATIONAL LAW

PART II THE SUBSTANCE OF INTERNATIONAL LAW

v

PART III THE SURROUNDINGS OF INTERNATIONAL LAW

Detailed Table of Contents

PART II THE SUBSTANCE OF INTERNATIONAL LAW

PART III THE SURROUNDINGS OF INTERNATIONAL LAW

Preface to the Second Edition

One of the perks of writing a textbook is that one may get the chance to correct errors, clarify things that have remained obscure, and present the reader with new materials and understandings. The current edition has corrected a few errors and typos and has hopefully clarified a few things that were obscure. It has also been updated in a general way by including recent materials (such as court cases), updating information about the status of treaties, and adding some references to recent (and not so recent) literature as well as recent events, from the annexation of Crimea by Russia to the curious phenomenon of Brexit. In addition, I have added a few pages on topics that were not, or insufficiently, covered in the previous edition, including sovereign debt restructuring, environmental protection in the Antarctic, and prompt release of vessels under the UN Convention on the Law of the Sea. Finally, each chapter except the final one ends with a short list of suggestions for further reading – this too is new.

I owe a great deal of thanks to all of those who have provided comments and feedback. Quite a few colleagues expressed their appreciation of the book's approach, and urged me to keep it in place in future editions. Some anonymous reviewers have made suggestions on the basis of a request by the publisher – these invariably proved helpful, and those reviewers will notice that quite a few of their suggestions have found their way into the text. Some readers (Oliver Diggelmann, Nikolaos Ioannides, John Palmer, and Winston Parker) took the trouble to contact me to tell me about typos, inaccuracies, and infelicities. The comments from students, in classrooms in Helsinki and elsewhere, proved extremely useful: if students don't get it, then it's time to rewrite. My wife Margareta read big chunks, and prevented me from making more errors than I would care to admit, while Gilda and Johan just make me happy. At the Press, I am indebted to my editors, in particular Marta Walkowiak and Valerie Appleby.

If there was one point coming out of the reviews commissioned by CUP, it was the common observation that the text was not detailed enough. One reviewer felt that human rights remained under-illuminated; someone else thought that the acquisition of territory deserved a chapter of its own, and yet another reviewer thought that I should pay more attention to the work of the United Nations. All are right of course, and all will continue to think that the text could use more detail. Sadly, though, adding a lot more detail would turn the book into something it was never meant to be. The trick is to combine the broad brush with an eye for detail; I have aimed to provide detailed information and analysis, but have also been mindful of the desire to keep the book readable.

It should perhaps also be borne in mind that a book such as this inevitably ends up compromising between two demands. On the one hand, it should explain how the law works. On the other hand, it should also state what the law says. The two sometimes come together, but sometimes also pull in opposite directions; at such moments, I have generally prioritized the explanatory dimension. Thus I sometimes provide classic case law if I think it is more illustrative than more recent decisions, and I sometimes devise hypothetical examples if real life examples are too complicated to serve as useful illustrations.

A challenge faced by most parents of young children is how to combine the demands of work and family life. It is safe to say that this edition would not exist without the contribution made by my parents-in-law, Lea and Markus. It is to them that this edition is dedicated.

Preface to the First Edition

This book has been a long time in the making. While the actual writing started in 2009 and took place, intermittently, until May 2012, the book reflects more than twenty years of teaching international law. The basic premise underlying it is that international law should not be studied as a vast and ever-increasing collection of rules, but is better approached as a way of thinking about and organizing the world. With that in mind, like all legal systems the international legal order can profitably be studied by asking four questions. First, there is the question of where the law comes from: what are its sources? Second, to what entities or individuals does the law apply or, in other words, what are its subjects? Third, what does the law do in cases of conflict (i.e. settlement), and, finally, what does the law actually say? What is its substance?

This book is organized with those four questions in mind. The first three, together pointing to the basic structure of the system, make up Part I of this book (Chapters 1–9): sources, subjects, and settlement, broadly conceived. This is the stuff all international lawyers (probably even all lawyers, in these days of globalization) will sooner or later be confronted with; all lawyers need to have some idea of how international law is made, in what circumstances states can be held responsible, how international tribunals function and whether or not specific entities are subject to international law.

The fourth question, asking about the substantive rules, makes up Part II (Chapters 10–15). It will be noticed that Part I is longer and more analytical than Part II. This is only natural: the most Part II can aspire to is to provide a basic description of the various branches of international law, without much detail. After all, international law spans, quite literally, the world, as well as most of the policy issues that one can think of. There is international law on topics as wide and diverse as international crime, international investment, international taxation, the movement of refugees, the protection of the environment and much, much more. Hence, a book such as this, limited in scope, can only cover the basics. Fortunately, though, there are wide bodies of literature available, as the footnotes testify, and for those who want more detailed generalist expositions there are at least three useful larger and more detailed general textbooks on the market. The interested reader could do worse than to pick one of these to read alongside the present book.[1]

While Parts I and II cover the four questions set out above (sources, subjects, settlement, and substance), the book does not stop after Part II. It also contains a, fairly brief, Part III (Chapters 16 and 17), addressing the context of international law. This addresses the circumstance that international law does not exist in a vacuum, but is closely related, on the one hand, to national legal systems (discussed in Chapter 16) and, on the other hand, to global governance, politics, and ethics (discussed in Chapter 17). As Joseph Weiler once suggested during a round-table discussion at New York University, present-day textbooks on international law should ideally reflect the circumstance that international law is part of a broader pattern of global governance, and not stick to describing a stilted world where all legally relevant rules are made by duly empowered diplomats, representing sovereign states. In Weiler's words, global governance 'is a coloring agent that suddenly illuminates phenomena that, under the normal spectacle of international law, you didn't see'.[2] This book hopes to reflect the two ideas that international law is of relevance to global governance, but sometimes struggles to come to terms with it. However, the format of this book does not allow for an in-depth discussion of the political context of international law: Part III remains necessarily brief. Readers with an interest in these matters may be well advised to read this book alongside a recent collection of articles edited by Crawford and Koskenniemi.[3]

This is a textbook on international law, and this simple fact has at least two important implications. First, since the aim is to outline the international legal order, the book is not set up as a commentary on current events. I accept that the reader may wish to see how the law is applied to specific events, and where possible this has been done, but without singling out specifically current events. Such comments on current events as there are serve purely illustrative purposes, if only because current events tend to have a limited shelf life; what is current today may be forgotten tomorrow.

Second, this is a book on international law, and while there is room for the argument that the European Union (EU) is part of international law, it does not address the EU separately, except where the practice of the EU is of relevance. Thus, there are fragments on the treaty practice of the EU, and a few paragraphs on the attitude of the EU to international law, but no detailed discussion of EU law, if only because others are far better qualified to discuss the EU than I am.[4]

---

[1] James Crawford, *Brownlie's Principles of Public International Law*, 8th edn (Oxford University Press, 2012); Malcolm Evans (ed.), *International Law*, 4th edn (Oxford University Press, 2014); and Malcolm Shaw, *International Law*, 7th edn (Cambridge University Press, 2014). Perhaps the most comprehensive single-volume treatise at the moment is in French: Patrick Daillier, Mathias Forteau, and Alain Pellet, *Droit International Public*, 8th edn (Paris: LGDJ, 2009), while a useful methodology and guide on how to do research is also in French: Olivier Corten, *Méthodologie du droit international public* (Brussels: Editions ULB, 2009).

[2] José E. Alvarez et al., 'The Shape of Global Governance', (2010) *NYU Law School Magazine*, 22–9, also available at http://blogs.law.nyu.edu/magazine/2010/roundtable-global-governance/ (visited 25 May 2012).

[3] James Crawford and Martti Koskenniemi (eds.), *The Cambridge Companion to International Law* (Cambridge University Press, 2012).

[4] The best general overview available is Paul Craig and Gráinne de Búrca, *EU Law: Text, Cases, and Materials*, 5th edn (Oxford University Press, 2011).

Finally, a note on sources. I have generally refrained from listing the specific places where treaties or other instruments can be found, for the solid reason that these instruments are easier to find these days by a quick Internet search than by going through the volumes of the United Nations Treaty Series (UNTS) or any domestic treaty series. However, most of the important treaties referred to in this book are available in a single collection.[5] With court decisions, I have generally aimed at listing a material source. With International Court of Justice (ICJ) decisions, this has been the ICJ Reports; with other cases, this has often (if not invariably) been the invaluable *International Law Reports* or its predecessor, the *Annual Digest*. Decisions of the European Court of Human Rights (ECtHR), moreover, are far more easily accessible on the Court's website[6] than in any published form.

Since this book is the product of more than twenty years of teaching, the number of people to whom I have become indebted is way too large to be listed. Still, a few need to be singled out. The late Bert Vierdag gave me my first official teaching job in 1990, at the University of Amsterdam. Martti Koskenniemi brought me to Helsinki six years later, and has been and remains a close friend and an immense influence. I have benefited from having some extremely good teachers, including Gerd Junne, Pieter Jan Kuijper, and Richard Lauwaars, and my approach to international law and the global order reflects their influences. Not only did they teach me properly about international law and international politics, they also taught by example about good teaching. And then there is the influence of more than twenty generations of students, at Amsterdam, Helsinki, and a variety of other places.

Many colleagues suggested things to read; I owe all of them a big 'thank you'. Antti Kivivuori and Alice Neffe provided me with specific materials. I am heavily indebted to Magda Kmak and Rain Liivoja, who read some of the draft chapters and provided useful comments, as did several anonymous reviewers for Cambridge University Press. Working with the Press has been, as always, a delight, thanks to the wonderful support offered by Finola O'Sullivan and Sinead Moloney. This book is dedicated to my wife Margareta and my children, Johan and Gilda.

---

[5] Malcolm D. Evans (ed.), *Blackstone's International Law Documents*, 10th edn (Oxford University Press, 2011); see also Jan Klabbers (ed.), *International Law Documents* (Cambridge University Press, 2016).
[6] At www.echr.coe.int/echr/.

Table of Cases

INTERNATIONAL FORA

GATT/WTO

General Court (EU, formerly Court of First Instance)

International Arbitral Awards

International Court of Justice

International Criminal Court (ICC)

International Criminal Tribunal for the former Yugoslavia (ICTY)

International Tribunal for the Law of the Sea (ITLOS)

Permanent Court of International Justice (PCIJ)

Netherlands

South Africa

United Kingdom

United States

Abbreviations

ADIZ	Air Defense Identification Zone
AIIB	Asian Infrastructure Investment Bank
ASP	Assembly of States Parties
BEPS	Base Erosion and Profit Shifting
BIT	bilateral investment treaty
CAR	Central African Republic
CARU	Comision Administradora del Rio Uruguay (Executive Commission on the River Uruguay)
CCAMLR	Convention for the Conservation of Antarctic Marine Living Resources
CISG	Convention on Contracts for the International Sale of Goods
CITES	Convention on International Trade in Endangered Species of Wild Fauna and Flora
CJAC .	Central American Court of Justice
CJEU	Court of Justice of the European Union
COP	conference of the parties
COPUOS	Committee on the Peaceful Uses of Outer Space
DSB	dispute settlement body (WTO)
DSU	dispute settlement understanding (WTO)
ECCC	Extraordinary Chambers in the Courts of Cambodia
ECHR	European Convention on Human Rights
ECT	Energy Charter Treaty
ECtHR	European Court of Human Rights
EEZ	exclusive economic zone
EFTA	European Free Trade Agreement
ENMOD	Environmental Modification Convention
ETS	European Treaty Series
EU	European Union
EULEX	European Union Rule of Law Mission in Kosovo
FATF	Financial Action Task Force
FRG	Federal Republic of Germany (former West Germany)
FYROM	Former Yugoslav Republic of Macedonia

FSIA	Foreign Sovereign Immunities Act
GATS	General Agreement on Trade in Services
GATT	General Agreement on Tariffs and Trade
GDR	German Democratic Republic (former East Germany)
IATA	International Air Transport Association
ICAO	International Civil Aviation Organization
ICC	International Criminal Court
ICCPR	International Covenant on Civil and Political Rights
ICESCR	International Covenant on Economic, Social and Cultural Rights
ICISS	International Commission on Intervention and State Sovereignty
ICJ	International Court of Justice (World Court)
ICRW	International Convention for the Regulation of Whaling
ICSID	International Centre for the Settlement of Investment Disputes
ICTR	International Criminal Tribunal for Rwanda
ICTY	International Criminal Tribunal for the former Yugoslavia
IDA	International Development Agency
IFC	International Finance Corporation
ILA	International Law Association
ILC	International Law Commission
ILO	International Labour Organization
IMCO	International Maritime Consultative Organization
IMF	International Monetary Fund
IMO	International Maritime Organization
IMT	International Military Tribunal (Nuremberg Tribunal)
INBAR	Organization for the Management of the Global Trade in Bamboo and Rattan Products
IOSCO	International Organization of Securities Commissions
ITC	International Tin Council
ITLOS	International Tribunal for the Law of the Sea
ITU	International Telecommunications Union
IWC	International Whaling Commission
MARPOL	International Convention for the Prevention of Pollution from Ships
MFN	most favoured nation
MIGA	Multilateral Investment Guarantee Agency
MOP	meeting of the parties
MoU	memorandum of understanding
NAFO	Northwest Atlantic Fisheries Organization
NATO	North Atlantic Treaty Organization
NGO	non-governmental organization
OECD	Organization for Economic Cooperation and Development
OSPAR	Convention for the Protection of the Marine Environment of the North-east Atlantic

PCA	Permanent Court of Arbitration
PCIJ	Permanent Court of International Justice
PISA	Programme on International Student Assessment
PLO	Palestine Liberation Organization
POP	persistent organic pollutant
R2P	responsibility to protect
SDR	special drawing right
SEC	US Securities Commission
SFRY	Socialist Federal Republic of Yugoslavia
SOLAS	International Convention for the Safety of Life at Sea
STL	Special Tribunal for Lebanon
STSL	Special Tribunal for Sierra Leone
TEU	Treaty on European Union
TFEU	Treaty on the Functioning of the European Union
TRIPs	trade-related aspects of intellectual property rights
UN	United Nations
UNCLOS	United Nations Conference on the Law of the Sea
UNCTAD	United Nations Conference on Trade and Development
UNEF	United Nations Emergency Force
UNEP	United Nations Environment Programme
UNESCO	United Nations Educational, Scientific and Cultural Organization
UNHRC	United Nations Human Rights Committee
UNITA	Uniao Nacional para a Independencia Total de Angola (Angolan rebel movement)
UNMIK	United Nations Mission in Kosovo
UNTAET	United Nations Administration in East Timor
UNTS	United Nations Treaty Series
VCLT	Vienna Convention on the Law of Treaties
VOC	Verenigde Oost-Indische Compagnie (United East India Company)
WHO	World Health Organization
WTO	World Trade Organization

PART I

The Structure of International Law

1

The Setting of International Law

INTRODUCTION

As anyone who has ever bought a product from abroad should realize, the purchase is possible because there are rules that make it so. As everyone who has ever hopped on an aircraft abroad, or sent a postcard abroad or watched a foreign television channel should realize, there are rules that facilitate doing so. These rules form part of a broader network of rules usually referred to as international law. International law is not just the law (if any) that deals with war and peace, or with genocide and human rights; it also encompasses rules on trade, on protection of the environment, on shipping and on the protection of refugees. Few of these rules are uncontroversial, and even fewer work perfectly, but the bottom line should be clear: the existence of international relations, of whatever kind, entails the existence of international law. As the ancient Romans knew, wherever there is a society, there will be law (*ubi societas, ibi jus*), and the rules regulating contacts within the society of states are generally called international law. It is these rules that form the topic of this book or, more precisely, this book is dedicated to providing a framework for the further study of those rules in detail, since there are far too many international legal rules to fit within the pages of a single volume.

More specifically, this book is dedicated to the study of public international law, as opposed to private international law. Whereas private international law regulates individual conduct with a transboundary element (international contracts, international marriages, or international traffic accidents, for example), public international law is often said to regulate relations between states. While saying so is still acceptable, it should come with the caveat that many of the rules of international law have an effect not only on states, but also on other entities, be they companies, individuals, or minority groups. Likewise, many of the rules are shaped not just between states but also involve representatives of international organizations (such as the United Nations – UN), or civil society organizations (such as Greenpeace).

Any international lawyer, whether she realizes it or not, works on the basis of a set of assumptions about what the world is like and, more specifically, what international law is like. In other words, all international lawyers utilize some kind of theory of international law. This can be a highly pragmatic theory, something to the effect that international law exists to serve peaceful relations between states and should be regarded from that perspective as a technical discipline, providing the tools for statesmen. This, arguably, is the dominant approach among international lawyers. It can also be a highly sophisticated and politically self-conscious theory, for example a theory holding that international law is the handmaiden of global capitalism, therewith complicit in oppression, and thus to be regarded with suspicion and a critical eye. It can be a theory viewing international law as a beacon of hope for the poor and oppressed – such a theory often undergirds the activities of those who specialize in human rights. And it can be a nationalist theory that starts with national self-interest, in which case international law is often viewed as an intruder, aiming to undermine national decision-making processes – such a view is not uncommon among social conservatives. Those who tend to view international law as either a tool for statesmen or as a beacon of hope tend to have a cosmopolitan outlook; they expect international law to be able to bring about a better world, and for them, 'sovereignty' is a four-letter word. By contrast, those who view international law as either intrusive or as the handmaiden of global capitalism tend to be less cosmopolitan; to them, 'sovereignty' is actually a useful shield.

Either way, whatever the lawyer does, whatever the lawyer writes, and whatever the lawyer thinks will in some way be based on an underlying set of ideas and assumptions about what the function of international law is, and what role it should play. International law, in other words, cannot be portrayed as politically innocent. This makes it imperative that a book such as this one starts with an overview of how international law has come about, what role it has played and what sort of role it could play.

THE SEVENTEENTH CENTURY

By general acclamation, the history of modern international law (international law as we know it) is usually said to have started in the seventeenth century.[1] That is not to say that there were no international rules before that date; the ancient Greek city states had already concluded treaties with each other on such matters as how best to treat prisoners of war; the Roman Republic devised an intricate system for dealing with foreign merchants; and, during the Middle Ages, when the city states of Italy were significant actors, the institutions of diplomacy developed, complete with embassies and diplomats and guarantees that their activities would not be interfered with by their host states.[2]

Still, the seventeenth century stands out, for a variety of reasons. One of these is that for much of the time preceding the seventeenth century, much of Europe tended to be organized in large empires, from the Roman Empire to the reign of Charlemagne. And since Europe, in those days, was thought to be congruent with the world at large, the result was that people did not think too much in terms of there being different political entities requiring a specific legal system to organize their relations. Instead, they tended

---

[1] For a useful collection of essays, see Bardo Fassbender and Anne Peters (eds.), *The Oxford Handbook of the History of International Law* (Oxford University Press, 2012).

[2] G. R. Berridge, *Diplomacy: Theory and Practice* (London: Prentice Hall, 1995).

to think of their empires as single entities, with the consequence that law was largely conceptualized as internal.[3]

Possibly the most relevant reason why the seventeenth century stands out is that in the year 1648, the Peace of Westphalia was concluded to mark the end of the Thirty Years War. In Münster and Osnabrück, two cities in today's Germany, the secular power of the pope, the leader of the Roman Catholic Church, came to a definitive end. It was agreed to confirm an earlier arrangement emanating from the 1555 Peace of Augsburg, to the effect that Europe would be divided into a number of territorial units, and that each of these units could decide for itself which religion to adopt: *cuius regio eius religio*. No outside interference was permitted, the result being the creation of sovereign states and, therewith, the birth of the modern state system.[4]

It was perhaps no coincidence that it was precisely the state that came out of the Middle Ages as the dominant form of political organization. Other entities (city states, feudal entities, or a league of trading posts such as the Hanseatic League) lost out, for, unlike states, they lacked full territorial control and, more important still, they lacked the capacity to guarantee commitments. What made the state dominant was that it had the authority to live up to its commitments, precisely by controlling territory.[5]

The second important event in the seventeenth century, as far as the development of international law is concerned, was the publication in 1625 of Hugo Grotius' *On the Law of War and Peace*. Grotius was already established as a leading intellectual,[6] and had been influential (much to the benefit of the Dutch East India Company, the Dutch vehicle for colonial exploitation) in shaping international law so as to uphold the freedom of the seas. This guaranteed free shipping for the Dutch fleet, and made it impossible for other countries, such as Spain, Portugal, and England, to claim authority over the high seas legitimately. And this, in turn, proved highly beneficial to Dutch trading interests. Indeed, as one commentator notes, among Grotius' innovations is his notion that all peoples have a right to trade; consequently, trading routes, such as the seas, ought to be free as well.[7] And all this, in turn, allowed Amsterdam to become the centre of global finance and paved the way for the Dutch Golden Century.

It is sometimes suggested that Grotius is the 'founding father' of international law, but such a claim is untenable. For one thing, international law was not invented by a single person, but grew out of the interactions of states and the commentaries of learned observers. Second, if there were a single creator, then there are a few other serious contenders.

---

[3] For an argument to this effect (albeit much more subtle), see J. M. A. Lenssen, 'Vroeg-Middeleeuws volkenrecht: Van Romeins Rijk tot Investituurstrijd', in A. C. G. M. Eyffinger (ed.), *Compendium Volkenrechtsgeschiedenis* (Deventer: Kluwer, 1989), 10–36.

[4] The connections between the Peace of Augsburg and the Peace of Westphalia are emphasized in C. G. Roelofsen, 'De periode 1450–1713', in Eyffinger, *Compendium*, 56–125, at 89–90. See also D. P. O'Connell, 'Territorial Claims in the Grotian Period', in C. H. Alexandrowicz (ed.), *Studies in the History of the Law of Nations* (Dordrecht: Springer, 1970), 1–15.

[5] The point is well made in Hendrik Spruyt, *The Sovereign State and Its Competitors* (Princeton University Press, 1994). See also Chapter 4 below.

[6] A fine biography in Dutch is Henk Nellen, *Hugo de Groot: Een leven in strijd om de vrede 1583–1645* (Amsterdam: Balans, 2007).

[7] Timothy Brook, *Vermeer's Hat* (London: Profile, 2008), at 67–8.

Two of those are the Spanish theologians Suarez and Vitoria, who preceded Grotius by a few decades. Vitoria in particular was highly instrumental in devising the moral justification for the creation of a legal system that would facilitate the spread of global capitalism.[8] Likewise a serious contender for paternity, a little over a century after Grotius, the Swiss Emeric de Vattel was the first (arguably) to have written a comprehensive manual on international law, to be used by the chancelleries of the world.[9]

However, this is not to deny Grotius' relevance. Grotius' significance resides in two circumstances. First, he forms a bridge between the classic naturalist way of looking at law and later positivist theorizing. Natural law thinking typically suggests that law is not made but found; it exists somehow in nature – it is often thought to be ordained by God – and can be recognized by the proper method of analysis or by those of the right faith. Positivism, by contrast, wary of the subjectivity inherent in such an approach, typically suggests that law is not given, but man-made; law is whatever states decide or agree that it is. Grotius' work encompassed elements of both viewpoints.

Second, Grotius may well have been the first to present a synthetic, comprehensive vision of international law.[10] *On the Law of War and Peace* addresses, as its title suggests, not only the law of armed conflict and aggression, but also such matters as the binding force of treaties. That is not necessarily to say, as is sometimes asserted, that Grotius developed the idea of an interconnected international community with its own legal system; instead, more modestly, he may well have been the first to lay down a specific set of binding international obligations, mostly inspired by the desire to lay down the limits to proper statecraft.[11]

COLONIALISM

It is no exaggeration to state that international law has been closely connected with imperialism and colonialism.[12] The emergence of early modern international law is comprehensible in the light of the struggle between European powers for influence elsewhere in the world. It has already been mentioned how Grotius contributed to the freedom of the seas, a freedom that stood his Dutch employers in good stead, as freedom of the seas allowed freedom of discovery and freedom to trade. These freedoms presupposed, however, that certain rules were considered to be in place in order to regulate relations with 'the natives' in continents such as the Americas and Asia.

---

[8] Martti Koskenniemi, 'Empire and International Law: The Real Spanish Contribution', (2011) 61 *University of Toronto Law Journal*, 1–36.

[9] As asserted by Marie-Hélène Renaut, *Histoire du droit international public* (Paris: Ellipses, 2007), at 114.

[10] Cornelis van Vollenhoven, *De drie treden van het volkenrecht* (The Hague: Martinus Nijhoff, 1918).

[11] Martti Koskenniemi, 'International Law and raison d'état: Rethinking the Prehistory of International Law', in Benedict Kingsbury and Benjamin Straumann (eds.), *The Roman Foundations of the Law of Nations: Alberico Gentili and the Justice of Empire* (Oxford University Press, 2010), 297–339.

[12] Recent studies exploring the colonialist legacy of international law include Martti Koskenniemi, *The Gentle Civilizer of Nations: The Rise and Fall of International Law 1870–1960* (Cambridge University Press, 2001), and Antony Anghie, *Imperialism, Sovereignty and the Making of International Law* (Cambridge University Press, 2004).

Among these rules was the rule that territories found overseas were to be regarded as not having been subject to sovereignty – as territory belonging to no one (*terra nullius*). In other words, stumbling on territory in Asia or the Americas, the European powers could proclaim that those territories belonged to them; the original inhabitants were, by and large, ignored. This required quite a balancing act, because these same original inhabitants were of the utmost importance when it came to making trading deals; the peoples of the Americas and Asia were, after all, deemed capable of concluding contracts with the Europeans, even contracts that would allow the Europeans exclusive trading rights in valuable commodities such as pepper or nutmeg. Hence an ambivalent picture emerges. For purposes of establishing sovereignty, the local population was often ignored, but, for commercial purposes, their consent was deemed vital, at least as an argument to convince competing European powers.

Much of the globe became the playground of the European powers, and at some point the non-European world (the New World, in a highly Eurocentric term) was literally divided between two of them. In 1493, the pope issued a papal bull (*Inter Caetera*) drawing a line through the Atlantic Ocean. Most of the territory to the west (with the exception of Brazil) was said to belong to Spain, while Portugal claimed some of the territories to the east. This was confirmed a year later in the Treaty of Tordesillas. With both countries further expanding east and west, they met again in the Pacific Ocean, which resulted in the Treaty of Saragossa, concluded in 1529 and effectively sealing the division of the world.[13]

Later, towards the end of the sixteenth century, England and Holland emerged as maritime powers, breaking the trading monopolies of the Portuguese in the Indian Ocean and thus also bringing the Spanish-Portuguese domination to an end. The Dutch, in 1602, created the Verenigde Oost-Indische Compagnie (United East India Company, VOC in abbreviated form),[14] and assigned it a trading monopoly. One important ramification was that the VOC came to exercise delegated governmental authority; it could acquire and administer territory, declare war and conclude treaties, and seize foreign ships. In 1603 this provoked an incident with Portugal, when the Dutch seized the Portuguese vessel *Santa Catharina*. In order to legitimate this act, the VOC asked Grotius to write on its behalf, which he duly did. In *Mare Liberum*, originally written as part of a larger work on prize law (*De Jure Praedae*) but separately published in 1609, Grotius argued that the high seas were not *terra nullius* (as the Spanish and Portuguese had implicitly presumed), but rather *terra communis*: common property, and thus not susceptible to occupation and sovereignty.

This in turn led to English protests, as the English insisted on exclusive rights to the high seas around the British Isles, therewith effectively advocating the idea that states could generate maritime zones. Negotiations between the English and the Dutch ensued (with Grotius a prominent member of the Dutch delegation), but to little avail. It was only in the mid-seventeenth century that the Dutch came round – without formally acknowledging as much – to the British position: John Selden's *Mare Clausum*, presented in 1635,

---

[13] Roelofsen, 'De periode 1450–1713', at 69.
[14] The English, incidentally, also had an East India Company, though this was less generously endowed with delegated state powers.

was finally grudgingly accepted. In fact, this signified that the British had become too strong to resist and that the balance of power had shifted; Spain and Portugal no longer reigned supreme, and Holland's position, too, was dwindling.

International law also played a marked role when it came to slavery, first by allowing and organizing it, and, later, in the course of the nineteenth century, by gradually arriving at a prohibition.[15] The abolition, curiously perhaps, was followed by the colonization of Africa. Whereas earlier Africa had been used as a vast reservoir of slave labour but without being colonized, once slavery and the slave trade had been legally abolished,[16] the European powers saw fit to conquer the continent in what has become known as the scramble for Africa.[17] In particular the French and English sublimated their animosities by occupying large tracts of land, with Germany, Portugal, and Belgium playing smaller roles. This is not to say that the latter were somehow less exploitative or more benign; in particular Belgium's reign in Congo (or rather, King Leopold's personal reign in Congo[18]) emptied the country of many of its riches.

Ironically perhaps, international law is also still trying to come to terms with the effects of decolonization. In the late nineteenth century the international community of states still effectively covered merely several handfuls of states, and the fifty states setting up the United Nations in 1945 were deemed to represent the 'vast majority of the members of the international community', in the words of the International Court of Justice (ICJ).[19] The subsequent emergence of newly independent states in various waves, mostly during the 1950s and 1960s, gave rise not only to questions of succession,[20] but also to questions of representation and substantive justice, as was recognized early on by some astute observers.[21]

INTERNATIONAL LAW AND THE GLOBAL ECONOMY

If colonialism was about trade and economic gain, which to some degree it was, this already suggests that, to a large extent, international law is in one way or another connected to the economy.[22] Sometimes this is obvious: institutions such as the World Trade Organization (WTO) or the International Monetary Fund (IMF) have been explicitly established to

---

[15] See e.g. Jenny S. Martinez, *The Slave Trade and the Origins of International Human Rights Law* (Oxford University Press, 2012).

[16] The slave trade still exists (despite its legal prohibition), and is currently often referred to as human trafficking.

[17] For a fine study in Dutch see H. L. Wesseling, *Verdeel en heers: De deling van Afrika 1880–1914* (Amsterdam: Bert Bakker, 1991).

[18] Leopold II has the dubious honour of probably being the only king in history whose personal property (i.e. what is now the Democratic Republic of the Congo) was annexed by the parliament of the country of which he was king because of his monstrous behaviour: he was called a 'greedy, grasping, avaricious, cynical, bloodthirsty old goat' by Mark Twain. See Simon Sebag Montefiore, *Monsters: History's Most Evil Men and Women* (London: Quercus, 2008), at 214.

[19] *Reparation for Injuries Suffered in the Service of the United Nations*, [1949] ICJ Rep. 174, at 185.

[20] Matthew Craven, *The Decolonization of International Law* (Oxford University Press, 2007).

[21] Among the first was B. V. A. Röling, *International Law in an Expanded World* (Amsterdam: Djambatan, 1960).

[22] See generally also Claire Cutler, *Private Power and Global Authority: Transnational Merchant Law in the Global Political Economy* (Cambridge University Press, 2003).

regulate aspects of economic life, and the various commodity arrangements so popular during the 1960s and 1970s to regulate markets in products such as coffee or cocoa sprang from more or less the same impulse to regulate economic life.

Less obviously perhaps, such phenomena as territorial rights or maritime demarcation owe much to economic concerns as well. Grotius had already advocated free trading routes, not so much out of a love of freedom (although that may have played a role as well), but also because freedom of the seas and free trade would bring enormous economic benefits – at least for the Dutch.

For much of the second part of the twentieth century, the cases that would reach the ICJ tended to be those involving the precise limits of territorial ownership, either on land or, more commonly, at sea. And they often found their cause in the discovery of oil and natural gas deposits; whereas states were not all that interested in establishing the precise boundaries of their jurisdictions earlier, they became a lot keener when they realized that they might be sitting on huge oil reserves.

This also marks the impotence of international law, though, at least on occasion; faced with the possibility of economic profit, states have been less than fully obedient to the classic non-intervention principle. As it could be economically beneficial to have friendly governments in place in states boasting oil reserves, so Western states made sure to help to put such friendly governments in place. In what is a sad recurrence in twentieth-century history, the British and the Americans have been instrumental in toppling various Iranian regimes; the French have played a dismal role in western Africa; and one might argue that the 1990 war between Iraq and Kuwait owed much to the United Kingdom again – the original boundary treaty at issue had been concluded in the 1930s by the British (ruling Kuwait) with themselves (effectively ruling Iraq as a mandate territory under auspices of the League of Nations).

In short, much (though not all) of international law is related to the economy; international law is, in part, the legal system regulating the global economy, in much the same way as it has been observed that domestic legal systems and law school curricula (at least in the Western world) from the late nineteenth century onwards were set up so as to facilitate the capitalist economy.

The rule of law, as the great German sociologist Max Weber observed, served to create legal and economic certainty – its precise content was long considered less relevant.[23] Giving effect to the idea of the rule of law, central topics to be studied in law schools were contract, property, civil procedure, torts and criminal law.[24] Something similar applies to international law, which, as T. E. Holland had already noted in the late nineteenth century, was effectively private law applied to public actors.[25] The central topics in international law emerging at the end of the nineteenth century included the law of treaties (still often deemed to be contract law writ large), the law of responsibility (modelled on tort law), acquisition of territory (the equivalent of property) and dispute settlement (which mimics

---

[23] Max Weber, *Economy and Society: An Outline of Interpretive Sociology*, ed. G. Roth and C. Wittich (Berkeley, CA: University of California Press, 1978).

[24] Duncan Kennedy, 'Legal Education and the Reproduction of Hierarchy', (1982) 32 *Journal of Legal Education*, 591–615, at 597.

[25] T. E. Holland, *The Elements of Jurisprudence*, 13th edn (Oxford: Clarendon Press, 1924), at 393–4.

civil procedure). Only criminal law remained missing, a situation often ascribed to the circumstance that international law does not emanate from a single sovereign authority. In a world of sovereign equals without overarching authority, so the argument goes, it is difficult to think of criminal law to begin with.

Over recent decades, however, international law has also come to embrace a version of criminal law, albeit with a twist; in international criminal law, the central actors are not states, but individuals.[26] This helps to perpetuate the idea that the legal order remains based on sovereign states; states cannot be imprisoned, but there is no obstacle to sending individuals acting in the name of the state to prison.

THE INTERNATIONAL LEGAL SYSTEM

The absence of a single overarching authority is perhaps the most noteworthy characteristic of international law. Indeed, for those who insist that law is only really law if and when it emanates from a single sovereign, international law cannot really be law. At best, as the nineteenth-century positivist thinker John Austin put it, international law can be seen as 'positive morality': it is more or less binding on states, but as a matter of morality, not as a matter of law.[27] While Austin's conclusion followed from the way in which he defined law and not so much from anything inherent in international law itself, and more recent theorists do not hesitate to refer to international law as 'law' proper, none the less Austin's point has struck a chord. How, indeed, does international law function if it has no sovereign authority? How are its rules made, in the absence of a legislator, and, perhaps even more puzzlingly, how can the system work in the absence, by and large, of a police force, a department of justice, a set of prosecutors and all the other characteristics we usually associate with legal systems? That is a relevant question because, the occasional headline news notwithstanding, international law seems to work reasonably well. Louis Henkin once put it memorably when he wrote that 'almost all nations observe almost all principles of international law and almost all of their obligations almost all of the time'.[28]

Various explanations can be offered for this state of affairs. One is that since states themselves make international law, they have little incentive to break it; it makes little sense to create a rule on Monday, only to ignore it on Tuesday or next Monday. Of course, circumstances may change, and if that happens states may be tempted to breach their obligations, but in the normal course of events this is not lightly to be presumed.

Related to this is the explanation of bureaucratic inertia. A civil servant who routinely implements an international legal norm five days a week will not all of a sudden tell herself that she should stop doing so. The implementation and application of law is very much a matter of habit and routine, and this is no different in international law. In other words, unless something dramatic happens (a new treaty, a new court ruling, a new government

---

[26] Chapter 12 below.

[27] John Austin, *The Province of Jurisprudence Determined*, ed. W. Rumble (Cambridge University Press, 1995 [1832]), e.g. at 124.

[28] Louis Henkin, *How Nations Behave: Law and Foreign Policy*, 2nd edn (New York: Columbia University Press, 1979), at 47 (emphasis omitted).

perhaps), states will continue to do what they are used to doing and this typically helps to strengthen international law. In addition, lawyers play a prominent role at foreign ministries and other government departments; it has been suggested (but this may be wishful thinking . . .) that their legal training instils in them a respect for the law and the professional reflex to accept its authority.

An important role is also played in international law by considerations of reciprocity.[29] If states A and B are at war, and A starts to mistreat B's citizens by violating the Convention on Prisoners of War, then B will be highly tempted to mistreat A's citizens as well, and may also start to violate that convention. Much the same applies in other branches of the law: if X opens Y's diplomatic mail, Y may do the same with X's diplomatic mail. Not all international law rests on this specific form of reciprocity, of course. It would be self-defeating to apply the same logic in cases of environmental damage, for instance ('If you pollute your rivers, then I shall pollute mine') or in respect of human rights ('If you torture your citizens, I shall torture mine'),[30] but that is not to deny that reciprocity can act as a powerful force in international law.

Another suggested explanation focuses on the role of legitimacy. A rule that is generally perceived as useful and that has been created in the proper manner may be seen as legitimate and thereby exercise a 'compliance pull'. States need not be reminded that they should adhere to such a rule; instead, they would want to adhere to it – it would be the right thing to do.[31]

Other considerations which may help to explain why international law is reasonably well complied with include the idea that states are few in number and are attached to their territories; they cannot escape from each other, and it is decidedly costly to be a pariah state. While bank robbers can flee from the law by escaping to another country (preferably one without extradition agreements[32]), states have no such option. They have to interact with each other, and when doing so, it helps to have a good reputation – no one wants to do business with a state that routinely violates its commitments. In social science parlance, there is a social sanction in place, which helps to stimulate law-abiding behaviour, as it is ultimately beneficial to be a member of the international community in good standing.[33]

This final point already suggests that international law is not completely devoid of sanctions. There is, admittedly, no international police force, and no international prison

---

[29] The seminal piece is Stanley Hoffmann, 'International Law and International Systems', in Klaus Knorr and Sydney Verba (eds.), *The International System: Theoretical Essays* (Princeton University Press, 1961), 205–37.

[30] The political scientist Robert Keohane helpfully distinguishes between specific and diffuse reciprocity: the latter would apply to common interests. Robert O. Keohane, 'Reciprocity in International Relations', reproduced in his *International Institutions and State Power: Essays in International Relations Theory* (Boulder, CO: Westview Press, 1989), 132–57.

[31] See generally, and in considerably more detail, Thomas M. Franck, *The Power of Legitimacy among Nations* (Oxford University Press, 1990). Franck similarly posited that a perception of the fairness of a rule may inspire law-abiding behaviour: Thomas M. Franck, *Fairness in International Law and Institutions* (Oxford: Clarendon Press, 1995).

[32] Note how this already suggests the significance of international law . . .

[33] Abraham Chayes and Antonia Handler Chayes, *The New Sovereignty: Compliance with International Regulatory Agreements* (Cambridge, MA: Harvard University Press, 1995).

where states can be locked up, but the social sanction of becoming a pariah state may be quite strong. In addition, international law does have some mechanisms to deal with violations, even if not all of these can properly be called 'sanctions', and here, too, reciprocity plays a prominent role.[34]

A practically relevant method of expressing dismay with another state's actions is the so-called retorsion. These are measures taken within the limits of the law and send the message that a state is not best pleased with another's actions. Typical examples would include recalling the ambassador 'for consultation',[35] or the breaking off of diplomatic relations altogether. Such activities send strong political messages, but do so without involving any breach of international obligations; the sanction is, so to speak, purely political. This is not the case with what used to be called reprisals, nowadays most often referred to by the more sterile term 'countermeasures'. These are characterized by their own illegality, but this illegality is rendered lawful if they are done in response to an earlier wrongful act committed by the other side.

An important related mechanism is well known from domestic contract law; if A violates a treaty, then B may do the same: *inadimplenti non est adimplendum*. The principle came before the Permanent Court of International Justice (PCIJ) in 1937, in a case between Belgium and the Netherlands concerning the regime relating to a river running through both countries. Belgium alleged that the Netherlands had violated a treaty commitment, and while the Court's majority rejected this claim, none the less Judge Anzilotti disagreed, and held in a dissenting opinion that Belgium would in turn have been entitled to do the same. He found the principle of *inadimplenti non est adimplendum* to be 'so just, so equitable, so universally recognized, that it must be applied in international relations also'.[36]

Other measures include self-defence and collective security action (including sanctions targeting individuals); and since the 1990s international law has even been in a position, on occasion, to imprison individuals who have committed war crimes and related acts; those convicted by the Yugoslavia and Rwanda tribunals can testify to this, even though it took the International Criminal Court (ICC) (in existence since 2002) a decade to decide its first substantive case. All this is better discussed elsewhere in this book, but it goes to show that the popular notion that international law is a system without sanctions is, at best, only partly true.

INTERNATIONAL LEGAL THEORIES

If Henkin was right when he suggested that states almost always adhered to almost all their obligations, then the question of whether international law is actually 'binding' would hardly appear relevant. What matters, one might say, is that international law seems to work; whether it does so because it is somehow binding, or for some other reason, is in

---

[34] This will be discussed further in Chapter 9 below.

[35] Thus, in April 2012, the Netherlands recalled its ambassador to Surinam (a former Dutch colony) after Surinam had adopted legislation providing an amnesty to individuals associated with gross human rights violations committed in the early 1980s.

[36] *Diversion of Water from the Meuse*, [1937] Publ. PCIJ, Series A/B, no. 70, at 50.

practical terms of little relevance. Yet the question whether international law is really 'binding' has occupied international lawyers since time immemorial and quite obviously, when judging a state's behaviour, it may matter whether the state was deemed to be bound by a rule of international law, or whether it merely violated a rule of comity or some social practice. A refusal by a state to put out the red carpet for a foreign head of state may violate a rule of etiquette, but is unlikely to end up before any court, for the simple reason that there is no rule of international law which says that one should welcome foreign heads of state with a red carpet.[37]

But even if it is accepted that international law is binding, the question arises where that law comes from. Earlier thinkers, before the Reformation and for quite some time thereafter, tended to think that international law was natural law; it was given by God, and could be recognized by those who adhered to the right religion. The problem with such a view turned out to be, eventually, that it was inherently subjective. Those of a different faith might reach different conclusions, and even people adhering to the same faith might come to different conclusions involving one and the same incident.

Hence, by the nineteenth century, the tide had turned a little, and naturalism had by and large been replaced by a more scientific-looking positivist approach, riding on the coat-tails of the emerging social sciences.[38] Positivism starts from the position that law does not hover about in nature but is, instead, man-made. In other words, the contents of law can be discovered by looking at what states actually do. This looked very sensible for a while, until people started to realize that if the law is what states do anyway, then it does not have much of a normative function.

The critical revolution in international law, spearheaded in the 1980s by David Kennedy at Harvard and Martti Koskenniemi in Helsinki, has made it clear that international law is in actual fact constantly in search of a compromise between the naturalist and the positivist traditions.[39] As Koskenniemi in particular has demonstrated, international law has to be both naturalist (in that it has to serve the common good of mankind, in today's version – the direct link to God is thought to have little credibility these days, and leaves unanswered the question whose God it concerns) and positivist (reflecting state practice and interests) at the same time. This is now structurally impossible: international law is not capable of being both naturalist and positivist at the same time. As a result, whenever someone invokes a naturalist argument it is vulnerable to a positivist critique, and vice versa.

By way of example, the naturalist may say that nuclear weapons are a terrible invention; the positivist may reply that even so, there is no treaty outlawing them. Should the positivist draw the conclusion that their use is therefore perfectly legal, the naturalist may respond that even though there is no treaty prohibiting nuclear weapons, there is no

---

[37] This is not to say they can be arrested at will; they will typically be immune from arrest, as will be discussed in Chapter 5 below.

[38] Mónica García-Salmones Rovira, *The Project of Positivism in International Law* (Oxford University Press, 2013); also Mark Mazower, *Governing the World: The History of an Idea* (London: Allen Lane, 2012).

[39] See in particular David Kennedy, *International Legal Structures* (Baden-Baden: Nomos, 1987), and Martti Koskenniemi, *From Apology to Utopia: The Structure of International Legal Argument* (Cambridge University Press, 2005 [1989]). Koskenniemi's work was reissued in 2005 by Cambridge University Press, with a new epilogue.

clear rule allowing for their use either – at no point has anyone actually been given permission to develop and use nuclear weapons. This discussion can go on forever and is, indeed, bound to go on forever, unless and until states reach some kind of agreement on what to do. Asking the ICJ for an opinion will prove useless in the absence of any clear political accord: all the Court can do (and did in fact do, when asked, in 1996)[40] is to declare either that the use of nuclear weapons is generally illegal, but sometimes legal, or the other way around. The trick then, of course, resides in finding out what the word 'sometimes' means. The consequence of all this, in Koskenniemi's words, is that international law is eventually the continuation of politics. It offers a framework and a vocabulary for the conduct of politics, but does not, and cannot, offer any solutions, precisely because it has to appeal both to justice and to everyday practice at the same time: 'Modern international law is an elaborate framework for deferring substantive resolution elsewhere: into further procedure, interpretation, equity, context, and so on.'[41]

If international law is inherently political, it seems to follow that its political positions can be elucidated. Some have studied how international law has been related to colonialism, or how it serves the needs of a global market economy. In turn, this has spurred activities to explore and use the emancipatory potential of international law more fully; after all, if international law is politics in disguise, then it follows that it can also be utilized for worthy causes. Karen Knop, for example, has studied how the right to self-determination has been used by disadvantaged groups in order to upgrade their status;[42] Hilary Charlesworth and Christine Chinkin have developed a feminist outlook on international law;[43] some scholars aim to develop a Marxist perspective on international law;[44] and the critical revolution has stimulated the emergence of scholars aiming to improve the plight of developing nations.[45] A useful side effect of all this is that few still believe in the fiction of a neutral, politically innocent international law. Where the political preferences of earlier international legal authors were hidden behind a vocabulary consisting either of impressive Latin phrases (*jus cogens*, *erga omnes*) or a quasi-scientific jargon in the case of positivism, the political preferences of such authors today are mostly out in the open.[46]

---

[40] *Legality of the Threat or Use of Nuclear Weapons*, advisory opinion, [1996] ICJ Rep., 226.

[41] Martti Koskenniemi, 'The Politics of International Law', (1990) 1 *European Journal of International Law*, 4–32, at 28.

[42] Karen Knop, *Diversity and Self-determination in International Law* (Cambridge University Press, 2002).

[43] Hilary Charlesworth and Christine Chinkin, *The Boundaries of International Law: A Feminist Analysis* (Manchester University Press, 2000).

[44] See e.g. Susan Marks (ed.), *International Law on the Left: Re-examining Marxist Legacies* (Cambridge University Press, 2008).

[45] This is known as the TWAIL movement, with TWAIL standing for Third World Approaches to International Law. For an excellent overview see Antony Anghie and B. S. Chimni, 'Third World Approaches to International Law and Individual Responsibility in Internal Conflicts', (2003) 2 *Chinese Journal of International Law*, 77–103. One example of TWAIL scholarship is Balakrishnan Rajagopal, *International Law from Below: Development, Social Movements and Third World Resistance* (Cambridge University Press, 2003).

[46] For further reflection, see Jörg Kammerhofer and Jean d'Aspremont (eds.), *International Legal Positivism in a Post-Modern World* (Cambridge University Press, 2014); Anne Orford and Florian Hoffmann (eds.), *The Oxford Handbook of the Theory of International Law* (Oxford University Press, 2016).

Since international law can be seen to continue political debate instead of settling it, it is no surprise that legal arguments have come to be invoked as political tools – a phenomenon sometimes referred to as 'lawfare'. In a sense, of course, this has always happened: if a state was deprived of an entitlement, it would try to find a legal argument to back up its claim. In this way, for example, the newly independent states of Latin America utilized legal argument to bolster their positions during much of the nineteenth century.[47] This usage has spread, however, in quite dramatic ways. One example (out of many) is the fall-out of Russia's annexation of the Crimea in 2014. Ukraine objected, as was to be expected, in some of the regular fora. Thus it looked for support (and found some) in the UN General Assembly, which adopted a resolution supporting Ukraine's territorial integrity.[48] Earlier it had looked, in vain, to the Security Council for support: as will be explained in chapter 4 below, five states (including Russia) enjoy a right of veto in the Security Council, making action by the Security Council against one of them highly unlikely.

But in addition to these fora, Ukraine has also been active elsewhere. It has brought cases against Russia, somehow relating to the annexation of Crimea, to the European Court of Human Rights;[49] it has reportedly prepared to start proceedings related to Crimea before the International Tribunal of the Law of the Sea,[50] and has even considered, it seems, starting proceedings before the International Court of Justice, on the basis of the Terrorism Financing Convention.[51] In addition, it has been raising issues concerning the Crimea with a diversity of international organizations. In the International Maritime Organization, it has complained about the safety of navigation in the Black Sea.[52] In the World Trade Organization, it has filed against Russia concerning importation of railway equipment. Little of this makes instrumental sense – Ukraine cannot seriously expect to win all its legal cases, if only because Russia has been very reluctant to accept the jurisdiction of international courts.[53] But Ukraine's activities do make sense as an emanation of 'lawfare': if you cannot beat Russia by military means, you might as well use the law to keep telling the world that Russia is acting as a bully. In this way, 'lawfare' is a tool for the smaller states against the bigger powers, but the risk is that the reverse may also happen.

If international law often continues political debate, then what often matters in addition to the precise rules and principles of international law are the identity and mindset of the people taking decisions, and the conditions under which this political debate can take place. This has generated an interest among international lawyers in political philosophy,

---

[47] Arnulf Becker Lorca, 'Sovereignty beyond the West: The End of Classical International Law', (2011) 13 *Journal of the History of International Law*, 7–73.

[48] UN General Assembly Resolution 68/282, 27 March 2014. Support was not overwhelming: no fewer than 58 states abstained and 24 did not vote. Most of these are from the Global South.

[49] http://www.humanrightseurope.org/2015/04/russia-court-extends-crimea-and-eastern-ukraine-case-deadline/ (last visited 7 March 2016).

[50] http://opiniojuris.org/2016/02/01/ukraine-prepares-to-take-russia-to-unclos-arbitration/ (last visited 7 March 2016).

[51] http://opiniojuris.org/2016/02/27/ukraine-v-russia-where-can-you-sue/ (last visited 7 March 2016).

[52] http://uk.mfa.gov.ua/en/press-center/news/42411-ukraine-calls-on-international-maritime-organization-to-respond-to-russias-illegal-actions-threatening-safety-and-security-of-navigation-in-black-sea (last visited 7 March 2016).

[53] See further chapter 8 below.

in particular in theories of deliberative democracy[54] as well as the republican tradition, which is often traced back to Machiavelli or even ancient Rome.[55] Noteworthy also is that some international lawyers (or lawyers generally) have started to look for guidance to the Aristotelian tradition of virtue ethics, a tradition where what matters is not only that rules exist, but also the character traits of the individuals who apply those rules.[56]

INTERNATIONAL LAW IN INTERNATIONAL RELATIONS THEORY

Whether or not one thinks that international law is useful often depends on the view one has of international politics generally, and it is common to distinguish three approaches.[57] First, self-proclaimed realists tend to view international law as largely irrelevant. For them, the international system is characterized by a struggle for power between states, and states will do anything to further their own interests. From this perspective states will only respect international law when it is in their interests to do so, and will disrespect it when it is not. Either way, international law does not do much work; it either reflects state interests or it is violated.[58]

Second, the liberal institutionalist approach to international affairs is not quite as ready to dismiss international law. Adherents to this approach tend to think that international law can be of relevance, at least if properly designed to take states' lust for power into account. Starting from similar premises as die-hard realists (states are primarily motivated by self-interest), they have identified that international law may be helpful in some walks of life, such as trade and investment, because legal rules tend to create certainty and create stable expectations. Law may help reduce transaction costs and for that reason alone it can be beneficial and serve a state's interests; while there may be costs involved (sometimes having to accept a negative court decision, for example), the benefits may outweigh them.[59] Thus a state that is a member of the WTO and regularly participates in trade negotiations does not

---

[54] See e.g. John Dryzek, *Deliberative Global Politics: Discourse and Democracy in a Divided World* (Cambridge: Polity, 2006).

[55] See e.g. Samantha Besson and José Luis Martí (eds.), *Legal Republicanism: National and International Perspectives* (Oxford University Press, 2009). See also M. N. S. Sellers, *Republican Principles in International Law: The Fundamental Requirements of a Just World Order* (New York: Palgrave Macmillan, 2006).

[56] See e.g. Jan Klabbers, 'Autonomy, Constitutionalism and Virtue in International Institutional Law', in Richard Collins and Nigel D. White (eds.), *International Organizations and the Idea of Autonomy* (London: Routledge, 2011), 120–40; Colin Farrelly and Lawrence B. Solum (eds.), *Virtue Jurisprudence* (New York: Palgrave Macmillan, 2008); Amalia Amaya and Ho Hock Lai (eds.), *Law, Virtue and Justice* (Oxford: Hart, 2013). I will return to this in Chapter 17 below.

[57] For a useful general overview, see Michael Byers, 'International Law', in Christian Reus-Smit and Duncan Snidal (eds.), *The Oxford Handbook of International Relations* (Oxford University Press, 2008), 612–31.

[58] The classic statement is Kenneth Waltz, *Theory of International Politics* (New York: McGraw-Hill, 1979), in which international law hardly warrants a footnote. The sentiment is sometimes echoed from within the legal community, where a rational choice perspective on international law ends up dismissing its value. Recent examples include Jack L. Goldsmith and Eric O. Posner, *The Limits of International Law* (Oxford University Press, 2005) and, far more sophisticated, Andrew T. Guzman, *How International Law Works: A Rational Choice Theory* (Oxford University Press, 2008). For a critique utilizing the same rational choice methodology, see Jens David Ohlin, *The Assault on International Law* (Oxford University Press, 2015).

[59] Some of the classic texts in this tradition include Stephen D. Krasner (ed.), *International Regimes* (Ithaca, NY: Cornell University Press, 1983) and Robert O. Keohane, *After Hegemony: Cooperation and Discord in the World Political Economy* (Princeton University Press, 1984).

need to worry, if it wants market access elsewhere, about whom it should talk to, what sort of access rules would be acceptable and even whether the other state will respect its commitments. WTO membership makes all these things easier and more predictable.[60] Hence, in certain circumstances, legal rules can have their advantages; the drawback, then, is that this helps to instrumentalize law. If other, non-legal mechanisms could have similar advantages or even be more beneficial for the user, then law would cease to play a role. It is no coincidence surely that one of the leading representatives of this tradition, Robert O. Keohane, has in recent years started to extol the virtues of legitimacy, not as an aspect of international law (as Franck, discussed in note 31, does), but rather as its replacement.[61]

A variation on realism and in some hands, on liberal institutionalism, is the law and economics approach, particularly prominent in US academia. This approach ('law as economics' as someone once quipped) takes its cue not so much from political science but, as the label suggests, from economics, in particular micro-economics. As economists tend to do when studying the behaviour of firms or consumers, law and economics scholars typically presume that states are rational actors, and presume that those rational actors behave so as to maximize their profits. On these premises, states will sometimes be inclined to adopt common rules, because common rules might lead to greater profit maximization than going it alone. In other circumstances, the analysis suggests, unilateral action may be preferable. In short, to the law and economics scholars all the world's a market, and while in good hands this approach is capable of generating illuminating insights,[62] its underlying premises need constantly to be interrogated. Is it really the case that states always act rationally?[63] And is it really the case that rationality goes hand in hand with profit maximization? And even if rationality and thinking in economic terms applies to trade law or investment law, how can it explain the worldwide prohibition of genocide or the near-universal acceptance of the Convention on the Rights of the Child? Moreover, there is the risk that such an approach ends up denying, or even actively undermining, the normative side of all things legal, because here in particular the risk of instrumentalization

---

[60] This helps explain the outcry when, in 2016, the US blocked the reappointment of one of the WTO's Appellate Body members, ostensibly because the person in question had been overly 'activist'. Surely, given that free trade and the WTO are greatly beneficial to strong trading nations such as the United States, it should not be so churlish as to try and stack the Appellate Body. See Arman Sarvaraian and Filippo Fontanelli, 'The USA and Re-appointment at the WTO: A 'Legitimacy Crisis?', at www.ejiltalk.org, 27 May 2016.

[61] See e.g. Allen Buchanan and Robert O. Keohane, 'The Legitimacy of Global Governance Institutions', (2006) 20 *Ethics and International Affairs*, 405–37.

[62] Some of the best work in this tradition is done by Trachtman. See e.g. Joel P. Trachtman, *The Economic Structure of International Law* (Cambridge, MA: Harvard University Press, 2008). Related recent developments include a focus on empirical studies and on behavioural incentives. See, respectively, Gregory Shaffer and Tom Ginsburg, 'The Empirical Turn in International Legal Scholarship', (2012) 106 *American Journal of International Law*, 1–46, and Anne van Aaken, 'Behavioral International Law and Economics', (2014) 55 *Harvard International Law Journal*, 421–81.

[63] The German-born political theorist Hannah Arendt observed, by contrast, that the field of international relations was precisely the one field where reduction to economic factors would be senseless, because the animosities and friendships between states are often inspired by other motives (such as religion, ethnicity, or history). See Hannah Arendt, 'What is Freedom?', reproduced in Hannah Arendt, *Between Past and Future* (London: Penguin, 1968), 143–71.

looms large: if the law does not maximize profits, then perhaps some other route ought to be chosen – perhaps even brute force.[64]

A third approach[65] among international relations scholars is the so-called constructivist approach, and this approach in particular takes international law very seriously.[66] Where the realists and, to some extent, the institutionalists tend to think of law as if all law were modelled on criminal law (commands, backed by sanctions), constructivists are more inclined to view international law as modelled on a private law conception; to their minds, international law is not just about prohibiting things, but also about facilitating behaviour. International law allows states to conclude alliances, and it helps to channel political dialogue; it makes a lot of difference whether an incursion by one state into a neighbouring state is discussed as an invasion, or as a humanitarian intervention or an exercise in self-defence. International law, in short, delivers the framework and vocabulary that helps make international politics possible. Without international law, there could not even be states, for how else can such entities be classified as states except on the basis of rules that say so? Law, in other words, helps to construct society, and is thus of immense importance.[67] The relevant question is not the realist question whether law constrains, but rather whether it enables, social life.

GLOBALIZATION, GLOBAL GOVERNANCE AND INTERNATIONAL LAW

The emergence of globalization[68] towards the end of the twentieth century has only strengthened the connection between law and economics. While globalization may encompass many different things and can even be considered ideology,[69] none the less there is general agreement that economic globalization is a key element in globalization, and that the existence of global economic relations demands a global legal framework.

---

[64] And then there is, obviously, the distributive question: whose profit is being maximized?

[65] The enumeration is not exhaustive: while the distinction between realists, liberal institutionalists, and constructivists is often made, there are other approaches possible. Some, for example, view international politics as the result of the interaction between internationalism and imperialism. Something of a manifesto is David Long and Brian C. Schmidt (eds.), *Imperialism and Internationalism in the Discipline of International Relations* (Albany NY: SUNY Press, 2005). Yet others view international affairs as exercises in imitation: see Roberto Farneti, *Mimetic Politics: Dyadic Patterns in Global Politics* (East Lansing MI: Michigan State University Press, 2015).

[66] Leading works in this tradition include Friedrich V. Kratochwil, *Rules, Norms, and Decisions: On the Conditions of Practical and Legal Reasoning in International Relations and Domestic Affairs* (Cambridge University Press, 1989), and Nicholas G. Onuf, *World of Our Making: Rules and Rule in Social Theory and International Relations* (Columbia, SC: University of South Carolina Press, 1989). An account combining constructivist thought with legal theory is Jutta Brunnée and Stephen J. Toope, *Legitimacy and Legality in International Law: An Interactional Account* (Cambridge University Press, 2010).

[67] See generally also Andrew Hurrell, *On Global Order: Power, Values, and the Constitution of International Society* (Oxford University Press, 2007); Friedrich V. Kratochwil, *The Status of Law in World Society: Meditations on the Role and Rule of Law* (Cambridge University Press, 2014).

[68] Useful introductions include Thomas Hylland Eriksen, *Globalization: The Key Concepts* (Oxford: Berg, 2007) and, highly readable, Alex MacGillivray, *A Brief History of Globalization* (London: Robinson, 2006). A rare study concerning the challenges globalization entails for international law is David J. Bederman, *International Law and Globalization* (New York: Palgrave Macmillan, 2008).

[69] See Jonathan Friedman, 'Globalization', in David Nugent and Joan Vincent (eds.), *A Companion to the Anthropology of Politics* (London: Blackwell, 2004), 179–97.

However, globalization affects more than the economy alone: it also affects cultural and social relations, it has given religious sentiments a new boost, and because globalization is often considered to make people feel insecure and alienated, it may also have sparked nationalist and regional feelings. With globalization comes localization, with social disembeddedness comes a desire to feel embedded again. We may all be watching *Dancing with the Stars* or *Big Brother*, but the cast has to be local; it is no fun for Finns to watch Japanese and no fun for the Japanese to watch Finns.[70]

More than this, globalization has also come to be accompanied by what is sometimes referred to as global governance: the exercise of authority, on the global level, outside regular legal structures.[71] This creates important challenges for international law. How should international lawyers assess the financial rules created by, for example, the Basel Committee, or accountancy rules developed by international accountancy boards? These are not easy to squeeze into the framework of traditional international law, yet they have a profound effect on the everyday lives of millions of people. Hence globalization and global governance pose challenges not just by throwing up new fields for regulation, but also, more fundamentally, by forcing international lawyers to rethink the tools of their trade. Globalization and global governance make it clear that many of the classic concepts and categories of international law (even concepts as fundamental as 'statehood' or 'treaty') may have become outdated. Indeed, if international law wants to continue to have something meaningful to say about the conduct of international politics, it will need to adapt itself to the changing world.[72]

To some extent, that process is going on as we speak. For the last two decades or so international lawyers have come to embrace an emerging international criminal law, aiming to curb the worst excesses of political crime worldwide, which is intimately related to global governance. Others have started to suggest that topics traditionally not considered to be part of international law should be given fresh consideration; perhaps international taxation is better seen as part of the international law of global governance than, as it stands, as the sovereign prerogative of states. Likewise, migration has become such a widespread phenomenon, and a phenomenon of such great economic importance in view of the remittances sent home by migrants, that international law can ill afford to leave the regulation of migration to domestic legal orders. After all, a legal order which allows capital, goods, and services to move freely across frontiers should perhaps also think about the movement of people, and not leave this to individual states. This might also help to propel labour law from its marginal position on the fringes of international law;

---

[70] See generally Saskia Sassen, *A Sociology of Globalization* (New York: Norton, 2007).

[71] Among the first to observe this were James N. Rosenau and Ernst-Otto Czempiel (eds.), *Governance without Government: Order and Change in World Politics* (Cambridge University Press, 1992), whereas a useful (political) framework is developed in Deborah D. Avant, Martha Finnemore, and Susan K. Sell (eds.), *Who Governs the Globe?* (Cambridge University Press, 2010). A pioneering legal study is Eyal Benvenisti, *The Law of Global Governance* (The Hague: Hague Academy of International Law, 2014).

[72] Weiler helpfully suggests a geological metaphor: different approaches do not radically replace each other, but instead a process of accretion takes place: J. H. H. Weiler, 'The Geology of International Law – Governance, Democracy and Legitimacy', (2004) 64 *Zeitschrift für ausländisches öffentliches Recht und Völkerrecht*, 547–62.

even though the International Labour Organization (ILO) has existed since 1919, labour law is not something with which international lawyers regularly occupy themselves.[73]

ETHICS AND INTERNATIONAL LAW

It is sometimes claimed that international law is not very ethical, but that is a debatable claim. Before the rise of the Westphalian system, the ethical contents of international law were not considered problematic. If international law was God-given, then by definition it would be ethical enough, and such debates as did take place largely involved the vexed question as to whether war was always wrong, or whether there were circumstances in which war, however nefarious, could none the less be considered just.[74]

Perhaps the main problem nowadays is not so much that international law and ethics have nothing to do with each other, but that different conceptions of the ethics of international law compete with each other. Thus some reacted furiously when the European Court of Human Rights (ECtHR) decided, in 2007, that it could not decide on a claim made by Kosovo citizens concerning the conduct of United Nations (UN) and NATO troops in Kosovo; the Court found that since the acts complained of were ultimately attributable to the UN, and since the UN was not a party to the European Convention on Human Rights, the Court therefore had no jurisdiction over those acts.[75] Hence, so the ethical argument goes, human rights were sacrificed. Yet the contrary finding would also have run into ethical problems; it would have amounted to punishing some of the UN's member states for activities of the UN itself, and that in itself might also be construed as unfair. In addition, it could have undermined the collective security function of the UN, which could have resulted in far greater unfairness down the line.[76]

Likewise, while one can interpret the *Arrest Warrant* case of the ICJ as a defeat for human rights (the Court held that a Congolese government minister was immune from prosecution despite his possible involvement in human rights violations),[77] one can also interpret it as a vindication for deliberative politics. Rules on immunity make it impossible to harass government members, thereby allowing international communication to take place without disturbance. And that too has an ethical quality in and of itself.

That said, the claim that global ethics has remained underdeveloped is fair enough.[78] Partly this results from the circumstance that moral philosophers tend to think about the ethical duties of individuals rather than of collectivities such as states. Indeed, it is

---

[73] See also Jan Klabbers, 'The Idea(s) of International Law', in A. S. Muller et al. (eds.), *The Law of the Future and the Future of Law* (Oslo: TOAEP, 2011), 69–80.

[74] The classic study is Michael Walzer, *Just and Unjust Wars*, 3rd edn (New York: Basic Books, 2000).

[75] For a sophisticated doctrinal critique, suggesting that attributing the acts to the UN should not automatically have absolved individual states, see Guglielmo Verdirame, *The UN and Human Rights: Who Guards the Guardians?* (Cambridge University Press, 2011).

[76] See joined cases *Behrami and Behrami* v. *France* (Application no. 71412/01), and *Saramati* v. *France and others* (Application no. 78166/01), decision of 2 May 2007, reproduced in 133 *International Law Reports*, 1.

[77] *Arrest Warrant of 11 April 2000* (*Democratic Republic of Congo* v. *Belgium*), [2002] ICJ Rep. 3; this will be further discussed in Chapter 5 below.

[78] See also Stanley Hoffmann, *Duties beyond Borders: On the Limits and Possibilities of Ethical International Politics* (Syracuse University Press, 1981).

contested whether collective actors have the capacity to act ethically to begin with, at least if by this is understood the capacity to be motivated by ethical reasons. One may say of an individual that she behaves charitably, but this is a more difficult judgement when collective actors are involved.[79]

Moreover, it is often posited that individuals have stronger obligations towards people close to them (family members, compatriots) than towards people elsewhere. As a result, much political ethics focuses on the duties of individuals within a delimited community, such as a village or a state. Still, this type of work has led to important insights, which at least ought to inform international law, such as the insight that global poverty is ethically unacceptable.[80] Some moral philosophers have started to analyse and discuss global ethics,[81] and international lawyers themselves have tried to find ways to express the fact that such activities as genocide, slavery, and torture are ethically wrong, and have come to use particular Latin phrases to express this sentiment (*jus cogens*), or even to hope that if international law can be seen as constitutionalizing it will automatically follow that such activities are prohibited.[82]

In short, it is not so much the case that international law is devoid of ethics, but rather that ethics itself is far from uniform: different ethicists follow different traditions and present different conclusions as to what exactly constitutes proper ethical behaviour, or whose behaviour counts, ethically speaking.

FINAL REMARKS: A CRITICAL PERSPECTIVE

The idea behind this book is to introduce, albeit in a nutshell, the entire corpus of international law, and to do so from a more or less critical angle. Among the main values of the critical approach is its methodology; it makes clear that international law always has to navigate between naturalism and positivism.[83] Thus the critical school has presented a useful tool for the explanation of international law – many of the uncertainties of international law can be traced back to the tension between

---

[79] For a useful set of papers exploring the moral agency of collective actors, see Toni Erskine (ed.), *Can Institutions have Responsibilities? Collective Moral Agency and International Relations* (New York: Palgrave Macmillan, 2003).

[80] See e.g. Thomas Pogge, 'Divided against Itself: Aspiration and Reality of International Law', in James Crawford and Martti Koskenniemi (eds.), *The Cambridge Companion to International Law* (Cambridge University Press, 2012), 373–97.

[81] See e.g. Charles S. Beitz, *Political Theory and International Relations* (Princeton University Press, 1999 [1979]); Simon Caney, *Justice Beyond Borders: A Global Political Theory* (Oxford University Press, 2005); Peter Singer, *One World: The Ethics of Globalization*, 2nd edn (New Haven, CT: Yale University Press, 2004).

[82] For a discussion of the latter see Jan Klabbers, Anne Peters, and Geir Ulfstein, *The Constitutionalization of International Law* (Oxford University Press, 2009), and Nico Krisch, *Beyond Constitutionalism: The Pluralist Structure of Postnational Law* (Oxford University Press, 2010). An attempt to justify international legal rules in moral (largely consequentialist) terms is Steven R. Ratner, *The Thin Justice of International Law: A Moral Reckoning of the Law of Nations* (Oxford University Press, 2015).

[83] This is, in a sense, unfair: many critical lawyers feel that their approach is not merely methodology, but also comes with political convictions, usually somewhat left of centre. Critical international lawyers have not merely unmasked the politics of international law, but also aim to participate in those politics. For illustration, see e.g. Marks, *International Law on the Left*.

naturalism and positivism, or between the community interest and the individual state interest, in more modern language.

One ramification is that, throughout this book, I will usually refrain from comments about whether the behaviour of states is lawful or unlawful. One of the fundamental teachings of the critical school is that legal rules tend to have uncertain content precisely because they need to navigate between positivist and naturalist positions (thus, they are 'indeterminate', in jargon) and, as a consequence, it is often impossible to identify a single right answer to any legal question. Instead, the more proper question to ask is whether behaviour can be legally justified; if state A sends its troops into neighbouring state B, it should be able to justify this in legal terms, and if the justification is strong enough, the behaviour can be deemed 'lawful'. Often enough, this judgement (whether in the hands of a court, other international lawyers,[84] or of the public at large) will take place on a sliding scale: behaviour is more or less justifiable in legal terms. Once a crucial point is passed (when the justification is not strong enough) the behaviour may be deemed unlawful.

By the same token, it is useful to remember that rules typically come with exceptions, and it takes a person or group of persons (such as a court) to decide whether to apply the rule or the exception; none of this takes place automatically. Likewise, rules tend to be both over-inclusive and under-inclusive: they will always cover events their drafters never thought of, and somehow manage not to cover some of the events to which they were intended to apply.[85] Hence, at the end of the day, international law is not carved in stone, but the product of a practice of argumentation, in which the individual characteristics of those evaluating the arguments, be they Foreign Office lawyers, judges, or even academics, play an important role.[86] With this in mind, it is time to start to discuss the structure, process, and contents of international law.

FURTHER READING

Antony Anghie, *Imperialism, Sovereignty and the Making of International Law*
(Cambridge University Press, 2004)
Antony Anghie and B. S. Chimni, 'Third World Approaches to International Law and
Individual Responsibility in Internal Conflicts', (2003) 2 *Chinese Journal of International
Law*, 77–103
Eyal Benvenisti, *The Law of Global Governance* (The Hague: Hague Academy of International Law,
2014)

---

[84] Schachter famously invoked an 'invisible college of international lawyers': if most international lawyers find behaviour unlawful, then it probably is. See Oscar Schachter, 'The Invisible College of International Lawyers', (1977) 72 *Northwestern University Law Review*, 217–26.

[85] The idea that rules are both over-inclusive and under-inclusive is authoritatively formulated in Frederick Schauer, *Playing by the Rules: A Philosophical Examination of Rule-Based Decision-Making in Law and in Life* (Oxford: Clarendon Press, 1991).

[86] See already Hersch Lauterpacht, *The Function of Law in the International Community* (Oxford University Press, 2011 [1933]), at 111.

Hilary Charlesworth and Christine Chinkin, *The Boundaries of International Law: A Feminist Analysis* (Manchester University Press, 2000)

Martti Koskenniemi, *From Apology to Utopia: The Structure of International Legal Argument. reissue with new epilogue* (Cambridge University Press, 2005 [1989])

Martti Koskenniemi, *The Gentle Civilizer of Nations* (Cambridge University Press, 2001)

Friedrich V. Kratochwil, *The Status of Law in World Society: On the Role and Rule of Law* (Cambridge University Press, 2014)

B. V. A. Röling, *International Law in an Expanded World* (Amsterdam: Djambatan, 1960)

2

The Making of International Law

INTRODUCTION

International law, so many claim, is predominantly made by states, and this still holds true in large measure. Since states are considered to be sovereign, it follows that there is no authority above them; and if there is no authority above them, it follows that law can only be made with their consent – otherwise the system would be authoritarian. Hence international law is often said to be a consent-based (or consensual) system.

International law does not have a specific document specifying how it is made; there is no treaty on the correct ways and processes for making international law. Instead, the Statute of the ICJ contains a listing of instruments that the Court may apply in deciding cases, and it is this listing that is often used as a starting point for a discussion of the sources of the law. This already suggests that the list is not exhaustive; it is possible that there are sources of law not mentioned in article 38 ICJ Statute. And indeed, recalling that the same list already graced the Statute of the PCIJ and was drafted in the early 1920s, it seems eminently plausible that in the years since then the possibilities for law-making have expanded. It is plausible to say that international organizations can make law, although one can also explain their resolutions as being treaty based, since the authority of such resolutions derives from the constitutive instrument of the organization. There is widespread discussion (if little truly conclusive) about the role of civil society and non-governmental organizations (NGOs) in the making of international law. And there are heated debates about whether states can make so-called 'soft law', and whether law can (and should be allowed to) arise through networks of civil servants and regulators.

In this chapter and the next the sources of international law will be discussed. The current chapter will concentrate on customary international law and general principles of law as well as sources of doctrine generally, whereas the next chapter will be devoted to the law of treaties. Before continuing, however, it is imperative to sketch first the basics of the system, and underline the role of consent. For while it may be the case that consent is of less importance nowadays than a century ago, it needs to be underlined that state consent is still of vital importance.

TWO SHIPS (OR PERHAPS THREE): *LOTUS* AND *WIMBLEDON*

On 2 August 1926, the steamships *Boz-Kourt* (flying the Turkish flag) and *Lotus* (French) collided on the high seas, off the Turkish coast. The *Boz-Kourt* was cut in two, eight Turkish nationals died, and the Turkish authorities started criminal proceedings against Lt Demons, first officer of the *Lotus*, as well as the captain of the *Boz-Kourt*, Hassan Bey. Both were found guilty by the Criminal Court of Istanbul and sentenced to a fine and some months' imprisonment.[1]

The fact that a French citizen (Demons) was being prosecuted in Turkey did not go down well with the French authorities, who claimed that Turkey lacked the required jurisdiction to prosecute a foreigner for acts committed outside Turkish territory. Turkey and France agreed to take the matter to the PCIJ, which in 1927 rendered its classic decision.[2]

The main question asked of the Court, as formulated by both parties together, was whether Turkey, in instituting proceedings against Lt Demons, had acted in conflict with principles of international law. In other words, the question was not whether Turkey had permission to start proceedings, but rather whether starting proceedings was prohibited. The Court actually agreed that this was the proper way to ask the question, for it was 'dictated by the very nature and existing conditions of international law'.[3]

The Court discussed the nature of international law as follows, in a famous paragraph:

> International law governs relations between independent States. The rules of law binding upon States therefore emanate from their own free will as expressed in conventions or by usages generally accepted as expressing principles of law and established to regulate the relations between these co-existing independent communities or with a view to the achievement of common aims. Restrictions upon the independence of States cannot therefore be presumed.[4]

Since no prohibition could be found in international law, the Court eventually decided that Turkey had not violated international law. There was simply no rule prohibiting Turkey from starting proceedings against Lt Demons in the circumstances of the case, and thus Turkey had done nothing wrong.

This proved to be a monumental decision, as much for its reasoning as for its outcome. The Court here laid down the idea of international law as a permissive system: behaviour must be considered permitted unless and until it is prohibited. The alternative, as argued by France, would have been to regard international law as a prohibitive system, where behaviour is only lawful if there is a rule that specifically allows it. Then again, it is easy to exaggerate the monumentality of the *Lotus* case. In most domestic societies, the same basic starting point applies; people can do as they please unless the law says they can't. We do not normally need specific rules telling us that we are allowed to walk on the sidewalk;

---

[1] *SS Lotus*, [1927] Publ. PCIJ, Series A, no. 10.

[2] A fine study of the contribution of the PCIJ to the formation of the international legal order is Ole Spiermann, *International Legal Argument in the Permanent Court of International Justice: The Rise of the International Judiciary* (Cambridge University Press, 2005).

[3] *SS Lotus*, at 18.   [4] Ibid.

instead, we are free to do so, unless there is a rule that prohibits walking on the sidewalk. As one of the basic principles of the modern *Rechtsstaat* puts it, *nullum crimen sine lege* (no crime without a law).

The *Lotus* case still echoes in international law. The Court's starting point (that states are permitted to do whatever they please unless it is prohibited) is still valid enough, although it is possible to claim that there are exceptions; surely committing genocide is wrong, even for those states that have never accepted the prohibition of genocide.[5] Some aspects of the decision were questionable. Thus the Court equated a Turkish ship with Turkish territory in order to establish a jurisdictional link, even though strictly speaking the territory on which the collision occurred was the high seas,[6] and arguably it concluded too rapidly that in cases of collision the affected state could exercise jurisdiction. Later treaties on the law of the sea limit the penal jurisdiction of states to the flag state or the state of nationality of the responsible officer, which suggests some dissatisfaction with the Court's broad jurisdictional sweep in the *Lotus* case.[7]

The *Lotus* case was decided by the casting vote of the Court's president, the Swiss lawyer Max Huber, known for his 'sociological jurisprudence' and generally positivist outlook.[8] Either way, the decision should not have come as a surprise; four years earlier, in its first ever contentious decision (the *Wimbledon* case), the PCIJ had strongly suggested the outlines of a positivist, permissive international legal order.

After the First World War the victorious powers negotiated the Versailles Treaty and then told Germany to consent to it. Under the treaty, the Kiel Canal, in northern Germany, was declared an international waterway; Germany could not block the passage of any ship, save in times of war. When Germany refused access, in 1921, to the steamer *Wimbledon*, flying the English flag and chartered by a French company, some of those victorious powers started proceedings in the PCIJ.[9] France, the United Kingdom, Italy, and Japan, joined by Poland, claimed that in refusing access to the SS *Wimbledon*, Germany had violated article 380 of the Versailles Treaty. One of Germany's counter-arguments, no doubt inspired by the awkward circumstance that Germany had not been allowed to participate in the drafting of the Versailles Treaty, was that the Versailles Treaty was difficult to reconcile with sovereignty. Surely concluding a treaty could not be equated with giving up sovereignty, yet this, Germany argued, was precisely what the internationalization of the Kiel Canal signified. Germany's argument invoked a powerful theoretical point. How is it even possible to have law in a system of sovereign states?

[5] The ICJ referred to this in *Reservations to the Convention on the Prevention and Punishment of the Crime of Genocide*, advisory opinion, [1951] ICJ Rep. 15, at 23, suggesting that the principles underlying the Genocide Convention 'are principles which are recognized by civilized nations as binding on States, even without any conventional obligation'.

[6] Obviously, a vehicle is not territory; a German car driving in the Netherlands is not a piece of German territory in the Netherlands.

[7] See article 1(1) of the 1958 Geneva Convention on the High Seas (450 UNTS 11), confirmed in article 97 United Nations Convention on the Law of the Sea (UNCLOS).

[8] Max Huber, *Die soziologischen Grundlagen des Völkerrechts* (Berlin: Rothschild, 1928 [1910]).

[9] *SS Wimbledon*, [1923] Publ. PCIJ, Series A, no. 1.

The Court effectively shot down Germany's argument. While it agreed that concluding a treaty could place restrictions on the exercise of sovereign rights, it disagreed with the position that sovereignty and international law were fundamentally irreconcilable, and instead suggested that sovereignty and international law went hand in hand: 'the right of entering into international engagements is an attribute of State sovereignty'.[10]

The two cases, *Lotus* and *Wimbledon*, together establish that in a horizontal order of sovereign equals international law is by no means impossible; indeed, it is precisely because states are sovereign that they can make international law. But the same sovereignty entails that rules can only be made on the basis of consent; the rules of international law emanate from the freely expressed will of sovereign states.

In other words, international law is often deemed a positivist system in that rules are created by consent of the states themselves, and do not flow from elsewhere. International law does not stem from religion (although historically this was often posited), or from considerations of morality, but instead stems from the acts of the system's subjects. That is not to say that 'natural law' has no place whatsoever; it is sometimes claimed that some rules are so important that they also exist without consensual foundations, and may even bind those states that have not accepted them. Such rules are known as *jus cogens* rules: peremptory rules from which no derogation is permitted, and examples often mentioned include the prohibitions of genocide, torture, slavery, and aggression.[11]

ARTICLE 38 ICJ STATUTE

After the Second World War the PCIJ was replaced by the ICJ. Drafted to become part of the Statute of the PCIJ, in 1920, article 38(1) ICJ provides as follows:

The Court, whose function is to decide in accordance with international law such disputes as are submitted to it, shall apply:
a. international conventions, whether general or particular, establishing rules expressly recognized by the contesting states;
b. international custom, as evidence of a general practice accepted as law;
c. the general principles of law recognized by civilized nations;
d. subject to the provisions of Article 59, judicial decisions and the teachings of the most highly qualified publicists of the various nations, as subsidiary means for the determination of rules of law.[12]

It is generally agreed that article 38 does not establish a rigid hierarchy of sources, in particular when it comes to the relationship between customary law and treaties; these can supersede each other and also, as the Court confirmed in 1986, exist alongside each

---

[10] Ibid., at 25. For further discussion see Jan Klabbers, 'Clinching the Concept of Sovereignty: *Wimbledon* Redux', (1998) 3 *Austrian Review of International and European Law*, 345–67.
[11] This will be further discussed in the next chapter.
[12] Article 59 ICJ Statute provides, in turn, that decisions of the Court are only binding on the parties to the dispute.

other.[13] That said, two elements of hierarchy can be seen in article 38. First, judicial decisions and the writings of the most highly qualified publicists are listed as subsidiary means only, and the reference to article 59 ICJ Statute further makes it clear that judicial decisions have no precedent effect in international law; decisions of the Court can only bind the parties to the dispute. This makes sense, of course; it follows from the organizing principle of sovereignty that the Court cannot make law, only apply it. Difficult as it may be to draw the line between applying the law and making law, what is clear none the less is that precedent effect would by definition involve law-making, and can thus not be accepted.

Second, there is also general agreement among international lawyers that general principles of law (mentioned in subparagraph (c)) have as their main function the filling of gaps. In other words, general principles will normally only be resorted to if there is a situation where there is neither an applicable treaty nor an applicable rule of customary international law. Thus put, it would seem that treaties and custom are the stronger sources, and that should perhaps not come as a surprise, as both rest (at least in theory) firmly on the consent of states.

TREATIES

Lord McNair, in his day the world's leading authority on the law of treaties, once described treaties as the only, and sadly overworked, workhorses of the international legal order.[14] If states want to make a deal (say, exchange territory), the only instrument at their disposal is the treaty. Likewise, they can effectively only use the treaty form if the ambition is legislative in nature (e.g. to protect against climate change or to guarantee human rights). The only instrument available to set up an institution such as the UN is, again, the treaty. Hence, a lot is demanded from treaties and, especially during the twentieth century, the treaty has become the dominant source of international law – or, if not of 'law' per se, then at least of rights and obligations.[15]

Accordingly, treaties can come in all forms and sizes. They can be bilateral but also multilateral; they can be highly solemn and cast in language with biblical overtones (think of the designation 'Covenant', which graced the constituting instrument of the League of Nations and is nowadays associated with two general and universal human rights instruments), but also highly informal. Typically, what matters is that states express their consent to be bound; in this way, being bound by treaty can be reconciled with the starting point of state sovereignty.

Treaties have been concluded and have operated since time (almost) immemorial, and it stands to reason that over the centuries rules have developed, in customary international

---

[13] *Military and Paramilitary Activities In and Against Nicaragua (Nicaragua v. USA)*, merits, [1986] ICJ Rep. 14, para. 176.

[14] A. D. McNair, *The Law of Treaties* (Oxford: Clarendon Press, 1961).

[15] On the distinction, see Sir Gerald Fitzmaurice, 'Some Problems Regarding the Formal Sources of International Law', in F. M. van Asbeck et al. (eds.), *Symbolae Verzijl* (The Hague: Martinus Nijhoff, 1958), 153–76.

law, on the conclusion of treaties, the effects and application of treaties, their validity, and their termination. These rules have been codified in the 1969 Vienna Convention on the Law of Treaties (VCLT), which applies to treaties concluded between states only. A later Vienna Convention was concluded (in 1986) to address treaties concluded with or between international organizations, but this has yet to enter into force. In the meantime, though, it is fair to say that treaties concluded with or between international organizations are governed, by and large, by the same customary rules underlying the 1969 Vienna Convention, and much the same applies to treaties involving yet other actors. Thus, a peace agreement following a civil war, if governed by international law (as is normally the case), or an agreement between a state and a mineral extraction company,[16] will typically be subjected to the customary law of treaties, and this, it is often claimed, is well-nigh identical to the 1969 Vienna Convention. These rules will be discussed in greater detail in the next chapter, as will the question of what exactly constitutes a treaty.

CUSTOMARY LAW

People living in groups engage in all sorts of practices, and it is probably the case that all societies recognize that in certain circumstances those practices can acquire the force of law.[17] This makes some practical sense; it may be easier to regard activities that people carry out anyway as law, instead of making written laws. While written law tends to be more precise, customary law has the advantage that precisely because it is based on social practices, it is usually deeply engrained in the everyday life of that society. In international law, characterized by the absence of a central legislator, customary law has traditionally played a very important role, and continues to do so. When treaties were still rare events, much of the law was based on the customs of the members of the international society – states.

Article 38 ICJ Statute defines customary law, in somewhat lapidary terms, as evidence of a general practice accepted as law. This is a bit curious (if not all that important) in that the custom is not, strictly, evidence of a general practice, but rather the other way around; the practice is evidence that there is a custom. Be this as it may, the definition provides two main requirements: there must be a general practice, and this general practice must be accepted as law or, as international lawyers tend to say, the general practice must be accompanied by *opinio juris*, a sense of legal obligation. Both requirements have their own complications, and the precise relationship between them is problematic as well.[18]

A General Practice

Societies differ from one another, and also over time; accordingly, it is difficult to say in the abstract when a practice is general enough to award it the status of a rule of customary

---

[16] See sole arbitrator Réné-Jean Dupuy, in *Texaco Overseas Petroleum Company and California Asiatic Oil Company* v. *Libya*, merits, reproduced in 53 *International Law Reports*, 420.

[17] David J. Bederman, *Custom as a Source of Law* (Cambridge University Press, 2010).

[18] See generally Anthony A. d'Amato, *The Concept of Custom in International Law* (Ithaca, NY: Cornell University Press, 1971).

international law. One would think that the practice of only a handful of states might not really qualify as 'general', but this would be mistaken. There is, for example, the possibility of regional customary law, confirmed as matter of principle in the 1950 *Asylum* case.[19] There may even be something like a custom between two states only, although here it might be more appropriate to speak of a set of historic rights and obligations.[20]

In earlier days it was sometimes thought that the formation of a customary rule could take quite some time. Without being very specific, Vattel noted in the eighteenth century that customary law consisted of customs and maxims 'consecrated by long use', which suggests quite a lengthy period of gestation, possible decades.[21] By contrast, the ICJ found in 1969 that 'even without the passage of any considerable period of time, a very widespread and representative [practice] might suffice of itself'.[22]

Likewise, it cannot be specified, in the abstract, how many instances of practice are required. Many incidents over a short period of time may be just as forceful as a handful of instances spread out over a long period of time, or even more so. Much may depend also on the precise issue area; it seems to be generally accepted that since there are few space activities to begin with, space law can develop without too many instances of practice, and it has even been suggested that in such a field 'instant custom' may develop.[23] In other walks of life, however, things may be different; in fields such as the law of the sea, there is more practice and therefore the demands on a new rule of custom may be considerably higher.

Another relevant question is whose practice is required. Obviously, landlocked states such as Austria and Switzerland will not have much practice when it comes to maritime affairs; consequently, a focus on their practice will not be very revealing. By the same token, the development of customary space law will owe more to the practices of the United States, Russia, and France than those of Sierra Leone or Norway. Consequently, what matters in particular is that those states whose interests are especially affected by a customary rule participate in its making.[24] If this seems difficult to reconcile with sovereign equality, none the less, given the very nature of custom as the normative reflection of practice, it could hardly be otherwise. The Belgian jurist Charles de Visscher, a long-time judge at the ICJ, once made an apt analogy with footprints in the sand; there are always

---

[19] *Asylum (Colombia/Peru)*, [1950] ICJ Rep. 266, esp. at 276–7. The Court accepted the possible existence of regional custom, but held that Colombia had failed to demonstrate the existence of the specific customary rule it relied on.

[20] See *Right of Passage over Indian Territory (Portugal v. India)*, [1960] ICJ Rep. 6, at 44, where 'the Court finds a practice clearly established between two States which was accepted by the parties as governing the relations between them, the Court must attribute decisive effect to that practice for the purpose of determining their specific rights and obligations'. One author even opines that custom as such does not exist in international law, but that all instances of custom are, in fact, recognitions of historic rights. See Ingrid Detter de Lupis, *The Concept of International Law* (Stockholm: Norstedts, 1987), at 115–16.

[21] Emer de Vattel, *The Law of Nations*, trans. T. Nugent (Indianapolis: Liberty Fund, 2008 [1758]), at 77.

[22] See *North Sea Continental Shelf Cases* (Germany/Denmark; Germany/Netherlands), [1969] ICJ Rep. 3, para. 73.

[23] See Bin Cheng, 'United Nations Resolutions on Outer Space: "Instant" Customary International Law?', reproduced in Bin Cheng (ed.), *International Law: Teaching and Practice* (London: Stevens & Sons, 1982), 237–62.

[24] The passage quoted above from the *North Sea Cases* continues 'provided it [the practice] included that of States whose interests were specially affected'. *North Sea Continental Shelf Cases*, para. 73.

'some who mark the soil more deeply with their footprints than others, either because of their weight, which is to say their power in this world, or because their interests bring them more frequently this way'.[25]

Perhaps the most controversial question concerning practice is what exactly counts as practice. Practice, after all, can take various forms; acting is practice, but so is speaking; philosophically at any rate, humans act through speech, and a lot also depends on the context. Saying 'I do' at a wedding ceremony is bound to give rise to different expectations from saying 'I do' when asked whether one likes a particular dish or whether one supports Manchester United.[26]

It is generally accepted that the material acts of states (thus, actively seizing foreign vessels, actually expropriating foreign property, or sending satellites into orbit) count as elements of state practice. It is also generally accepted that the legislative acts of states, and their legal practices generally, may qualify as state practice. Thus, if many states enact a law for the protection of fish stocks up to 200 miles off their coasts, and if they actively prosecute violators, then at some point the conclusion may be warranted that this is a general practice with the potential to crystallize into a rule of customary international law.

More controversial is whether mere statements may qualify as state practice. If state representatives proclaim before international audiences that the state in question condemns torture, is this to be counted as state practice, or merely an example of talk being cheap? If the head of government of a state declares to his parliament that the state will never expropriate foreign property, is this to be regarded as state practice, or rather as a public statement, without any probative value unless the state actually enacts a law protecting against expropriation? And what if a state votes in an international meeting; is voting to be regarded as acting, on the same level as the material act, or is voting closer to mere speech? In short, the evidences of custom are, and will remain, controversial.

Accepted as Law

Complications are compounded by the second main requirement of custom; not only must there be a general practice, but this practice must also be accepted as law (*opinio juris*). This makes sense; there are many practices which are deemed useful or pleasant in one way or another, but which it would be silly to try and enforce in a court of law, or to ask for compensation upon violation. Thus, it might be customary to welcome visiting foreign dignitaries by rolling out the red carpet, but few would think of such a rule as a rule of law; it has force, but has not been 'accepted as law'. The requirement of *opinio juris* therewith plays the useful role of separating law from other normative control systems, such as etiquette or morality, or of separating legally warranted behaviour from merely politically expedient behaviour.

---

[25] Charles de Visscher, *Theory and Reality in Public International Law*, trans. P. Corbett, rev. edn (Princeton University Press, 1968 [1957]), at 155.

[26] On speech act theory, see J. L. Austin, *How to Do Things with Words*, 2nd edn (Oxford University Press, 1975); John R. Searle, *Speech Acts* (Cambridge University Press, 1969).

How, then, to recognize *opinio juris*? In fact, the evidences of *opinio juris* are often identical to those of state practice; enacting a law, concluding a treaty, engaging in a legal practice may all count both as evidence of state practice, and as evidence of the sentiment that the behaviour is legally warranted. In addition, it is generally acknowledged that resolutions adopted by international organizations (in particular the UN General Assembly, whose resolutions do not formally bind the UN's membership) or at international conferences may, their non-binding status notwithstanding, reflect *opinio juris*.

THE METHOD OF CUSTOM: THE *PAQUETE HABANA*

Difficult as all this seems, in practice it transpires that with common sense one can go a long way. A good way to illustrate the identification of a rule of customary international law is an old decision, from the year 1900, of the US Supreme Court, in the *Paquete Habana* case.[27] This arose out of the Spanish-American war, in 1898. The *Paquete Habana* and the *Lola* were Cuban fishing vessels and, since Cuba was still ruled by Spain, seen by the United States as enemy ships. A US gunboat seized the vessels in 1898, after they had been at sea for nearly a month (the crews were unaware that war had broken out). They were sold by auction for the princely sums of $490 and $800. The original owners claimed that the United States had no right to seize foreign fishing vessels, even in times of war. The case reached the US Supreme Court, which was thus given the task of trying to verify whether the capture of foreign fishing vessels in times of war was in accordance with international law.

The Court studied the matter carefully, and was able to cite orders by the English king Henry IV, from the early fifteenth century, to the effect that fishing vessels were not to be seized in wartime. The Court found similar decrees or orders from other countries (France, the United States itself), and unearthed a number of treaties between England and France, France and Holland, and the United States and Prussia, all of them stipulating in essence that fishing vessels were exempt from seizure in times of war. And this was not just a matter of law on paper; the Supreme Court found that local courts would habitually apply the rule and exempt foreign fishing vessels from seizure.

The Court also found some exceptions. France, for instance, at one point had withdrawn the exemption for fishing vessels, due to abuse by its enemies, but the overwhelming evidence of the practice investigated by the Court pointed to the existence of a general practice, and thus a rule of customary international law. This was confirmed by the opinions of the writers of general textbooks on international law, including jurists from countries such as Portugal, Italy, Spain and Argentina. In the end, the Supreme Court concluded that the capture had been unlawful, and that the proceeds of the sale (the $490 and $800) should be restored to the original owners, as well as costs and damages.

The case is highly instructive for the methodology used by the Supreme Court. First, it is noticeable that it does not separate practice from *opinio juris*; it takes at face value that the

---

[27] *Paquete Habana*, 175 US 677, US Supreme Court, 8 January 1900. Another interesting aspect, to be discussed in Chapter 16 below, is that international law was deemed to be part of US law, and thus had to be applied by the Supreme Court.

two elements of custom are closely related and evidenced by legal materials, such as royal orders, legislation, treaties and court decisions. This makes sense, of course; it would be very curious for a state to issue a law or decree while denying the legal relevance of the law or decree thus enacted.

It is also useful to note that the Court looks at the practice of various states but, at the same time, that the number of states is quite limited. The Court cites orders and treaties involving England, France, Holland, the United States and Prussia, but not many more countries. Then again, those states would have arguably been among the most important ones, in particular when it came to maritime affairs (although surely, by that criterion, Portugal and Spain should not be left out). And to alleviate any doubts, as a subsidiary means, to invoke the language of article 38 ICJ Statute, the Court also looked at the opinions of the most highly qualified publicists.

CONSENT AND THE PERSISTENT OBJECTOR

As a matter of theory, since international law is supposed to be about sovereign states, customary international law too is said to rest on the consent of states. Where other instruments may be consented to expressly, however, a state's consent to custom is thought to be tacit or implied. The standard position is this. If a state notices that a new rule of customary law is in the process of being created, and it feels unable to accept it, it should make its opposition known. By objecting persistently, the state can ensure that it does not become bound. What is more, if many states object persistently, together they can prevent the rule from coming into being.

The leading case on what constitutes persistent objection is the 1951 *Fisheries* case.[28] At issue was the question of whether the United Kingdom had accepted Norway's practice of delimiting its maritime zones not by measuring directly from the coastline,[29] but by drawing straight, artificial baselines from the outer edges of a number of islands and rocks off the coast (the so-called *skjaergaard*). The net result was that by doing so, Norway increased the width of its maritime zones. When English fishermen were arrested for fishing in Norway's territorial sea (which was wider than would have been the case had Norway used the normal method of delimitation), the United Kingdom started proceedings before the ICJ.

Norway justified its unorthodox practice essentially on a combination of two grounds: necessity and history. First, Norway's curious coastline (the *skjaergaard*) consists of a messy formation of islands, rocks, reefs, and islets, some 120,000 in total, which makes the regular method of delimitation very difficult, and would result in the near-total absence of any territorial sea. As a result (and this is the historical argument), Norway had for many years engaged in the drawing of straight baselines, had announced this to the world at large in various royal decrees and at various international meetings, and could thus claim a historic right to do so. In order to make this argument work, Norway could point out that already, in 1812, it had issued a royal decree announcing that it would draw straight baselines. It had

---

[28] *Fisheries* (*United Kingdom* v. *Norway*), [1951] ICJ Rep. 116.
[29] This will be further discussed in Chapter 13 below.

repeated this at various times during the nineteenth and twentieth centuries, the most recent one dating from 1935. No states had objected.

The United Kingdom, in turn, claimed that it was not aware of the Norwegian decrees or the subsequent practice of Norway, and therefore it could not have objected, but this argument lacked credibility: 'As a coastal State on the North Sea, greatly interested in fisheries in this area, as a maritime Power traditionally concerned with the law of the sea . . . the United Kingdom could not have been ignorant.'[30]

The case suggests strongly that the Court recognizes that persistent objections can block the formation of rights vis-à-vis others; had the United Kingdom objected persistently to Norway's claim, it is possible that the Court could have found that Norway had a historic right, but one that was not binding on the United Kingdom. Strictly speaking, though, a historic right is not the same as a general customary rule, since historic rights, by their very nature, can only belong to one state at a time. However, since states are sovereign and therefore consent is needed, it also follows that the theory of custom must allow for the possibility that states do not consent, and will therefore not be bound. Any other construction would be incompatible with the basic structure of the system.[31]

A NORMATIVE PROBLEM, OR TOWARDS MODERN CUSTOM

Customary law owes its recognition to the circumstance that it reflects what states do. But what if states breach an existing custom? Does this imply that the existing rule is weakened and possibly a new one is being formed? Or what if the practice of states is morally difficult to accept? If many states commit acts of torture, is the conclusion then inevitable that torture is allowed under customary international law, or can it still be said that torture is not permissible under customary international law? Here, the distinction between material acts and verbal acts, made above, is of relevance, as it is this distinction which allowed the ICJ to come to terms with the problem of immoral acts in the *Nicaragua* case.[32]

The case arose out of Nicaragua's claim that the United States had used force against it by helping to train opposition groups, by assisting others in small invasions into Nicaragua, and by laying mines in some of Nicaragua's ports and attacking oil installations and a naval base. Since the ICJ was barred from testing the legality of the US behaviour against the UN Charter (which clearly prohibits the use of force) for technical reasons,[33] it had to identify whether there existed a prohibition on the use of force in customary international law.

In doing so, the ICJ was confronted with the problematic (some would say hypocritical) situation that while many states publicly claim that they will not use force and hold it to be illegal, none the less history is replete with instances in which states actually use

---

[30] *Fisheries*, at 139.
[31] Having said that, the doctrine is only rarely invoked, which suggests either that many states do not follow all developments very closely or that they tend to agree by and large on new practices crystallizing into customary international law. See Jonathan I. Charney, 'The Persistent Objector Rule and the Development of Customary International Law', (1985) **56** *British Yearbook of International Law*, 1–24.
[32] See *Nicaragua*. [33] To be discussed below, in Chapter 8, 152.

force. State practice thus seemed to allow for the use of force. The Court, however, was not too bothered by this:

> The Court does not consider that, for a rule to be established as customary, the corresponding practice must be in absolutely rigorous conformity with the rule. In order to deduce the existence of customary rules, the Court deems it sufficient that the conduct of States should, in general, be consistent with such rules, and that instances of State conduct inconsistent with a given rule should generally have been treated as breaches of that rule, not as indications of the recognition of a new rule.[34]

In other words, what matters most is what states say they do. If they generally proclaim that the use of force is illegal, then the occasional use of force does not affect the existing customary rule. The classic maxim that, with respect to custom, 'law breaking is an essential method of law making',[35] no longer holds true completely; law-breaking is best seen as a violation, not as the beginning of a new custom, as long as states agree that the old rule is still worth keeping. Likewise, if states generally proclaim that torture is illegal, if they prohibit torture in their constitutions and penal codes and prosecute those who commit acts of torture, then it can be said that torture is prohibited under customary international law. Things will be different if acts of torture are accompanied by statements that the torture was justified, or necessary, or acceptable, or even desirable. In such a case, at some point in time customary law will no longer prohibit torture; breaking the law will have resulted in making new law.

The methodological importance of the Court's approach in *Nicaragua* can hardly be overstated. Instead of inductively looking at state practice and drawing conclusions, it started from the other end; it deduced the existence of a rule from the existence of *opinio juris*, and then suggested that contrary state practice was not really all that relevant as long as states continued to uphold the rule verbally. This has greatly facilitated the finding that morally desirable rules (think of human rights) can be considered as customary international law, but has done so by creating, so to speak, a virtual reality. Custom is no longer based on what states actually do, but partly at least based on what they say to do, even if they act differently.[36]

ON LAW-BREAKING AND LAW-MAKING

The customary process, and the possible normative relevance of wrongful behaviour, can perhaps best be understood by means of a (morally less explosive) example: the formation of the customary right to claim sovereignty over the continental shelf. The continental shelf is, technically, that part of the land mass where it continues under the sea. In some cases, it hardly exists – the sea floor will fall sharply. In other cases,

---

[34] *Nicaragua*, para. 186.

[35] J. G. Merrills, *Anatomy of International Law* (London: Sweet & Maxwell, 1976), at 8.

[36] For an attempt to reconcile the two approaches, see Anthea Roberts, 'Traditional and Modern Approaches to Customary International Law: A Reconciliation', (2001) 95 *American Journal of International Law*, 757–91.

the change is less abrupt, and this, in turn, might make it possible to find and exploit reserves of oil and natural gas.[37]

Among the first to realize this (and among the first with the technology to make it happen) was the United States, and US president Harry Truman issued a proclamation in 1945 according to which the continental shelf off the US coast would fall under the jurisdiction of the United States: 'the Government of the United States regards the natural resources of the subsoil and sea bed of the continental shelf beneath the high seas but contiguous to the coasts of the United States as appertaining to the United States, subject to its jurisdiction and control'.[38]

In principle, this had the potential to violate existing international law. The continental shelf and the water above it extend into what were known as the high seas, and the high seas, so it had been commonly held since the days of Grotius, cannot be subject to any state's jurisdiction. Hence other states could have regarded this as incompatible with their own rights on the high seas, and could have claimed that the Truman Proclamation was illegal. However, other states decided that they wanted to do the same as the United States, and started to make similar proclamations. Thus the United Kingdom made similar claims on behalf of Jamaica and the Bahamas,[39] and various states in Latin America and in the Persian Gulf area followed suit. While the contents of the claims varied (with some claiming full sovereignty, instead of functional jurisdiction as Truman had done), their core was invariably that some kind of jurisdiction was claimed, and this core, so Lord Asquith noted in September 1951 in the *Abu Dhabi* arbitration, was 'acquiesced in by the generality of Powers, or at least not actively gainsaid by them'.[40]

However, Lord Asquith was in 1951 not yet convinced that the rule had become part of customary international law, even though he thought it would be desirable, since the world appeared to be running out of oil. He concluded, in notable language, that

> there are in this field so many ragged ends and unfilled blanks, so much that is merely tentative and exploratory, that in no form can the doctrine claim as yet to have assumed hitherto the hard lineaments or the definitive status of an established rule of International Law.[41]

Not long thereafter, however, the continental shelf became the topic of a multilateral convention, which finally eradicated any doubts; in the space of roughly a decade, the potentially law-breaking Truman Proclamation had given rise to a new rule of law, and when the *North Sea Continental Shelf* cases came before the ICJ in 1969, the ICJ went so far as to refer to coastal state rights over the continental shelf as being 'inherent'.[42]

---

[37] See further Chapter 13 below.

[38] The text of the Truman Proclamation is available at the American Presidency Project of the University of California at Santa Barbara, at www.presidency.ucsb.edu/ws/index.php?pid=12332 (visited 20 August 2010).

[39] In fact, the United Kingdom had already concluded a treaty on behalf of Trinidad with Venezuela to much the same effect in 1942. See R. R. Churchill and A. V. Lowe, *The Law of the Sea*, 3rd edn (Manchester University Press, 1999), at 142–3.

[40] *Petroleum Development Ltd* v. *Sheikh of Abu Dhabi*, award by Lord Asquith of Bishopstone, September 1951, in 18 *International Law Reports*, 144, at 154.

[41] Ibid., at 155.   [42] *North Sea Continental Shelf* cases, para. 19.

GENERAL PRINCIPLES OF LAW

Article 38 ICJ Statute also allows the ICJ to have recourse to the general principles of law, recognized by civilized nations. The latter part of the sentence (addressing civilized nations) is a throwback to the early twentieth century, when it was still common to distinguish between civilized and not so civilized nations. Nowadays that distinction is seriously frowned on, although in the literature sometimes a similar distinction is made between liberal states (i.e. states that operate under the rule of law, are democratically organized, and respect human rights) and illiberal regimes.[43]

If treaties and custom are traceable to a state's express consent to be bound, this is less obvious with general principles. These are often viewed authoritatively as general notions that form part of the legal system and can be applied in a variety of settings, and it is this characteristic that distinguishes them from rules.[44] Thus the prohibition on murder is a rule which can only be applied if a murder occurs; it offers little help in cases of shoplifting or insider trading. And if it is established that a murder has taken place, the rule can be applied, and whatever consequences it spells out may take place.

By contrast, principles are far more open ended, and can be applied in a variety of settings. Thus the principle that 'no one shall benefit from their own wrong' can be applied in murder cases (the murderer shall not inherit his victim's fortune or be entitled to keep the victim's wallet), but also with respect to shoplifting or insider trading (the perpetrator shall not be allowed to keep the proceeds) and even to military invasions. Generally, then, principles do not immediately specify a particular outcome to a case, but may help to point the way. They are thereby eminently useful for filling possible gaps in the law.[45] If there is no applicable customary rule or treaty provision, then resort to a general principle of law can be helpful.

The notion of general principles includes such things as the notion of good faith, as well as generally accepted ideas that no one shall be judge in their own cause, that people shall not be sentenced twice for the same act, and that there shall be no crime without a law.[46] Those principles are not, in any direct sense, 'adopted' or 'legislated'; instead, they form part of most, perhaps all, legal systems of the world. It would, after all, be difficult to conceive of a legal order based on bad faith, or one where double jeopardy was the norm. Since these principles are not adopted or legislated, they cannot be traced back to expressions of consent by states, and it is probably for that reason that the ICJ has never decided a case solely and expressly on the basis of a general principle of law. Doing so would render it vulnerable to the critique that the state losing out never accepted the principle in question, and this is something the Court is no doubt keen to avoid.

---

[43] Among the most extreme is Fernando Tesón, *A Philosophy of International Law* (Boulder, CO: Westview, 1998). More sensibly, the great philosopher John Rawls has claimed that a distinction between liberal and illiberal can be made, but that the latter should not be ostracized: John Rawls, *The Law of Peoples* (Cambridge, MA: Harvard University Press, 1999).

[44] This owes much to Ronald Dworkin, *Taking Rights Seriously* (Cambridge, MA: Harvard University Press, 1978).

[45] On gaps, see Ulrich Fastenrath, *Lücken im Völkerrecht* (Berlin: Duncker & Humblot, 1990).

[46] The leading study is still Bin Cheng, *General Principles of Law as Applied by International Courts and Tribunals* (Cambridge University Press, 2006 [1953]).

That said, the ICJ sometimes uses notions that come very close, and gives these a prominent place. An example is the idea of equity, which often plays a role in maritime delimitation. Confronted with an island just off another state's coast (think of the British Channel Islands off the French coast), the Court can decide that the island should not be given full weight when delimiting the maritime boundary, for giving it full weight could be unfair; it would leave the coastal state with very small maritime zones.

General principles of law are sometimes conceptualized as a sort of 'custom lite', as rules which are perhaps a bit more 'necessary' (necessity, of course, is always in the eye of the beholder) than other rules, and for which therefore there would apply less strict demands on state practice and *opinio juris*.[47] This would make it possible to also hold actors other than states bound to such 'general principles', for it remains unclear to what extent customary international law (created as it is between states) can be considered binding on entities other than states. Still, conceiving of general principles as 'custom lite' is perhaps not advisable, partly because it undermines traditional custom (whose strength is precisely that it is embedded in social practices), and partly because it tends to circumvent consent, and experience suggests that actors are generally not very keen on adhering to rules to which they have not consented.

UNILATERAL DECLARATIONS

The World Court has on several occasions suggested that unilateral statements by states may well come to bind those states. It has done so if the statement is made in the context of long-standing negotiations,[48] but also in the absence of such a framework. Clearly, not all unilateral declarations will come to have binding effect. Some statements are best seen as declarations of fact or expressions of political opinions, such as an act of recognition. While a state that has formally recognized another state cannot later deny having done so, the recognition as such does not give rise to tangible rights or obligations.[49] Sometimes statements can also be little more than political outbursts; a presidential address labelling genocide in a neighbouring country as a 'disgrace' will not have legal effects, unless the labelling is accompanied by some kind of promise ('it is a disgrace, and we shall intervene to bring it to an end').

The leading cases on unilateral declarations are the *Nuclear Tests* cases.[50] After France had started nuclear testing in French Polynesia and some of the fall-out landed in Australia and New Zealand, the latter countries claimed that France had interfered with their sovereign right to be free from nuclear materials on their territories. They asked the Court to order France to stop testing, and this placed the Court in a difficult position, for while it

---

[47] Among the more sophisticated examples to date is Olivier de Schutter, 'Human Rights and the Rise of International Organisation: The Logic of Sliding Scales in the Law of International Responsibility', in Jan Wouters et al. (eds.), *Accountability for Human Rights Violations by International Organisations* (Antwerp: Intersentia, 2010), 51–128.

[48] *Legal Status of Eastern Greenland*, [1933] Publ. PCIJ, Series A/B, no. 53.

[49] The leading study is by Eric Suy, *Les actes unilateraux en droit international public* (Paris: LGDJ, 1962).

[50] There were two of these, almost identical: *Nuclear Tests (Australia v. France)*, (1974) ICJ Rep. 253, and *Nuclear Tests (New Zealand v. France)*, (1974) ICJ Rep. 457.

was no doubt the case that states did not have to accept nuclear fall-out, it was also true that there was no general rule against nuclear testing – and even if there had been a general rule, it was by no means certain that it would be binding on France.

Fortunately, several French government officials (including the president and members of the government) had made public declarations to the effect that if things went well, testing could soon come to an end. Thus, the President's Office had issued the statement that 'in view of the stage reached in carrying out the French nuclear defence programme France will be in a position to pass on to the stage of underground explosions as soon as the series of tests planned for this summer is completed'.[51] And France's Foreign Minister had told the UN General Assembly that 'We have now reached a stage in our nuclear technology that makes it possible for us to continue our programme by underground testing, and we have taken steps to do so as early as next year.'[52] The Court would come to interpret these statements as promises, as they seemed to indicate an intention to be bound on the part of France; France had thus promised to stop testing. Australia and New Zealand could thus rely on this promise, which effectively meant that the case no longer had an object.

The *Nuclear Tests* decision is vulnerable to legal criticism. Thus one may well wonder, as some have done, whether unilateral statements are a recognized mode of law-making to begin with.[53] Then again, if promises can be generally binding, there seems no reason to exclude promises made by states from creating obligations.[54] More serious, then, is the question whether France actually intended to be bound: many of its statements were in conditional form ('if p, then q'), rather than strict promises ('we shall q'). And the Court conveniently ignored that in addition to an order to stop France's testing, the applicants had also requested the Court to declare that testing nuclear weapons was incompatible with applicable rules of international law – by deciding the way it did, the Court never got around to deciding on the general legal issue.

But, in all likelihood, that was precisely what the Court was after; it could not say anything on the basis of general law, as there was arguably no general law. A finding that nuclear testing was prohibited would lack proper legal foundation and run the risk of being ignored by the major nuclear powers. Conversely, a finding that nuclear testing was perfectly legal would also lack a proper legal foundation,[55] and upset all non-nuclear powers. Hence the best thing the Court could do was to make sure that the case would go away without upsetting anyone, and this it brilliantly achieved.

---

[51] *Nuclear Tests* (Australia), para. 34.   [52] Ibid., para. 39.

[53] Alfred P. Rubin, 'The International Legal Effect of Unilateral Declarations', (1977) **71** *American Journal of International Law*, 1–30.

[54] Indeed, in 2006 the ILC issued a set of Guiding Principles on unilateral declarations in which it accepted that declarations 'publicly made and manifesting the will to be bound may have the effect of creating legal obligations.' See 'Guiding Principles Applicable to Unilateral Declarations of States Capable of Creating Legal Obligations', in (2006) *Yearbook of the International Law Commission*, vol. II, part 2, 159–66.

[55] Except perhaps by reliance on the *Lotus* doctrine; what is not prohibited (i.e. nuclear testing) is therefore permitted. Surely, though, this would be an unsatisfactory foundation for a judgment on such a politically sensitive matter, and it may also be contended that precisely in the law of armed conflict, the presumption is reversed, due to the so-called De Martens clause (this will be discussed in Chapter 11 below).

OTHER POSSIBLE SOURCES AND THE RENEWAL OF SOURCES DOCTRINE

The two major sources of international law – custom and treaty – both work on the assumption of regular, formalized contact between regular, formalized entities: states. In theory (often left implicit), the idea is that states act through formally designated organs and representatives and come to some form of agreement (either in writing or by means of their practices), and that their agreements should have legal effect. In such an idealized world, there would not be much need or much room for other sources. Moreover, such a model has the great benefit that it is nicely reconcilable with democratic theory; after all, states act through governments, and governments can be controlled by parliaments and, ultimately, by the electorate. Thus, in theory, the making of international law could be subjected to democratic scrutiny, and it is surely no coincidence that in most democratic states the conclusion of treaties is subject to parliamentary approval – in particular if those treaties can come to be directly effective in the domestic legal orders.[56] Otherwise, after all, a piece of domestic law could with impunity be set aside by the government by means of concluding a contradictory treaty.

The world of global governance, however, no longer fits this stylized model – and like all models, it never completely reflected reality anyway. Many dealings between states take place in other ways, for instance on the level of individual governmental departments (the ministry of trade, the ministry of health), lower governmental authorities (provinces, cities) or agencies on different functional levels (central banks, water boards).[57] Moreover, it is also clear that much authority is exercised by entities that are not related to states; this applies to large companies, but equally to non-governmental entities that may have no formal authority but whose authority rests on their expertise on a given topic, or on the fact that they are known as principled actors who may command some form of respect.[58] The big challenge for international lawyers is to come to terms with the activities of such actors and, somehow, to decide when their work gives rise to international law, and when it does not. Clearly Greenpeace, Human Rights Watch, Transparency International, the One World Trust and similar actors exercise quite a bit of influence and set standards of desirable behaviour. Clearly, the Basel Committee exercises a lot of influence on the financial sector, and sets standards as to desirable behaviour. And clearly, the practices of traders are of great influence in the commercial sector in the form of a so-called *lex mercatoria*, whether or not they are confirmed by states.

In addition, many intergovernmental organizations (from the UN and the World Bank to the African Union or the Inter-American Tropical Tuna Commission) set standards concerning what, to their minds, constitutes desirable action. While many of the instruments arising from international organizations are formally non-binding recommendations, in some cases it is nevertheless possible for international organizations to take binding

---

[56] This will be further discussed in Chapter 16 below.

[57] The leading study is Anne-Marie Slaughter, *A New World Order* (Princeton University Press, 2004).

[58] A useful framework is developed by political scientists Deborah D. Avant, Martha Finnemore and Susan K. Sell (eds.), *Who Governs the Globe?* (Cambridge University Press, 2010).

decisions and even to engage in law-making activities, depending on the powers that have been given to these organizations or have been appropriated by them.[59]

Governance, in short, no longer follows the classic modernist model but, in a useful phrase, has become 'network governance'.[60] How, then, to assess the products of these kinds of governance in legal terms? Many international lawyers have adopted the phrase 'soft law' to denominate normative utterances that do not neatly fit the listing of article 38 ICJ Statute, but the term 'soft law' is misleading and unhelpful. It is misleading to speak of soft law as this phrase suggests that law can come in varying degrees of 'bindingness'; as if a treaty, properly concluded between state representatives, were more binding than, say, standards developed by the Basel Committee. It is, moreover, unhelpful to refer to soft law, in that it still does not say anything about why some expressions come to be seen as law and therewith demand some kind of compliance (however soft perhaps), whereas others need not be so regarded.[61]

The heart of the problem is that international law lacks a proper criterion for distinguishing between law and non-law. Traditionally, following the statist model, this was hardly an issue; the only validity requirement that was needed was the consent of states, and this could be explicit (as with treaties) or tacit (with custom). But where political action, including governance, is no longer the sole prerogative of states and their duly authorized representatives, a different criterion of validity is required. Some have proposed a behavioural criterion:[62] normative statements are law when they are respected (when they have 'normative ripples') – but this lacks analytical rigour. After all, it is perfectly possible for a valid treaty provision to be ignored; surely, this cannot mean that the treaty provision is not law. Moreover, this would also entail that the law cannot be known in advance; one would have to see whether a rule was respected before it could be considered law, and this, ultimately, would be difficult to reconcile with the requirements of the rule of law. After all, people should know what the law says before they act, and not have to wait to find out whether their behaviour will, ultimately, be found illegal.[63]

Others have suggested that the question of whether something is law or not is really not all that relevant, and perhaps even smacks of a 'politics of definition';[64] whoever gets to define law (and legal validity) puts himself in a position of authority. What matters, on this view, is not so much whether something is 'law', but whether transgressions of norms

---

[59] Thus it is generally accepted that the EU can make law in the form of regulations, and that the UN Security Council can take binding administrative decisions. Whether the latter can also 'legislate' is debated, and debatable.

[60] For a useful analytical discussion on these two models, see Maarten A. Hajer, *Authoritative Governance: Policy-Making in the Age of Mediatization* (Oxford University Press, 2009).

[61] See generally Jan Klabbers, 'The Redundancy of Soft Law', (1996) 65 *Nordic Journal of International Law*, 167–82. Also worth considering is that, typically, domestic constitutions do not create procedures to be followed when making soft law: hence, typically, soft law can be made without democratic control.

[62] A monumental attempt is José E. Alvarez, *International Organizations as Law-Makers* (Oxford University Press, 2005).

[63] One influential formulation of the rule of law (without using the term) is Lon L. Fuller, *The Morality of Law*, rev. edn (New Haven, CT: Yale University Press, 1969).

[64] Boaventura de Sousa Santos, *Toward a New Legal Common Sense*, 2nd edn (London: Butterworths, 2002), at 91. Similarly, Anderson dismisses the quest for a validity requirement as 'liberal legalism': Gavin Anderson, *Constitutional Rights after Globalization* (Oxford: Hart, 2005), esp. at 40–4.

provoke some kind of community reaction. Again, then, the perspective becomes *ex post facto*. This may be useful for the social scientist looking to explain behaviour, but is less helpful to the lawyer, whose task is to facilitate, constrain and evaluate behaviour.

In this light, perhaps the better view (however 'legalistic' perhaps) is to propose a 'presumption of binding force'; normative utterances should be presumed to give rise to law, unless and until the opposite can somehow be proven.[65] Thus, banking rules adopted by the Basel Committee or fisheries standards set under the auspices of the Inter-American Tropical Tuna Commission should be considered as law, unless it can be demonstrated that no normative effects were intended, or that not all relevant stakeholders were involved in the process of setting the standards.

This presumptive thesis will have the benefit of being workable (in that one can hardly imagine a legal order working on the presumption that normative utterances have no legal significance unless otherwise proven) and of allowing for participation by the relevant actors, whether they are states or not. Additionally, and not unimportantly, it would seem that international courts have traditionally worked on the basis of this presumption, and continue to do so; they typically allow for commitments to be highly informal, and tend only to dismiss the legal force of instruments if those instruments are clearly not intended to give rise to rights or obligations. Thus, the Court of Justice of the European Union (CJEU) could dismiss a claim based on an agreement concluded between the EU's Commission and the US Department of Commerce and the United States Trade Representative on technical barriers to trade, since the agreement specified that the parties would implement it 'on a voluntary basis'. This, then, clearly rebuts the presumption that the agreement would give rise to rights and obligations, and the Court acted accordingly.[66] On the other hand, on this presumptive theory, the International Tribunal for the Law of the Sea (ITLOS) attached legally binding force to regulations adopted by the International Seabed Authority,[67] and likewise, a WTO panel had no problem accepting the binding force of standards developed under auspices of the Inter-American Tropical Tuna Commission: these tribunals presumed these regulations and standards to have legal effect, and found no evidence to rebut that presumption.[68]

FINAL REMARKS

Legal systems need rules that help them to identify which rules form part of that system and those which do not, but which might be useful social or ethical norms or otherwise

---

[65] See, in far greater detail, Jan Klabbers, 'Law-Making and Constitutionalism', in Jan Klabbers, Anne Peters, and Geir Ulfstein, *The Constitutionalization of International Law* (Oxford University Press, 2009), 81–124.

[66] Case C-233/02, *France* v. *Commission*, [2004] ECR I-2759. For further discussion and examples, see Jan Klabbers, 'International Courts and Informal International Law', in Joost Pauwelyn, Ramses A. Wessel, and Jan Wouters (eds.), *Informal International Lawmaking* (Oxford University Press, 2012), 219–40.

[67] *Responsibilities and Obligations of States Sponsoring Persons and Entities with Respect to Activities in the Area*, advisory opinion, ITLOS, 1 February 2011.

[68] *United States – Measures Concerning the Importation, Marketing and Sale of Tuna and Tuna Products*, WTO, DS381, panel report circulated 15 September 2011.

influence the behaviour of actors, albeit without the imprimatur of law. Traditionally, international lawyers specified that this rule was the consent of states; anything states consented to, as law, would become recognized as a source of international law. It could hardly be otherwise in a system of sovereign states – one cannot hold states bound against their will.

Yet the old system is losing vitality in the wake of the emergence of actors other than states and with 'network governance' complementing traditional diplomatic intercourse. It is no coincidence that international lawyers have, since the 1960s or thereabouts, started to reconsider sources doctrine, first in order to come to terms with the role of the UN General Assembly in world affairs,[69] and more recently to come to terms with the increasing number of possible instruments adopted and the apparent authority and influence of actors other than states.[70] There is even a semantic shift; the term 'law-making' has come to replace the more traditional term 'sources doctrine', presumably because 'law-making' carries more dynamic and politically astute overtones.[71] 'Sources' suggest that the law springs from somewhere, in much the same way as a river may have its source in a mountain stream; 'law-making', on the other hand, evokes a less pastoral image, and is far more suggestive of law being man-made and, possibly, coming in many different guises.

Be that as it may, sources doctrine cannot be done away with.[72] While the penumbra may be under discussion, sources doctrine (or law-making) at its core stands for the translation of political agreement between the relevant actors into legally enforceable rights and obligations. The next chapter will provide a closer look at what has arguably become the most relevant instrument through which international law is made: the treaty.

FURTHER READING

José E. Alvarez, *International Organizations as Law-Makers* (Oxford University Press, 2005)

Bin Cheng, *General Principles of Law as Applied by International Courts and Tribunals* (Cambridge University Press, 2006 [1953])

Alan Boyle and Christine Chinkin, *The Making of International Law* (Oxford University Press, 2007)

Jan Klabbers, Anne Peters, and Geir Ulfstein, *The Constitutionalization of International Law* (Oxford University Press, 2009)

Joost Pauwelijn, Ramses Wessel, and Jan Wouters (eds.), *Informal International Law* (Oxford University Press, 2012)

Anthea Roberts, 'Traditional and Modern Approaches to Customary International Law: A Reconciliation', (2001) **95** *American Journal of International Law*, 757–91

Anne-Marie Slaughter, *A New World Order* (Princeton University Press, 2004)

Eric Suy, *Les actes unilateraux en droit international public* (Paris: LGDJ, 1962)

---

[69] See e.g. Jorge Castaneda, *Legal Effects of United Nations Resolutions* (New York: Columbia University Press, 1969).

[70] G. J. H van Hoof, *Rethinking the Sources of International Law* (Deventer: Kluwer, 1983).

[71] G. M. Danilenko, *Law-making in the International Community* (Dordrecht: Martinus Nijhoff, 1994); Alan Boyle and Christine Chinkin, *The Making of International Law* (Oxford University Press, 2007).

[72] And, arguably, positivist approaches are experiencing something of a resurgence. See e.g. Jean d'Aspremont, *Formalism and the Sources of International Law* (Oxford University Press, 2011), and Jörg Kammerhofer, *Uncertainty in International Law* (London: Routledge, 2011).

3

The Law of Treaties

INTRODUCTION

Treaties have been concluded from the moment there were entities of whom it could be said that they engaged in international relations, and have been concluded in a variety of forms. It is well documented that the ancient Greek city states concluded treaties with each other on such things as access to courts or treatment of prisoners of war, while the Louvre museum in Paris has on display the so-called Amarna letters, pieces of correspondence (chiselled on stone tablets) from the fourteenth century BCE by the rulers of Syria and Palestine to pharaoh Amenophis IV (better known perhaps as Akhenaton, husband of Nefertiti).

It was quickly discovered that such agreements are best considered as somehow giving rise to binding obligations: *pacta sunt servanda*. Anything else would have been counter-productive; there is little point in concluding agreements if the premise is that no binding force will ensue. The rule *pacta sunt servanda* is thereby an indispensable rule, a rule of natural law in the sense that without it no system of law can be conceived.[1] Still, binding as treaties may be, for a long time it was thought expedient to underline the binding force of treaties by practical means. A particularly gruesome guarantee was the exchange of 'witnesses'; individuals were held hostage until such time as the treaty had been performed. More innocent was the practice of invoking the help of higher powers; for a long time, treaty-making was formalized by means of an oath.

Over time, a number of rules grew and crystallized concerning the making of treaties, their effects and application, their validity, and their termination. These rules formed the basis of the drafting of the 1969 VCLT which, on its entry into force in 1980, to a large extent reflected customary international law, albeit with the addition of a few salient novelties, such as the notion of *jus cogens* – peremptory norms from which no derogation was permitted. The Vienna Convention, therewith, has become the leading instrument on the law of treaties, even though it limits its scope to treaties concluded between states. Treaties concluded between international organizations (or between a state and an

---

[1] The classic rendition of this argument was Sir Gerald Fitzmaurice, 'Some Problems Regarding the Formal Sources of International Law', in F. M. van Asbeck et al. (eds.), *Symbolae Verzijl* (The Hague: Martinus Nijhoff, 1958), 153–76.

international organization) are governed by the terms of the 1986 Vienna Convention on the Law of Treaties with or between International Organizations. This latter instrument, while not in force, is itself thought largely to reflect customary international law, and follows the 1969 convention almost to the letter.

The drafters of the 1969 Vienna Convention made two important conceptual choices. One was almost natural; having been prepared within the International Law Commission (ILC) by four lawyers hailing from the United Kingdom and well versed in Anglo-Saxon contract law,[2] the Vienna Convention almost naturally came to reflect a contractual outlook rather than a more public-law-inspired outlook. This has important ramifications; some of its rules are very useful when treaties resemble contracts, but are less useful for those treaties that more closely resemble legislation – think of human rights treaties, or treaties for the protection of the natural environment.[3]

The second choice was probably equally vital; instead of focusing on the substance of treaties (the treaty as obligation), the drafters concentrated on the form of treaties (the treaty as instrument). This was, to some extent, a considered choice. One of the ambitions was to formalize rules on signature and ratification – it goes without saying, however, that one cannot sign or ratify an obligation; one can only sign or ratify the instrument that contains the obligation. An important consequence is that the Vienna Convention says little about the consequences of a breach of obligations; this was left to the law on state responsibility.

Most of the rules of the Vienna Convention were, or have become, customary international law. While the convention limits itself to treaties concluded between states, this does not mean that treaties with or between other entities end up in a legal vacuum; clearly, one can apply the rules of the Vienna Convention with relative ease to agreements with rebel movements or with multinational companies. It is also useful to realize that most of the rules are residual in nature; states are free to depart from them by mutual agreement, for example if they wish to create their own rules on interpretation or on how to amend their treaty. This is underlined by article 5 VCLT, leaving international organizations free to develop their own rules. But where states do not think of alternative rules, they can fall back on the Vienna Convention's rules. Still, as a result, it is sometimes difficult to argue that the Vienna Convention is 'violated'; it may simply be the case that the parties have contracted out of the Vienna Convention's rules.[4]

TWO BASIC PRINCIPLES

The law of treaties is based on two foundational principles. The first of these is a logical corollary to the concept of state sovereignty; treaties need to be based on the free consent of

---

[2] Special rapporteurs Brierly, Fitzmaurice, and Waldock were British; the fourth, Sir Hersch Lauterpacht, was not, but had spent some three decades in the United Kingdom by the time he was elected to the ILC.

[3] The distinction is explored by Bruno Simma, 'From Bilateralism to Community Interest in International Law', (1994/VI) 250 *Recueil des Cours*, 221–384; see also Matthew Craven, 'Legal Differentiation and the Concept of the Human Rights Treaty in International Law', (2000) 11 *European Journal of International Law*, 489–520.

[4] For much the same reason it may even be difficult to think of the Vienna Convention regime as embodying customary international law, but this is a jurisprudential point perhaps better left for a different occasion.

states as discussed in the previous chapter. This much was recognized by some of the earlier decisions of the PCIJ, in particular perhaps the *Lotus* case.[5]

The second foundational principle specifies, however, that the freedom of states is not unlimited; once consent to be bound has been expressed and the treaty has entered into force, the treaty shall be kept by the parties in good faith – *pacta sunt servanda*, codified in article 26 VCLT. The law no longer insists on exchanging witnesses or proclaiming oaths to underscore the binding force of treaties, but still, the message is clear: once in force, treaties are supposed to be performed. This too is said to follow from sovereignty, but stresses the responsible side of sovereignty, premised as it is on the thought that states know what they are getting themselves into when concluding treaties. Treaty-making, as the PCIJ held in the 1923 *Wimbledon* case, is an emanation of sovereignty, and the responsible sovereign sticks to his word.[6] Even contrary domestic law, as article 27 VCLT makes clear, is not a valid excuse for failing to perform a treaty obligation, at least not under international law. Thus the Vienna Convention proclaims its own priority over domestic law; confusingly though, domestic law may beg to differ and proclaim itself superior to international law – in such a case, no meta-rule is available to say which one is right.

THE CONCEPT OF TREATY

The Vienna Convention defines treaties as agreements in written form, concluded between states and governed by international law, whatever the number of instruments involved and whatever their particular designation. The latter point makes it clear that treaties can come under all sorts of names, ranging from the very solemn (covenant, charter), via the average (treaty, convention, pact, protocol) to the downright pedestrian (agreed minutes, exchange of notes, memorandum of agreement or understanding).[7] The designation, in other words, makes no legal difference, although the choice of a solemn label may indicate that such an agreement is deemed to be of great political significance. There is sometimes said to be one important exception, though; according to some, the choice for the label 'memorandum of understanding' (MoU) would signify an intention not to be legally bound, and thus be of great legal relevance. I will return to this below.

The definition's reference to the number of instruments merely means that treaties can come both in the form of a single instrument, and in the form of correspondence, in much the same way as offer and acceptance, taken together, can form a contract in most contract law systems. Typically, such correspondence will be conducted between a government and an embassy and, typically, this is seen as a fine practical way to conclude treaties of limited political significance.

The circumstance that treaties need to be in written form is peculiar to the Vienna Convention, and results from the Convention's above-mentioned focus on the form of treaties. Article 3 VCLT quickly adds, however, that this is without prejudice to the legal force of oral agreements. Likewise, the requirement that it must concern treaties concluded

---

[5] *SS Lotus*, [1927] Publ. PCIJ, Series A, no. 10.   [6] *SS Wimbledon*, [1923] Publ. PCIJ, Series A, no. 1.
[7] See generally Denys P. Myers, 'The Names and Scope of Treaties', (1957) 51 *American Journal of International Law*, 574–605.

between states results from the scope of the Vienna Convention; again, it is perfectly possible that instruments not concluded by states are none the less treaties – it is just that such treaties will not be governed by the Vienna Convention.

The only really relevant requirement, then, is that treaties are only treaties if governed by international law. Traditionally, this was useful for delimiting treaties from instruments between states governed by one or the other domestic legal system. One can imagine, for instance, that the lease of a building by the United Kingdom in Germany for the purpose of housing the UK embassy takes the form not of a treaty, but of a contract governed by German law. Hence such an agreement, despite being concluded between states, would fall outside the scope of the Vienna Convention.

In recent decades (since the 1950s, somewhat hesitantly),[8] the conviction has grown among international lawyers that the requirement that treaties be 'governed by international law' can also be used to separate treaties from non-legally binding instruments; the idea has become popular that in addition to treaties, states can also conclude other instruments: political agreements, morally binding agreements, or 'soft law' agreements. The idea has arisen that since somehow the intentions of states seem to be relevant, states can intend to submit their agreements either to the international legal order or to some other normative order, and it is here that the above-mentioned MoUs come in. Designating an agreement as an MoU, so the argument goes, would manifest a mutual intention not to be legally bound but, instead, to be bound merely on the political or moral level.[9]

While this argument possibly first gained serious popularity among practitioners in the UK Foreign and Commonwealth Office, it has been embraced by other foreign ministries as well. This should not come as a surprise; for government officials, it adds a useful tool to their toolbox, as the advantages of such MoUs would seem to include enhanced flexibility and, perhaps most importantly, the possibility of circumventing domestic parliamentary participation in the conclusion of treaties. After all, there are many national constitutions that insist that treaties should be subjected to parliamentary approval; but few constitutions say anything at all about politically or morally binding agreements such as, possibly, MoUs. Hence government officials gain considerable freedom of action this way.

As a legal matter, however, it is perhaps useful to spell out that the distinction between treaties and MoUs has not been approved by the ICJ. Quite the contrary: the relevant case law would seem to deny such a distinction. In *Aegean Sea Continental Shelf*, the ICJ saw no problem in treating a press communiqué as a binding treaty possibly conferring jurisdiction on the Court.[10] In *Qatar* v. *Bahrain*, in 1994, the Court even seemed flatly to refuse to

[8] The classic piece is J. E. S. Fawcett, 'The Legal Character of International Agreements', (1953) 30 *British Yearbook of International Law*, 381–400. Earlier arguments concerning gentlemen's agreements typically operated on the assumption that morally binding relations would be created between individuals (who were deemed to be gentlemen, after all), rather than between states.

[9] Anthony Aust, 'The Theory and Practice of Informal International Instruments', (1986) 35 *International and Comparative Law Quarterly*, 787–812; see also Anthony Aust, *Modern Treaty Law and Practice* (Cambridge University Press, 2000), Ch. 3.

[10] *Aegean Sea Continental Shelf* (Greece v. Turkey), jurisdiction, [1978] ICJ Rep. 3. See also, more recently, *Pulp Mills on the River Uruguay* (Argentina v. Uruguay), [2010] ICJ Rep. 14, paras. 138–140 (treating a press communiqué as a legally binding treaty).

acknowledge the possibility of there being any relevant alternative to the classic treaty format; the Court strongly suggested that when states enter into commitments, the only possible form for those commitments is the treaty, despite objections by Bahrain's Foreign Minister that he had never intended, when concluding an agreement with Qatar, actually to conclude a legally binding document.[11]

Still, as noted, the practice of many states suggests that even though courts might disagree and there are theoretical and philosophical problems with thinking in terms of intending to create moral or political obligations, states conclude many agreements which they hold to be creative not of legal obligations, but of more flexible political or moral obligations. This takes place in several ways. Sometimes it is thought that MoUs are the result of conscious policy choices. Thus, on this line of reasoning, states can choose whether to cast their agreement in treaty form (thus making it legally binding) or in MoU form (keeping it outside the realm of law altogether). They will do so, typically, on a cost–benefit analysis, weighing the benefits of flexibility against the costs of a less robust commitment.[12]

In other cases the non-binding claim may result from the circumstances of conclusion. Increasingly, agreements are concluded outside the regular diplomatic channels by civil servants and others who may not carry the required authorization ('full powers' – see below), meeting in informal meetings or networks. Sometimes also norms and standards may emerge from bodies which lack law-making powers. Thus civil servants from various departments may meet and agree on guidelines in their field; banking standards are set, to some extent, by networks of central bankers; likewise, the insurance industry has developed semi-binding standards to regulate the insurance sector, while accountancy standards emanate from the international accountancy industry.[13] All these norms and standards have in common that they are not unequivocally cast in traditional treaty form; all of them also have in common that they exercise normative guidance, and one way to explain this is to point out that this normative guidance is not legal in nature (precisely because of the disrespect for law-making formalities) and thus must stem from something else. Either way, though, it is undeniable that such 'twilight' norms are increasingly being created, precisely because of the flexibility they seemingly offer; they create commitments that are not unduly rigid, according to proponents.

THE CONCLUSION OF TREATIES

While treaties are concluded on behalf of states (or other entities), states are abstractions, and need people of flesh and blood to perform the legally relevant acts. This raises the

---

[11] *Maritime Delimitation and Territorial Questions between Qatar and Bahrain* (*Qatar* v. *Bahrain*), jurisdiction and admissibility, [1994] ICJ Rep. 112. For further discussion, see Jan Klabbers, *The Concept of Treaty in International Law* (The Hague: Kluwer, 1996).

[12] See e.g. Charles Lipson, 'Why are Some International Agreements Informal?', (1991) 45 *International Organization*, 495–538; Kal Raustiala, 'The Form and Substance of International Agreements', (2005) 99 *American Journal of International Law*, 581–614; Andrew T. Guzman, *How International Law Works: A Rational Choice Theory* (Oxford University Press, 2008).

[13] The most authoritative overview is Anne-Marie Slaughter, *A New World Order* (Princeton University Press, 2004).

question of who can perform such acts. Obviously, this prerogative rests with the head of state; he or she, after all, is traditionally thought to be the personification of the state. For practical reasons, it has also long been evident that heads of government, too, could conclude acts relating to the conclusion of treaties; in particular where the role of the head of state is largely a ceremonial function, as is the case in many monarchies, this is a useful addition.

Since the 1933 *Eastern Greenland* case it has been clear that international law also treats foreign ministers as having the power to bind their states. This was not immediately obvious; after all, historically foreign ministers have occupied a somewhat 'clerical' position, reflected for instance in the designation 'secretary of state'. Still, in *Eastern Greenland*, the PCIJ found that a verbal statement given by Norway's Foreign Minister Ihlén to Denmark, to the effect that Norway would not contest Danish sovereignty over Eastern Greenland, was binding on Norway; someone in his position, so the Court argued, could be relied on by others.[14] The Vienna Convention reflects all this in article 7, and adds that ambassadors and representatives at conferences or organizations also have powers to bind the state, albeit less far-reaching ones than heads of state and government and foreign ministers. Their powers are limited to negotiating with the states (or conferences or organizations) to which they are accredited; thus the US ambassador to Russia cannot rely on his position to negotiate a treaty with Mexico while holidaying in Acapulco.

Others are supposed to present so-called full powers, documents emanating from the competent domestic authorities (typically the foreign ministry), specifying that the person concerned is empowered by his home state to participate in various acts relating to the conclusion of treaties. Sometimes the full powers may include authority to sign; in other cases it may be limited to negotiating – this depends on the degree of confidence the local authorities have in the person concerned, and on what their domestic law says about treaty-making.

Still, as if to underline the flexibility of the law of treaties, full powers may also be dispensed with (article 8 VCLT). If it is clear that representatives of states A and B can trust each other in saying who they are, there is no particular need to present full powers. This typically plays a role in relations between neighbouring states; one can imagine that, say, high-ranking officials at the environment ministries of Finland and Sweden, meeting several times a year to discuss all sorts of things, will get to know each other (and their respective responsibilities and competences) really well. In such circumstances, it would be awkward to ask for full powers.

Confusingly, the two main ways of expressing consent to be bound by treaties are signature and ratification. This is confusing because the signature plays a double role; it can express consent to be bound in treaties that are considered of little political significance, but it is also often merely the first step towards ratification, signifying that agreement on a text is reached without expressing the state's consent to be bound.

It used to be the case that signature involved a promise to ratify. Centuries ago, when absolute monarchs still reigned widely, kings, princes, and emperors would send

---

[14] *Legal Status of Eastern Greenland*, [1933] Publ. PCIJ, Series A/B, no. 53.

plenipotentiaries abroad to negotiate treaties (the term 'full power' derives from 'plenipotentiary'), and would have to submit the resulting document to their rulers for approval. It was widely assumed, however, that plenipotentiaries would carefully consider the monarch's wishes while negotiating abroad – if only to prevent imprisonment or worse on return. As a result, there was a clear expectation that the monarch in question would accept the treaty, and consequently something of a duty to ratify existed, albeit one that could not always be realized.[15]

This has proved untenable with the rise of parliamentary democracy; a duty to ratify would be difficult to reconcile with democratic considerations. At the same time, an increasingly perceived need for flexibility and speed has diminished the attraction of ratification. In 1929 the PCIJ could still hold that if a treaty remained silent on how consent to be bound should be expressed, this would mean that ratification was required.[16] Nowadays, however, it would seem that the rule has been reversed; if a treaty remains silent, mere signature probably suffices. If and when a treaty provides for ratification, then this is 'of vital importance', to cite the ICJ;[17] but if no such provision is made, then the default rule would seem to be that signature suffices.

This does not mean that the state which signs can do as it pleases in the time before ratification or, as the case may be, between ratification and entry into force of a treaty. Article 18 VCLT (known as the 'interim obligation') suggests that such a state may not engage in behaviour which would 'defeat the object and purpose' of the treaty concerned. This does not amount to a full commitment just yet, for obviously ratification would then become a meaningless act. Moreover, the signatory is free at all times to make known an intention not to become a party (to 'unsign', as the US government put it when making it clear, in 2002, that it had no intention of ratifying the Statute of the ICC), but article 18 does create a good faith obligation not to undermine the treaty's *raison d'être*.

The interim obligation is one of those provisions that works well with contractual arrangements, but less well with law-making treaties. One can imagine that if state A purchases military equipment from state B, B should not do anything to destroy that equipment before the treaty enters into force; this would radically alter the balance of concessions underlying the arrangement. The same logic, however, cannot be applied to law-making treaties; signing a torture convention and quickly engaging in torture just before its entry into force cannot be said to change the balance of concessions; it cannot be said to 'defeat the object and purpose' of the treaty. If anything, it underlines that the treaty is still necessary.

It is no coincidence, then, that courts have redefined article 18 when it comes to law-making treaties, and have focused not so much on the effect of behaviour, but rather on whether the acts complained of manifested nasty intentions. A useful example is the *Opel Austria* decision of the EU's CFI (now known as its General Court) in 1998.[18] Confronted

---

[15] The seminal study is J. Mervyn Jones, *Full Powers and Ratification* (Cambridge University Press, 1946).

[16] *Territorial Jurisdiction of the International Commission of the River Oder*, [1929] Pub. PCIJ, Series A, no. 23.

[17] *Ambatielos (Greece v. United Kingdom)*, preliminary objections, [1952] ICJ Rep. 28, at 43.

[18] Case T-115/94, *Opel Austria GmbH v. Council*, [1997] ECR II-39.

with the question of whether the imposition of a tariff by the EU Council on a product coming from Austria just days before doing so would be prohibited by means of the European Economic Area (EEA) agreement, the Court focused not on whether this tariff would defeat the very *raison d'être* of the EEA agreement, but rather whether the Council had a good reason for imposing the tariff at that particular moment. The EEA agreement established economic ties between fifteen states, created institutional integration and would deeply intervene in the economies of the states concerned. In such a case it was pointless to ask whether a single tariff would 'defeat the object and purpose' of such an agreement, for the answer should be obvious; such a single act would never be able to meet that particular test.[19]

If states wish to apply their agreement immediately, even before domestic procedures have finished, they can do so: article 25 VCLT allows for the provisional application of treaties.[20] Note that this does not mean that the treaty enters into force quickly: it merely, but importantly, means that the treaty's regime will be applied prior to its entry into force. The institution of 'provisional application' raises some questions relating to the nature of the rights and obligations under treaties that are provisionally applied, and has been under discussion in the ILC since 2013. To date, special rapporteur Juan Manuel Gómez-Robledo has devoted four reports to the matter.[21] The matter has proved to be particularly difficult in investment arbitration, with several arbitrations under the Energy Charter Treaty revolving around the legal effects of this treaty during the period of provisional application.[22] Typically, provisional application is based on a provision in the treaty itself,[23] but sometimes also in a specific protocol.[24] Sometimes a state may also declare unilaterally that it shall apply the provisions of a treaty regime provisionally, pending entry into force.[25]

RESERVATIONS

Arguably the most important provisions of the Vienna Convention are those dealing with reservations to treaties – that is, unilateral acts by which individual states wish to modify or exclude part of a treaty.[26] This is relevant because it allows states to commit themselves at

---

[19] Jan Klabbers, 'How to Defeat the Object and Purpose of a Treaty: Toward Manifest Intent', (2001) 34 *Vanderbilt Journal of Transnational Law*, 283–331.

[20] See generally René Lefeber, 'The Provisional Application of Treaties', in Jan Klabbers and René Lefeber (eds.), *Essays on the Law of Treaties: A Collection of Essays in Honour of Bert Vierdag* (The Hague: Martinus Nijhoff, 1998), 81–96.

[21] A related phenomenon is 'anticipatory application' of treaties, in which domestic courts apply treaties (if circumstances allow) that will soon enter into force for the state concerned.

[22] This will be further discussed in Chapter 15 below.

[23] See, e.g., article 45 of the Energy Charter Treaty, or article 41 of the Straddling Fish Stocks Agreement (further discussed in Chapter 13 below).

[24] Thus the erstwhile General Agreement on Tariffs and Trade (GATT) was applied on the basis of a Protocol of Provisional Application between 1947 and 1995 – see also Chapter 15 below.

[25] Syria requested permission from the OPCW to do so pending entry into force of the Chemical Weapons Convention in 2013. If this looks virtuous, it should be remembered that not so long before, Syria had been widely accused of using chemical weapons against its own population, and may thus have had a good reason to generate some attractive publicity.

[26] Note that with bilateral treaties, reservations are rare: a proposed reservation is better regarded, in contractual terms, as a new offer.

no cost; it allows them to join regimes without having to make dramatic domestic policy changes if they do not want to, and is thus a tool for flexibility. In colloquial terms, it allows states to have their cake and eat it too.

It remains, to a large extent, up to the parties to a treaty to decide how to handle reservations. If reservations are deemed intolerable, then the states concerned can simply agree that no reservation is permitted.[27] States may also agree, when drafting a treaty, that reservations are allowed to some provisions but not to others.[28] In both cases the treaty text will govern the matter. Problems may arise, however, if the treaty remains silent on reservations, either because the negotiators never got round to addressing the issue or, more likely, because they were unable to agree on whether to allow them. In such cases, the question whether a reservation is permissible is referred to general international law, and in practice this means, nowadays, that the regime of the Vienna Convention is invoked.

Before the Second World War the general rule on reservations was, in essence, simple: states could make reservations to treaties, provided those reservations were accepted by all their treaty partners. This entailed a requirement of unanimity, and thereby handed a veto to all treaty partners. The rise of human rights treaties after the Second World War, however, suggested that there was a drawback to this way of doing things; it might result in states not joining regimes despite their participation being very useful. Things came to a head with the conclusion, in 1948, of the Genocide Convention. The General Assembly of the UN (sponsoring this convention) was uncertain how to deal with proposed reservations made by the USSR and its allies. These related to article IX of the convention, and concerned the possible role of the ICJ in enforcing it. Since these states had never recognized the jurisdiction of the ICJ, they were reluctant to grant the ICJ jurisdiction to enforce the Genocide Convention. This essentially resulted in two camps. One camp favoured the universality of the regime, and argued for inclusion of the USSR and its allies, even at the cost of diminishing the integrity of the regime. The other side, by contrast, claimed that integrity was of the utmost importance; it was no good having different rules for different parties.

The stalemate was broken by the ICJ, holding in a classic advisory opinion that unless the parties themselves agreed otherwise, reservations to treaties should be deemed permissible as long as they were consistent with the object and purpose of the treaty concerned. *In casu*, then, the outcome was easy to predict; the object and purpose of the Genocide Convention can plausibly be described as preventing and punishing the crime of genocide. While it might be useful to employ the ICJ for purposes of enforcement, this is not thought to be absolutely pivotal; there might be other ways to enforce the convention, and indeed, the convention had high expectations of the role of domestic courts.[29]

---

[27] An example is Article XXII of the Chemical Weapons Convention, which states: 'The Articles of this Convention shall not be subject to reservations.' Reservations to annexes to the Convention are in principle acceptable, however.

[28] A classic example, discussed by the ICJ in the *North Sea Continental Shelf* cases was article 12 of the 1958 Convention on the Continental Shelf, which read in relevant part that 'any state may make reservations to articles of the Convention other than to articles 1 to 3 inclusive'.

[29] *Reservations to the Convention on the Prevention and Punishment of the Crime of Genocide*, advisory opinion, [1951] ICJ Rep. 15.

It might be argued that the Court was, to some extent, seduced by the simplicity of the situation before it; its test of compatibility with a treaty's object and purpose might be more difficult to apply with treaties whose object and purpose could not so easily be reduced to a single desideratum.[30] Thus one would either have to accept that treaties might have multiple objects and purposes (what, for example, would be the object and purpose of the Treaty establishing the European Union (TEU)?), or accept that the identification of object and purpose would be possible only on an unhelpfully high level of abstraction. One might well suggest that the object and purpose of the ECHR is to protect human rights, but that does not offer much help when judging whether a reservation limiting, for example, the freedom of assembly of designated terrorist organizations would be justified.

None the less, the ruling of the ICJ found its way into the VCLT, but without the drafters being able to solve another problem inherent in the ICJ's approach. How does one determine whether a proposed reservation is compatible with the object and purpose of a treaty? One option is to have a unified, centralized system for doing so, but no such system exists. As a result, the determination is made by all treaty partners individually, with the obvious result that some can be vehemently opposed to a reservation which for others is perfectly acceptable. The Vienna Convention, in effect, sketches four different sorts of response in article 20.

The first of these is simply acceptance. A state can expressly accept a reservation made by another state. This is, however, rare. More common is the second position: a state remains silent. Perhaps it feels that it agrees with the reservation but sees no need to spell it out; or perhaps it never even gets around to properly investigating what it thinks of the proposed reservation. A small state such as Iceland may not have all that many people working at the treaty section of its foreign office and will have to prioritize its activities.[31] If a state remains silent, then article 20, paragraph 5 VCLT ascribes consent to its position; if a state does not react within twelve months, it is considered to have accepted the proposed reservation.

Things get decidedly more problematic with the third position: states may object to a reservation but without wishing to jeopardize their treaty relations with the reserving state. In such a case, and curiously enough, the VCLT determines that despite the objection, the relations between the two states will include the reservation.[32] In other words, the reserving state gets what it wants, despite the objections of its counterpart. Indeed, the reserving state gets what it wants no matter what the response is: explicit acceptance, silence or objection.

Only under the fourth position are things different, for here the reserving state does not get what it wants. If the treaty partner specifies that it does not accept a proposed reservation and does not wish to have treaty relations with the reserving state, only then does the reservation have no effect. Indeed, the entire treaty remains without effect between those two states, something which is only plausible on the presumption that the treaty can be carved up into so many bilateral sets (dyads) of rights and obligations. This is a fair

---

[30] See generally Jan Klabbers, 'Some Problems Regarding the Object and Purpose of Treaties', (1997) 8 *Finnish Yearbook of International Law*, 138–60.

[31] Standard international law joke (not terribly funny, but so be it): 'Have you heard that Iceland's legal department recently doubled in size?' 'Oh, has it?' 'Yes, from one to two lawyers.'

[32] This was confirmed in the *Anglo-French Continental Shelf Arbitration*, reported in (1979) 18 *International Legal Materials*, 397.

assumption with some treaties. For instance, a multilateral treaty on extradition typically creates sets of bilateral relations between states A and B, A and C, B and C, and so on. It is far more problematic, however, with treaties aiming to create a more or less unified regime; think, for instance, of human rights treaties, or treaties relating to the commons (such as the law of the sea). Here something gets lost if the treaty is considered as a bundle of bilateral relations; the prohibition on torture cannot meaningfully be cast in terms of relations between France and Belgium, France and Germany, Belgium and Germany; and rules on the protection of the marine environment likewise cannot always plausibly be recast as sets of bilateral rights and obligations. As a result, states are reluctant to indicate that they wish to have no relations at all with a reserving state, even if they feel strongly that a proposed reservation is highly problematic.

In short, the Vienna Convention's regime on reservations is said to be tilted in favour of the reserving state; the reserving state usually gets what it wants, so much so that many have claimed that allowing for reservations ends up 'ruining' treaty regimes.[33] It is no accident, then, that several attempts have been undertaken to shift the balance somewhat and ensure that the reserving state does not always get away with making pernicious reservations.

The most prominent of these attempts resides in the case law of the ECtHR (and earlier also the European Commission of Human Rights, now defunct). In a string of cases in the 1980s, the Court, following the Commission's lead, suggested that since it could make binding determinations on the scope of the rules of the European Convention, it followed logically that it could also make determinations concerning the permissibility of reservations. It did so most famously with regard to a Swiss reservation in *Belilos*, holding that the power to decide on reservations was inherent in its judicial function.[34] The UN Human Rights Committee (HRC), entrusted with the task of overseeing compliance of states with the International Covenant on Civil and Political Rights (ICCPR), thought that this was an extremely useful idea, and claimed much the same power for itself. In this case, however, states vehemently objected, precisely because the HRC performs no judicial function; it may make recommendations to states, but cannot make any binding determinations.

A second attempt to restore the balance between reserving states and their partners was pioneered by the Nordic states, which started to add to their objections the statement that the reserving state 'shall not benefit' from its reservation. In other words, the Nordic states aimed to rewrite the Vienna Convention's regime by specifying different legal consequences to be attached to objections to reservations. This, too, is problematic. For one thing, it is not up to the Nordic states to start to rewrite the Vienna Convention (although the Nordic initiative has been picked up more widely by other European states – the initiative has been endorsed, for example, by legal advisers of the member states of the Council of Europe); but, more fundamentally, it would also mean that reservations could be separated (severed) from the instrument of ratification to which they were

[33] See e.g. Liesbeth Lijnzaad, *Reservations to UN Human Rights Treaties: Ratify and Ruin?* (Dordrecht: Martinus Nijhoff, 1994).

[34] *Belilos* v. *Switzerland* (Application no. 10328/83), judgment of 29 April 1988, 88 *International Law Reports*, 635.

attached, the result being that a state would become bound without the reservation on which it insisted. And such a result is highly unlikely to be acceptable to sovereign states.[35]

A third attempt, then, has been to bring the matter to the attention of the ILC, the body responsible for drafting the Vienna Convention in the first place. The ILC appointed one of its members, Alain Pellet, as special rapporteur on reservations to multilateral treaties.[36] Pellet's general position is that it is undesirable to change the convention's regime on reservations; according to Pellet, the problem lies not so much in the Vienna Convention's rules, but in the absence of agreement among states. States make reservations, most probably, when they cannot get their way during the negotiations; they lose out, and the only way to protect themselves is by making reservations. To offer a simplistic example, if all states agreed on subordinating the rights of women to sharia law (or of having women's rights prevail over sharia law), Islamic states would feel no need to make reservations safeguarding the sharia from intervention in the form of treaties. Hence, the problem resides, predominantly, in the absence of agreement. Even then, it would be up to states themselves to create rules against reservations; as noted, nothing prevents states from prohibiting reservations to the treaty they are about to conclude, or to agree that reservations to some articles are prohibited. Often enough, though, states cannot even agree on such provisions, let alone on matters of substance. In short, reservations, so Pellet suggests, are the price to pay for living in a world of pluralism.

In the end the ILC, led by Pellet, drafted a Guide to Practice on reservations which, for the most part, follows the Vienna Convention's regime.[37] Still, on some points it provides clarification. Thus it describes compatibility with object and purpose in fairly detailed terms: 'A reservation is incompatible with the object and purpose of a treaty if it affects an essential element of the treaty that is necessary to its general tenour [sic], in such a way that the reservation impairs the *raison d'être* of the treaty.'[38] Perhaps most remarkably, though, the Guide to Practice adopts the position that an impermissible reservation is by definition invalid, independent from any objections.[39] In doing so, it effectively adopted the position upheld in the literature by some British scholars.[40]

---

[35] Jan Klabbers, 'Accepting the Unacceptable? A New Nordic Approach to Reservations to Multilateral Treaties', (2000) 69 *Nordic Journal of International Law*, 179–93. Goodman advocates severability and suggests that this should be no problem if states propose reservations as negotiating chips and do not mean them seriously at any rate; but there is no empirical evidence that states do not 'mean' their reservations. See Ryan Goodman, 'Human Rights Treaties, Invalid Reservations, and State Consent', (2002) 96 *American Journal of International Law*, 531–60.

[36] Pellet produced a series of reports, published in the *Yearbook of the International Law Commission*, starting in 1995.

[37] UN Doc. A/CN.4/L.779 of 19 May 2011.

[38] Ibid., point 3.1.5. It also provides further guidance on how to identify object and purpose in point 3.1.5.1.

[39] Ibid., points 4.5.1 and 4.5.2.

[40] These operated on the basis of the idea that where reservations are impermissible, they are by definition invalid, and acceptance or non-acceptance does not enter into the picture. While this approach is theoretically attractive, it is hard to see (and the Guide to Practice does not shed light on this) how impermissibility could be established except by gauging the reactions of treaty partners. The seminal article is D. W. Bowett, 'Reservations to Non-restricted Multilateral Treaties', (1976–77) 48 *British Yearbook of International Law*, 67–92.

If states could all agree on the wisdom of taking certain courses of action, or prohibiting others, there would be no need for reservations to begin with. But the fact of the matter is that states do not agree, and one of the ways to make cooperation and coexistence possible in the face of deep disagreement is the faculty of making reservations. There are other techniques available as well, perhaps the most prominent being the creation of differentiation within treaty regimes. This plays a prominent role within the EU (whose member states are free not to join the common currency, for example),[41] and has an increasingly prominent role in the field of international environmental law, where states accept 'common, but differentiated responsibilities'. Indeed, one of the reasons why reservations are virtually unknown to international environmental regimes resides precisely in the circumstance that such regimes create different obligations for different parties, all in a bid to accommodate political differences of opinion.

INTERPRETATION

Once a treaty enters into force, the struggle over what the treaty means only begins in earnest, and much of that struggle takes the shape of debates, currently, about the proper way of interpreting a text.[42] The very process of interpretation can roughly be seen as having three distinct aims. On one reading, interpretation is about discovering the objective meaning of a treaty; in a second variation, interpretation is not so much about discovering what a text means, but rather about what its drafters had in mind when drafting it. And on a third reading, interpretation is predominantly concerned with realizing the goals of the drafters.

These are subtle, but vital differences in emphasis, and it should not come as a surprise that they have given rise, traditionally, to three distinct methods of interpretation. The first is known as the textual approach, aiming to elucidate the objective meaning of the text. This comes with at least two disadvantages, however.[43] First, it would seem to presuppose that words have an inherent meaning of their own, whereas the philosophy of language suggests that this is not the case; an ashtray is not called 'ashtray' because it is inherently an ashtray, but rather because there exists a linguistic convention that 'ashtray' is the proper word to use when describing a receptacle for the leftovers and remnants of cigarettes. Moreover, it is by no means prohibited to use ashtrays for the deposit of, say, pieces of chewing gum, or orange peel, so we might as well have called it a 'gumtray' or a 'peeltray'.[44] Second, and of greater practical relevance, since treaties are often concluded against a background of profound disagreement (they are 'disagreement reduced to writing', in Allott's gloriously accurate phrase[45]), often enough the terminology used is

---

[41] See generally Filip Tuytschaever, *Differentiation in European Union Law* (Oxford: Hart, 1999).

[42] See generally Richard Gardiner, *Treaty Interpretation* (Oxford University Press, 2008).

[43] A possible further disadvantage is that a strict textual approach might be unnecessarily limiting. By way of example: the UN Charter clearly speaks of the UN Secretary General as a man. 'He shall be the chief administrative officer' (art. 97), and what matters is 'his opinion' (art. 99). Surely, though, this should not be taken as meaning that the position is open only to men.

[44] This is based, ever so loosely, on Ludwig Wittgenstein, *Philosophical Investigations*, trans. G. E. M. Anscombe (Oxford: Blackwell, 1953).

[45] Philip Allott, 'The Concept of International Law', (1999) 10 *European Journal of International Law*, 31–50.

not all that unequivocal. A wonderful example of what lawyers are keen to refer to as 'constructive ambiguity' is the phrase 'sustainable development', to be found in quite a few documents on environmental issues largely because no one has a clue as to its meaning, and everyone can thus read their own preferred meaning into the phrase.[46]

The second approach, focusing on the intent of the drafters, is referred to as the historical method. This comes with the great drawback that it leaves everything static; why should a treaty concluded in, say, 1928, be interpreted in 2018 as if it were still 1928? Another problem is that relying on legislative intent may rule out the political desires or ambitions of states that did not exist independently when the treaty was drafted, and thus had no influence over its meaning. By way of example, the UN currently counts 193 member states, only fifty-one of which participated in the drafting of the Charter; the rest, for the most part, did not exist as independent states in 1945, and thus had no input whatsoever. And third, the historical method presupposes both that historical records are available, and that everyone agrees on what qualifies as historical records (*travaux préparatoires*) to begin with. Yet both are problematic since for many treaties the negotiating records are not available; the treaties establishing the EU are a prominent case in point. And even if the actual record of negotiations were available, would one also have to look at domestic records, such as cabinet notes on the position to adopt when negotiating the treaty, or instructions to negotiators or statements of purpose planted in the press? In short, there would be no end to the things to take into account.[47]

Third, then, there is the teleological approach, concentrating not so much on the literal intentions of the drafters, but rather on what the drafters aimed to achieve. On this reading, it would arguably be acceptable to find that a treaty on extradition concluded in the 1930s also covered such things as computer crime, even though the computer had yet to be invented, or to interpret a human rights treaty as covering also, say, the right to a sexual identity, even though the text as such did not immediately support this. The drawback then will be obvious; an interpretation that is too teleological (from the Greek *telos*, goal) runs the risk of becoming unrecognizable to its parties, and may thereby lose some of its political legitimacy.

The Vienna Convention, in article 31, produces a sensible compromise between the textual and teleological approaches, and stipulates that treaties shall be interpreted in accordance with the ordinary meaning to be given to the words in their context and in the light of the treaty's object and purpose. The historical approach is explicitly relegated to secondary status, precisely because of the problems outlined above, and can only legitimately be used if the general rule leaves the meaning unclear, or leads to manifestly absurd results. Sensibly, interpretation should take into account the context of a treaty, which is further delimited as including subsequent practice of the parties and subsequent agreement between the parties.[48]

---

[46] See also Chapter 14 below.

[47] For a general discussion see Jan Klabbers, 'International Legal Histories: The Declining Importance of *Travaux Préparatoires* in Treaty Interpretation?', (2003) 50 *Netherlands International Law Review*, 267–88. Moreover, this would lead to parallel negotiations: negotiating not just the treaty text itself, but also negotiating the text that will become the negotiating record.

[48] This has been taken up by the ILC in 2008, with Georg Nolte first heading a study group and later acting as special rapporteur. See Georg Nolte (ed.), *Treaties and Subsequent Practice* (Oxford University Press, 2014). Note that subsequent practice is less relevant when it comes to interpreting judgments. As the ICJ

Still, not too much should be made of rules on interpretation.[49] Interpretation is to some extent an art rather than a science, and is most assuredly a political enterprise; typically, if not invariably, interpretation serves to bolster a conclusion reached on the basis of intuition or political preference, rather than as the mechanistic application of a set of rules to a set of facts in a political vacuum.[50] Indeed, one would need to interpret those facts themselves to begin with. Is a detonation by a suicide bomber in Israel an act of terror or an act of resistance? Is the dropping of bombs on someone else's territory an act of aggression, or lawful self-defence, or perhaps even carried out as an act of humanitarianism? Only against the background of such a determination can the relevant texts be meaningfully analysed and discussed.

That is not to say that interpretation is a free-for-all. Interpretation is probably best seen as a social practice, typically taking place between like-minded persons who have some idea of what counts as plausible and what counts as implausible. Without being conclusive, environmentalists probably have some reasonably specific ideas as to what people usually have in mind when talking of 'sustainable development', ideas they derive from earlier authoritative interpretations, from being familiar with discussion in policy circles, and so on. Typically, the human rights lawyer having to look at sustainable development will be unfamiliar with those things; she is not a part of the same 'interpretative community',[51] and is thus likely to entertain different ideas and, quite possibly, likely to seek refuge behind rules on interpretation, precisely because such rules seem to offer a unified method for looking at an unfamiliar text.

THE APPLICATION OF TREATIES

The Vienna Convention, probably rightly, treats interpretation as an aspect of the application of treaties, surrounding its provisions on interpretation (arts. 31–33) by articles dealing with application more strictly. Like all legal rules, treaties too can potentially have legal effects along four dimensions: space, time, persons, and subject matter. The convention is practically silent on subject matter, leaving states with great freedom to contract; they can conclude treaties on all sorts of topics, the one caveat being that they cannot conclude treaties which would conflict with *jus cogens* norms (more on this below).

As far as space goes, the Vienna Convention creates a presumption that treaties apply in principle to the entire territory of a state, unless the treaty provides otherwise. This is of

---

explained in 2013, what matters is what the Court actually decided, 'not what the parties subsequently believed it had decided.' *Request for Interpretation of the Judgment of 15 June 1962 in the Case Concerning the Temple of Preah Vihear* (Cambodia v. Thailand), [2013] ICJ Rep. 281, para. 75.

[49] See e.g. Jan Klabbers, 'On Rationalism in Politics: Interpretation of Treaties and the World Trade Organization', (2005) 74 *Nordic Journal of International Law*, 405–28.

[50] See also Ingo Venzke, *How Interpretation Makes International Law: On Semantic Change and Normative Twists* (Oxford University Press, 2012).

[51] This very useful notion was pioneered by literary theorist Stanley Fish. See for instance Stanley Fish, *Doing What Comes Naturally: Change, Rhetoric, and the Practice of Theory in Literary and Legal Studies* (Oxford: Clarendon Press, 1989). For an application to international law, see Ian Johnstone, *The Power of Deliberation: International Law, Politics and Organization* (Oxford University Press, 2011).

particular relevance to colonial states; treaties concluded by, say, the Netherlands will also apply to the Dutch Antilles (an island group in the Caribbean), unless the treaty says otherwise. Often enough treaties do so, of course; the EU treaties are a prominent example of a set of treaties explicitly not applicable to the Dutch Antilles. It was also on this basis that it was decided, in the 1980s, that the EU treaties would no longer apply to Greenland (which is, after all, part of Denmark).

The regime relating to the working of treaties over time is more complicated. The starting point is easy; there will be a presumption that treaties have no retroactive effect, unless the treaty provides otherwise. Things get more difficult, though, in the light of the circumstance that treaties can be concluded which affect each other's operation. For example, it is by no means impossible that an extradition treaty may collide with a human rights convention,[52] or that human rights law or environmental law may collide with trade law,[53] or that the obligations of a member state of the European Union under EU law may conflict with its obligations towards some other state under an air traffic agreement or an investment agreement.[54] Such a conflict of norms can be treated as a matter of successive treaties, and this is largely how the Vienna Convention approaches the matter, thereby focusing on the temporal aspect. Under article 30 VCLT, if the parties to all those treaties are identical, then the later in time (*lex posterior*) will prevail.[55]

Things get really difficult, though, when the parties are not identical (A has obligations towards B, and later, irreconcilable ones, towards C), because in such a case, one cannot simply apply a temporal provision. To stipulate that the later in time prevails would do an injustice to the first treaty partner (B),[56] whereas applying the earlier in time would be an injustice to C. While article 30(4) VCLT displays a small preference for the *lex posterior*, this only applies to relations between those states that are parties to the later in time. As a result, the consensus position is arguably what has become known as the 'principle of political decision': state A should choose whether to honour its commitments towards B or C, and compensate the 'losing' party.[57]

It would, hypothetically, have been possible to approach treaty conflict not as a temporal matter, but as one of hierarchy, or as a matter of substance. The hierarchy idea is embedded in article 103 of the UN Charter which, in turn, has been confirmed by article 30(1) VCLT: in the case of conflict between obligations arising under the UN Charter and those arising under any other agreement, obligations arising under the

[52] On treaty conflict generally, see Guyora Binder, *Treaty Conflict and Political Contradiction: The Dialectic of Duplicity* (New York: Praeger, 1988), and Seyed Ali Sadat-Akhavi, *Methods of Resolving Conflicts between Treaties* (Leiden: Martinus Nijhoff, 2003).

[53] The leading study is Joost Pauwelyn, *Conflict of Norms in International Law: How WTO Law Relates to Other Rules of International Law* (Cambridge University Press, 2003).

[54] See generally Jan Klabbers, *Treaty Conflict and the European Union* (Cambridge University Press, 2008).

[55] Not necessarily always though; much depends on what the treaties themselves stipulate, and it is not impossible that especially in procedural fields (extradition, recognition of judgments, criminal assistance, consular matters) existing rules continue to exist alongside later rules. Hence, a treaty conflict may occur with one and the same party.

[56] See already the dissent by Judge Van Eysinga in *Oscar Chinn*, [1934] Publ. PCIJ, Series A/B, no. 63.

[57] Possibly the first formulation hereof is Manfred Zuleeg, 'Vertragskonkurrenz im Völkerrecht. Teil I: Verträge zwischen souveränen Staaten', (1977) 20 *German Yearbook of International Law*, 246–76.

UN Charter shall prevail.[58] It is generally thought that this is what makes UN sanctions possible; member states cannot undermine sanctions by suggesting that they have other, contrary, treaty obligations towards the targeted state. To some extent, the idea of hierarchy is also honoured by paragraph 2 of article 30 VCLT. This paragraph recognizes the possibility that treaties may grant priority to other existing (or future) treaties. Often, article 351 of the Treaty on the Functioning of the European Union (TFEU) is cited as an example, and while this is understandable on the basis of its text, the CJEU has done its best to narrow down its practical scope, to such an extent that article 351 has been stripped of much of its content.[59]

Alternatively, treaty conflict can be approached as a matter of substantive (as opposed to temporal) conflict; in this case, the classic maxim *lex specialis derogat lex generalis* often warrants application. However, the VCLT did not opt for this possibility, if only because this would have been difficult to reconcile with the VCLT's approach to treaties as instruments rather than obligations. While judicial tribunals on occasion apply the *lex specialis* rule,[60] this is not unproblematic. How to determine which treaty is the special one, and which the general one? One can do this by looking at the topic, but also by looking at the number of parties involved – and the results may well be different. Moreover, the *lex specialis* rule may even lead to unpalatable results. Thus, by way of example, it might suggest that a bilateral extradition treaty prevails over a multilateral human rights treaty, and that is a conclusion many people would intuitively reject.

It would seem fair to say that the law of treaties does not offer a one-size-fits-all solution to address treaty conflict, and this is probably a good thing; any such solution would end up doing an injustice to at least one of the parties involved, and the absence of a general rule allows wise political decisions to be taken.[61] The one risk is that associated with fragmentation;[62] there is a danger that WTO panels will look first and foremost to WTO law, at the expense of other concerns; human rights lawyers might look first and foremost to human rights law; labour lawyers first and foremost to labour law, and so on. With this in mind, some have read a so-called 'principle of systemic integration' into the rules on interpretation; as interpretation ought to take place against the background of the relevant rules of international law, so tribunals and other bodies should do their best to take rules from other regimes into account.[63]

When it comes to the personal dimension of treaties, the Vienna Convention is fairly clear; treaties are only binding on the parties to them (as article 26 stipulates) and can create

---

[58] A useful analysis is Rain Liivoja, 'The Scope of the Supremacy Clause of the United Nations Charter', (2008) 57 *International and Comparative Law Quarterly*, 583–612.

[59] See generally Klabbers, *Treaty Conflict*.

[60] For an insightful discussion, see Anja Lindroos, 'Addressing Norm Conflicts in a Fragmented Legal System: The Doctrine of *Lex Specialis*', (2005) 74 *Nordic Journal of International Law*, 27–66.

[61] This is further elaborated in the excellent study by Surabhi Ranganathan, *Strategically Created Treaty Conflicts and the Politics of International Law* (Cambridge University Press, 2015).

[62] See generally Andreas Fischer-Lescano and Gunther Teubner, *Regime-Kollisionen: Zur Fragmentierung des globalen Rechts* (Frankfurt am Main: Suhrkamp, 2006).

[63] Most authoritatively Martti Koskenniemi, *Fragmentation of International Law: Difficulties Arising from the Diversification and Expansion of International Law. Report of the Study Group of the International Law Commission* (Helsinki: Erik Castrén Institute, 2007).

neither rights nor obligations for third parties without their consent. Articles 35 and 36 specify that with respect to obligations, such consent must be express and in writing; with rights, the regime is more relaxed, in that consent may also be expressed by acting in accordance with the right. Thus if an international waterway (such as the Suez Canal) is opened for ships of all nations, merely making use of the waterway is sufficient to express consent to having been granted a right.[64]

However, while the Vienna Convention is fairly clear, there is a grey area. There may be situations where the behaviour of two or more states creates a so-called objective regime, a regime that non-parties would be expected to respect, even without their consent. This is not a matter of rights or obligations per se; it rather concerns the creation of a regime or an entity.[65] A good example is the creation of the Antarctic regime in 1959. Twelve states with an interest in the Antarctic decided between themselves to set up a cooperative scheme in the area, and not to recognize anyone else's territorial claims.[66] This then raised the question of why third parties would be bound to respect this, and the most plausible answer, finding some support in the leading case of the ICJ on the objective existence of international organizations,[67] was that the states concerned created a regime for the greater good of mankind, and could thus legitimately expect others to honour their creation. Other examples may include nuclear-free zones, or the position of Berlin after the Second World War, or the maritime grave established after the sinking of the *MS Estonia* in 1994 between Finland, Sweden and Estonia.[68]

TREATY REVISION

While the term 'revision' in the context of changing treaties over time is loaded (it was the term used by Hitler's Germany in connection with the Versailles Treaty), it aptly collects various ways in which treaties may change over time. The most formal way of doing things is through amendment, and under the terminology of the Vienna Convention (article 40), amendment by definition involves all parties to the original treaty. If some parties only are concerned with attempts to revise a regime, the convention speaks of a modification between those parties *inter se*. Such modification is generally permitted as long as it does not deprive others of rights under the original version of the treaty concerned, and as long as it is compatible with the treaty's object and purpose.

Amendment (as well as modification) goes through different stages. A first is that an amendment must actually be proposed. Typically, a meeting of the parties is then convened,

---

[64] The seminal study is Christine Chinkin, *Third Parties in International Law* (Oxford University Press, 1993).

[65] The leading study is Eckart Klein, *Statusverträge im Völkerrecht* (Heidelberg: Springer, 1980).

[66] Bruno Simma, 'The Antarctic Treaty as a Treaty Providing for an "Objective Regime"', (1986) 19 *Cornell International Law Journal*, 189–209.

[67] *Reparation for Injuries Suffered in the Service of the United Nations*, advisory opinion, [1949] ICJ Rep. 174, esp. at 185 (the UN existed objectively because it was created by a large number of states, 'representing the vast majority of the members of the international community'). See also Chapter 5 below.

[68] On this last, see Marie Jacobsson and Jan Klabbers, 'Rest in Peace? New Developments Concerning the Wreck of the M/S Estonia', (2000) 69 *Nordic Journal of International Law*, 317–22.

at which the amendment may be adopted by majority rule, and, if so, the typical final stage is the ratification of the amendments adopted. Hence states are asked twice for their opinion, once while adopting the amendment, and once while deciding to approve ratification of the amendment.[69]

The main legal question that then arises is what happens if an amendment is indeed ratified by most parties, but not by all. Here, the situation differs from treaty to treaty, and it is the treaty concerned that controls the issue – the Vienna Convention's rules on the topic are residual. Some treaties specify that amendments only enter into force on unanimous acceptance. Others provide that amendments enter into force for all parties, even though acceptance by a majority suffices for the amendment to enter into force; this, for instance, is the case with the UN Charter.[70] And yet others suggest that amendments only enter into force for the states that accept them, with the result that those not accepting them remain bound by the old version of the treaty – this is also the default option of article 40(4) VCLT. Needless to say, this is not always very practicable, as it creates two regimes within one. Arguably a better option (though a bit drastic) is to provide that those who do not accept the amendment cease to be parties.

Most importantly, many treaties change over time by means of less formal methods. Treaties are interpreted on a daily basis, and those interpretations may be subject to change. Moreover, treaties may establish organs whose practice may shed light on the scope of the treaty's provisions and on how they are to be applied, and with treaties establishing international organizations there is the distinct possibility of treaty expansion by means of the so-called implied powers doctrine, which suggests that organizations may have competencies that are not explicitly written down in the constituent treaty (this is sometimes referred to as 'mission creep').[71] The net result is that even without formal amendment or modification, treaties may become unrecognizable: few people present at the creation of NATO in 1949 would recognize today's NATO as the organization they helped to create. To some extent this is a good thing, no doubt; it allows treaties to adapt themselves to changing circumstances. The drawback, however, is that informal change is not conducive to stability, and may trample on the procedural guarantees written into the treaty. It is no coincidence that the CJEU has cautioned against relying too much on informal change if this would circumvent existing procedures for amendment.[72]

Typically, amendments will not affect those who are not parties to begin with, and bilateral treaties, if amended, will remain bilateral. There are, however, exceptions possible: in 1957, under Council of Europe auspices, the European Convention on Extradition was concluded, a multilateral treaty amending a network of existing bilateral agreements. The operative provision is article 28(1), holding that the 1957 Convention shall 'supersede the provisions of any bilateral treaties, conventions or agreements governing extradition between any two Contracting Parties'.

---

[69] The leading study is Ralph Zacklin, *The Amendment of the Constitutive Instruments of the United Nations and Specialized Agencies* (Leiden: Brill, 2005 [1968]).

[70] See article 108 UN Charter, with the caveat that acceptance by the permanent members of the Security Council is required.

[71] See also Chapter 5 below.   [72] Case 43/75, *Defrenne* v. *Sabena*, [1976] ECR 455.

VALIDITY AND INVALIDITY

As alluded to before, the Vienna Convention's provisions on the factors that may invalidate a treaty relate to defects in a state's consent to be bound, with one arguable exception; the *jus cogens* provision of article 53 stipulates that a treaty can be void if there is a problem with its substance.[73] Articles 46 to 50 list factors that may invalidate a treaty, but need not do so per se; the parties can also agree that although something went wrong, they none the less want to hold on to their treaty, and do not want to see it invalidated. It is different with articles 51–53; if the circumstances mentioned there occur, the treaty will automatically be invalid. Here invalidity, in other words, operates by law.[74]

Things that may render a treaty invalid under articles 46 to 50 include such activities as bribery, errors in the conclusion of treaties (but not linguistic errors, understandably), negotiators acting outside their instructions and, possibly, although not mentioned explicitly, bad faith. An example of the latter, often mentioned, is how Hitler approached the infamous 1938 Munich agreement; as he never intended to keep his side of the deal, the agreement should not be considered valid.[75] Most of these grounds of invalidity have, so to speak, a high James Bond quality; they seem to occur more often to the scriptwriters of espionage movies than in real life.[76]

Still, article 46 is of some interest, as it provides that in certain specific instances a violation of domestic treaty-making rules may result in the invalidity of a treaty. Noteworthy is the negative formulation. Such a violation of domestic procedure 'may not be invoked', except in specific circumstances, if it concerns a rule of fundamental importance and if the violation was manifest. While the Vienna Convention does not define what it means by 'rule of fundamental importance', the notion is probably broader than only the rules laid down in domestic constitutions, for the good reason that not all states have constitutional provisions on treaty-making.[77] On the other hand, an instruction in an interdepartmental circular or memo probably will not qualify as 'of fundamental importance' for purposes of article 46.

The bigger cognitive problem, though, resides in the definition of 'manifest violation'; a violation is manifest if it is objectively evident that the treaty partner, acting in good faith, should have known that the state concerned was violating its own domestic provisions. This will be rare, for the good reason that those domestic provisions are rarely clear enough even to lawyers well versed in those domestic systems. By way of example, the US Constitution provides that treaties require the advice and consent of the Senate. It is also generally

---

[73] The leading monograph predates the Vienna Convention: Edoardo Vitta, *La validité des traits internationaux* (Leiden: Brill, 1940).

[74] For a general overview see Jan Klabbers, 'The Validity and Invalidity of Treaties', in Duncan Hollis (ed.), *The Oxford Guide to Treaties* (Oxford University Press, 2012), 551–75.

[75] See e.g. Paul Reuter, *Introduction au droit des traités*, 3rd edn, ed. Ph. Cahier (Paris: Presses Universitaires de France, 1995).

[76] Aust pointedly notes that in his thirty years with the British Foreign Office, he never came across a serious issue of invalidity. Aust, *Modern Treaty Law*, 252.

[77] The Netherlands deconstitutionalized its rules in the early 1990s and replaced them by means of a lower-ranking State Act. For discussion, see Jan Klabbers, 'The New Dutch Law on the Approval of Treaties', (1995) 44 *International and Comparative Law Quarterly*, 629–43.

accepted, however, that there are treaties which do not have to pass the Senate; the president can do some things on his own, and can also, on the basis of congressional authorization, conclude so-called executive agreements. The big debate, then, is on where the border between the two resides, and this is something that divides US constitutional lawyers.[78] And if those US specialists cannot be certain, how likely is it that their treaty partners can be certain? In short, it will rarely, if ever, be 'objectively manifest' to state A that state B is violating its own rules on treaty-making, and it is no coincidence that in the one case where this was argued before the ICJ, the ICJ flatly rejected the argument.[79]

Articles 51 and 52 deal with issues of somewhat 'higher' politics. The basic thought is that treaties procured on the basis of coercion are void. Article 51 specifies the fairly unlikely situation of coercion of state representatives (this is unlikely because there are many people involved in treaty-making – coercion of only one of them might not be enough), whereas article 52 addresses the more interesting scenario of coercion of the state. The standard example is, of course, a military invasion so as to procure consent. As coercion is difficult to reconcile with free consent, this is obviously problematic. The question at the Vienna Conference though was whether the notion of coercion would, or should, also cover instances of economic or political pressure. For instance, how does one rate the scenario in which state A threatens to withhold development aid unless state B opens its markets, accepts a new boundary, or joins a military alliance? And if one should feel that this is unpalatable, how about the situation where A threatens to withhold development aid unless B ratifies a human rights convention? In particular, the developing nations argued in Vienna that such cases also constituted coercion. However, article 52 is limited to military pressure, on the theory that if it were also to take economic or political pressure into account, there would be very few valid treaties left. To soften the blow, a declaration was attached to the Final Act of the Vienna Conference holding that exercising economic and political pressure was to be condemned, but without this leading to tangible legal consequences.

In this light, a curious case is formed by peace treaties, such as the Treaty of Versailles. After all, such treaties are almost by definition the result of coercion; with the Versailles Treaty, no negotiations with Germany ever took place. Instead, Germany was confronted with a fait accompli: either approve, or face the consequences, those consequences being military action. So how does international law handle this sort of situation? Clearly, to argue that peace treaties are invalid in view of the use of force involved would be unsatisfactory. Hence the one answer international lawyers usually come up with relates to the legality of the war that gave rise to the peace treaty; if force is used in violation of the UN Charter (i.e. if the aggressor wins), it is coercion and invalidity results; whereas if force is used in conformity with the UN Charter, the resulting peace treaty will not be regarded as having been concluded by means of coercion.

The most eye-catching provision on invalidity is without a doubt the *jus cogens* rule: a treaty concluded in violation of a 'peremptory norm' is void. Such peremptory norms are

---

[78] See e.g. Michael J. Glennon, *Constitutional Diplomacy* (Princeton University Press, 1990).
[79] *Land and Maritime Boundary between Cameroon and Nigeria (Cameroon v. Nigeria; Equatorial Guinea intervening),* [2002] ICJ Rep. 303.

norms that are accepted as such ('peremptory norms' meaning norms from which no derogation is permitted) by the international community of states as a whole. Obviously, then, this presents a fairly high hurdle for the creation of peremptory norms. Some norms are universally accepted – think of the sanctity of diplomatic mail, or the right of innocent passage in the law of the sea[80] – but are not seen as peremptory; states are free to 'contract out' of such norms. Other norms may have a greater chance of being regarded as peremptory (in particular human rights norms) but may not be accepted as peremptory by the international community of states as a whole. While the Western world treasures freedom of religion, for instance, in other parts of the world it is common to have state religions or even theocracies. While unanimous acceptance is not required, acceptance by a fairly large number of states seems necessary; moreover, those states should represent all major ethical traditions.

This finds its reason in the following idea. Certain types of behaviour go against the international *ordre public*; international law should not enforce what Alfred von Verdross, in a pioneering piece, referred to as 'forbidden treaties'.[81] In much the same way that domestic legal orders will refuse to enforce contracts to commit murder, so too international law should refuse to recognize certain treaties as going against public order. Not surprisingly, while the idea has a long tradition in natural law thinking, it resurfaced with the rise of Nazism in the 1930s, and, equally unsurprisingly, the norms typically regarded as falling within this category would include such norms as the prohibition of slavery and of genocide, as well as the prohibition of torture. Aggression, too, is often mentioned, but only on the understanding that this refers to use of force which does not serve a lawful purpose; use of force in self-defence is clearly tolerated, and the same argument can in certain circumstances be made with respect to the use of force to preserve self-determination or as an intervention for humanitarian purposes.[82]

As noted, *jus cogens* is a controversial category, mainly because the notion introduces a vertical element – a public law element – to the global legal order and might interfere with considerations of state sovereignty, perhaps even to the point of diluting the very system of international law.[83] It is also noteworthy that the ICJ, until recently, did its utmost to avoid even using the term, despite having several opportunities to do so.[84] Only in 2006, in the

---

[80] The latter is discussed in Chapter 13 below.

[81] Alfred von Verdross, 'Forbidden Treaties in International Law', (1937) 31 *American Journal of International Law*, 571–7.

[82] See e.g. Lauri Hannikainen, *Peremptory Norms (Jus Cogens) in International Law: Historical Development, Criteria, Present Status* (Helsinki: Finnish Lawyers' Publishing Company, 1988).

[83] The classic rendition is Prosper Weil, 'Towards Relative Normativity in International Law?', (1983) 77 *American Journal of International Law*, 413–42. In particular, the French government has not hesitated to voice its concerns: for the French position; see Olivier Deleau, 'Les positions francaises á la Conférence de Vienne sur le Droit des Traités', (1969) 15 *Annuaire Français de Droit International*, 7–23.

[84] In its *Nuclear Weapons* opinion, for instance, it designated certain principles of the law of armed conflict as 'intransgressible'; taken literally, that would suggest *jus cogens* status without using the words. See *Legality of the Threat or Use of Nuclear Weapons*, advisory opinion, [1996] ICJ Rep. 226, para. 79 (note that in para. 83, the Court explicitly stated that it did not wish to address the possible *jus cogens* character of the norms concerned).

Armed Activities case, did the Court for the first time apply the concept when it described genocide as being 'assuredly' prohibited as a matter of *jus cogens*.[85]

The precise consequences of the characterization of a norm as *jus cogens* remain, however, unclear. What is clear is that a treaty concluded in violation of such a norm will be void, in accordance with article 53 of the Vienna Convention;[86] hence, a treaty between Holland and Belgium to commit genocide will be invalid, and rightly so. But international law so far has not spelled out any other consequences. Some possible consequences might appear logical extensions of article 53; if a treaty violating *jus cogens* is void, then the same should apply to other legal instruments, such as Security Council resolutions.[87] But that said, the Court has consistently refused to base its jurisdiction on a *jus cogens* norm, maintaining a clear distinction between the legal character of a rule and the Court's own jurisdiction.[88] Moreover, the Court has been unwilling to allow *jus cogens* norms to take priority over jurisdictional immunities.[89]

TERMINATION AND SUSPENSION

While an invalid treaty is one that has no legal effects whatsoever, a terminated treaty is one whose legal effects have come to an end. This may happen through various means. Obviously, the easiest way to accomplish this is when the parties agree that their treaty must come to an end; sometimes, however, a treaty may also terminate by the operation of law. Suspension is a different phenomenon, in that it does not signify the termination of a particular instrument, but rather the temporary deactivation of a treaty's regime. However, the modalities are much the same as for termination.

To achieve termination by agreement, states have various techniques at their disposal. They can agree beforehand that the treaty will be of limited duration, and include an expiry clause. Or they can provide (but this is rare) that the treaty will be terminated once the common object has been achieved. This may work with respect to, say, a project between two states to build a dam in a boundary river, but only if the treaty to build the dam is replaced by a treaty to manage and maintain it. Even strictly contractual agreements hardly come to an end upon performance. As a theoretical matter it is awkward to insist that a treaty for exchange of territories stops existing once those territories have

---

[85] *Armed Activities on the Territory of the Congo (New Application: 2002) (Democratic Republic of Congo v. Rwanda)*, jurisdiction and admissibility, [2006] ICJ Rep. 6, para. 64.

[86] And, importantly, assuming that the norm can also be applied to states that are not parties to the Vienna Convention or which, like the French, have more or less persistently objected to the very category of *jus cogens*.

[87] This came before the ICJ in 1993, when Bosnia suggested that an arms embargo imposed by the Security Council made it impossible for Bosnia to defend itself against the far better armed Serbs, and therewith contributed to genocide. *Application of the Convention on the Prevention and Punishment of the Crime of Genocide (Bosnia and Herzegovina v. Serbia and Montenegro)*, further requests for the indication of provisional measures, [1993] ICJ Rep. 325.

[88] See e.g. *Armed Activities*, para. 64. By contrast, the Court of First instance of the EC (now known as its General Court) has based certain powers of judicial review on the legal character of the norms concerned. See e.g. Case T-315/01, *Kadi v. Council*, [2005] ECR II-3649.

[89] *Jurisdictional Immunities of the State (Germany v. Italy; Greece Intervening)*, [2012] ICJ Rep. 99.

been exchanged; it is more likely to lead a dormant existence, but can be referred back to if and when problems arise.[90]

Other techniques include the replacement of an old treaty by a newer one between the same parties; the old one must be considered terminated. Article 59 of the Vienna Convention also suggests that an older one can be terminated by a new agreement to terminate, regardless of whether the new one has provisions to replace the old one. And there is even the possibility of desuetude (disuse); here, too, however, consent plays an important role. A treaty that has not been applied by parties for a long time because none of them wants to apply it may be considered to have fallen into disuse – a possible example is the 1907 Hague Convention Relative to the Opening of Hostilities, which insists on a declaration of war as a condition for the legality of war. But where a treaty is not applied simply because the circumstances for its application do not arise, the desuetude conclusion cannot nearly as easily be drawn. By way of example, an extradition treaty needs to be activated by means of extradition requests; those only make sense if criminal suspects are presumed to be in the country. If no such situation arises, there is no occasion to apply the extradition agreement, but this says nothing about whether the parties wish to get rid of the agreement.

Things may be different when the parties cannot agree on the desirability of terminating a particular treaty. In such a case, the Vienna Convention offers three possible justifications for unilateral termination, provided (at least following the letter) that certain procedural requirements are met which in practice would imply termination by agreement.[91] The first of those is the classic contractual idea that violation by A means that B may be released from its obligations (*inadimplenti non est adimplendum*),[92] but with a twist: only a 'material breach' may be invoked.[93] That provokes the question of how article 60 defines 'material breach', and it is here that doubts creep in, for article 60 speaks of violations of provisions essential for the accomplishment of the treaty's object and purpose. Hence it is not the gravity of the breach that counts, but the importance of the provision breached. While one can sympathize with the thought behind this, it has proved unworkable in practice. Typically, when tribunals discuss article 60, they conceptualize it as referring to grave breaches, rather than breaches of important provisions.[94]

An interesting aspect of article 60 is that it recognizes that some multilateral treaties have a public law character, and cannot be reduced to bilateral sets of rights and obligations. It does so by granting all parties to the treaty the right to act in response to a material breach. Whereas traditionally only the directly injured party could respond, under paragraph 2 the

---

[90] Such treaties are sometimes referred to as dispositive, suggesting that no further relations are needed. This would seem to be misleading.

[91] The classic study is Arie E. David, *The Strategy of Treaty Termination: Lawful Breaches and Retaliation* (New Haven, CT: Yale University Press, 1975).

[92] It was embraced with great enthusiasm by Anzilotti J in his dissent in the *Meuse* case: the principle was 'so just, so equitable, so universally recognized, that it must be applied in international relations also'. *Diversion of Water from the Meuse*, [1937] Publ. PCIJ, Series A/B, no. 70, at 50.

[93] See generally Shabtai Rosenne, *Breach of Treaty* (Cambridge University Press, 1985).

[94] As was anticipated by Bruno Simma, 'Reflections on Article 60 of the Vienna Convention on the Law of Treaties and its Background in General International Law', (1970) 20 *Österreichische Zeitschrift für öffentliches Recht und Völkerrecht*, 5–83.

other parties (not directly injured, so not the victims of invasion, or recipients of trade embargoes or any such action) may unanimously decide to terminate the treaty or suspend its operation in response to the breach.[95]

At first sight, article 60, paragraph 5 also takes the special position of multilateral treaties into account. It suggests that if A violates a human rights treaty, this violation does not give B or C a right to terminate the treaty, and rightly so; the cure would be worse than the disease. However, by limiting itself to treaties of a humanitarian character, it ends up suggesting that with other 'law-making' treaties, this logic does not apply. Surely, a decision by state A to dump nuclear waste in the Atlantic should not grant states B and C an excuse to terminate an environmental agreement; a decision by A to produce chemical weapons should not provide B and C with an argument to terminate their commitment to the Chemical Weapons Convention, for much the same reasons as treaties of a humanitarian character are singled out. These treaties aspire to give effect to a perceived community interest, and cannot usually be reduced to bilateral sets of rights and obligations.

Article 61 can be discussed with far greater brevity; it allows for termination on a supervening impossibility of performance, and therewith performs much the same function as *force majeure* or Act of God clauses may do in contract law; if due to natural circumstances it becomes impossible to perform a treaty, then it might be wiser to consider it as terminated, or at least consider its regime as suspended. This might apply, for instance, to a treaty utilizing a boundary river for irrigation purposes; if the river runs dry, there is not much left to apply, provided of course that the river's drought was not directly caused by one of the parties. If state A secretly pumps the river dry, or diverts its course upstream, article 61 does not apply. That said, with the influence man-made activities have on the weather, it is not entirely clear where to draw the line between natural and man-made occurrences; if a dry river can be attributed to global warming, is it still a natural occurrence?[96]

The most spectacular way of terminating a treaty is by invoking a fundamental change of circumstances, the popular plaything of *Realpolitiker* from Bismarck to de Gaulle, and beyond.[97] The great attraction of this doctrine (also known as the *rebus sic stantibus* doctrine) is that it suggests that treaties are only binding as long as they are convenient; once they become inconvenient (rationalized as the result of changing circumstances) it is permissible to terminate them. Hence, *pacta* may well be *servanda*, but only up to a point. While it is no doubt prudent for international law to possess such a safety valve in case circumstances do indeed change fundamentally, it is no coincidence that courts have always been reluctant to apply it to the case before them. After all, doing so might open up Pandora's box; once article 62, containing the rule that treaties can be terminated upon a fundamental change of circumstances, has been applied, more and more cases may follow.

---

[95] The seminal article is D. H. N. Hutchinson, 'Solidarity and Breaches of Multilateral Treaties', (1988) 59 *British Yearbook of International Law*, 151–215.

[96] Probably not, but then the problem of attribution arises in another guise; who can be blamed for global warming?

[97] See already Erich Kaufmann, *Das Wesen des Völkerrechts und die Clausula Rebus Sic Stantibus* (Tübingen, 1911).

The ICJ, for instance, has been very reluctant, typically applying the criteria laid down by article 62 for successful invocation with great restraint. Those criteria boil down to three important elements. First, the circumstances concerned must have been an essential basis for the parties' consent; second, the change must have been unforeseen; and, third, the change must 'radically transform the extent of the obligations still to be performed under the treaty'. Those are awkward formulations, precisely because so much is at stake.

When Iceland in the early 1970s argued that revolutionary changes in fisheries technology released it from fisheries agreements with the United Kingdom and Germany, the ICJ did not quite agree. Without pronouncing itself on the merits, it strongly stated that the *rebus* doctrine could not, on its own, affect jurisdictional provisions in a treaty.[98] More importantly, when Hungary argued that a fundamental change in environmental awareness, in conjunction with the fall of communism, ought to release it from a treaty with Slovakia to build a possibly harmful dam in the Danube river, the Court suggested that the changes had not been entirely unforeseeable, and did not affect the basis on which the treaty had been concluded. Moreover, the Court added that the bilateral treaty at issue contained extremely useful revision provisions; where such provisions exist, surely catering to changed circumstances should not pose any problems.[99]

There is one case where a court actually upheld an appeal to the *rebus* doctrine: the decision of the CJEU in the *Racke* case, in 1998. Here, the issue was whether the EU had lawfully suspended a free trade agreement with Yugoslavia upon the outbreak of civil war in that country. The Court found that indeed the EU had acted lawfully, for the circumstances underlying the treaty had been peace and stable state institutions. Neither of these applied any longer, so it was no wonder that the EU no longer saw 'the point' of the treaty.[100]

That decision is vulnerable to criticism, as it casts its net far too wide; well-nigh all treaties presuppose peace and stable state institutions, with the obvious exception of treaties on the law of armed conflict (these serve little function in peacetime situations). Moreover, it is somewhat incongruous to note that where the Vienna Convention explicitly excluded armed conflict from its scope, the Court re-introduces it through the *rebus* doctrine.[101] Still, fortuitously, Pandora's box has not yet been opened, perhaps due to the self-restraint of politicians or, more probably perhaps, to the circumstance that few international lawyers are even aware of the *Racke* decision. And those who report it tend to downplay its significance.[102]

---

[98] *Fisheries Jurisdiction (UK v. Iceland)*, jurisdiction, [1973] ICJ Rep. 3, esp. paras. 40–3. The Court repeated the same in the parallel case between Germany and Iceland, [1973] ICJ Rep. 49, paras. 40–3.

[99] *Gabcikovo-Nagymaros Project* (Hungary/Slovakia), [1997] ICJ Rep. 7, para. 104.

[100] Case C-162/96, *A. Racke GmbH & Co. v. Hauptzollamt Mainz*, [1998] ECR I-3655, esp. para. 57.

[101] Article 73 VCLT holds, *inter alia*, that the VCLT is without prejudice to questions arising from the outbreak of hostilities.

[102] Aust, *Modern Treaty Law*, at 241–2, suggests that the ECJ approached the matter as one of judicial review and found, on a cursory review, that the EU Council had not engaged in a manifest violation of any rule of law.

FINAL REMARKS

While treaties are usually portrayed, in traditional fashion, as stemming from a 'meeting of the minds', usually incorporating a quid pro quo, it is probably more useful to think of treaties as, in Philip Allott's phrase, 'disagreement reduced to writing'. Thus considered, all of a sudden the existence of reservations makes sense; thus considered, it makes sense that states are arguing loudly not only over what should go into their treaties, but also on how those treaties should be interpreted, and by whom. And thus considered, it makes sense to have rules stipulating that a fundamental change of circumstances may release states from their treaty obligations. The classic idea that politics only plays a role during negotiations, and gives way to law once a treaty has been concluded, is patently false.

Some ironic testimony to this is the circumstance that the elaborate procedural provisions of the Vienna Convention (articles 65 and 66) to settle cases where states unilaterally invoke grounds of invalidity or termination are among the deadest letters ever written. The procedures of articles 65 and 66 have never been used and, in all likelihood, never will be used, precisely because they aim to capture things which cannot be captured. States will not invoke invalidity out of concern for the other state's domestic treaty-making procedures under article 46, as the procedural provisions presuppose; instead, they will (if at all) invoke invalidity because they are unhappy with a treaty, and if their counterpart's treaty-making procedure offers a legal way out, then so be it. The Vienna Convention's drafters intuitively sensed as much; they tried to make sure, by means of article 42 of the convention (allowing invalidity or termination only on the grounds mentioned in the convention, thus trying to establish a closed system), that no impertinent arguments could creep in.[103] But alas, no such luck; politics can be steered and guided, but never tamed.

In fact, steering the political process is a continuous challenge, and it should not come as a surprise that since the VCLT entered into force in 1980, the ILC has been asked to have a fresh look at several of the VCLT's regimes, all of them with strong political overtones. The ILC has had a fresh look at reservations, resulting in the Guide to Practice adopted in 2011, is currently looking at provisional application and at the effects of the passage of time on the rules of interpretation, and may soon start looking at *jus cogens*. All this is testimony to the circumstance that this seemingly dry and technical part of international law is actually the playground of politics.

FURTHER READING

Olivier Corten and Pierre Klein (eds.), *The Vienna Conventions on the Law of Treaties: A Commentary* (Oxford University Press, 2011)

Arie E. David, *The Strategy of Treaty Termination: Lawful Breaches and Retaliations* (New Haven, CT: Yale University Press, 1975)

Duncan Hollis (ed.), *The Oxford Guide to Treaties* (Oxford University Press, 2012)

---

[103] Jan Klabbers, 'Reluctant Grundnormen: Articles 31(3)(c) and 42 of the Vienna Convention on the Law of Treaties and the Fragmentation of International Law', in Matthew Craven, Malgosia Fitzmaurice, and Maria Vogiatzi (eds.), *Time, History and International Law* (Leiden: Martinus Nijhoff, 2007), 141–61.

Jan Klabbers, *The Concept of Treaty in International Law* (The Hague: Kluwer, 1996)

Liesbeth Lijnzaad, *Reservations to UN Human Rights Treaties: Ratify and Ruin?* (Dordrecht: Martinus Nijhoff, 1994)

A. D. McNair, *The Law of Treaties* (Oxford: Clarendon Press, 1961)

Surabhi Ranganathan, *Strategically Created Treaty Conflicts and the Politics of International Law* (Cambridge University Press, 2015)

Edoardo Vitta, *La validité des traités internationaux* (Leiden: Brill, 1940)

4

The Subjects of International Law

INTRODUCTION

The laws of China, as commonly understood, apply to all persons and legal entities in China; it is often said that these form the subjects of Chinese law. By the same token, the question arises to whom, or to which entities, international law applies. What, in other words, are the subjects of international law? This is a topic of great controversy, partly because of the relevance of subjects doctrine. Rights and obligations must apply to someone – it is through subjects doctrine that these rights and obligations under international law are allocated.[1]

The main subjects of international law are states, and for centuries states were held to be the only subjects of international law, save perhaps for a few oddities (the Holy See, the Maltese Order) which would be considered subjects of international law for historic reasons and, it seems, because states generally treated them as subjects. This focus on states still applies, and makes for difficult discussions on the legal standing of other entities. It is now generally recognized that entities such as intergovernmental organizations (e.g. the UN, the EU, the IMF, or the WTO) are to be regarded as subjects of international law – and this was ultimately confirmed by the ICJ in the 1949 *Reparation* opinion,[2] holding that the UN had to be considered as such. Yet this was not always the case; early observers made great efforts to come to terms with the status of the League of Nations,[3] some treating the League as an oddity similar to the Holy See.[4]

The global legal order, by now, clearly counts states and international organizations among its subjects, but the question arises whether other entities are so recognized as well. This is a tricky question, as international law has no formal criteria for admission to 'subject

---

[1] See generally Jan Klabbers, '(I Can't Get No) Recognition: Subjects Doctrine and the Emergence of Non-state Actors', in Jarna Petman and Jan Klabbers (eds.), *Nordic Cosmopolitanism: Essays in International Law for Martti Koskenniemi* (Leiden: Martinus Nijhoff, 2003), 351–69.

[2] This will be further discussed below.

[3] See e.g. Lassa Oppenheim, 'Le caractère essentiel de la Société des Nations', (1919) 23 *Revue Générale de Droit International Public*, 234–44; John Fischer Williams, 'The Status of the League of Nations in International Law', in John Fischer Williams, *Chapters on Current International Law and the Law of Nations* (London: Longman, Green & Co., 1929), 477–500.

[4] J. H. W. Verzijl, *International Law in Historical Perspective*, Vol. II: *International Persons* (Leiden: Sijthoff, 1969), at 303–5.

status' or, what in practice amounts to much the same, for international legal personality. As we shall see, even with states themselves, the picture is not entirely clear; it is not always clear when and how states come into existence, for the purposes of international law.

As a practical checklist, one may ask oneself whether an entity enjoys direct rights or obligations under international law. If so, it is probably safe to say it ranks as a subject of international law, at least to the extent (and here some circularity sets in) of those same rights or obligations. From this perspective, there is little doubt that individuals are usually seen as subjects of international law (and not as mere objects for international legal regulation), as individuals may enjoy rights directly under international law, in particular in the form of human rights standards, but also under international humanitarian law (the law applicable on and around the battlefield) or under refugee law. It is also increasingly recognized that individuals may owe obligations directly under international law; the emergence of international criminal law in particular suggests as much. The position of the individual in international law will be discussed in more detail in Chapter 6 below.

But individuals do not always act alone; they also tend to organize themselves in all sorts of political, social or economic groups. Oppressed individuals within a state may come to form a national liberation movement; in recent history, the Palestine Liberation Organization (PLO) is among the best known. Individuals who share an ethnic or linguistic background may come to be seen – or regard themselves – as minorities, national minorities, as a people, or an indigenous people. Individuals may band together and form companies; if successful, these companies may operate globally, as is the case with Microsoft, Apple or Shell. People live together in political communities other than states: in particular cities are starting to play a role in global politics, and thus sooner or later need to be accommodated in the system of international law.[5] And individuals may be driven by ideals and band together to rally for a political cause: to promote environmental protection, for instance, or to draw attention to human rights abuses. In those cases, they may form a so-called non-governmental organization (NGO), with leading examples including Greenpeace and Amnesty International.

All of these clearly play a role in global politics, as the chapter on law-making above has already indicated; one cannot meaningfully think about global affairs without acknowledging the important role played by Amnesty International when it comes to human rights, or think about Iraq without acknowledging the position of the Kurds or think about the global economy without thinking of Microsoft, Apple or Shell.[6] Yet none of these is unequivocally accepted as a subject of international law. Instead, the very category has become something of a political aspiration, and that should not come as a surprise, for recognition as a subject of international law, or recognition of a group's legal personality,

---

[5] See, e.g., Helmut Philipp Aust, 'Auf dem Weg zu einem Recht der globalen Stadt? "C40" und der "Konvent der Bürgermeister" im globalen Klimaschutzregime', (2013) 73 *Zeitschrift für ausländisches öffentliches Recht und Völkerrecht*, 673–704. Some of the more important cities these days are built around airports: see John Kasarda and Greg Lindsay, *Aerotropolis: The Way We'll Live Next* (London: Penguin, 2012).

[6] A useful collection on non-state actors is Andrea Bianchi (ed.), *Non-state Actors and International Law* (Farnham: Ashgate, 2009).

amounts to a certain degree of acceptance of its goals.[7] It is for this reason that states are very reluctant to recognize that terrorist groups such as Al Qaeda or Islamic State[8] be seen as subjects of the law; being accepted as a subject implies recognition of political legitimacy, for that is precisely what recognition is about. As this passage illustrates, it is well-nigh impossible to discuss subject status without referring to recognition; below we will see that this applies even to the status of states.

For the moment suffice it to say that the checklist test (does an entity possess rights or obligations under international law?) may still be as good as it gets. Following this test, it would seem that minorities can be regarded as subjects, for they have at least the right to be free from discrimination. By the same token peoples are subjects to the extent that they enjoy a right to self-determination; companies are subjects to the extent that their investments tend to be protected under international law, and NGOs are increasingly recognized as having a right to speak at international conferences, bring matters to the attention of international tribunals (often, but not exclusively, as a so-called friend of the court, *amicus curiae*), or even, more broadly, having a right to participate in the making of international law.[9]

An important corollary is that the status of legal subject may be very limited, and that the very exercise of a legal right may constitute subject status while simultaneously being evidence of it. A good example resides in agreements concluded to stop civil conflict or to set up some peace enforcement mechanism. Such an agreement may have to include local warring groups that, normally, will not have any status under international law. Yet, without them, the agreement is pointless; as a political matter, their participation is needed.[10]

STATES

States are the main subjects of international law and are generally considered to be sovereign, implying that they need not accept any authority from above or from anyone else unless they choose to do so. Importantly, though, sovereignty is not a natural concept, but is, instead, socially constructed.[11] Moreover, sovereignty itself does not signify very much; it does not, in and of itself, give rise to rights or obligations.

States are, in their generally recognized form of today, a relatively recent phenomenon. In the Middle Ages and after, the dominant form of political organization was the city state, and a little later independent leagues such as the Hansa (a group of trading cities located predominantly around the Baltic Sea) appeared. Yet the state became the dominant form of

---

[7] Jan Klabbers, 'The Concept of Legal Personality', (2005) 11 *Ius Gentium*, 35–66.

[8] On the rise of the latter, see Michael Griffin, *Islamic State: Rewriting History* (London: Pluto, 2016).

[9] See generally Alan Boyle and Christine Chinkin, *The Making of International Law* (Oxford University Press, 2007). For a comprehensive overview of the international legal position of NGOs see Anna-Karin Lindblom, *Non-governmental Organisations in International Law* (Cambridge University Press, 2006).

[10] The agreement by which the EU undertook the administration of Mostar (in Bosnia) in the mid-1990s involved the participation of the local community of East Mostar, as well as that of West Mostar. For the purposes of this particular agreement, these entities were considered to have legal personality under international law, precisely because without them the agreement would have been useless.

[11] See e.g. F. H. Hinsley, *Sovereignty* (London: Watts & Co., 1966), and Thomas J. Biersteker and Cynthia Weber (eds.), *State Sovereignty as Social Construct* (Cambridge University Press, 1996).

political organization, largely because it had one big advantage over its competitors; states together could guarantee that their authority would be uninterrupted, whereas the authority of city states, for instance, never covered the countryside surrounding the city. Hence, from a systemic perspective, the state had attractions that its competitors did not.[12]

This is reflected in the criteria that international law posits for statehood.[13] These are often derived from a convention concluded in the 1930s, in Montevideo: the American Convention on Statehood.[14] Article 1 lists four requirements that are often considered to be a good starting point for any discussion of statehood, and often considered as codifying customary international law, even though the circle of parties was limited to the American states, and even though many observers would agree that the Montevideo list is incomplete and outdated. Following the Montevideo Convention, states should have a population, territory, a government, and the capacity to enter into relations with other states.

Population

The first requirement listed in the Montevideo Convention is that a state needs to have a population. How the population got there is considered irrelevant, as is the question of how it multiplies itself (this may be of relevance with respect to the Holy See's possible claims to statehood).[15] Likewise, it is considered irrelevant whether the population is large (China, India), or small; even Nauru and Vanuatu, with a few tens of thousands of inhabitants, are considered fully fledged states. The 'mini-states' of Europe (Andorra, Monaco, Liechtenstein, San Marino) are also generally considered states; they have all the attributes of statehood, although they sometimes 'outsource' some of a state's tasks. Thus, Liechtenstein's defence tasks are handled by Switzerland, but this circumstance alone is not seen to diminish Liechtenstein's statehood, even though it negatively affected Liechtenstein's request to be admitted to the League of Nations in 1920.[16]

Territory

Second, states should have territory; without territory, there can be no state.[17] The idea of a cyberstate, then – a state without territory – is difficult to conceive of under the requirements of international law. That is not to say that a territory should be completely fixed; a core territory suffices, even if the boundaries remain disputed – and wisely so, as most states have boundary disputes with their neighbours; this even applies between such calm

---

[12] Hendrik Spruyt, *The Sovereign State and its Competitors* (Princeton University Press, 1994).

[13] The leading study is James Crawford, *The Creation of States in International Law*, 2nd edn (Oxford University Press, 2006).

[14] The convention was concluded in 1933 and entered into force in 1934.

[15] That said, a German court held in 1978 that population must refer to 'an essentially permanent form of communal life in the sense of sharing a common destiny'. In the case at hand, the population of the self-proclaimed Duchy of Sealand, occupying an abandoned oil platform off the United Kingdom coast, did not qualify as such. *In re Duchy of Sealand*, Administrative Court Cologne, 3 May 1978, reproduced in 80 *International Law Reports* 683.

[16] The League did not accept Liechtenstein for precisely this reason, but much later it turned out to be no impediment for admission to the UN. Liechtenstein joined the latter in 1990.

[17] And territory is generally understood as part of the surface of the earth – artificial platforms, even if attached to the earth, do not qualify: see *In re Duchy of Sealand*.

and settled states as the Netherlands and Germany, or the Netherlands and Belgium. And some states have boundaries that are so controversial that a requirement of fixed boundaries would be hopelessly unrealistic; Israel may qualify as an example. The only important criterion, then, is the existence of a core territory; other than that, international law posits no demands on territory, and refrains, for instance, from indicating minimum or maximum sizes. The notion of territory encompasses internal waters and the territorial sea.[18]

Effective Government

The criteria of territory and population are, one could say, more or less formal in nature; a state either has them (in whatever quantity) or does not. The two remaining criteria are more substantive, though. Arguably the most important requirement is that in order to qualify for statehood, a state must have an effective government, although the Montevideo Convention itself does not use the adjective 'effective'. None the less, this follows the logic of arbitrator Huber's opinion in the *Island of Palmas* arbitration; for Huber, effective government (in this case in connection with title to territory rather than statehood as such) served to allow other states to contact someone if things were going wrong. In other words, if a territory lacks effective government, there is no one to contact or hold responsible should, for instance, one of your citizens get mugged. The underlying idea is that a state can be accepted as such only when it is in a position to guarantee that law and order, in whatever precise form, will be upheld.[19]

That is not to say that international law is very concerned with the precise form of government; as long as law and order can be guaranteed, international law is satisfied. As a logical consequence of the sovereign equality of states, there is no specific form of government prescribed. This is controversial, of course, as it means that nasty dictatorships are treated in the same way as enlightened democracies, and it is no coincidence that on occasion attempts are made to influence the form of government. In the nineteenth century this took the form of making a distinction between civilized and uncivilized states. On this basis the Ottoman Empire and Japan could be kept on the margins of international law. While this appeal to a standard of civilization has largely disappeared, a faint echo can still be heard in article 38 of the ICJ Statute, which accepts 'general principles of law recognized by civilized nations' as a source of international law.

More recently, it has been proposed that only liberal democracies be recognized as proper states,[20] sometimes even to the effect of completely excluding non-liberal regimes.[21] This is not without problems though. First, it remains unclear who is to determine whether a regime qualifies as a liberal democracy, and on the basis of what standards. Second, more pragmatically perhaps, some of the world's major powers might not qualify. Yet to treat these as second-class subjects is politically awkward. Hence, sometimes a somewhat softer

---

[18] This will be further discussed in Chapter 13 below.

[19] *Island of Palmas Case* (*USA* v. *Netherlands*), sole arbiter Max Huber, 2 *Reports of International Arbitral Awards*, 829.

[20] See e.g. John Rawls, *The Law of Peoples* (Cambridge, MA: Harvard University Press, 1999).

[21] An extreme rendition is Fernando Teson, *A Philosophy of International Law* (Boulder, CO: Westview, 1998).

stance is chosen, for instance by suggesting that while the law does not insist on liberal democracy, it nevertheless recognizes an 'emerging right to democratic governance'.[22]

Capacity to Enter into International Relations

This was a helpful requirement in the days of colonialism, and the Montevideo Convention, being concluded in the 1930s, could not avoid being a child of its time. The hallmark of colonialism was precisely that while colonized territories might have enjoyed considerable autonomy, they were typically not considered to be capable of entering into relations with other states without consent from the metropolitan state. Sometimes this basic idea was ignored when it was politically expedient to do so. Thus, India (a British colony) and the Philippines (a US colony) both enjoyed independent relations prior to independence; India, for instance, was a member of the League of Nations, despite only gaining independence after the League's demise.

Colonialism gave rise to various types of relations between colonizer and colonized, and did so in hugely unreliable terminology. Some territories were nominally independent, but protected by Western powers; such territories would, not untypically, be referred to as protectorates. A lighter form of sovereignty was often described as 'suzerainty'. Some Western powers had 'overseas departments', whereas others would have 'dominions'. 'Colony' would be the generic term, but 'crown colony' was not unheard of either. In short, this kind of label often owed much to internal, domestic political or administrative considerations, and did not necessarily say much about the precise legal relationship between colonizer and colonized. The League of Nations added to the confusion by creating mandate territories (administered by Western powers,[23] but subject to the League's authority), a practice that would be continued by the United Nations as trusteeships until the last formally designated trusteeship (Palau, as part of the Pacific Islands) gained independence in 1994.

Nowadays the requirement that a state must have the capacity to enter into international relations is not considered all that relevant, although it provides services with respect to federal states in particular; it makes it clear that while the United States is a state for purposes of international law, its component elements (Texas, Arkansas, Iowa, etc.) are not. Beyond this, Craven is not wrong when he describes this requirement as 'a conclusion rather than a starting point'.[24]

RECOGNITION OF STATES (OR GOVERNMENTS)

The Montevideo Convention not only listed the requirements for statehood but also referred to recognition of statehood, and in doing so drew attention to what is arguably the most

---

[22] Thomas M. Franck, 'The Emerging Right to Democratic Governance', (1992) 86 *American Journal of International Law*, 46–91.

[23] These were, for the better part, former German and Ottoman territories and would, for the better part, come to be administered by the United Kingdom and France. The one geographical exception was South Africa, which was given authority over what is nowadays Namibia, but it seems justifiable to treat the South Africa of the 1920s and 1930s as a Western power.

[24] Matthew Craven, 'Statehood, Self-determination, and Recognition', in Malcolm Evans (ed.), *International Law*, 3rd edn (Oxford University Press, 2010), 203–51, at 220.

complicated, and assuredly the most politicized, aspect of statehood: recognition. Recognition gives rise to quite a bit of confusion, and does so partly because it is unclear what exactly is recognized: a state or a government? The legality of a government, or its practical existence (recognition *de jure* or de facto)? Moreover, it remains unclear what the precise legal effects of recognition are.[25]

To start with the latter, at least the Montevideo Convention was consistent in its approach when it embodied the so-called declarative theory of recognition and provided that recognition was of no legal relevance whatsoever. Under this declarative theory, the act of recognition should be used merely to specify that in the opinion of other states, entity X meets the requirements of statehood. Thus, an act of recognition can declare that entity X is indeed a state, but given that X meets the requirements, such a declaration is not, strictly speaking, necessary.

The rival theory is the so-called constitutive theory, which posits, in a nutshell, that since the community of states is essentially a political community, membership is dependent on acceptance by the existing members, in much the same way as membership of exclusive country clubs or Manhattan condos may depend on acceptance by existing members. In this view, recognition is vital; even if all four requirements are royally met, an entity that is not recognized will have a hard time existing, as Biafra found out to its dismay. In 1967 it proclaimed independence after a bloody war of secession with Nigeria, only to discover that it did not meet with recognition from more than a handful of states – and within three years after proclaiming independence, Biafra became a part of Nigeria again.

While lawyers tend to prefer the declaratory theory (which aims to strip the law from political elements), there is some reason to believe that in practice, the constitutive theory may be the stronger one, if only because it is next to impossible for a state to survive without recognition. At least in this sense, recognition is often constitutive. Moreover, the one thing that is clear is that recognition is, essentially, a political act; state X decides whether it recognizes entity Y as a state, and may do so for a host of reasons. Obviously, it may do so because it thinks that entity Y meets all requirements of statehood, but it may also do so for different reasons, e.g. because it appreciates the government running entity Y, or because Y has just seceded from X's arch-enemy, or because it feels that the people of entity Y are entitled to their own state on the basis of a right to self-determination (this will be discussed elsewhere),[26] or even simply because entity Y is located on top of oil or natural gas reserves and should thus be treated with kid gloves. By the same token, recognition may be withheld for political reasons: when the slaves of Haiti created their own state in the late eighteenth century and proclaimed independence from France, recognition was not forthcoming: states feared uprisings in other states, and bowed to French pressure not to recognize the new state.[27] In short, while recognition may owe something to the criteria

---

[25] See generally also Stefan Talmon, *Recognition of Governments in International Law, with Particular Reference to Governments in Exile* (Oxford: Clarendon Press, 1998).

[26] See Chapter 6 below.

[27] Liliana Obregón, 'Haiti and the Cosmopolitan Imagination', in Mónica García-Salmones and Pamela Slotte (eds.), *Cosmopolitanism in Enlightenment Europe and Beyond* (Brussels: Peter Lang, 2013), 159–79, at 172.

of statehood, it is an illusion to think that states will decide on the basis of legal criteria alone whether or not to recognize. It would be more accurate to say that the legal criteria offer some guidance (and few entities are recognized without scoring at least reasonably well on some of the requirements), but that decisions on whether to recognize or not are eminently political decisions, predominantly guided by political motivations.[28]

As the previous paragraph suggests, matters are complicated by the circumstance that when states engage in recognition, it is not always with a view to recognizing statehood. Often what really matters is not so much statehood, but rather the sort of government that the new state has. The most dramatic example took place after the Second World War, when Germany was divided in two, the Federal Republic of Germany (FRG, West Germany) and the German Democratic Republic (GDR, East Germany). Communist states were reluctant to recognize the FRG, despite its meeting the requirements of statehood, whereas Western states were highly reluctant to recognize the GDR. The stalemate only came to an end in 1973.

Recognition of governments can also take place either *de jure* or de facto, and here it is the intention of the recognizing state that decides. *De jure* recognition signifies that a government has risen to power in a legitimate way; de facto recognition, on the other hand, signifies that while a government may be in power and thus constitute a negotiating partner, the recognizing state is not very pleased with the way the government came into power. The classic example relates to British recognition of Nazi authority in Czechoslovakia; the British were pragmatic enough to recognize that the Nazis were in charge, yet still voiced their dissent at the illegitimate way in which they had assumed power.[29]

To a large extent, the value of recognition is symbolic; state X accepts entity Y as one of its equals. In practice, it may not have all that much effect on relations between states, as intergovernmental relations also occur without recognition; many states have treaty relations with entities they are reluctant to recognize.[30] Entering into treaty relations does not constitute implied recognition, and most definitely does not constitute implied recognition when the treaty partners themselves exclude this. It is none the less probably accurate to state that entering into diplomatic relations will constitute implied recognition, as the formalization of diplomatic relations presupposes the sort of political validation that otherwise comes from recognition.

While recognition is, in principle, a unilateral act, which affects bilateral relations, it is nowadays accepted that admission into the UN marks something like collective recognition;[31] a state admitted as a member of the UN is accepted as a legitimate member

---

[28] Sometimes even mundanely so: Britain's prime minister Neville Chamberlain wrote to his sister in the mid-1930s that Italy's rule over Abyssinia would at some point have to be recognized: 'we had better give it while we can get something in return for it'. Cited in Norman A. Graebner and Edward M. Bennett, *The Versailles Treaty and Its Legacy: The Failure of the Wilsonian Vision* (Cambridge University Press, 2011), at 157.

[29] This sounds rather benign, but can also be put differently; the British were displeased with the Nazi rise to power, but did not want to take a principled stand and thus decided to afford recognition de facto, so as to allow trade and commerce to continue unimpeded.

[30] The classic study is B. R. Bot, *Nonrecognition and Treaty Relations* (Leiden: Sijthoff, 1968).

[31] The seminal study is John Dugard, *Recognition and the United Nations* (Cambridge: Grotius, 1987).

of the community of states, if only because admission into the UN signifies approval by at least two-thirds of the UN's member states including the five major powers on the Security Council.[32] When one of the permanent members of the Security Council refuses to admit an applicant, sometimes compromises will be looked for: faced with the reluctance in 2011 of the United States to admit Palestine as a regular UN member state, the General Assembly granted Palestine the status of non-member observer state.[33] The political sensitivity thereof resides in the use of the word 'state': this is something the United States, aiming to protect Israel, does not appreciate. Either way, collective recognition by the UN does not amount to individual recognition by each and every UN member state; the symbolic validation of recognition is considered to be too important to be left to a collective organ.[34]

The legal effects of recognition, as noted, do not so much extend to the level of intergovernmental relations; treaty relations will take place with or without recognition. Rather, recognition and non-recognition first and foremost affect the lives of individuals. Thus if a state has not yet recognized South Sudan (which gained independence in July 2011, and became a UN member a few days later), it may be that South Sudanese passports are not accepted as valid, or that marriages or other administrative acts performed under South Sudanese law are not accepted as valid. It is important to note, however, that the validity abroad of those acts does not depend only on recognition of the state concerned; during the 1970s, Haiti – recognized by the United States – gained some fame as a place where Americans could acquire a divorce much more quickly than in the United States and without having to specify grounds, only to find out later that such a 'Haitian divorce' was not always accepted in the United States.[35]

Perhaps the relevance of recognition can be best illustrated by juxtaposing two recent cases. The first of these concerns South Sudan, which seceded from Sudan in 2011. Before secession South Sudan was a more or less autonomous part of Sudan, but two horrendous civil wars suggested that there was little love lost between the central government in Khartoum and the people of South Sudan. A referendum about secession took place in early 2011; some 98 per cent of the electorate voted for independence, and independence was declared on 9 July 2011. On 14 July South Sudan was admitted into the UN, and had been recognized already by some eighty individual states. The first of these, importantly, was Sudan, which thereby signified that the secession of South Sudan occurred with Sudanese consent. Recognition by Sudan was quickly followed by that of regional power Egypt and by Germany, at the time president of the UN Security Council. Other major powers (China, the United States, Russia) followed suit, thereby indicating that in the eyes of the global powers South Sudanese statehood was desirable.

---

[32] The procedure is listed in article 4 UN Charter.

[33] General Assembly Resolution 67/19 of 4 December 2012. The status is rare: the only other entity accepted as a non-member observer state is the Holy See, since 1964.

[34] Moreover, it probably does not apply to other universal organizations: admission to the United Nations Educational, Scientific and Cultural Organization (UNESCO) is not seen as collective recognition, partly because there is no screening by the superpowers in the form of the Security Council. The threat of the United States to stop funding UNESCO after the latter admitted Palestine in 2011 is a salutary reminder.

[35] The procedure was immortalized in the Steely Dan song 'Haitian Divorce'. The chorus ran: 'Oh – no hesitation, no tears and no heartbreaking, no remorse. Oh – congratulations, this is your Haitian divorce.'

The situation of Kosovo provides a sobering contrast. Kosovo was part of the Socialist Federal Republic of Yugoslavia (SFRY) and, after the latter's break-up, of Serbia. Its population is, however, largely of different ethnicity, which in practice meant the regular occurrence of discrimination and gross human rights violations, including such ethnic cleansing that NATO air forces bombed Serbia to induce it to stop, in 1999. Kosovo was administered for a while by the UN Mission in Kosovo (UNMIK), and declared independence in 2008. Yet general recognition has not been forthcoming; in July 2011 Kosovo is recognized by seventy-six states and by Taiwan, but while these states include the United States, the United Kingdom, Germany, and France, important major powers are missing; in particular, China and Russia have so far not recognized Kosovo as an independent state and neither has Serbia. Recognition by the state being seceded from is of major importance in cases of secession; as the case of South Sudan illustrates, the consent of the 'parent state' makes life a lot easier. The circumstance that Kosovo has declared independence is, somehow, of little relevance; the ICJ found, in 2010, that such unilateral declarations of independence are not unlawful under international law, but refrained from going any further.[36]

Kosovo is part of what used to be Yugoslavia, and the break-up of Yugoslavia during the early 1990s has provided international lawyers with lots of material on statehood, recognition, and state succession. In particular two developments stand out, both related to the EU. First, in order to assist it in its policy formulation, the EU established the so-called Badinter Commission (named after its chairperson, French lawyer Robert Badinter). This commission issued a number of highly relevant opinions on issues such as state dissolution, the applicability of the right to self-determination and how this affects the earlier internal boundaries and state succession. These opinions, while not strictly speaking binding, have provided much impetus for the further development of international law.[37] For instance, the Badinter Commission declared that the principle of *uti possidetis*, holding that earlier internal boundaries in principle continue to exist after independence or dissolution, should be seen as a binding general principle. While it had first been applied in the context of the decolonization of Latin America and later in Africa,[38] the commission suggested that it should also be applied in Europe.[39]

Second, in late 1991 the EU adopted a set of guidelines for recognition of the new states in eastern Europe, which can be seen to have added considerably to the requirements for statehood or, at any rate, for legitimate statehood. The EU stipulated that new states should only be recognized if they respected existing boundaries, if they accepted disarmament

---

[36] *Accordance with International Law of the Unilateral Declaration of Independence in Respect of Kosovo,* advisory opinion, [2010] ICJ Rep. 403. To be sure, the Court did answer the question before it, and was not asked by the General Assembly to spell out what the consequences of a declaration of independence could be.

[37] For a useful overview see Matthew Craven, 'The European Community Arbitration Commission on Yugoslavia', (1996) 66 *British Yearbook of International Law,* 333–413.

[38] For more details, see Jan Klabbers and René Lefeber, 'Africa: Lost between Self-determination and *Uti Possidetis*', in Catherine Brölmann et al. (eds.), *Peoples and Minorities in International Law* (Dordrecht: Martinus Nijhoff, 1993), 37–76.

[39] Badinter Commission (formally the Arbitration Commission of the Conference on Yugoslavia), Opinion no. 3, 11 January 1992, reproduced in 92 *International Law Reports,* 170.

commitments, guaranteed the rights of minorities and displayed a commitment to democracy, the rule of law and human rights. The Badinter Commission subsequently applied these guidelines in determining whether the former Yugoslav republics should be recognized. The political relevance of the EU guidelines seems to support the constitutive theory; a state should only be recognized if it meets with political and legal requirements held dear by existing states.[40] And yet the Badinter Commission itself stated unequivocally, some two weeks before the guidelines were issued, that 'the effects of recognition ... are purely declaratory'.[41] What this suggests is not so much that either theory is correct, but rather that recognition is an intensely political affair, and probably combines elements of both theories, in mixtures that vary with the circumstances of the particular case.

ACQUISITION OF TERRITORY

If territory is such an important element of statehood, and goes hand in hand with sovereignty, then how do states acquire their territory? On this topic, international law owes much to the Roman law of property, as this body of law was dominant in Europe at a time when the European discovery voyages – the travels of Columbus, Magellan, Vespucci, Tasman, and others – set off.[42]

A first mode of acquiring territory, long since discarded, was discovery. It is generally accepted that discovery gave rise to an inchoate title, which could be perfected by further acts. Needless to say, this only worked on the presumption that the discovered territory was uninhabited or, more likely, that the original inhabitants were somehow of lesser status than their European discoverers.

Either way, discovery as a possible mode of acquiring territory was relatively short-lived, if only because the emergence of international relations started to put a premium on actual possession and effective government.[43] This, in turn, was rendered necessary in order to protect the rights of foreign travellers, as arbiter Huber memorably claimed in his famous *Island of Palmas* opinion.[44] In this case, at issue was sovereignty over an island located between the Philippines (long a Spanish colony) and Indonesia, a Dutch colony. When after the US–Spanish war the Philippines changed hands and became a US colony, a dispute arose over Palmas. The Spanish had discovered it and could thereby claim title, but the Dutch had actually occupied and administered it. At the 'critical date' (the moment of cession in 1898), so Huber argued, the law prescribed that discovery alone was not sufficient; the exercise of effective government was far more important. Hence Huber decided that title to the island rested with the Netherlands. In doing so Huber not only

[40] The EU guidelines are reproduced in (1992) 31 *International Legal Materials*, 1486.
[41] Badinter Commission, Opinion no. 1, 29 November 1991, in 92 *International Law Reports* 162, at 165.
[42] The classic study is Robert Y. Jennings, *The Acquisition of Territory in International Law* (Manchester University Press, 1963). A more recent contribution is Marcelo G. Kohen, *Possession contesté et souveraineté territoriale* (Paris: Presses Universitaires de France, 1997).
[43] Not to mention its (lack of) morality; Crawford dismisses the thesis that discovery could give rise to title as 'ethnocentric'. Crawford, *Creation*, at 271.
[44] *Island of Palmas*. For a critical contemporary analysis, see W. J. B. Versfelt, *The Miangas Arbitration* (Utrecht: Kemink en Zoon, 1933). Miangas was the Dutch name given to the island, Palmas the Spanish.

gave fresh impetus to the law on territory, but also to international law more generally. The idea that the relevant law was the law at the 'critical date' presupposed that the law could develop. A once valid title could thus be superseded in the light of later events, and this stirred up quite a bit of controversy.[45]

Moreover, it is not always obvious what the 'critical date' in any given dispute is. Huber, in *Palmas*, opted for the date of cession, and that seems sensible enough. But had he opted for the date of discovery as critical, the picture would have changed dramatically, and likewise if he had opted for the date of first settlement, or the date on which the dispute was brought. The point is that international law does not contain any rule outlining how to identify the 'critical date', and much thus comes to depend on the sensibilities and inclinations of those who get to decide.

The notion of effective government, emphasized by Huber in *Palmas*, owed much to two concepts borrowed from Roman law. Under *occupatio* (occupation), someone assumes ownership over a good that was not earlier subject to ownership. In territorial cases this refers to the taking of *res nullius* – no man's land. Under *prescriptio* (prescription), on the other hand, ownership is assumed despite rival claims; the Dutch settling on the Island of Palmas is a fine illustration. In both cases, the relevant consideration would be the exercise of authority over an extended period of time, accompanied by the will to do so (*animus occupandi*), and preferably uncontested.

Currently, occupation and prescription (never mind discovery) are no longer considered terribly relevant, partly because the use of force is strongly prohibited under international law. It follows that military conquest is unlikely to result in title to territory; if a title is unlawfully procured it will not immediately be accepted, although over time acquiescence may come to do its legalizing work: a conquest that has met with general acceptance (or resignation) tends to harden into title.[46]

While there are still territories over which sovereignty is uncertain,[47] in most cases there will at least be some recognized form of governmental authority on display. This applies to well-nigh all territorial disputes of the last decades, whether Iraq's invasion of Kuwait in 1990, Israel and the occupied territories, or even the Falklands war of the early 1980s between the United Kingdom and Argentina, once memorably described as 'two bald men fighting over a comb'. That said, though, a redrawing of boundaries is quite common after major wars, resulting in changes in ownership. The United States considerably enlarged its territory following disputes with Spain and, later, Mexico

---

[45] This became known as the doctrine of inter-temporal law. For useful discussion see T. O. Elias, 'The Doctrine of Intertemporal Law', (1980) 74 *American Journal of International Law*, 285–307.

[46] Crimea, annexed by Russia in 2014, may come to prove the point. While initially the annexation was greeted with indignation, opposing voices are heard less and less often, something influenced no doubt by the fact that the annexing state happens to be one of the world's major powers. China's role in Tibet suggests a similar scenario.

[47] And at least one stretch of rocky desert located between Egypt and Sudan yet rejected by both: Bir Tawil 'appears to be the only place on the planet that is both habitable and unclaimed'. Alastair Bonnett, *Unruly Places: Lost Spaces, Secret Cities, and Other Inscrutable Geographies* (Boston: Houghton Mifflin Harcourt, 2014), at 73.

around the turn of the twentieth century, whereas in Europe the boundaries of a country such as Poland repeatedly shifted throughout that century.

If occupation and prescription are potentially modes of territorial acquisition involving the use of force, more peaceful modes also exist. Historically of some importance is cession – one state handing over territory to another, usually in exchange for a sum of money or, on occasion, for another piece of territory. Relevant examples include the sale of Alaska by Russia to the United States in 1867, or the 1803 Louisiana Purchase by which the United States acquired almost a quarter of its current territory from the French. Famously, the Dutch traded their possession New Amsterdam for a nutmeg-rich part of Indonesia and the guarantee of undisturbed ownership of a bauxite-rich strip of land in South America, nowadays known as Surinam. New Amsterdam was traded with the British, was renamed New York and the rest, as they say, is history.[48]

Peaceful as cession may be, it can none the less play a forceful role in oppression. It has been noted, for instance, that much of the colonization of Africa in the late nineteenth century involved cession;[49] native rulers ceded their territories to the European newcomers, sometimes in exchange for European backing of their own claims to local power.

In some cases, territory is not sold, but rather leased. Thus the United Kingdom leased Hong Kong from China, and the United States has leased Guantánamo Bay from Cuba. The basic idea with such a construction is that sovereignty is separated from the exercise of sovereign acts (including the exercise of jurisdiction). Thus Hong Kong remained Chinese territory (and reverted back to China in 1997), but sovereign acts would be performed by the United Kingdom. Such constructions have historically given rise to controversial situations. One example is the US involvement with the Panama Canal, going back to a treaty concluded in 1903;[50] on the basis of a set of treaties concluded between Panama and the United States in 1977, the canal was to be restored under Panamanian authority as of 1999, but on promise of its permanent neutrality. A more recent variation is sometimes referred to as 'land-grabbing': states lease (or sometimes purchase) territory in other states as if they would be private investors, often for purposes of food security.[51]

Another peaceful way of acquiring territory, from one perspective at least, is to submit territorial disputes to adjudication and leave it to a court or arbitrator to decide. In one sense, of course, the courts will not hand out territory but, being mouthpieces of the law, merely decide what the law says and who can be considered the legal owner; on the other hand, since the law is not always all that clear to begin with, and legal claims often overlap, it can also be maintained that the courts do more than just apply existing law, and actually

---

[48] For a fine discussion of the lingering and positive influence of the Dutch in New York, in particular in spreading liberal values, see Russell Shorto, *The Island at the Center of the World* (New York: Random House, 2005).

[49] Crawford, *Creation*, at 266.

[50] The colourful history of this treaty is recounted with gusto in Vaughan Lowe, *International Law* (Oxford: Clarendon, 2007), at 66.

[51] For brief critical discussion, see Jochen von Bernstorff, 'The Global "Land-Grab", Sovereignty and Human Rights', (2013) 2 *ESIL Reflections*, issue 9.

decide, on occasion, on ownership.[52] Indeed, many of the cases that reach the ICJ or international arbitral tribunals have to do with boundaries – in particular maritime boundaries – and territory, so much so that there exists a rich and detailed jurisprudence. It is precisely because all geographical situations tend to be unique that the assistance of a tribunal is needed; if all that was required was the application of general rules, states could figure it out for themselves. Hence there is some merit in suggesting that adjudication is a mode of acquisition of territory.[53]

Mother Nature may sometimes lend a hand or, on occasion, do the opposite. States can acquire territory through such processes as accretion or sedimentation. Yet states can also lose territory with the general rising of sea levels following global warming and some, such as the Maldives or the Netherlands (what's in a name . . .), are at risk of losing substantial chunks of territory if rising sea levels continue.

INTERNATIONALIZED TERRITORY

Political circumstances sometimes give rise to what, for want of a better term, may be referred to as internationalized territory; territory placed under the authority of a group of states acting together (this applied, for instance, to Berlin after the Second World War) or under the authority of an international organization.[54] Recent examples include the administration of East Timor and Kosovo under auspices of the UN, but the practice is considerably older. Sometimes this concerns territory within a single state but with law and order guaranteed by outside forces (the Memel territory and the Saarland between the two world wars), sometimes this may also concern territory that is internationalized so as to grant a state access to the open sea (this applied, after the First World War, to Danzig) or to govern a contested area in a time of deep political cleavage (Berlin between 1945 and 1990, arguably). As mentioned, moreover, the League of Nations created mandate territories, former colonies administered by other states but under ultimate supervision of the League.

A different manifestation is the regime concerning the Antarctic. While several states had made claims over parts of the Antarctic, in 1959 they and a few others came together and decided to 'freeze' those claims and instead administer the Antarctic together; an elaborate system was set up, and was complemented by a few more specific treaties in later years.[55] Legally it is not self-evident that this could happen; effectively, the original twelve parties to the Antarctic Treaty decided to exclude other possibly interested states, although the

---

[52] The boundary between Iraq and Kuwait was drawn, following Iraq's invasion of and subsequent withdrawal from Kuwait, by the Security Council. This was controversial because it is not at all certain that the Council has the legal power to decide on boundary and territorial questions. For a brief discussion, see Jan Klabbers, 'No More Shifting Lines? The Report of the Iraq–Kuwait Boundary Demarcation Commission', (1994) 43 *International and Comparative Law Quarterly*, 904–13.

[53] A curious example is the 2007 *Abyei* arbitration, a dispute not between two states but between a state and a liberation movement, brought on the basis of an arbitration agreement. PCA, Case No. 2008–07, *Abyei Arbitration* (Sudan/Sudan People's Liberation Movement/Army), final award of 22 July 2009. The oil-rich area is located in what are now the borderlands between Sudan and South Sudan, and still contested.

[54] See generally Ralph Wilde, *International Territorial Administration: How Trusteeship and the Civilizing Mission Never Went Away* (Oxford University Press, 2008).

[55] See generally Keith Suter, *Antarctica: Private Property or Public Heritage?* (London: Zed Books, 1991).

treaty would later come to encompass some of these. Such constructions create situations or regimes between groups of states which will affect others without their consent. Typically, as long as those other states acquiesce in the situation, there is not much of a problem, and sometimes such acquiescence is bound to occur if major powers are involved, or if the 'objective regime' is created by a universal international organization such as the UN. In other settings, though, states that are not involved may well object, as creating such an objective regime effectively amounts to limiting the scope for non-participants.[56]

STATEHOOD: CONTINUITY AND CHANGE

Once a state exists, there is a very strong presumption that it will continue to exist. Most pertinently, the reduced effectiveness of government does not affect its statehood; even Somalia, whose government was for a long time either ineffective or non-existent from the early 1990s, continued to be considered as a state, albeit perhaps a 'failed state'.[57] While this raises all sorts of practical legal questions (to whom does one send an extradition request if government is ineffective?), none the less the presumption of continuity is extremely strong, and understandably so; if ineffectiveness of government led to loss of statehood, then quite a few established states might be at risk. During 2011–2012, for example, Belgium was without a government for more than a year following its latest elections. It is not so much the case that the country was ungoverned (the previous government will typically maintain a caretaker function), but it does signify a level of instability and, thereby, ineffectiveness.

However, it is possible for statehood to change, and at least four methods of change can be discerned. South Sudan illustrates that a new state may come into being on the basis of secession. This can be done peacefully, but sometimes also following a bloody civil war; the secession of Bangladesh from Pakistan in the early 1970s is emblematic. Likewise, sometimes secession follows an international war; Belgium was first separated from the Netherlands following Napoleon's defeat, and it finally gained independence in 1830. The main characteristic of secession is that the old parent state continues to exist, and continues to do so under the same name and with the same legal identity, but with a reduced territory.

A second mode of state succession is decolonization. Under this process, based on the problematic ethics of colonialism, a hundred or so former colonies have gained independence, mainly during the 1950s and 1960s.[58] While this resembles secession, a defining distinction is that the former colonies are based elsewhere in the world and are not contiguous with the metropolitan area. More than regular annexation or territorial aggrandizement, colonialism came to be regarded as evil; as a result, there are some

---

[56] See generally Bruno Simma, 'The Antarctic Treaty as a Treaty Providing for an "Objective Regime"', (1986) 19 *Cornell International Law Journal*, 189–209. See also the brief discussion of objective regimes in the previous chapter.

[57] See generally Riikka Koskenmäki, 'Legal Implications Resulting from State Failure in Light of the Case of Somalia', (2004) 73 *Nordic Journal of International Law*, 1–36.

[58] See generally Matthew Craven, *The Decolonization of International Law* (Oxford University Press, 2007).

differences in the legal situation of former colonies as compared to seceded states such as South Sudan or Eritrea (which seceded from Ethiopia in the early 1990s).[59]

Third, states may merge or unite or, if they had already formed a unity at some earlier point in history, be reunited. This, arguably, is the case with Germany since the absorption of the former GDR into the FRG in 1990. Other examples include Yemen (a merger of North Yemen and South Yemen since 1990) and Tanzania (bringing together Tanganyika and Zanzibar since 1964). On a longer historical view, many currently existing states owe their existence to smaller entities coming together. This applies, for instance, to the Netherlands (which started life as the United Provinces) and federations such as the United States, but also to states such as Italy and Germany, which, until far into the nineteenth century, consisted of a number of smaller entities.

Finally, states may dissolve. This happened in recent years with the Socialist Federal Republic of Yugoslavia and, arguably, with the USSR as well, although the treatment of the Russian Federation casts some doubt on this characterization. After all, a hallmark of dissolution would seem to be the total break-up of the previous state, with none of the new states continuing the identity of the old state. Yet, while the dissolution of the USSR was largely treated this way, a special position was carved out for the Russian Federation, presumably so as not to complicate membership of the UN Security Council. After all, should the USSR disappear completely, then so would its position on the Security Council. As a result, the precise composition of the Security Council would be opened up, which might result in awkward political situations for France and the United Kingdom, whose membership of the Council can no longer be said to rest on their global political power (if it ever could). Hence it was thought better to treat Russia as a special case, and the solution to accept Russia as the legal continuation of the USSR (with smaller territory and different name, but otherwise the same entity) was adopted by the Security Council meeting in 1992 at the highest political level.[60]

The Russia episode suggests that the influence of political considerations also colours the law on state succession. To some extent this cannot be avoided, not only because the creation of states is such a highly political affair, but also because state succession can come about in so many different forms, from secession to dissolution. As a result, it has proved very difficult to formulate general principles. The most important attempt to do so is the 1978 Vienna Convention on Succession of States in Respect of Treaties, which aims to govern the effect of state succession on treaty relations. The problematique will be obvious; would a treaty concluded by the former USSR continue to bind successor states, such as Ukraine or Belarus? And if so, does this also apply to the Baltic states, which can claim with some force that their absorption into the USSR was based on annexation?[61]

On the one hand, there is much to be said for continuity of treaties. After all, in particular when it comes to human rights treaties, it would be rather awkward to hold that people are

---

[59] This will be further discussed below.

[60] Tellingly, the UN Charter still lists the 'Union of Soviet Socialist Republics' as one of the Council's permanent members: article 23 UN Charter.

[61] On the latter, see Lauri Mälksoo, *Illegal Annexation and State Continuity: The Case of the Incorporation of the Baltic States by the USSR* (Leiden: Martinus Nijhoff, 2003).

protected on Monday but no longer on Tuesday simply because a state succession has occurred.[62] The same consideration may well apply to disarmament treaties; the international community has an interest in seeing that the disarmament commitments of the USSR continue to be binding on Ukraine and Belarus.

On the other hand, assuming the continuity of treaties would effectively mean that new states would be under legal obligations to which those states never consented. While this is justifiable with respect to systemic rules such as those relating to treaty-making or state responsibility (secondary rules, in the terminology of legal philosopher H. L. A. Hart[63]), it is less easily justifiable with respect to substantive obligations; why would a new state be under an obligation, say, to provide market access to foreign imports, while older states only incurred such an obligation on the basis of explicit consent?

As a result, the 1978 Vienna Convention does not say all that much. Newly independent states (i.e. former colonies, but not states that have seceded from neighbouring states) may start their existence with a 'clean slate'; under article 16, treaties do not devolve upon them merely because they were in force for the metropolitan state. Here, the 1978 Convention pays tribute to decolonization, and aims to compensate, so to speak, former colonies for the injustices of colonialism. In cases of merger or unification, however, the presumption is that existing treaties continue to remain in force (article 31) unless the parties concerned agree on a different solution, and much the same applies to a separation (be it secession or dissolution) under article 34. Importantly, state successions do not affect boundary treaties or 'other territorial regimes', according to articles 11 and 12, and the convention is without prejudice to questions arising from military occupation (article 40).

As noted, the Vienna Convention relates to the effects of state succession on treaties; it says nothing about customary international law or, for that matter, rights and obligations created in other ways. These matters continue to be controversial; on the basis of the 1978 Convention it remains uncertain whether, for example, Security Council sanctions would devolve upon a new state, or even whether a newly independent state remains bound by customary human rights obligations resting on the metropolitan state.

The 1978 Convention has met with little overt support in state practice, perhaps partly because its drafters were highly motivated by the injustices of colonialism at a time when colonialism had already come to an almost complete end; the drafting was memorably characterized by a prominent international lawyer as 'looking back in anger'.[64] The convention needed a mere fifteen ratifications to enter into force, and even this low number took sixteen years to achieve: the convention entered into force in 1996 and, in July 2016, still has only twenty-two parties, quite a few of them new states such as Montenegro, Slovenia, Croatia, Serbia, the Czech Republic and Slovakia.

None the less, the convention does have its use, in that it establishes guidelines for the handling of state successions. The guidance it provides is not very detailed, perhaps, and to

---

[62] For an authoritative formulation, see Menno Kamminga, 'State Succession in Respect of Human Rights Treaties', (1996) 7 *European Journal of International Law*, 469–84.

[63] H. L. A. Hart, *The Concept of Law* (Oxford: Clarendon Press, 1961).

[64] My memory insists that the characterization is Bruno Simma's but, alas, does not tell me where exactly he wrote these words.

some extent not geared towards the sort of situations that may be expected to emerge (focusing as it does mainly on decolonialization), but it does have the great merit of providing diplomats and statesmen with a vocabulary for discussing issues of state succession and with a number of legal presumptions. In practice, typically, states will decide on these issues on the basis of mutual agreement, but the agreement is reached against a background provided by the convention's rules.

A succession of states not only affects treaty relations; it also affects such matters as a state's property, its debts, and its archives. This is of great political relevance: property may include nuclear arsenals, and archives may include the records of nasty secret services. On these topics, a separate convention was concluded in 1983 (the Vienna Convention on State Succession in Respect of State Property, Debts and Archives), but this has yet to enter into force. Its existence in legal limbo is not considered to be much of a problem though, practically speaking; cases of state succession in respect of these matters tend to be dealt with on the basis of agreement between the states concerned at any rate, and it could hardly be otherwise.[65]

Obviously, once a state ceases to exist, so does its nationality; since there is no Soviet Union any longer, neither can there be Soviet citizens. What, then, happens to citizens of a state that becomes subject to a succession? The ILC of the UN has adopted a number of articles on the topic but no general multilateral convention exists as yet. Under these articles, adopted in 1999 and endorsed by the General Assembly,[66] the main political impetus is to prevent statelessness from occurring;[67] as a result, the guiding presumption, laid down in article 5, is that individuals will have the nationality of the state on whose territory they habitually reside. Hence former Soviet citizens will have acquired Ukrainian nationality if they live in Ukraine, Moldovan nationality if they live in Moldova, and so on.

This hardly solves all problems, however. In particular, the Soviet practice of Russification (sending ethnic Russians to live in other parts of the USSR, often as soldiers) has given rise to quite a backlash, in particular in the Baltic states. These states claimed to have been illegally annexed for some fifty years; the former Soviet soldiers were seen as occupying forces and therefore were to be sent back to Russia rather than given local nationality, and acquisition of nationality was made dependent on command of the local language.

---

[65] Thus in 1994 Ukraine gave up its nuclear weapons (inherited from the USSR) in exchange for a guarantee of the inviolability of its territory by means of the so-called Budapest memorandum, involving the United States, Russia, and the United Kingdom. For legal analysis see Thomas D. Grant, 'The Budapest Memorandum of 5 December 1994: Political Engagement or Legal Obligation?', (2014) 34 *Polish Yearbook of International Law*, 89–114. While the 2014 annexation of Crimea is difficult to reconcile with the Budapest Memorandum, the legal analysis is complicated by the claim that the Budapest memorandum might not constitute a legally binding agreement. On this, see Chapter 3 above.

[66] They are available at http://untreaty.un.org/ilc/texts/instruments/english/commentaries/3_4_1999.pdf (last visited 22 July 2011).

[67] In this it follows the European Convention on Nationality (European Treaty Series, ETS, no. 166), concluded under the auspices of the Council of Europe in 1997. This convention lays down, in article 18, a number of principles that govern nationality in cases of state succession, including the prevention of statelessness.

Finally, membership of international organizations is also affected by a succession of states.[68] The basic principle is that membership is personal (i.e. state-specific), so once a state ceases to exist, so, too, does its membership of an international organization. The main general exception here concerns the financial institutions (IMF, World Bank, etc.), where membership is not considered personal, and understandably so; otherwise a heavily indebted member state could decide to dissolve and thereby escape liability. The fact that membership is personal implies that new states, following a succession, are expected to apply for admission as new member states, and this is indeed what has largely happened following the European wave of succession in the 1990s. When Czechoslovakia broke up, the two new states (the Czech Republic and Slovakia) both generally applied for admission to a number of international organizations, as did the new states arising from the ashes of the former USSR[69] and SFRY. The one exception was the new Germany, which was generally considered to be the continuation of the older FRG, with added new territory. Here then the main legal questions arose about the GDR's outstanding membership fees; after some negotiations, these were eventually taken care of by the new Germany.[70]

INTERNATIONAL ORGANIZATIONS

Next to states, it is generally accepted that international organizations play a pivotal role in global affairs and, therewith, in international law.[71] International organizations are usually defined as intergovernmental organizations, created by states, usually by means of a treaty, in order to exercise a task or function that states themselves are unable or unwilling to perform. Examples range from organizations for the exercise of collective security (the UN) and those devoted to trade (WTO) or development (World Bank) to more mundane issues such as the management of the global market for bamboo and rattan products (INBAR) or the provision of forestry research in Europe (European Forest Institute).

The first international organizations were created with a view to managing problems of communication, be it on international waterways (the Rhine Commission, established in 1815, is one of the first) or with a view to other means of communication: postal traffic, telegraph messages, and railway traffic.

Yet international organizations started to become important players in particular after the First World War, when their potential to manage global security (League of Nations) and global labour relations (ILO) was tested: a prominent observer speaks in this connection of the years 1919–1920 as marking a 'move to institutions'.[72] Organizations would further

---

[68] The leading study is Konrad Bühler, *State Succession and Membership in International Organizations: Legal Theories versus Political Pragmatism* (The Hague: Martinus Nijhoff, 2001).

[69] But see the discussion of the Russian Federation in the UN, above.

[70] See generally Jan Klabbers et al. (eds.), *State Practice Regarding State Succession and Recognition* (The Hague: Martinus Nijhoff, 1999).

[71] See generally Jan Klabbers, *An Introduction to International Organizations Law*, 3rd edn (Cambridge University Press, 2015); H. G. Schermers and Niels M. Blokker, *International Institutional Law: Unity within Diversity*, 5th edn (Leiden: Martinus Nijhoff, 2011), and Evelyne Lagrange and Jean-Marc Sorel (eds.), *Traité de droit des organisations internationales* (Paris: LGDJ, 2013).

[72] David Kennedy, 'The Move to Institutions', (1987) 8 *Cardozo Law Review*, 841–988.

gain in popularity after the Second World War, with the creation of the UN, global economic institutions such as the IMF, the World Bank, the General Agreement on Tariffs and Trade: (GATT) (now the WTO), and a mushrooming of regional organizations, in particular in Europe (Benelux, Council of Europe, NATO, EU).[73]

The leading theory about international organizations is referred to as functionalism, and can already be discerned in some of the earliest writings.[74] The underlying idea is that whereas states are organized on a territorial basis, organizations are built around functions. They are often considered to have such rights, powers, privileges, and immunities as are necessary to enable them to exercise those functions, and nothing more.[75]

It is undisputed that organizations perform significant functions in global governance; the world would be a decidedly different place (and probably a far worse place) without the existence of international organizations. Even international law itself would look very different; as German authors Matthias Ruffert and Christian Walter maintain, much international law is created by or within international organizations.[76] Air law would look different without the standards set by the International Civil Aviation Organization (ICAO) in respect of, for example, airport safety. Maritime law would be radically different without the efforts of the International Maritime Organization (IMO), and labour law owes much to the ILO. The World Health Organization (WHO), likewise, has been highly instrumental in the near eradication of tuberculosis and the fight against other diseases, from malaria and HIV/AIDS to avian flu, swine flu, and Ebola fever.

In the end, many human activities are somehow within the province of an international organization, but there are two significant exceptions: environmental protection and financial regulation. This signifies the absence of broad political agreement on whether and how to protect the environment or regulate the work of the financial sector. As a result, the environment generally is part of a programme conducted by the UN (United Nations Environment Programme, UNEP, headquartered in Nairobi, Kenya – this unorthodox location itself already suggests that environmental protection has not been a huge priority), whereas otherwise relatively informal entities (often referred to as meetings or conferences of the parties – MOPs or COPs) are created under sectoral agreements, with separate regimes for such topics as the protection of the ozone layer, transport of hazardous materials, and airborne pollution.[77] The financial sector, in turn, is highly fragmented, with separate entities dealing with development (World Bank, regional investment banks), banking regulation (Basel Committee), debt relief (Paris Club, IMF),

[73] For a comprehensive political history of international organizations see Bob Reinalda, *Routledge History of International Organizations: From 1815 to the Present Day* (London: Routledge, 2009).
[74] See in particular Paul S. Reinsch, *Public International Unions, Their Work and Organization: A Study in International Administrative Law* (Boston, MA: McGinn & Co., 1911). For synthesis and critique, see Jan Klabbers, 'The EJIL Foreword: The Transformation of International Organizations Law', (2015) 26 *European Journal of International Law*, 9–82.
[75] The powers of international organizations will be addressed in the next chapter.
[76] See Matthias Ruffert and Christian Walter, *Institutionalisiertes Völkerrecht* (Munich: Beck, 2009).
[77] See generally Robin R. Churchill and Geir Ulfstein, 'Autonomous Institutional Arrangements in Multilateral Environmental Agreements: A Little-noticed Phenomenon in International Law', (2000) 94 *American Journal of International Law*, 623–59. See also Chapter 14 below.

control over securities markets (IOSCO), and so on; one prominent commentator speaks of a 'dizzying array' of entities involved, with many of them again aiming to operate in the 'twilight zone' between law and non-law.[78]

Organizations are the creatures of their member states, and those states are usually represented in a plenary organ, such as the UN General Assembly or the WTO Ministerial Conference. Such plenary organs are typically organs for debate and discussion rather than quick decision-making; they are platforms for political leaders to manifest themselves on the global stage.

Since plenary organs will usually only be in session once a year or even less often, many organizations will have an executive organ to handle urgent matters and, possibly, matters within their own delimited sphere of competence. A typical example is the UN Security Council, whose main task is to secure international peace and security. In order to give effect to that task, it can be called together at short notice, and its relatively small size (fifteen members, five of which are permanent while the others serve two-year terms) facilitates the possibility of taking decisions. Most decisions require a majority of nine votes, including the 'concurring vote' of the permanent members. This is known as the latter's veto right, and is a constant topic of debate, in that many feel that a privileged position for a handful of states is unfair. While the privileged position of the five permanent members (China, France, Russia, the United Kingdom, and the United States) is historically understandable, in particular in the light of the role of the Council in maintaining peace and security, it has none the less lost quite a bit of its legitimacy. For one thing, the permanent five are not usually involved in UN peacekeeping efforts, and it is at least arguable that France and the United Kingdom should no longer be seen as superpowers, having been surpassed by states such as Germany and Japan. These last two also contribute considerably more to the UN budget than do France and the United Kingdom. The EU could possibly also claim superpower status in its own right but, as it is not a state, it cannot join the UN: UN membership is only open to states.[79]

Virtually all international organizations, no matter how small, will have an administrative organ, a secretariat, whose tasks will include the execution of decisions of the policy-making organs and the preparation of meetings, translation of documents, and so on. This has given rise to the emergence of an international bureaucracy, often with an agenda of its own. Many hold that the task of the secretariat is to think of the common interest (as opposed to member state interests) and, where necessary, play a political role in thinking of new ideas, new approaches, and new initiatives, while safeguarding the organization's mission.[80] The best-known example, in all likelihood, is the invention of UN peacekeeping in the 1950s by Secretary-General Dag Hammarskjöld and some of his

---

[78] See Chris Brummer, 'How International Financial Law Works (and How It Doesn't)', (2011) 99 *Georgetown Law Journal*, 257–327. See also Chapter 15 below.
[79] See generally Thomas D. Grant, *Admission to the United Nations: Charter Article 4 and the Rise of Universal Organization* (Leiden: Martinus Nijhoff, 2009).
[80] The classic study is Thomas G. Weiss, *International Bureaucracy* (Lexington, MA: Lexington Books, 1975).

closest associates.[81] That said, the bureaucracy can also play a stifling role; political scientists have used bureaucracy theory to explain the UN's inertia during the Rwandan genocide.[82]

There is no general right of admission to international organizations; each organization can set its own rules on whom to admit and how admission should take place. The UN, for example, by virtue of article 4 of the Charter, is open to 'peace loving states' who, in the judgement of the UN, are 'able and willing' to carry out their obligations under the Charter.[83] Admission takes place by decision of the General Assembly, on the recommendation of the Security Council and this means, as a practical matter, that unless an aspirant state has the backing of the five permanent members of the Council, it will not be admitted.[84]

The North Atlantic Treaty (establishing NATO) holds in article 10 that new members may join on being invited by the collective membership. This idea of invitation to membership reached the ICJ in 2011. Greece and the Former Yugoslav Republic of Macedonia (FYROM), not the closest of friends as both lay claim to the label 'Macedonia', had concluded an agreement (the Interim Accord) in 1995 in which Greece[85] had promised not to object to FYROM's applications for membership in a number of international organizations, including NATO. Greece reneged on its commitment and NATO decided not to extend an invitation to FYROM. The question arose whether NATO's decision could be attributed to Greece, but the Court rejected that proposition: the proper question was 'whether the Respondent violated the Interim Accord as a result of its own conduct'.[86]

While the constitutions of international organizations often remain silent on withdrawal by member states, none the less it is widely acknowledged that if a member state no longer wants to be a member state, it might be best for all concerned to let it withdraw,[87] and some organizations create an explicit provision to that effect. The League

---

[81] For a fine analysis see Anne Orford, *International Authority and the Responsibility to Protect* (Cambridge University Press, 2011).

[82] Michael Barnett and Martha Finnemore, *Rules for the World: International Organizations in Global Politics* (Ithaca, NY: Cornell University Press, 2004). In greater detail: Michael Barnett, *Eyewitness to a Genocide: The United Nations and Rwanda* (Ithaca, NY: Cornell University Press, 2002).

[83] In *Admissions I*, the ICJ held that these criteria are exhaustive, albeit open to interpretation. See *Admission of a State to the United Nations (Charter, Article 4)*, advisory opinion, [1948] ICJ Rep. 57. See generally Grant, *Admission to the United Nations*.

[84] In *Admissions II*, this procedure was deemed an essential manifestation of checks and balances between the two main organs: the Assembly cannot admit new members without Security Council recommendation. See *Competence of the General Assembly for the Admission of a State to the United Nations*, [1950] ICJ Rep. 4.

[85] Groucho Marx would have been amused: since Greece was reluctant to recognize FYROM's claims regarding the use of the label 'Macedonia', the agreement referred to Greece as the Party of the First Part, with FYROM being listed as the Party of the Second Part.

[86] *Application of the Interim Accord of 13 September 1995 (Former Yugoslav Republic of Macedonia v. Greece)*, [2011] ICJ Rep. 644, para 42. The Court would indeed hold that Greece had breached its obligation towards FYROM. The case illustrated the complex relationship between organizations and their member states; the leading study is Catherine M. Brölmann, *The Institutional Veil in Public International Law: International Organisations and the Law of Treaties* (Oxford: Hart, 2007).

[87] For insightful discussion see J. H. H. Weiler, 'Alternatives to Withdrawal from an International Organization: The Case of the European Economic Community', (1985) 20 *Israel Law Review* 515–31.

of Nations allowed for withdrawal, a facility gladly used by Germany and Japan in the 1930s.[88] In 2016, the withdrawal clause in the Treaty establishing the EU reached the newspapers when the British people, by referendum, voted to leave the EU: Brexit. This means that article 50 TEU will have to be activated, which, in turn, will set in motion lengthy and complicated negotiations between the EU and the United Kingdom. At the time of writing, it seems that the results of the referendum have caught the proponents of Brexit by surprise – few seem to have an idea what to do next.

THE UNITED NATIONS

Among international organizations a special place is reserved for the United Nations. Set up in 1945, it is generally considered to be the most important organization, for a variety of reasons. One of these has to do with the scope of its activities; the UN occupies itself with nearly all aspects of international life, and can thus be said to be an organization of general jurisdiction. While its main task is, arguably, to provide for international peace and security, it also functions as a platform for discussion on numerous other topics, and it is telling that some twenty other universal international organizations are formally linked to the UN, forming what is sometimes referred to as the 'UN family'. Moreover, the UN comprises well-nigh all states in the world; at present, it has 193 member states – only a handful of very small states remain outside, as well as some entities whose statehood is debated (Kosovo, Palestine, and Taiwan, for instance).

As a matter of law, the UN has another element that elevates it above other organizations. Under article 103 of the UN Charter, obligations for member states arising under the Charter 'shall prevail' over other, competing obligations.[89] Thus the UN occupies a hierarchically superior position, so much so that it is sometimes said that the UN Charter functions as the constitution of the community of states.[90] While such claims are more easily made than substantiated, they are not without a kernel of truth.

The UN comprises six principal organs. The General Assembly is its plenary. It cannot adopt law (it is not a global legislature), but as an assembly of 193 states, its voice tends to get heard. Its predominant role is to discuss matters of global justice, and while its resolutions formally do not give rise to legal obligations, they can be highly authoritative. Perhaps the main example is the Universal Declaration of Human Rights which, its non-binding character notwithstanding, sparked the international human rights revolution after its adoption by the General Assembly in 1948.

The UN's executive organ is the Security Council, composed of fifteen member states. As noted, five of these (China, France, the Russian Federation, the United Kingdom and the United States) occupy a permanent seat, and have a right of veto; decision-making

---

[88] See generally Alison Duxbury, *The Participation of States in International Organisations: The Role of Human Rights and Democracy* (Cambridge University Press, 2011).

[89] For a useful discussion, see Rain Liivoja, 'The Scope of the Supremacy Clause of the United Nations Charter', (2008) 57 *International and Comparative Law Quarterly*, 583–612.

[90] See e.g. Bardo Fassbender, *The United Nations Charter as the Constitution of the International Community* (Leiden: Martinus Nijhoff, 2009).

generally takes place with the consent (or at least absence of opposition) of these permanent members. In addition, ten member states are elected for a period of two years, representing the world's geographical regions. While non-permanent membership does not last very long, states regard membership as highly prestigious and campaign seriously in order to be elected every now and then.

The five permanent members owe their special position to the outcome of the Second World War; it reflects the power configurations prevailing in 1945. Consequently, it is often argued that the composition of the Council is outdated, and the Council is also considered not very representative, leading to the argument that perhaps important southern states (Brazil, India, South Africa) ought to have a permanent seat, in order to make the Council more representative.

Technically, the Council has no legislative powers. It can adopt decisions that are binding on the member states by virtue of article 25 UN Charter, but the original idea was that such decisions would be administrative in nature, rather than legislative. Thus the Council can order military action, but cannot adopt a global tax, or order states to conduct an environmental impact assessment prior to starting up industrial projects. That said, the dividing line between administrative and legislative measures is a thin one, and the Council is sometimes accused of adopting a quasi-legislative role. It is also in this connection that the call for reform of the Council's composition is most often heard.[91]

The UN also comprises a secretariat, headed by the Secretary-General, currently the South Korean diplomat Ban Ki Moon and from 2017 his Portuguese successor António Guterres. The secretariat is ordained to be impartial but, that said, the Secretary-General does have a role to play beyond mere administration; his task (thus far, all incumbents have been male, representing different geographical parts of the globe following a rotation scheme[92]) includes bringing matters to the attention of the Security Council.[93]

Additionally, the UN consists of the Economic and Social Council, responsible for coordinating the activities of the UN family, among other things. The Trusteeship Council was responsible for supervising the administration of trusteeship territories, but has fairly little to do since the last of these territories, Palau, gained independence and became a member state of the UN in 1994. Finally, the sixth principal organ is the ICJ. In other words, there is a strong institutional connection between the leading organization and the World Court.

OTHER SUBJECTS

If states are the original subjects of international law and have full capacity, and if international organizations, too, in principle have full capacity under international law,

---

[91] Jan Klabbers, 'Reflections on the Politics of Institutional Reform', in Peter G. Danchin and Horst Fischer (eds.), *United Nations Reform and the New Collective Security* (Cambridge University Press, 2010), 76–93.

[92] In spring 2016, campaigning for a new Secretary-General to replace Ban started in earnest, and there was much talk of it being eastern Europe's turn, and high time for a female Secretary-General. In the event the Portuguese António Guterres was chosen.

[93] An excellent collection of articles concerning the role of the Secretary-General is Simon Chesterman (ed.), *Secretary or General? The UN Secretary-General in World Politics* (Cambridge University Press, 2007).

the legal status of other entities is less clear and less extensive. Often enough, the legal rights or obligations of other entities are determined by political exigencies; a local community, or a liberation movement, or an indigenous people, may conclude such treaties as are necessary to achieve a lasting settlement, or be involved in such actions as are compatible with its political status and position. Little can therefore be said in general terms, except perhaps to repeat that legal subject status is often constituted by the very act it legitimizes.

NGOs play an increasingly important role in international law. Under the Geneva conventions, humanitarian organizations, and in particular the International Committee of the Red Cross (set up under Swiss law), may be given certain tasks relating to the protection of prisoners of war.[94] Other NGOs have, without necessarily enjoying a formal right of initiative, been instrumental in encouraging states to conclude conventions, none more so perhaps than the International Campaign to Ban Landmines, whose activism resulted in the 1997 Mine Ban Treaty.[95] More generally, states and international organizations often rely on NGOs to provide them with information concerning, for example, environmental disasters or human rights violations.

Indigenous people, too, have certain rights under international law. Often having been chased away from their ancestral lands, the rights of indigenous people to those ancestral lands have gradually come to be recognized. While the colonizers upheld the fiction that the lands were either *terra nullius* at the time of colonization, or uncultivated and thus akin to *terra nullius*, in the 1992 *Mabo* case the Australian High Court rejected this argument, holding instead that the English claim to sovereignty over the Murray Islands (now Australia) in 1879 was no longer tenable. Brennan J put it as follows: 'If the international law notion that inhabited land may be classified as *terra nullius* no longer commands general support, the doctrines of the common law which depend on (this doctrine) can hardly be retained.'[96] Importantly, the Court did not go so far as to claim that the colonization had been illegal at the time but, using arbiter Huber's doctrine of inter-temporal law[97] to good effect, did claim that it had fallen out of step with modern conceptions of justice.

The position of indigenous people is not only discussed in connection with claims on native lands, but also with respect to their customs. The special relationship with native lands may have ramifications when it comes to such diverse topics as environmental protection and intellectual property. It is widely thought, for instance, that some indigenous peoples have knowledge of the medicinal qualities of plants and herbs unmatched by that of Western pharmacy, yet intellectual property law facilitates what is sometimes referred to as 'biopiracy' – the patenting of traditional knowledge by Western pharmaceutical companies.[98]

---

[94] Articles 9 and 10 of the Geneva Convention Relative to the Treatment of Prisoners of War.

[95] The ICBL and its leader, Jody Williams, were jointly awarded the 1997 Nobel Peace prize.

[96] *Mabo and Others* v. *Queensland* (no. 2), 3 June 1992, reproduced in 112 *International Law Reports* 457, at 490. In dismissing the idea that inhabited territories could have been regarded as *terra nullius*, the High Court followed the ICJ in *Western Sahara*, advisory opinion, [1975] ICJ Rep. 12.

[97] Under this doctrine, facts and claims must be assessed against the law as it has developed. Huber relied on this idea in the *Island of Palmas* arbitration, discussed above.

[98] For a brief discussion see Carlos Correa, *Intellectual Property Rights, the WTO and Developing Countries: The TRIPS Agreement and Policy Options* (London: Zed Books, 2000), at 171–3.

Other entities may occupy a historical position as subject of international law. This is the case, for instance, with the Holy See, which can conclude treaties (so-called 'concordats') and also has diplomatic missions; the Holy See's representative is not referred to as an ambassador, but as a nuncio. The Holy See is often allowed to participate in the negotiation of multilateral conventions, enjoys diplomatic relations with many states and is a party to such general international law documents as the 1961 Vienna Convention on Diplomatic Relations. It is not a member of the UN, however (instead, its status is that of an observer non-member state), and opinions are divided as to whether it would be eligible for membership under the provisions of article 4 UN Charter, which not only stipulates that aspiring members must be states (this alone is doubtful) but must also be willing and able to give effect to the obligations involved in membership.

FINAL REMARKS

The link between statehood and territory has traditionally been based on the underlying theory that territory is best seen as analogous to property; it can be bought and sold, perhaps even occupied, and can possibly be taken away in case of misbehaviour. Historically, that theory has served a useful purpose for Western countries looking to justify their expansion, but has always remained awkward. What to do with the inhabitants of territory changing hands? Generally speaking, they could hardly always be moved, although in some cases widespread exchanges of population have taken place.[99] The more popular option, then, was always just to ignore the plight of the inhabitants.

It is worth noting that the theory analogizing territory with property is increasingly coming under threat. In fact, the only entities whose authority is based on territory are states; with others, ranging from international organizations to NGOs and companies, the basis is not so much territory, rather it is functional. Indeed, some theorists have proclaimed that this trend will only continue, and that the big challenge for international lawyers is not so much to guarantee cooperation and communication between states, but rather between functional 'regimes': the trade regime, the security regime and other functional regimes.[100]

And some have noted that the state itself is deterritorializing, due to functional disaggregation of the state into functional units (ministries, agencies, etc., each having its own international role to play)[101] and, ironically perhaps, as a result of the state's own arrogance. States increasingly separate their territory from their authority or jurisdiction, as such diverse examples as Guantanamo Bay (the United States considering its prisoners there to be outside its jurisdiction) and Christmas Island (Australia refusing to treat immigrants arriving there as possible refugees) make clear. Yet, as arbiter Huber pointed out in *Island of Palmas*, unless a state accepts responsibility for things happening in its territory, the very title to that territory becomes difficult to justify.

---

[99] See, among others, Mark Mazower, *Dark Continent: Europe's 20th Century* (London: Penguin, 1998).

[100] See in particular Andreas Fischer-Lescano and Gunther Teubner, *Regime-kollisionen. Zur Fragmentierung des Globalen Rechts* (Frankfurt am Main: Suhrkamp, 2006).

[101] Anne-Marie Slaughter, *A New World Order* (Princeton University Press, 2004).

Be that as it may, subjects doctrine in international law is politically highly significant, yet difficult to get a handle on. What is clear is that states, once recognized, are full subjects, and that international organizations are capable of performing, in principle, many international legal acts. Yet the key word, in most cases, is recognition; international law lacks formal criteria (or, more accurately, such formal criteria as it has are insufficient), the result being that an entity that is not recognized as bearing rights or obligations under international law will have a tenuous legal position. Recognition is the homage that politics pays to law; once recognized, law governs international relations, but the decision on who gets to participate, and in what way, is only tangentially regulated by international law. This is often deplored, but it could hardly be otherwise, precisely because there is so much at stake; as noted, it is through the notion of subjects that actual rights tend to be allocated.

FURTHER READING

James Crawford, *The Creation of States in International Law*, 2nd edn (Oxford University Press, 2006)

John Dugard, *Recognition and the United Nations* (Cambridge: Grotius, 1987)

Andreas Fischer-Lescano and Gunther Teubner, *Regime-Kollissionen: Zur Fragmentierung des globalen Rechts* (Frankfurt am Main: Suhrkamp, 2006)

Robert Jennings, *The Acquisition of Territory in International Law* (Manchester University Press, 1963)

Jan Klabbers, *An Introduction to International Organizations Law*, 3rd edn (Cambridge University Press, 2015)

Jan Klabbers, 'The EJIL Foreword: The Transformation of International Organizations Law', (2015) 26 *European Journal of International Law*, 9–82

Marcelo G. Kohen, *Possession contesté et souveraineté territoriale* (Paris: Presses Universitaires de France, 1997)

Anne-Marie Slaughter, *A New World Order* (Princeton University Press, 2004)

5

Jurisdiction, Powers, and Immunities

INTRODUCTION

States, being sovereign, can in principle do within their territories as they please: they can legislate as they please, they can prosecute anyone who violates their laws, and they can lock up anyone who commits a crime. In international law language, it is often said that states have jurisdiction over their territories, and that this jurisdiction is, in principle, exclusive and unlimited.

In practice, needless to say, things are not quite as dramatic. While it is true to say that states enjoy jurisdiction, they sometimes have to compete with other states to be able to prosecute the same acts. Moreover, historically the practice has been built that states shall not subject other states and their representatives to their jurisdiction, hence the existence of state immunity (also referred to as sovereign immunity) and of diplomatic privileges and immunities. This chapter will address the jurisdiction of states as well as its functional equivalent: the powers of international organizations. Jurisdiction and powers help to determine what it is that states and international organizations are legally entitled to do, and are therefore indispensable complements to the discussion in the previous chapter.

FIVE PRINCIPLES

States can typically claim jurisdiction on the basis of five (overlapping) principles.[1] Importantly, these are not laid down in any multilateral treaty, or even found in domestic legislation. There is no provision in Dutch criminal law specifying that Dutch criminal law is based on the principle of territoriality or some suchlike idea. What typically happens is that a national criminal code (or any other code) specifies a list of offences, and academic commentators subsequently deduce that this particular code evidences one or the other of international law's principles. Moreover, while international law allows domestic law to be based on any of these principles or a combination, it does not bind states. States are under no obligation, for instance, to accept the principle

---

[1] See generally Cedric Ryngaert, *Jurisdiction in International Law* (Oxford University Press, 2008).

of universal jurisdiction, except and to the extent that a treaty may provide for universal jurisdiction in respect of a particular crime.[2]

That said, many treaties are concluded precisely with a view to coordination in case of jurisdictional conflicts. As we will see, this applies, for instance, to what happens in case of collisions on the high seas, but it applies more generally as well; many treaties of private international law serve first and foremost to allocate jurisdiction over private transactions with a transboundary element.

The first three principles correspond, roughly, to the three defining elements of statehood; since a state is defined by having territory, a population, and a government, its jurisdiction enables it to exercise authority over territory, over its population, and so as to protect its government. In addition, since some territory (and a lot of water) is outside the jurisdiction of any single state, some ideas had to be developed to cover events happening in the interstices between state jurisdictions. This led to the emergence of a principle of universality as well as the idea that on board ships and aircraft, flag-state jurisdiction applies. Finally, some states have accepted a principle of passive personality of jurisdiction – but this is a fairly recent invention which is not only considered politically controversial, but is also difficult to justify in functional terms.

Territoriality

The *fons et origo* of jurisdiction of states is the principle of territoriality, signifying that sovereignty and territory go hand in hand. The main idea is that states can exercise authority over all acts that take place on their territory through legislation, and prosecute all those who violate the laws in force on that territory. This is a pretty straightforward matter, as long as the notion of territory is clearly demarcated.

Things may get more difficult when two or more states are involved, and the archetypal example is that of a man standing in state A and shooting someone across the border in state B.[3] In such a case it is generally accepted that both states can claim jurisdiction: A can do so on the basis of the theory that the behaviour originated in its territory (subjective territoriality), whereas B can invoke objective territoriality – the effects of the action were felt in B.

The controversial decision of the PCIJ in the *Lotus* case was based on objective territoriality; after a Turkish ship and a French ship had collided on the high seas, the Court held that the effects of the collision were felt by Turkey, and therefore Turkey could claim jurisdiction. What makes this less than persuasive (given the facts of the case) is that the Court could only do so by ignoring the fact that the collision took place on the high seas; it equated the Turkish ship with Turkish territory. This has therefore been corrected by treaty,

---

[2] And this is exceptional in its own right; universal jurisdiction is the only one of the principles that sometimes finds itself explicitly mentioned, perhaps because as a legal principle it is still considered controversial.

[3] This kind of thing may happen in particular near border checkpoints, either to keep people out or to prevent them from leaving. For one example among surprisingly many, see http://www.sandiegouniontribune.com/news/2010/jun/08/mexico-anger-high-as-us-border-patrol-kills-teen/ (visited 22 April 2016). Typically, though, in these cases the shooter is a state official, which diminishes chances of prosecution.

abandoning the territorial analogy altogether; under the law of the sea, in the case of collisions taking place on the high seas, the states that can exercise jurisdiction are the flag state of the ships concerned, or the state of nationality of the accused.[4]

Nationality

If the principle of territoriality is undisputed, so, too, is the principle of nationality; states can claim authority over their nationals (including for purposes of prosecution) no matter where they are.[5] A well-known example is that US nationals are under a duty to pay taxes to the United States, even if they reside elsewhere, but the more common field of application is criminal law; the Dutch suspect of a murder committed in Japan can be prosecuted by the Dutch authorities. Whether this is smart is a different matter; it seems likely that the production of evidence and the questioning of witnesses may be easier in Japan than in Holland, but that takes nothing away from the circumstance that the Dutch have the right to prosecute. In the case of dual nationality (individuals who are nationals of two states), both states would be entitled to claim their authority, although in practice there will usually be a dominant nationality whose state will be keener to claim authority than the other.

Jurisdiction on board ships and aircraft is linked to the nationality of these vehicles.[6] This entails that the legislation of the laws of the country of nationality (the 'flag state') apply on board. A KLM stewardess is not allowed to serve alcohol to individuals under 18 years of age, in accordance with Dutch law.[7] Likewise, being born aboard a US aircraft means that the newborn child will acquire US nationality, as in the United States nationality is linked to place of birth.[8]

Protection

It is also generally accepted that states can claim jurisdiction over activities that endanger them, even if those activities take place elsewhere and are ascribed to non-nationals. For instance, a group of Russians printing counterfeit US dollars in a basement in Hamburg, Germany, could be subject to the authority of the United States on the basis of this principle. Territoriality would point to Germany and nationality to Russia, but the United States could claim jurisdiction by arguing that the national interest was at stake; after all, the influx of large amounts of counterfeit money could have serious economic effects. Other examples of crimes which might trigger the protective principle are such matters as the planning of a *coup d'état*, or immigration fraud (smuggling people in or out of a

---

[4] Article 97 of the 1982 UNCLOS.

[5] The theoretical basis has always been a bit unclear. In 1953, a British military tribunal suggested that specific legislation was required to extend the jurisdiction of British courts over acts committed by British subjects abroad. See *R. v. Page*, UK Courts-Martial Appeal Court, 10 November 1953, reported in 20 *International Law Reports* 188.

[6] See e.g. article 92 UNCLOS.

[7] KLM is the Dutch national airline, and on a flight from Helsinki to Amsterdam (2 October 2014) a KLM stewardess confirmed that the flights are operated with the help of a flight manual which sets out and refers back to Dutch law.

[8] See also the next chapter.

country, usually smuggling in), or possibly also attacks on diplomats abroad.[9] Some manifestations are rather broad, and shade into the passive personality principle (discussed below): in 1932, Mexico's Supreme Court upheld protective jurisdiction over a foreigner who had affected 'the legal interests of a Mexican citizen'.[10]

Passive Personality

Controversial is the principle of passive personality, even if it has been applied by courts for a considerable period of time.[11] It holds that a state can prosecute anyone who harms its nationals, no matter where this occurs. If the nationality principle is based on the nationality of the suspect, the passive personality principle takes the nationality of the victim as its starting point, and in doing so it has resurrected the classic idea that injuring a citizen of a state is akin to injuring that state (the idea underlying the institution of diplomatic protection, discussed in Chapter 8 below).

The passive personality principle is highly controversial, as it sends a message to the other state that its legal system is not good enough; a crime committed against Italians in, say, Norway, could under this idea better be dealt with in Italy than in Norway. For that reason the principle is not generally accepted, with, for example, British courts stating unequivocally that 'the murder of a British citizen by a non-British citizen outside the United Kingdom would not constitute an offence in respect of which the United Kingdom could claim extra-territorial jurisdiction ... the United Kingdom courts only have jurisdiction to try a defendant where he has committed a murder outside the United Kingdom if he is a British citizen, regardless of the nationality of the victim.'[12]

Universality

The most interesting and imaginative of the principles is that of universal jurisdiction. Under this idea, some crimes are so abhorrent that all states can legislate and prosecute, regardless of the involvement of their territory or nationals. Historically, this is often said to have evolved in response to the emergence of piracy; pirates, after all, tend to reside on the high seas, out of the reach of any territorial jurisdiction, and pirate groups may comprise individuals of many nationalities, making prosecution on the basis of nationality highly arbitrary. Hence universality arose to prevent piracy from benefiting from the cracks inevitable in a system based primarily on territorial sovereignty.[13]

More recently, universality has been utilized in connection with gross violations of human rights, and possibly the most influential in this respect is the decision of the US

[9] The latter is laid down in the 1973 Convention on the Prevention and Punishment of Crimes against Internationally Protected Persons, article 3.
[10] *In re González*, Mexico, Supreme Court, 21 July 1932, reported in 6 *Annual Digest* 151.
[11] See e.g. *Crown* v. *Yerizano*, Saghalien District Court, Japan, September 1926, reported in 3 *Annual Digest* 149: the court exercised jurisdiction over a crime committed by a foreigner abroad against someone believed to be Japanese.
[12] *In re Augusto Pinochet Ugarte*, England, Divisional Court, Queen's Bench Division, 28 October 1998, reported in 119 *International Law Reports* 27, para. 33.
[13] Universality has historically also been said to apply to attacks on ambassadors, following a similar logic.

Court of Appeals for the Second Circuit in *Filártiga* v. *Peña-Irala*.[14] Dr Filártiga's son had been tortured and killed in Paraguay by the then chief of police of Asuncion, Peña-Irala. When Filártiga moved to New York, Peña-Irala was also there (as an illegal alien); consequently, Filártiga tried to interest the US authorities in prosecuting Peña-Irala, but they declined, claiming that US courts would lack criminal jurisdiction over crimes committed in Paraguay, by a Paraguayan, against another Paraguayan. In despair, Filártiga brought a civil case on the basis of a largely dormant piece of legislation, the 1789 Alien Tort Claims Act which provided for jurisdiction over torts (not crimes) committed 'in violation of the law of nations or a treaty of the United States'.[15]

The lower court declined, not being sure about its jurisdiction, but the Court of Appeals decided to apply the Alien Tort Claims Act. It thereby exercised universal jurisdiction, deciding a case without there being any grounding in any of the other principles. The one thing left for the court to do was to hold that torture (the act of which Peña-Irala was suspected) was indeed a 'violation of the law of nations'. In the end, it awarded a huge sum of money to Filártiga, but by then (oh irony of bureaucracy), Peña-Irala was no longer in the country; he had been deported as an illegal alien by the immigration authorities.

The *Filártiga* decision started off a flurry of litigation in the United States based on gross human rights violations committed elsewhere and by non-US nationals,[16] to the extent that in 2004 the US Supreme Court decided to put a limit on it by holding that the Alien Tort Claims Act covered only serious violations of the most widely accepted human rights. In the case at hand it concerned the abduction of someone involved in the Mexican drugs trade; this 'deprivation of liberty' lasted less than a day, and was therefore, according to the Court, not serious enough to be considered a violation of customary international law and thus covered by the Alien Tort Claims Act.[17] One other limitation had always been implicit in the flurry of cases; typically, the cases were brought by individuals who had taken up residence in the United States, so there would be some connection to that country.

This left open the question how strong the connection to the United States should be, and that question was explicitly addressed in the 2013 *Kiobel* case, requiring a very strong connection.[18] The Supreme Court held, by narrow majority,[19] that the general presumption against extraterritorial application of US legislation also covers the Alien Tort Claims Act, despite the circumstance that the ATCA is a jurisdictional statute, not a substantive one. There was nothing in its drafting history, according to the majority opinion, which

---

[14] *Filártiga* v. *Peña-Irala*, 630 F.2d 876 (Second Circuit of Appeals, 30 June 1980), reproduced in 77 *International law Reports* 169.

[15] For a fine analysis see Anne-Marie Burley (Slaughter), 'The Alien Tort Statute and the Judiciary Act of 1789: A Badge of Honor', (1989) 83 *American Journal of International Law*, 461–93.

[16] See generally Craig Scott (ed.), *Torture as Tort: Comparative Perspectives on the Development of Transnational Human Rights Litigation* (Oxford: Hart, 2001).

[17] *[José Francisco] Sosa* v. *Humberto Alvarez-Machaín*, 542 US 692 (2004), US Supreme Court, 29 June 2004.

[18] *Kiobel et al.* v. *Royal Dutch Petroleum Co. et al.*, 569 US ___ (2013), US Supreme Court, 17 April 2013).

[19] The minority was unhappy with the way the Court's response was framed in terms of the presumption against extraterritoriality, but agreed with the outcome that some kind of connection to the United States would be desirable. In the case at hand, the activities complained of had been carried out in Nigeria, by foreign companies, and against individuals who, at the time, had been living in Nigeria.

suggested that the Act was meant to apply to situations taking place abroad (except in relation to piracy), and application to acts taking place abroad could have nasty foreign policy repercussions. Surprisingly perhaps, at no point did the majority opinion address the circumstance that earlier cases had been less strict concerning the connection to the United States, although the minority suggested that just like pirates, human rights violators acting in violation of the 'law of nations' could be 'fair game' and subject, in principle, to US jurisdiction.[20] Even then, though, the minority opinion agreed that in the case at hand the link was not strong enough. As a result, some have commented that *Kiobel* marks the end of the exercise of universal jurisdiction by the United States.[21]

Whether that is an accurate assessment remains to be seen, if only because *Kiobel* addresses remedial jurisdiction without paying attention to prescriptive jurisdiction. The exercise of prescriptive jurisdiction (i.e. making laws that affect other states) is by no means excluded after *Kiobel*. Be that as it may, other states too have facilitated proceedings on the basis of universality. Thus, Belgium's genocide law of 1993 allowed claims with no connection to Belgium to be brought. While this takes the philosophy behind universality seriously, it does mean that sometimes politically awkward cases can be brought by people who have visited Belgium solely in order to file a complaint, as if Belgium were a juridical supermarket. Thus cases were brought against Israel's Prime Minister Ariel Sharon for his involvement in massacres in Palestinian refugee camps in Lebanon, and against leading US officials, including the first President Bush for the bombing of Baghdad in the early 1990s. Belgium amended its law in 2003 so as to introduce some connection to the country itself, hoping thereby to stop the flow of politically sensitive cases.

Universal jurisdiction sounds a wonderful idea, as it helps to bring an end to impunity for gross human rights violations. Yet there are some drawbacks. It is noticeable, for instance, that many of the cases brought in the United States in the wake of *Filártiga* were brought against individuals or regimes already ousted from power. Universal jurisdiction thus runs the risk of becoming an exercise in 'looking back in anger'. There are also all sorts of practical concerns; the trial in Finland of an individual suspected of having participated in the 1994 Rwanda genocide[22] meant that the local Finnish court and prosecutor had to go on a field trip to Rwanda for a number of weeks, in order to interview witnesses and gather evidence. Obviously, wealthy countries may be able to afford this, but poorer states may not; therefore the exercise of universal jurisdiction runs the risk of becoming a fig leaf for the exercise of political power – rich Western states prosecuting those individuals who offend the standards of those rich Western states.[23]

---

[20] For a scathing critique, see Ralph G. Steinhardt, '*Kiobel* and the Weakening of Precedent: A Long Walk for a Short Drink', (2013) 107 *American Journal of International Law* 841–5, at 841: 'what is law in *Kiobel* isn't clear and what is clear in *Kiobel* isn't law'.

[21] See e.g. Julian G. Ku, '*Kiobel* and the Surprising Death of Universal Jurisdiction under the Alien Tort Statute', (2013) 107 *American Journal of International Law* 835–41.

[22] For more details, see Rain Liivoja, 'Dish of the Day: Justice sans frontières à la Finlandaise', (2010) 1 *Helsinki Review of Global Governance*, 20–3, and Rain Liivoja, 'This Court Sentences You . . . : Trial Court Delivers Judgment in the First Finnish Genocide Case', (2011) 2 *Helsinki Review of Global Governance*, 34–5.

[23] For a critique partly along these lines, see Magdalena Kmak, *The Scope and Application of the Principle of Universal Jurisdiction* (Helsinki: Erik Castrén Institute, 2011).

For these reasons, universal jurisdiction is bound to remain controversial, and it is notable that while the principle is undoubtedly accepted (hence international law permits states to exercise universal jurisdiction), few treaties actually make universal jurisdiction compulsory. A proposal to make the ICC work on the basis of universal jurisdiction was explicitly rejected; it now works mainly on the basis of the territoriality and nationality principles.[24]

It is of some importance to distinguish universal condemnation of a crime from the possibility of universal jurisdiction. Perhaps the most instructive example can be found in the Genocide Convention, which prohibits genocide – possibly the clearest example of a *jus cogens* norm – but does not provide for universal jurisdiction: article VI specifies that those suspected of genocide 'shall be tried by a competent tribunal of the State in the territory of which the act was committed', or possibly by an international criminal tribunal. Hence the convention gives pride of place to the principle of territoriality. Still, states may legislate so as to prosecute genocide wherever it has occurred; but the point is that they are not obliged to do so by the Genocide Convention. In other words, while the substance of a rule may be universally accepted, its enforcement may still be fragmented.

EXTRATERRITORIAL JURISDICTION

It follows from the above that states sometimes claim jurisdiction over acts occurring outside their boundaries. If any of the other principles can be invoked, then this causes few problems, but sometimes the exercise of extraterritorial jurisdiction is rendered problematic. Perhaps the best-known example relates to the reach of US anti-trust law. Traditionally, the US courts have assumed jurisdiction over acts done elsewhere (and considered legal elsewhere) if those acts would affect the US market; this has become known as the 'effects doctrine'. European states have resisted this practice for a while, up to the point of prohibiting European companies from cooperating with US judicial procedure (for instance, providing them with an excuse to refuse to present evidence) in the form of so-called 'blocking statutes'.[25] Yet, under the slogan 'if you can't beat them, join them', the CJEU itself has started to be as aggressive as the US courts; in the classic *Woodpulp* case, it fined four large wood pulp producers for violating EU competition rules, despite the circumstance that all four were, at the time, located outside the EU.[26]

Of increasing political relevance is the reach of international human rights law. Typically, human rights treaties provide protection, in the words of article 1 of the ECHR, 'to everyone within their jurisdiction'. In layman's terms, one would expect this to mean that protection was not limited to a state's territory, strictly speaking, but also extended to other settings: for instance when a state has temporarily leased territory, or when a state is occupying another state, or even when the state is engaged in activities inside another state.

---

[24] This will be further discussed in Chapter 12 below.

[25] Seminal is A. V. Lowe, 'Blocking Extraterritorial Jurisdiction: The British Protection of Trading Interests Act, 1980', (1981) 75 *American Journal of International Law*, 257–282.

[26] Joined cases 89, 104, 114, 116, 117, and 125–129/85, *Ahlström and others* v. *Commission* [1988] ECR 5193 (*Woodpulp*).

The ECtHR has addressed the matter, but in somewhat haphazard fashion. In *Loizidou* it accepted that the reach of the convention included territory under occupation; in the case at hand, it held that in principle Turkey might be responsible for its behaviour in the Turkish part of Cyprus.[27] In *Bankovic*, however, it held that the reach of the convention did not extend outside the states parties to the convention; the behaviour of NATO member states in the former Yugoslavia was therefore not covered by the convention.[28] The Court thereby seemed to suggest that the 'legal space' created and protected by the convention was, in principle, limited to the parties' territories.

Possibly a feature distinguishing both cases is that whereas in *Loizidou* both Cyprus and Turkey were parties to the convention, and activities thus had to fall within the jurisdiction of one of them, the former Yugoslavia at issue in *Bankovic* was not a convention party. Hence the inhabitants of the latter had no pre-existing rights under the convention. Such a conceptualization makes some sense if the focus rests, indeed, on the question for whom the convention creates rights. Alternatively, however, one may also approach the matter as one of obligations of states: for whom does the convention create obligations? Such a focus might suggest a broader reach for the convention.[29] After all, surely certain obligations – in particular the obligation to refrain from nasty behaviour, sometimes referred to as 'negative obligation' – should not come to a halt at the boundary post.[30] In its more recent case law the Court does not go quite that far, but seems to have accepted at least the proposition that with public power comes responsibility. It has held the United Kingdom responsible for the behaviour of UK troops in Iraq on the basis that the United Kingdom (together with the United States) exercised effective control over Iraq at the relevant moment,[31] and on the same basis held the Netherlands responsible for a human rights violation occurring at a boundary checkpoint in Iraq controlled by the Dutch.[32]

The European Court of Human Rights has also repeatedly held that states remain responsible for acts committed by agents of other states but on their territory. Thus, in *El Masri*, it held the former Yugoslav Republic of Macedonia responsible for treatment suffered at the hands of US CIA agents at Skopje airport and beyond,[33] and in *Abu Zubaydah*, it held Poland responsible for allowing human rights violations to take place in a secret US prison on Polish territory.[34] Earlier, it had found the same principle to apply in relation to the acts

---

[27] *Loizidou* v. *Turkey*, preliminary objections (application no. 15318/89), judgment of 23 March 1995, paras. 62–4.

[28] *Bankovic and others* v. *Belgium and others*, admissibility (application no. 52207/99), decision of 12 December 2001, esp. para. 80.

[29] Brilmayer comes close to such a conceptualization. See Lea Brilmayer, 'From "Contract" to "Pledge": The Structure of International Human Rights Agreements', (2006) 77 *British Yearbook of International Law*, 163–202.

[30] See likewise Marko Milanovic, *Extraterritorial Application of Human Rights Treaties: Law, Principles, and Policy* (Oxford University Press, 2011).

[31] *Al-Skeini and Others* v. *United Kingdom* (application no. 55721/07), judgment of 7 July 2011, paras. 149–50.

[32] *Jaloud* v. *The Netherlands* (application no. 47708/08), judgment of 20 November 2014, para. 152.

[33] *El Masri* v. *Former Yugoslav Republic of Macedonia* (application no. 39630/09), judgment of 13 December 2012, para. 206. El Masri had been arrested in Skopje, handed over to CIA agents, and was transported, without any form of process, to a secret detention facility in Afghanistan.

[34] *Husayn (Abu Zubaydah)* v. *Poland* (application no. 7511/13), judgment of 24 July 2014, para. 449.

of non-recognized entities on a state party's territory: the state remains responsible for 'acquiescence or connivance' on the part of its authorities.[35] And without being very generous in argumentation, it has also assumed that the international zone of an airport remains under the jurisdiction of the state on whose territory the airport is located: 'Despite its name, the international zone does not have extraterritorial status.'[36]

Things are also problematic when military troops are located abroad and become involved in common crimes. On the one hand, one could argue that, for instance, a murder taking place on a foreign army base falls within the jurisdiction of the host state; after all, it is that state's territory, and it has a strong and legitimate interest in upholding law and order there. On the other hand, one could also claim that the sending state has a legitimate interest in seeing that military law and discipline are unaffected by the interference of what are, effectively, foreign courts. Consequently, it has been argued that such a situation requires special treatment; it cannot neatly be captured in terms of the five principles outlined above.[37]

CONCURRENT JURISDICTION

If states can claim jurisdiction on the basis of several distinct principles, it would also logically seem to follow that several states may be able to claim jurisdiction over one and the same act. Imagine, for instance, a shooting spree on San Marco Square in Venice, Italy, with a Bulgarian gunman taking the lives of three German tourists and a Brazilian diplomat. In this hypothetical example, jurisdiction could be claimed by Italy (territoriality principle) and Bulgaria (nationality principle), and perhaps also by Brazil (if protection of diplomats is considered to fall within the protective principle) and Germany (if the passive personality principle is accepted). A claim based on the universality principle is less likely, however, as this principle is not usually invoked for common crimes. If, however, the Bulgarian gunman claimed to represent a political movement and the act were considered one of terrorism, then perhaps the universality principle could also be relied on – provided that it is considered to encompass acts of terrorism.

Sometimes concurrent jurisdiction is created by treaty. An example hereof is how, in 1980, the Belgian Court of Cassation upheld the proposition that Belgian courts could exercise jurisdiction over drugs trafficking charges on the arrest of the suspects in a moving train, going from Paris, France, to Amsterdam in the Netherlands, and passing through Belgium. At the moment of the arrest, the train had still been in France, but Belgian courts could exercise jurisdiction on the basis of the 1962 border control agreement between

---

[35] *Ilascu* v. *Moldova and Russia* (application no. 48787/99), judgment of 8 July 2004, para. 318 (relating to acts of Transdniestria).

[36] *Amuur* v. *France* (application no. 19776/92), judgment of 25 June 1996, para. 52. Domestic courts also tend to consider the transit zones of airports as part of their territory for purposes of the exercise of criminal jurisdiction. See e.g. *Public Prosecutor* v. *Jean O.*, Austria, Supreme Court, 15 October 1981, reported in 77 *International Law Reports* 483.

[37] Rain Liivoja, 'An Axiom of Military Law', doctoral thesis, University of Helsinki, 2011.

France and Belgium, which explicitly created the authority to exercise jurisdiction in the train 'in the same manner as on their own territory'.[38]

In cases of concurrent jurisdiction, it may be quite a hassle to figure out which state has the stronger claim. In the normal course of events, the best cards are held by the state holding the suspect in custody. After all, unless states want to conduct trials *in absentia* (which they are usually reluctant to do), they cannot really proceed without a suspect. Thus states will have to ask for extradition – this will be further discussed in Chapter 12 below, but here it can already be spelled out that some treaties, aiming to prevent 'safe havens', stipulate an obligation either to prosecute or to extradite (*aut dedere, aut judicare*). One example can be found in the 1999 Terrorism Financing Convention, which specifies that a state will, if it does not extradite an offender, 'be obliged, without exception whatsoever and whether or not the offence was committed in its territory, to submit the case without undue delay to its competent authorities'.[39] States can also waive any jurisdictional claims they may have, and allow others to proceed.[40]

THE POWERS OF INTERNATIONAL ORGANIZATIONS

States are based on territory and have a population of their own; hence states can exercise authority (or jurisdiction) on those two bases. International organizations, by contrast, lack their own territory, and lack their own population; it follows that their authority (in particular their authority to legislate) must find a different basis. The leading theory is that organizations are established on a functional basis;[41] their authority derives, in one way or another, from their function or functions, and this is usually captured by claiming that international organizations can exercise legal powers.[42] The member states set up an organization to perform a certain function (be it collective security, as with the UN, or the promotion of global health, as with the WHO), and in order to give effect to that function the organization must be able to exercise some authority.

Usually this is captured in terms of a doctrine of 'attributed' or 'conferred' powers or competences; the member states may clearly specify in the treaty setting up the organization what the powers of the organization and its organs are. Thus the member states of the UN have conferred on the UN Security Council the 'primary responsibility for the maintenance of international peace and security', and have done so by means of article 24 UN Charter. They have, likewise, given the UN the power to promote 'higher standards of living' and respect for human rights (article 55 UN Charter), or, more specifically, the power to conclude agreements with other international organizations (article 57 UN Charter).

[38] *Lo Yin Ling and Man Kin Ping*, Belgium, Court of Cassation, 16 April 1980, reported in 82 *International Law Reports* 104.
[39] Article 10 of the International Convention for the Suppression of the Financing of Terrorism.
[40] See e.g., by implication, *Re Gadois Deceased*, Paris Court of Appeal, France, 14 December 1953, reported in 20 *International Law Reports* 186.
[41] Jan Klabbers, 'The EJIL Foreword: The Transformation of International Organizations Law', (2015) 26 *European Journal of International Law*, 9–82.
[42] See generally Viljam Engström, *Constructing the Powers of International Institutions* (Leiden: Martinus Nijhoff, 2012).

While the conferred powers can be rather broad, as the above examples suggest, none the less the scope of powers of organizations would be easy to verify if those powers were limited to those explicitly granted by member states. In that case, the question 'Can organization A engage in activity X?' could be answered relatively simply by checking its constituting treaty. In reality, however, things get more complicated, as organizations are often said not merely to have powers that are explicitly granted, but also powers that can be implied by their constituting treaties. These are not written down explicitly, but are none the less considered necessary for the organization.

This 'implied powers' doctrine comes in two guises. One school of thought, tracing the doctrine back to federalist political theory, maintains that an implied power is a power necessary to give effect to an explicit power. Thus, a power to decide on legal claims may involve (imply) the power to create a mechanism or organ for deciding such claims.[43] The broader approach, though, connects implied powers not with explicit powers, but with the functions of the organization. Under this theory, the organization will have any powers that may be necessary for it to achieve its goals.

This broader theory is based on the ICJ's 1949 *Reparation for Injuries* opinion, in which the Court held that the UN had a right to bring claims against a non-member state because this would enable it to carry out its functions, despite the fact that its constituting document said not a word about the power to bring claims.[44] The case arose after an UN-appointed mediator, the Swedish Count Folke Bernadotte, had been assassinated while trying to help settle the dispute surrounding the creation of Israel in 1946–7. It was unclear who would cover burial costs and related hospital costs, and the UN feared that it would hardly be able to engage in keeping the peace if this was the sort of cost it was always going to have to bear. Hence, since the assassination was attributed to the underground Zionist group Irgun, headed by Menachim Begin,[45] the UN wondered whether it could claim compensation from Israel. The Charter remained silent about the UN bringing claims (of any kind), so it fell to the Court to decide on the question, and, as noted, the Court formulated a broad implied powers doctrine.

The doctrine is so broad, indeed, that it has come to justify all sorts of activities being undertaken by international organizations, providing much of the legal justification of what in other contexts is referred to as 'mission creep'. The UN, for instance, can utilize the doctrine so as to justify its involvement in drugs trafficking. After all, the drugs trade is often used to finance military or guerrilla uprisings; hence the function of upholding international peace and security warrants an interest in drugs trafficking, despite the absence of any reference to it in the UN Charter. The underlying theory, then, is that the drafters of the Charter would surely have inserted a clause on drugs trafficking if only they had thought of it. Drafters are not, alas, omniscient, but none the less, as the Court has

---

[43] *Interpretation of the Greco-Turkish Agreement of December 1st, 1926*, advisory opinion, (1928) Publ. PCIJ, Series B, no. 16.

[44] *Reparation for Injuries Suffered in the Service of the United Nations*, advisory opinion, [1949] ICJ Rep. 174.

[45] In one of the wonderful ironies of history, Begin would three decades later be prime minister of Israel. In that capacity he concluded a peace agreement with Egypt and received the Nobel Peace Prize.

repeated time and again, an implied power arises 'by necessary intendment'.[46] Thus, even an implied power can rhetorically be traced back to the wishes of the drafters and thereby to the consent of the organization's member states.

It is useful to distinguish between the capacity of an international organization to engage in activities, and its competences or powers. Under general international law, international organizations have the capacity to perform all sorts of acts; they can (and do) conclude treaties, they can open missions in the world's political capitals, and even, in some circumstances, bring legal claims, although they cannot bring cases to the ICJ.[47] Generally speaking though, the capacity of organizations is reined in by their limited competences. Thus, unless the implied powers are stretched beyond breaking point, an organization devoted to forestry research cannot engage in military missions. It may have the capacity under international law to do so, but will lack the competence. However, this is not unique to international organizations; some states have limited their power to act by means of their constitutions. Thus, since the Second World War, both the Japanese and the German constitutions have provided that these states cannot participate in military operations, despite the fact that under international law they would have the capacity to do so – provided, of course, the military operation was itself lawful.[48]

SOVEREIGN IMMUNITIES

Mankind has learned the hard way that negotiations between states would be made extremely difficult if whenever a negotiator was sent, he was put in prison or killed – this would not be conducive to productive diplomatic relations. Hence, over time, the practice grew of providing states and their plenipotentiaries with protection against the authorities of the state with which they were supposed to do business, and these have found recognition in the law of immunities. It is generally accepted that states themselves can be immune from prosecution in other states, as can their representatives (diplomats and others), and much the same applies to international organizations.

For centuries, states were held to be absolutely immune, meaning, in effect, that states could not be prosecuted before the courts of other states. The underlying theory owed much to the idea that domestic courts should be used for disputes between individuals, but that disputes involving states – international disputes proper – should somehow be settled on the international level, through diplomacy, or by means of an international tribunal.

This worked fine when states and their rulers were deemed identical; when Louis XIV proclaimed 'L'état, c'est moi', he made some sense to his contemporaries. States and their

---

[46] In this way, the ICJ approved of the creation of an administrative tribunal by the UN in *Effect of Awards of Compensation made by the United Nations Administrative Tribunal*, advisory opinion, [1954] ICJ Rep. 47, and of peacekeeping by the UN in *Certain Expenses of the United Nations (Article 17, Paragraph 2, of the Charter)*, advisory opinion, [1962] ICJ Rep. 151. For further discussion, see Jan Klabbers, *An Introduction to International Organizations Law*, 3rd edn (Cambridge University Press, 2015).

[47] Under article 34 ICJ Statute, only states can do so.

[48] Article 9 of the Japanese Constitution of 1946 provides, in part, that 'land, sea, and air forces . . . will never be maintained'. The German constitution envisages a purely defensive role for its armed forces, although Germany may participate in collective security systems as well.

sovereigns were really one and the same, and it stood to reason that no sovereign ruler would have to endure the indignity of a trial abroad. The position could hold until the twentieth century, when states started to take on an increasing number of functions, including the operation of state companies. This now opened the possibility of state companies reneging on their contracts with impunity for, being instruments of the state, they could benefit from the state's absolute immunity. In particular after the Russian revolution of 1917, when well-nigh all commercial relations would be state activities, the spectre loomed larger.[49]

This prompted a number of states slowly to resort to a different approach; states would still be immune as regards their governmental acts (*acta jure imperii*), but not for their commercial acts (*acta jure gestionis*), a position set out with some clarity in a letter written by acting US Attorney General Jack Tate in 1952. That makes eminent sense, at first sight; why accept the immunity of a state in a case of breach of contract? It soon appeared, however, that this distinction between governmental and commercial acts created a problem of its own: how to tell the difference? Some states proposed to look at the object of the transaction: if the act was done for the public good, then it was a governmental act, and thus immunity should apply. Other states preferred to look at the nature of the transaction: if an act was by its nature a commercial transaction, regardless of its purpose, then it had to be classified as commercial, and thus immunity should not apply.

It would seem that this second approach (of looking at the nature of the transaction) has become the more generally accepted, and probably for good reason. After all, the 'purpose test' is vulnerable to the criticism that it lacks sharpness; one may well expect most commercial activities of a government to have a public purpose, whether it be the purchase of army boots for its soldiers or the lease of computer equipment for its *fonctionnaires*. Governments presumably engage in few, if any, transactions for private purposes, hence the 'purpose test' would offer wide loopholes, and still come very close to absolute immunity in practice.

It is important to note that international law does not prescribe anything here; instead, it is permissive. It permits states to adopt absolute immunity; likewise, it permits them to adopt a system of relative immunity. In many states, then, sovereign immunities are regulated by domestic legislation, also because in the absence of a universally applicable convention many terms will require further detailed definition. In the United States, for instance, the relevant law is the 1976 Foreign Sovereign Immunities Act (FSIA), which confirms that states can claim immunity except for commercial activities. It also provides that states may waive their immunity, and holds that no immunity applies to certain activities related to terrorism. For purposes of the FSIA, a foreign state includes its organs and political subdivisions, and in order to establish what counts as a commercial activity, the FSIA holds that the nature of the transaction is decisive. Importantly, the FSIA subjects itself to the supremacy of existing treaties, which means, in effect, that the

---

[49] The leading study is Hazel Fox and Philippa Webb, *The Law of State Immunity*, 3rd edn (Oxford University Press, 2013).

immunities of embassies granted under the Vienna Convention on Diplomatic Relations are not affected by the FSIA.[50]

Attempts to harmonize the various practices of states have so far not been very successful. The European Convention on State Immunity, concluded in 1972, has yet to enter into force, and the more recent and more universal UN Convention on the Jurisdictional Immunities of States and their Property, concluded in 2004, still has some way to go before it acquires the required number of instruments of ratification; thirty are needed, whereas only twenty-one have been forthcoming as at April 2016.

Part of the problem is that the realization has dawned that there is a category of acts that defy classification as either 'official' or 'private'. Think, for instance, of human rights violations; these are rarely carried out for private reasons, and can thus not be considered *acta jure gestionis*. Yet it would be awkward to accept human rights violations as official government business, to which immunity applies. While there is case law to this effect from domestic courts, in relation to such acts as torture[51] and even the Holocaust[52] it is difficult to think of such acts as being *acta jure imperii* and thus entitled to sovereign respect.

In a 2012 decision, the ICJ none the less – and rather controversially – upheld the immunity of a state for gross human rights violations. After Italy's Court of Cassation had held, in the 2004 *Ferrini* case,[53] that state immunity could not apply when *jus cogens* was violated, Germany (the state concerned) complained to the ICJ that denying immunity violated international law and the Court agreed. It argued that substantive norms (such as, *in casu*, the prohibition of forced labour), even if they were recognized as *jus cogens*, operated differently from procedural devices, such as the rules on state immunity. In other words, according to the Court there was no conflict between *jus cogens* and rules on state immunity, and thus no sense in which either could be considered to be superior: 'The two sets of rules address different matters.' According to the Court, the rules on immunity determine whether a national court has jurisdiction, but that question is different from the question concerning the lawfulness of the activities at issue.[54]

HEADS OF STATE AND OTHERS

Derived from the idea of sovereign immunity is the idea that the leaders of states are still immune from jurisdiction, at least while in office. This was confirmed as the state of customary international law in the 2002 *Arrest Warrant* case: heads of state, heads of

---

[50] For an in-depth discussion, see Sean D. Murphy, *Principles of International Law* (St Paul, MN: West/ Thomson, 2006), 266–84.

[51] *Siderman de Blake* v. *Argentina*, 965 F.2d 669, US Ninth Circuit Court of Appeals, 22 May 1992.

[52] *Princz* v. *Federal Republic of Germany*, 26 F.3d 1166, US DC Circuit Court of Appeals, 1 July 1994.

[53] *Ferrini* v. *Federal Republic of Germany*, Court of Cassation, Italy, judgment of 11 March 2004, in 128 *International Law Reports*, 658.

[54] *Jurisdictional Immunities of the State* (*Germany* v. *Italy*; Greece Intervening), [2012] ICJ Rep. 99, para. 93. The Italian Constitutional Court decided later that the human rights guarantees offered by Italy's constitution prevail over contrary international law, therewith effectively ignoring the ICJ's judgment. See Judgment no. 238, judgment of 22 October 2014, further discussed in Chapter 16 below.

government, and foreign ministers are immune from prosecution, at least while in office.[55] Having left office, their immunity for sovereign acts performed while in office continues to apply, but much depends, obviously, on how 'sovereign acts' is defined.

The question of the immunities of heads of state and other political leaders gained considerable political momentum during the 1990s with, first, the creation of the ad hoc tribunals for Yugoslavia and Rwanda and, second, the arrest of General Pinochet, the former dictator of Chile, in a hospital in London. Attention was focused on the possibility of prosecuting political leaders for their contribution to mass atrocities. Pinochet had headed a regime that was known to have had a highly cavalier attitude to human rights, and part of the idea behind the ad hoc tribunals was to prosecute precisely the political leadership: the likes of Slobodan Milosevic in Yugoslavia, and Rwanda's Jean Kambanda, who was prime minister of the country during the 1994 genocide. Article 7 of the International Criminal Tribunal for the former Yugoslavia (ICTY) Statute lifted the immunity of political leaders, including heads of state and government, as did article 6 of the International Criminal Tribunal for Rwanda (ICTR) Statute. This allowed the prosecution of Kambanda and Milosevic, and while the former was indeed sentenced to life imprisonment, the latter died during the proceedings against him.

The fact that the statutes of the ICTY and the ICTR explicitly lifted the immunity of political leaders[56] can be seen as an affirmation that without such provision, the customary rule is still that immunity applies. This presented a problem in the *Pinochet* case.[57] Pinochet, who had ruled Chile with an iron fist between 1973 and 1990, was wanted by a Spanish court in order to be tried on charges of torture, kidnapping, and mass disappearances. When arrested in London, he invoked head of state immunity; as a former head of state, he suggested, he was immune from prosecution by any domestic court. The House of Lords would, eventually, disagree. Basing itself on the 1984 Torture Convention, which creates universal jurisdiction for torture and says nothing at all about immunity, it suggested that the very creation of universal jurisdiction would be nullified if immunities prevailed. Hence the Torture Convention had to be construed so as to lift immunities, at least once political leaders had left office.[58]

DIPLOMATIC PRIVILEGES AND IMMUNITIES

Diplomats represent their state abroad, and in order to do so properly, should be free from concerns about harassment or arrest. For that reason, international law has long recognized that diplomats, their immediate families, and others working or at an embassy, enjoy certain privileges and immunities, and those rules, customary in origin, have largely been

---

[55] *Arrest Warrant of 11 April 2000* (*Democratic Republic of Congo* v. *Belgium*), [2002] ICJ Rep. 3, esp. para. 61.

[56] See also article 27 ICC Statute, which does the same in more explicit terms.

[57] The *Pinochet* case is, actually, a string of cases. The one most relevant for present purposes is *Regina* v. *Bow Street Metropolitan Stipendiary Magistrate, ex parte Pinochet Ugarte* (no. 3), House of Lords, 24 March 1999, reproduced in 119 *International Law Reports*, 135.

[58] For a highly readable account see Philippe Sands, *Lawless World: America and the Making and Breaking of Global Rules* (London: Allen Lane, 2005), 23–45.

codified in the 1961 Vienna Convention on Diplomatic Relations. The convention entered into force in 1964, and had no fewer than 190 parties as of April 2016, making it one of the most widely ratified international conventions.[59]

The convention makes a distinction between four kinds of persons: there are the diplomats proper (circularly defined as those 'having diplomatic rank'), the technical and administrative staff, the service staff, and the private staff. All of them boast some level of privileges and immunities, but the level for diplomats is higher than for the other categories. In addition, the convention devotes a number of provisions to the diplomatic mission and other non-personal objects, such as correspondence.

Diplomatic relations are established by mutual consent, and the accreditation of the head of mission depends on his or her acceptance by the host state. States need not provide reasons for refusal to accept certain individuals, and are at liberty to declare individual diplomats *persona non grata*, again without having to provide reasons. This is, in a way, the price to pay for immunity; diplomats are immune from prosecution, but if suspected of crimes they can always be expelled. That said, sending them off is often done for more or less political reasons; if state A declares someone *persona non grata*, state B may be tempted to reciprocate.

The mission (i.e. the embassy) is inviolable; domestic authorities may not enter except with the ambassador's permission or, in extreme cases, the permission of the sending foreign minister.[60] This is a strict obligation, and often upheld in even the most extreme circumstances. One example is that when in the early 1980s shots were fired from the Libyan embassy in London, killing a police officer, the United Kingdom none the less refrained from invading the premises. The inviolability extends to the furnishings and property, as well as to the means of transport of the mission, and also applies to the private residence of diplomats. Likewise, archives and documents of the mission are inviolable, and the mission enjoys free communication for all official purposes. This includes the inviolability of diplomatic mail and the diplomatic bag.

Diplomatic agents (those who are 'of diplomatic rank') enjoy immunity from criminal jurisdiction in the receiving state, as well as immunity from administrative and civil jurisdiction, except in certain narrowly defined circumstances (e.g. when the diplomat acts as executor of someone's will). They are also inviolable; they may not be arrested and should this happen, they should be promptly released. Diplomats are also exempt from social service charges in the receiving state, and from all dues and taxes (again, with some narrow exceptions). That does not mean that they are exempt from taxes altogether; typically, being employed by their home state, they pay taxes to their home states. Much the same applies to the family of the diplomat, defined as those 'forming part of his [*sic*] household'.

---

[59] An excellent guide is Eileen Denza, *Diplomatic Law: Commentary on the Vienna Convention on Diplomatic Relations*, 4th edn (Oxford University Press, 2016).

[60] This helps to explain why people sometimes seek refuge from prosecution in an embassy – an action that is not to be confused with arbitrary detention. A prominent current example is that of WikiLeaks founder Julian Assange, who has been in the Ecuadorian embassy in London since 2012. The UK authorities cannot enter the embassy, and Ecuador is not under any strict obligation to send him away.

Much the same also applies to the technical and administrative staff (secretaries, translators, etc.), except that their immunity from prosecution extends only to official acts. Members of the service staff (such as drivers) enjoy official act immunity, exemptions from taxation on their salaries and exemptions from social service charges, and private servants of the mission (such as a nanny) enjoy a more limited scope; their exemptions only extend to taxes on their salaries, plus whatever the receiving state is willing to grant them.

All this is subject to an important principle – the principle of nationality discrimination. If it happens to be the case that a driver, or even a diplomat, is a national of the receiving state, his or her situation is governed by the laws of the receiving state. No immunities are provided for in the Vienna Convention, with the exception of the case of diplomats; in the rare case that these are nationals of the receiving state, their immunity from jurisdiction, and inviolability, only extends to official acts performed in the exercise of their functions.

In much the same way as diplomats representing states can claim privileges and immunities, so too can officials of international organizations or state delegates to such organizations.[61] While there is no equivalent treaty to the 1961 Vienna Convention, most international organizations have headquarters agreements with their host states which outline the immunities and privileges of staff, delegates and the organization itself, and some conventions of a more general nature exist. Thus the status of the UN in the United States depends partly on the 1946 General Conventions on Privileges and Immunities of the UN and partly on the UN–US headquarters agreement, as well as on applicable domestic legislation.

Typically, the status of international civil servants and delegates to organizations is quite comparable to that of state diplomats and embassies, but the underlying theory is more clearly spelled out as 'functional'; organizations, their staff and delegates have such privileges and immunities as are necessary to enable the organization to function.[62] That said, there is considerable uncertainty concerning the theoretical basis of the immunity of state diplomats, and a strong case can be made that here, too, the defining hallmark is a functionalist one. At the very least, it is by now commonly accepted that a diplomatic mission abroad is not a small bit of territory of the sending state; this so-called 'exterritorial' theory is widely discarded, and only resurfaces occasionally in airport bestsellers such as *The Da Vinci Code*.

FINAL REMARKS

The jurisdiction of states is a topic of vital, if sometimes somewhat neglected,[63] importance; it determines the limits of the state's authority, whether this is legislative authority or

---

[61] See generally Klabbers, *Introduction*, 130–53.

[62] See P. H. F. Bekker, *The Legal Position of Intergovernmental Organizations: A Functional Necessity Analysis of their Legal Status and Immunities* (Dordrecht: Martinus Nijhoff, 1994).

[63] The leading monograph is Ryngaert, *Jurisdiction*, while authoritative general studies include F. A. Mann, 'The Doctrine of Jurisdiction in International Law', (1964/I) 111 *Recueil des Cours*, 9–162.

enforcement authority. In other words, China cannot legislate over Switzerland, and Bulgaria cannot prosecute a German shoplifter for shoplifting in Nigeria. Likewise, the scope of activities of international organizations is hemmed in by the concept of competences; the WHO is not in a position to adopt rules on the liberalization of trade or ask an opinion on the legality of nuclear weapons,[64] and the WTO cannot issue vaccination passports or approve a loan to build a dam in Mauritania.

This means, of course, that jurisdiction and competences are often contested, and often become the subject of international litigation. The ICJ has developed the concept of powers of international organizations in a string of cases, and has dealt with state jurisdiction on quite a few occasions as well, whether it concerns the jurisdiction to prosecute a collision on the high seas (the *Lotus* case),[65] or the jurisdiction to grant nationality (*Nationality Decrees*),[66] or the jurisdiction to prosecute high-ranking state officials (*Arrest Warrant*).[67]

By extending the scope of their jurisdiction, states may attempt to engage in global governance; the further the legislative powers of state X reach, the more it can control behaviour worldwide. Hence, in particular where global regimes are absent, the extraterritorial reach of state jurisdiction serves as the functional equivalent of global governance. Needless to say, jurisdiction thereby becomes an instrument in the hands of powerful states, and it is no coincidence that the exercise of jurisdiction based on the principle of universality is often criticized on precisely that basis.

Either way, jurisdiction is inherent in statehood, and powers, while not inherent perhaps,[68] are vital to the functioning of international organizations. This sets states and international organizations apart from other subjects of international law; these may have rights under international law, but cannot be said to enjoy jurisdiction. The next chapter will discuss at some length the legal position of what is, according to some, the real subject of international law: the individual.

FURTHER READING

P. H. F. Bekker, *The Legal Position of Intergovernmental Organizations: A Functional Necessity Analysis of Their Legal Status and Immunities* (Dordrecht: Martinus Nijhoff, 1994)

Eileen Denza, *Diplomatic Law: Commentary on the Vienna Convention on Diplomatic Relations*, 4th edn (Oxford University Press, 2016)

Viljam Engström, *Constructing the Powers of International Institutions* (Leiden: Martinus Nijhoff, 2012)

---

[64] *Legality of the Use by a State of Nuclear Weapons in Armed Conflict*, advisory opinion, [1996] ICJ Rep. 66.

[65] *SS Lotus* [1927] Publ. PCIJ, Series A, no. 10.

[66] *Nationality Decrees Issued in Tunis and Morocco (French Zone)*, advisory opinion, [1923] Publ. PCIJ, Series B, no. 4.

[67] *Arrest Warrant*.

[68] The theory of inherent powers of international organizations would hold that organizations can engage in all kinds of activities unless explicitly prohibited. Such a theory has been proposed, but has not met with general acceptance. Its main proponent is Finn Seyersted, *Common Law of International Organizations* (Leiden: Martinus Nijhoff, 2008).

Hazel Fox and Philippa Webb, *The Law of State Immunity*, 3rd edn (Oxford University Press, 2013)

F. A. Mann, 'The Doctrine of Jurisdiction in International Law', (1964/I) 111 *Recueil des Cours* 9–162

Marko Milanovic, *Extraterritorial Application of Human Rights Treaties: Law, Principles, and Policy* (Oxford University Press, 2011)

Cedric Ryngaert, *Jurisdiction in International Law*, 2nd edn (Oxford University Press, 2015)

Craig Scott (ed.), *Torture as Tort: Comparative Perspectives on the Development of Transnational Human Rights Litigation* (Oxford: Hart, 2001)

6

The Individual in International Law, Including Human Rights

INTRODUCTION

For centuries, international law did not think of individuals in other than a highly abstract sense. Individuals were citizens of states; international law was the law between states, and that was it. Individuals, so the phrase went, were objects of international law, but not subjects; they were not considered to be capable of bearing rights and obligations under international law.

And saying that individuals were objects of international law did not take things very far. States could treat their citizens as they pleased. It was only with citizens of other states that states had to respect some basic principles. Thus, if an alien (the term is telling in its own right, evoking creatures from outer space) was injured, then international law could come into play; the state could be held responsible if it was complicit in mistreatment of an individual, or if it failed to protect an individual. And if an alien's property was confiscated or expropriated, again the state could be held responsible and perhaps be under a duty to compensate. Beyond this, however, international law did not address the position of individuals, and this state of affairs lasted until well into the twentieth century.

This chapter aims to discuss the emergence of the individual as a subject of international law by concentrating on the rights individuals nowadays enjoy under international law.[1] This means, first and foremost, a discussion of international human rights law, but also a brief discussion of individuals as refugees and as migrants. In addition, this chapter devotes some attention to individuals as members of social groups other than states: as peoples, minorities, or indigenous peoples. It is also useful to point out, at this juncture, that individuals not only have rights under international law but also have obligations; the emergence of international criminal tribunals makes it clear that individuals can be prosecuted, under international law, for such heinous activities as committing war crimes or committing genocide. A substantive discussion of this is, however, best left to a later chapter.[2]

---

[1] For a general overview see Kate Parlett, *The Individual in the International Legal System: Continuity and Change in International Law* (Cambridge University Press, 2011).

[2] Chapter 12 below.

FROM SLAVERY TO HUMAN RIGHTS

Possibly the first issues which directed the attention of international law to the plight of individuals were slavery and the slave trade. In the early nineteenth century, several states, including the United Kingdom and the United States, enacted legislation to abolish the slave trade, and by the end of the century slavery had become generally outlawed in the western hemisphere. This was partly done for humanitarian reasons, no doubt, but partly also because slavery distorted global competition. Then again, it has also been argued that the United Kingdom's sponsorship of abolitionism actually cost its imperial economy dearly.[3]

Either way, by the end of the nineteenth century slavery had become taboo. The 1885 General Act of the Berlin Conference, known for having regulated the 'scramble for Africa',[4] contained in article 9 a provision emphasizing that slave trading was prohibited in international law, and that the African territories 'may not be used as a market or means of transit for the trade in slaves'. This was followed five years later by the Brussels Conference, more specifically devoted to ending slavery, where the preamble of the Declaration of the General Act underlined in a somewhat paternalistic tone that what followed was 'a collection of measures intended to put an end to the Negro Slave Trade by land as well as by sea, and to improve the moral and material conditions of existence of the native races'. And by 1926 a Slavery Convention could be concluded under auspices of the League of Nations, roundly condemning slavery and the trade in slaves.

The same League of Nations was instrumental in creating the first instruments for the protection of minorities. This was a direct consequence of the Versailles Peace after the First World War; the map of Europe had been redrawn to such an extent that the new boundaries started to include ethnic minorities, or new states had been created that were amalgams of different ethnic groups thrown together, exemplified by the proclamation, in 1918, of the Kingdom of Serbs, Croats and Slovenes (which quickly would become known under the easier name Yugoslavia).[5] While the intention of stimulating the self-determination of nations and peoples in Europe had come to nought, at least the sentiment inspired the conclusion of treaties for the protection of these national minorities; states were only allowed to join the League of Nations once they had committed to minority protection.[6]

Still, this was a far cry from thinking of the individual as a subject of international law, and it is useful to point out that to the extent that the minorities treaties and the Slavery Convention could be seen as protecting human beings, they did so by treating humans as groups (rather than individuals), and by casting humans as victims. This latter point, treating humans as victims, would prove to be persistent; much human rights law is still

---

[3] Jenny Martinez, 'Antislavery Courts and the Dawn of International Human Rights Law', (2008) 117 *Yale Law Journal*, 550–641, and, in greater detail, Jenny Martinez, *The Slave Trade and the Origins of International Human Rights Law* (Oxford University Press, 2012).

[4] A fine study (in Dutch) is H. L. Wesseling, *Verdeel en heers: De deling van Afrika, 1880–1914* (Amsterdam: Bert Bakker, 1991).

[5] See generally Margaret Macmillan, *Paris 1919: Six Months that Changed the World* (New York: Random House, 2001).

[6] For critical historical discussion, see Mark Mazower, *Dark Continent: Europe's 20th Century* (London: Penguin, 1998).

based on the same idea, and much international criminal law (to be discussed elsewhere in this book) is likewise based on the idea that nasty people should be locked up so that they cannot make more victims. The period after the Second World War did, however, see a changing attitude on the first point. Humans started to be seen not just as members of groups, but as individuals in their own right; this marked the birth of international human rights law,[7] even if it did not yet mark the emergence of the global human rights phenomenon.[8]

The underlying idea, sensible in an era marked by totalitarianism, was that individuals needed to be protected against their own governments; consequently, the dominant conceptualization of human rights has been that they apply in relations between government and governed, rather than in relations between individuals. In more recent years, however, the idea has gained ground that human rights can also play a relevant role in private relations and that actors other than states may be legally bound to respect human rights law.[9]

This new idea still had a hesitant start. The UN Charter contains only a few lukewarm references to human rights. Ensuring respect for human rights is one of the purposes of the UN, and articles 55 and 56 provide the UN with the tools to formulate human rights policies. The first breakthrough, however, would come in 1948, when on 10 December the General Assembly adopted arguably its most important resolution ever: the Universal Declaration of Human Rights. Adopted as a General Assembly resolution, the Universal Declaration is technically not considered as a legally binding document; its force *qua* instrument is that of a recommendation. Its influence has, however, proved to be enormous.

The Universal Declaration, drafted by a committee chaired by Eleanor Roosevelt, the widow of US President Franklin Roosevelt, and comprising representatives of a variety of ideologies, contains a set of rights said to be of a universal character. These comprise classic, well-established notions such as the freedoms of expression, of religion, and of assembly, but also less obvious ones, such as the right to have paid holidays. Initially, commentators were sceptical, none more so perhaps than the American Anthropological Association, which emphasized, in a statement on the draft version of the Universal Declaration, issued in 1947, that since cultures across the world were different and highly varied, it would be unlikely that any set of rights could actually meaningfully be considered 'universal'.[10] Yet many have later reached the conclusion that the Universal Declaration stimulated states to guarantee human rights in their national constitutions and legislation, leading to the conclusion that some of its provisions have crystallized into customary

---

[7] For a useful overview, see Paul Gordon Lauren, *The Evolution of International Human Rights: Visions Seen* (Philadelphia, PA: University of Pennsylvania Press, 1998).

[8] For a powerful and sophisticated (if not always subtle) argument that the international human rights revolution only took off in the 1970s, see Samuel Moyn, *The Last Utopia: Human Rights in History* (Cambridge, MA: Harvard University Press, 2010). For further reflections on the possible relevance of the ban on the slave trade as the starting point of human rights, see Philip Alston, 'Does the Past Matter? On the Origins of Human Rights', (2013) 126 *Harvard Law Review*, 2043–81.

[9] See the highly influential works by Andrew Clapham, *Human Rights in the Private Sphere* (Oxford: Clarendon Press, 1993), and *Human Rights Obligations of Non-State Actors* (Oxford University Press, 2006).

[10] The American Anthropological Association came to reconsider its position in 1999. For an intelligent discussion see Karen Engle, 'From Skepticism to Embrace: Human Rights and the American Anthropological Association from 1947–1999', (2001) 23 *Human Rights Quarterly*, 536–59.

international law. Moreover, the Universal Declaration was given teeth by means of two treaties negotiated under auspices of the UN: the ICCPR and the International Covenant on Economic, Social and Cultural Rights (ICESCR).

This division into two documents became a political necessity during the Cold War. While the Universal Declaration still considered human rights to be part of a single whole ('indivisible'), the years after 1948 marked a political division. Western states in particular emphasized the relevance of the classic civil and political rights, ranging from freedom of expression to the prohibition of torture; these would allow people to be free, and to take part in democratic politics. The communist bloc and parts of the developing world were, however, critical; what good is freedom of information if people are illiterate? What good is freedom of assembly if people are too hungry and undernourished even to think of attending meetings? Hence, while the West sponsored civil and political rights, the Eastern bloc sponsored the primacy of economic, social, and cultural rights. The same division would quickly become manifest in Europe in the years immediately after the adoption of the Universal Declaration; in 1950 Western European states would conclude the European Convention on Human Rights (ECHR), predominantly a set of political and civil rights.[11] It was only in 1962 that a (fairly limited) set of social rights would follow, in the form of the European Social Charter.

The legal differences between the two sets of rights need not be exaggerated, but two aspects warrant mention. First, civil and political rights are often considered to be rights that do not require any government action; the prohibition of torture, so the argument goes, implies that states should abstain from torture, and freedom of religion implies that states should not interfere when people aim to exercise their religion. By contrast (so the argument continues), economic, social, and cultural rights, such as the right to housing, or the right to education, demand that states actively initiate policies; a right to education implies that schools are built, for instance, and that teachers get paid. The distinction, however, in this pure form, is more apparent than real. Freedom of religion need not just mean that governments abstain from intervening; it may also imply that they sponsor the building of places of worship for religious minorities, while the prohibition of torture at the very least means that police officers must be instructed and trained in how to behave properly.

Still (and this is the second aspect worth mentioning), part of the distinction is of some practical legal relevance. Typically, civil and political rights can be formulated with greater precision, and thus be enforced with greater ease. A provision such as article 3 ECHR, holding that 'No one shall be subjected to torture' is easier to enforce than a provision to the effect that 'States shall, within their resources, ensure adequate housing'. As a result, states with monist systems[12] tend to find it easier to allow civil and political rights to be directly effective in their legal orders. However, this is not to say that economic and social rights are completely unenforceable: the South African Constitutional Court provided, in *Grootboom*,

[11] It has moreover been suggested, rather plausibly, that the European focus on civil and political rights functioned as a tool in Cold War politics. See Moyn, *Last Utopia*, at 79.
[12] A monist state is a state that allows international law to be directly effective within its own legal order, and thus enforceable by its domestic courts. See Chapter 16 below.

a welcome illustration of how such rights, too, can be enforced, by conceptualizing them as bundles of procedural rights (see below). Thus, while a right to housing cannot guarantee that everyone has a house, it can guarantee that when housing is available, everyone should have access to accommodation, and that people cannot be evicted from their homes in an inhumane manner.[13]

Partly to escape the problems inherent in distinguishing between two different classes of rights, some treaties have been concluded addressing only a single right or, alternatively, aiming to protect specific sets of individuals. There are thus specialized conventions against torture, against racial discrimination, against discrimination of women, and on the rights of migrant workers; and the most ratified treaty to date worldwide is the Convention on the Rights of the Child.[14]

THE INSTITUTIONALIZATION OF HUMAN RIGHTS

It is one thing to say that all humans enjoy human rights, and do so by virtue of human dignity, as the Universal Declaration puts it in its opening article. It is quite a different matter to make those rights become a reality, and it is at least arguable that international human rights law continues to have problems in this respect. The many human rights treaties in existence have not been able to prevent terrible massacres in places as diverse as Rwanda, Argentina, or the former Yugoslavia.[15] More recently, Sudan and Syria illustrate that all is not (yet?) well, and the responses during 2015–16 to the refugee influx into Europe may also suggest that the impulse to respect human dignity is, on occasion, rather suspended.

The most developed system of human rights protection is, quite possibly, offered by the ECHR.[16] Joining the convention, as almost fifty European states have done, automatically implies accepting the jurisdiction of the ECtHR, and over the years this Court has decided thousands of cases, with many thousands more still waiting to be decided. The Court comprises a judge from each of its member states, appointed for a period of six years, and typically works in chambers composed of smaller numbers of judges, with the so-called Grand Chamber, consisting of seventeen judges, as its highest institution. Individuals can petition the Court if they feel that they have been the victim of a violation of one of the rights guaranteed in the convention or in one of its protocols, provided they have exhausted local remedies;[17] they must file within a reasonable period of time; the claim may not be made anonymously; and may not be 'manifestly ill-founded'. The latter sees to it that

---

[13] *Government of the Republic of South Africa and others* v. *Irene Grootboom and others*, South Africa, Constitutional Court, judgment of 4 October 2000.

[14] Many relevant human rights instruments are collected in Jan Klabbers (ed.), *International Law Documents* (Cambridge University Press, 2016). Since South Sudan and Somalia became parties to the Convention in 2015, the United States is the only state that has not joined the regime.

[15] For a balanced account, see Susan Marks and Andrew Clapham, *International Human Rights Lexicon* (Oxford University Press, 2005).

[16] The ICJ does not address human rights very often, but a rare exception is the *Case Concerning Ahmadou Sadio Diallo* (*Republic of Guinea* v. *Democratic Republic of Congo*), [2010] ICJ Rep. 639.

[17] This entails that the individual must have first tried to find relief in the courts of the state concerned. See also Chapter 8 below.

nonsensical claims are weeded out; a claim, for instance, that a prison sentence violates someone's freedom of movement, is untenable, although, if the sentence results from an unfair trial, it may have some traction.

The convention guarantees the right to life, prohibits torture, slavery, and forced labour, protects habeas corpus and a fair trial, protects against retroactive penal legislation and contains the classic freedoms: of expression, assembly, religion, and private and family life. While, for instance, the torture prohibition is generally considered to be absolute ('non-derogable'), states are allowed to make exceptions when it comes to the classic freedoms, provided they do so by law and provided doing so is 'necessary in a democratic society'. This makes some sense, of course; freedom of expression should not become freedom to incite racial hatred; freedom of assembly cannot mean the freedom to plot against a democratically elected government. States are also allowed to declare a state of emergency under article 15 of the convention, which results in the suspension of some of the rights guaranteed in the convention. France did so in 2015 after a terrorist attack in Paris had killed some 130 people, while Turkey invoked article 15 following a failed (and, some suggest, staged) *coup d'état* in July 2016.

The convention has proved to be a 'living instrument', in two ways. One is that by means of protocols, a number of other human rights have been added; this applies, for instance, to the right to property which, interestingly, was absent from the original convention. Other rights include the right to education (thereby suggesting that the distinction between the two classes of rights is rather porous), the right to free elections, the right to freedom of movement and the prohibition of expulsion of nationals. The Sixth Protocol abolishes the death penalty.

These protocols are binding only for states that have ratified them, with the result that some states have more stringent human rights obligations under the convention regime than others. With the creation of substantive rights, this is awkward but not problematic. It is different, though, with protocols aiming to rearrange the institutional set-up of the Court. These, by their very nature, demand ratification by all contracting parties. This applied most famously to Protocol 11, which created a complete overhaul of the Court and entered into force in 1998.

The second way the scope of human rights protection has increased is by means of the Court's interpretations. The classic example is the 1975 *Golder* case, where the Court interpreted that the right to a fair trial, mentioned in article 6 ECHR, would also include a right to have access to courts. This was by no means self-evident, given the wording of article 6, which seems to limit the right to a fair trial only to a situation when a claim has been brought, thus excluding the very right to bring a claim.[18] In his dissenting opinion, Judge Fitzmaurice suggested that this broader interpretation would run the risk of taking the convention away from what the member states had in mind.[19]

[18] The opening sentence of article 6, paragraph 1: 'In the determination of his civil rights and obligations or of any criminal charge against him, everyone is entitled to a fair and public hearing within a reasonable time by an independent and impartial tribunal established by law.'

[19] *Golder* v. *United Kingdom*, Application no. 4451/70, judgment of 21 February 1975.

Human rights are less institutionalized outside Europe, although in particular the Americas have seen spectacular developments since the dictatorial regimes of the 1970s and 1980s have been toppled. The Inter-American Court of Human Rights can adjudicate inter-state complaints (as can the ECtHR), but also has the power to decide in individual cases, at least with respect to states that have accepted the right of individual petition. In addition, it has issued a few influential advisory opinions, for instance on the scope of reservations to the Inter-American Convention on Human Rights.

In Africa the leading instrument is the Banjul Charter of Human and People's Rights, concluded in 1981, which has the unique feature of concentrating also on the rights of groups and underlines that individuals also have duties towards the communities in which they live. In more recent years, this has come to be accompanied by an African Court of Human Rights, established by means of a protocol to the Banjul Charter and in operation since 2004.[20] In Asia, the member states of the Association of Southeast Asian Nations (ASEAN) adopted the ASEAN declaration on human rights in 2012, an instrument considered by some as potentially watering down well-entrenched substantive rights.

Perhaps most interesting is the situation within the UN. The two International Covenants both have their own monitoring bodies; the Human Rights Committee oversees the implementation of the ICCPR, whereas the Committee on Economic, Social and Cultural Rights oversees the implementation of the ICESCR. In both cases, their opinions are considered to be non-binding; both can entertain individual complaints (and do so with some regularity), but neither can make binding decisions, as they lack the power to do so. Part of their influence, then, stems not so much from a developed case law, but rather from the circumstance that those committees function as bodies of independent human rights experts: their statements on what constitutes, for instance, the right to water, tend to be viewed as highly authoritative.

Politically more sensitive is the role of the UN in formulating human rights. Almost literally since its creation, the UN had a Commission on Human Rights – it was out of this Commission that the Universal Declaration emerged. As a sub-organ of the Economic and Social Council, it was composed of representatives of the UN's member states, to be elected from the UN's total membership. As a result of the inevitable politics and horse-trading ('if you vote for me here, I'll support you elsewhere') involved, the Commission came to include many states whose own human rights records were far from unblemished and this, in turn, diminished the Commission's moral authority considerably; it hardly inspires confidence to be lectured on human rights by a state that itself has huge human rights problems.

The remedy then seemed simple: disband the Human Rights Commission, and create a new body. This is what eventually happened in 2006, when the new Human Rights Council

---

[20] A useful overview of the development of the Banjul Charter is Inger Österdahl, 'The Surprising Originality of the African Charter on Human and Peoples' Rights', in Jarna Petman and Jan Klabbers (eds.), *Nordic Cosmopolitanism: Essays in International Law for Martti Koskenniemi* (Leiden: Martinus Nijhoff, 2003), 5–32.

was created by the UN General Assembly.[21] Inevitably, however, some of the same old problems have re-emerged; this new body, too, is composed of the representatives of member states, and while a decent human rights record is a formal requirement for being elected, in practice it seems that not all that much has changed. For instance, in 2016, the Council's members include human rights stalwarts such as China and Russia, as well as a state such as Qatar, with a somewhat problematic record of treating migrant workers.

THE APPLICATION OF HUMAN RIGHTS

Historically, it seems fair to say that human rights were born so as to protect individuals from their governments, and rhetorically they are powerful tools. Human rights are often said to be universal, and sometimes said to be absolute, in that no contrary behaviour can be tolerated. In practice, though, governments need not necessarily fear the workings of human rights law too much, and to some extent may even benefit; being found to act in conformity with human rights standards provides a government with a strong aura of legitimacy. Moreover, human rights often cannot be taken literally, but need instead to be reconceptualized as procedural norms.

When two human rights clash, courts often have no choice but to weigh the claims and try to find an equitable balance. This is often referred to as 'human rights balancing', and finds philosophical support in the works of legal theorists such as Ronald Dworkin and Robert Alexy.[22] The underlying idea is that rights can rarely be absolute; my freedom of expression is limited by your right to be free from racial hatred, and your freedom of religion is met by my right to be free from proselytization. In such circumstances, it makes some sense to try and balance the two rights. Yet this automatically also means that different authorities may balance in different ways; as a matter of principle, your right to be free from racial hatred still means that my freedom of expression is limited, but the limits may differ from place to place. A judge in Amsterdam may interpret the same right, issued under the same convention, differently from a judge in, say, Vienna, Chicago, or Odessa. This means, if nothing else, that the universality of human rights exists more on the level of abstraction than on the concrete level; the exercise of the right will have to take local contexts and circumstances into account. It may also come to mean – more seriously perhaps – that balancing becomes an excuse for limiting rights.

A lot also comes to depend on what exactly is balanced against what – balancing is extremely vulnerable to judicial manipulation. A decent illustration is the problematic decision of the European Court of Human Rights in *Perincek* v. *Switzerland*. Mr Perincek is a populist Turkish politician, who tours Europe claiming that the Armenian genocide of 1915 was never really a genocide. He was prosecuted in Switzerland and found guilty of genocide denial, but the ECtHR disagreed, suggesting that his freedom of expression must

[21] General Assembly Resolution 60/251. For a brief discussion, see Jan Klabbers, 'Reflections on the Politics of Institutional Reform', in Peter G. Danchin and Horst Fischer (eds.), *United Nations Reform and the New Collective Security* (Cambridge University Press, 2010), 76–93.

[22] Ronald Dworkin, *Taking Rights Seriously* (Cambridge, MA: Harvard University Press, 1978); Robert Alexy, *Theorie der Grundrechte* (Frankfurt am Main: Suhrkamp, 1994 [1985]).

be balanced against the sentiments of the relatives of those who died in the genocide. The Court found it had little problem in letting freedom of expression prevail: prosecuting Mr Perincek was not shown to be 'necessary in a democratic society for the protection of the honour and the feelings of the descendants of the victims of the atrocities dating back to 1915 and subsequent years'.[23] On this logic, though, no genocide denial can ever be prosecuted: the 'honour and the feelings of the descendants' can never be expected to outweigh the individual's right to express himself freely, following the Court's construction.

It should also be realized that rights themselves cannot and do not decide on their application; this is always done by people (judges, administrators, policymakers), and therefore inevitably involves political judgement. As a result, the suggestion that rights are apolitical must be firmly rejected; reasonable people may have reasonable disagreements on the scope of rights, and on whether to apply the right or invoke its exceptions.[24]

Much the same applies, in a stronger way perhaps, to the doctrine of the margin of appreciation, as developed by the ECtHR. This entails the ECtHR accepting determinations made by national authorities regarding, for instance, local situations, and will allow national authorities quite a bit of leeway in determining how to behave. The leading case involves a British publisher, Richard Handyside.[25] He found himself prosecuted for violating the UK Obscene Publications Act after publishing a Danish book (*The Little Red Schoolbook*, which explained sex to teenagers) in Britain; the British authorities deemed the publication obscene, and an affront to British morality. Handyside's argument that *The Little Red Schoolbook* had been successfully published in a number of other states parties to the ECHR was to no avail; the Strasbourg Court found that Britain was best placed to assess the attitudes of the British people on matters of public morals, and if the British authorities were of the opinion that *The Little Red Schoolbook* would meet with opposition in Britain, then it was not for the ECtHR to substitute its own opinion for that of the British authorities. Hence, under this doctrine, the local authorities enjoy considerable leeway.

The point to note is that the Court could have decided otherwise. It could have held that since *The Little Red Schoolbook* was deemed perfectly acceptable in other states parties to the convention, therefore the British should overcome their anxieties and accept the publication. If it did not offend Danes, Dutch or Germans, then why should it offend the British? Still, the Court chose not to do so, and instead created a policy space for local authorities to act as they see fit, limiting the Court's scrutiny to manifestly unjust situations.[26]

---

[23] *Perincek* v. *Switzerland*, application No. 27510/08, judgment of 17 December 2013, para. 129. The Grand Chamber upheld the decision in its judgment of 15 October 2015. Note also how the Court avoids the use of the word 'genocide', speaking of 'atrocities'. In fact, the Court came dangerously close to genocide denial itself. For a critique, see Jan Klabbers, 'Doing Justice: Bureaucracy, the Rule of Law and Virtue Ethics', *Rivista di Diritto di Filosofia* (forthcoming).

[24] The seminal piece is Martti Koskenniemi, 'The Effect of Rights on Political Culture', in Philip Alston (ed.), *The EU and Human Rights* (Oxford University Press, 1999), 99–116.

[25] *Handyside* v. *United Kingdom* (Application no. 5493/72), ECtHR, judgment of 7 December 1976.

[26] On the margin of appreciation doctrine, see e.g. George Letsas, *A Theory of Interpretation of the European Convention on Human Rights* (Oxford University Press, 2007).

Many human rights have a difficult time being applied in a specific manner. Human rights cannot be analogized to, say, contractual rights or intellectual property rights; those are rights that a court can guarantee in a meaningful way. But how can a court possibly guarantee the right to life, as mentioned in article 2 ECHR? Surely, courts cannot prevent people from getting killed, from contracting diseases, and so on. The answer sometimes found hinges on a proceduralization of the right in question. While it is difficult to say anything sensible about life, at least the right to life can be understood as entailing, for instance, an obligation on the part of a government to launch an investigation into suspicious deaths, as well as an obligation resting on authorities never to 'shoot to kill' when aiming to arrest someone.[27] This proceduralization not only helps to flesh out the right to life; it also functions, almost perversely, as a way to limit the scope of the right to life. Construed as a set of procedural obligations, it means that the ECtHR does not need to take a stand on the great and controversial moral issues involving life, such as abortion, euthanasia or assisted suicide.[28]

While this proceduralization is visible in connection with civil and political rights, it is even more obviously present with economic, social, and cultural rights. Thus important elements of the right to water, as formulated by the Committee on Economic, Social and Cultural Rights, include the idea that water be accessible without discrimination, that water must be of sufficient quality, and that it must be available. This last is difficult to enforce, but at the very least entails that states must have a water strategy, and must draw up legislation on water.[29] Similarly, a proceduralization of this kind allowed the South African Constitutional Court to enforce the right to housing in the above-mentioned *Grootboom* case.[30]

GROUP RIGHTS

Individual rights are often said to be based on human dignity; it is the dignity of each individual, qua individual, that needs to be protected. One forceful line of criticism is that individuals do not exist in a vacuum. Individuals are inevitably defined by the groups of which they are a part: their families most obviously, but also the communities in which they grow up. A focus on individuals and their rights, so the critique goes, will ensure that individuals become alienated from their communities, will become ever so many little islands adrift in an ocean.[31] The remedy then, for some, is to complement individual rights by recognition of the value of community, for example by means of recognizing group rights.

---

[27] See e.g. *McCann and others* v. *United Kingdom* (Application no. 18984/91), ECtHR, judgment of 27 September 1995.

[28] See also the discussion in Clare Ovey and Robin C. A. White, *Jacobs and White European Convention on Human Rights*, 3rd edn (Oxford University Press, 2002), 53–6.

[29] General Comment no. 15 (2002), Committee on Economic, Social and Cultural Rights, UN Doc. E/C.12/2002/11.

[30] To be sure, in *Grootboom* the Court relied primarily on rights as guaranteed in South Africa's Constitution rather than international documents, but the basic idea is much the same.

[31] For a forceful critique, see Alasdair MacIntyre, *After Virtue: A Study in Moral Theory*, 2nd edn (London: Duckworth, 1985). A good overview of the discussion is offered by Shlomo Avineri and Avner de-Shalit (eds.), *Communitarianism and Individualism* (Oxford University Press, 1992).

It is sometimes claimed that civil and political rights form the first generation of human rights, while economic, social, and cultural rights make up the second generation. Following this enumeration, the term 'third-generation human rights' refers to collective rights. The first manifestations thereof were the minorities treaties concluded in the aftermath of the First World War, and the treaties bringing an end to slavery.[32] After the Second World War an important milestone was the Genocide Convention. Following the Holocaust, the General Assembly drew up a resolution against genocide, followed two years later by a convention. This 1948 Genocide Convention aims, quite simply, to prevent and punish genocide, which is defined as committing violent acts 'with intent to destroy, in whole or in part, a national, ethnical, racial or religious group, as such'. The legal difficulties here are twofold. First, it would seem that violence against other groups does not qualify as genocide (there is no reference for instance to destruction of 'political groups'), and, second, it tends to be difficult to prove the 'intent to destroy'. Often, mention is made of a 'specific intent' (*dolus specialis*) which goes above and beyond the intentions already present in the acts of violence themselves. Thus, article II provides that 'deliberately inflicting' certain conditions on a group is an example of an act which may amount to genocide; the word 'deliberately' already refers to a state of mind. Given these weighty obstacles, it should come as no surprise that courts are rather careful in qualifying activities, however nasty, as genocide. Still, the ICJ has held that the massacre of some 8,000 Muslim men and boys in Srebrenica, in 1995, constituted genocide, and in doing so followed earlier determinations made by the ICTY.[33]

Other collective rights include the right to self-determination (discussed later in this chapter), but also, it is sometimes claimed, such rights as the right to a clean environment. Indigenous peoples may have collective rights to enjoy their culture (think, for instance, of reindeer herding in Lapland). Minorities may have a right to be educated in their native language and perhaps even, in some cases, a right to political autonomy or self-government within the framework of an existing state. One of the most important intellectual problems here is to define the group in question. Provided that a minority has a right to autonomy, how to determine who is part of the minority? Is that a geographical area, such as Kosovo, or does it encompass, rather, ethnic communities (e.g. the Serbian community in Kosovo)?

Another issue is how the group right relates to individual rights; is a religious minority entitled to force its religion on young adults who have been born to religious parents but want to leave the church without leaving the community altogether? Such an issue arose in Canada in the 1970s, when Canada's Indian Act of 1876 made it impossible for a Canadian First Nation woman, Sandra Lovelace, to return to the tribe of her birth after her divorce from a non-First Nation man. The UN Human Rights Committee felt that it did not seem

---

[32] Note how this already suggests the limited utility of labels: surely, the 'third generation' here preceded the first and second generations.

[33] *Application of the Convention on the Prevention and Punishment of the Crime of Genocide (Bosnia and Herzegovina v. Serbia and Montenegro)*, [2007] ICJ Rep. 43, para. 297. The atmosphere is well captured by Dutch journalist Frank Westerman, *De slag om Srebrenica: de aanloop, de val, de naschok* (Amsterdam: Bezige Bij, 2015).

that 'to deny Sandra Lovelace the right to reside on the reserve [was] reasonable, or necessary to preserve the identity of the tribe'.[34]

The legal provision at issue in this case was article 27 ICCPR, which aims to protect the collective right of a group to enjoy its culture by means of creating an individual right for members of the group. On the one hand, doing so is understandable, especially in a convention generally geared towards protecting individual rights. On the other hand, by focusing on individuals enjoying a collective good, the provision neatly illustrates the tension between individualist and communitarian thought, reflecting the wider philosophical divide referred to above.

SELF-DETERMINATION

Individuals derive much of their identity from the groups in which they are embedded. While we are born alone and die alone, in the meantime we are part of a family, a community, go to school together, and so on. Hence some have argued that an insistence on individual rights alone is not enough; since individuals derive their identity from the groups they are a part of, such groups may also require protection.

This sentiment is all the more prominent if and when such groups are under threat. A minority within a state being abused by a majority may need legal protection, and, increasingly, such protection has been looked for in international law. Arguably the main example (and the most extreme example) of such a group right is the right to self-determination. This entails that identifiable groups have a right to determine for themselves how they wish to be politically organized. Under the influence of the decolonization process, the right to self-determination became enshrined in the two UN human rights covenants of 1966, and was confirmed as one of the main principles of international law in a Declaration of Principles adopted by the General Assembly in 1970.[35] Under this Declaration, self-determination can take the form of independent statehood, association, or integration with another state, or some other political status. It is generally considered a rule of customary international law, and the ICJ has referred to self-determination as an *erga omnes* principle.[36] Clearly then, it is an important principle, yet its contents remain less than clear.

There are two major problems usually associated with self-determination. The first is the identification of the 'self': who bears the right to self-determination?[37] One might think of groups sharing some objective factor such as the same language, ethnicity, or history, but this does not quite work as planned. Surely, Australians and Americans share the same language (they are 'divided by a common language', as it is sometimes said), but few would think they were one people. The history of the Catalans is intricately interwoven with Spanish history, yet the Catalans feel strongly different from the Spanish.

---

[34] *Sandra Lovelace* v. *Canada*, Communication no. 24/1977, para. 17, Human Rights Committee, Communication of 30 July 1981.
[35] General Assembly Res. 2625 (XXV).   [36] *East Timor* (*Portugal* v. *Australia*), [1995] ICJ Rep. 90, para. 29.
[37] See generally James Summers, *Peoples and International Law* (Leiden: Martinus Nijhoff, 2007).

Hence, where objective factors are under-inclusive or over-inclusive, attention shifts to 'subjective' factors; a people is a people if this is the group's self-identification. But this, in turn, may create authoritarian overtones; what if the group includes individuals who do not feel the same way? Should their individual self-determination give way to the collective feeling of their neighbours? Moreover, and more to the point perhaps, it has been noted that groups are often socially constructed;[38] they are not authentically existing communities, but have been created by means of mass media, propaganda and selective history lessons.[39]

The second problem with self-determination is that the main claim related to it is a claim of secession, but that in turn is difficult to reconcile with the stability of existing statehood. With the exception of decolonization (where the right to self-determination did not do much work),[40] international law is reluctant to break up existing states, for doing so might destabilize the global order.[41] Hence the right of self-determination of one group may conflict with the right to continued statehood of another group, and in the absence of any hierarchy in international law, the result is often bloodshed rather than peaceful secession. In the end, it may be more fruitful to regard the right of self-determination not so much as leading to a right of secession,[42] but as leading to either 'internal self-determination' (i.e. full respect for the human rights of the members of the breakaway group) or as a right to political participation on equal terms for the minority.[43]

NATIONALITY

Most individuals are nationals (citizens) of a single state, and will become so by virtue of the circumstances of their birth. There is little international law on the topic; instead, international law by and large leaves the granting of nationality to domestic law, and typically, domestic law chooses one of two main methods for granting nationality. The first and most widespread method holds that children will acquire the nationality of their parents, regardless of where they are born. Thus, nationality follows the bloodlines: *jus sanguinis*. As a result, children born of Dutch parents will become Dutch nationals, even if they are born abroad.

The leading alternative, practised in particular by the United States, is to grant national-ity to everyone born on a state's territory: *jus soli*. Thus a child born in the United States

---

[38] See in particular Benedict Anderson, *Imagined Communities*, rev. edn (London: Verso, 1991).

[39] The French philologist Ernest Renan has already written, more than a century ago, that forgetfulness, perhaps even errors, may be essential in the forging of nations. See Ernest Renan, *Qu'est-ce qu'une nation?*, ed. S. Sand (Paris: Flammarion, 2011 [1882]), at 56.

[40] Martti Koskenniemi, 'National Self-determination Today: Problems of Legal Theory and Practice', (1994) 43 *International and Comparative Law Quarterly*, 241–69.

[41] For the same reason, where states do break up, none the less old internal boundaries continue to exist. This is known as the principle of *uti possidetis*, which played a major role in the decolonization of Latin America and Africa and the dissolution of the USSR and Yugoslavia. It was accepted as a general rule of international law by the ICJ in the case concerning the *Frontier Dispute* (Burkina Faso/Mali), [1986] ICJ Rep. 554. See also the brief discussion in Chapter 4 above.

[42] So also Canada's Supreme Court, *Re Secession of Quebec*, judgment of 20 August 1998, reported in 115 *International Law Reports*, 536.

[43] Jan Klabbers, 'The Right to be Taken Seriously: Self-determination in International Law', (2006) 28 *Human Rights Quarterly*, 186–206.

will automatically acquire US nationality, even if her parents are French, German, or Chinese. This applies in principle even if the parents are only in transit in the United States, or find themselves on board US aircraft or ships.

International law does not yet[44] have to say much about the granting of nationality, except by setting limits to the freedom of states. Thus, as the PCIJ held in 1923, it was unacceptable for France to grant French nationality to all inhabitants of the French zones in Morocco and Tunis, for this also affected people who already had a nationality.[45] The other main setting in which international law enters the picture is in situations of dual nationality, where it has been held that, for the purposes of a state defending an individual's right, that individual must be its national and the link between state and individual must be 'genuine'.[46]

For, obviously, in a globalizing world, it is increasingly likely that children will be born with more than one nationality. Those born of parents with different nationalities may already become dual nationals; the same applies to children born in the United States of non-US parents. Moreover, waves of immigration have led to large groups of individuals with two nationalities. Many states tend to regard this as difficult, on the (questionable) theory that individuals can have loyalties only towards a single state at any given moment in time. Whereas during the 1990s some relaxation on this score was visible (states increasingly seeming to accept dual citizenship),[47] the current trend in western Europe, under the influence of hard-nosed populist politicians, is to be strict on dual nationality; if people emigrate, for instance, and take on the nationality of their new state of residence, they may automatically lose their old nationality. Taking on a new nationality, at the same time, is made more difficult; in many states; individuals have to take examinations to show some knowledge of the local history and culture, or mastery of the local language. Simultaneously, however, some states (such as the Comoros) have started to 'sell' their citizenship to the stateless so as to raise badly needed funds,[48] while other states are advertising their citizenship: one can procure citizenship of Grenada for US$200,000 plus application, processing, and due diligence fees. Dominican citizenship comes slightly cheaper, and can be yours for US$100,000 plus fees.[49]

All of this would not be a problem if it were not for the fact that nationality comes with rights. Thus nationality determines whose passport the individual can carry;[50] the right to

---

[44] It has been noted, though, that a change is under way in that international law is slowly starting to concern itself with issues of nationality and citizenship. See Peter J. Spiro, 'A New International Law of Citizenship?', (2011) 105 *American Journal of International Law*, 694–746.

[45] *Nationality Decrees Issued in Tunis and Morocco (French Zone)*, advisory opinion, [1923] Publ. PCIJ, Series B, no. 4.

[46] *Nottebohm (Second Phase) (Liechtenstein v. Guatemala)*, [1955] ICJ Rep. 4; the details are discussed in Chapter 8 below.

[47] See e.g. Thomas M. Franck, *The Empowered Self: Law and Society in the Age of Individualism* (Oxford University Press, 1999).

[48] Atossa Araxia Abrahamanian, *The Cosmopolites: The Coming of the Global Citizen* (New York: Columbia Global Reports, 2015).

[49] This information was found in an advertisement published in the British Airways' in-flight magazine, in July 2016. The company behind it is called Global Partners; see https://csglobalpartners.com/ (visited 19 August 2016).

[50] This was not always the case. For an entertaining history of the passport, see Martin Lloyd, *The Passport: The History of Man's Most Travelled Document* (Stroud: Sutton Publishing, 2003).

diplomatic protection can only be extended to nationals; and political rights (such as the right to vote) are often tied to nationality. One exception (of sorts) is created by EU law, which has invented its own notion of citizenship, complementary to national citizenship. Under EU law, nationals of EU states residing elsewhere in the EU can take part in some elections, but not in the main national elections; EU citizens in distress outside the EU may be able to ask for help from the consulates or embassies of other member states, and it is arguable that EU citizenship also comes to affect the right to diplomatic protection.[51]

THE RIGHT TO HAVE RIGHTS? STATELESS PERSONS, REFUGEES AND MIGRANTS

The German political theorist Hannah Arendt famously suggested that human rights are often dependent on notions of citizenship; before the introduction of human rights in international instruments, human rights were typically only granted to citizens of states. Thus people may have human rights under French law, or under US law, but their position is a lot trickier if they are not members of any political community. The stateless, so Arendt claimed (and for many years she was stateless herself, having fled Nazi Germany via France to settle in the United States[52]), are not members of any community, and thus have few or no rights, and most assuredly no rights relating to participation in public affairs, such as the right to vote or to run for office. On such a reading, the relevant question is whether people have 'the right to have rights' to begin with.[53]

One way in which some human rights instruments have tried to solve this problem is to provide for human rights protection not just to citizens of contracting parties, but to everyone who comes within the jurisdiction of the instrument concerned. Thus article 1 ECHR provides that the parties 'shall secure to everyone within their jurisdiction' the rights enshrined in the convention. The Court, in turn, has interpreted this broadly, but not in unlimited fashion. Thus it has held that the convention has a reach outside the territories of the parties as such; it has accepted that it has jurisdiction for example over government acts in occupied territories.[54] On the other hand, it has denied this jurisdiction when behaviour is attributable to international organizations. When parties act through international organizations (e.g. NATO or the UN), their behaviour may be attributable to those organizations.[55]

The human rights of those who have left their native communities tend to be problematic. Under the Refugee Convention only those who flee for fear of political persecution may qualify as refugees and therewith obtain refugee status. This leaves two large groups in the cold. First, those who flee for economic reasons (to escape poverty, malnutrition, famine,

---

[51] For a brief discussion, see Annemarieke Vermeer-Künzli, 'Exercising Diplomatic Protection: The Fine Line between Litigation, Demarches and Consular Assistance', (2006) 66 *Zeitschrift fur auslandisches öffentliches Recht und Völkerrecht*, 321–50.

[52] See the wonderful biography by Elizabeth Young-Bruehl, *Hannah Arendt: For Love of the World*, 2nd edn (New Haven, CT: Yale University Press, 2004).

[53] Hannah Arendt, *The Origins of Totalitarianism* (San Diego: Harvest, 1979), 290–302.

[54] Chapter 5 above.

[55] Joined cases *Behrami and Behrami* v. *France* (Application no. 71412/01) and *Saramati* v. *France and others* (Application no. 78116/01), ECtHR, judgment of 2 May 2007.

droughts, or floods) are not to be considered refugees within the meaning of the Refugee Convention. Second, the Refugee Convention only applies to those who cross boundaries; those who remain within their own states are considered to be 'internally displaced persons'.

The 1951 Refugee Convention was born out of the Second World War and, originally, was limited to protecting those who had fled the Nazi horrors and the Stalinist terror. When it became clear that political repression was not only occurring in Europe, the convention was complemented by a protocol concluded in 1967, which broadened the protection to other settings.

The central provision of refugee law is the prohibition of *non-refoulement*, laid down in article 33, paragraph 1 of the Refugee Convention and sometimes said to be *jus cogens*:

> No Contracting State shall expel or return ('refouler') a refugee in any manner whatsoever to the frontiers of territories where his life or freedom would be threatened on account of his race, religion, nationality, membership of a particular social group or political opinion.

While this would seem to be generally adhered to, none the less states often send refugees back to the state to which they first fled. Thus a Rwandan refugee making his way to Denmark via Uganda cannot be sent back to Rwanda, but can be sent back to Uganda. As a result, some of the world's poorer states (such as Pakistan and Lebanon) have absorbed millions of refugees, with the rich West carrying but a small part of the burden. Moreover, some of those Western states have started to treat refugee applications offshore, on the questionable argument that the *non-refoulement* principle only applies to refugees who have already entered their territory, or have assigned the first screening of potential refugees to private companies, such as airlines. In such cases, individuals may be sent away before actually being able to present their case, and since they are sent off by private companies, there is no administrative decision they can appeal to, and the state can escape responsibility by claiming that the decision was made by a private company.[56]

While the conclusion of the Refugee Convention was undoubtedly a humanitarian achievement, none the less the reluctance of states to create such a convention shines through many of its provisions. Article 2, for instance, points out that refugees have responsibilities towards the state that accepts them, and article 9 authorizes a suspension of the rights of refugees in times of emergency.

Since the scope of human rights instruments is typically determined on the basis of a state's jurisdiction rather than its territory pure and simple, refugees may find protection under human rights conventions; for instance, when located in a state party to the ECHR, refugees should be given access to courts under its article 6. Much the same applies to migrants; migrants, too, are, as a general matter, protected by the human rights instruments prevailing in the country where they reside, but it has been observed

---

[56] See the fine study by Thomas Gammeltoft-Hansen, *Access to Asylum: International Refugee Law and the Globalisation of Migration Control* (Cambridge University Press, 2011).

that such instruments do little to take the peculiar situation of migrants into account.[57] For that reason, a special convention on migrants' rights has been concluded which, however, adds little to general human rights law and has met with a lukewarm response on behalf of states. Indeed, one major problem is that not a single migrant-receiving state has ratified the convention, with the result that for all practical purposes the convention misses its target.[58]

Since most people work for a living, want to work for a living, or have worked for a living until retirement, labour rights form an important, and highly necessary, special group of rights.[59] While here too much is left to domestic law, some labour standards have been formulated, on the international level, under the auspices of the ILO, which has been in existence since the end of the First World War. The creation of the ILO was inspired, no doubt, by the fear that working people would en masse opt for communism unless their situation were improved, and the unique feature of the ILO is that it encompasses not just representatives of its member states, but also of employer and employee organizations (trade unions).[60]

While the ILO has sponsored many conventions (and these are, in truth, rather well adhered to, being implemented in domestic legislation), arguably the most notable achievement has been the formulation of a set of core labour standards. This takes the form of a (non-binding) declaration,[61] but with the aspiration of great authority.[62] In essence, these core standards include freedom of assembly and the right to collective bargaining, non-discrimination in employment and occupation, and prohibitions on child labour and forced labour. Notably, this is a fairly minimal set of principles; the declaration does not mention such things as a right to paid holidays,[63] maternity leave, minimal safety requirements, or a minimum wage.[64]

Most of the international law relating to labour issues is still domestically oriented, aiming to embed rights for the domestic workforce. Laudable as that is, it falls short of protecting migrant workers. In order to fill that gap and facilitate the creation of workers' rights for migrants, some academics have posited a concept of 'transnational labour

---

[57] For an excellent study of how law shapes our conception of individuals, see Catherine Dauvergne, *Making People Illegal* (Cambridge University Press, 2008).

[58] See also Vincent Chetail, 'The Human Rights of Migrants in General International Law: From Minimum Standards to Fundamental Rights', (2013) 28 *Georgetown Immigration Law Journal*, 225–55.

[59] For a journalistic account of the sometimes desperate circumstances of ordinary working life in one of the richest nations of the world, see Barbara Ehrenreich, *Nickel and Dimed: Undercover in Low-Wage USA* (London: Granta, 2001).

[60] For this reason, Cox labels the ILO as a corporatist manifestation on the international level. Robert W. Cox, *Production, Power, and World Order: Social Forces in the Making of History* (New York: Columbia University Press, 1987).

[61] www.ilo.org/declaration/thedeclaration/textdeclaration/lang-en/index.htm (last visited 7 December 2011).

[62] For critical discussion see Philip Alston, '"Core Labour Standards" and the Transformation of the International Labour Rights Regime', (2004) 15 *European Journal of International Law*, 457–521.

[63] This was, rather optimistically perhaps, included in the Universal Declaration of Human Rights.

[64] Sometimes labour protection follows on the heels of a disaster: the garment industry aimed to provide safety in Bangladesh only after a collapsing building had killed more than 1,100 workers. Being concluded between trade unions and brands and retailers, the Bangladesh accord neatly illustrates the conceptual challenges international law is facing. The accord is reproduced in Klabbers (ed.), *International Law Documents*.

citizenship', in order to 'facilitate the free movement of people while preventing the erosion of working conditions in the countries that receive them'.[65]

FINAL REMARKS

There can be no doubt that the individual should be central to international law. States, after all, are but abstractions, and of relatively recent origin at that. However, whether this means that individuals should be accepted and recognized as 'subjects' of international law, seems a bit beside the point. It might be more important to create decent international legal rules for individuals, allowing them to live freely and determine their own futures without fear of subjugation, and without having to starve. Being a 'subject' of any legal system is merely academic shorthand, and in itself not worth much unless accompanied by certain legal rights.

Moreover, to the extent that the label 'subject' is often seen to refer mostly to human rights, it misses the point that for refugees, migrants, workers, and the unemployed, the rules available in current international law are not all that helpful; typically, the determination of refugee status is left to domestic authorities on the basis of domestic law and typically, a refugee applying for asylum must be able to navigate the domestic bureaucracy and be able to convince local officials that, indeed, she should be seen as a refugee. This in turn requires, as has been noted, something of a schizophrenic position; the refugee must present herself as destitute, yet at the same time she must be articulate enough to present a credible and consistent scenario.[66]

In short, while it is plausible to say that the individual has come to be recognized as a subject of international law, such a claim on its own does not say all that much. A decent international legal order must not only recognize individuals as subjects, but also provide individuals with decent levels of protection and opportunities, regardless of where they live and regardless of whether they are refugees, migrants, or internally displaced persons.

FURTHER READING

Benedict Anderson, *Imagined Communities*, rev. edn (London: Verso, 1991)

Andrew Clapham, *Human Rights in the Private Sphere* (Oxford: Clarendon Press, 1993)

Catherine Dauvergne, *Making People Illegal* (Cambridge University Press, 2008)

Thomas Gammeltoft-Hansen, *Access to Asylum: International Refugee Law and the Globalisation of Migration Control* (Cambridge University Press, 2011)

Alasdair MacIntyre, *After Virtue: A Study in Moral Theory*, 2nd edn (London: Duckworth, 1985)

---

[65] Jennifer Gordon, 'Transnational Labor Citizenship', (2007) 80 *Southern California Law Review*, 503–88, at 504–5.

[66] For a fine discussion in these terms, see Kristin Bergtora Sandvik, 'On the Social Life of International Organisations: Framing Accountability in Refugee Resettlement', in Jan Wouters et al. (eds.), *Accountability for Human Rights Violations by International Organisations* (Antwerp: Intersentia, 2010), 287–307.

Jenny Martinez, *The Slave Trade and the Origins of International Human Rights Law* (Oxford University Press, 2012)

Samuel Moyn, *The Last Utopia: Human Rights in History* (Cambridge, MA: Harvard University Press, 2010)

Peter J. Spiro, 'A New International Law of Citizenship?', (2011) 105 *American Journal of International Law*, 694–746

7

The Law of Responsibility

INTRODUCTION

'Responsibility' is the term used by international lawyers to denote the idea that some entity can be blamed for undesirable behaviour. The main form, relatively well settled, is the responsibility of states. It was confirmed by the PCIJ in the 1920s, in the *Chorzow Factory* case, that the possibility of being held responsible was the price to pay for being able to participate in international law.[1] Consequently, it would seem that, in principle, all subjects of international law can be held responsible for their behaviour, not just states, but also international organizations, liberation movements, and even NGOs. That said, however, specific responsibility regimes have only been developed with respect to states, international organizations, and individuals, and even then much of the law is rather sketchy and incipient. To some extent, the gap is being filled by speaking of accountability (as opposed to responsibility) of companies and NGOs, in addition to corporate social responsibility. It is worth pointing out, though, that on these topics hard and fast legal rules are few and far between. The only firmly established set of rules in existence relates to the responsibility of states, and these rules will be central to this chapter. In addition, some attention will be paid to the responsibility or accountability of other actors.

As a terminological matter, responsibility is usually (but not always) distinguished from liability and accountability. Liability usually denotes the existence of a financial obligation; someone is liable to pay compensation. Hence a finding of responsibility may come with a finding of liability; X is responsible for wrongdoing, and thus liable to pay compensation. Alternatively, parties can agree that regardless of who is responsible for some mishap, liability shall rest with a particular state. This is the case, for instance, within NATO: responsibility for certain NATO acts may rest with NATO itself (depending on the circumstances), but liability is assigned, by treaty, to particular member states.[2]

---

[1] *Factory at Chorzów (Claim for Indemnity) (Germany v. Poland)*, merits, [1928] Publ. PCIJ, Series A, no. 17, at 47 *(Chorzów Factory* Case).

[2] The relevant agreement is, mostly, NATO's 1951 Status of Forces Agreement. For in-depth discussion, see Kirsten Schmalenbach, *Die Haftung internationaler Organisationen* (Frankfurt am Main: Peter Lang, 2004) 537–539.

Accountability is the broadest of the terms, and in its more sophisticated versions may signify the existence of a relationship whereby someone is held to explain and justify their behaviour to someone else.[3] This may involve the law of responsibility, but need not: one can also meaningfully speak of democratic accountability, for example where a person is expected to justify her behaviour to a parliament rather than before a court. In international law generally, the link between responsibility and courts is best taken lightly; while many courts exist, compulsory jurisdiction is rare; hence responsibility is often also discussed in diplomatic practice, and not just before a court or tribunal.

FROM CUSTOM TO CODIFICATION

Systematic thinking about state responsibility started to emerge with the rest of investment arbitration in the Americas in the second half of the nineteenth century, and came to exist in the form of a detailed corpus of customary rules.[4] Given its immense importance to international law, at least in the public view (after all, to many people, law and enforcement are much the same thing), the thought arose after the Second World War that it might be a good idea to attempt to codify the customary rules into a neat and tidy convention on state responsibility. This, however, proved easier said than done. As it turned out, the law on state responsibility is riddled with a host of political, conceptual, and philosophical issues, some of which will be discussed below. As a result, it took the ILC almost four decades to settle on a number of articles on state responsibility, with the final version being steered through under the guidance of special rapporteur James Crawford.[5] The idea of actually codifying the rules and concluding a convention has more or less been abandoned. Now that the ILC has managed to agree on a number of rules, it is feared that submitting these to an international conference will only result in states trying to tamper with them and undoing the entire edifice. Hence the ILC has brought the rules on state responsibility to the attention of the General Assembly which, in turn, has formally endorsed them. The articles are thought to reflect customary international law to a large extent and are considered highly authoritative.

An important analytical point is that the ILC articles are based on a distinction between primary and secondary norms of international law, a distinction possibly borrowed from the influential legal theory of H. L. A. Hart.[6] According to this distinction, primary rules are the substantive obligations of states: the prohibition of genocide, the prohibition of aggression, the right of innocent passage in territorial waters, or the tax exemptions enjoyed by diplomats. By contrast, the rules on state responsibility, like those of the law

---

[3] Very useful is Ebrahim Elnoor and Edward Weisband (eds.), *Global Accountabilities: Participation, Pluralism, and Public Ethics* (Cambridge University Press, 2007).

[4] For a fine discussion see Tzvika Nissel, 'A History of State Responsibility: The Struggle for International Standards (1870–1960)', doctoral thesis, University of Helsinki, 2016.

[5] James Crawford, *The International Law Commission's Articles on State Responsibility: Introduction, Text and Commentaries* (Cambridge University Press, 2002). A classic critique of the entire project is Philip Allott, 'State Responsibility and the Unmaking of International Law', (1988) 29 *Harvard International Law Journal*, 1–26.

[6] H. L. A. Hart, *The Concept of Law* (Oxford: Clarendon Press, 1961).

of treaties, are counted among the secondary rules: rules that determine how primary rules are created, interpreted, or enforced. The reason for the ILC to make this distinction was to allow it to focus on responsibility itself; otherwise, its project on responsibility would constantly have been diverted by attempts not only to tell states how to enforce their obligations, but also to tell them what those obligations were.[7]

While the ILC's articles are of general scope, they are without prejudice to the possibility that special regimes have their own rules on what to do in cases of violation. Thus the rules on state responsibility in EU law depart considerably from the general rules formulated by the ILC, so much so that it is sometimes held that the EU is a 'self-contained' regime, more or less hermetically sealed off from international law. By the same token, the WTO system departs on some points from the general system, as do the regimes set up by human rights conventions.

STATE RESPONSIBILITY: TWO BASIC PRINCIPLES

The general articles on state responsibility as formulated by the ILC are, it could be said, based on two foundational principles. The first of these is that states can be held responsible for acts[8] that are attributable to them. The second basic idea is that states can only be held responsible for internationally wrongful acts – that is, acts that are somehow committed in violation of an international obligation incumbent on the state.

Attribution

The idea that states can be held responsible for acts that are attributable to them in itself responds to a vexed philosophical problem. States do not have souls or minds; they are collective actors and, as such, have no psyche, and thus can hardly be accused of criminal intent or negligence. To the extent that these are states of mind, it is difficult to apply them to collective actors. Hence, as collective actors, it is by no means certain that states have what philosophers refer to as moral agency – the capacity to think in terms of right and wrong and act accordingly.[9] None the less, the idea that states can be held responsible for acts attributable to them is generally regarded (if it is considered to begin with) as a useful legal fiction, since it is often desirable that someone be held responsible and, for instance, be given the chance to rectify a situation. Since most international-law-related activities are beyond the powers of single individuals, it is useful to employ the idea that states may be held responsible, at least for activities that are attributable to states.

---

[7] Crawford, *State Responsibility*, at 14–16.

[8] The notion of 'acts' is also thought to cover 'omissions', but this is not always easy to operationalize. Sometimes not respecting a duty to act results in a clear omission leading to responsibility (e.g. failing to protect diplomatic premises), but it is difficult to think of legally relevant omissions in the absence of a clear duty to act, and this plagues in particular the law of international organizations. For discussion see Jan Klabbers, *Sins of Omission: The Responsibility of International Organizations for Inaction*, NYU Jean Monnet Working Paper 2/2016.

[9] For a useful discussion of some of the issues involved, though not discussing states much, see Toni Erskine (ed.), *Can Institutions Have Responsibilities? Collective Moral Agency and International Relations* (New York: Palgrave Macmillan, 2003).

This has the important corollary that states are, as a matter of principle, not responsible for the activities of private parties. If a serial killer in Japan happens to kill a foreigner, the responsibility of Japan is not at stake, unless (as will be discussed below) Japan somehow is implicated. If an action bears no relation to the state, the state cannot, and will not, be held responsible.

The state will be held responsible, however, for the acts of its organs and its officials, even those who act outside their proper competences (*ultra vires*). The underlying theory is that the state must control its officials and organs, if only because no one else can. Thus an act of torture committed by a rogue police officer in contravention of local law will none the less engage the responsibility of that state; an act of plundering by military troops, against clear instructions, will none the less engage the responsibility of the state concerned.

Of course, the state cannot be expected also to control the acts of its officials in their spare time. Should a police officer, on his day off, be engaged in extortion of tourists, the state can hardly be held responsible, although things may change when the police officer is wearing his uniform and uses his badge in order to facilitate the extortion. Such instances are among the many borderline cases in the law of state responsibility, and reasonable people may disagree on whether the state incurs responsibility in these circumstances.

An important consideration is that responsibility is determined on the basis of international law. Domestic law considerations are not decisive: thus a state cannot hide behind its constitutional provisions for escaping responsibility for the acts of constitutionally independent organs, such as courts or parliaments. Should a parliament be late in implementing a mandatory obligation, it is no excuse to say that the state cannot control its parliament; should a court commit a blatant denial of justice in a case involving a foreigner or violate international law in a judgment,[10] it is no excuse to claim that courts are constitutionally independent.

Internationally Wrongful Act

Under the articles on state responsibility, states can only be held responsible for acts that violate their international legal obligations. In the case of an allegation of a treaty violation, this presupposes that the state is a party to the treaty in question. If it is not, no legal obligation is incumbent upon it, and hence it cannot be held responsible, even if the behaviour in question is quite obnoxious. This implies that states cannot be held responsible for activities that are harmful or cause damage, but are none the less legal. An obvious example may concern the execution under the death penalty of a foreigner; a state which accepts the death penalty (and is not a party to any treaty outlawing it) cannot be held responsible for the execution of a convicted criminal, even though the execution causes harm in the most literal way.[11]

---

[10] For a fairly recent example see *Jurisdictional Immunities of the State (Germany* v. *Italy: Greece Intervening)*, [2012] ICJ Rep. 99.

[11] This is not to say that no responsibility can occur for acts involved in the trial or sentencing of the individual concerned, since here other legal obligations may be involved and may have been violated.

In other words, international law does not utilize a system of strict (or absolute) liability; the wrongful act is an essential requirement. There are exceptions, however. Thus it is generally accepted that states are responsible for damage caused by satellites sent into orbit, even if launching and maintaining satellites is perfectly legal. This is explicitly provided for in the 1972 Convention on International Liability for Damage Caused by Space Objects, article 2: 'A launching State shall be absolutely liable to pay compensation for damage caused by its space object on the surface of the Earth or to aircraft in flight.'

Likewise, it is possible to bring a complaint under GATT/WTO law against a state for causing economic damage, even without applicable rules being violated, as long as benefits under the trading regime are at stake.[12] States are also sometimes considered responsible for damage caused under some environmental agreements (for instance relating to transportation of ultra-hazardous materials), even without a violation, although explicit treaty provisions to this effect are rare. One (possible) example is the 1960 Organization for Economic Cooperation and Development (OECD) Paris Convention on Third Party Liability in the Field of Nuclear Energy, which holds that private parties can sue for damages in case of a nuclear incident. In such a case, the operator of the nuclear facility can be sued. The operator need not necessarily be a state, however, so it cannot with great conviction be said that this entails state responsibility.

Generally, then, damage or harm is not treated as a precondition; what matters is the violation of an international obligation, whether this creates material damage or not. The idea here is that damage is not always manifested in material ways but can also be conceptualized as a violation of someone's rights, or as moral damage. Especially in the politically sensitive world of international relations, situations may arise which are clear violations even without causing material damage; an intrusion into air space, for instance, constitutes a violation of international law without necessarily creating material damage.

RESPONSIBILITY AND PRIVATE ACTS

As mentioned, states cannot be held responsible for the purely private acts of their citizens. Yet situations may occur where a state may incur what may be termed 'indirect' responsibility. This is the case, for instance, if a state 'acknowledges and adopts' illegal private acts,[13] or fails to prevent them in violation of an international legal obligation.

The leading case is the 1980 *Tehran Hostages* case.[14] In 1979, groups of so-called militant students took part in the Iranian Revolution and occupied the US embassy in Tehran, as well as US consulates in Tabriz and Shiraz, and held their staff hostage for more than a year. Since those 'militant students' were private persons, the state of Iran did not incur responsibility for the seizing of the embassy, but it did incur responsibility for a number of related circumstances. For instance, as the ICJ held, the Iranian authorities had been under an

---

[12] This is, in other words, an example of where a special regime (the trading regime) departs from the general rules.

[13] Articles on State Responsibility, article 11.

[14] *United States Diplomatic and Consular Staff in Tehran (USA v. Iran)*, [1980] ICJ Rep. 3 (*Tehran Hostages*).

obligation, derived from diplomatic law,[15] to provide protection to the embassy, but were nowhere to be found when the seizure occurred, and undertook no steps to bring the situation to a speedy end. In fact, Ayatollah Khomeini, Iran's leader at the time, applauded the hostage-taking as a useful way of exercising pressure on the United States and decided to perpetuate it; this, then, the Court argued, transformed the acts of private citizens into acts of the state.[16]

There can be little doubt that state responsibility cannot be escaped by 'outsourcing' government activities to private actors. While theoretically the division between public and private acts is fluid, none the less conduct will be attributable to the state if a person or group of persons is acting 'on the instructions of, or under the direction or control of', the state.[17] This may cover the activities of state companies (although here the 'corporate veil' may render analysis more difficult), but also irregular armed bands and, arguably, private military companies or mercenaries. The main intellectual problem here is to determine the precise standard for determining the degree of state involvement.

While the ICJ, in the 1986 *Nicaragua* case,[18] applied a fairly strict standard, insisting that the acts of Nicaragua's contras were only attributable to the United States in those instances where the United States had actually been in 'effective control' of the contras (which is stricter than, say, supporting them or financing them), a decade later the ICTY in *Tadic* applied a looser test, finding that 'overall control' of Serbia over the acts of irregular troops was sufficient to attribute conduct to the Serbs.[19] The ICJ responded in its 2007 *Genocide* judgment by suggesting that the overall control test adopted by the ICTY was unsuitable for purposes of state responsibility, although it may have been of use in determining whether the conflict in Yugoslavia was in fact an international conflict.[20] In the Court's view, 'the "overall control" test is unsuitable, for it stretches too far, almost to breaking point, the connection which must exist between the conduct of a State's organs and its international responsibility'.[21] In other words, under the overall control test, even a fairly slender connection could suffice to attribute responsibility to a state for acts of others. This overall control test the Court must now have deemed politically unwise; in a world of sovereign states, one cannot too lightly hold states responsible for the conduct of others.

A special case is provided by insurrectional movements.[22] These are by definition not state organs; after all, their very aim is to overthrow the state or, alternatively, to secede. Hence their conduct is unlikely to be attributable to the sitting government representing the state. In order to prevent a vacuum, then, international law prescribes that the state will be held responsible should the insurrectionists succeed; if they manage to take over the state (or create a new one), the state will be responsible for their acts. Matters are unclear, however, with respect to the conduct of unsuccessful insurrectionists; as these do not come

---

[15] Article 22, 1961 Vienna Convention on Diplomatic Relations.   [16] *Tehran Hostages*, para. 74.
[17] Articles on State Responsibility, article 8.
[18] *Military and Paramilitary Activities in and Against Nicaragua (Nicaragua v. USA)*, merits, [1986] ICJ Rep. 14, para. 115.
[19] *Prosecutor* v. *Dusko Tadic*, case IT-94-1-A, judgment of 15 July 1999, paras. 120–2.
[20] *Application of the Convention on the Prevention and Punishment of the Crime of Genocide (Bosnia and Herzegovina v. Serbia and Montenegro)*, [2007] ICJ Rep. 43, para. 404 (*Genocide*).
[21] *Genocide*, para. 406.   [22] Articles on State Responsibility, article 10.

to form governments and thus possibly incur state responsibility, their responsibility – if any – must be grounded on a different basis.

CIRCUMSTANCES PRECLUDING WRONGFULNESS

In domestic law there may be circumstances which help to justify behaviour that would otherwise be illegal, and international law, too, knows a number of circumstances which can be invoked by a state to justify behaviour that would otherwise amount to a wrongful act and thus give rise to state responsibility. These are assembled under the general heading 'circumstances precluding wrongfulness', and listed in articles 20–25 of the Articles on State Responsibility. An important theoretical point is that the circumstances merely preclude wrongfulness; they serve as justifications for wrongful acts in certain circumstances, but they do not make the original obligation go away.

Perhaps the most obvious of these is if conduct takes place with the consent of a state. Thus the permission by a state to use its airspace 'legalizes' what would otherwise be illegal conduct. Equally obvious is that self-defence, provided it is lawful, constitutes a circumstance precluding wrongfulness.[23] And, as noted above, an act that takes place in response to another state's wrongful conduct (this used to be known as reprisal, but is nowadays often referred to as a lawful countermeasure) may well be justified. In these three cases (consent, self-defence, countermeasures), conduct is responsive to another state's conduct.

The more interesting scenarios are those where wrongfulness is precluded due to the existence of what might be considered an objective situation. This applies, for example, in the case of *force majeure*, a turn of events beyond the control of the state, making performance of an obligation impossible. One can think of earthquakes, droughts, or floods, but also the outbreak of an insurrection. What matters most of all is that the state could not perform, even if it wanted to.

This distinguishes *force majeure* from two similar grounds: distress and necessity. Distress relates to situations where alternative courses of action exist, but would demand sacrifice of the actor concerned. Typical examples would involve aircraft landing without authorization on foreign territory in order to avoid crashing, or ships entering territorial waters in order to seek shelter from extreme weather conditions.

Necessity, finally, is the most 'political' ground, as it aims to justify behaviour that would otherwise be wrong as necessary to protect a vital state interest. Examples are varied, and may range from setting on fire a ship that leaks oil in order to prevent large-scale pollution, to expropriating foreign property in order to feed military troops. Needless to say, the ground of 'necessity' lends itself to easy abuse, and therefore comes with strict conditions; under article 25 of the Articles on State Responsibility, the national interest at stake must be 'an essential interest' which must be under 'grave and imminent peril', and the conduct concerned must be relatively harmless towards the state to which the obligation is owed or the international community as a whole.

---

[23] The precise criteria for lawful self-defence will be discussed in Chapter 10 below.

Moreover, it is of note that the provision is negatively formulated; necessity may not be invoked unless an essential interest is under grave and imminent peril. The ICJ confirmed in its 1997 *Gabcikovo-Nagymaros* case that necessity was best approached narrowly. In this case, Hungary had invoked a state of necessity ('ecological necessity') in order to justify non-performance of its 1977 treaty with Czechoslovakia on building a dam in the River Danube. The Court, in what can only be seen as a word of warning, cautioned against invoking necessity lightly; invoking necessity as a justification implies that the behaviour would be wrongful to begin with, would trigger the responsibility of the state concerned, and possibly give rise to a valid claim for compensation.[24]

CONSEQUENCES OF RESPONSIBILITY

Traditionally, international law singles out three possible forms of reparation for injury.[25] Ideally, the state in the wrong will provide restitution and restore the situation as it would have existed without the wrongful act. Since the latter depends on conjecture, article 35 of the Articles on State Responsibility has opted for the easier-to-apply restoration of the *status quo ante* – without having to imagine what would have happened had the wrongful act not taken place. Failing this, reparation may take the form of compensation, and sometimes satisfaction is considered sufficient (articles 36 and 37 of the Articles on State Responsibility). It is also possible to end up with a combination of any of these. Importantly, the underlying assumption here is that reparation is not seen as punishment, or as setting a deterrent example. The function of reparation is not to punish, but to repair, and this, in turn, is based on the idea that it is somehow inappropriate to punish the sovereign.

Restitution is the main form of reparation – at least in theory and sometimes also in practice. Should property have been unlawfully seized, it can always be returned; likewise, prisoners unlawfully detained can be released. Restitution therefore includes the cessation of the wrongful act but, logically, this will often also have to precede it. In case of an invasion, for instance, the first priority will be to stop the invasion; only thereafter will restitution possibly come into play.

If the property is already destroyed, or prisoners have been killed, there is obviously no longer any possibility of return. It goes without saying that often situations will be of this kind; in case of environmental damage, or deaths on the battlefield, the *status quo ante* cannot be restored. Here, then, compensation may provide a useful alternative. According to special rapporteur Crawford, the function of compensation 'is to address the actual losses incurred as a result of the internationally wrongful act'.[26] Consequently, compensation should also cover losses of profits, if and where appropriate, but since the function of reparation is not to punish, international law does not generally provide for punitive damages.

The third form reparation may take is known as satisfaction, and, as article 37 of the Articles on State Responsibility holds, this 'may consist in an acknowledgement of

---

[24] *Gabcikovo-Nagymaros Project (Hungary/Slovakia)*, [1997] ICJ Rep. 7, para. 48.
[25] See *Chorzów Factory*, although the Court in that case did not specifically single out satisfaction.
[26] Crawford, *State Responsibility*, at 219.

the breach, an expression of regret, a formal apology or another appropriate modality'. As this list suggests, satisfaction is mostly considered useful in connection with moral damage that cannot be quantified and thus cannot give rise to compensation in a meaningful way. Again, the idea of punishment is abandoned, and article 37 prescribes that satisfaction shall not be humiliating; apologizing is okay, but grovelling goes too far.

RESPONSIBLE TO WHOM?

In the system of international law, characterized as it is by the coexistence of sovereign equals, obligations are typically conceptualized as being owed towards another state or a group of other states. Typically, even under multilateral treaties, treaty relations are seen as dyadic in nature; even under, say, the UN Convention on the Law of the Sea (UNCLOS), Germany owes obligations to Austria, to Denmark, to Brazil, and so on. Hence, despite the multilateral form of the treaty, the obligations are typically seen as giving rise to bilateral relations.

It follows that the law of state responsibility also thinks primarily in terms of bilateral obligations: should a German ship enter Brazil's internal waters, then Germany commits an internationally wrongful act towards Brazil, but not towards Denmark or Austria. Hence Germany is responsible to Brazil, and will be expected to make reparations to Brazil.

All this sounds plausible with respect to many situations, but sometimes it does not. For instance, the above logic does not apply to human rights treaties; the torture of a Turkish prisoner by Turkish authorities will harm the prisoner, rather than the other parties to a human rights convention. Hence human rights treaties do not neatly fit the bilateral model, and much the same applies to other treaties that are based on some kind of consideration of the interest of the international community (treaties establishing international organizations, environmental treaties). Hence, where the common interest of the international community is at stake, or where a collective interest is at stake, article 48 of the Articles on State Responsibility also allows others to invoke the responsibility of the state carrying out the wrongdoing.[27]

This goes some way towards recognizing a public element in the system of international law. In particular the idea that 'any' state can invoke responsibility for the interests of the international community marks a minor revolution. It effectively signals that with some obligations, any state, whether injured or not, can act against the state carrying out the wrongdoing, and that is a far cry from the traditional 'horizontal' system of bilateral relations.

The same philosophy that undergirds *jus cogens* in international law (the existence of community interests) has thereby also entered the law on state responsibility. This did not happen overnight; a first hint to this effect was presented by the ICJ in the 1970 *Barcelona Traction* case, where it launched the idea that some obligations are not just owed towards one's treaty partners or other individual states under customary international law, but also

---

[27] Similarly, article 60 of the VCLT allows others than the directly injured state to take action in case of a material breach of treaty.

owed towards the international community of states as a whole – so-called obligations *erga omnes*.[28] According to the Court, it concerned, for instance, obligations not to hold people in slavery or engage in racial discrimination, and not to commit aggression or commit genocide.[29] The concept of *erga omnes* obligations was launched *obiter* (the Court did not need to say this to decide the case at hand)[30] and initially did not attract much attention, but over time has come to be regarded as one way in which the common interest may find protection. While the ICJ has consistently maintained that the violation of an *erga omnes* obligation does not, in and of itself, provide the ICJ with jurisdiction,[31] the Articles on State Responsibility now make clear that violations of such obligations can be addressed in diplomatic practice.

In *Construction of a Wall*, the ICJ spelled out some of the consequences of a breach of an *erga omnes* obligation; all states are under an obligation to refrain from recognizing the illegal situation; they are under an obligation not to render aid or assistance to the state carrying out the wrongdoing, and to ensure that state's compliance.[32]

The idea of allowing any state – and not just a directly injured state, if any – to intervene in order to stop gross injustices (genocide, ethnic cleansing) retains a strongly seductive quality. Yet, as Koskenniemi suggests, such a wide avenue for countermeasures may open the door for the great powers to establish domination in the name of community values. After all, as the experience in Syria, ongoing at the time of writing, suggests, interveners are states such as the United States, France or Russia, rather than, say, Nepal, Eritrea or Honduras.[33]

Even more controversial than the idea of *erga omnes* obligations was the idea, launched by the ILC at some point during the drafting of the Articles on State Responsibility, that states could commit crimes and thus be held criminally responsible.[34] This was controversial not just because it also presupposed a public law element (like *jus cogens* and *erga omnes*), but also because it would introduce a punitive element; it is one thing to ask a state to make reparation, but quite another to hold it criminally responsible. This then also created the question of the proper punishment; if a state commits a crime (rather than a wrongful act or tort), then what can be done against the state? One can, and should,

---

[28] See generally Christian J. Tams, *Enforcing Obligations Erga Omnes in International Law* (Cambridge University Press, 2005).

[29] *Barcelona Traction, Light and Power Company, Limited (Belgium v. Spain)*, [1970] ICJ Rep. 3, para. 34.

[30] Rumour has it that the *dictum* was inserted so as to remedy the backlash suffered by the Court after a very narrow decision in 1966 had denied jurisdiction in a case brought by Liberia and Ethiopia on behalf of Namibia. Rumour also has it that the *dictum* was the brainchild of Judge Manfred Lachs; the latter rumour is reported in Antonio Cassese, *Five Masters of International Law* (Oxford: Hart, 2011), at 80.

[31] See e.g. *East Timor (Portugal v. Australia)*, [1995] ICJ Rep. 90, para. 29: while the Court confirmed that the principle of self-determination was of *erga omnes* character, it none the less argued 'that the *erga omnes* character of a norm and the rule of consent to jurisdiction are two different things'. See generally Jan Klabbers, 'The Scope of International Law: Erga Omnes Obligations and the Turn to Morality', in Matti Tupamäki (ed.), *Liber Amicorum Bengt Broms* (Helsinki: Finnish ILA Branch, 1999), 149–79.

[32] *Legal Consequences of the Construction of a Wall in the Occupied Palestinian Territory*, advisory opinion, [2004] ICJ Rep. 136, para. 159.

[33] Martti Koskenniemi, 'Solidarity Measures: State Responsibility as a New International Order?', (2001) 72 *British Yearbook of International Law*, 337–56.

[34] This is carefully discussed in Nina H. B. Jorgensen, *The Responsibility of States for International Crimes* (Oxford University Press, 2000).

obviously, ask it to cease its conduct; one should also ask it to provide reparation, but what more can be done within the international legal system? It would be unthinkable to put a state or its government in prison, or order a government to abdicate. Eventually, given this problem of identifying proper punishment, the notion of holding states criminally responsible was largely given up. What is left is the idea that when *jus cogens* norms are violated, states should not assist the wrongdoing state or recognize as lawful the situation created thereby. Other than that, the concept of crimes of states has left little trace in the Articles on State Responsibility, although criminal responsibility is not rejected on principle by special rapporteur Crawford.[35]

RESPONSIBILITY OF INTERNATIONAL ORGANIZATIONS

The collapse of the International Tin Council (ITC) in the 1980s suggested that legal questions could arise about the responsibility of international organizations. Until then, this was rarely given any serious thought; organizations were set up to exercise functions delegated by their member states, so if they happened to do something wrong, the member states could, at least in theory, be held responsible. Hence, for a long time, it was thought that a responsibility regime for international organizations was not really necessary. Yet when the debtors of the ITC approached the ITC's member states for compensation after the Council became insolvent, those member states invoked the separate legal personality of the Council in order to escape liability; since the Council was a legal person, its debts were its own, and not attributable to the member states, and this position was confirmed, albeit somewhat hesitantly, by the English courts, in which much of the litigation took place.[36]

As a result, international lawyers began to think seriously about a set of rules on the responsibility of international organizations, and the ILC began work on the topic in 2000, when it appointed its member Giorgio Gaja as special rapporteur on the topic. Gaja's work was made extremely difficult by two considerations pulling in opposite directions. On the one hand, the rules on responsibility must, substantively, follow the rules on state responsibility; it would be awkward to have two completely different responsibility regimes. Thus Gaja has made it clear that the same two basic principles apply; organizations can be held responsible for internationally wrongful acts that are attributable to them. On the other hand, as much as it is desirable to follow the rules on state responsibility, the ILC has to grapple with the circumstance that while international organizations are typically composed of states and perform functions delegated by states, they are not identical to states. They differ in some fundamental respects; they have no territory of their own; they lack sovereign jurisdiction and lack the sort of officials whose acts often give rise to responsibility – organizations usually have no police officials and no military of their own.

---

[35] Crawford, *State Responsibility*, 16–20.
[36] For further discussion, see Jan Klabbers, *An Introduction to International Organizations Law*, 3rd edn (Cambridge University Press, 2015), 312–15.

There are other circumstances as well which make the development of a set of rules highly problematic. Thus international organizations are usually parties to only a few treaties, hence it may be difficult to accuse an organization of committing an internationally wrongful act for, as noted, this presupposes the existence of a binding legal obligation.[37] And while international organizations are bound, as the ICJ posited in 1980, by the 'general rules of international law',[38] it is not self-evident that this covers all possible rules of customary international law, or merely customary rules that facilitate the existence of international law (such as the law of treaties). Hence it might be the case that there are not all that many international law rules that organizations can violate to begin with.[39]

Likewise, attribution is problematic, largely because organizations do not have their own troops or officials. For instance, a fairly typical scenario with respect to UN peacekeeping is that the UN authorizes its member states to go on a mission, and that the interested member states together form troops which tend to operate under national rules of engagement. Should, for instance, a Canadian peacekeeper violate international humanitarian law, it is by no means obvious whether responsibility should rest with the UN, with his national state or even with the individual peacekeeper. And even if the acts were attributable to the UN, this might not necessarily result in justice being done.

A sobering example is the decision of the ECtHR in *Behrami and Saramati*, in 2007.[40] Here the issue concerned the responsibility for conduct of UN troops in Kosovo, which had led to some (alleged) human rights violations. The victims of these violations brought cases against some of the UN's member states most closely involved, in particular France and Norway – under the ECHR, this is the most obvious route. The Court's finding that the conduct was attributable to the UN therewith created the curious problem that the Court also had to find the case inadmissible; the UN is not a party to the ECHR, and thus the Court has nothing to say about the UN's conduct. Here then, attribution of conduct to the UN resulted, in effect, in a 'leaking away' of responsibility.[41]

In 2011, the ILC adopted a set of articles on the responsibility of international organizations.[42] To the extent that the articles follow the Articles on State Responsibility, they are

---

[37] Discussions include Kristina Daugirdas, 'How and Why International Law Binds International Organizations', (2016) 57 *Harvard International Law Journal* (forthcoming) and Jan Klabbers, 'The Sources of International Organizations Law', in Samantha Besson and Jean d'Aspremont (eds.), *Oxford Handbook of the Sources of International Law* (Oxford University Press, forthcoming).

[38] *Interpretation of the Agreement of 25 March 1951 between the WHO and Egypt*, advisory opinion, [1980] ICJ Rep. 73.

[39] Sometimes organizations unilaterally declare that they consider themselves legally bound by sets of rules. On this basis, the UN Secretary-General proclaimed in the 1990s that the UN would respect international humanitarian law; see also Chapter 11 below.

[40] Joined cases *Behrami and Behrami* v. *France* (Application no. 71412/01) and *Saramati* v. *France and others* (Application no. 78116/01), ECtHR, judgment of 2 May 2007. For insightful discussion, see Guglielmo Verdirame, *The UN and Human Rights: Who Guards the Guardians?* (Cambridge University Press, 2011), 108–13.

[41] More generally, this is sometimes referred to as the problem of the 'many hands': where many actors are involved in conduct, it is sometimes difficult to figure out who is responsible for which part of the group's work. For insightful discussion, see Mark Bovens, *The Quest for Responsibility* (Cambridge University Press, 1998).

[42] For useful discussion see Maurizio Ragazzi (ed.), *Responsibility of International Organizations: Essays in Memory of Sir Ian Brownlie* (Leiden: Martinus Nijhoff, 2013).

authoritative, and possibly have the force of customary international law. Or, more accurately perhaps, to the extent that they reflect the principles underlying the regime on state responsibility, the draft articles on the responsibility of international organizations carry great authority. Yet the main international organizations are not very interested in having firm and detailed rules on responsibility to begin with, and the most active organization in the international legal order (the EU) would much prefer to carve out a separate niche for itself.[43]

Given these uncertainties, it is perhaps no coincidence that both the International Law Association (ILA)[44] and individual academics[45] have launched proposals arguing that international organizations can best be held accountable (the word 'responsibility' is studiously avoided as being too closely related to state responsibility and the ILC's approach) by borrowing notions from administrative law. This helps to overcome the problem of insisting on internationally wrongful acts; broad principles of administrative law, so the reasoning goes, would be applicable not so much because organizations had become parties to them, but simply because they were sensible and mostly procedural in nature. After all, who could possibly object to transparency in decision-making, broad participation in decision-making, or the use of proportionality in applying the law? This may look like a promising avenue, but, as has been pointed out, many of these administrative law principles originate largely in the United States and Europe and are thus not beyond political suspicion.[46] Moreover, who will decide what constitutes broad participation in decision-making? How will proportionality actually be determined? Even such neutral-looking devices as administrative law principles may still give rise to profound political disagreement and widely differing interpretations.

INDIVIDUAL RESPONSIBILITY

In contrast to the responsibility of international organizations which, as noted, has come to be recognized as a topic for study and debate only since the 1980s, international law has for centuries recognized something akin to the responsibility of individuals for their conduct. This has mostly been limited to conduct on the battlefield; history is replete with examples of individuals who have been tried after conflicts for their behaviour during those conflicts, and the Versailles Treaty concluding the First World War

---

[43] Pieter Jan Kuijper and Esa Paasivirta, 'The EC and the Responsibility of International Organizations', (2004) 1 *International Organizations Law Review*, 111–38.

[44] ILA, 'Accountability of International Organisations: Final Report', in International Law Association, *Report of the Seventy-First Conference Berlin* (London: ILA, 2004), 164–241. The ILA, incidentally, is an association of respected professionals (academics as well as practitioners) active in the field of international law, but without any official standing.

[45] This refers to an approach that has gained fame under the heading 'Global Administrative Law'. Something of a manifesto is Benedict Kingsbury, Nico Krisch, and Richard B. Stewart, 'The Emergence of Global Administrative Law', (2005) 68 *Law and Contemporary Problems*, 15–61, while an authoritative overview is Sabino Cassese (ed.), *Research Handbook on Global Administrative Law* (Cheltenham: Edward Elgar, 2016). See further also Chapter 17 below.

[46] See e.g. B. S. Chimni, 'Co-option and Resistance: Two Faces of Global Administrative Law', (2005) 37 *New York University Journal of International Law and Politics*, 799–827.

explicitly stated as much with respect to the former German Emperor, Kaiser Wilhelm II. He was to be publicly arraigned 'for a supreme offence against international morality and the sanctity of treaties'.[47]

The underlying theory was neatly formulated by the Nuremberg Tribunal, when it held that states are abstractions that cannot act except by means of people of flesh and blood. It follows that when states commit an internationally wrongful act, it is possible to single out the 'responsible' individuals and try them as individuals. In principle, taking this theory to the extreme, there are few wrongful acts that cannot be traced back – attributed – to individuals. Aggression is usually the result of commands from a political leader; prosecute the leader, and all will be well.

The hallmark of individual responsibility under international law is that individuals will be held responsible directly under international law – without domestic law functioning as an intermediary. Where state responsibility is often practised on the diplomatic level ('state X holds state Y responsible'), doing so makes little sense as regards individual responsibility. Individual responsibility responds to the urge actually to punish those who commit serious crimes under international law, and thereby almost by definition presupposes the existence of international courts and tribunals. These exist, but mainly in the sphere of international humanitarian law and international criminal law; think, for instance, of the ICC, or the Nuremberg Tribunal, or the ICTY and the ICTR. It is largely for transgression of these bodies of primary rules (to revert to the ILC terminology) that individuals can be held responsible under international law; other bodies of primary rules have yet to develop a responsibility regime.

On a theoretical level, it should perhaps be noted that individual responsibility differs from state responsibility and international organization responsibility in that the distinction between primary and secondary rules hardly works. Many of the rules on individual responsibility (the secondary rules) are actually to be found within the primary rules; the requirement of *mens rea*, or criminal intent, is to be found typically in international criminal law. In fact, there are no secondary rules on individual responsibility – a circumstance which strengthens the impression that individual responsibility is often based on a spur of the moment assessment rather than following a well-established set of rules. That impression is further strengthened by the fact that many of the tribunals tend to be ad hoc; they are typically created in the immediate aftermath of an attack or humanitarian crisis, exercising a highly specific jurisdiction. This applies to such entities as the Extraordinary Chambers in the Courts of Cambodia, the Special Court for Sierra Leone and the Special Tribunal for Lebanon,[48] as well as entities such as the (erstwhile) ICTY and the ICTR or the scheduled Kosovo Relocated Specialist Judicial Institution, which will be housed in The Hague and will look into serious crimes

---

[47] Versailles Treaty, article 227. The Kaiser fled to the Netherlands which, not being a party to the Versailles Treaty, did not surrender him.

[48] This last is particularly curious, in that it has been set up to deal with the deaths of twenty-two individuals in an attack.

allegedly committed by members of the Kosovo Liberation Army during the struggles of 1999–2000.[49] The first, and thus far only, permanent institution is the ICC.[50]

SHARED RESPONSIBILITY?

As already alluded to above, the coexistence of different systems of responsibility sometimes makes for uncomfortable decision-making, and brings its own bucket of philosophical problems with it. These include issues of causation: how, for example, to assign responsibility for global problems that are the result of individual states (or even individuals) all doing things that are not necessarily illegal? The standard example is climate change, caused by all of us, yet by no one in particular.[51]

In a sense, of course, states (and international organizations) are abstractions, only capable of acting through individuals, so from that perspective it would be sensible just to target the responsible individuals. Yet doing so ignores the circumstance that individuals, no matter how nasty or evil, often cannot work in isolation. Focusing on individual responsibility then misses the point that many evil acts can only take place because of the existence of an institutionalized system of terror. To put it starkly, Hitler's orders during the Holocaust would have been ineffective if others had not obeyed them. Hitler could execute his policies because others agreed, followed him, and faithfully did what he told them to do and sometimes more. A focus on individual responsibility tends to hide from view the extent to which individuals and political structures are combined to disastrous effect.

There is, moreover, a second factor at work here, in that often the behaviour of high-ranking state officials need not be inspired by nasty or evil motives. The German political theorist Hannah Arendt has brilliantly drawn attention to what she called the 'banality of evil'; evil can sometimes result from nasty motives, but can also, in large bureaucracies, result from the banality of pushing papers.[52] Arendt closely followed the trial of Adolf Eichmann, a high-ranking official in Nazi Germany, responsible for coordinating the transport of Jews to extermination camps. Eichmann may or may not have been a zealous anti-Semite;[53] what mattered is that he thoughtlessly signed papers sending huge numbers of people to their deaths, taking pride in doing his job properly. A focus on individual responsibility has problems capturing this type of evil, precisely because it is not born out of evil motives but may almost inhere in the existence of rational bureaucracy.

Thus a focus on individual responsibility ignores the underlying framework that sometimes facilitates gross crimes. Conversely, a focus on state responsibility tends to ignore the

---

[49] It will be composed of international judges, but will apply Kosovo law. See further https://www.government.nl/latest/news/2016/01/15/kosovo-court-to-be-established-in-the-hague (visited 25 July 2016).

[50] See Chapter 12 below.

[51] A useful discussion of the various issues is André Nollkaemper and Dov Jacobs (eds.), *Distribution of Responsibilities in International Law* (Cambridge University Press, 2015).

[52] Hannah Arendt, *Eichmann in Jerusalem: A Report on the Banality of Evil* (London: Penguin, 1963).

[53] This is disputed, perhaps partly because his crimes would be easier to explain if he could be depicted as an evil monster. On this, see Jan Klabbers, 'Just Revenge? The Deterrence Argument in International Criminal Law', (2001) 12 *Finnish Yearbook of International Law*, 249–67.

role, sometimes decisive, of individuals. Nazi Germany would have been different, and most probably less bloody, without Hitler, Goering, and Himmler, and it seems a bit awkward to hold a state (and therewith, by association, its entire population) responsible for the misdeeds of what is usually an elite group of political leaders. Yet state structures are often involved, so one cannot just focus on individuals, because doing so might mean that a state gets off the hook.

The risk, then, is that the focus can constantly oscillate between state responsibility and individual responsibility, to such an extent that eventually no one is held responsible or to such an extent that both are held responsible in ways that are deemed unjust. Things are further complicated by the possible addition of a third layer of responsibility: that of international organizations. While it is no doubt possible, technically, to develop reasonable rules of attribution to address single cases, the risk of responsibility leaking away looms large, and perhaps the adaptation of an old maxim is of use: where everyone can be responsible, no one is.

FINAL REMARKS

The law of responsibility is a vital area of international law and, what is more, is an area in great flux. While the rules on state responsibility are reasonably settled, those on the responsibility of international organizations are under development, and the law on individual responsibility, it sometimes seems, is trying to run before it has learned how to walk.

The law of responsibility is also quite a fascinating area, in particular because it opens up avenues for deep reflection. There is, as mentioned, the very idea of moral agency; do non-human entities have moral agency? Other difficult questions abound. Can responsibility ever be collective, as both state responsibility and international organization responsibility presuppose, or is collective responsibility the aggregate of individual responsibilities?[54]

Even on the more technical level there are difficult and, as yet, unresolved issues. Think only of the question of when an internationally wrongful act commences; is planning a wrongful act in itself already wrongful? What if the wrongful act is unsuccessful? And how is one to assess a continuous violation (for instance, a foreign invasion) – is that a single wrongful act? Or rather a series of single wrongful acts? Or is the continuous wrongful act somehow different in kind from other wrongful acts?[55]

One final remark: it is arguably no coincidence that issues of responsibility and accountability have recently come to occupy a prominent place in international legal discussions – discussions on responsibility and accountability have tended to be few and far between. This is no longer the case, and it may well be that accountability has become such a hot topic because there is such great uncertainty concerning both the sources and subjects of international law and global governance. Where no one can be certain any longer whether

---

[54] On this issue, see Larry May, *Sharing Responsibility* (University of Chicago Press, 1992).
[55] The seminal piece is Joost Pauwelyn, 'The Concept of a "Continuing Violation" of an International Obligation: Selected Problems', (1995) 66 *British Yearbook of International Law*, 415–50.

norms are 'legal' and whether those from whom the norms emanate have law-making authority, it stands to reason that attention focuses on the output side; at least there may be merit in trying to hold actors to account if their behaviour is questionable.[56]

FURTHER READING

Sabino Cassese (ed.), *Research Handbook on Global Administrative Law* (Cheltenham: Edward Elgar, 2016)

James Crawford, *The International Law Commission's Articles on State Responsibility: Introduction, Text and Commentaries* (Cambridge University Press, 2002)

James Crawford, Alain Pellet, and Simon Olleson (eds.), *The Law of International Responsibility* (Oxford University Press, 2010)

Ebrahim Elnoor and Edward Weisband (eds.), *Global Accountabilities: Participation, Pluralism, and Public Ethics* (Cambridge University Press, 2007)

Jan Klabbers, *Sins of Omission: The Responsibility of International Organizations for Inaction*, NYU Jean Monnet Working Paper 2/2016

André Nollkaemper and Dov Jacobs (eds.), *Distribution of Responsibilities in International Law* (Cambridge University Press, 2015)

Maurizio Ragazzi (ed.), *Responsibility of International Organizations: Essays in Memory of Sir Ian Brownlie* (Leiden: Martinus Nijhoff, 2013)

Guglielmo Verdirame, *The UN and Human Rights: Who Guards the Guardians?* (Cambridge University Press, 2011)

---

[56] For further reflections along these lines, see Jan Klabbers, 'From Sources Doctrine to Responsibility? Reflections on the Private Lives of States', in Pierre d'Argent et al. (eds.), *Les limites du droit international: Essais en l'honneur de Joe Verhoeven* (Brussels: Bruylant, 2015), 69–85.

8

International Courts and Tribunals

INTRODUCTION

The sovereignty of states means that it has been considered very difficult to hold states to account before a court. This is still reflected in the idea that states enjoy sovereign immunities in domestic law, one of these being immunity from prosecution; as we have seen in an earlier chapter, states cannot be held to account in the courts of another state for their official acts.[1]

If states cannot be held to account before a domestic court, it stands to reason that their acts can be adjudicated before international tribunals, but this has taken a long time to develop. States have been reluctant to subject themselves to the jurisdiction of international tribunals and, by and large, continue to be reluctant to do so. While international courts are quite numerous in the early twenty-first century (at the latest count, there are some 125 in existence, in all sorts and varieties),[2] adjudication took a long time to develop and is still often considered as onerous. States tend to prefer to settle their differences by political means, and in a sense, this is as it should be; much as in private relations between individuals, courts should be a medium of last resort. This chapter will discuss briefly dispute settlement by political means, discuss arbitration and, at considerable length, discuss the ICJ.

SETTLING DISPUTES

The UN Charter obliges its member states to settle their disputes peacefully, and does so in various ways. One of these ways is that the peaceful settlement of disputes is listed among the founding principles of the UN in article 2, paragraph 3 of the Charter, and is followed,

---

[1] Chapter 5 above.

[2] For an authoritative overview see Ruth MacKenzie, Cesare Romano, and Yuval Shany (eds.), *The Manual on International Courts and Tribunals*, 2nd edn (Oxford University Press, 2010). On concurrent jurisdiction over the same case, see Yuval Shany, *The Competing Jurisdictions of International Courts and Tribunals* (Oxford University Press, 2003).

in the next paragraph, by the prohibition of the use of force.[3] Article 33 UN Charter adds a list of possible ways to settle disputes peacefully, most of these being of a political nature.

While it should be obvious that these means of settling disputes cannot have a technical meaning (with the possible exception of the 'legal' means, arbitration, and adjudication, which will be discussed below), it is perhaps useful to describe briefly how they tend to be used in diplomatic practice. 'Negotiation' typically involves two parties who, by trying to talk things through, aim to reach a solution to their dispute. They may, and usually will, do so by means of invoking legal arguments ('You are not entitled to hold military manoeuvres in front of my coast', or 'I am entitled to capture drugs smugglers in my territorial waters'), but there is no particular expectation that such disputes will be settled on the basis of law alone. That said, to reach a settlement by means of coercion would be difficult to defend; typically, a whole range of arguments, including legal arguments, will play out in any dispute.

If the two parties are incapable of reaching an accommodation, they may try to enlist the services of a third party. This can be a third state, but it can also be a trusted individual: the pope has acted in such a way, as have several heads of state and, more recently, the Secretary-General of the United Nations. Such third-party involvement can take several forms.

If the parties refuse to communicate directly with each other, the third party may offer his (or her, or its) 'good offices'; it can offer itself as a channel for communication. An example may reside in a particularly explosive debate during the 1980s concerning territorial sovereignty over oil-rich islands between Qatar and Bahrain, in the Persian Gulf; while neither trusted the other enough to be in conversation, both trusted Saudi Arabia enough to act as a go-between or, more romantically, a *postillon d'amour*. Qatar would send notes to Saudi Arabia asking the latter to pass them on to Bahrain, and the replies would come via the same route. In the end, Saudi Arabia was able to persuade both states to submit the matter to the ICJ.

It may also be the case that there is not just a disagreement between two states on, for example, an alleged violation of a legal rule, but that they cannot even agree on what actually happened. In such cases, a third party may be entrusted with a fact-finding task, trying to present an authoritative version of the facts leading up to the dispute. Sometimes this is left to trusted individuals; it is more common nowadays to establish a fact-finding commission. One example is that the Human Rights Council of the UN established a Commission of Inquiry on the Syrian Arab republic in 2011 to investigate possible violations of international humanitarian law.[4] Article 33 of the UN Charter speaks, indeed, of 'enquiry'.

Where the third party becomes actively engaged in the negotiations, and for instance assumes a role by submitting possible solutions, it is common to speak of 'mediation'. A possible example (but this is difficult to confirm) may be the role played by Algeria in settling the 1979 hostage crisis between Iran and the United States. When Iranian revolutionaries had stormed the US embassy and were holding US personnel hostage, and after aborted rescue missions by the United States, a stalemate seemed to ensue. Eventually,

---

[3] This prohibition will be discussed in Chapter 10 below.
[4] Human Rights Council Resolution S-17/1, 12 August 2011.

representatives of Iran and the United States met in Algiers, Algeria's capital, and agreed on releasing the hostages and on how the private claims of many individuals and companies were to be settled.

It is likely that Algeria mediated, although Algeria has been reluctant to acknowledge such a role. The reason is eminently political: mediation would imply a serious degree of cooperation with the United States. Yet, in the volatile climate of Arab politics, Algeria would not wish to be accused of being overly friendly with the United States, let alone of being its handmaiden.

An even more intense role for third parties than that envisaged by mediation is their role in 'conciliation'. Here, the third party acts almost like a tribunal, hearing evidence, reading memorials, and presenting a recommendation based on the evidence as presented. The difference from the work of a regular court is that the third party is not, actually, a court, and that its recommendation is not binding. A noteworthy example is the *Jan Mayen* conciliation, allowing Norway and Iceland to settle their dispute over Jan Mayen Island and the resources to be found in the surrounding waters and seabed.[5]

Finally, article 33 UN Charter also mentions that disputes may be referred to regional organizations for a solution. In the systematics of the article, this is not very illuminating (as it does not specify the role the organization may play), but the idea behind it is quite simply that sometimes regional organizations are well placed to offer good offices or mediate between neighbouring states. Note, however, that none of these terms is truly a term of art; it is telling that the ICJ used both 'mediation' and 'good offices' to describe the involvement of Saudi Arabia in the dispute between Qatar and Bahrain.[6]

For the lawyer, the two more interesting methods of peaceful settlement mentioned in article 33 UN Charter are arbitration and adjudication (i.e. the use of a court or tribunal).[7] They have one important thing in common: they are based on the consent of states. This is a logical corollary of state sovereignty; the sovereign state need not accept any authority from above, unless it has itself consented thereto. What separates arbitration from adjudication is that arbitration is by definition ad hoc (arbitral panels are set up to decide a single case or a set of related cases, whereas courts are meant to be permanently available), and as a result, the parties usually have more influence on the composition of the arbitral panel and the law it will apply.

ARBITRATION

Modern arbitration in international law is often traced back to the 1794 Jay Treaty.[8] The treaty followed the earlier peace treaty between Great Britain and its former colonies

---

[5] The report of the Conciliation Commission, dated 19–20 May 1981, is reproduced in 62 *International Law Reports*, 108.

[6] *Maritime Delimitation and Territorial Questions between Qatar and Bahrain (Qatar v. Bahrain)*, [1994] ICJ Rep. 112, para. 16.

[7] Incidentally, the terms 'court' and 'tribunal' can be used interchangeably; there does not seem to be a serious difference between the two.

[8] Treaty of Amity, Commerce, and Navigation, concluded in 1794. John Jay was the US Secretary of State at the time.

in the United States after the United States gained independence, and specified that some of the questions that had not been dealt with, or which had not been clear, should be submitted to peaceful settlement by a commission. This included parts of the course of the boundary with Canada, still ruled by Britain (article 5 Jay Treaty), and the settlement of damages to citizens of both parties (articles 6 and 7). The boundary question was to be settled by a commission consisting of three members: one appointed by His Britannic Majesty, one by the US president, and the third by the two commissioners together. The damages question was to be submitted to a five-member panel, composed in a similar way, and could be decided by a majority of three (provided at least one of the commissioners appointed by each state was part of that majority).[9] The parties agreed to accept the awards as final and binding.

Important as the *Jay* Arbitration was, it did not deal with matters of life and death. A sterner test for the potential of international arbitration came with the *Alabama Claims* arbitration between, again, the United States and Great Britain in 1872, based on the 1871 Treaty of Washington. During the American civil war, Britain had declared its neutrality but had none the less supplied the Confederates (the 'South') with warships (including the CSS *Alabama*, which had been built in Britain), which caused great damage to the Northern action. The arbitral panel found unanimously that Britain was liable for US losses, and awarded $15,500,000 to the United States in damages.

The experience suggested that arbitration could become a useful and, above all, peaceful means of dispute settlement, even in matters often associated with 'high politics', such as national security. This sentiment led to the creation, at the first Hague Peace Conference in 1899, of the Permanent Court of Arbitration (PCA), which, despite its name, is not actually a court. It is best regarded as an international organization that facilitates arbitration, and it does so by keeping a roster of available individuals ready for appointment as arbitrators. These individuals have been accepted in advance, and the availability of their names on a list can possibly speed up the process of arbitration; it makes it more difficult for parties to block arbiters proposed by the other side. Having accepted them in advance, they cannot then claim that certain individuals are unacceptable.

Some of international law's leading cases of the early twentieth century have been solved via the PCA, an example being the *Island of Palmas* arbitration, decided by sole arbiter Max Huber in 1928.[10] With the emergence of the PCIJ and ICJ the PCA fell into relative disuse for a while, but in recent years it has been increasingly active, deciding, for instance, on issues arising during the war between Ethiopia and Eritrea. An important component, moreover, is that PCA arbitrations nowadays often deal with investment claims between a company and a state.

As the above already suggests, the disputing parties exercise quite some influence on the arbitration panel's composition. Typically, they each appoint one or two arbiters, who together appoint a third (or fifth), although sometimes a sole arbiter is preferred. The parties sometimes also indicate which law the panel is to apply, unless this is clear from the case

[9] There is no majority requirement mentioned with respect to the boundary issue.
[10] This is discussed in Chapter 4 above.

itself, for instance, if arbitration is brought under a particular convention which has to be applied. Arbitration leads to binding and final awards, although sometimes parties try to appeal to the ICJ. Arbitration is by definition ad hoc; once the award is rendered, the panel will dissolve. That said, some tribunals have had a long-standing existence dealing with a single series of related claims, perhaps none more so than the Iran–US Claims Tribunal, set up in 1981 to address the claims arising out of the taking of American hostages in Tehran following Iran's Islamic Revolution. The tribunal consists of nine arbiters, three appointed by the United States, three appointed by Iran, and three neutrals, and decides its cases in chambers of three arbiters (with one from each group).

If only to indicate the Humpty-Dumpty nature of legal terms, the Badinter Commission, set up on behalf of the EU to advise it on legal matters during the conflict in the former Yugoslavia, was officially referred to as the Arbitration Commission. None the less, its opinions were not considered binding, and its composition differed from regular arbitration panels in that two of its members were appointed by Yugoslavia's federal presidency and three by the EU.[11]

ADJUDICATION AND THE ICJ

Possibly the first ever international court (i.e. a judicial body set up for an unlimited duration, with the task to apply international law) was the Central American Court of Justice (CJAC).[12] Its existence was short lived, though, and it did not survive the outbreak of the First World War. None the less, it did decide a handful of cases, mostly involving boundary arrangements in Central America, and in the process said some interesting things about issues of wider significance, such as treaty conflicts.

However, the jurisdiction of the CJAC was geographically limited; it could only settle disputes between Central American states. The first more or less universal court was the PCIJ, the predecessor of the current ICJ. The ICJ is still the most relevant international tribunal, despite its fairly small caseload, for a combination of two reasons.[13] First, it is universal in terms of the states whose disputes it can settle; these include states from all continents. This, however, is not quite unique; much the same applies to ITLOS, located in Hamburg, the WTO's panels and Appellate Body, and the ICC.

What sets the ICJ (and before it the PCIJ) apart is, second, that it is a court of general jurisdiction; it can, in principle, adjudicate claims on all sorts of topics, ranging from maritime delimitation to violations of the law of armed conflict, and ranging from environmental claims to claims involving financial issues. Where the ICC's jurisdiction is limited to

---

[11] This is also discussed in Chapter 4 above. Its first opinion, rendered on 29 November 1991, on whether Yugoslavia was in the process of dissolving, is reproduced in 92 *International Law Reports*, 162. It gave an opinion on its own competence and the non-binding nature of its decisions, in response to objections raised by Yugoslavia's authorities, on 26 May 1993, reproduced in 96 *International Law Reports*, 713.

[12] But note the existence of anti-slavery courts already during the 1870s. See Jenny Martinez, 'Antislavery Courts and the Dawn of International Human Rights Law', (2008) 117 *Yale Law Journal*, 550–641.

[13] For a rich and detailed account see Robert Kolb, *The International Court of Justice* (Oxford: Hart, 2013).

international criminal law, and that of the WTO to international trade law, the jurisdiction of the ICJ is, in principle at any rate, substantively unlimited.

In addition to the above-mentioned more or less universal courts there exist a number of regional courts.[14] The best known of these are, quite possibly, the CJEU, and the ECtHR; their jurisdiction is limited to issues arising under their constituent treaties, to which only European states are party. Much the same applies elsewhere: there is an Inter-American Court of Human Rights, as well as an African Court of Human and Peoples' Rights, and various regional trade organizations may have their own judicial or quasi-judicial bodies; the EFTA Court, operating within the European Free Trade Area, is an example, as is the Andean Court of Justice (operating between a number of states in Latin America). There is little point in discussing all existing international courts and tribunals in detail, if only because all courts will have their own rules as to when they can exercise jurisdiction, concerning the admissibility of complaints or concerning their legal procedure. Instead, the remainder of this section will be devoted, by and large, to an in-depth discussion of the ICJ.

The ICJ, as mentioned, was preceded by the PCIJ, set up in the aftermath of the First World War. The PCIJ was based on a Statute, and was loosely (but only loosely) related to the League of Nations. Its Statute provided that it could render two types of decision: first, decisions in contentious cases between states, and, second, advisory opinions on the request of an international organization. The PCIJ issued a number of noteworthy and still influential judgments and opinions, of which the *Lotus* and *Wimbledon* cases are arguably the most famous.[15] It did not survive the outbreak of the Second World War, however, and formally ceased to exist in 1946.

Where the PCIJ was only loosely linked to the League of Nations (which meant, for instance, that the League was not in a position to help enforce PCIJ decisions), the ICJ is officially one of the six principal organs of the UN, on a par with the Security Council and the General Assembly. It still operates, by and large, on the basis of the PCIJ's Statute, slightly revised in 1945 and now included as an integral part of the UN Charter.

The ICJ is based in The Hague, in a building appropriately referred to as the Peace Palace, and consists of fifteen 'titular' judges. There is no nationality requirement involved, other than that no two judges shall be nationals of the same state (article 3 ICJ Statute). In practice, however, it transpires that the five permanent members of the Security Council always have a judge of their nationality on the ICJ, and this makes some geopolitical sense; it would be difficult for a number of judges drawn exclusively from small countries to persuade the superpowers of the evil of their ways. The ICJ owes its legitimacy not merely to being impartial and to legal brilliance, but also to being politically acceptable.

A curious feature that may help to bolster this political acceptability is that states involved in a dispute before the Court are allowed (if they have no titular judge on the bench) to appoint an ad hoc judge of their own choosing. Thus, in a dispute between

---

[14] A useful overview of international adjudication is offered by Daniel Terris, Cesare Romano, and Leigh Swigart, *The International Judge: An Introduction to the Men and Women Who Decide the World's Cases* (Oxford University Press, 2007).

[15] These are discussed in Chapter 2 above.

Liechtenstein and the United States, Liechtenstein would be allowed to appoint an ad hoc judge, who would merely add to the number of judges. And if neither party has its own titular judge, then both can appoint an ad hoc judge, so that the maximum number of people on the bench at any time can be seventeen. This helps to persuade the state concerned that its arguments are being taken seriously by the Court and illustrates graphically that the law is, in part, about equality of arms.[16] Typically, but not invariably, the ad hoc judge is a national of the state appointing him or her, and it is probably no coincidence that the ad hoc judge often votes for the state that appointed him or her, but there are examples to the contrary.[17]

There are few requirements about the composition of the Court. Judges must be 'of high moral character' and either be lawyers qualified for highest judicial office in their own states, or be 'jurisconsults of recognized competence in international law' (article 2 ICJ Statute). The latter clause allows states to nominate lawyers with vast experience in their foreign office but less in a judicial function; often the US judge tends to come from the State Department, and the same applies to the French judge. The only other requirement can be found in article 9 ICJ Statute. The Court as a whole should reflect the main forms of civilization and the principal legal systems of the world. This means in practice that the Court will comprise judges from western and eastern Europe, the Middle East, Latin America, sub-Saharan Africa, and Asia; much of the nominating process takes the form of negotiating between the various regions of the world.

Judges are appointed by the General Assembly and the Security Council following a complicated and highly politicized procedure which occupies no fewer than nine articles of the ICJ's Statute (articles 4–12 ICJ Statute). Typically, the individuals chosen tend to be male, and of a somewhat advanced age; few judges have been appointed when they were still in their forties. The first permanent female judge to be appointed was Dame Rosalyn Higgins, of British nationality and formerly a professor at the London School of Economics; Higgins is also the first female president of the Court, having presided from 2006 until 2009. The first female ad hoc judge was Suzanne Bastid, whose father, Jules Basdevant, was himself a judge at the ICJ.[18] At the time of writing, the Court includes three female judges, two of them nationals of the two major powers: Joan Donoghue of the United States and China's Xue Hanqin. The third female judge currently on the bench is Uganda's Julia Sebutinde.

Judges are appointed for a period of nine years and reappointment is possible; two terms are by no means rare, and some judges have been on the bench for over a quarter of a

---

[16] For a brief discussion of the way in which the Court operates, see Rosalyn Higgins, 'Remedies and the International Court of Justice: An Introduction', in Malcolm Evans (ed.), *Remedies in International Law: The Institutional Dilemma* (Oxford: Hart, 1998), 1–10.

[17] One example is the position of ad hoc judge Riphagen, appointed by Belgium, in *Barcelona Traction, Light and Power Company, Limited (Belgium v. Spain)*, [1970] ICJ Rep. 3.

[18] Bastid was appointed as an ad hoc judge by Tunisia in *Application for Revision and Interpretation of the Judgment of 24 February 1982 in the Case concerning the Continental Shelf (Tunisia/Libyan Arab Jamahiriya) (Tunisia v. Libya)*, [1985] ICJ Rep. 192. For the record, she voted against Tunisia on most of the issues before the Court. The only other female ad hoc judge to date has been Christine van den Wyngaert, appointed by her native Belgium in *Arrest Warrant of 11 April 2000 (Democratic Republic of Congo v. Belgium)*, [2002] ICJ Rep. 3.

century.[19] Staggered elections take place every three years, when some of the judges are replaced or reappointed. This ensures that not all judges are replaced at the same time and guarantees continuity. The judges decide on an individual basis (as opposed to the collegiate decision-making found in some other international tribunals, most notably the CJEU). If the votes are tied, the casting vote of the president – who is appointed by the Court – will be decisive. This happened, for instance, in the famous *Lotus* case and, much later, in the advisory opinion on the legality of nuclear weapons. The votes can be tied for several reasons. Sometimes judges fall ill; sometimes they have to recuse themselves for having been involved in a dispute as counsel or adviser of one of the parties before being called to the bench; and sometimes there is an odd number of titular judges complemented by one ad hoc judge.

The Court normally sits in plenary, but is also allowed to sit in chambers. This has the advantage for the parties to the dispute that they can exercise some influence on the composition of the chamber, since the establishment of a chamber will usually be done only on request of the parties. This also immediately reveals what many consider to be a disadvantage; on one of the few occasions when the ICJ actually set up a chamber on the parties' request, the chamber, deciding a dispute between two Western states, was nigh-on fully composed of Western judges.[20] This does little to stimulate trust in the impartiality of the Court. The attempt by the Court to establish a permanent chamber for the settlement of environmental disputes has met with little success; states have refrained from making use of the facility and the chamber was more or less formally dissolved in 2006.[21]

Judges can append a separate opinion to a judgment. In such a case, they tend to agree with the outcome of the case but not with the majority's reasoning. They can also append a dissenting opinion, spelling out why they think the majority got it wrong. These separate and dissenting opinions are a goldmine for academic international lawyers, and sometimes become almost as authoritative as the majority decision.

The ICJ can only hear cases between states, as article 34 ICJ Statute stipulates; other entities may well be considered subjects of international law, but have no access to the Court. This is particularly problematic with respect to the actions of international organizations; these sometimes exercise powers that are similar or identical to those of states, yet cannot be involved in proceedings before the ICJ. It is telling that after NATO bombed Belgrade, in the late 1990s, in an attempt to stop the ethnic cleansing in Kosovo, Serbia could not start proceedings against NATO, but only against a number of NATO's member states individually.[22]

Article 35 ICJ Statute specifies that the Court is open to parties to its Statute. This provision has lost much of its relevance now that membership of the UN (and therewith

---

[19] This applies to Japan's Shigeru Oda (1976–2003) and Poland's Manfred Lachs (1967–1993).

[20] *Delimitation of the Maritime Boundary in the Gulf of Maine Area (Canada/United States)*, [1984] ICJ Rep. 246, with the judges coming from Italy (President Ago), France (Judge Gros), Germany (Judge Mosler), the United States (Judge Schwebel) and Canada (ad hoc Judge Cohen).

[21] The Court in 2006 decided not to elect any members to the chamber.

[22] See e.g. *Legality of Use of Force (Serbia and Montenegro v. Belgium)*, [2004] ICJ Rep. 279. These attempts came to naught, incidentally, mostly for want of jurisdiction.

of the Statute) is close to universal, but used to be of some relevance; non-parties may be allowed to participate, but only under conditions set by the Security Council. During the 1950s, this applied to proceedings brought by Liechtenstein and Switzerland; both states had remained outside the UN at the time.

Court cases involving states can analytically be divided into five stages.[23] Courts must, typically, figure out whether they have jurisdiction to decide the complaint, and whether the complaint is admissible. Before doing so, they may indicate whether interim measures of protection are called for. Thereafter, they can proceed to the merits, and perhaps separately decide on compensation. Of these five stages, little of general relevance can be said about the merits of a dispute; this depends, after all, on the facts of the case. The other four stages call for some discussion, though, and it will be convenient to start with the Court's jurisdiction.

JURISDICTION

There is no such thing in international law as truly compulsory jurisdiction. The tourist travelling in Italy and committing a felony is by definition subject to the jurisdiction of Italian courts, whether she likes it or not, but in international law, this is not the case; states will have to consent to the jurisdiction of international courts and tribunals. In some cases, they do so by joining a regime that has a court with compulsory jurisdiction. This applies, for instance, to the European Union, and since the late 1990s also to the ECHR. In such a case, the consent is embedded, so to speak, in the act of joining the regime; the regime and its court form part of one and the same package.

In most cases, however, joining a regime does not automatically subject a state to the jurisdiction of a court that may operate within that regime. For instance, under the various UN human rights conventions, a state can be a party without accepting the optional protocol that would provide the quasi-judicial treaty bodies[24] with the jurisdiction to hear cases. This does not mean, of course, that states can ignore the conventions at issue; the obligations under the convention are binding under international law, but cannot be enforced by an international tribunal unless the state itself consents to that tribunal's jurisdiction.

With the ICJ, there are various ways in which parties can accept the Court's jurisdiction and therewith accept that the Court has the power to render a decision, either in their favour or against them. These are, by and large, listed in article 36 ICJ Statute, and paragraph 1 of article 36 alone already lists three possible 'heads of jurisdiction': 'The jurisdiction of the Court comprises all cases which the parties refer to it and all matters specially provided

---

[23] Like most classifications, this one, too, is questionable. Sometimes a sixth stage can be discerned: a request to interpret an earlier judgment. It transpires that a long period of time may pass between the original judgment and the request for interpretation, as evidenced by the fifty years at issue in *Request for Interpretation of the Judgment of 15 June 1962 in the Case concerning the Temple of Preah Vihear (Cambodia v. Thailand)*, [2013] ICJ Rep. 281.

[24] Such bodies, such as the Human Rights Committee overseeing implementation of the ICCPR, are often called 'quasi-judicial', in that while their work resembles that of a court, their 'verdicts' are not considered to be legally binding.

for in the Charter of the United Nations or in treaties and conventions in force.' Other heads of jurisdiction included the optional clause, transferred jurisdiction, and the rare institution of *forum prorogatum*.

All Cases Which the Parties Refer to It

Perhaps the easiest way for the ICJ to assume jurisdiction is if the parties can agree to submit their dispute to the ICJ. If so they conclude an agreement to bring their case to the ICJ, and ideally, such a 'special agreement', as it is sometimes called (or *compromis*, in French), will dispel all doubts. This happens often enough; quite a few cases reach the Court this way.

Sometimes, though, one of the parties brings a case to the Court, claiming that an agreement exists which suggests that the other side has accepted the Court's jurisdiction.

If the other side objects, the Court will have to verify the reality of both states' acceptance of its jurisdiction, and it tends to err on the side of caution. If the Court is not certain, it sometimes dismisses the case. The underlying reason is that if a state is not convinced that the matter should go to the ICJ, it will not be very inclined to respect any judgment, especially not if the judgment goes against it. In such a situation, it might be better to have no judgment than to have a judgment that will be disrespected.

A good illustration of the Court's reluctance is the 1978 *Aegean Continental Shelf* case, involving Greece and Turkey.[25] The two states have a long history of less-than-friendly relations, and one of the bones of contention is the status of the waters and continental shelf surrounding some Greek islands just off the Turkish coast. This flared up again when, in the early 1970s, Turkey started to hand out oil concessions to companies on territory that Greece claimed as Greek. Normal negotiations came to naught, but by 1975 both parties managed to agree on the text of a press communiqué which envisaged the possibility of seizing the ICJ if other matters, still to be tried, were to fail. The wording was, however, ambiguous. On the one hand, the communiqué suggested that the dispute as regards the continental shelf should be resolved 'by the International Court at The Hague';[26] on the other hand, the parties also decided to speed up the schedule for bilateral negotiations. This led the Court to find eventually that Greece had 'jumped the gun';[27] it had brought the case unilaterally, on the basis of the communiqué, without Turkey having actually approved such a course of action. When Greece brought the case, in 1976, negotiations were still going on.

The Court has also specified that if there is indeed a commitment to seize the ICJ discernible in the text of a *compromis*, then the subjective intentions of the two parties at the time of concluding the *compromis* are of little further significance. In particular, the argument, put forward by Bahrain, that its *compromis* with Qatar to submit a dispute on the continental shelf to the ICJ was never intended to be legally binding, was done away

---

[25] *Aegean Sea Continental Shelf*, [1978] ICJ Rep. 3. To be sure, Greece also invoked another basis for the jurisdiction of the Court – this one too failed.
[26] Ibid., para. 97.   [27] Ibid., para. 105.

with rapidly by the Court.[28] In this case, then, the Court did find that both parties had accepted its jurisdiction, even though one of them later tried to deny this.

All Matters Specially Provided For in the Charter

When the UN Charter was drafted, it was for a while thought to be useful if the Security Council could order states to submit their dispute to the ICJ. At the end of the day, however, this idea failed to meet with sufficient support; no doubt, many states were afraid to be forced to The Hague in this way, and the communist states that existed in those days always felt that the Court was the handmaiden of global capitalism, and therefore refused to recognize its jurisdiction. As a result, there is, quite literally, nothing in the Charter that would provide the Court with the jurisdiction to decide contentious cases.[29] It would have been useful to delete the Charter reference from the wording of article 36, but this never happened. Hence, this sentence is a classic example of a 'dead letter' provision.

All Matters Specially Provided For ... in Treaties and Conventions in Force

Quite a few treaties envisage that when a dispute arises concerning the interpretation or application of the treaty in question, the ICJ may be seized. Perhaps the best-known example is article IX of the Genocide Convention, which provides in relevant part, 'Disputes between the Contracting Parties relating to the interpretation, application or fulfilment of the present Convention ... shall be submitted to the International Court of Justice at the request of any of the parties to the dispute.'

This became a well-known provision when a number of communist states signalled their intention to lodge a reservation against article IX on ratifying the Genocide Convention. This led to heated debates whether reservations to jurisdictional clauses were permissible when the convention itself was silent on reservations, to an advisory opinion of the ICJ, and eventually to a new regime on treaty reservations, more or less codified in the VCLT.[30]

The typical formula in a jurisdictional clause provides the ICJ with jurisdiction in case of a dispute involving 'interpretation or application' of a convention. This often evokes the predictable argument that while two parties may have a dispute under a convention, the dispute does not concern interpretation or application of that convention, and thus does not come within the Court's purview. Usually, the Court makes short shrift of such an argument, for the good reason that at some level there will be few disputes that are not about interpretation or application of a convention.

Sometimes the jurisdictional clause is laid down in a substantive treaty provision; sometimes also it can be part of an optional protocol. The latter is the case, for instance, with the 1963 Convention on Consular Relations. The convention itself does not contain a

---

[28] *Maritime Delimitation and Territorial Questions between Qatar and Bahrain (Qatar v. Bahrain)*, jurisdiction and admissibility, [1994] ICJ Rep. 112, para. 27; Having signed a commitment, 'the Foreign Minister of Bahrain is not in a position subsequently to say that he intended to subscribe only to a "statement recording a political understanding", and not to an international agreement'.

[29] The Charter does provide the Court with jurisdiction to render advisory opinions upon requests by international organizations, in article 96 UN Charter.

[30] See for more detail Chapter 3 above.

jurisdictional clause, but its optional protocol does. The political reason for doing so is to allow states to join the treaty even though they are reluctant to submit disputes to the ICJ. In such a case, they can simply refrain from accepting the optional protocol, and there is no need to make a reservation (which might be undesirable for other reasons). It also implies that states can withdraw from the protocol without having to withdraw from the treaty; an example hereof is the US withdrawal from the protocol to the Consular Convention after the ICJ had held three times within a handful of years that the United States had violated the right of foreigners to consular assistance in case of arrest.[31]

Article 36, paragraph 1 provides that the jurisdictional clause must be embedded in a treaty or convention 'in force'; obviously, a clause in a treaty that has never entered into force, that has been lawfully terminated or that is regarded as invalid should not be held against a state. However, this is eventually for the Court to decide; it cannot accept the proposition that unilateral treaty termination will also bring an end to any jurisdictional clause, especially if at issue is whether the unilateral termination is lawful or not. The Court held as much in the early 1970s, after Iceland had attempted to terminate an agreement with the United Kingdom, including the clause that the United Kingdom invoked to seize the ICJ.[32]

It may be the case that a treaty clause is the only way to seize the Court, even if the underlying wrongful act has little directly to do with the treaty concerned. In order to bring its case, then, a state is forced to make its claim fit the treaty, so to speak. A particularly poignant example arose after Russia had invaded Georgia, in 2008. Georgia brought a case to the ICJ, but in the absence of any other jurisdictional connection, could only do so on the basis of the Convention on the Elimination of Racial Discrimination, which contains a jurisdiction clause. This created the odd spectacle of complaining about invasion and the use of force as a series of acts of racial discrimination; while the Court sympathized with Georgia's plight, it felt that it could not meaningfully exercise its jurisdiction.[33]

The Optional Clause

The technically most complicated basis for the Court to assume jurisdiction resides in the so-called optional clause jurisdiction.[34] The underlying idea is simple enough: the drafters of the Statute, in the early 1920s, were convinced that the world would be a better place if all states were to accept, without further ado, the ICJ's jurisdiction as compulsory. In order to achieve this, all states were invited (in article 36, paragraph 2 ICJ Statute) to declare their acceptance of the Court's jurisdiction as compulsory. If it then happened that a dispute was brought involving two states that had both issued such a declaration, it followed that the Court would have jurisdiction without anyone having to go to the trouble of taking further steps.

---

[31] The last of these was *Avena and Other Mexican Nationals (Mexico v. USA)*, [2004] ICJ Rep. 12.

[32] *Fisheries Jurisdiction (United Kingdom v. Iceland)*, jurisdiction, [1973] ICJ Rep. 3.

[33] The racial discrimination convention envisages negotiations before seizing the ICJ, and the Court was not convinced that Georgia had seriously attempted to negotiate with Russia. *Application of the International Convention on the Elimination of All Forms of Racial Discrimination (Georgia v. Russian Federation)*, preliminary objections, [2011] ICJ Rep. 70.

[34] See generally Gunnar Törber, *The Contractual Nature of the Optional Clause* (Oxford: Hart, 2015).

This seemed like a good idea at the time, but much of the sting was removed by allowing states to insert all sorts of conditions and clauses (see article 36, paragraph 3 ICJ Statute) and since the system works on the basis of reciprocity (following paragraph 2), the ICJ can only work on the basis of the lowest common denominator, and even then at present only seventy-two states have such a declaration in force. If state A has accepted the Court's jurisdiction from 1 January 2000, and state B has done so from 1 January 2008, then disputes between A and B arising between 2000 and 2008 are excluded from the scope of the ICJ's jurisdiction; A may have accepted the jurisdiction over such a dispute, but B has not. The Court once defined it as follows: 'Reciprocity in the case of Declarations accepting the compulsory jurisdiction of the Court enables a Party to invoke a reservation to that acceptance which it has not expressed in its own Declaration but which the other Party has expressed in its Declaration.'[35]

States have seen fit to insert other conditions as well. Thus some optional clause declarations exclude disputes with particular groups of states. In its 2014 declaration,[36] the United Kingdom, for example, excludes disputes 'with any country which is or has been a Member of the Commonwealth' – this narrows it down considerably, as the Commonwealth currently comprises fifty-three states. The United States, when it still maintained its declaration in force, had carved out an exception for disputes involving multilateral treaties with other American states; the Court could only apply these, in accordance with the US declaration, if all parties to the treaty affected by the decision were also parties to the case before the Court. The ICJ accepted this in the *Nicaragua* case, and excluded the UN Charter from its deliberations; clearly, since the prohibition on the use of force was among the issues, all UN members would have to be parties to the dispute under the terms of the US declaration, since all were affected by a decision on the prohibition on the use of force. The ICJ therefore proceeded to discuss the case predominantly on the basis of customary international law.[37]

Sometimes states may be inclined to exclude issues that they anticipate to be controversial. A well-known example is that when Canada introduced environmental legislation to cover a part of the high seas not clearly within its coastal jurisdiction, it immediately amended its optional clause declaration so as to exclude the new legislation from being tested before the ICJ.[38]

Most problematic has been, however, what has become known as the 'automatic reservation'. These are clauses in a declaration by which a state claims that it will accept the ICJ's jurisdiction except for matters falling within that state's domestic jurisdiction or related to its national security, to be decided by that state itself. Obviously this grants the state concerned an enormous discretion; hypothetically, it could invade another state but escape

---

[35] *Interhandel (Switzerland v. United States)*, preliminary objections, [1959] ICJ Rep. 6, at 23.
[36] The text of the UK's declaration is reproduced in Jan Klabbers (ed.), *International Law Documents* (Cambridge University Press, 2016).
[37] *Military and Paramilitary Activities In and Against Nicaragua (Nicaragua v. USA)*, jurisdiction of the Court and admissibility of the application, [1984] ICJ Rep. 392.
[38] The Court came to accept this in the *Fisheries Jurisdiction* case (*Spain v. Canada*), jurisdiction, [1998] ICJ Rep. 432.

scrutiny by claiming that the matter was related to its national security or domestic jurisdiction. Here too, however, reciprocity applies, which means that a state with such an automatic reservation, should it bring a case against another state, cannot prevent that other state from invoking its own automatic reservation against it.

This became clear in the 1957 *Norwegian Loans* case. Norway had allegedly defaulted on certain government loans, to the detriment of French investors. Both states had issued an optional clause declaration, with the French declaration containing an automatic reservation, stating that its declaration did 'not apply to differences relating to matters which are essentially within the national jurisdiction as understood by the Government of the French Republic'. The Court held that 'the Norwegian Government is entitled, by virtue of the condition of reciprocity, to invoke the reservation contained in the French Declaration', and found that it did not have the jurisdiction to adjudicate upon the dispute.[39]

The case inspired one of the more famous separate opinions by an international judge. Judge Hersch Lauterpacht agreed with the Court that it was without jurisdiction, but went a step further and argued that the French reservation concerning its national jurisdiction was contrary to the Court's Statute which provides, in article 36, paragraph 6, that decisions on jurisdiction shall be taken by the Court, not by individual states. As a result of this, the French reservation was invalid, according to Lauterpacht. What is more, the French reservation was an integral part of the French declaration, and could not be severed. This meant that the entire French declaration was invalid and therewith that France had never validly accepted the Court's jurisdiction to begin with.[40]

Since optional clause declarations are unilateral undertakings by states, they are free to amend or withdraw them at any time. The Court has held, however, that amendments or withdrawals cannot take immediate effect. This came to the fore in the complicated *Nicaragua* case. The United States had issued an optional declaration in 1946, in which it stipulated that it would respect a six-month period of notice in case of withdrawal. Just before Nicaragua initiated proceedings against the United States on 9 April 1984, the United States informed the Court on 6 April 1984 that it would amend its declaration, so as to exclude disputes 'with any Central American State', with immediate effect. The Court would have none of it, and controversially held that not only was this difficult to reconcile with the United States' own undertaking to respect a period of notice of six months in case of withdrawal (note, however, that the 1984 letter amounted to an amendment, not a withdrawal), it was also difficult to defend in more general terms. These declarations, so the Court found, while unilateral, none the less 'establish[ed] a series of bilateral engagements'.[41] Hence, good faith dictated that they should be treated by analogy to treaties without a termination provision, and a reasonable time for withdrawal had to be respected. The Court did not specify what this reasonable time would amount to, but drily observed 'that from 6 to 9 April would not amount to a "reasonable time"'.[42]

---

[39] *Certain Norwegian Loans* (*France* v. *Norway*), [1957] ICJ Rep. 9, at 27.
[40] Ibid., at 43–59 (Lauterpacht J, separate opinion).   [41] *Nicaragua*, jurisdiction and admissibility, para. 60.
[42] Ibid., para. 63.

In one curious case in the early 1950s, Italy brought a case against France, the United Kingdom, and the United States (it is in itself rather unusual to have more than one respondent state) concerning an amount of gold that had been looted by Germany during the Second World War. After proceedings were instigated, arbitration decided that the gold belonged to Albania. Thereupon Italy itself suggested that the Court lacked jurisdiction, and the Court agreed: since at the heart of the case there was a dispute between Italy and Albania, the Court found it could not decide such a dispute without the consent of Albania.[43]

Transferred Jurisdiction

Although in strict law the PCIJ and the ICJ are separate entities and it cannot be said that the ICJ is legally the continuation of the PCIJ, none the less the two institutions have in common their function as the world's only international court of general jurisdiction, and they work on the basis of (by and large) the same constituent document: the Statute. Accordingly, cases that were initially referred to the PCIJ, for instance by means of a treaty provision, are considered transferred to the ICJ. This is provided for in article 37 ICJ Statute, and much the same is said in article 36, paragraph 5, with respect to optional clause declarations. Of course, with the passage of time, there are fewer and fewer treaties or declarations still in force that would confer jurisdiction on the PCIJ.

Forum Prorogatum

In the late 1940s, English ships sailing off the Albanian coast through the Corfu Channel ran into mines. Human lives were lost, and quite a bit of material damage ensued. Britain responded in two ways. It started a minesweeping operation a few weeks later, and it initiated proceedings before the ICJ against Albania, the state it held responsible. Doing so involved, potentially, a formidable jurisdictional hurdle; Albania had never accepted the jurisdiction of the ICJ; there was no treaty clause that provided for jurisdiction, and initially no *compromis* was concluded.[44]

Still, Albania decided to go along with the proceedings: it filed memorials, and even appointed an ad hoc judge. In the circumstances, the Court decided that, based on Albania's behaviour, Albania had accepted the Court's jurisdiction in this particular case.[45] This is sometimes referred to as *forum prorogatum*.[46]

Under article 38 of the Rules of Court as drawn up in 1978, it is also possible to start proceedings against a state that has not yet accepted the Court's jurisdiction. If the respondent state accepts the invitation, the Court can exercise its jurisdiction based on this ad hoc acceptance. The first (and, thus far, only) time this has been used involved a dispute

---

[43] *Monetary Gold Removed from Rome in 1943 (Italy v. France, UK and USA)*, preliminary questions, [1954] ICJ Rep. 19, at 32. See also the discussion of third parties below.

[44] Note that the parties concluded a *compromis* while the proceedings were ongoing, on 25 March 1948.

[45] *Corfu Channel*, preliminary objections, [1948] ICJ Rep. 15.

[46] It is sometimes related to estoppel, a notion that signifies that if one consistently gives the impression to agree on a certain course of conduct (and perhaps benefits from doing so), one cannot later claim never to have done so. The *locus classicus* is the *Temple* case, in which the ICJ held that Thailand had given Cambodia the impression that it accepted a boundary line, and could not subsequently deny this. *Temple of Preah Vihear (Cambodia v. Thailand)*, [1962] ICJ Rep. 6.

between Djibouti and France. The former brought a case; France had earlier withdrawn its optional clause declaration, but none the less accepted the Court's jurisdiction in the case brought by Djibouti. As the Court explained: 'The deferred and *ad hoc* nature of the Respondent's consent, as contemplated by Article 38, paragraph 5, of the Rules of Court, makes the procedure set out there a means of establishing *forum prorogatum*.'[47]

ADMISSIBILITY

Curiously, the Statute of the ICJ contains little on the admissibility of complaints. The background is, most likely, the consideration that since the Court's jurisdiction is based on the consent of states, it would be rather unlikely for states to consent to cases which they would consider frivolous. Moreover, some of the regular conditions of admissibility of complaints have no application in disputes between states. One such general condition is that courts will not normally hear cases that are brought by anonymous plaintiffs,[48] but, surely, such a condition is quite unthinkable in an inter-state dispute.

None the less, customary international law recognizes some limits to the freedom of states to bring complaints to The Hague. The two most relevant ones, for practical purposes, are the exhaustion of local remedies rule, and the rule concerning the nationality of complaints. A possible third rule is more elusive, and might relate to the time factor; it would be surprising if the Court were to entertain a complaint by France, to the effect that the conduct of British troops at Waterloo, in 1815, had violated international humanitarian law. That is not to say that historical facts are excluded before the Court; quite the contrary, for especially in territorial cases and boundary disputes the Court is often called on to analyse historical documents and interpret historical facts.[49] It is merely to say that the legality of those documents and facts will not easily come before the Court unless they play a role in an ongoing dispute.[50] Arguably, the Court sees itself primarily as a settler of disputes rather than, for instance, concerned with the development of international law; given this self-image, there is little place for looking at disputes that have lost their currency.[51]

Moreover, in circumstances where one state does something against another, it would be inappropriate to insist on legal niceties in order not to listen to complaints. If state A invades state B, state B should have access to Court rather than be encouraged to retaliate. If the effects of an industrial disaster in state C spread to state D and caused considerable damage, it stands to reason that state D should have access to Court, and not be forced to take the law into its own hands. In other words, if the situation is at the inter-

---

[47] *Certain Questions of Mutual Assistance in Criminal Matters (Djibouti v. France)*, [2008] ICJ Rep. 177, para. 63.

[48] This is stipulated as an admissibility requirement in the ECHR.

[49] In *Minquiers and Ecrehos*, the Court did not shy away from going back to the early middle ages. *Minquiers and Ecrehos case (France/United Kingdom)*, [1953] ICJ Rep. 47.

[50] Malcolm Shaw, 'A Practical Look at the International Court of Justice', in Evans, *Remedies*, 11–49.

[51] That said, there does not appear to be a time limit for asking the Court to render an *interpretation* of a judgment, although there are some substantive limits concerning requests for a *revision*, recorded in article 61 ICJ Statute.

state level alone, there is something proper about not allowing conditions of admissibility to intervene and possibly prevent a peaceful, judicial solution.

The only situations, then, where admissibility conditions tend to come into the picture is when states exercise what is often referred to as diplomatic protection[52] on behalf of their nationals. This may occur, for instance, when the possessions of a national are expropriated by another state without proper compensation, or where a national has been subject to human rights violations. The right to exercise diplomatic protection is a right that is often said to belong to the state; on this line of thought, the individual concerned has no right to be protected, and the state can deny a request for protection on policy grounds. That said, it has been suggested in recent years that, if serious human rights violations are at issue, the state should always exercise diplomatic protection. This position has not yet been accepted as part of positive international law, but some movement in this direction seems inevitable.[53]

Exhaustion of Local Remedies

The main rule is that states cannot bring cases to the ICJ unless the individual (or entity) concerned has tried all relevant legal remedies in the state where the wrong has occurred. Thus, in the case of an expropriation, the individual must first petition the local courts, all the way up to the highest court, before her state of nationality can step in. This is based on two policy considerations. First (this was affirmed by the ICJ in the 1959 *Interhandel* case), it gives the accused state a chance to rectify things before the matter is taken to the international level.[54] Second, it prevents diplomatic channels from clogging up.

Useful as the rule is, there is one major exception, and that is when it is clear that local remedies will be ineffective. For instance, it would have been highly unfair to insist that Jews should exhaust local remedies in Germany during the Nazi era; in those circumstances, it would have been clear that effective court proceedings would never materialize.[55]

The Nationality of Complaints

Policy considerations dictate that states can only bring complaints on behalf of their nationals, be they individuals or companies. Otherwise, individuals or companies might involve in 'state-shopping', or possibly bring multiple cases via multiple states. In the background is, moreover, the idea that the wrong against the individual or company is an affront against the dignity of the state of nationality; violating the rights of an Australian amounts to an indignity against Australia, but not any other state.[56]

---

[52] For the record, this refers to protection by diplomats, rather than protection of diplomats.

[53] In 2006, the ILC adopted a set of (draft) articles on diplomatic protection, prepared by Special Rapporteur John Dugard. The articles are reproduced in Klabbers, *International Law Documents*.

[54] *Interhandel*, at 27: 'it has been considered necessary that the State where the violation occurred should have an opportunity to redress it by its own means'. The Court specifically refers to the rule as a 'well-established rule of customary international law'.

[55] In *Nicaragua*, the Court also stipulated that there is no need to exhaust available international methods – such as the Central American Contadora process – before seizing the ICJ. *Nicaragua*, jurisdiction and admissibility, para. 108.

[56] *Mavrommatis Palestine Concessions*, [1924] Publ. PCIJ, Series A. no. 2, at 12, where the PCIJ held: 'By taking up the case of one of its subjects and by resorting to diplomatic action or international judicial

The nationality of complaints came most prominently to the fore in the mid-1950s, in the *Nottebohm* case.[57] Friedrich Nottebohm, born in Germany, had spent many years in Guatemala when the Second World War was about to break out. Still a national of Germany, he decided to apply for Liechtensteinian nationality through his brother, who happened to live there. After a quick procedure, Liechtenstein granted him its nationality, but when he tried to return to Guatemala he was arrested as a German 'enemy alien' and had to spend the rest of the war in a camp in the United States. Moreover, his profitable coffee plantation had been nationalized by the Guatemalan authorities after these had declared war on Germany – the nationalization was probably Guatemala's only wartime act of any significance.

After the war, Nottebohm asked Liechtenstein to initiate proceedings on his behalf before the ICJ, and Liechtenstein agreed. The ICJ, however, made short shrift of Liechtenstein's complaint. Without putting it in so many words, it felt that Nottebohm had acquired Liechtensteinian nationality through a debatable procedure and for dubious reasons; a 'genuine link' between Nottebohm and Liechtenstein did not exist.

This was a curious decision, if only because the granting of nationality is usually left to states; it is not for the ICJ to decide on the validity of naturalization. Moreover, the 'genuine link' requirement had, until then (and, in fairness, also since then), largely been used in cases of dual nationality; in such cases, the state with the most genuine link may act on behalf of the individual.[58]

Most puzzlingly, perhaps, if Nottebohm was not effectively a national of Liechtenstein, then what was he? He had never acquired Guatemalan nationality, but it would seem his German nationality came to an end when he acquired the nationality of Liechtenstein. This would have rendered him stateless, in which case Guatemala should not have been able to deport him as an 'enemy alien' and nationalize his property.[59] Then again, it probably did not help his cause that he had signed the letter applying for Liechtensteinian nationality with an enthusiastic 'Heil Hitler'.[60]

The same nationality rule also applies to companies; a state may only extend diplomatic protection to companies that have its nationality. This raises the issue of how the nationality of a company is determined, and this issue reached the Court in 1970, in *Barcelona Traction*. A subsidiary of a Canadian company, Barcelona Traction had suffered from some actions by the Spanish government, and asked Canada to bring a claim on its behalf. Canada, however, refused. Subsequently, the company approached Belgium, on the theory that since almost 90 per cent of the shares were held by Belgians, one might as well regard Belgium as the national state of the company. The Court disagreed. Without firmly deciding how a company acquires nationality (it mentioned two possibilities: headquarters, or state of registration), it none the less made it clear that this could not depend on the nationality

proceedings on his behalf, a State is in reality asserting its own rights – its right to ensure, in the person of its subjects, respect for the rules of international law.'

[57] *Nottebohm (Liechtenstein v. Guatemala)*, second phase, [1955] ICJ Rep. 4.

[58] In addition, the genuine link is used to establish the nationality of ships and aircraft.

[59] Knop also notes that the Court 'did not follow the logic of the genuine link all the way through'. See Karen Knop, 'Statehood: Territory, People, Government', in James Crawford and Martti Koskenniemi (eds.), *The Cambridge Companion to International Law* (Cambridge University Press, 2012), 95–116, at 99.

[60] As reported in Antonio Cassese, *Five Masters of International Law* (Oxford: Hart, 2011), at 62.

of the shareholders, if only because shares can be sold very quickly and across boundaries and, moreover, are usually held by a variety of people from a variety of backgrounds. Hence the Court rejected Belgium's claim against Spain.[61]

INTERIM MEASURES OF PROTECTION

It may sometimes happen that the Court is asked to order a state to stop behaving in a certain way, so as not to endanger any rights prior to a final decision by the Court. Such a request for an interlocutory order was presented, for instance, by Paraguay in 1998, when the United States was about to execute a Paraguayan citizen (Angel Breard) who had been convicted of rape and murder but, so Paraguay argued, had not had the benefit of consular assistance, in violation of US obligations under the 1963 Consular Convention. Obviously, if Mr Breard were to be executed, the case before the ICJ would no longer have a point. Hence, to protect Paraguay's right, Paraguay asked for interim measures of protection, and the Court ordered the United States to stay the execution.[62]

This sparked some discussion on the legal nature of interim measures. Under a purely textual interpretation of the operative provision (article 41 ICJ Statute), it would seem that such measures are not binding; the Court is said to have the power to 'indicate' interim measures (and 'indicate' is not a very 'hard' verb) and, moreover, merely specifies that measures 'ought to be taken' by the parties. Taken together, this would signify that interim measures are in the nature of recommendations more than anything else, and this was indeed one of the arguments used by the United States to go ahead and execute Mr Breard as scheduled.

However, this is not the only possible reading of article 41 ICJ Statute. A more functional approach would argue that since the article is concerned with protecting the rights of the parties during proceedings, they must by their very nature be compulsory. This holds true even more strongly in light of the circumstance that final decisions by the ICJ are binding. What is the point of issuing a binding final decision if a party has been allowed to undermine it by destroying rights during proceedings? Not surprisingly, many observers found this the more convincing view, and the Court itself adhered to it in a later, similar case involving the planned execution in the United States of two German nationals; it unequivocally held that interim measures issued under article 41 ICJ Statute are binding.[63]

Traditionally, the Court has been somewhat reluctant to order interim measures of protection, but this may partly also have been due to the circumstance that until the 1990s, few cases came before the Court where the protection of rights pending litigation was at issue. A Court that is asked to establish a boundary, for instance, need not order protective measures, unless one of the parties bolsters its argument by the use of force.

---

[61] *Barcelona Traction.*
[62] *Vienna Convention on Consular Relations (Paraguay v. USA)*, Order, [1998] ICJ Rep. 248. For a brief comment, see Jan Klabbers, 'Executing Mr Breard', (1998) 67 *Nordic Journal of International Law*, 357–64.
[63] *LaGrand (Germany v. USA)*, [2001] ICJ Rep. 466.

Moreover, on those occasions when it had granted interim protection, few parties complied.[64] The Court's rough guideline seems to be that no protective measures will be ordered unless something irreversible may otherwise happen. Thus it ordered such measures in cases where individuals awaited the death penalty, in cases involving nuclear testing,[65] and in cases involving gross human rights violations,[66] but not, for instance, when sanctions ordered by the Security Council were at issue.[67]

The Court's reluctance may partly be explained by the problem of jurisdiction. The problem is this. If it turns out, on closer scrutiny, that the Court lacks jurisdiction to decide the case, then any order of interim measures transgresses the Court's competence, as it cannot claim authority over states without their consent, and an order of interim measures presupposes authority. As a result, the Court will only order interim measures in those cases where it can satisfy itself quickly that it may have jurisdiction (prima facie jurisdiction, i.e. jurisdiction at first sight).

COMPENSATION

Technically, the Court has the possibility, if it finds that one of the parties has violated its obligations under international law and the other has suffered financial or other losses, to order compensation. This, however, is relatively rare, at least before the ICJ;[68] among the few cases where the Court did so was its very first case, in 1923 (as the PCIJ): the *Wimbledon* case, where it presented a precise calculation of damages payable, including interest.[69] Likewise, in *Corfu Channel*, it ordered Albania to pay the United Kingdom £843,947 by way of compensation, based on the recommendations of experts.[70] Sometimes the Court is content to issue a declaratory judgment; the mere finding that the other side has violated the law must be considered sufficient satisfaction.

Often, though, the outcome is some form of settlement. This is obvious in cases of boundary delimitation; the delimitation here is the judgment, and much the same can apply to cases where the Court decides on title to territory. A kind of settlement can also be seen in those cases where the Court finds that both parties had violated their obligations, as happened in *Gabcikovo-Nagymaros*.[71] Sometimes the Court may decide that the plaintiff

---

[64] See generally Constanze Schulte, *Compliance with Decisions of the International Court of Justice* (Oxford University Press, 2004), at 399, noting that in most cases 'non-compliance was the rule, rather than the exception'.

[65] *Nuclear Tests (Australia v. France)*, Order, [1973] ICJ Rep. 99.

[66] *Application of the Convention on the Prevention and Punishment of the Crime of Genocide (Bosnia and Herzegovina v. Serbia and Montenegro)*, Order, [1993] ICJ Rep. 3.

[67] *Questions of Interpretation and Application of the 1971 Montreal Convention Arising from the Aerial Incident at Lockerbie (Libya v. USA)*, Order, [1992] ICJ Rep. 114 *(Lockerbie* case).

[68] By contrast, investment arbitration often revolves around compensation, with investors arguing for compensation after seeing the value of their investment diminished by governmental actions.

[69] *SS Wimbledon*, [1923] Publ. PCIJ, Series A, no. 1. The Court held that Germany was to pay France the sum of 140,749 French francs and 35 centimes, at an interest rate of 6 per cent per annum. Note, though, that this only concerned France (which had actually suffered some material damage); the other applicant states were not to be compensated.

[70] *Corfu Channel*, assessment of the amount of compensation, [1949] ICJ Rep. 244.

[71] *Gabcikovo-Nagymaros Project (Hungary/Slovakia)*, [1997] ICJ Rep. 7.

has got what it wanted if the respondent state has modified its behaviour,[72] and sometimes the Court decides that the parties should further negotiate in order to reach a settlement – it may then instruct them, with some precision, as to the factors they ought to take into account.[73] And then sometimes parties reach an agreement on how to settle their dispute before the Court can order compensation; thus, in *Nicaragua*, after the judgment itself had been rendered, the Court started to think about compensation when the news arrived that Nicaragua and the United States had reached a settlement.

MISCELLANEOUS ISSUES

Non-appearance

It is generally considered smart for parties to appear before the Court, even if and when they feel the Court lacks jurisdiction. By appearing, after all, they are in a position to argue their own case and make sure that the Court hears all relevant facts and is informed of all relevant legal considerations. That said, though, there is no obligation for parties to appear, and the ICJ Statute even contains a provision (article 53) ordering the Court, in case of non-appearance, to make sure that the applicant's claim is 'well founded in fact and law'. During the 1970s in particular states tried to make a point by refusing to appear.[74] Thereafter, however, the practice of non-appearance fell out of favour. Perhaps the fact that the Court agreed with Turkey in *Aegean Sea Continental Shelf*,[75] despite Turkey's absence, managed to convince states of the Court's impartiality.

Third Parties and the Court

International legal disputes are typically structured and conceived of as bilateral disputes; A and B have a dispute, the Court decides who is right, and that is it. Article 59 ICJ Statute spells this out, just to be on the safe side; the decision of the Court is binding only on the parties. Indeed, the seriousness of this idea is underlined by stating it in the negative: the decision, so article 59 provides, 'has no binding force except between the parties'. Hence a decision is not supposed to affect any third parties.

In reality, of course, states do not live in a vacuum, and many of the Court's findings will have some effect on third parties. Thus, for example, a finding that the proclamation of a specific maritime zone has become customary international law, is a finding that affects all states, as such a rule of customary law will apply, most probably, to all of them.

None the less, there may be cases where the link is an even closer one. If a state feels that it has an interest of a legal nature in a case, it may ask for permission to intervene, in order

---

[72] This occurred, famously, in the *Nuclear Tests* cases (*Australia* v. *France*) (*New Zealand* v. *France*), [1974] ICJ Rep. 253, 457, discussed in greater detail in Chapter 2 above.

[73] *North Sea Continental Shelf (Germany/Denmark; Germany/Netherlands)*, [1969] ICJ Rep. 3.

[74] Iceland in the *Fisheries Jurisdiction* cases, France in *Nuclear Tests*, Turkey in *Aegean Sea Continental Shelf*, and Iran in *United States Diplomatic and Consular Staff in Tehran* (*USA* v. *Iran*), [1980] ICJ Rep. 3, all refused to appear.

[75] *Aegean Sea Continental Shelf*.

to protect its interest (article 62 ICJ Statute).[76] The most likely scenario, depending on geographical circumstances, is where the Court is asked to define a territorial regime, yet doing so will inevitably affect the position of the third party; think for instance of three states located at different ends of a lake or sea. In such circumstances the Court has been willing to allow intervention;[77] otherwise, though, it has been reluctant. On one occasion, it also allowed two distinct cases to be joined; Denmark and Holland had both agreed separately with Germany to submit their dispute concerning the continental shelf in the North Sea to the Court, and the Court saw no problem in treating it as one case, aided no doubt by the consideration that it could hardly decide the cases separately at any rate.[78]

More recently, the Court saw itself confronted with the curious situation that two contending parties had both started independent proceedings against each other: Costa Rica had started proceedings against Nicaragua, and Nicaragua had started proceedings against Costa Rica. In both cases, moreover, the Court felt that the disputes were closely related, addressing the same geographical concerns and invoking the same instruments in support of the claims. When Nicaragua asked for the two cases to be treated jointly, the Court agreed, despite Costa Rica's objections: given the similarities involved, and based on the principle of the 'sound administration of justice' and the 'need for judicial economy', the Court found it appropriate to join the proceedings.[79]

The construction of disputes as essentially bilateral also implies that the Court has thus far refused to accept anything coming close to an *actio popularis*. It did so, amid great controversy, in 1966, when it held that Liberia and Ethiopia lacked the standing to start proceedings against South Africa over its administration of South West Africa.[80] The circumstance that South Africa had been given the power to do so by the League of Nations, and that Liberia and Ethiopia had been the League's only two African member states, was not sufficient, according to the Court; their own interests were not at stake, and they could not bring a case on behalf of the oppressed people of South West Africa.[81]

Finally, in 1995 the Court made it clear that even a so-called *erga omnes* principle was not able to afford the Court with jurisdiction in the absence of a clear jurisdictional grant. This arose in the *East Timor* case, where Portugal brought a case against Australia for Australia's part in oppressing the people of East Timor and denying their self-determination. East Timor was, at the time, annexed by Indonesia, and the boundary treaty

---

[76] For useful discussion, see John G. Merrills, 'Reflections on the Incidental Jurisdiction of the International Court of Justice', in Evans, *Remedies*, 51–70.

[77] *Land, Island and Maritime Frontier Dispute (El Salvador/Honduras)*, Application by Nicaragua for Permission to Intervene, [1990] ICJ Rep. 92.

[78] In the pertinent order, the Court held that Denmark and the Netherlands 'are in the same interest'. *North Sea Continental Shelf* cases *(Denmark/Federal Republic of Germany; Netherlands/Federal Republic of Germany)*, order of 26 April 1968, [1968] ICJ Rep. 9, at 10.

[79] *Construction of a Road in Costa Rica along the San Juan River (Nicaragua v. Costa Rica)*, joinder of proceedings, [2013] ICJ Rep. 184.

[80] *South West Africa (Ethiopia v. South Africa; Liberia v. South Africa), Second Phase*, [1966] ICJ Rep. 6.

[81] Part of the controversy resided not only in South Africa's nasty apartheid regime (in rejecting the case, it looked as if the Court condoned apartheid), but also in the circumstance that it had earlier hinted that it would have the jurisdiction to proceed. *South West Africa (Ethiopia v. South Africa; Liberia v. South Africa)*, preliminary objections, [1962] ICJ Rep. 319.

concluded between Indonesia and Australia adversely affected the East Timorese. Since the Timorese were denied self-determination, and since self-determination had to be regarded as an *erga omnes* principle, so Portugal argued, a claim against Australia was fully justified. The Court, however, disagreed, finding that any judgment in the case would automatically affect Indonesia. Hence it could only proceed with Indonesia's consent, yet Indonesia had not accepted the Court's jurisdiction in any form.[82]

ADVISORY OPINIONS

Under article 65 ICJ Statute, international organizations may ask the ICJ for an advisory opinion 'on any legal question'.[83] Under article 96 UN Charter, the Security Council and the General Assembly are empowered to do so, and other organizations may do so as well, provided they are authorized to do so by the General Assembly. The reach of these requests is limited to legal questions related to the activities of international organizations or their organs, and in the past this facility has been used by, among others, the Intergovernmental Maritime Consultative Organization (IMCO, nowadays the IMO) and the WHO, whereas the ILO repeatedly asked for advisory opinions from the PCIJ.

The Court maintains a strong line that it should, in principle, provide such opinions when requested, and has only twice declined to do so. The first time was in 1923, when the League of Nations submitted the question of Eastern Carelia to the PCIJ. Since this was in essence a conflict between Finland and the USSR, and the USSR, moreover, was neither a member state of the League of Nations nor a party to the PCIJ's Statute, the Court felt uncomfortable addressing the situation; it would have amounted to deciding a contentious complaint without having the jurisdiction (over the USSR) to do so.[84]

The second time came when the Court was asked by the WHO to decide on the legality of nuclear weapons. The Court held that the request was *ultra vires*, as the WHO's competence was limited to health issues, not disarmament, and the legality of the use of certain weapons would have no bearing on their health effects; nuclear weapons are not good for the health, whether their use is legal or illegal. As a result, the Court lacked advisory jurisdiction. The Court's task was made somewhat easier in that a similar request had been lodged by the General Assembly itself; rejecting the WHO's request would not come at the price of leaving the legality of nuclear weapons completely undiscussed.[85]

The background of the facility of asking for advisory opinions has to do with the circumstance that organizations have no standing before the ICJ (they cannot, literally, sue or be sued), yet may be confronted with legal issues relating to their work. Indeed, it would be fair to say that much of the law of international organizations has been fleshed

---

[82] *East Timor (Portugal v. Australia)*, [1995] ICJ Rep. 90. It is often suggested that in doing so, the Court applied a principle first formulated in the *Monetary Gold* case.

[83] The classic study is Kenneth J. Keith, *The Extent of the Advisory Jurisdiction of the International Court of Justice* (Leiden: A.W. Sijthoff, 1971).

[84] *Status of Eastern Carelia*, [1923] Publ. PCIJ, Series B, no. 5.

[85] *Legality of the Use by a State of Nuclear Weapons in Armed Conflict*, advisory opinion, [1996] ICJ Rep. 66. For discussion, see Jan Klabbers, 'Global Governance at the ICJ: Re-reading the WHA Opinion', (2009) 13 *Max Planck Yearbook of United Nations Law*, 1–28.

out precisely by means of advisory opinions, such as the highly influential *Reparation for Injuries* case, in which the ICJ specified that international organizations may often justify their activities on the basis of powers that can be implied from their functions, even though not explicitly granted in their constituent documents.[86]

This also suggests that despite being non-binding, advisory opinions can be highly authoritative. This has sometimes prompted international organizations (the General Assembly in particular) to request also opinions on issues that are not immediately related to the position or status of the organization itself, but come close to being in the nature of disputes involving states that would be unwilling to accept the court's jurisdiction. A possible example is the *Western Sahara* opinion, addressing sovereignty over this African area. The dispute involved three states (Morocco, Spain, and Mauritania), but the Court justified the exercise of its advisory function by the argument that the dispute had arisen within the General Assembly and therefore the Assembly needed assistance in deciding how to proceed.[87] Likewise, in the *Israeli Wall* opinion, it held that since the UN has an obvious responsibility relating to peace and security, the fact that the request reflected a dispute between Israel and Palestine did not make it improper for the Court to accept the request.[88]

Perhaps confusingly, some advisory opinions of the ICJ may be considered 'binding', namely those which are brought on the basis of a provision in a legal instrument other than the ICJ Statute.[89] This was used, for instance, in the case involving the position of a UN special rapporteur, Mr Cumuraswamy;[90] the request was brought not on the basis of article 65 ICJ Statute but on the basis of the General Convention on the Privileges and Immunities of the UN, which specified in its section 30 that if the Court were asked for an advisory opinion, the ensuing opinion would be regarded as 'decisive'.

JUDICIAL REVIEW?

When in 1992 Libya seized the ICJ to complain about sanctions imposed on it by the Security Council, the Court became embroiled in a long-standing discussion on whether or not it had the power legally to review the acts of other organs of the UN. The sanctions were imposed following the explosion of a PanAm flight over the town of Lockerbie, Scotland, suspected to have been ordered by Libya. Libya complained that the sanctions regime ignored its position under the 1971 Montreal Convention, which allows it either to extradite the suspects or to prosecute them. The sanctions disregarded the possibility of prosecution

---

[86] *Reparation for Injuries Suffered in the Service of the United Nations*, advisory opinion, [1949] ICJ Rep. 174; see also Chapter 5 above.

[87] *Western Sahara*, advisory opinion, [1975] ICJ Rep. 12, esp. para. 34.

[88] *Legal Consequences of the Construction of a Wall in the Occupied Palestinian Territory*, advisory opinion [2004] ICJ Rep. 136, para. 49.

[89] See generally Roberto Ago, '"Binding" Advisory Opinions of the International Court of Justice', (1991) 85 *American Journal of International Law*, 439–51.

[90] *Difference Relating to Immunity from Legal Process of a Special Rapporteur of the Commission on Human Rights*, [1999] ICJ Rep. 62. In the earlier *Mazilu* opinion, Mr Mazilu's home state had made a reservation stating that it would not accept the binding nature of the opinion; hence, in his case, the opinion remained advisory only, despite having been brought on the same basis. See *Applicability of Article VI, Section 22, of the Convention on the Privileges and Immunities of the United Nations*, [1989] ICJ Rep. 177.

in Libya, and thus were, so Libya argued, in violation of international law. The Court was called on to order the United States and the United Kingdom to withdraw the sanctions.[91]

The Court, however, did not rise to the bait. In response to Libya's request for provisional measures, it seemed to give some priority to the Security Council sanctions over the 1971 Montreal Convention, but without saying anything final.[92] Hence the question of whether the Court could review the legality of Security Council acts was left open.

On the other hand, even though the UN Charter does not provide for review, and the Court has explicitly claimed it has no power to review,[93] it none the less seems to do so with some regularity. It could hardly be otherwise; any request to spell out the legal consequences of acts of the Council or, for that matter, any other organ of the UN, presupposes some power of review. The question, then, is not so much whether the Court has the power of judicial review, but how it should exercise this power, over which acts, and on whose request.[94]

FINAL REMARKS

Among the core functions of international law is that of facilitating the peaceful settlement of disputes. International courts and tribunals play an important role in doing so, but cannot be expected to replace the role of political agreement. Yet sometimes this is forgotten; sometimes the ICJ is asked to resolve a highly charged political issue, and therewith replace the role of politicians. A prime example is that the Court was requested in the mid-1990s to decide on the legality of nuclear weapons. The issue had divided politicians and the public at large since the 1940s, without their being able to reach any form of agreement. In such circumstances, the Court could not be expected to present a coherent and convincing legal solution, as the ICJ's finding indeed made clear; it held that generally, the use of nuclear weapons was illegal, except in extreme circumstances of self-defence, and without further discussing what such extreme circumstances could consist of. In other words, the use of nuclear weapons is illegal, except when it is allowed.[95]

However, courts play a useful role, if only to channel political disputes. Arcane as discussions about the jurisdiction of the Court or the admissibility of complaints may seem, they are often sublimated political debates. This useful role is not the sole province of the ICJ, though; other courts, international and domestic, play an important role as well.

It has long been a matter of debate whether the ICJ can be expected to be more than a settler of disputes. Many observers feel that the ICJ should not limit itself to settling disputes, but also has a certain responsibility when it comes to developing international law. After all, its judgments can be highly authoritative, and in the absence of an

---

[91] Libya could not directly bring a case against the UN or the Security Council, and thus had to proceed against the two permanent members of the Council most closely involved.

[92] *Lockerbie*, Order.

[93] *Legal Consequences for States of the Continued Presence of South Africa in Namibia (South West Africa) notwithstanding Security Council Resolution 276 (1970)*, advisory opinion, [1971] ICJ Rep. 16, para. 89.

[94] See generally Jan Klabbers, 'Straddling Law and Politics: Judicial Review in International Law', in R. St. J. MacDonald and D. M. Johnston (eds.), *Towards World Constitutionalism* (Leiden: Martinus Nijhoff, 2005), 809–35.

[95] *Legality of the Threat or Use of Nuclear Weapons*, advisory opinion, [1996] ICJ Rep. 226.

international legislature, what better organ to help develop the law than the world's leading court? Others may point out, though, that this would give the Court a political task, for which it is perhaps not particularly well equipped. That said, there can be little doubt that, as a matter of fact, the ICJ does contribute to the development of international law – for better or for worse.[96]

The debate has recently assumed a new – and perhaps more appropriate – guise; academics have raised the issue of in whose name international courts generally legitimize their authority.[97] Do they do so in the name of the world community, however amorphous the latter may be? Or do they merely speak on behalf of the parties to the case before them? In particular the emergence of international criminal tribunals suggests a move towards deciding cases in the name of the world community, as this might be the most proper way to legitimize their authority.

FURTHER READING

Armin von Bogdandy and Ingo Venzke, 'In Whose Name? An Investigation of International Courts' Public Authority and Its Democratic Justification', (2012) 23 *European Journal of International Law*, 7–41

Malcolm Evans (ed.), *Remedies in International Law: The Institutional Dilemma* (Oxford: Hart, 1998)

Kenneth J. Keith, *The Extent of the Advisory Jurisdiction of the International Court of Justice* (Leiden: A. W. Sijthoff, 1971)

Robert Kolb, *The International Court of Justice* (Oxford: Hart, 2013)

Hersch Lauterpacht, *The Development of International Law by the International Court* (Cambridge University Press, 1982 [1958])

Constanze Schulte, *Compliance with Decisions of the International Court of Justice* (Oxford University Press, 2004)

Yuval Shany, *The Competing Jurisdictions of International Courts and Tribunals* (Oxford University Press, 2003)

Daniel Terris, Cesare Romano and Leigh Swigart, *The International Judge: An Introduction to the Men and Women Who Decide the World's Cases* (Oxford University Press, 2007)

[96] See already Hersch Lauterpacht, *The Development of International Law by the International Court* (Cambridge University Press, 1982). The first version of this book was published in 1934. The issue was more recently revisited by Christian J. Tams and James Sloan (eds.), *The Development of International Law by the International Court of Justice* (Oxford University Press, 2013).

[97] Armin von Bogdandy and Ingo Venzke, 'In Whose Name? An Investigation of International Courts' Public Authority and Its Democratic Justification', (2012) 23 *European Journal of International Law*, 7–41.

9

Sanctions, Countermeasures, and Collective Security

INTRODUCTION

Popular wisdom has it that international law is a system without sanctions. This nugget of wisdom was popularized by the legal theorist John Austin, writing in the early nineteenth century that international law was little else but 'positive morality'. There were rules applicable in the relations between states, but these hardly added up to something that could meaningfully be considered 'law', for true law, so Austin suggested, consists of emanations from a sovereign backed up by force.[1] International law, not having a sovereign and not being based on the centralized use of force, therefore could not be considered as law. At best, international rules could be morality, and since these rules were sometimes written down they could qualify as 'positive', but that was as far as Austin was willing to go.

While highly critical of Austin, the legal philosopher H. L. A. Hart, in his classic *The Concept of Law* written in the latter half of the twentieth century,[2] none the less reached a fairly similar conclusion; to his mind, international law was, in a way, law, but did not add up to a legal system properly speaking, largely because rules relating to how international law is made and enforced seemed to be lacking. Again, then, the relative dearth of sanctions seemed to suggest that international law was not really law, and even to this day the legal nature of international law is sometimes questioned. To those who equate law with punishment, international law must seem problematic indeed.

Yet it would be a mistake to think that international law has no sanctions whatsoever, and an even bigger mistake to think that international law does not work because it lacks sanctions, if only because anthropological evidence suggests that there are many other reasons why people (including states) obey the law, not just the fear of sanctions.[3]

Still, it used to be quite accurate to claim that international law lacked centralized sanctions. Traditionally, international law has accepted at least three kinds of responses to state behaviour that can be qualified as sanctions. First, there is the idea that a breach by one side releases the other side from its obligations; second, there is the so-called retorsion;

---

[1] John Austin, *The Province of Jurisprudence Determined*, ed. W. Rumble (Cambridge University Press, 1995 [1832]).
[2] H. L. A. Hart, *The Concept of Law* (Oxford: Clarendon Press, 1961).   [3] See also Chapter 1 above.

and third, international law has traditionally accepted the institution of reprisal or *represaille*. All three have in common that they are responses by individual states to wrongful actions that somehow affect them. In such a system, centralized sanctions for a long time did not exist, unless one agreed, with Kelsen, that when a state engages in, for instance, a reprisal, it acts as an organ of the international community and with a mandate from that community, so to speak.[4] Many have felt, however, that this theoretical position is a bit too contrived.

If sanctions have typically been seen as 'self-help', to use a term once in vogue to describe the system,[5] it is also the case that international lawyers have always dreamt of centralized sanctions; centralized sanctions would make the system complete, would allow it to graduate from a 'primitive' to a 'developed' legal system. Such a system is still a long way off, but the twentieth century has witnessed the rise of a system of collective security, first and rather hesitantly with the League of Nations, and since 1945 more firmly with the UN. The current chapter will address the various forms of sanctions available to states.

INADIMPLENTI NON EST ADIMPLENDUM

It is a well-known principle of contract law (any system of contract law, most likely) that a violation of a contract by party A potentially releases party B from any outstanding obligations. This is based on elementary fairness; it would be hopelessly unfair if party A were allowed to benefit from a contract without providing something in return.

The same rule applies in international law: if state A acts in breach of a treaty, then state B can use this as a reason not to perform its side of the bargain. The underlying theory of course is precisely that treaties are the result of a bargain; A provides something to B, and hopes to receive something else in return. As Anzilotti J put it in 1937, not without a sense of pathos but with great justification, 'I am convinced that the principle underlying this submission (*inadimplenti non est adimplendum*) is so just, so equitable, so universally recognized, that it must be applied in international relations also.'[6] Anzilotti then went on to state that this was clearly one of those general principles of law, recognized in the Court's Statute.

Even though the principle clearly exists and fulfils a useful function in international law, it is not resorted to all that often. The underlying reason is that for the principle to work effectively, both parties must be convinced that the treaty is best terminated; party A does so by breaching it, and party B by invoking the breach so as to justify non-performance and therewith, in effect, causing termination. This begs the question though; if both parties really want to terminate the treaty, then there are easier, less damaging mechanisms available. They can agree on termination with immediate effect, or agree to ignore the treaty and let it fall into disuse (desuetude).

---

[4] Hans Kelsen, *Principles of International Law* (New York: Rinehart & Co., 1952).

[5] This was the term used for example by Michael Akehurst, *A Modern Introduction to International Law*, 6th edn (London: Unwin Hyman, 1987).

[6] *Diversion of Water from the Meuse*, [1937] Publ. PCIJ, Series A/B, no. 70, dissenting opinion Anzilotti J, at 50.

What is more likely, however, is that one of them breaches it, but the other does not view non-performance or termination as the proper remedy. Such a situation arose in the curious *Rainbow Warrior* case. French secret service officials had bombed a Greenpeace ship lying in port in New Zealand. The ship, the *Rainbow Warrior*, was damaged as a result, and one person (a Dutch-Portuguese photographer) lost his life. New Zealand pressed charges against two French officials and, faced with the prospect of its officials serving time in New Zealand, France intervened and asked for a diplomatic solution. As a result, an agreement was concluded under which the two would be incarcerated for a period of three years on a French military base in French Polynesia, and could only be removed with New Zealand's permission.

It so happens that, with both individuals, France violated the treaty; both were taken off the military base without New Zealand's consent. New Zealand, obviously, objected. The point for present purposes, however, is that the relief sought by New Zealand was not the termination of the treaty; instead, New Zealand argued that the two should sit out their remaining time. What makes the final award curious is that the arbiters disagreed; by the time the final decision was rendered, the three years earmarked for incarceration had expired.[7]

The situation in which New Zealand found itself in *Rainbow Warrior* will often occur; it will only be in rare cases that termination of a treaty is the preferred response to a breach of the treaty by the other side. Moreover, the *inadimplenti non est adimplendum* principle is almost by definition limited to bilateral treaties. If it has any application at all with respect to multilateral treaties, it must be a different kind of application; a breach by A of an obligation towards B does not mean that B can unilaterally terminate the treaty, since doing so would also affect the legal position of C, D, and others. Even a suspension (let alone termination) by B of its relations with A under the treaty might be difficult, since potentially this could affect C, D, and others as well.[8] Suspending a trade agreement, for instance, may lead to trade diversion; suspending an environmental agreement may lead to environmental degradation. Hence the only feasible conclusion is that *inadimplenti non est adimplendum* may serve as something of a sanction, but is naturally of limited scope, applying first and foremost to bilateral treaty relations, and even then only in fairly rare circumstances.[9]

RETORSION

Perhaps the most ubiquitous of sanctions known to international law is the retorsion (and yes, it is traditionally spelled this way, rather than as 'retortion'). A retorsion is, essentially,

---

[7] *Rainbow Warrior* (*New Zealand* v. *France*), award of 30 April 1990, reported in 82 *International Law Reports*, 499, esp. para. 114.

[8] But see article 60 VCLT, which offers this as a possibility. That said, article 60 is not particularly well drafted. See generally Bruno Simma and Christian Tams, 'Article 60 – Convention de 1969', in Olivier Corten and Pierre Klein (eds.), *Les Conventions de Vienne sur le droit des traités. Commentaire article par article* (Brussels: Bruylant, 2006), 2131–76.

[9] It is not usually discussed in the context of customary international law, perhaps for the good reason that customary international law is almost by definition multilateral in form and would thereby give rise to the same problems as arise with multilateral treaties, even though bilateral custom is not excluded.

an unfriendly act made in response to an injurious act done by another state. Examples abound, but perhaps the best known is the breaking off of diplomatic relations or recalling ambassadors. Doing so is considered perfectly legal, but unfriendly, and will thus normally need an excuse; and the usual excuse is that the measure is retaliatory in nature, done in response to an unfriendly act. Other examples of retorsion may include the expulsion of aliens, the imposition of travel restrictions or restrictions on imports or exports, or the suspension of development aid (at least where these are not founded on the basis of a legal obligation).

There is some debate about whether the retorsion only covers acts done in response to unfriendly but still legal acts, or whether it also covers acts done in response to activities that were themselves illegal under international law. The better view is no doubt that the hallmark of the retorsion resides not so much in what it is a response to, but rather in its own legality; what characterizes the retorsion is that it remains within the law. In the language of state responsibility, the retorsion is not a 'circumstance precluding wrongfulness' for the simple reason that the act is not wrongful.

REPRISALS AND COUNTERMEASURES

The absence of any wrongfulness in case of a retorsion is what sets it apart from the reprisal or, in the somewhat anodyne terminology favoured these days, countermeasures. For it is the defining characteristic that countermeasures are in themselves illegal acts which become justified by being a response to an earlier violation by the other side, and, for this reason, countermeasures are listed among the 'circumstances precluding wrongfulness' in the Articles on State Responsibility.[10] In other words, an illegal act may become 'legal', so to speak, by being done in response to an earlier violation of international law. Needless to say, though, this is subject to strict conditions (these will be discussed shortly).

Historically, countermeasures were known as 'reprisals', and could come in essentially two forms; they could be non-forcible, or they could involve the use of force ('belligerent reprisals'). As international law gradually, during the first half of the twentieth century,[11] came to frown on the use of force in any circumstances, it stands to reason that the belligerent reprisal, too, fell into disrepute, and it is by now commonly accepted that reprisals may not involve the use of force. In order to make this abundantly clear, in all likelihood, the term 'reprisal' has largely been relegated to the dustbin of history and replaced by the term 'countermeasures'.

One of the classic cases involving (at that time still) reprisals is the *Naulilaa* case, an arbitral award settling a dispute between Portugal and Germany in 1928.[12] In October 1914 a German military column had crossed the border of South West Africa (then a German colony) and entered Angola, then a Portuguese colony, without authorization from the Portuguese authorities. The column was intercepted by Portuguese forces and conducted to Fort Naulilaa in Angola. At Naulilaa, a dispute occurred between the Portuguese

---

[10] As discussed in Chapter 7 above.   [11] This will be discussed in Chapter 10 below.
[12] *Naulilaa (Portugal v. Germany)*, Special Arbitral Tribunal, 31 July 1928. Reported in 4 *Annual Digest*, 526.

and the Germans which resulted in the death of three German officers. In response, German troops attacked a number of Portuguese forts and posts and conquered the fort at Naulilaa. When Portugal complained before a special arbitral tribunal set up under the Versailles Treaty, the tribunal investigated whether Germany's act could qualify as a reprisal, and formulated three conditions. First, reprisals may be legitimately exercised only when preceded by a wrongful act. *In casu*, because the Germans had been killed by accident, the tribunal held that this condition was not met. Second, a reprisal must be preceded by a request to redress the injury. Germany should first have entered into talks with Portugal in order to reach a settlement; the tribunal considered that simply warning Portugal that its posts and forts would be attacked was not sufficient. And third, reprisals must remain proportional: 'Reprisals which are altogether out of proportion with the act which prompted them, are excessive and therefore illegal.'[13]

These three criteria were by and large confirmed in a more recent arbitration – quite possibly the first to use the term 'countermeasures' systematically. It concerns the *Air Services Agreement* case, which arose out of a dispute between France and the United States. The parties had concluded an air services agreement in 1946 and supplemented it in 1960, providing among other things for landing and disembarking rights for certain designated carriers. When Pan American Airlines started to behave in a way which the French felt was in contravention to the agreement (changing to a smaller aircraft in London, instead of flying larger aircraft straight to Paris), they prohibited PanAm passengers from disembarking, effectively banning PanAm from flying to Paris. The United States retaliated by preventing certain French flights from landing in the United States. The matter was submitted to arbitration, with one of the questions being whether the US response had been lawful.

The tribunal, having confirmed a general right to take countermeasures in case of a violation by another state, found that the first condition for the lawfulness of countermeasures was that they had to be proportional. This in itself, so the tribunal suggested, was to some extent a matter of appreciation; it does not suffice just to compare one side's financial losses with those of the other side. Instead, one should also take into account the positions of principle involved. In the end, it found that the measures taken by the United States did 'not appear to be clearly disproportionate when compared to those taken by France'.[14]

Whereas the *Naulilaa* award stipulated that a countermeasure should be preceded by an unsatisfied demand, the *Air Services Agreement* tribunal upheld a somewhat different position. While it upheld the value of resorting to negotiations and consultations, none the less it found that such obligations do not prohibit the resort to countermeasures, and argued that proper use of countermeasures can actually stimulate negotiations.[15] The United States imposed its countermeasures while the *compromis* to resort to arbitration was already under negotiation (but not yet concluded). The panel found that taking

---

[13] Ibid., at 527. The International Court confirmed these conditions (while shunning the term 'reprisal') in *Gabcikovo-Nagymaros Project (Hungary/Slovakia)*, [1997] ICJ Rep. 7, paras. 82–86.

[14] *Air Services Agreement of 27 March 1946*, award of 9 December 1978, reported in 54 *International Law Reports*, 303, para. 83.

[15] Ibid., paras. 89–90.

countermeasures during negotiations was not prohibited and could even be helpful, although the parties should take the greatest care not to escalate their dispute: 'Counter-measures therefore should be a wager on the wisdom, not on the weakness of the other Party.'[16] Still, the right unilaterally to take countermeasures comes to an end once the judicial or arbitral procedure has been set in motion.[17]

While the *Air Services Agreement* case unequivocally confirmed the relevance, in the context of countermeasures, of there being an earlier violation by another state, and equally unequivocally confirmed the relevance of the proportionality requirement, it reinterpreted the 'unsatisfied demand' requirement to some extent and in a fairly subtle manner by claiming that consultations and countermeasures could go hand in hand. As a matter of legal technique, it is noteworthy perhaps that the tribunal cast its requirement in terms of whether or not countermeasures were prohibited; it is not unlikely that the question of whether they had actually been permitted could have resulted in a different answer. Either way, the requirements have been codified (if that is the proper term to use) in articles 51 and 52 of the Articles on State Responsibility: article 51 gives pride of place to proportionality, while article 52 adds the requirement of an unsatisfied demand com-bined with the required offer of negotiations.

The Articles on State Responsibility add, in article 22, yet another important requirement: countermeasures are, in principle, only allowed against a state responsible for an earlier internationally wrongful act. The exception might be found, it seems, in article 54 *juncto* article 48, and concerns treaties protecting a collective interest or *erga omnes* obligation; in such cases other treaty partners, and indeed any state, can invoke the wrongdoing state's responsibility, possibly even including countermeasures. However, the ILC was hesitant to deduce a general right to take countermeasures in these circumstances, and the formulation of article 54 reflects this; the provisions on countermeasures are 'without prejudice' to a possible right to act in the common interest.

COLLECTIVE SECURITY

In domestic societies, it is usually the case that law and order have been centralized: a particular crime will be met with police investigations, possibly with a prosecutor pressing charges before a court, possibly followed by centrally imposed fines or prison sentences – all this to prevent vendettas and blood feuds. In international law, it is not the case that such a well-oiled system of collective security exists, although international lawyers have since the seventeenth century dreamed of such a system. Following the First World War, the League of Nations Covenant came close to providing for a collective security mechanism, but did so still in hesitant terms. Its article 11 provided, in relevant part:

> Any war or threat of war, whether immediately affecting any of the Members of
> the League or not, is hereby declared a matter of concern to the whole League, and the
> League shall take any action that may be deemed wise and effectual to safeguard

[16] Ibid., para. 91. [17] Ibid., para. 96.

the peace of nations. In case any such emergency should arise the Secretary General shall on the request of any Member of the League forthwith summon a meeting of the Council.

The language suggests that collective sanctions and collective security were seen to go hand in hand or, in other words, that collective sanctions concerned first and foremost the scourge of war. For other violations of international law, no collective sanctions were as yet envisaged. Note also that article 11 did not specify which organ of the League should take the action, or what sort of measures could be taken. Combined with the easy option of withdrawal from the League (Germany and Japan left the League before measures could be taken),[18] this resulted in a collective security mechanism that was not very successful. Article 16 of the Covenant provided, moreover, that the League's member states could take economic sanctions against aggressor states, but left both decision-making and execution to the member states themselves. Needless to say, given its decentralized nature, the system did not work too well; on the one occasion where the League actually agreed to impose sanctions on an aggressor state (when Italy invaded Abyssinia, today's Ethiopia), few member states could be bothered to implement them.[19]

The international community got a second chance when drafting the UN Charter and, in all fairness, created a much more effective system. The lead role is played by the UN Security Council, and at the heart of the system is article 39 UN Charter; if the Security Council identifies a threat to peace, a breach of the peace, or an act of aggression, it can order measures to be taken.

Those measures fall into three broad groups. First, under article 40 UN, the Council can take provisional measures, in order to safeguard the rights of the parties. This has, in practice, not had much impact; the Council has rarely indicated provisional measures but has, instead, moved on to order measures under articles 41 or 42 UN Charter. These measures under article 41 or 42 have the same conserving effect as provisional measures, and can be ordained for any period of time. Thus the provisional measures envisaged in article 40 serve little purpose – their job can be done just as well by the measures mentioned in articles 41 and 42 UN.

Article 41 refers, generally, to measures not involving the use of armed force, and lists a number of possible examples: severance of diplomatic relations, complete or partial interruption of economic relations, postal relations, and so on. Important to note is that the wording is clearly non-exhaustive; measures under article 41 'may include' economic sanctions and the like, but may also consist of measures not mentioned in article 41. Even the creation of international war crimes tribunals – the ICTY and the ICTR – has been justified under article 41, meeting with the stamp of approval of one of those tribunals itself.[20]

---

[18] The Covenant's very opening article, article 1, advertised the possibility of withdrawal. This is not unlike getting married with the divorce papers already drafted, just in case . . .

[19] For a scathing contemporary critique, see E. H. Carr, *The Twenty Years' Crisis 1919–1939* (London: Macmillan, 1983 [1939]), esp. at 118–19.

[20] ICTY, Case IT-94-1, *Prosecutor* v. *Dusko Tadic*, decision on interlocutory appeal, 2 October 1995. Whether it was smart to let the ICTY decide on the legality of its own creation is doubtful, though. For a good general discussion of the creation of in particular the ICTY, see Gary J. Bass, *Stay the Hand of Vengeance: The Politics of War Crimes Tribunals* (Princeton University Press, 2000).

Article 42 even allows for forcible measures. The original idea was that member states of the UN would place troops at the UN's disposal, and that those troops would act at the behest of the Security Council to implement forcible measures. This was never realized, though: whereas the creation of a UN rapid deployment force is a staple of discussions on UN reform, no such force has ever been created. As a result, the typical scenario is that the Council authorizes member states to take any action necessary to repel an aggressor state. Those member states then send their own troops while agreeing on some form of unified command (often referred to as 'coalitions of the willing'), and those troops themselves continue to operate as national troops, acting under national rules of engagement and remaining subject to national military law.

The system hinges on the role of the Security Council, for it is only if the Council identifies a threat to the peace, breach of the peace, or act of aggression, that the system is activated.[21] If the Council does not make such a finding, then no collective action will take place. It is here that the veto right of the five permanent members is often complained about. While the Council might be quick to find that the behaviour of, say, Libya activates the collective security mechanism, the Council had since 1945 remained silent when China invaded Tibet, when the United Kingdom and France attacked Egypt over the nationalization of the Suez Canal, when the USSR invaded Hungary, Czechoslovakia, or Afghanistan, or when the United States was at war in Vietnam or invaded Grenada or Panama. A history of the postwar world based solely on Security Council records would provide a highly distorted picture.

The veto is often complained about, but its creation was based on the solid thought that if the global community wants peace and security to be restored and maintained, it will need troops to do so; the veto is the price to pay for saddling five states with the responsibility of taking care of peace and justice.[22] The vagueness of article 11 of the League of Nations Covenant had proved unworkable; a more elaborate and concrete system was needed.

The system's first test arose on the occasion of an attack by North Korea on South Korea, in 1950. The Council first determined that the attack constituted a breach of the peace, and demanded cessation of hostilities.[23] When that failed, the Council subsequently recommended that the members of the UN 'furnish such assistance to the Republic of Korea as may be necessary to repel the armed attack and to restore international peace and security in the area'.[24] Having observed a willingness of UN member states to come to the rescue of South Korea, the next resolution recommended that such national troops should be made

---

[21] The terminology looks more precise than its handling in practice justifies: the Council usually limits itself to observing a 'threat to the peace'. For discussion, see Jan Klabbers, 'Intervention, Armed Intervention, Armed Attack, Threat to Peace, Act of Aggression, and Threat or Use of Force: What's the Difference?', in Marc Weller (ed.), *The Oxford Handbook of the Use of Force in International Law* (Oxford University Press, 2015), 488–506.

[22] Notably, discussions during the 1940s indeed spoke of the responsibility of the major powers to maintain peace; the special position of the permanent members was widely seen as a responsibility rather than a privilege. See Jan Klabbers, 'Reflections on the Politics of Institutional Reform', in Peter G. Danchin and Horst Fischer (eds.), *United Nations Reform and the New Collective Security* (Cambridge University Press, 2010), 76–93.

[23] Security Council Res. 82 (1950).   [24] Security Council Res. 83 (1950).

available to a unified command led by the United States, requested the United States to take charge, and authorized the use of the UN flag, so as to symbolize that the military intervention would be carried out on the authority of the UN.[25]

What made this possible to begin with was the curious USSR policy of boycotting Security Council meetings. The USSR took the voting provision of article 27, paragraph 3 UN rather literally; any action by the Security Council requires the 'concurring vote' of the five permanent members and thus, so it must have thought, as long as it was absent, the Council could not take any valid decisions. While in strict law this was a solid argument (given the dictionary meaning of 'concurring'), none the less the Council called the Soviet Union's bluff and decided to go ahead without its approval. As a result, over time the notion of 'concurring vote' in article 27 came to mean that absence or abstention still qualified as 'concurring'; the veto, in other words, must be express.[26]

Either way, the Korea crisis set the tone. What is particularly noteworthy is that UN interventions are 'recommended' or, nowadays, 'authorized', not 'ordered'; the Council determines that an 'article 39 situation' exists, and then recommends or authorizes action. The UN action against Iraq, for instance, following the latter's invasion of Kuwait in 1990, was similar in nature; the Council 'authorizes Member States . . . to use all necessary means to uphold and implement Resolution 660 (1990) and all subsequent relevant resolutions and to restore international peace and security in the area'.[27]

More recently, the same applied to the UN action in Libya, following the civil uprising there and the government's use of force against civilians. The Security Council, in Resolution 1973 (2011), authorized its member states 'to take all necessary measures . . . to protect civilians and civilian populated areas under threat of attack in the Libyan Arab Jamahiriya, including Benghazi, while excluding a foreign occupation force of any form on any part of Libyan territory'.[28]

Usually, the mandatory language used in Security Council resolutions under Chapter VII of the Charter is limited to the aggressor state; the Council may 'demand' that Iraq cease its actions, but will only 'recommend' or 'authorize' its other member states to step in and take positive measures. The exception is formed by what may be termed the imposition of negative measures. Thus, in respect of Libya in 2011, the Council decided to impose a flight ban. The reason why a flight ban can be imposed, while military action can only be authorized, resides in the circumstance that a flight ban demands little implementing action and is therefore practically easier to achieve and, importantly, at little political cost. Military action may mean that men and women come home in body bags; consequently, this is a decision best left to domestic political authorities.

---

[25] Security Council Res. 84 (1950).

[26] This would be approved by the ICJ in 1971, in response to a claim by South Africa that the Council had taken invalid decisions regarding its treatment of Namibia. *Legal Consequences for States of the Continued Presence of South Africa in Namibia (South West Africa) Notwithstanding Security Council Resolution 276 (1970)*, advisory opinion, [1971] ICJ Rep. 16.

[27] Security Council Res. 678 (1990). Resolution 660 (1990) was the first resolution adopted following the invasion, condemning it and demanding Iraq's immediate withdrawal from Kuwait.

[28] Security Council Res. 1973 (2011), para. 4.

By contrast, a decision to impose a flight ban involves far fewer political costs, and can therefore with greater confidence be taken by the Council itself.[29]

In recent years, the Council has often been called on to provide collective security, and it seems fair to say that its work can take on various different dimensions. These may range from preventing warring factions from continuing their fighting (the traditional peacekeeping idea), to endorsing mechanisms for reconstruction, and pretty much everything in between. Thus, to take just one recent example from 2016,[30] in a lengthy resolution the Council endorsed the position of Faustin-Archange Touadéra as president of the Central African Republic (CAR) and expressed the need for a democratic political process; it aimed to protect human rights (with special reference to sexual abuse) and called on parties to cease violating them; it renewed the mandate of the peacekeeping mission operation in CAR; it highlighted the need for protection of civilians as well as UN personnel, and urged the provision of humanitarian assistance. It further hoped to stimulate security sector reform, as well as disarmament along with repatriation of displaced persons, expressed support for the rule of law and condemned the illicit trafficking in natural resources. Finally, there was a specific call on French forces to provide operational support to the UN operation – in recognition of the circumstance that peacekeeping forces often lack the sort of equipment and training that the Big Powers can provide.[31]

Indeed, on the basis of Chapter VII, the Security Council has authorized numerous activities in order to combat or prevent 'threats to the peace'. It sometimes encourages member states to cooperate with each other and responsible international organizations so as to make sure that chemical weapons do not fall into the hands of terrorist groups.[32] Sometimes also it approves of a larger role for regional international organizations: the EU and NATO operate in Bosnia with the explicit blessing of the Council.[33] Sometimes it allows action to be taken against activities not always considered to constitute military attacks, as when it endorsed action against piracy off the Somali coast.[34] And sometimes its resolutions ooze a little despair: a resolution adopted in late June 2016 calls upon the parties to the conflict in the Middle East to implement 'immediately' a resolution first adopted in 1973.[35]

Such decisions are, under article 25 of the Charter, binding on the UN member states, as these have agreed to 'accept and carry out' decisions of the Security Council 'in accordance with the present Charter'. While this clearly suggests that decisions of the Council are binding, it is unclear whether this refers to all decisions of the Council. What is clear is that recommendations from the Council are just that – recommendations. But what is unclear is whether the words 'in accordance with the present Charter', as written in article 25, refer to

[29] A fine study of the Security Council is David L. Bosco, *Five to Rule Them All: The UN Security Council and the Making of the Modern World* (Oxford University Press, 2009).
[30] Security Council Res. 2301 (2016), adopted 26 July 2016.
[31] For first-hand accounts of the UN's involvement (or non-involvement) with the Rwandan genocide, interspersed by very sobering thoughts on practical obstacles and the UN bureaucracy, see Michael Barnett, *Eyewitness to a Genocide: The United Nations and Rwanda* (Ithaca, NY: Cornell University Press, 2002), and Roméo Dallaire, *Shake Hands with the Devil: The Failure of Humanity in Rwanda* (New York: Carroll & Graf, 2003).
[32] Security Council Res. 2298 (2016).   [33] See, e.g., Security Council Res. 2247 (2015).
[34] See, e.g., Security Council Res. 2184 (2014).   [35] Security Council Res. 2294 (2016).

decisions of the Council, or to implementation by member states; must those decisions be in accordance with the Charter, or must implementation be in accordance with the Charter? (This will be further discussed below.)

The standard practice of 'authorizing' action provokes at least two fundamental legal issues. The first is this: if the UN merely 'authorizes' action, can it still be called UN action? The practical answer is that 'it depends', and it depends particularly on the scope of UN control. If the action is in reality an action by a single state (or a group of states) without any UN involvement, then the action can hardly be deemed UN action.[36] Even then, though, UN authorization may help to legitimate what would otherwise be possibly unlawful use of force.

The second relevant question is whether the authorization is limited in time. The typical practice of the Council is to leave this open. Often enough, it is difficult to reach political agreement on the need to intervene; discussions on the duration of the intervention would considerably complicate things, so that often no time limit is specified. As a result, bringing an intervention to an end might require a separate Council decision, which, as usual, would be subject to the veto; hence often no decision is taken and things are just left to peter out. This created an awkward situation when, in 2003, the United States and United Kingdom invaded Iraq and claimed, in justification, that they were doing so to give effect to Council resolutions from the early 1990s. The underlying argument was that these decisions had never been revoked, and were thus still valid. This particular argument has met with abundant criticism, and rightly so; the Council could not have intended to authorize an attack in 2003 almost wholly unrelated to the events that had given rise to the intervention in 1990.[37]

TRIGGERING COLLECTIVE ACTION

As noted, the collective security system is activated if the Security Council identifies a threat to the peace, a breach of the peace, or an act of aggression, yet these notions are not defined in the Charter. So what do they mean? The easy answer would be to refer back to general international law and say that, for instance, an act of aggression is whatever international law says it is, but this is not of much help; the international community has been trying to define aggression since the early twentieth century, but without much success.[38]

In practice, therefore, the Council has quite a bit of leeway. If it were to decide, tomorrow, that the depletion of fishing stocks off the west African coast formed a threat to the peace, then so be it; depletion of fishing stocks may then be seen as a threat to the peace. In fact, while the most obvious scenario involves the use of armed force, the Council has not limited itself to the obvious international armed conflicts. It has, for instance, classified the conflict

---

[36] For useful discussion see Tarcisio Gazzini, *The Changing Rules on the Use of Force in International Law* (Manchester University Press, 2005), 43–54.

[37] See e.g. A. V. Lowe, *International Law* (Oxford University Press, 2007), at 273.

[38] For a fine overview, see Bengt Broms, 'The Definition of Aggression', (1977/I) 154 *Recueil des Cours*, 299–400.

in Libya as 'a threat to international peace and security',[39] and above piracy has already been mentioned as a threat to the peace.

A statement emanating from the Council, and issued on the occasion of its first ever meeting at the level of heads of state and government (it normally meets at the ambassadorial level) indicates just how far the notions of article 39 can go. Having noted that peace is more than just the absence of armed conflict, the Council proceeded by suggesting also that 'non-military sources of instability in the economic, social, humanitarian and ecological fields have become threats to peace and security'.[40] This opened the door for holding that large refugee flows may come within the scope of article 39, as might HIV/Aids or climate change.[41]

A more traditional approach was fostered by the General Assembly, trying in 1974, after lengthy negotiations, to fill the gap left by the absence of any definition in article 39 UN Charter. The Assembly adopted a 'definition of aggression' which, however, proved less than successful. It stipulated that a number of individual events (invasion, bombing, blockade, etc.) would constitute aggression. This of course runs the risk that any of these activities would automatically be condemned, regardless of the circumstances and the intention behind them (think of bombing in self-defence), so the definition had to be rescued by a saving clause; those acts do not constitute aggression if they are in accordance with the UN Charter.[42] And that meant that the international community was right back where it started; the Charter is not very precise on what constitutes aggression, so any definition referring back to the Charter can only be considered circular and, eventually, inadequate.[43]

As a result, the Security Council still enjoys great latitude under article 39, and so far at any rate no Council determination has been declared invalid or illegal, and it is difficult to see how it could. Since there is no delimitation in the Charter with respect to article 39 findings, it is hard to find any limits that the Council could transgress. This in turn, though, is disquieting, and sometimes suggested as a good reason to establish a system of judicial review of Security Council acts.[44]

Importantly, there is no obligation for the Council to identify a threat to the peace, a breach of the peace, or an act of aggression, as the victims of Rwanda's 1994 genocide found out the hard way. The Council has the discretion to identify or not identify an 'article 39' situation, and non-identification can have many causes. This follows not so much from the wording of

---

[39] Security Council Res. 1973 (2011).   [40] UN Doc. S/23500, 31 January 1992.

[41] With the last two, the Council has hinted that there is a connection with the maintenance of peace and security, but without as yet actively claiming that they constitute a threat to the peace. See Security Council Res. 1308 (2000) with respect to HIV/Aids, and Presidential Statement 2011/15 on climate change, where the Council in guarded terms 'expressed its concern that possible adverse effects of climate change may, in the long run, aggravate certain existing threats to international peace and security'. In Resolution 2177 (2014), it also suggested action against the spread of the Ebola virus, although without explicitly referring to the virus as a 'threat to the peace' or anything similar. The European refugee crisis, which started in 2015 and is currently ongoing, seems by and large to have escaped the Council's attention.

[42] In addition, force used against colonial domination was clearly deemed justifiable under the definition of aggression. See General Assembly Res. 3314 (XXIX).

[43] For the classic critique see Julius Stone, 'Hopes and Loopholes in the 1974 Definition of Aggression', (1977) 71 *American Journal of International Law*, 224–46.

[44] See also the brief discussion in the previous chapter.

article 39 ('The Security Council shall determine'), but rather from the nature of the provision; conduct only amounts to a threat to peace, breach of the peace or act of aggression if the Council says so – and no one can correct the Council's assessment.

An obvious reason for non-identification would be the involvement of one of the permanent members of the Security Council, but other reasons too may play a role. For instance, the absence of any action on Rwanda in 1994 has been ascribed to the bureau-cratic inertia dominating the UN at the time; the UN had just been involved in some problematic operations and did not want to burn its fingers again.[45]

A somewhat similar situation occurred a year later in Srebrenica (Bosnia): the UN had identified a safe area for Muslim refugees, but when this was under Serbian attack the Dutch peacekeepers did little to avert the action, and it appears that the necessary air support had been ruled out by France and the United States.[46] As a result, some 8,000 people died, an action later characterized by the ICJ as 'genocide'. Here at least the Dutch courts have been able to hold the Netherlands partly responsible for failing to protect, while some of the Serbian political and military leaders have been tried by the ICTY.[47]

THE ROLE OF THE GENERAL ASSEMBLY

As noted, the UN-authorized action in Korea, in 1950, was greatly facilitated by the absence of the USSR from Council meetings. As the Council went ahead even without the Soviet Union's concurring vote, the expectation grew that the Soviet Union would not let this happen again. Consequently, many expected that the Council would, in the near future and given the general background formed by the Cold War, rarely if ever be in a position to take measures to maintain or restore international peace and security – the USSR would be keen to prevent its client states from being targeted, and something similar might apply to the other permanent members.

As a result, the sentiment grew that perhaps the General Assembly, the UN's plenary body, should devise a mechanism to step in, in those cases where the Council was stymied by the veto. In November 1950, a few months after the Council had authorized the Korea action, the Assembly adopted its Uniting for Peace resolution. The main idea was that, within the limits of its powers, the Assembly, too, could authorize the use of force against aggressor states. However, since the powers of the Assembly are limited to recom-mendations (except on topics internal to the running of the UN *qua* organization),[48]

---

[45] See Michael Barnett and Martha Finnemore, *Rules for the World: International Organizations in Global Politics* (Ithaca, NY: Cornell University Press, 2004); see also Barnett, *Eyewitness to a Genocide*.

[46] An excellent study (in Dutch) is Frank Westerman, *De slag om Srebrenica: de aanloop, de val, de naschok* (Amsterdam: Bezige Bij, 2015).

[47] The Dutch Supreme Court, in *The Netherlands* v. *Nuhanovic*, upheld a Court of Appeals decision finding the Netherlands to be partly responsible: see case 12/03324, decision of 6 September 2013. The Hague District Court reached a similar finding in case C/09/295247 HA ZA 07–2973, *Mothers of Srebrenica* v. *The Netherlands and the United Nations*, decision of 16 July 2014. The immunity of the United Nations was steadfastly upheld.

[48] For instance, the Assembly has the budgetary power in the UN, and can decide (on Council recommendation) on admission or expulsion of member states.

it follows that the Assembly cannot 'order' peace operations, but can at best recommend them. Given the practice of the Council to authorize operations, this distinction is of greater theoretical than practical value. However, where the Council can, by virtue of article 25, impose operations against a member state even against that state's will, Assembly operations need the consent of the state concerned.

The most important legacy of the Uniting for Peace resolution, beyond its formal invocation, was that it provided the starting shot for the practice of peacekeeping. Peacekeeping is not formally regulated in the Charter, but has been created in practice, a typical example of the UN utilizing an implied power.[49] Based on the consent of the warring parties, peacekeepers have been active all over the globe, sometimes for short periods of time, sometimes also for longer periods; the UN thus has a presence on the island of Cyprus going back to the early 1960s, and is even still present in Korea, to oversee the truce separating North Korea from South Korea. Peacekeeping has also developed over the years, and may sometimes (depending on the precise mandate) include nation-building and even territorial administration. The best-known examples of the latter are the UN's administration over East Timor prior to the independence of this former Portuguese colony (UNTAET, 1999–2002) and the administration of Kosovo until 2008 (UNMIK; this is now replaced, by and large, by the EU-sponsored EULEX mission).

The biggest political problem arises not so much out of peacekeeping itself, but relates to its financing. Two of the permanent members of the Security Council in the late 1950s and early 1960s launched the objection that the operations in Suez and Congo were *ultra vires*, as they went beyond the powers explicitly granted to the General Assembly. As a result, they argued that peacekeeping should not be paid for from the regular UN budget; one could not expect member states to carry the burden for invalid action. The General Assembly referred the matter to the ICJ for an advisory opinion, and in the 1962 *Certain Expenses* case the Court reached two important conclusions.

First, Assembly authorized action is not against the Charter per se; while the Council has been given 'primary responsibility' (article 24 UN Charter) for the maintenance of international peace and security, this does not preclude other organs from acting, as the existence of a primary responsibility leaves open the possibility of there being a secondary responsibility. Second, the Court held that the Assembly itself was best placed to decide whether or not it had the power to act, and even if the power to act were beyond the Assembly, it would not therefore also be beyond the UN at large. Consequently, peacekeeping activities could legitimately be part of the regular UN budget. In practice, though, the French/Soviet point hit home; peacekeeping authorized by the Assembly is normally dealt with in separate budgets, and paid for by those member states willing to shoulder the financial burden.[50] It is also, typically, engaged in by poorer states, keen to use the opportunity to gain some income, some training, and perhaps even equipment.

---

[49] See Chapter 5 above.
[50] *Certain Expenses of the United Nations (Article 17, Paragraph 2, of the Charter)*, advisory opinion, [1962] ICJ Rep. 151.

PEACEKEEPING

The idea of peacekeeping was put to the test in 1956, when after Egypt had announced the closing of the Suez Canal, it was attacked by France and the United Kingdom. The Security Council did not respond (both France and the United Kingdom having a veto right in the Council), so Secretary-General Hammarskjöld ended up acting under the Uniting for Peace resolution when he established the UN's peacekeeping force, the United Nations Emergency Force (UNEF). In response, the Assembly recommended the sending of troops, to act as a buffer. Although the United Kingdom and France quickly withdrew, the troops remained stationed in Egypt to keep the peace until 1967, when the Egyptian government made it clear that it no longer consented to having UN troops on its territory. The Assembly also acted during the independence struggle in the Congo. While the unexpected withdrawal of Belgium, the colonial power, had activated the Council to authorize a mission, after a number of months the Council vetoed an extension. The Assembly stepped into the vacuum thus created.[51]

The UN's Secretary-General from 1953 until his death in 1961, Dag Hammarskjöld, formulated a number of principles of peacekeeping. It is a temporary action, to be carried out in complete impartiality, without the five permanent members of the Security Council delivering troops, under unified UN command and, most importantly perhaps with a view to its political acceptability, it requires the consent of the host state.[52] In the Suez affair, this meant that the peacekeepers were stationed in Egypt with the permission of the Egyptian president, Gamal Abdel Nasser; accordingly, when Nasser later changed his mind, the peacekeepers left.

This became the template for many, many activities; at any given moment nowadays, there are some fifteen or so peacekeeping missions active across the world. In some cases, the limited duration never quite materialized; the peacekeeping mission on Cyprus has been ongoing since 1964, while the peacekeepers in Lebanon have been on the spot since 1978.

The impartiality requirement sometimes proved difficult to maintain; in a fundamental way, it is difficult to stay impartial in the face of naked aggression, and even more pointedly, staying impartial in such a case may well amount to taking sides, however implicitly. Perhaps the most poignant example is Srebrenica. This was designated as a safe haven for Muslim refugees in Bosnia in the mid-1990s, to be protected by a Dutch battalion of peacekeepers. The result is well known; faced with a Serbian attack, the Dutch refused to use weapons to defend the refugees (peacekeepers are supposed only to use weapons to defend themselves), the refusal resulting in the massacre of an estimated 8,000 men and boys.[53]

Over the years, the concept of peacekeeping has evolved considerably, especially since it became clear that merely keeping the peace would do little to solve the underlying political issues, and would do little to help restore war-torn communities. Hence it has become customary to speak not merely of peacekeeping, but also of peace-building: in late 2006,

---

[51] Georges Abi-Saab, *The United Nations Operation in the Congo 1960–1964* (Oxford University Press, 1978).
[52] Manuel Fröhlich, *Political Ethics and the United Nations: Dag Hammarskjöld as Secretary-General* (London: Routledge, 2008), at 155.
[53] See also above.

the UN created a new sub-organ (the Peacebuilding Commission) to address the issue. This had proved necessary because peace-building, or even the setting up of a temporary government apparatus in the form of an international administration mission, gives rise to all sorts of legal and political issues.[54]

The two best-known administrations to date are those set up after East Timor gained a quick independence and was found almost completely to lack a governmental infrastructure (UNTAET), and UNMIK, set up in Kosovo to postpone the political decision whether Kosovo should be independent or should remain part of Serbia. Such missions encounter issues relating to which law shall apply in the territory, who exercises police functions, whether regular immunities of international staff should apply, and many, many more,[55] requiring political guidance.

INDIVIDUAL SANCTIONS

Since the UN is an international organization consisting of member states, it stands to reason that the addressees of its decisions should be expected to be, first and foremost, those member states, and indeed this used to be the case. Decisions, whether taken by the Council or the Assembly, were invariably addressed to the member states, for the simple reason that, on any classic conception of international organization, the UN has no authority over anyone but its members. This is, in fact, confirmed by the UN Charter itself, which provides in article 2, paragraph 6 that the UN shall seek the assistance of non-member states in activities related to peace and security; it cannot simply presume that those states are bound by whatever the UN decides.[56]

Yet, since the early 1990s, the UN Security Council in particular has also started to address others than its member states, perhaps inspired by an ICJ dictum from the early 1970s.[57] A first episode concerned the imposition of sanctions on the Angolan rebel movement UNITA, and doing so directly, rather than by pointing out that Angola would be under sanctions and therewith also UNITA.[58]

More common, and less controversial, is to refer to other international organizations, in particular regional organizations. Thus, by way of example, Resolution 1973 (2011) requests that the member states of the League of Arab States participate in the action against Libya (paragraph 5) and provides for various forms of coordination involving the League of Arab States (paragraphs 8, 11).

---

[54] Klabbers, 'Reflections'.

[55] See e.g. Ralph Wilde, *International Territorial Administration: How Trusteeship and the Civilizing Mission Never Went Away* (Oxford University Press, 2008).

[56] And this, in turn, is an emanation of the classic *pacta tertiis* principle: treaties create neither rights nor obligations for third parties.

[57] See *Namibia*, where the Court found that it was incumbent on all states (not just UN members) to give effect to a certain Security Council resolution, and tried to found this on the *erga omnes* theory. For a critique, see Jan Klabbers, 'The Scope of International Law: *Erga Omnes* Obligations and the Turn to Morality', in Matti Tupamäki (ed.), *Liber Amicorum Bengt Broms* (Helsinki: Finnish ILA Branch, 1999), 149–79.

[58] Security Council Res. 834 (1993).

But the most common form of sanctions at present is for these to affect individuals and legal persons.[59] This is a reply, of sorts, to the classic criticism that sanctions against states are not terribly precise; they tend to victimize the population, without actually getting at the individuals who are considered to be involved in oppression or aggression.[60] Hence, the invention of so-called targeted sanctions, or smart sanctions. These are not, legally, addressed to individuals – the main addressees are still the member states. But it is clear that targeted sanctions have as their aim the establishment of limits on the freedom of movement of individuals, and it is obviously necessary that those individuals are identified by name. The typical procedure is for the Council to impose sanctions relating to a particular situation and to create a 'sanctions committee' to oversee the implementation. This committee then also singles out individuals to whom the sanctions may apply, usually on the basis of a proposal from one of its members. As a result, individuals become blacklisted and may find that their accounts are frozen.[61]

This practice has provoked a lot of criticism over the last couple of years, not least because the way in which individuals become blacklisted has none of the formal guarantees of a fair trial; if the members of the sanctions committee agree that someone should be blacklisted, then so be it. Little is presented by way of evidence, and indeed there are few standards for reviewing the legality of sanctions to begin with; a suspicion that someone may be implicated in, for example, financing terrorism tends to suffice, and such a feeling may all too easily arise from an individual sending money to a relative in Afghanistan or Yemen. Moreover, once an individual is on the blacklist, the UN has no legal procedures available for contesting the blacklisting. Hence it is often suggested that in imposing sanctions on individuals, the UN violates their human rights by not offering the guarantees of a fair trial, and by not offering any possibility for appeal.[62]

Often (if not invariably) these individual sanctions are ordered in connection with terrorism, and this applies also to the most famous case to date, the case of Mr Kadi. Mr Kadi is a Saudi Arabian businessman who found, to his dismay, that he was put on the blacklist. As a result, his accounts in the EU[63] were frozen on the basis of an EU regulation implementing the Security Council decision and decisions from the relevant sanctions committee. Mr Kadi forcefully disagreed, and went to the EU courts to contest the legality of the sanctions, citing that the sanctions violated his human rights (fair trial, access to justice, and the right to property). The first court (then known as the EU's Court of First

---

[59] International sanctions may be implemented or complemented by national authorities. In the USA, an important role is played by the Treasury Department's Office of Foreign Assets Control (OFAC), in existence since 1950; the list of individuals on the receiving end of sanctions – the OFAC list – is colloquially known as the 'Oh F**k' list, apparently to signify how difficult it is to be removed from it.

[60] For a scathing critique, see Scott Veitch, *Law and Irresponsibility: On the Legitimation of Human Suffering* (London: Routledge, 2007).

[61] The best overview to date is Jeremy Matam Farrall, *United Nations Sanctions and the Rule of Law* (Cambridge University Press, 2007).

[62] In addition, freezing accounts may be construed as a violation of the right to enjoy one's property, at least if done without the guarantee of a fair trial.

[63] The EU feels that implementing Security Council sanctions is a task properly belonging to it rather than to individual member states, despite the fact that the EU is not a member of the UN (and could not be, since it is not a state).

Instance) disagreed with him, for a variety of reasons.[64] Mr Kadi then appealed to the CJEU, which famously held that since the measures concerning Mr Kadi were taken by the EU, they should be in accordance with EU constitutional standards. These standards included respect for human rights, and since the measures against Kadi violated some of his human rights as guaranteed in the EU, it followed that the EU measures had to be considered (in part) invalid.[65]

That was, and is, a controversial decision; in deciding solely on the basis of EU law, the Court all but ignored the international law context of the case; it ignored the circumstance that the source of the measure was not the EU administration, but the Security Council. Moreover, it saddled the EU member states with an immense problem; under EU law, they could not give effect to these sanctions; yet under international law (article 25 UN) they were bound to give effect to those same sanctions.[66]

What the case illustrates above all is the procedural incompleteness of international law, at least on this point.[67] The human rights invoked by Mr Kadi are fairly generally recognized and are also part of the UN legal system (this applies at least to the right to a fair trial and the right to have access to justice).[68] But what is lacking at the level of the UN is a procedure to have those rights enforced against the UN itself: such a procedure is available in the EU, hence Mr Kadi had little choice but to bring his case to the EU courts, despite the awkward circumstance that, in effect, the EU was merely implementing Security Council measures.[69]

The *Kadi* case is probably best seen as a warning (or invitation, if you will) from the CJEU to the Security Council, to the effect that the Council should strive to improve the human rights aspects of its targeted sanctions procedures, lest these remain unacceptable to important political entities such as the EU.[70] Whether this is a wise move is debatable. Some posit that the Security Council too is bound to respect human rights, and there is nothing wrong with domestic courts pointing this out,[71] whereas others may warn that doing so might open a Pandora's box; surely, one cannot leave international peace and security depending on the workings of hundreds or even thousands of local courts, regardless of whether they are located in Luxembourg or Tehran, The Hague or Washington D.C., Karlsruhe or Pyongyang?

---

[64] Case T-315/01, *Kadi* v. *Council and Commission*, [2005] ECR II-3649.

[65] Joined cases C-402/05 P and C-415/05 P, *Kadi and Al Barakaat* v. *Council and Commission*, [2008] ECR I-6351.

[66] See generally Jan Klabbers, *Treaty Conflict and the European Union* (Cambridge University Press, 2008).

[67] I am indebted to Margareta Klabbers for pointing this out.

[68] Things are less certain with respect to the right to property which, famously, is not covered by the UN-sponsored ICCPR.

[69] A different question is whether regular models of review, known from domestic settings, have much traction in the setting of Security Council sanctions. For discussion, see Devika Hovell, *The Power of Process: The Value of Due Process in Security Council Sanctions Decision-Making* (Oxford University Press, 2016).

[70] The Council has actually done this, up to a (fairly limited) point: it has created an Office of the Ombudsperson to address requests by those who would like to be removed from sanctions lists. See https://www.un.org/sc/suborg/en/ombudsperson (visited 1 August 2016).

[71] The most sophisticated argument to date in favour of this proposition is Antonios Tzanakopoulos, *Disobeying the Security Council: Countermeasures against Wrongful Sanctions* (Oxford University Press, 2011).

LIMITS TO THE SECURITY COUNCIL?

The *Kadi* episode in particular has breathed new life into an older debate as to whether there are any limits to what the Security Council can do. During the Cold War, this was not under discussion; the Council made few decisions, paralysed as it often was by the United States' and the Soviet Union's adherence to the veto, and even fewer decisions that would be deemed controversial. But since the end of the Cold War, the Council has become very active, and some of its decisions have even come close to being legislative in nature. This applies above all to its decisions on combating international terrorism.

As a result, debate has been sparked on whether the Council can do as it pleases, or whether it is subject to legal limits.[72] As noted above, the Charter itself is not very clear on the topic; article 25 suggests that members are bound to give effect to Council action 'in accordance with the present Charter', but it remains unclear whether this refers to Council action, or to the obligation of the members to implement Council action; linguistically, both interpretations are possible.

As a result, many commentators resort to functional arguments or, as the case may be, to policy arguments. One group maintains that it is unthinkable that the UN, endowed with the task of maintaining peace and security and, implicitly, with the task of helping to make the world a better place, would be at liberty to transgress human rights standards. Surely it would be an anomaly if the UN sponsored human rights treaties and held governments to account for unjust behaviour, while all the time ignoring human rights standards itself.

This school of thought finds some support in the case law of the ICJ, in particular perhaps the *Effect of Awards* opinion, in which the Court held that the creation of a staff tribunal for the UN was justified in the light of its task to help ensure global justice.[73]

The other school of thought points out that limits on the Security Council are not all that easy to reconcile with the very idea behind the Council; the Council was set up like a fire department, with the task of quelling fires at short notice and no matter the circumstances. If there had been any idea about limits, those would have been expressly mentioned in the Charter, and at any rate should not make the Council's primary task too difficult.

Both sides have a point; the Council was originally set up as a fire department, with little or no regard to legal limits, and the UN has indeed developed in directions perhaps not immediately foreseen by the drafters of its Charter. It is here that the shoe starts to pinch; the idea that the Council respects legal limits is often directed not so much against its swift political responses, but rather against those activities which presuppose a longer-term perspective. Much of the criticism originated when the Council started to engage in (quasi-)legislative activities; after the Lockerbie incident, it came close to rewriting extradition law,[74] and its approach to terrorism too has been closer to that of a legislature than of

---

[72] The related question of whether judicial review over Security Council acts is possible is briefly discussed in the previous chapter.

[73] *Effect of Awards of Compensation made by the United Nations Administrative Tribunal*, advisory opinion, [1954] ICJ Rep. 47.

[74] This will be discussed in Chapter 12 below.

an administrative organ.[75] Obviously, a legislative body should respect legal limits, and should be more or less representative of its constituency. It is no coincidence, then, that the Council has attracted a lot of criticism; the five permanent members are hardly representative any longer (if they ever were), and in issuing legislation one just cannot ignore the dictates of the rule of law. While the latter is a fluid and contested notion,[76] what is clear is that the concept of rule of law implies some respect for individual rights, and puts a premium on matters such as transparency.[77]

FINAL REMARKS

If sanctions were often considered the Achilles heel of international law, this can no longer be said to be the case (if it ever could). Indeed, the worry now is often that the Council in particular is too eager in handing out sanctions, targeting individuals on the basis of procedures that are not very transparent, and often on the basis of flimsy evidence as well. Ironically, the literature has started to discuss second-order sanctions – sanctions against the main dispenser of sanctions if the main dispenser gets it wrong. The *Kadi* case can be seen as a central event here, and is mostly interpreted as the CJEU sending a warning signal to the Security Council, while the literature aims to rationalize this by eulogizing disobedience of the Council.

Whether this is smart remains to be seen; anthropological evidence and philosophical argument suggest that people or institutions do not just obey the law out of fear of sanctions. Instead, they internalize norms, and come to apply them because these norms are considered just, or effective, or reasonable, and perhaps because those people and institutions feel that living a good life is, in part, a matter of obeying the law. Sanctions are useful and can themselves be expressions of fairness, but a political community whose members act solely out of fear for sanctions is a dictatorship.

FURTHER READING

Georges Abi-Saab, *The United Nations Operation in the Congo 1960–1964* (Oxford University Press, 1978)

Michael Barnett, *Eyewitness to a Genocide: The United Nations and Rwanda* (Ithaca NY: Cornell University Press, 2002)

David L. Bosco, *Five to Rule Them All: The UN Security Council and the Making of the Modern World* (Oxford University Press, 2009)

Roméo Dallaire, *Shake Hands with the Devil: The Failure of Humanity in Rwanda* (New York: Carroll and Graf, 2003)

---

[75] For an in-depth discussion see Jose E. Alvarez, *International Organizations as Law-Makers* (Oxford University Press, 2005).

[76] For a useful overview, see Brian Z. Tamanaha, *On the Rule of Law: History, Politics, Theory* (Cambridge University Press, 2004).

[77] An inspiring vision on the rule of law is formulated (albeit not under that heading) by Lon L. Fuller, *The Morality of Law*, rev. edn (New Haven, CT: Yale University Press, 1969).

Jeremy Matam Farrall, *United Nations Sanctions and the Rule of Law* (Cambridge University Press, 2007)

Manuel Fröhlich, *Political Ethics and the United Nations: Dag Hammarskjöld as Secretary-General* (London: Routledge, 2008)

Scott Veitch, *Law and Irresponsibility: On the Legitimation of Human Suffering* (London: Routledge, 2007)

Marc Weller (ed.), *The Oxford Handbook of the Use of Force in International Law* (Oxford University Press, 2015)

PART II

The Substance of International Law

10

Use of Force

INTRODUCTION

When after the Napoleonic wars of the early nineteenth century the Prussian major-general Carl von Clausewitz famously wrote that war was the continuation of policy by other means,[1] he had a point. Throughout the ages, war had been conducted without many legal obstacles being placed in its way, and there was a strong sentiment that going to war, for whatever reason, was perfectly legal. Admittedly, many felt that this was an undesirable state of affairs, and theologians and lawyers alike had aspired to limit the possibility of resorting to war by making a distinction between just wars and unjust wars, but state practice had proved rather resilient. And understandably so: distinguishing between just and unjust wars presupposes a working conception of justice, and since justice is itself a highly contested concept, it follows that reasonable people could disagree about whether a war would be just or unjust.[2]

Earlier generations of international lawyers insisted on a rigid distinction between war and peace; the two would be entirely different conditions, governed by different sets of rules. Some of this is still visible in today's international law; there are specific rules on how to behave during war (such as the 1949 Geneva Conventions) which have little application during peacetime. Still, the rigidity of that earlier distinction no longer applies; war and peace have come to be seen as more fluid conditions, sometimes governed by specific rules, but sometimes also by general rules.[3] There is little doubt, for instance, that human rights law continues to apply even in wartime.[4]

Still, as a general rule, warfare is nowadays prohibited. Under the UN Charter, there is a well-nigh total ban on the use of force, with only one recognized exception other than the

---

[1] Carl von Clausewitz, *On War*, trans. J. J. Graham (London: Wordsworth, 1997 [1832]), at 22: 'War is a mere continuation of policy by other means ... war is not merely a political act, but also a real political instrument, a continuation of political commerce, a carrying out of the same by other means.'

[2] The seminal study is Michael Walzer, *Just and Unjust Wars*, 3rd edn (New York: Basic Books, 2000).

[3] For a general argument on the fluidity of war and peace and the way law helps to construct war, see David Kennedy, *Of War and Law* (Princeton University Press, 2006).

[4] *Legal Consequences of the Construction of a Wall in the Occupied Palestinian Territory*, advisory opinion, [2004] ICJ Rep. 136, para. 106.

possibility of engaging in collective security acts: the right to self-defence. That is not to say, though, that the use of force has become a thing of the past; armed conflicts still occur, as do civil conflicts and armed interventions, and much legal argument goes into debating whether such acts can be justified on the basis of customary international law.

This suggests that the law on the use of force is made up of two different regimes; the Charter regime, and the customary regime which, according to many observers, may be more flexible than the Charter regime. This chapter will discuss both regimes, but will start by sketching the development of the ban on the use of force from the late nineteenth century onwards. In addition, I will address the changes taking place in the use of force, with force increasingly being used by non-state actors such as terrorist groups.

ABOLISHING WAR

In 1899 the first Hague Peace Conference took place, organized (as its title suggests) in the Dutch city of The Hague, but having been convened by the Russian Tsar Nicholas II. This conference was of great importance for a variety of reasons, not least that it was one of the first times a conference of more or less universal scope took place. Earlier conferences tended to be limited to the European powers, which, somewhat arrogantly, presumed that whatever they decided would be of universal validity. But in The Hague, there was also a notable presence of states from Asia and Latin America.

The first Hague Conference saw the adoption of a number of treaties, mostly related to controlling the means of warfare (*jus in bello*)[5] rather than the right to wage war (*jus ad bellum*). None the less, one of the conventions provided for the pacific settlement of disputes, and created a Permanent Court of Arbitration to address legal issues between states, therewith positing, it seemed, a viable alternative to warfare: in case of a dispute, it would always be possible to activate the PCA, which was to be 'accessible at all times'.[6] And indeed, some of the celebrated international law cases were settled by the PCA, including the *Island of Palmas* arbitration.[7]

The Second Conference of 1907 went a bit further still, and while it too resulted in a fair number of instruments on controlling the means of warfare, it also led to two instruments that aimed to regulate recourse to war itself. The first of these was the so-called Drago–Porter Convention, in which the parties agreed not to go to war in order to reclaim contractual debts owed to their nationals. This had been quite an issue in the preceding century, but many felt that contractual debts constituted too flimsy a reason to justify the large-scale use of force, and perhaps sensed there to be something inappropriate in using public funds (armies) for private gain.

The second relevant treaty concluded in 1907 was the Convention on the Opening of Hostilities. Under this convention, war should not be commenced without a reasoned declaration of war, or an ultimatum accompanied by a conditional declaration of war.

---

[5] This will be further discussed in the next chapter.
[6] Convention (I) for the Pacific Settlement of International Disputes, article 20. This convention was to be replaced by a similar but larger one concluded at the 1907 Conference.
[7] Discussed in Chapter 4 above.

Moreover, the existence of a state of war should be announced to neutral powers. The idea was to turn war into a legalized, technical state of being, but it is arguable that the convention eventually had the opposite effect. Since surprise attacks may be of great military advantage, states would often enough engage in armed conflict but stop short of calling this 'war'. Perhaps perversely, the convention thereby did little to stop warfare or make it succumb to legal rules. Instead, it stimulated the issuing of declarations of war so as to secure material advantage; Guatemala declared war on Germany in the 1940s so as to justify the taking of enemy property, including the prospering coffee plantation of Mr Nottebohm.[8] In recent decades, the declaration of war has fallen into disuse, so much so that some have argued that the 1907 Convention on the Opening of Hostilities is best regarded as terminated by *desuetudo*.[9]

A further step in the outlawing of war came with the establishment of the League of Nations, after the First World War. Not only did the Covenant of the League of Nations set up a system of collective security, it also created an obligation on member states to resort to arbitration in case of a dispute. Under article 12 members of the League were not allowed to go to war prior to resorting to arbitration, judicial settlement, or involvement of the League Council. They agreed 'in no case to resort to war until three months' after the award, judgment, or report. History suggests that this did little good, and that the League's collective security guarantee was not terribly successful either; aggressive states could simply withdraw from the League and thereby escape if they felt these obligations to be overly onerous.

None the less, the 1920s were characterized by strong pacifist sentiments, and understandably so, after the massive carnage of the First World War.[10] By the end of the decade, in 1928, states gathered once more to prohibit warfare, this time spurred on by France and the United States in the form of the so-called Kellogg–Briand pact. In this treaty, the parties 'condemn recourse to war for the solution of international controversies, and renounce it, as an instrument of national policy in their relations with one another'. Hence the Pact aspired to a total ban on war, and while it quickly became very popular, attracting many instruments of ratification, eventually it would not be able to prevent Japan from invading China, Italy from going into Abyssinia, or Germany from occupying Czechoslovakia and Austria and thereafter invading Poland and much of western Europe. Still, it provided one of the legal bases for holding high-ranking Nazis responsible for crimes against peace in the well-known Nuremberg proceedings after the end of the Second World War.[11]

THE UN CHARTER

Already during the Second World War, allied governments felt that the use of force should be outlawed. The 1941 Atlantic Charter, for instance, a high-level political statement issued

---

[8] This led to the famous *Nottebohm* case, discussed in Chapter 8 above.

[9] E. W. Vierdag, *Oorlogsverklaring* (inaugural address), University of Amsterdam, 1992.

[10] For a fine study of the prevailing political and social climate, see Daniel Gorman, *The Emergence of International Society in the 1920s* (Cambridge University Press, 2012).

[11] Chapter 12 below.

by UK Prime Minister Winston Churchill and US President Franklin Roosevelt, pointed out that states should abandon the use of force, 'for realistic as well as spiritual reasons'.[12] Interestingly, this Atlantic Charter was already aimed at the 'use of force', a concept that is considerably broader than 'war'. And since states had come to shun the formal declaration of war, such a broader concept was considered useful, so as to avoid giving states the possibility to hide behind claims that their behaviour did not, technically, amount to war.

This was followed by the UN Charter, which lays down an almost absolute prohibition of the use of force in article 2, paragraph 4, and is important enough to be quoted in full: 'All Members shall refrain in their international relations from the threat or use of force against the territorial integrity or political independence of any State, or in any other manner inconsistent with the Purposes of the United Nations.' Those purposes of the UN are listed in article 1, and are very broad as well; they include the maintenance of international peace and security, the development of friendly relations, and international cooperation. In short, there are not a lot of manifestations of the use of force thinkable that would be consistent with the purposes of the UN, and that would not go against the 'territorial integrity or political independence' of states.

This broad prohibition found almost immediate support from the ICJ, deciding the *Corfu Channel* case in 1949.[13] Mines in the Corfu Channel, under Albanian jurisdiction, had cost the lives of several British sailors, and the Court would hold Albania responsible even though Albania claimed it had not itself laid those mines.[14] More to the point, however, a British response action in order to sweep for mines in the Corfu Channel several weeks later was also roundly condemned by the Court. The United Kingdom offered two justifications, and both were rejected by a unanimous (on this point) ICJ.

First, the United Kingdom suggested that its minesweeping operation ('Operation Retail') had as its main function the gathering of evidence. The Court dismissed this as a new theory of intervention which manifested a 'policy of force' that could easily be abused, and which would seem to be reserved for powerful states only. Second, the United Kingdom classified the operation as one of 'self-help' or 'self-protection',[15] but this too was rejected, as the minesweeping operation violated Albania's territorial integrity regardless of the intentions behind it.[16] Without overtly relying on the new Charter (possibly for the good reason that Albania had not yet been admitted into UN membership – this would only happen in 1955), the Court none the less confirmed that the prohibition of the use of force was to be taken seriously.

Article 2, paragraph 4 UN Charter prohibits not only the actual use of force, but also the threat of force. This has proved difficult to operationalize (Is a military manoeuvre along the

---

[12] Atlantic Charter, recital 8.   [13] *Corfu Channel*, merits, [1949] ICJ Rep. 4.

[14] The precise ground for Albania's responsibility has always been somewhat less than fully concise; the Court referred to 'elementary considerations of humanity, even more exacting in peace than in war; the principle of the freedom of maritime communication; and every State's obligation not to allow knowingly its territory to be used for acts contrary to the rights of other States'. *Corfu Channel*, at 22.

[15] The term 'self-defence' was studiously avoided, quite possibly because several weeks separated the original incident and the UK's response, and the more time that expires between attack and response, the less plausible it is that this response can be classified as self-defence.

[16] *Corfu Channel*, at 35.

border to be regarded as a threat of force? How does a policy of deterrence fare?), but still suggests that the drafters were keen on creating as comprehensive a prohibition as possible.[17] What also speaks for this interpretation is that the right to be free from the use of force is not merely reserved for member states, but applies to all states. This is no longer much of an issue (since nearly all states in the world are UN members), but was not to be taken for granted in 1945.

Still, article 2, paragraph 4 is not entirely 'waterproof'. One thing to note is that the prohibition only affects the activities of states 'in their international relations'. Hence, as a legal matter, the use of force within states is not captured, and this state of affairs can be ascribed to the view, still prevailing in 1945, that whatever happens within a state is not the concern of international law. It also became clear, during the drafting of the Charter at the 1945 San Francisco conference, that somehow the right of self-defence needed to be acknowledged – this would find a place in article 51 UN Charter, and will be discussed below.

Perhaps surprisingly, the ICJ has rarely had the opportunity in contentious proceedings to say much about the use of force and self-defence as regulated in the Charter. Many cases of aggression have been brought before the Court, but often the Court had to conclude that it lacked the jurisdiction to proceed. This occurred, for instance, in the wake of several aerial incidents involving the Western states on the one hand and the USSR and some of its allies on the other;[18] it occurred when Serbia brought charges against a number of individual NATO member states for their participation in the intervention to end the human rights violations in Kosovo, and most recently this applied to the conflict between Georgia and Russia. In other cases, the parties decided either to withdraw the complaint[19] or to settle out of court.[20]

In yet other cases, the Court, while having jurisdiction, was not in a position to apply the UN Charter due to restrictions on its jurisdiction. In *Nicaragua*, the United States had famously insisted on a so-called 'multilateral treaty reservation' in its acceptance of the Court's jurisdiction; the Court could, in disputes involving multilateral treaties, only apply

---

[17] Stürchler, in the leading monograph on the topic, sensibly holds that the Charter contains an inherent tension. It expects states to be ready to defend themselves, but this very same readiness can be seen as a threat by others. Nikolas Stürchler, *The Threat of Force in International Law* (Cambridge University Press, 2007).

[18] See e.g. *Aerial Incident of October 7th, 1952 (USA v. USSR)*, Order, [1956] ICJ Rep. 9; *Aerial Incident of March 10th, 1953 (USA v. Czechoslovakia)*, Order, [1956] ICJ Rep. 6; *Aerial Incident of September 4th, 1954 (USA v. USSR)*, Order, [1958] ICJ Rep. 158, and *Aerial Incident of 7 November 1954 (USA v. USSR)*, Order, [1959] ICJ Rep. 276. These cases all involved alleged attacks on aircraft, and thus could have come within the ambit of the law on the use of force. Several other aborted cases involved Bulgaria, which, however, at the relevant time had not been admitted into the UN and was thus technically not bound by article 2, paragraph 4 UN Charter. See *Aerial Incident of July 27, 1955 (Israel v. Bulgaria)*, preliminary objections, [1959] ICJ Rep. 127; *Aerial Incident of 27 July 1955 (UK v. Bulgaria)*, Order, [1959] ICJ Rep. 264; *Aerial Incident of 27 July 1955 (USA v. Bulgaria)*, Order, [1960] ICJ Rep. 146.

[19] *Border and Transborder Armed Actions (Nicaragua v. Honduras)*, Order, [1992] ICJ Rep. 222, despite the Court having found jurisdiction; *Border and Transborder Armed Actions (Nicaragua v. Costa Rica)*, Order, [1987] ICJ Rep. 182; *Armed Activities on the Territory of the Congo (Democratic Republic of Congo v. Rwanda)*, Order, [2001] ICJ Rep. 6, and *Armed Activities on the Territory of the Congo (Democratic Republic of Congo v. Burundi)*, Order, [2001] ICJ Rep. 3.

[20] *Aerial Incident of 3 July 1988 (Iran v. US)*, Order, [1996] ICJ Rep. 9.

these multilateral treaties if all parties possibly affected by the judgment were also parties to the proceedings. As a result, the Court was forced to decide on the basis of customary international law, and found that the customary prohibition on the use of force continued to exist alongside the Charter prohibition.[21]

By the time the *Oil Platforms* case arose,[22] the United States had terminated its acceptance of the court's compulsory jurisdiction (it did so in the aftermath of *Nicaragua*). Consequently, the Court, in *Oil Platforms*, saw its jurisdiction limited to application of the 1955 Treaty of Amity concluded between Iran and the United States – again, then, the UN Charter escaped scrutiny. And the first decision of the Court involving the use of force involved Albania, at the time not yet a member of the UN and thus not bound by the Charter's provisions. As a result, there is only one contentious case, really, where the Court had the opportunity to pay some attention to the Charter provisions involving the use of force: the 2005 judgment in *Armed Activities* between the Democratic Republic of Congo (DRC) and Uganda.

In *Armed Activities*, the Court held that article 2, paragraph 4 UN was a 'cornerstone' of the Charter, and that the provision on self-defence had to be read narrowly; it did not 'allow the use of force by a State to protect perceived security interests' beyond the wording of article 51,[23] although the Court stopped short of saying that an 'armed attack' must indeed already have occurred. While Uganda argued that it had occupied towns and airports in the DRC not for the purpose of overthrowing the DRC government but for its own perceived security needs, the Court did not accept that argument, and held that Uganda, in doing so, had violated the principles of non-intervention and the non-use of force: Uganda's unlawful military intervention amounted to a 'grave violation of the prohibition of the use of force expressed in article 2, paragraph 4, of the Charter'.[24]

SELF-DEFENCE

The Charter, as discussed in a previous chapter, envisaged the creation of a system of collective security, spearheaded by the Security Council. Since the permanent members of the Security Council were given a veto, some of the smaller states, in particular in Latin America, feared that their big neighbour state could abuse its privilege by returning to the nineteenth-century Monroe doctrine under colour of Security Council approval. Hence these smaller states sought some form of guarantee that the collective security mechanism would not make it impossible for them to act in self-defence.[25]

The resulting provision is article 51 UN Charter, which allows states their 'inherent' right of self-defence, but only, it seems, until the Security Council steps in; the article aims to

---

[21] *Military and Paramilitary Activities In and Against Nicaragua (Nicaragua v. USA)*, merits, [1986] ICJ Rep. 14, para. 176.

[22] *Oil Platforms (Iran v. USA)*, [2003] ICJ Rep. 161.

[23] *Armed Activities on the Territory of the Congo (Democratic Republic of Congo v. Uganda)*, [2005] ICJ Rep. 168, para. 148.

[24] Ibid., para. 164.

[25] Stephen C. Schlesinger, *Act of Creation: The Founding of the United Nations* (Boulder, CO: Westview, 2003).

find a balance between collective security and individual (or collective) self-defence. Perhaps for this reason, the condition under which self-defence may be exercised is rather strict; self-defence may be engaged in 'if an armed attack occurs'. This suggests a tension with the prohibition laid down in article 2, paragraph 4, which, as discussed, does not just outlaw the use of force but also the threat thereof. Moreover, to insist on the actual occurrence of an armed attack, so it is claimed, is difficult to reconcile with real-life demands. Taken literally, article 51 is, in the words of Tom Franck, an 'idiot rule': it can be applied by 'idiots', in that the only determination that needs to be made is whether, in fact, an armed attack has occurred.[26] Yet one can hardly expect states to wait until an armed attack occurs before defending themselves; indeed, small states (think Belgium or Belize) could be completely wiped out by a single armed attack, especially if nuclear weapons were used; surely the Charter cannot have intended to negate any right to self-defence in such a case?

For this reason, it may be claimed that article 51 cannot mean what it says, and does not say what it means, and one may point to the customary right of self-defence, which, so the argument goes, would be broader than the right as formulated in article 51 UN. It is generally accepted that the customary requirements are authoritatively formulated in correspondence between the United States and the United Kingdom following the British attack on an American ship, the schooner *Caroline*, in 1837. The *Caroline* had been used to transport supplies to Canadians rebelling against British domination, and was consequently attacked by the British while lying in harbour. US Secretary of State Daniel Webster claimed, in correspondence with UK representative Lord Ashburton, that the attack on a ship lying in harbour could not be justified under the heading of self-defence, for self-defence was only allowed in cases in which the 'necessity of that self-defence is instant, overwhelming, and leaving no choice of means, and no moment for deliberation'.[27] The threat, in other words, must be 'imminent'.

The important thing to note is that Webster's definition, while strict, is not quite as strict as article 51 UN Charter, and leaves open the possibility of what is sometimes referred to as 'anticipatory self-defence': self-defence in anticipation of an attack that is about to happen. Even the Webster definition, however, does not allow for so-called 'pre-emptive self-defence', let alone 'preventive self-defence': self-defence now with the putative aim of preventing a strike by the other state which may or may not otherwise take place at some unspecified later point in time.[28] However, such arguments have been made, most notably by the United States, both to justify its actions against terrorist groups[29] and more generally as part of its national security strategy, aiming to deal with threats before they actually become threats.[30] The risk will be obvious; far from

---

[26] Thomas M. Franck, *The Power of Legitimacy among Nations* (Oxford University Press, 1990), 75–7.

[27] Letter from Webster to Lord Ashburton, 6 August 1842, available at http://avalon.law.yale.edu/ 19th century/br-1842d.asp#web1 (visited 25 January 2012).

[28] On terminology see Ashley S. Deeks, 'Taming the Doctrine of Pre-Emption', in Marc Weller (ed.), *The Oxford Handbook of the Use of Force in International Law* (Oxford University Press, 2015), 661–77.

[29] See the discussion in Christine Gray, *International Law and the Use of Force*, 2nd edn (Oxford University Press, 2004), at 171.

[30] A. V. Lowe, *International Law* (Oxford: Clarendon Press, 2007), at 277.

contributing to the outlawing of force, a doctrine of preemptive self-defence might give powerful states an almost unlimited licence to use force.[31]

Leaving the doctrine of pre-emptive self-defence aside, it is generally accepted that in order for self-defence to be lawful, two conditions must be met: necessity and proportionality. Together they imply that self-defence may not be punitive; the point of self-defence is to repel an attack, not to pursue the attacker.[32] For much the same reason, self-defence may justify a temporary military occupation, but cannot justify long-term occupation, let alone annexation.[33] Moreover, it seems highly implausible that an act taking place long after the initial event can still be regarded as self-defence: once the attack has been repelled, or the attacker has stopped for some other reason, it would seem that the possibilities for lawful self-defence have come to an end.

In its 2003 *Oil Platforms* judgment, the World Court held that the requirement of necessity was more than just a phrase. Confronted with possible minelaying by Iran, the United States responded by attacking Iranian oil platforms on two separate occasions. This, the Court felt, was inappropriate, as there had been little evidence to suggest that those platforms had been used for military activities or had served as the basis for Iran's alleged mine-laying. Instead, as the United States in part conceded, the platforms had been 'targets of opportunity'; this rendered the attack on them unnecessary for purposes of invoking the customary law on self-defence.[34] The Court's analysis also suggests, quite naturally, that necessity and proportionality are cumulative criteria; since the United States had been unable to show necessity, its self-defence argument had already failed.[35]

Self-defence is most obviously used when one state invades another, but can also be directed against less large-scale events, although the ICJ has suggested that it has 'no relevance' when the threat is an internal one.[36] Consequently, it is generally accepted that self-defence can be used against intrusions of airspace by military aircraft, as well as against aggressive behaviour from warships, and quite obviously against invasions. Somewhat more controversial is whether a state has the right to defend itself if merchant ships under its flag are the subject of an attack, although most observers would probably accept this.[37] It could also be argued that shootings from an embassy building could be considered an armed attack activating the right to self-defence, but when such a situation actually occurred in London in 1984, the UK government declined to attack the embassy concerned, and probably wisely.

---

[31] A UK committee chaired by Sir John Chilcott concluded in July 2016 that there were serious doubts concerning the legality of the invasion of Iraq by the UK (and by implication the USA) in 2003. See Sir John's statement, http://www.iraqinquiry.org.uk/the-inquiry/sir-john-chilcots-public-statement/ (visited 20 August 2016).

[32] Gray, *Use of Force*, at 121.   [33] Ibid., at 126.   [34] *Oil Platforms*, para. 76.

[35] The Court did engage in a hypothetical proportionality analysis, and found that one of the US responses could have been proportional, but the second was not. *Oil Platforms*, para. 77.

[36] *Construction of a Wall*, para. 139. While the Court is no doubt correct in the abstract, it is less clear whether the threat invoked by Israel in the case at hand should be considered as a purely internal situation.

[37] Tarcisio Gazzini, *The Changing Rules on the Use of Force in International Law* (Manchester University Press, 2005), 135–7.

Much more controversial is the situation when the attack is not immediately attributable to another state; terrorist attacks may form the clearest example, but so are attacks by irregular bands. The argument can work in two ways. First, since state responsibility can only be triggered by an act attributable to a state, it could be claimed that aggression by non-state actors could not activate the right to self-defence. This, however, seems plausible only on a conception of self-defence as somehow being linked to the law on state responsibility,[38] whereas it could be equally plausible to regard self-defence as a right belonging to the state no matter whether the aggressor is actually a state. This second, more functionalist, understanding is confirmed by article 51 of the Charter, which at no point limits the right of self-defence to being applicable only to attacks by states.[39]

While extreme, state practice following the attacks on New York's World Trade Center on 11 September 2001 (9/11) suggests much the same. The Security Council, in resolutions 1368 (2001) and 1373 (2001), recognized that states have a right of individual and collective self-defence against terrorist attacks. Additionally, it seems to have been accepted that self-defence is also allowed against states harbouring terrorists or complicit in terrorism. Trapp sensibly explains this with the help of the doctrine of necessity in the law of self-defence: if and when self-defence is necessary, it can also be exercised against a state somehow collaborating with a terrorist group. However, if the state concerned does its utmost to track down and prosecute the terrorists, then acts of self-defence against that state are not justifiable.[40]

It also seems accepted that self-defence against terrorism can take the form of pre-emptive killing of known terrorists or, less obviously, individuals strongly suspected of terrorist activities. This is commonly referred to as 'targeted killings'. While there is a strong presumption that individuals ought not to be killed, few states would argue in favour of an absolute prohibition on killing known terrorists, and the absence of outrage following the killing of Osama bin Laden in 2011 confirms as much. Usually, attention focuses on related legal questions, such as whether the state in which the killing has taken place has consented thereto,[41] or whether the amount of collateral damage (e.g. innocent bystanders getting killed in the process) is acceptable.[42]

Things are different when attacks can actually be attributed to a state, and here the relevant case law reveals two lines of thought. The narrow reading stems from the ICJ in the *Nicaragua* case. Confronted with the question whether the acts of armed groups within Nicaragua could be attributed to the United States, the Court formulated that the

---

[38] And thus having to meet the two main requirements for state responsibility: an internationally wrongful act, attributable to a state. For such a conceptualization, see Gazzini, *Changing Rules*, at 129.

[39] See also Daniel Bethlehem, 'Self-Defense against an Imminent or Actual Armed Attack by Nonstate Actors', (2012) 106 *American Journal of International Law*, 770–7.

[40] Kimberley N. Trapp, 'Can Non-state Actors Mount an Armed Attack?', in Weller (ed.), *Oxford Handbook*, 679–96. See also Bethlehem, 'Self-Defense'.

[41] After all, such a targeted killing, if done abroad (as is usually the case) involves the exercise of public power by foreign authorities, and thereby can be construed as intervention.

[42] Blum and Heymann report that even human rights bodies have not categorically condemned targeted killings in all circumstances, despite the obvious fact that targeted killings can only with difficulty be reconciled with the right to life. Gabriella Blum and Philip Heymann, 'Law and Policy of Targeted Killing', (2010) 1 *Harvard National Security Journal*, 145–70.

relevant standard was one of 'effective control'; if it could be proved that the activities of the so-called Contras, a rebel group supported by the United States, were 'effectively controlled' by the United States, then the United States would incur responsibility and Nicaragua would eventually be justified in directing its self-defence against the United States.[43]

The Court upheld this rather strict approach in the *Armed Activities* case. Although in the latter case it did not find that the aggressive acts of a rebel group could be attributed to Uganda, it did reach the conclusion that providing training and military support to such a group may violate certain other international obligations, such as the obligation to refrain from organizing or instigating civil strife or the overthrow of regimes. These obligations, so the Court specified, are 'declaratory of customary international law'.[44]

By contrast, in the *Tadic* case, a different tribunal (the ICTY) posited that 'effective control' was too strict a test, and that the looser test of 'overall control' would be more appropriate.[45] What the ICTY aimed to convey is that states should be held responsible for groups acting on behalf of and with the connivance of a state, even if they are not acting on a direct order. This, so the ICTY held, would be more in line with the law on state responsibility which, after all, holds states responsible even for the *ultra vires* acts of their officials and organs.[46] In a later case, the ICJ took issue with the 'overall control' test developed in *Tadic*, and found it 'unsuitable, for it stretches too far, almost to breaking point, the connection which must exist between the conduct of a State's organs and its international responsibility'.[47]

It is sometimes posited that self-defence may also take the form of attempts to rescue nationals abroad. On such a view, self-defence is justified not only when a state's territory is under attack, but also when its nationals (residing abroad) are under attack. Others claim that rescuing nationals abroad would be an independent right under customary international law, independent of any connection to the state's right to defend itself. The matter is controversial, and the law unclear. Sometimes such interventions meet with vehement objections; at other times, states seem by and large to acquiesce. Much depends on the precise circumstances of the case; intervening to rescue nationals from war-torn settings may meet with more sympathy than doing the same in quiet Denmark.[48] Rescuing nationals abroad was also one of the arguments used by Russia when annexing Crimea in 2014, but the argument would have been much stronger had Russian nationals actually been at

---

[43] *Nicaragua*, para. 115. The ICJ eventually held that the control by the United States fell short of meeting this standard.

[44] *Armed Activities*, para. 162.

[45] *Prosecutor* v. *Dusko Tadic*, case IT-94-1-A, judgment of 15 July 1999, paras. 120–2.

[46] ICTY judge Antonio Cassese would later add, in an interview, that this less strict test also had the advantage of turning what otherwise could have been classified as an internal conflict limited to Bosnia and the Bosnian Serbs, into an international conflict, thereby triggering the full applicability of international humanitarian law. See J. H. H. Weiler, 'Nino – In His Own Words', (2011) 22 *European Journal of International Law*, 931–46, at 942–3.

[47] *Application of the Convention on the Prevention and Punishment of the Crime of Genocide (Bosnia and Herzegovina* v. *Serbia and Montenegro)*, [2007] ICJ Rep. 43, para. 406.

[48] For a useful discussion see Gray, *Use of Force*, 126–9.

risk in Ukraine. As it happened, various international observers found no evidence of any systemic maltreatment, rendering the argument rather spurious.[49]

Article 51 envisages both individual and collective self-defence, and thereby allows for the creation of self-defence alliances. The leading example thereof is (or was, perhaps) the North Atlantic Treaty Organization (NATO), set up in 1949 to defend the West against the perceived Soviet threat, and itself giving rise to the creation of the Warsaw Pact in 1955. Article 5 NATO stipulates that an armed attack against one of its members may be seen as an armed attack against all of them, and gives the other members the right (but not the obligation)[50] to come to the defence of the state under attack. During the Cold War article 5 was never used; the Soviet threat never became acute enough. But famously, article 5 was invoked after the attack on the twin towers on 9/11; NATO's member states agreed that 9/11 constituted an attack on the United States and that therefore they were legally justified in helping the United States to defend itself.

While alliances such as NATO arrange for collective self-defence *ex ante*, it is also possible to organize collective self-defence ad hoc, once an armed attack has indeed occurred. This does, however, presuppose, as the ICJ made clear in the *Nicaragua* case, that the state under attack actually asks for assistance. *In casu* the United States justified its incursions into Nicaragua by claiming to act on behalf of El Salvador in collective self-defence; El Salvador, however, had not asked the United States to do so, and consequently, this was an argument the ICJ could not accept; otherwise, it would give states a blank cheque to intervene.[51]

It has always been assumed that armed attacks would involve kinetic force: weapons, tanks, aircraft, bombs. A relatively recent phenomenon, however, is the possible non-kinetic use of force, better known under the heading 'cyberattack'.[52] This provokes a host of new questions: how even to recognize a cyberattack? And how to respond to it? A complicating factor might be that the computer networks involved are often in private hands: is an attack on a large bank, for example, to be seen as an attack within the meaning of international law, and does it trigger the right to self-defence, or at least countermeasures, for the state where the bank is located? If it does (and most would probably agree that it does), then what counts as proportionality? Can an attack on a bank be met with a counter-attack on a hospital? The law here is still in development, so much so that it remains unclear whether existing legal principles can be adapted to this new phenomenon, or whether it demands the creation of entirely new ideas, rules and principles.[53]

---

[49] Much the same can be said of the other arguments invoked by Russia, including the use of force by invitation: while admittedly there had been an invitation (later withdrawn) by then-president Yanukovych, at no point had Ukraine's government stopped functioning. For a fine discussion of these and other arguments, see Thomas D. Grant, 'Annexation of Crimea', (2015) 109 *American Journal of International Law*, 68–95.

[50] As Glennon once put it nicely, this provision thereby contains a clear 'element of noncommitment in the commitment'. Michael Glennon, *Constitutional Diplomacy* (Princeton University Press, 1990), at 214.

[51] *Nicaragua*, paras. 232–8.

[52] For a useful overview of the issues, see Michael N. Schmitt, 'The Use of Cyber Force and International Law', in Weller, *Oxford Handbook*, 1110–30.

[53] For thoughtful reflection see Antonia Chayes, *Borderless War: Civil Military Disorder and Legal Uncertainty* (Cambridge University Press, 2015).

HUMANITARIAN INTERVENTION

It is sometimes posited that even though the Charter does not specify it in so many words, states are none the less entitled to use force for humanitarian reasons. The most widely discussed recent instance of such a humanitarian intervention was NATO's intervention in the former Yugoslavia in 1999, to compel Serbia to stop committing atrocities against the population of Kosovo.

Humanitarian interventions are highly controversial, for a variety of reasons. The main reason is, no doubt, that humanitarian intervention lends itself to large-scale abuse. It is next to impossible to draw up formal guidelines to justify such an intervention; should a hundred or two hundred persons be massacred first? Or should many thousands of individuals be massacred? Can it be used against states that do not actively kill off their populations but none the less commit many other grave human rights violations? And if so, where to draw the line? And then there is the question of sacrifice; can states be expected to place their own soldiers at risk in order to save the lives of strangers? It is perhaps no coincidence that the Kosovo intervention almost completely consisted of bombardments; little action on the ground implies little risk for one's own troops, but does increase the possibility of mistakes and imprecision.[54]

Added to this is the problem that few states have the military capacity to intervene for humanitarian reasons. It may well be hypothesized that the United States and other large powers are better placed to do so than, say, Costa Rica or Niger. Hence humanitarian intervention can quickly become the prerogative of powerful states, providing them with an excuse to exercise domination. Moreover, what has always remained unresolved is whether humanitarian intervention is a right that states possess, or a right that belongs to oppressed populations, or perhaps even an obligation on states that have the capacity to intervene in other states.

That is not to say that there may not be situations where, indeed, the atrocities are so large-scale as to shock the world's moral conscience. The Kosovo intervention may well serve as a bona fide example. Even so, most commentators have described it as illegal; in the absence of authorization by the Security Council, the general position seems to be that humanitarian intervention is prohibited, but that if it occurs and seems morally justified or legitimate, the world community grudgingly accepts it.[55] This is in itself not unproblematic either; it shifts the discussion from a legal debate to a debate about morality, but without providing further guidance as to when intervention would be justified and under what conditions.[56]

---

[54] As Orford recalls, NATO's campaign killed an estimated five hundred Yugoslav civilians. Anne Orford, *Reading Humanitarian Intervention* (Cambridge University Press, 2003), at 193.

[55] See e.g. Bruno Simma, 'NATO, the UN, and the Use of Force: Legal Aspects', (1999) 10 *European Journal of International Law*, 1–22.

[56] And it is perhaps useful to point out that moral philosophers are also divided about when to exercise humanitarian intervention. Some present it as a fairly absolute moral obligation, even if the chances of success are slender, whereas for others the chance of bringing atrocities successfully to an end is part and parcel of the very concept; without a decent chance of success, one should not even try. The latter approach is endorsed by Peter Singer, *One World: The Ethics of Globalization*, 2nd edn (Yale University Press, 2004),

Perhaps for this reason the debate has taken on a new dimension since the Canadian-sponsored International Commission on Intervention and State Sovereignty (ICISS) launched the idea of states having a responsibility to protect oppressed people, including against their own governments, in 2001.[57] Under this idea, popularly abbreviated as R2P, states have the responsibility to protect individuals. Where they fail to exercise this responsibility within their own boundaries, others are entitled to step in, at least when it concerns genocide or ethnic cleansing. What distinguishes R2P, as formulated by the Commission, from the more traditional idea of humanitarian intervention is not just a change of vocabulary (shifting the focus from rights to responsibilities) but resides also, and perhaps more importantly, in attention to prevention and in particular reconstruction. Under R2P the international community should not just intervene to stop ongoing atrocities, but should also help to prevent atrocities from occurring and be involved in rebuilding war-torn societies, if necessary by means of establishing a long-term presence.

This has spurred one prominent observer, Anne Orford, to identify R2P as possibly the most significant normative development in international affairs since the conclusion of the UN Charter; it provides a justification for putting states under international supervision, thereby changing the nature of sovereignty. Under R2P, so Orford suggests, sovereignty becomes conditional, and ultimately subjected to approval by the international community.[58]

TERRORISM

As noted earlier, article 2, paragraph 4 UN Charter prohibits the use of force in international relations, but because its wording limits this prohibition to apply solely to international relations, it has long been recognized that article 2, paragraph 4 UN does little to prohibit civil wars. Judged by its wording, moreover, and a logical corollary of having been laid down in an instrument concluded between states, the prohibition of the use of force is binding only on the member states of the UN. While it would not be plausible to state that therefore other actors can use force to their heart's delight, it none the less suggests a gaping hole in the framework of the international legal regulation of the use of force. What to do with force used by non-state actors? And, in particular, what to do when force is used by terrorist groups?

International law has always found it problematic to present a universally accepted definition of terrorism, despite attempts to do so going back to the 1920s, in the aftermath of the First World War.[59] Part of the problem is, no doubt, that terrorism tends to be politically motivated (however perverse the motives may be), resulting in the circumstance that what some regard as acts of terrorism may be regarded by others as romantic acts of resistance; as the cliché goes, one man's terrorist is another man's freedom fighter.

137–9, whereas proponents of the more absolute view include Andrew Altman and Christopher Heath Wellman, *A Liberal Theory of International Justice* (Oxford University Press, 2009), at 104.

[57] ICISS, *The Responsibility to Protect* (Ottawa: International Development Research Centre, 2001).

[58] Anne Orford, *International Authority and the Responsibility to Protect* (Cambridge University Press, 2011). To be sure, this brief description hardly does justice to her sophisticated argument.

[59] After all, the assassination of Archduke Franz-Ferdinand of Austria in Sarajevo, in 1914, which triggered the outbreak of the First World War, may be seen as an act of terrorism.

What adds to the difficulties is that, for some, terrorism is by definition limited to the acts of non-state actors, whereas others feel that states too can engage in terrorist acts.[60]

Since a general definition has remained out of reach, the international community has aspired to combat terrorism in two other ways. The first of these has been, since the early 1970s, to focus on the prohibition of specific acts of terrorism, regardless of the motivation behind them or the status of the perpetrator. This resulted in the conclusion, in 1970, of the Hague Convention for the Suppression of Unlawful Seizure of Aircraft, and, in 1971, of the Montreal Convention for the Suppression of Unlawful Acts against the Safety of Civil Aviation. Under article 3 of the latter convention, the states parties undertake to make a number of offences punishable by severe penalties, and in order to prevent the possibilities of offenders fleeing to safe havens, the 1971 Convention also stipulates (in article 7) that states are obliged either to prosecute or extradite suspects.

Later conventions would follow similar patterns. Thus, in 1979, a Convention against the Taking of Hostages was concluded, and following the notorious *Achille Lauro* affair in 1985 (the taking of a ship by terrorists),[61] the Convention for the Suppression of Unlawful Acts against the Safety of Maritime Navigation was concluded in 1988. A decade later saw the conclusion of the 1998 International Convention for the Suppression of Terrorist Bombings.[62]

If one strand of the approach to prohibiting terrorism has been to concentrate on specific acts of terror, the other strand, of more recent origin, has been to focus not so much on terrorist activities themselves, but on acts related to and facilitating terrorism. Emblematic is the conclusion of the 1999 International Convention for the Suppression of the Financing of Terrorism, which makes it a punishable offence to provide or collect funds for terrorist activities.[63]

Some regional initiatives likewise focus not so much on terrorism itself, but on ancillary activities.[64] Thus the Council of Europe sponsored the conclusion of the 2005 Convention on the Prevention of Terrorism, which contains provisions on recruitment of terrorists, training of terrorists, and public provocation. The 1977 Council of Europe Convention for the Suppression of Terrorism mainly aims to create a special regime for terrorism in extradition law,[65] stipulating for instance that terrorist acts cannot qualify as 'political offences' and thus result in terrorism suspects escaping from extradition.[66]

---

[60] See generally Jan Klabbers, 'Rebel with a Cause? Terrorists and Humanitarian Law', (2003) 14 *European Journal of International Law*, 299–312.

[61] See the discussion in Antonio Cassese, *Violence and Law in the Modern Age*, trans. S. Greenleaves (Princeton University Press, 1988), 62–75.

[62] Additionally, there are similarly structured conventions on crimes against internationally protected persons, on the physical protection of nuclear material, on acts of violence at civilian airports, and on the safety of fixed platforms on the continental shelf.

[63] For discussion see Anthony Aust, 'Counter-terrorism: A New Approach', (2001) 5 *Max Planck Yearbook of United Nations Law*, 285–306.

[64] For a brief discussion of the EU's counter-terrorism regime, see Jan Klabbers, 'Europe's Counter-terrorism Law(s): Outlines of a Critical Approach', in Malcolm Evans and Panos Koutrakos (eds.), *Beyond the Established Legal Orders: Policy Interconnections between the EU and the Rest of the World* (Oxford: Hart, 2011), 205–24.

[65] The convention was updated by means of a protocol concluded in 2003.

[66] Extradition law will be discussed in Chapter 12 below.

Despite this flurry of activity, and despite the circumstance that most of the relevant conventions have attracted many ratifications, the attack on New York's World Trade Center on 11 September 2001 suggested that there were still holes in the network of conventions, allowing terrorists to operate from a handful of states. In order to counter this, the Security Council controversially adopted its Resolution 1373 on 28 September 2001, a good two weeks after 9/11. Following Resolution 1373, member states of the UN are under an obligation to 'prevent and suppress the financing of terrorist acts', criminalize the collection of provision of funds, freeze assets, refrain from all kinds of support to terrorist acts, deny safe haven, and prosecute and punish terrorist suspects.

Remarkably, thereby, the Security Council created a binding set of legal obligations for all its member states, going beyond what many hold to be the limits of its powers, and breaking through the classic idea of state sovereignty, according to which states cannot be obliged to do things without their consent. While it could be argued that states gave their consent when they joined the UN and agreed to 'accept and carry out' the decisions of the Security Council, in accordance with article 25 UN Charter, the counter-argument would be that in Resolution 1373 the Council comes so close to legislating that it acts *ultra vires* – and member states cannot be expected to 'accept and carry out' *ultra vires* decisions.[67]

As noted above, for some terrorism may also be the work of states, but most observers intuitively hesitate to accuse states of terrorism, reserving the term instead for acts done by non-state actors such as Al Qaeda or Islamic State. In the latter conception, there remains the problem of how to act when terrorist groups act from the territory, and perhaps even with the connivance, of states. In other words, can states be held responsible for terrorist acts committed by non-state actors, and if so, under which circumstances? In line with the general law on state responsibility,[68] it would seem that states can be held responsible either if terrorist acts can be attributed to them (for instance, if the state exercises effective control over them) or, more likely perhaps, for failing to prevent terrorist acts.[69]

In the end, as this brief survey suggests, perhaps the main intellectual problem with terrorism in international law is that it is so difficult to classify – it defies well-nigh all traditional categories of international law.[70] Terrorists commit crimes, but are not ordinary criminals; they typically act not out of greed or lust, but for political reasons. They take part in international hostilities, but are not usually regarded as regular armed forces either. Terrorist groups may be extremely well organized, but they are not states, and while their acts may affect states deeply, it is difficult for states to find a response. Terrorists may be

---

[67] The two positions are well reflected in Matthew Happold, 'Security Council Resolution 1373 and the Constitution of the United Nations', (2003) 16 *Leiden Journal of International Law*, 593–610, and Eric Rosand, 'The Security Council as "Global Legislator": Ultra Vires or Ultra Innovative?', (2004–5) 28 *Fordham International Law Journal*, 542–90.

[68] This is discussed in Chapter 7 above.

[69] See generally Tal Becker, *Terrorism and the State: Rethinking the Rules of State Responsibility* (Oxford: Hart, 2006), and Marja Lehto, *Indirect Responsibility for Terrorist Acts: Redefinition of the Concept of Terrorism Beyond Violent Acts* (Leiden: Martinus Nijhoff, 2009). For self-defence against terrorism, see the remarks earlier in this chapter.

[70] See similarly Andrea Bianchi, 'Terrorism and Armed Conflict: Insights from a Law and Literature Perspective', (2011) 24 *Leiden Journal of International Law*, 1–21.

seen to violate human rights, but may also require protection through human rights law. With long-standing terrorist groups, it may be the case that the only way to end terror is to come to political recognition of the group's desires and the legitimacy of their gripes, yet this is something states are extremely reluctant to do. And while it may be useful to combat terrorism by punishing terrorists, it may also be useful (perhaps even more so) to combat terrorism by fighting the root causes of terrorism – if these can be identified to begin with.

THE END OF ARMED CONFLICT

The end of armed conflict is not always a neatly regulated affair. The history books may be full of important peace treaties (and most treaties making their way into the history books tend to be peace treaties, from Westphalia to Versailles), but not all armed conflict comes to an end by means of a peace treaty. Typically, during armed conflict, there may be negotiated ceasefires and armistices and, equally typically, it may be the case that at the end of armed conflict there may be a formal surrender. Thus, on 5 May 1945, Germany formally surrendered to a Canadian general in the Dutch town of Wageningen in order to mark the end of the occupation of the Netherlands. Yet a formal peace treaty has never been concluded.

Nor did the war between Iraq and Kuwait result in a peace treaty. Instead, and uniquely, the war was concluded by means of a resolution of the Security Council, spelling out the legal consequences for Iraq of its aggression.[71] Under the terms of this resolution, the territorial boundary between the two states is confirmed to be the boundary laid down in a treaty concluded in 1963; Iraq is placed under strict disarmament obligations; and Iraq is held liable for any losses sustained as a result of the invasion and occupation of Kuwait. The language is revealing; at one point, concerning nuclear weapons, the Security Council decides 'that Iraq shall unconditionally agree'.

The relevance of peace treaties is not to be overestimated; where a peace treaty is in place, the state of war has formally been ended and, hence, acts involving the use of force will require a new justification. Where no peace treaty is concluded, by contrast, there is room for the argument that the states are formally still at war, and that acts of force are to be regarded as legitimate wartime acts. Hence the great symbolic and practical significance of some of the peace treaties concluded by Israel, for example with Egypt (in 1979) and Jordan (1994).

In much the same way that declarations of war have become rare in inter-state conflict, so the term 'peace treaty' has come into disuse in relations between states. Euphemisms such as 'agreement on the normalization of relations' tend to be preferred. Still, this takes nothing away from the circumstance that peace treaties continue to be concluded, and are often also concluded following civil conflicts. Typically, such agreements do not merely bring conflicts to an end, but also contain provisions on reconstruction and transitional justice.[72]

---

[71] Security Council Res. 687 (1991).
[72] See generally Christine Bell, 'Peace Agreements: Their Nature and Legal Status', (2006) 100 *American Journal of International Law*, 373–412.

FINAL REMARKS

The prohibition of the use of force is no doubt one of the major achievements of international law. Even if often 'honoured in the breach', it is none the less of great significance that force is no longer considered acceptable, except in certain very limited circumstances, most notably in self-defence and under the auspices of the UN. This does not mean, and cannot mean, that aggression will never occur; in much the same way as the domestic law on murder cannot prevent all murders, so too the international prohibition of the use of force cannot be expected to bring an end to all violence.

Having said that, violence and oppression can come in several guises, and people get killed not just during armed conflict and other bursts of violence, but also due to extreme poverty and malnutrition. This has met with some recognition in recent years: security is not just the absence of armed conflict, but also the provision of conditions for people to lead decent lives.

FURTHER READING

Andrea Bianchi, 'Terrorism and Armed Conflict: Insights from a Law and Literature Perspective', (2011) 24 *Leiden Journal of International Law*, 1–21

Antonia Chayes, *Borderless War: Civil Military Disorder and Legal Uncertainty* (Cambridge University Press, 2015)

Carl von Clausewitz, *On War*, trans. J. J. Graham (London: Wordsworth, 1997 [1832])

Christine Gray, *International Law and the Use of Force*, 2nd edn (Oxford University Press, 2004)

David Kennedy, *Of War and Law* (Princeton University Press, 2006)

Anne Orford, *International Authority and the Responsibility to Protect* (Cambridge University Press, 2011)

Michael Walzer, *Just and Unjust Wars*, 3rd edn (New York: Basic Books, 2000)

Marc Weller (ed.), *The Oxford Handbook of the Use of Force in International Law* (Oxford University Press, 2015)

11

The Law of Armed Conflict

INTRODUCTION

The previous chapter discussed in some detail when states can legally use force, and held that nowadays they can do so either under the banner of collective security (with UN Security Council authorization) or in self-defence. Classically, the law relating to the right to wage war is known as the *jus ad bellum*, and it has occupied philosophers and lawyers for centuries.[1] In much the same way as there are rules on when force can be used, there are also rules on how force can legally be used: *jus in bello*. Some even go so far as to say that the phase of reconstruction after hostilities have come to an end is subject to a special legal regime: *jus post bellum*.[2] The *jus ad bellum* has been discussed in the previous chapter; the current one will be devoted to the *jus in bello* and, to a limited extent, to the emerging *jus post bellum*.

As the previous chapter also suggested, the distinction between war and peace is not nearly as clear-cut as it once may have been, and the term 'war' itself is often avoided, on the theory that it is too politically loaded.[3] War is rarely declared these days (if at all), and armed hostilities can come in varying grades of intensity, ranging from minor boundary incursions to full-blown attacks. As a result, it is difficult to say where peace ends and war begins. Moreover, it is no longer considered to be the case that peacetime rules are more or less automatically suspended once hostilities break out; certainly the fact that Iraq and the United States were at war did not affect their membership of the UN, and nor did it suspend their obligations under human rights conventions or environmental treaties.

Nor is it the case that war is an activity beyond the pale of law. The classic maxim *inter arma silent leges* ('when the weapons speak, the law is silent') was probably always more of a rhetorical flourish than an accurate description, for warfare is a highly regulated activity. This chapter will focus on the rules that limit the effects of warfare, but these are far from

---

[1] Michael Walzer, *Just and Unjust Wars*, 3rd edn (New York: Basic Books, 2000).
[2] Carsten Stahn, '"Jus ad bellum", "jus in bello" ... "jus post bellum"? – Rethinking the Conception of the Law of Armed Force', (2007) 17 *European Journal of International Law*, 921–43.
[3] David Kennedy, *Of War and Law* (Princeton University Press, 2006).

the only rules applicable; any army in action will have transport contracts, and v
reckon with labour law as well as with rules about payments or rules abou
accountability, and so on.[4]

INTERNATIONAL HUMANITARIAN LAW

The law of armed conflict has, historically, often been divided into two groups. A first group
of instruments contains restrictions on the conduct of hostilities. These were formulated, to
a large extent, during the two peace conferences organized in The Hague in 1899 and 1907
on the instigation of Tsar Nicholas II,[5] and are accordingly often referred to as The Hague
law. Second, the laws of armed conflict contain provisions to protect victims – that is,
people not taking active part in combat, including those who have been imprisoned or
shipwrecked; these have largely been laid down in four conventions concluded in Geneva
in 1949 (following earlier conventions concluded in Geneva), under the auspices of the
International Committee of the Red Cross (ICRC), and are hence often referred to as
the Geneva law. The total body of rules also comprises two additional protocols to the
Geneva Conventions, concluded in 1977 and updating the law (Protocol I) and relating to
non-international armed conflicts (Protocol II), as well as, arguably, a number of conventions targeting specific types of weapons – the latter are often considered as part of the
Hague law.[6] Thus the 1993 Chemical Weapons Convention outlaws the production, stock-
piling, and use of chemical weapons, and a similar instrument exists with respect to
biological weapons, concluded in 1972. Outlawing certain types of weapons too has a
respectable pedigree; the 1868 St Petersburg Declaration outlawed the use of so-called
'dumdum' bullets. It is generally acknowledged that the laws of armed conflict have as their
purpose making war and armed conflict somewhat more bearable; the law has a humanitarian mission. Consequently, it has become commonplace to refer to this body of rules as
international humanitarian law.[7]

This is not to say that international humanitarian law only originated around the turn of
the twentieth century. It has been recorded that rules on how to conduct armed conflict go
back a long way in time; the ancient Greeks had rules on how to behave during warfare
and, reportedly, in ancient China, the practice was for the date and place of battle to be
agreed beforehand, making war the equivalent of the gentlemanly duel.[8] Vattel, writing in
1758, pointed to quite a few rules relating to warfare, and did so by relying on authorities
from earlier times, from ancient Greek philosophers to writers such as Grotius. The rules

---

[4] Ibid. See also David Kennedy, 'Lawfare and Warfare', in James Crawford and Martti Koskenniemi (eds.),
The Cambridge Companion to International Law (Cambridge University Press, 2012), 158–83.
[5] It has been suggested that the Tsar was inspired mostly by financial concerns; an impoverished Russia would
not be able to keep up a high level of military expenses. See Chris af Jochnick and Roger Normand,
'The Legitimation of Violence: A Critical History of the Laws of War', (1994) 35 *Harvard International Law
Journal*, 49–95. Dutch lawyer Tobias Asser received the 1911 Nobel Peace Prize for his contribution to the
organization of these conferences.
[6] In 2005, a third additional protocol was concluded, relating to the use of an additional emblem.
[7] See generally Jean Pictet, *Humanitarian Law and the Protection of War Victims* (Leiden: Sijthoff, 1975).
[8] Stephen C. Neff, *War and the Law of Nations: A General History* (Cambridge University Press, 2005), at 22–5.

that Vattel noted ranged from respecting the life of enemy soldiers on surrender to the injunction not to maltreat '[w]omen, children, feeble old men, and sick persons' and to treat prisoners of war decently. He also noted that weapons ought not to be poisoned; this was prohibited 'by the law of nature, which does not allow us to multiply the evils of war beyond all bounds'.[9] A first attempt to codify the laws of armed conflict was made by Columbia University law professor Francis Lieber during the US civil war, and promulgated by US president Abraham Lincoln in 1863. These Lieber Instructions (often also referred to as the Lieber Code) would come to influence the law considerably.

The sentiment identified by Vattel – not to multiply the evils of war – still informs the law of armed conflict. The law is based on the thought that warfare may be inevitable, but should not cause unnecessary suffering, and two principles in particular are said to play a key role. The first is the principle of distinction; combatants and civilians should be treated separately, as should military and civilian targets. This is pivotal, and means that civilians and civil objects may never be the object of attack – only combatants and military objects may be targeted. The second is, indeed, the principle not to cause unnecessary suffering to combatants. The ICJ has underlined the relevance of these principles in its opinion on the legality of nuclear weapons, referring to them as 'intransgressible principles of international customary law'.[10]

These two principles have been fleshed out in the rules of the law of armed conflict, and the Geneva Conventions aim to protect the wounded and sick members of armed forces (Convention I); the wounded, sick and shipwrecked members of armed forces at sea (Convention II); prisoners of war (Convention III); and the civilian population (Convention IV). These rules can be very detailed. Thus, prisoners of war 'must at all times be humanely treated', and the detaining power must take care of their maintenance and health.[11] Civilian enemy hospital staff 'shall be respected and protected',[12] and an occupying power has the duty, within 'the means available to it', to ensure food and medical supplies to civilians.[13] Perfidy is prohibited,[14] and forcible displacement of the civilian population only allowed if its security or 'imperative military reasons' make this necessary.[15]

International humanitarian law aims not only to protect civilians from being killed or hurt by direct military activities, its protection also extends to works and installations, cultural objects, and the environment. Thus, under Additional Protocol I, it is prohibited to commit hostile acts against 'historic monuments, works of art or places of worship' (article 53). Dams, dykes, and nuclear power plants should not be attacked if doing so may result in 'severe losses among the civilian population' (article 56), and the natural environment should be protected against 'widespread, long-term and severe damage' (article 55). While Additional Protocol I brings a number of protected objects together, they have also been protected in separate treaties.

---

[9] Emer de Vattel, *The Law of Nations*, trans. T. Nugent (Indianapolis: Liberty Fund, 2008 [1758]), book III. The quotes are from paragraphs 145 and 156 respectively.
[10] *Legality of the Threat or Use of Nuclear Weapons*, advisory opinion, [1996] ICJ Rep. 226, para. 79.
[11] Geneva Convention III, articles 13, 15.   [12] Geneva Convention IV, article 20.   [13] Ibid., article 55.
[14] Additional Protocol I, article 37.   [15] Additional Protocol II, article 17.

Thus cultural property finds protection in a convention concluded in 1954, which broadly encompasses buildings, works of art, archaeological sites, and even books, as well as the places where cultural property may be located, such as museums and libraries. A convention concluded in 1977 prohibits the military (or other hostile) use of environmental modification techniques, defined as 'any technique for changing – through the deliberate manipulation of natural processes – the dynamics, composition or structure of the Earth, including its biota, lithosphere, hydrosphere and atmosphere, or of outer space'.[16]

Among the more intriguing aspects of international humanitarian law are questions relating to its precise scope. Some of the earlier conventions provided, in harmony with prevailing general international law, that particular instruments would only apply if both parties to the conflict were also parties to the convention concerned – the so-called *si omnes* clause. Thus, the 1868 St Petersburg Declaration which, its designation notwithstanding, was a treaty, provided that it was 'compulsory only upon the Contracting or Acceding parties thereto in case of war between two or more of themselves'. Needless to say, such a clause would do little to alleviate needless suffering, and quickly came to be seen as difficult to reconcile with the humanitarian mission of the law.

Instead, the law moved in the other direction, aiming to provide as much protection as possible, and in doing so it departed from the basic presumption that international law was a permissive system where everything was allowed unless specifically prohibited (the *Lotus* doctrine).[17] Arguably the most noteworthy feature of international humanitarian law, from a systemic point of view, is that the law is intended to form a single, seamless whole without any gaps. Since it might be difficult to achieve this in the light of the circumstance that the drafters of treaties are sadly not omniscient, Professor Friedrich von Martens (a Russian delegate, hailing from what is today Estonia)[18] proposed the introduction of a general savings clause. The preamble to the 1899 Convention (II) with Respect to the Laws and Customs of War on Land holds, in relevant part:

[I]n cases not included by the Regulations ... populations and belligerents remain under the protection and empire of the principles of international law, as they result from the usages established between civilized nations, from the laws of humanity, and the requirements of the public conscience.[19]

In various formulations, this Martens clause came to be included in later instruments, outlining that humanitarian law aims to protect no matter the circumstances;[20] if no rule can immediately be identified, then one just has to dig a little deeper and see whether

---

[16] Environmental Modification (ENMOD) Convention, article II.   [17] Chapter 2 above.

[18] For a wonderful fictional account, see the novel by Jaan Kross, *Professor Martens' Departure*, trans. Anselm Hollo (London: Harvill, 1994 [1984]).

[19] In *Corfu Channel*, the ICJ relied on a variation of this formula to hold, in the absence of a clear rule, that Albania could be held responsible for the presence of mines in the Corfu Channel. *Corfu Channel Case*, merits, [1949] ICJ Rep. 4.

[20] Note also that while treaties generally may be terminated on a material breach committed by a party, this does not apply, under article 60, paragraph 5 of the Vienna Convention, to treaties 'of a humanitarian character'.

protection can be based on morality, on common usage, or on whether public opinion would find the behaviour acceptable.[21]

The broad scope of humanitarian law is also manifested in the circumstance that the four Geneva Conventions of 1949 comprise a few 'common provisions' – that is, provisions that are laid down in identical form in all four conventions. Common article 1 states it in unequivocal terms: 'The High Contracting Parties undertake to respect and to ensure respect for the present Convention in all circumstances.' Common article 2 elaborates by rejecting the *si omnes* clause discussed above, and additionally holds that the conventions apply even if not all parties to the conflict are parties to the relevant convention, even if not all have recognized the state of war, and also in times of occupation. Perhaps the best-known of these, though, is common article 3, to which we shall now turn.

INTERNATIONAL AND NON-INTERNATIONAL CONFLICTS

The distinction between international and non-international armed conflicts (i.e. international war and civil war) has long been considered of vital importance. After all, if it is really the case that international law regulates first and foremost the relations between states, then it follows that international law cannot claim much authority over civil wars; these were, in the grander scheme of things, to be dealt with by domestic law – if at all. Moreover, states were always fearful that by applying international legal rules to entities that were not states (whether terrorist groups or breakaway factions or local groups run by warlords), they might end up legitimizing those entities; applying international law in such situations may be seen as bestowing political legitimacy on such groups. And, in addition, it is not always clear whether small-scale events, such as a domestic riot or disturbance, should trigger the applicability of international humanitarian law.

The distinction between international and non-international armed conflict was always problematic, for various reasons. The first reason is simply cognitive: how can such a distinction be drawn in practice? Many civil wars, after all, contain some international element; perhaps one side to the conflict receives arms from abroad; perhaps another side makes use of foreign troops. Partly, the law has responded by insisting on a regime of impartiality or neutrality; in non-international conflicts, intervention by outsiders was considered prohibited, at least in the form of support to rebel groups.

Moreover, conflicts may start as civil war but soon become international; if one of the factions breaks away and forms its own state, then what was a civil war all of a sudden becomes an international conflict. Likewise, if the rebels are recognized as belligerents, the conflict could be seen as internationalized. This internationalization was considered quite problematic, for example with the break-up of Yugoslavia during the early 1990s, and

---

[21] This, at least, is the usual narrative, but it is worth noting that Martens represented Russia and may thus have striven to protect Russian interests, and that the inherent lack of concreteness of the Martens clause may well promote great power interests: absent specific limitations on behavior, who is to say that a great power acts in conflict with the 'requirements of the public conscience'? For such an alternative – and compelling – reading, see Rotem Giladi, 'The Enactment of Irony: Reflections on the Origins of the Martens Clause', (2014) 25 *European Journal of International Law*, 847–69.

the reason why it was considered so is that international law only comes to apply in full once a conflict is considered international. Hence the applicability of international humanitarian law comes to depend, to a great extent, on the characterization of the conflict. Thus it is of great relevance how conflicts are framed.

Finally, the distinction was always problematic in the light of the humanitarian mission of international humanitarian law. After all, innocent bystanders probably could not care less whether the conflict in which they are caught up should be characterized as international or non-international, as long they are offered some protection, and this applies all the more so given that, typically, civil wars are more cruel and bloody than international armed conflicts.[22] As the late Antonio Cassese, a former president of the ICTY, summed it up in an interview, referring to 'this stupid distinction': 'A rape is a rape, a murder is a murder, whether it is committed within the framework of an international armed conflict, a war proper, or a civil war.'[23]

Common article 3 provides that the Geneva Conventions also guarantee basic protection in conflicts of a non-international character. This has been referred to as a 'mini-convention' within the conventions, and has proved of great relevance as the majority of conflicts following the Second World War have been internal conflicts, to which otherwise no international legal rules would have been applicable. While this suggests a strongly humanitarian sentiment, none the less it does have its limits; the protection of common article 3 covers mostly civilians and those who are *hors de combat*; combatants are not covered, on the theory that in a non-international conflict, there is no such thing as combatant status – combatant status only applies to international conflicts. And so as to underline the point that bestowing legitimacy on non-state actors remains a vital consideration, the article ends by providing that the legal status of the parties to the civil war shall not be affected by the application of its provisions. In other words, treating civilians of the 'enemy' side decently does not bestow any recognition on that other party.

Even so, the 'mini-convention' of common article 3 was considered as insufficient in the light of the preponderance of civil conflicts and the cruelty with which these can be fought, spurring states to conclude a separate treaty extending much of international humanitarian law to civil conflicts. This second additional protocol of 1977 still does fairly little to protect those who take active part in the hostilities (then again, this hardly differs from the situation in international conflicts). Otherwise, too, its scope is remarkably limited; it covers only internal wars between the regular armed forces and other armed groups, provided these exercise control over territory and are highly organized, and that is a high standard to meet. Hence conflicts between various factions are not covered, and neither are smaller 'internal disturbances and tensions'.[24]

---

[22] It may be interesting to speculate whether the cruel nature of many civil wars is the result precisely of the inapplicability of much of international humanitarian law.

[23] J. H. H. Weiler, 'Nino – In His Own Words', (2011) 22 *European Journal of International Law*, 931–45, at 942.

[24] Article 1, paragraph 2 of Additional Protocol II. Very critical on the limited scope of Additional Protocol II is Frits Kalshoven, *Zwijgt het recht als de wapens spreken?* (The Hague: Staatsuitgeverij, 1985), 122–9.

PROPORTIONALITY AND MILITARY NECESSITY

Much as international humanitarian law may aim to protect people, it also has to cater for the demands of warfare, and some even go so far as to suggest that the main task of international humanitarian law resides in the legitimation of military violence; prohibiting some acts makes other acts seem acceptable.[25] Many provisions come with the caveat that behaviour is prohibited unless dictated by 'military necessity', 'military demands' or similar formulations, and it is generally accepted that behaviour during armed conflict is subject to a general proportionality requirement.[26] For example, under the 1954 Hague Convention on Cultural Property, cultural property is generally respected, but military necessity constitutes an exception.[27]

Military necessity and proportionality, although often and easily conflated, are analytically distinct. An action that is deemed necessary for military purposes may still be disproportionate, and vice versa. Thus, bombing a bridge and therewith cutting off a supply route for enemy arms may well be necessary for military reasons, but doing so at the moment when hundreds of civilians are fleeing across the same bridge is likely to render the action disproportionate.

The general idea behind military necessity is simple enough; the law proposes that there be a balance between the military demands and the protection of human lives. Yet how exactly this balancing should occur is controversial and difficult to specify in the abstract.[28] In particular, the problem is to figure out what the standard of measurement should be. Is it the contribution to the military purpose of a specific action? Or its contribution to the military operation as a whole? Taking the lives of twelve civilians may be acceptable when measured against the objective of liberating a state; but taking the same twelve lives is less acceptable when measured against the objective of destroying a television broadcasting facility.

The requirement of proportionality, in turn, is a response to the infinite variety of possible activities during armed conflict. It is impossible and unworkable to prohibit all of them in specific legal rules, and what is nasty in some circumstances may be acceptable in others. Hence, as Cannizzaro brilliantly puts it, 'proportionality thus makes it possible to cover an ample spectrum of conduct in a relatively small number of quite simple rules, which, moreover, evolve over time in correspondence to the development of social custom'.[29] There is, however, a price to pay: the price of a lack of abstract precision. Much depends on how proportionality is operationalized; the larger the objective, the more activities will be seen as proportional.[30] That said, most specialists would agree

---

[25] Af Jochnick and Normand, 'Legitimation of Violence'.

[26] The leading article is Judith G. Gardam, 'Proportionality and Force in International Law', (1993) 87 *American Journal of International Law*, 391–413.

[27] Article 4, 1954 Hague Convention on Cultural Property.

[28] Jan Klabbers, 'Off Limits? International Law and the Excessive Use of Force', (2006) 7 *Theoretical Inquiries in Law*, 59–80.

[29] Enzo Cannizzaro, 'Proportionality in the Law of Armed Conflict', in Andrew Clapham and Paola Gaeta (eds.), *The Oxford Handbook of International Law in Armed Conflict* (Oxford University Press, 2014), 332–52.

[30] Green inadvertently captures the ambivalence when writing that 'the standard of measurement is always the contribution to the military purpose of the particular action or the operation as a whole'. See L. C. Green, *The Contemporary Law of Armed Conflict* (Manchester University Press, 1993), at 331.

that the relevant standard is the advantage of the action in the light of the attack as a whole, rather than parts of it.

Both military necessity and proportionality are eminently flexible concepts. It has been argued, for example, that the bombing of a city so as to undermine morale can constitute a legitimate activity,[31] and many have suggested that the use of nuclear weapons during the Second World War was eventually justified because it helped to shorten the war and thereby saved many lives. None the less, under article 51 of Additional Protocol I there can be little doubt that such indiscriminate attacks are nowadays prohibited.

While proportionality cannot be defined in the abstract, the balancing must none the less take place in good faith, and it is not impossible that actors might end up being held to account *ex post facto* in subsequent war crimes proceedings. A corollary is the idea of doing the least possible damage, including when it comes to killing people. A strong argument can be made that whenever the choice is between capture and killing, capture should be chosen, and when the choice is between serious and light wounding of enemy combatants, the law ordains that light wounding suffices.[32]

ARMS AND WEAPONS

During the Middle Ages, when sieges of fortresses were common, defending troops would sometimes pour boiling oil over advancing enemy soldiers.[33] This was obviously most unpleasant and hardly chivalrous, and at some point the practice was outlawed. Typically, the point where weapons become outlawed is the point at which they can easily be replaced by newer technologies; some lament that much of the law relating to restrictions on the types of weapons that can be used merely prohibits yesteryear's weaponry.[34]

Be that as it may, as with international law generally, the agreement of states is pivotal, and over the years states have reached agreement on outlawing many different types of weapon, ranging from the dumdum bullets that were the subject of the 1868 St Petersburg declaration to bacteriological and chemical weapons. One of the political problems here is that of trust; if I agree to get rid of my chemical weapons, can I be sure that my possible future enemies will do the same? Hence the possibility of verification is sometimes built into treaties outlawing weaponry. For instance, the Chemical Weapons Convention allows for inspections of chemical facilities in its states parties, and even knows the possibility of so-called 'challenge inspections', to be carried out at the request of another party to the convention.[35] By contrast, the 1972 Biological Weapons Convention lacks a verification mechanism, partly because biological products are also in common, regular use and inspection would be too interventionist, according to some governments.

---

[31] For discussion, see Sheldon M. Cohen, *Arms and Judgment: Law, Morality, and the Conduct of War in the Twentieth Century* (Boulder, CO: Westview, 1989), at 110–12.

[32] For such an argument, see Ryan Goodman, 'The Power to Kill or Capture Enemy Combatants', (2013) 24 *European Journal of International Law*, 819–53. Much of the argument is based on article 35 of Additional Protocol I (1977), which suggests that the right to choose methods and means of warfare is 'not unlimited' and that causing 'superfluous injury or unnecessary suffering' are prohibited.

[33] As reported in Green, *Contemporary Law*, at 26.

[34] Af Jochnick and Normand, 'Legitimation of Violence'.   [35] Article IX Chemical Weapons Convention.

Perhaps most debated are nuclear weapons, whose potential for destruction is unparalleled. Having been used twice in recorded history (nuclear bombs were dropped on the Japanese cities of Hiroshima and Nagasaki in August 1945), the legality of nuclear warfare has long occupied the minds of politicians and lawyers alike. In 1995 the General Assembly of the UN submitted the question of the legality of nuclear weapons to the ICJ, which responded somewhat enigmatically. Having (not surprisingly) been unable to find a treaty outlawing nuclear weapons, the Court addressed whether their use would be compatible with fundamental principles of environmental law, human rights law, humanitarian law, and other branches of international law, and while it held that international humanitarian law applied to nuclear weapons, it none the less reached the conclusion (by the narrowest possible majority, with President Bedjaoui's casting vote being decisive) that 'generally' the threat or use of nuclear weapons was in conflict with the principles of international humanitarian law but, so the Court continued, 'the Court cannot conclude definitively whether the threat or use of nuclear weapons would be lawful or unlawful in an extreme circumstance of self-defence, in which the very survival of a State would be at stake'.[36]

This conclusion is hardly surprising. If states are fundamentally disagreed on a topic, it is not for the Court to decide it for them. While there is some truth in the proposition that all political questions have legal aspects, the task of the Court is not to create this law in the face of political opposition, in particular not if that opposition includes those states that actually have the technology and resources to produce nuclear weapons. A finding that nuclear weapons would be perfectly legal would have been politically unpalatable, but a finding that their use would be absolutely prohibited would have been equally difficult to defend.

That said, in *Shimoda et al.* v. *The State*, the Tokyo District Court in 1963 reached the conclusion that the use of nuclear weapons was in fact illegal under international law, at least if used in indiscriminate aerial bombardments. This did not, however, result in compensation or damages; the peace treaty between the United States and Japan ruled out this possibility, with Japan having waived the option of exercising diplomatic protection on behalf of its citizens.[37]

Currently, there is some debate as to whether the use of drones is allowed under international law. Drones are unmanned aerial vehicles, capable of being used with great precision in order to hit their target, and, by being unmanned, of doing so with no physical risk whatsoever to those who use them. They are reported to have been instrumental in the targeted killings of individuals, and have sometimes ended up killing civilians instead of their targets. One authority concludes that while the use of drones during armed conflict may be legal (depending on the circumstances and the way they are used), it is extremely unlikely that their use outside this context would pass the test of legality; it is bound to

[36] *Legality of the Threat or Use of Nuclear Weapons*, advisory opinion, [1996] ICJ Rep. 226, para. 105 E.
[37] The decision is available, in English translation, on the website of the ICRC: http://www.icrc.org/IHL-NAT.NSF/39a82e2ca42b52974125673e00508144/aa559087dbcf1af5c1256a1c0029f14d!OpenDocument (last visited 29 December 2011).

conflict with elementary human rights concerns.[38] Thus far, drones have mainly been used by a single state (the United States), which therefore could consider itself invulnerable to drone attacks by others and thus may not have been overly interested in legal regulation. The more other states can develop the technology, however, the more vulnerable the United States, too, will become.[39]

Military experts are also highly concerned about cyber warfare. While cyber-attacks are unlikely to kill people directly, they may result in sabotage of financial systems or electricity grids, and thereby lead to deaths indirectly; lack of power in a hospital can have dire consequences. Hacking, moreover, may become (or already be) a new instrument of espionage. While international humanitarian law traditionally has little mercy for spies,[40] it might be difficult to apprehend hackers, especially if they were located far away, in the relative safety of their own states. Indeed, it might be next to impossible to learn their identity, which renders cyber warfare problematic; even if a cyber-attack takes place, how does one know who the attacker is?[41]

INTERNATIONAL HUMANITARIAN LAW AND INTERNATIONAL ORGANIZATIONS

It is increasingly common for international organizations to play a role in armed conflict, be it as peacekeeping forces or, more actively, by helping to curb aggression. The UN authorized Operation Desert Storm, in 1990, to oust Iraq from Kuwait; the UN and NATO have been active in recent years in Afghanistan, and the UN, NATO, and the EU have all played a role in the territory of the former Yugoslavia. This raises the obvious question whether international organizations are bound to respect the rules of international humanitarian law.

That question is easier to ask than it is to answer, as organizations are not among the parties to the relevant conventions. To argue that they are bound by those conventions because most or all of their member states are bound is tantamount to rejecting the idea that organizations have their own identity and legal personality,[42] but to argue that they are free to act as they see fit would undermine the applicability of international humanitarian law and might be seen as an invitation to the other party to the conflict to do the same, and thereby be counterproductive.[43]

---

[38] Thus Philip Alston, the UN special rapporteur on extrajudicial, summary, or arbitrary executions in an addendum to his 2010 report to the UN Human Rights Council. See UN Doc. A/HRC/14/24/Add.6.

[39] Drones are often used for targeted killings, discussed in the previous chapter.

[40] Under Additional Protocol I, article 46, spies are not normally entitled to be treated, on capture, as prisoners of war.

[41] Both drones and cyberattacks are insightfully discussed in Antonia Chayes, *Borderless Wars: Civil Military Disorder and Legal Uncertainty* (Cambridge University Press, 2015).

[42] On the relevance hereof, see Jan Klabbers, *An Introduction to International Organizations Law*, 3rd edn (Cambridge University Press, 2015).

[43] For a discussion of the application of customary international law to international organizations see Olivier de Schutter, 'Human Rights and the Rise of International Organisation: The Logic of Sliding Scales in the Law of International Responsibility', in Jan Wouters et al. (eds.), *Accountability for Human Rights Violations by International Organisations* (Antwerp: Intersentia, 2010), 51–128.

The non-governmental Institut de Droit International (a group of highly respected international lawyers) adopted a resolution in 1975 urging the UN to deliver a statement that it considered itself bound by the 1949 Geneva Conventions,[44] and the UN Secretary-General duly complied, albeit a little late; in 1999, Secretary-General Kofi Annan issued a bulletin outlining observance by UN forces of international humanitarian law.[45] The precise format is legally ambivalent; the document is referred to as a 'bulletin', but the legal status of the instrument is not entirely clear.[46] It does not explicitly incorporate the entire corpus of international humanitarian law, and as a unilateral declaration, it is not immediately clear when and under what circumstances it can be renounced. None the less, the bulletin does list a number of the basic principles of international humanitarian law, and suggests that UN forces will act in conformity with these. The EU, in 2005, adopted guidelines on promoting compliance with international humanitarian law, but without actually proclaiming itself bound. Instead, the EU suggests that since its member states are bound by the relevant conventions, there is little necessity for the EU also to proclaim itself bound.[47]

However, even if international organizations can be considered bound by international humanitarian law, the structure of both those organizations and of the missions they engage in makes the attribution of responsibility difficult. Thus, some of the UN's work in the former Yugoslavia is carried out by NATO which, in turn, means that NATO's member states deploy troops, often subject to national rules of engagement. If an individual peacekeeper violates a rule of international humanitarian law, the question is often whether this is his or her own responsibility, whether it involves the state concerned, whether it involves NATO, and whether it involves the UN. In the controversial *Behrami and Saramati* case, the ECtHR argued that the behaviour of NATO troops was ultimately attributable to the UN, and since the UN was not a party to the ECHR, the Court found the claims inadmissible.[48]

INTERNATIONAL HUMANITARIAN LAW AND PRIVATIZATION

Similar issues concerning the attribution of conduct may come to the fore when warfare is conducted by private entities. Traditionally, these were mercenaries: individuals would make themselves available, for a fee, to fight for a prince or king. While this was convenient in that the king did not need to call on his subordinates to wage war, none the less it came with a drawback; mercenaries could not be relied on to have much loyalty to the king or prince they were fighting for, and might be expected to switch allegiance if offered a higher fee by the enemy. Hence, the term 'mercenary' tends to carry negative connotations. Machiavelli did not care much for them:

---

[44] The text is reproduced in Dietrich Schindler and Jiri Toman (eds.), *The Laws of Armed Conflict*, 2nd edn (Alphen aan den Rijn: Sijthoff, 1981), 819–20.

[45] UN Doc. ST/SGB/1999/13.

[46] Arguably, the bulletin is based on the authority of the Secretary-General to issue binding instructions to UN staff.

[47] OJ, 23 December 2005, C327/4. This is, incidentally, a curious position for the EU to take, as it suggests that the EU is merely the aggregate of its member states, without any separate identity or personality.

[48] joined cases *Behrami and Behrami* v. *France* (application no. 71412/01) and *Saramati* v. *France and others* (application no. 78166/01), decision of 2 May 2007, reported in 133 *International Law Reports*, 1.

Mercenaries and auxiliaries are useless and dangerous ... For mercenaries are disunited, thirsty for power, undisciplined, and disloyal ... The reason for all this is that there is no loyalty or inducement to keep them on the field apart from the little they are paid, and this is not enough to make them want to die for you.[49]

Perhaps as a result, mercenaries are not protected under international humanitarian law; they need not be treated as prisoners of war, need not be repatriated once conflict comes to an end and can be prosecuted for every activity they have engaged in during their employment. The UN has sponsored a Convention against the Recruitment, Use, Financing and Training of Mercenaries, in force since 2001, which essentially criminalizes acts related to mercenarism.[50] Mercenaries must be distinguished from foreign volunteers, the best-known examples of which are probably the French Foreign Legion or the British Gurkhas; the latter are a recognized part of the British army.

More common than the use of mercenaries these days is the use of so-called private military companies, and this owes much to the changing nature of armed conflict. Private military companies tend to be engaged not so much on the battlefield itself (although this is not excluded), but are typically endowed with responsibilities for ancillary tasks such as the protection of convoys, the organization of logistics, or the security of prisoner camps. Moreover, since there is but a fine line between warfare and postwar reconstruction, private companies may often be engaged in the latter while ten miles down the road conflict still rages.

Either way, the main legal issue here is that of responsibility, and that became painfully clear after news and graphic pictures spread in 2004 about misconduct in the Abu Ghraib prison, in US-occupied Iraq; employees of a private military company were seen to abuse prisoners while conducting interrogations on the assignment of the US government. In such circumstances, there may be (at least) three bases for holding the state responsible, despite the circumstance that the private company is not a state organ.[51] First, the private company may be exercising governmental authority; second, it may be operating under state control; and third, the state has a due diligence obligation to make sure that no human rights violations (or other violations of international law) occur within its jurisdiction.[52]

FOREIGN OCCUPATION

If it is true that war and peace are difficult to distinguish these days, this also applies when hostilities have ceased, either temporarily or on a more permanent basis. Hostilities can stop temporarily in the case of foreign occupation; in such a case, the law of occupation is

---

[49] Niccolò Machiavelli, *The Prince*, trans. G. Bull (London: Penguin, 2004 [1531–32]), at 51–2.

[50] UN Doc. A/Res/44/34, 4 December 1989.

[51] The law of state responsibility is discussed in Chapter 7 above.

[52] For a fine study see Katja Creutz, *Transnational Privatised Security and the International Protection of Human Rights* (Helsinki: Erik Castrén Institute, 2006). On the use of private entities to engage in governmental functions and US law, see Paul R. Verkuil, *Outsourcing Sovereignty* (Cambridge University Press, 2007).

triggered, and continues to apply as long as the occupation continues or, more pragmatic-ally, as long as the occupation is recognized as constituting occupation and does not become normalized. Thus, sometimes politically sensitive situations arise. Is China occupy-ing Tibet, or has Tibet become part of China? Is Israel an occupying force in the Gaza strip or on the West Bank, or are these now generally seen as part of Israel? Were the Baltic states occupied by the USSR, or had they become part of the USSR? Emotions can run high here, and the law lacks clear criteria for distinguishing between occupation and annexation, and also the time factor may come to play a role; what starts out as (illegal) occupation may come to be legalized by the passage of time in conjunction with acceptance, acquiescence, and recognition.

Occupation is often linked to warfare, but can also result from threats to use force, as the German occupation of Bohemia and Moravia in 1939 suggests, or as a by-product of a peace agreement; this applied, for instance, to the allied control of the Rhineland after the Versailles Treaty. What matters is, as Benvenisti puts it, that 'the trigger for international regulation is not the mode of assuming control by the occupant but the temporary suspension of the sovereign's authority'.[53] Either way, the occupying power cannot just do as it pleases; it has to respect certain international legal norms towards the civilian population, most notably those derived from international humanitarian law and human rights law. With that in mind, the law of occupation is activated without delay, as soon as active combat has come to an end, or even earlier, once the territory has been placed under authority of the occupying army, even though it may still meet with resistance.

The key legal provision is still article 43 of the 1907 Hague Regulations – Benvenisti refers to it as 'a sort of mini-constitution for the occupation administration'.[54] The article provides that the occupant 'shall take all the measures in his power to restore and ensure, as far as possible, public order and safety, while respecting, unless absolutely prevented, the laws in force in the country'. If it may be argued that article 43 is geared mostly to the interests of the displaced sovereign, and somewhat less to the plight of the civilians in the occupied territory, the balance is somewhat restored by the Fourth Geneva Conven-tion of 1949, which contains a number of provisions (section III) specifically aimed at protecting the civilian population. Thus, article 50 addresses childcare and education, article 53 prohibits the destruction of property, and article 55 sees to the supply of food and medication. These provisions are not absolute; after all, Geneva Convention IV generally applies to situations of armed conflict, and hence the duties of the occupying power tend to be circumscribed by military necessity (if explicitly mentioned) and the means available to the occupying power. However, in *Construction of a Wall*, addressing the behaviour of Israel in the occupied Palestinian territory, the ICJ suggested that these qualifiers must be interpreted strictly; the Court was not convinced, in that case, that destruction of property was 'rendered absolutely necessary by military operations'.[55]

---

[53] Eyal Benvenisti, *The International Law of Occupation*, 2nd edn (Oxford University Press, 2012), at 3.
[54] Ibid., at 69.
[55] *Legal Consequences of the Construction of a Wall in the Occupied Palestinian Territory*, advisory opinion, [2004] ICJ Rep. 136, para. 135.

JUS POST BELLUM AND POST-CONFLICT GOVERNANCE

If the *jus ad bellum* relates to the transition from peace to war and the *jus in bello* regulates conduct during war, then what about the transition back to peace? It is increasingly recognized that international law may have a role to play here, but also that the available vocabulary and rules are not all that helpful. Hence there have been several calls for recognition of a separate body of rules to regulate and assist the period immediately following the end of armed conflict: a *jus post bellum*.

One cluster of ideas involving this *jus post bellum* focuses on the post-conflict peace itself; the peace agreement should include all stakeholders in order to be legitimate; there should not be onerous reparations or harsh punishment imposed on states for having committed aggression; individual responsibility is preferable to collective responsibility; some attention should be paid to reconciliation between the warring factions or states, and human rights ought to be recognized as basic foundations for the peace settlement.[56]

A broader strand, though, moves towards post-conflict governance: the idea that, after a conflict, the area in question is best governed, at least for a while, under international auspices.[57] The core of this idea revolves around state-building; from the ashes of an armed conflict, a new state must be built. Hence administrative institutions must be set up, legal instruments must be adopted, and, mundane or not, somehow provision must be made for the garbage to be picked up on a regular basis. And these things are best left, so the argument goes, to the international community, as only the international community can be considered impartial.

As an idea, this is not entirely new. It may be recalled that after the First World War, various former colonies were deemed not yet fit to stand on their own feet, and came to be administered as mandate territories, governed by a different state under the ultimate auspices (if not necessarily much control) of the League of Nations; the UN repeated the model when it created its trusteeship system. A more relevant predecessor, though, is the governance, directly by the League, of the Saarland, caught between France and Germany; the League also placed a number of contested cities (such as Danzig, Fiume) under tutelage and, reportedly, the city of Tangier, in Morocco, was under international administration even before the League of Nations came into existence.[58] More recently, following independence from Indonesia, East Timor was placed under international administration for a number of years in the late 1990s, and Kosovo, whose territorial status is as yet undecided, has been governed for a number of years by UNMIK and, since UNMIK's demise, has been under tutelage of the EU by means of the latter's EULEX mission.

---

[56] This follows Stahn, 'Rethinking'.

[57] Anne Orford, *International Authority and the Responsibility to Protect* (Cambridge University Press, 2011), briefly discussed in Chapter 10 above.

[58] See generally Outi Korhonen, Jutta Gras, and Katja Creutz, *International Post-conflict Situations: New Challenges for Co-operative Governance* (Helsinki: Erik Castrén Institute, 2006).

International law may also have a role to play after dictatorship comes to an end, in situations that are sometimes referred to as 'transitional justice'.[59] Here, important questions may arise not only as to whether the dictatorial regime should, *ex post facto*, be held criminally liable and on what basis,[60] but also how to move on. Typically, the state concerned will be in need of a new constitution, but also in need of a new system of private law, in particular if the end of the dictatorship is accompanied by a shift in political ideology, as occurred in the eastern Europe of the 1990s. In such circumstances, international organizations such as the IMF and the World Bank can offer advice, but this too can have political and distributive ramifications; it has been argued, for instance, that such policy advice has seriously contributed to gender inequality throughout eastern Europe.[61]

WARS AGAINST PHENOMENA

A peculiar, and somewhat unsavoury, issue concerning the law's applicability has arisen in recent years in connection with wars without readily identifiable enemies. This applies, in some contexts, to the proclaimed war on drugs, but mostly to the war on terror. The reasoning goes something like this. Drugs and terrorism are unacceptable and should be fought. Regular police operations are deemed unsatisfactory, ineffective or unproductive; hence war has to be declared against these phenomena.

The net result of this is that wars on drugs and terror tend to be fought in the interstices between legal regimes, and this has become most visible perhaps with respect to the war on terror.[62] Regular criminal law and the legal guarantees that come with it under the rule of law (such as the right to a fair trial) do not apply; after all, there is a war to be fought. However, since the particular enemy is not a particular entity but rather a phenomenon, the rules of international humanitarian law may not apply either. This has proved to be quite a potent justification for incarcerating individuals suspected of terrorism, or suspected of aiding and abetting terrorist activities, in particular at Guantanamo; those incarcerated were characterized as 'unlawful enemy combatants' (a category unknown in international humanitarian law) and initially deprived of habeas corpus and not considered to be prisoners of war either. Following litigation before the US Supreme Court, however, at least some legal rights of the prisoners have started to be recognized.

Thus, in *Hamdan* v. *Rumsfeld*, Osama bin Laden's former driver had been tried before a military commission set up at Guantanamo, but this failed to satisfy the US Supreme

[59] See generally Ruti G. Teitel, *Transitional Justice* (Oxford University Press, 2000).
[60] In the *German Border Guards* case, the ECtHR upheld a conviction of GDR leaders on the basis of the GDR's commitments under international human rights law. Even though the GDR leaders acted in conformity with GDR law, that body of law itself was deemed to depart from the GDR's international commitments. See *Streletz, Kessler and Krenz* v. *Germany* (application nos. 34044/96, 35532/97 and 44801/98), ECtHR, judgment of 22 March 2001.
[61] Kerry Rittich, *Recharacterizing Restructuring: Law, Distribution and Gender in Market Reform* (The Hague: Kluwer Law International, 2002).
[62] See also the discussion in Chapter 10 above.

Court, which held that the procedures envisaged by these military commissions violated both US law and the Geneva conventions. The Bush administration had deemed the individuals concerned to be embroiled in an international conflict but without international humanitarian law being applicable; the Supreme Court now held that the conflict was non-international in character (after all, it was not a conflict between states) and thus triggered the applicability of common article 3, and common article 3, so the Supreme Court continued, warrants that individuals be tried by a 'regularly constituted court'; this then excludes military commissions.[63]

FINAL REMARKS

It is a truism to claim that the laws of armed conflict and the laws of peace have become increasingly close, so much so that the legal vocabulary has recently been enriched with the term 'lawfare', contracting law and warfare.[64] Military operations are embedded in legal frameworks, many of them originally written for peacetime purposes, while situations of war and peace may be difficult to disentangle. In such situations, much comes to depend on how issues and situations are classified and categorized, and in the absence of clear categories, this in turn gives rise to a 'politics of framing'; qualifying the situation of Tibet, for instance, as one of occupation, gives rise to a different legal situation from classifying it as the regular exercise of territorial sovereignty.[65]

This, in turn, entails that difficult moral decisions may need to be made by political leaders, but that is, in a sense, nothing new. The law of armed conflict has rarely been about the mechanical application of hard and fast rules; instead, it has often been imbued with a sense of morality, perhaps even chivalry.[66] And that is a good thing too for, as Michael Walzer has observed, the laws of armed conflict 'leave the cruelest decisions to be made by the men on the spot with reference only to their ordinary moral notions or the military traditions of the army in which they serve'.[67]

FURTHER READING

Eyal Benvenisti, *The International Law of Occupation*, 2nd edn (Oxford University Press, 2012)

Judith G. Gardam, 'Proportionality and Force in International Law', (1993) 87 *American Journal of International Law*, 391–413

Rotem Giladi, 'The Enactment of Irony: Reflections on the Origins of the Martens Clause', (2014) 25 *European Journal of International Law*, 847–69

---

[63] *Hamdan* v. *Rumsfeld*, 548 US 557, US Supreme Court, 29 June 2006, at 62–8. In a later decision, the Supreme Court held that US constitutional guarantees also extended to the prisoners at Guantanamo; see *Boumediene* v. *Bush*, 553 US 723, US Supreme Court, 12 June 2008.

[64] See also the brief discussion in Chapter 1 above.

[65] On the politics of framing generally, see Nancy Fraser, *Scales of Justice: Reimagining Political Space in a Globalizing World* (New York: Columbia University Press, 2009).

[66] See generally Rain Liivoja, 'Regulating Military Conduct: The Intersection of Law and Honour', in Jan Klabbers and Touko Piiparinen (eds.), *Normative Pluralism and International Law: Exploring Global Governance* (Cambridge University Press), 143–65.

[67] Walzer, *Just and Unjust Wars*, at 152.

Chris af Jochnick and Roger Normand, 'The Legitimation of Violence: A Critical History of the Laws of War', (1994) 35 *Harvard International Law Journal*, 49–95

David Kennedy, *Of War and Law* (Princeton University Press, 2006)

Kerry Rittich, *Recharacterizing Restructuring: Law, Distribution and Gender in Market Reform* (The Hague: Kluwer Law International, 2002)

Ruti G. Teitel, *Transitional Justice* (Oxford University Press, 2000)

Michael Walzer, *Just and Unjust Wars*, 3rd edn (New York: Basic Books, 2000)

12

International Criminal Law

INTRODUCTION

There are close connections between international humanitarian law and international criminal law. Perhaps the most obvious of these is the circumstance that war crimes trials have played a major role in the development of what is commonly referred to as international criminal law. Yet it seems useful and justifiable to treat the two bodies of law separately, for on the one hand, as the previous chapter has sought to show, humanitarian law covers more than war crimes, crimes against humanity, genocide, and aggression, and international criminal law, by the same token, covers more than humanitarian law as well. Hence the two branches overlap, but are not identical, and it cannot be said that one subsumes the other. What makes international criminal law particularly fascinating is that it assigns responsibility to individuals, and thereby breaks through the classic structure of international law.

The current chapter will address the role of the International Criminal Court (ICC) and war crimes trials, but will also pay some attention to more ordinary forms of crimes with transboundary elements, and will discuss the forms of cooperation states have developed in combating crime. Even though the term 'international criminal law' is usually reserved for war crimes and the like, it should not be forgotten that there is a vast body of legal instruments dealing with international cooperation in combating other crimes. The chapter will also contain a discussion of the law of extradition, as the classic form of inter-state cooperation in criminal matters.

WAR CRIMES TRIALS AND THE ICC

Throughout history it has often been the case that once a war had come to an end, the victorious powers would quickly mete out 'justice' by executing enemy leaders or, more charitably perhaps, ordering them into exile, as happened to Napoleon. If there were trials, they would be conducted by national courts, trying foreigners suspected of war crimes and, one may surmise, often enough finding them guilty.

This would occasionally even apply after civil war. A famous example is how Henry Wirz, a Confederate camp commander during the US civil war, maltreated prisoners of war and was later tried by a military commission in Washington; he was hanged in 1865.[1] As the case suggests, it was sometimes considered possible to prosecute individuals for crimes committed during war and civil conflict, even on the basis of a set of rules that was normally thought to be applicable to states rather than individuals. That said, acts of violence during civil war were usually treated as common crimes, at least until the ICTY made it clear, in *Tadic*,[2] that the notion of war crimes could usefully be employed during non-international conflicts as well as international ones.

Perhaps the most important innovation of the International Military Tribunal (IMT) established in Nuremberg after the Second World War was that this was an international tribunal, set up by the four Allied powers after the war, and devoted to the prosecution of some of the major Nazi war criminals. That this would happen was by no means self-evident; reportedly, the UK prime minister, Winston Churchill, was rather keen simply to execute the Nazi leaders, although he felt that German officers should be tried.[3]

Being international was not the only innovative aspect of the IMT; also unique was the extent of its jurisdiction. The major war criminals would be prosecuted on three possible counts: crimes against peace, war crimes, and crimes against humanity. Of these three, war crimes formed the least problematic category, for it made intuitive sense that war crimes could be committed by individuals, and there was historical precedent to back this up. To prosecute individuals for crimes against peace, however, was somewhat unorthodox. This group of crimes was defined as the planning and waging of war, typically an activity that, before Nuremberg, was considered a governmental activity; states could wage war, but it was less obvious that individuals could do so.[4]

The most controversial aspect, however, was the prosecution for crimes against humanity. This involved murder, extermination, enslavement, and deportation of the civilian population 'whether or not in violation of the domestic law of the country where perpetrated'.[5] In other words, international law now came to interfere with the freedom of states to treat their own populations as they saw fit. It is very likely that the category of crimes against humanity did not exist prior to the Nuremberg proceedings, and that hence the prosecution of individuals on this basis stood in tension with the principle of legality (*nullum crimen sine lege*). None the less, as Hersch Lauterpacht explained to one of the legal advisers at the UK Foreign Office, while 'crimes against humanity' constituted an innovation it affirmed that international law was not just the law between states but was

---

[1] Antonio Cassese, *Violence and Law in the Modern Age*, trans. S. Greenleaves (Princeton University Press, 1988), at 124–5.

[2] See the discussion in Chapter 11 above.

[3] For a highly readable first-hand account see Telford Taylor, *The Anatomy of the Nuremberg Trials* (London: Bloomsbury, 1993), at 29–32.

[4] The IMT was followed by a number of trials conducted by the occupying US authorities, also in Nuremberg. On these, the seminal study is Kevin Jon Heller, *The Nuremberg Military Tribunals and the Origins of International Criminal Law* (Oxford University Press, 2011).

[5] See article 6 of the Charter of the International Military Tribunal, reproduced in Dietrich Schindler and Jiri Toman (eds.), *The Laws of Armed Conflict*, 2nd edn (Alphen aan den Rijn: Sijthoff, 1981), 825–31.

also 'the law of mankind'; this was 'an innovation which the outraged conscience of the world and an enlightened conception of the true purposes of the law of nations impel [the Allied powers] to make immediately operative'.[6]

Possibly in an effort to render the crimes against humanity category less explosive, the drafters of the IMT Charter added the rider that prosecution could only take place for such crimes if committed in connection with the Second World War or with crimes against peace and war crimes; this narrowed the scope considerably. Either way, the outcome of the Nuremberg trials was widely seen as satisfactory; a number of high-ranking Nazis received the death penalty; others were imprisoned (including the enigmatic Albert Speer, Hitler's architect)[7] and three of the suspects were acquitted.[8]

Ever since the Nuremberg (and Tokyo[9]) trials, the creation of a permanent international criminal court has ranked high on the wish-list of international lawyers but, for many years, without much success. While isolated proceedings took place after several conflicts, including the court-martial in 1970 of US Lt Calley by the US authorities after the massacre at My Lai, Vietnam, a permanent international court seemed out of reach. The mood changed though in the early 1990s, when the UN Security Council twice in quick succession created ad hoc tribunals: one to deal with the atrocities in the former Yugoslavia (ICTY), and one to deal with the genocide in Rwanda (ICTR). These were set up to prosecute individuals for their participation in those atrocities, with a narrowly circumscribed jurisdiction and initially even very limited funding.[10] When it was suggested around the same time that a tribunal be created to deal with international crimes such as drugs trafficking, the time seemed ripe for a permanent international criminal court. In 1998, a number of states concluded the Rome Statute of the International Criminal Court; it entered into force in 2002, and in 2016 comprises 124 states.[11] Notably, though, many of the bigger military powers are missing; while Germany, France and the United Kingdom are parties, Russia, China, India, Israel and, notoriously, the United States are not.[12] The links between the ICC and its Assembly of States Parties (ASP) is a close one: the Assembly not only decides on the appointment of judges and other officials of the ICC, but also has a number of working

---

[6] Hersch Lauterpacht writing to Patrick Dean in August 1945, quoted in Elihu Lauterpacht, *The Life of Hersch Lauterpacht* (Cambridge University Press, 2010), at 274.

[7] Speer is the subject of a fascinating biography by Gitta Sereny, *Albert Speer: His Battle with Truth* (London: Picador, 1995).

[8] These would, however, be tried on different counts by local German denazification courts and found guilty. One of them, Hjalmar Schacht, was acquitted on appeal, and established himself as a successful financial adviser of various governments; he had managed Germany's central bank under Hitler. For details, see Taylor, *Anatomy*, at 612–14.

[9] In Tokyo, responsible Japanese political and military leaders were tried before a Tribunal composed of judges from all states (or their colonial masters) invaded by Japan. For a lovely and lively discussion, see B. V. A. Röling and Antonio Cassese, *The Tokyo Tribunal and Beyond* (Cambridge: Polity Press, 1993).

[10] Both were closed at the end of 2015, and have been replaced by the International Residual Mechanism for Criminal Tribunals, created by UN Security Council Resolution 1966 (2010).

[11] The drafting is reflectively discussed in Immi Tallgren, 'We Did It? The Vertigo of Law and Everyday Life at the Diplomatic Conference on the Establishment of an International Criminal Court', (1999), 12 *Leiden Journal of International Law*, 683–707.

[12] On the position of these states see Jan Klabbers, 'The Spectre of International Criminal Justice: Third States and the ICC', in Andreas Zimmermann (ed.), *International Criminal Law and the Current Development of Public International Law* (Berlin: Duncker and Humblot, 2003), 49–72.

groups on general issues (such as cooperation between the ICC and states), and can adopt amendments (subject to ratification) without the need for a review conference.

The jurisdiction of the ICC comprises four distinct categories of offence: individuals may be prosecuted for genocide, war crimes, crimes against humanity, and the crime of aggression. Ironically, in the light of the impetus to the ICC project, the crime of drugs trafficking is not included; the ICC is limited to what might be called 'political crimes' – that is, crimes committed in a political context rather than, for instance, out of greed.[13] All four categories have been given detailed definitions; the list of acts constituting war crimes alone covers some four pages, and all four are subject to further refinements in the form of 'elements of crime'; which are to be adopted by the Assembly of State Parties to add greater precision. This immediately suggests the tightrope on which the ICC has to balance. On the one hand, it is the embodiment of the 'end of a culture of impunity'; whenever and wherever political leaders misbehave, there will be a call that they be tried before the ICC. Yet, on the other hand, as a permanent criminal tribunal, the ICC must strictly adhere to the idea of legality. Where ad hoc tribunals (such as Nuremberg) derive part of their legitimacy from being a response to recent atrocities and can thus afford to 'improvise', a permanent court cannot afford this luxury. The hallmark of a permanent criminal apparatus is that subjects must know at all times for what exactly they can be held to account, and this, in turn, demands that crimes be defined *ex ante*, in great detail, and with great precision. It was precisely on grounds of legality (insufficient evidence, unreliable witnesses) that ICC Trial Chamber V decided in 2016 to vacate the charges against two Kenyans suspected of crimes against humanity.[14]

The personal jurisdiction of the ICC is limited; it has jurisdiction over nationals of its state parties and over the territories of its state parties. The idea of universal jurisdiction was floated during the negotiations, but eventually defeated, in particular on US insistence; the United States worried that its soldiers, active all over the world, might come to be prosecuted before the ICC, and is still concerned even about the territorially based jurisdiction, as this would imply that US soldiers could be prosecuted for actions committed in the territory of one of the parties to the ICC Statute. Still, as Schabas explains, turning vice into virtue, the absence of universal jurisdiction may have been good for the ICC; if it were to have universal jurisdiction, then whether a state would ratify or not would be irrelevant. Hence the limited jurisdiction creates an incentive for states to ratify the Statute.[15]

Either way, US fears about the ICC always seemed a mite exaggerated, as the hallmark of the ICC is what is referred to as the principle of complementarity. Under article 17 ICC, one of the conditions of admissibility is that a case must not be prosecuted, or seriously

---

[13] That said, there have been calls to regard the acts of police or security forces against drugs trafficking as war crimes or crimes against humanity. See e.g. Kimberly Curtis, 'Will the International Criminal Court Take on the Mexican Drug War', at http://www.undispatch.com/will-international-criminal-court-take-mexican-drug-war/ (visited 14 August 2016). In a sense, moreover, drugs trafficking has a strong political element: states tend to be less concerned with the plight of users than with the economic and political power generated by trade in narcotics.

[14] ICC 01/09–01/11, *Prosecutor* v. *William Ruto and Joshua Sang*, decision of 5 April 2016.

[15] William A. Schabas, *An Introduction to the International Criminal Court*, 4th edn (Cambridge University Press, 2011), 64–8.

investigated, elsewhere. If proceedings are pending or have been completed before a national court (regardless of the outcome), then the case will be inadmissible before the ICC, unless the state concerned is unable or unwilling 'genuinely' to prosecute or investigate. It seems that this latter point plays a role in the ongoing examination of the situation in Georgia, where the behaviour of Russian troops is also under scrutiny.[16]

Uniquely among international criminal tribunals, which usually deal with past atrocities, the temporal jurisdiction of the ICC is prospective; only cases committed after the ICC's entry into force may be heard, hence only cases committed after 1 July 2002 or after the entry into force of the Rome Statute for that particular state. This again suggests the pivotal importance of the legality principle: *nullum crimen sine lege*. The principle is explicitly laid down in article 22 ICC, while article 23 lists its corollary: *nulla poena sine lege* (no punishment without law).

The Court's jurisdiction can be triggered in three ways, in accordance with article 13 ICC Statute. First, states parties to the Statute may refer a situation to the prosecutor. Second, the Security Council of the UN, acting under Chapter VII of the UN Charter, may refer a situation to the prosecutor, and, third, the prosecutor may start investigations *proprio motu*. This last possibility is quite an innovation, although in order to proceed, the prosecutor must get the green light from the ICC's pre-trial chamber.

High as expectations for the ICC were, its first substantive judgment was only rendered in 2012, despite the ICC having been in existence for almost a decade. In March 2012 the DRC rebel leader Thomas Lubanga was convicted of enlisting and conscripting child soldiers. He was later sentenced to fourteen years' imprisonment, and in 2015 was transferred from The Hague to a DRC prison.[17] In 2014, Germain Katanga, also hailing from the Democratic Republic of Congo, was convicted of crimes against humanity and war crimes and sentenced to twelve years' imprisonment,[18] while in 2016 a third individual was convicted. The DRC rebel leader Jean-Pierre Bemba was found guilty of crimes against humanity and war crimes committed in the Central African Republic in 2002 and 2003, and sentenced to eighteen years' imprisonment.[19]

The fact that few convictions have so far been issued (only three in almost fifteen years) does not mean that the ICC's judges have been sitting idly by; they have fleshed out quite a bit of the practical workings of the ICC, deciding on a number of aspects of prosecution and trial. Still, given the dearth of actual judgments, perhaps the greater relevance of the ICC to date is its symbolic value.[20] Its very existence shows the world that some forms of political

---

[16] ICC 01/15. Like the United States, Russia is not a party to the Rome Statute; its troops are under investigation for acts committed on Georgian territory, and possibly not fully addressed by legal proceedings in Russia.

[17] ICC-01/04–01/06, *Prosecutor* v. *Thomas Lubanga Dyilo*.

[18] ICC-01/04–01/07, *Prosecutor* v. *Germain Katanga*.

[19] ICC-01/05–01/08, *Prosecutor* v. *Jean-Pierre Bemba Gombo*.

[20] I have elsewhere called it a 'simulacrum' of global governance: see Jan Klabbers, 'Hannah Arendt and the Languages of Global Governance', in Marco Goldoni and Christopher McCorkindale (eds.), *Hannah Arendt and the Law* (Oxford: Hart, 2012), 229–47, at 234. A simulacrum is something which imitates the appearance of something else without having its substantive characteristics, as the notion was developed by the French philosopher Baudrillard. See Jean Baudrillard, *Simulacra and Simulation*, trans. S. Glaser (Ann Arbor, MI: University of Michigan Press, 1994).

crime are simply unacceptable. This may not exercise much of a deterrent effect,[21] but is none the less often considered to be a useful reminder to political leaders that while they may be lucky and get away with nasty behaviour, they can no longer count on it. Moreover, there is a widely held sentiment that courts such as the ICC are important with a view to offering the victims of the crimes the chance to get their stories heard, to provide some closure, and perhaps even financial compensation. With this in mind, a Trust Fund for Victims is attached to the ICC, and convicted suspects may come to be liable to pay reparation. Still, all things considered, the ICC is quite an expensive enterprise: its programme budget for 2015 was some €130 million.[22]

It is also useful to note that while the ICC is the only permanent international criminal tribunal, its creation has not stopped the establishment of ad hoc tribunals. There are in existence special, temporary tribunals to deal with situations that have taken place in Cambodia,[23] Sierra Leone,[24] and Lebanon,[25] to name just a few, while in addition national courts may be created or utilized for the prosecution of (former) political leaders. Some tribunals are purely international, some are purely national and some are so-called hybrids, consisting of a mixture of local and international judges.

Inasmuch as the creation of tribunals is considered desirable to bring an end to impunity, sometimes the alternative of a truth commission is used. The basic idea is not to have individuals stand trial, but to find out what happened,[26] and achieve a national reconciliation. The most famous example, and generally seen as a success, was South Africa's Truth and Reconciliation Commission, set up to come to terms with South Africa's history of apartheid. Still, it is sometimes suggested that there is a tension between impunity and reconciliation; the latter may involve the granting of amnesties, which, some argue, are in violation of customary international law.[27] That is a rather far-fetched legal argument, in that human rights law typically says little about amnesties and none of the leading instruments actively prohibits the granting of amnesties. On the

---

[21] Jan Klabbers, 'Just Revenge? The Deterrence Argument in International Criminal Law', (2001) 12 *Finnish Yearbook of International Law*, 249–67.

[22] https://asp.icc-cpi.int/iccdocs/asp_docs/Resolutions/ASP13/ICC-ASP-13-Res1-ENG.pdf (visited 3 August 2016).

[23] The Extraordinary Chambers in the Courts of Cambodia (ECCC) has been set up to investigate the atrocities committed by the Khmer Rouge during its time in power in Cambodia, from 1975 until 1979.

[24] The jurisdiction of the Special Tribunal for Sierra Leone (STSL) related to the civil war raging in the country during the 1990s. The Tribunal closed its work in 2013, but a small Residual Special Tribunal has been created to take care of outstanding legal tasks, ranging from managing the archives to supervision of prison sentences.

[25] Curiously, perhaps, the Special Tribunal for Lebanon has been set up to investigate a single incident costing twenty-two lives, including that of the then prime minister, Rafik Hariri. It consists of eleven judges, has been in existence since 2009, and in 2016 is trying its first case, *Prosecutor* v. *Ayyash et al.* (case STL-11-01). In the meantime, a contempt trial has been completed: case STL-14-06/T/CJ, *Prosecutor* v. *Akhbar Beirut S.A.L. and Ibrahim Al Amin*.

[26] This is something trials are not particularly good at, as historical narratives typically end up being filtered by rules on what constitutes legally admissible evidence. For a brilliant study on this issue, see Lawrence Douglas, *The Memory of Judgment: Making Law and History in the Trials of the Holocaust* (New Haven, CT: Yale University Press, 2001).

[27] The seminal article is Diane Orentlicher, 'Settling Accounts: The Duty to Prosecute Human Rights Violations of a Prior Regime', (1991) 100 *Yale Law Journal*, 2537–615.

other hand, there is room for the argument that blanket amnesties are unacceptable, as they merely serve to shield suspects from justice.[28]

Popular as international criminal tribunals have become in circles of Western liberals, none the less some have attracted considerable political opposition. Some of this has come from obvious corners: one can imagine why Serbians, largely seen as the aggressors in the conflict in the former Yugoslavia, have been critical of the ICTY. Critiques of the ICC have been different, though: some have raised concerns about the ICC targeting mainly Africans: the three convicted individuals thus far all hail from the Democratic Republic of Congo, and many of the pending proceedings and outstanding indictments also involve Africans. To some extent this reflects the fact that African countries have enthusiastically ratified the ICC Statute, in ways that do not apply in quite the same magnitude elsewhere. As observed above, the ICC's reach is limited to territorial and national jurisdiction, and with states such as Russia and China being non-parties, proceedings against Russians or Chinese individuals are near-impossible. The concern is, however, that it may also reflect prosecutorial policy; perhaps to allay such fears, recent investigations and preliminary examinations include situations in Georgia, Colombia, and Ukraine. There is also a preliminary investigation under way of incidents happening in the occupied Palestinian territory, including East Jerusalem, on the basis of an acceptance of jurisdiction issued by Palestine under article 12(3) ICC Statute, before it actually became a party to the Statute.[29]

CORE CRIMES

It is generally acknowledged that the jurisdiction of the ICC comprises what are often referred to as 'core crimes': genocide, war crimes, crimes against humanity, and the crime of aggression. Yet prosecuting these four crimes is by no means easy. For one thing, to a large extent they are the work of groups; it is next to impossible for a single individual to commit genocide or aggression. Yet the ICC was created precisely with a view to prosecuting individual offenders, on the underlying theory, no doubt, that states too often get away with nasty behaviour and are, at any rate, abstractions, composed of individuals.

The international legal prohibition on genocide[30] goes back to 1948, when the Genocide Convention was concluded, in the aftermath of the Holocaust. Under the convention, the killing of groups of people by reason of their race, nationality, ethnicity, or religion is prohibited, as well as causing serious bodily harm, preventing births, transferring children,

---

[28] For an excellent study of punishment and alternative ways of reconciliation, see Mark A. Drumbl, *Atrocity, Punishment, and International Law* (Cambridge University Press, 2007).

[29] The Court's jurisdiction was accepted on 1 January 2015; a day later Palestine acceded to the ICC Statute, which has been in force for it since 1 April 2015. All this presupposes that Palestine is considered a state (see article 125 ICC Statute). While the depository of the ICC Statute, the UN Secretary-General, seems to have accepted Palestine's accession as valid, it may still be declared invalid in proceedings by the ICC itself – although this seems unlikely in the extreme.

[30] The term was coined by Raphael Lemkin. For a sketch of his relevance, see Mark Mazower, *No Enchanted Palace: The End of Empire and the Ideological Origins of the United Nations* (Princeton University Press, 2009).

and creating conditions intended to destroy the group. The decisive criterion here is the so-called 'specific intent' or *dolus specialis*; the intention not just to kill people (this is bad enough, of course, but does not make the killing of large numbers of people genocide), but to kill them with the 'intent to destroy, in whole or in part, a national, ethnical, racial or religious group, as such', as article 2 Genocide Convention puts it.[31] This is difficult to prove, and the ICJ rejected genocide allegations by Croatia about genocide committed by Serbs against Croatians and, conversely, Serbian claims about Croatian genocide committed in Croatia, precisely for this reason.[32] In the end, there are relatively few authoritative findings of genocide. The ICJ held that the killing of some 8,000 Muslim men in Srebrenica, in 1995, constituted genocide,[33] a conclusion already reached earlier by the ICTY.[34]

There is also widespread agreement that the Armenian genocide of 1915 truly constituted genocide although, as a legal matter, the Genocide Convention did not yet exist at the time.[35] When in 2011 the French authorities proposed a law making the denial of genocide a punishable crime, Turkey (widely held responsible for the Armenian genocide) responded furiously, suggesting that what had happened did not constitute genocide, although it acknowledged that many had died. The episode suggests that an accusation of genocide is diplomatically awkward; genocide constitutes the 'crime of crimes' and is not an accusation that states will shake off lightly.

The prohibition of crimes against humanity was, as explained above, an innovation of the Nuremberg proceedings, but has rapidly become accepted as part of positive international law. In the ICC Statute, crimes against humanity involve a number of acts (murder, extermination, rape, sexual slavery, torture, enforced disappearance and a host of other acts) that form part of 'a widespread or systematic attack directed against any civilian population'. Here, too, a separate element of intent (sometimes referred to as the 'contextual element' or 'mental element') must be present, although it is probably less strict than with genocide; for a suspect to be guilty of crimes of humanity, he or she must have 'knowledge of the attack'. Without this, the suspect may be guilty of murder or rape, or even of war crimes, but not of crimes against humanity.[36]

---

[31] Note that this leaves other mass killings unmentioned. The president of the Philippines, Rodrigo Duterte, has called on his nationals to kill drug users and dealers, expecting up to 100,000 deaths. This might well be genocide in any sociological sense, but does not meet the legal definition, as drug users are not singled out on the basis of their race, religion, and so on. Obviously, then, the risk is that because it does not meet the legal definition, it is not taken seriously: this would manifest a rather dramatic impoverishment of our moral vocabulary. The story is reported at https://www.theguardian.com/world/2016/aug/02/more-than-700-killed-in-less-than-three-months-in-filipino-drugs-crackdown (visited 3 August 2016).

[32] *Application of the Convention on the Prevention and Punishment of the Crime of Genocide (Croatia v. Serbia)*, judgment of 3 February 2015, ICJ Rep. paras. 440–1 and 515, respectively.

[33] *Application of the Convention on the Prevention and Punishment of the Crime of Genocide* (*Bosnia and Herzegovina v. Serbia and Montenegro*), [2007] ICJ Rep. 43.

[34] Case IT-98-33-T, *Prosecutor v. Radislav Krstic*, para. 598.

[35] Rather embarrassingly, the European Court of Human Rights cast some doubts on the qualification of the Armenian genocide as genocide in *Perincek v. Switzerland* (application no. 27510/08), judgment of 17 December 2013. See also the discussion in Chapter 6 above.

[36] Schabas, *Introduction*, at 114–15.

International criminal law and international humanitarian law meet in the category of war crimes, as these essentially consist of violations of international humanitarian law.[37] Indeed, part of the definition of war crimes in the ICC Statute refers to war crimes as comprising grave breaches of the Geneva Conventions of 1949, as well as other serious violations of the laws and customs applicable in international armed conflict as well as non-international armed conflicts. Still, the ICC Statute also lists some 'new' war crimes, including attacks on peacekeeping missions and the use of human shields.[38] In August 2016, moreover, proceedings started in the case against Ahmad Al Mahdi, who is charged with having committed war crimes, in particular the destruction of historical and religious monuments in Mali.

As with crimes and criminal law generally, a decisive factor is criminal intent (*mens rea*). In many cases, act and intent will go together (it is difficult to imagine pillaging a town by accident or through negligence), but in some cases this does not necessarily hold true. For instance, the accidental destruction of property may not qualify as a war crime, but the intentional destruction of such property most probably will. As article 30 ICC Statute explains, a person has intent when he or she 'means to engage in the conduct' or 'means to cause' a consequence (or is aware that the consequence will occur in the normal course of events).

In order to enhance legal certainty, the Assembly of States Parties to the ICC has drawn up lengthy lists breaking down the elements of the various crimes over which the ICC has jurisdiction. Thus, in order to be convicted for the war crime of an unlawful attack on civilians under article 8(2)(b)(i) ICC Statute, the suspect must have directed such an attack, must have done so with civilians as object, and must have done so intentionally, and the attack must have taken place in the context of an international conflict and the suspect must have been aware that the conflict was going on.

Aggression constitutes a special case, in several respects. First, during the original negotiations, the parties could not reach agreement on a definition, and thus agreed to return to the issue after the ICC's entry into force. The absence of agreement was not, actually, all that surprising; as one of the previous chapters indicated, international law has never been able to present an airtight agreed definition of aggression,[39] for the reason that while all aggression involves the use of force, some uses of force may be more acceptable than others. One can define problems away by labelling the 'acceptable' uses as self-defence, or independence struggle, or liberation, but this merely begs the question and shifts the problem.

None the less, at the 2010 review conference in Kampala, the ICC parties reached some form of agreement on what constituted aggression, effectively by defining aggression as the use of force in contravention of the UN Charter and borrowing examples first drawn up by the General Assembly in its 1974 resolution containing a definition of aggression.[40] The crime of aggression, then, consists in the 'planning, preparation, initiation or

---

[37] Marco Sassòli, 'Humanitarian Law and International Criminal Law', in Antonio Cassese (ed.), *The Oxford Companion to International Criminal Justice* (Oxford University Press, 2009), 111–20.

[38] Schabas, *An Introduction*, at 136–7.   [39] Chapter 10 above.   [40] General Assembly Res. 3314 (XXIX).

execution' of an act of aggression by a person in a position to exercise control over the political or military actions of a state. Even so, this agreement (constituting a new article 8*bis* ICC Statute) was subject to ratification by thirty states parties to the ICC,[41] and even then will still need a further decision by the Assembly of States Parties to activate the Court's jurisdiction. Under the Kampala agreement, such a decision can at the earliest be reached after 1 January 2017, as agreed.

A special problem relating to the crime of aggression was, moreover, the safeguarding of the role of the Security Council which, under Chapter VII of the UN Charter, has the authority to determine the existence of threats to the peace, breaches of the peace, or acts of aggression. Hence the prosecutor can only start *proprio motu* investigations into the crime of aggression once it is clear that the Security Council agrees with the identification of the act of aggression, or at least does not disagree.[42]

INDIVIDUAL RESPONSIBILITY

Traditionally, under international law, if something were to go wrong, the state would be held responsible, at least for behaviour attributable to it.[43] Mostly, of course, acts of genocide or violations of humanitarian law would be attributable to the state, yet the institution of state responsibility has often been deemed somewhat ineffective for such crimes. After all, states are abstractions, acting through people of flesh and blood, so what could be more reasonable than to hold individuals responsible for such crimes? Thereby, war crimes tribunals break through the classic horizontal, inter-state structure of international law.

Yet holding individuals responsible is no easy task, as war crimes, crimes against humanity, genocide, and aggression are typically collective acts, engaged in by groups of people. Moreover, such crimes often take place in the context of hierarchically organized operations, with some individuals being in a position to order others to behave in a certain manner. In order to be fair, then, it is essential to figure out which part of the activity was engaged in by which individual.[44] International law addresses this issue in essentially three different ways.

First, as confirmed in article 25 ICC Statute, it aims to identify individual culprits. Individuals can be prosecuted under article 25 for committing crimes, whether individually or jointly, but also for aiding and abetting, or, with genocide, for public and direct incitement. Individuals can also be prosecuted for attempting aborted crimes, unless they acted in such a manner as to prevent the crime from taking place or completely abandoned the criminal effort.

Second, individuals can be prosecuted for having ordered crimes (as confirmed by article 25 ICC Statute) as well as for being in command of groups that have committed

---

[41] This number was reached in June 2016, when Palestine submitted the thirtieth instrument of ratification. For useful discussion, see Jennifer Trahan, 'Implications of the 30th Ratification of the International Criminal Court's Crime of Aggression Amendment by Palestine', at www.opiniojuris.org, 30 June 2016 (visited 4 August 2016).

[42] Article 15*bis* ICC Statute, as amended.   [43] This is discussed in Chapter 7 above.

[44] See generally Larry May, *Sharing Responsibility* (University of Chicago Press, 1992).

crimes. This command responsibility,[45] laid down in article 28 ICC Statute,[46] can go very far, as is illustrated by the case of General Yamashita. After the Second World War, the Japanese general was found guilty by a US military commission[47] (with the verdict upheld by the US Supreme Court)[48] for having commanded troops engaged in war crimes in the Philippines, even though at the material time he was isolated from his troops and could not have exercised much direct influence on their activities.[49] Such a construction is not ideal; it seems a little unfair to punish individuals for behaviour they never took part in and could not realistically have controlled. None the less, it is probably inevitable; otherwise, military leaders could all too easily escape prosecution. After all, high-ranking military leaders and political commanders rarely get their own hands dirty. That said, General Yamashita's case was rather extreme; he was found guilty because a man in his position simply 'must have known' of atrocities; later cases, as well as Additional Protocol I to the Geneva Conventions,[50] suggest that 'should have known' might be a more appropriate standard, which would effectively result, if successful, in a conviction for negligence.[51]

Third, following orders may help to mitigate eventual punishment or even constitute a full defence. Under the ICC Statute, the defence of superior orders will rarely apply to genocide and crimes against humanity,[52] and otherwise only if the order was backed by legal obligation, if the person concerned did not know the order was unlawful, and the order was not 'manifestly unlawful'. The idea of 'unlawfulness' must no doubt be seen broadly, covering not just the domestic law of the state of nationality of the accused but also international law; the ECtHR upheld criminal penalties instituted against former East German border guards for crimes committed in the service of East Germany's government. While their acts may have been lawful under East German law, they were deemed to be unlawful in light of East Germany's obligations under international human rights law.[53]

Perhaps the biggest risk involved in relying on individual responsibility is that by focusing on the individual perpetrators, the state itself manages to escape scrutiny. The ICC Statute aims to undercut this by providing that issues of individual responsibility shall not affect state responsibility,[54] but as a general construction this may be too facile. While the ICTY has meted out punishment on Serbians, Croats, and Bosnians alike

---

[45] See generally Guénaël Mettraux, *The Law of Command Responsibility* (Oxford University Press, 2009).

[46] The ICC discussed article 28 ICC Statute extensively in *Bemba*.

[47] *In re Yamashita*, US Military Commission, 7 December 1945, reported in 13 *Annual Digest*, 255.

[48] *In re Yamashita*, US Supreme Court, 4 February 1946, reported in 13 *Annual Digest*, 269.

[49] Some of the atrocities committed by Japan during the Second World War are described in Iris Chang, *The Rape of Nanking: The Forgotten Holocaust of World War II* (London: Penguin, 1997).

[50] Article 86, para. 2 Additional Protocol I.

[51] As the ICC confirmed in *Bemba*, what is relevant is not so much the formal or legal capacity of the commander, but his or her 'material ability to act'. *Bemba*, para. 199.

[52] Article 33, para. 2 holds that orders to commit genocide and crimes against humanity are 'manifestly unlawful'.

[53] *Streletz, Kessler and Krenz* v. *Germany* (application nos. 34044/96, 35532/97 and 44801/98), ECtHR, judgment of 22 March 2001.

[54] Article 25, para. 4 ICC Statute.

concerning the violence taking place in the former Yugoslavia in the early 1990s, their states have hardly been held responsible.[55]

This may, in a sense, be inevitable, in particular in the light of the changing nature of armed conflict; where force is increasingly used by irregular bands, by troops acting in cahoots with a state but not under its effective control, it becomes so much harder to hold states responsible, precisely because it may be difficult to attribute behaviour to the state. The ICTY tried to overcome this, in *Tadic*, by holding that a loose form of 'overall control' by Serbia over the Bosnian Serbs would suffice to establish attribution, but the ICJ respectfully disagreed. In the 2007 *Bosnia* judgment, it held that the connection was insufficient, and instead clung to the older, and more stringent, attribution test laid down in the 1986 *Nicaragua* case, where it held that control by a state over irregular bands must be 'effective control' not merely 'overall control'.[56]

Critics of war crimes proceedings often point out that such proceedings may end up in 'victor's justice', or even 'show trials', possibly at odds with the presumption of innocence.[57] Historically, such charges have a point; Nuremberg, for instance, was limited to the prosecution of Germans, leaving aside atrocities committed by the USSR, the United Kingdom, or the United States. Moreover, the onset of the Cold War entailed that while the IMT in Nuremberg paid attention to German aggression and war crimes, it paid fairly little attention to the Holocaust.[58] It has also been noted that the ICTY pointedly refused to look into allegations that the 1999 bombing of Belgrade by NATO aircraft might be difficult to reconcile with international humanitarian law,[59] while the ICTR has sometimes been accused of one-sidedness as well.[60] In order to overcome the possible charge of politicization, the ICC Statute states unequivocally that everyone 'shall be presumed innocent until proved guilty': the onus rests on the prosecutor to prove the guilt of the accused, and guilt must be established 'beyond a reasonable doubt'.[61]

TRANSBOUNDARY POLICE COOPERATION

Crime control has always been regarded as one of the essential tasks of the sovereign state, and is still very much a national affair. Yet here, too, international cooperation is not lacking, and much international cooperation is spearheaded by the United States, to the

---

[55] In the 2007 *Bosnia* case, Serbia was eventually held responsible for failure to prevent genocide and failure to cooperate fully with the ICTY, but not for having committed genocide.

[56] See the discussion in Chapter 7 above, with references.

[57] See e.g. Martti Koskenniemi, 'Between Impunity and Show Trials', (2002) 6 *Max Planck Yearbook of United Nations Law*, 1–35. One of the classic monographs is Judith Shklar, *Legalism: Law, Morals, and Political Trials* (Cambridge, MA: Harvard University Press, 1986 [1964]).

[58] Germany was, after the war, a much-needed ally against the USSR, and thus there was little point in highlighting the atrocities committed by the Nazis.

[59] Following in-depth investigations, the prosecutor found no grounds to start proceedings, being satisfied that no deliberate targeting of civilians or unlawful military targets had taken place. See ICTY press release PR/P.I.S./510-e, available at http://www.icty.org/sid/7846 (last visited 12 May 2012).

[60] Rory Carroll, 'Genocide Tribunal "Ignoring Tutsi Crimes"', *Guardian*, 13 January 2005.

[61] Article 66 ICC Statute.

extent that international crime control has been called 'one of the most important – and one of the most overlooked – dimensions of US hegemony in world politics'.[62]

One reason why international crime control operates below the radar is that much of it is done by its immediate practitioners (police offers, prosecutors), rather than through high-level political initiatives. A telling example is that Interpol started its existence, in the 1920s,[63] as a gathering of police officers, and that its member states still predominantly send police officers as delegates to meetings of Interpol's plenary body, its General Assembly.[64]

Another reason why international crime control is so often overlooked is that it is highly dispersed, or decentralized. There are different treaties in place dealing with different topics, ranging from regimes on piracy and privateering and slavery and slave trade to cooperation to combat drugs trafficking or the trade in endangered species, or in small weapons. Some of the more recent emanations engage with money laundering and bribery, resulting sometimes in the outlawing of activities that used to be considered as more or less regular business practices.[65]

This recharacterization of activities ('reframing') is not uncommon; activities that at some point were regarded as relatively benign come to be criminalized, usually under auspices of a leading state that sees its market leadership threatened. The drugs trade poses a good example; during the nineteenth century, when the United Kingdom was the leading supplier of opium, it even engaged in a war (the Opium War) in order to get China to open its markets. As one observer explains, 'the opium trade was treated as an economic issue – an important element in overcoming Britain's trade deficit with China'.[66] Now that the global north does not produce drugs but consumes them, the trade in drugs is treated as a matter of national security, justifying even a high-profile and expensive 'war on drugs'.

The drugs trade provides a good example of how international crime control can be organized. The central legal instrument is the 1988 UN Convention against Illicit Traffic in Narcotic Drugs and Psychotropic Substances. The convention obliges the parties to criminalize a vast range of activities related to drugs, ranging from production and manufacture to sale, importation, and exportation, including the management and finan-cing of these activities. The convention also obliges its parties to attach sanctions, including imprisonment and fines. If the parties want to, they may also provide for treatment or rehabilitation of drug users, but these are optional; the criminal sanctions, on the other hand, are compulsory.[67]

---

[62] Peter Andreas and Ethan Nadelmann, *Policing the Globe: Criminalization and Crime Control in International Relations* (Oxford University Press, 2006), at 10.

[63] A first meeting took place in 1914, but not much happened until the early 1920s.

[64] For a useful study of Interpol as an international organization see Rutsel Martha, *The Legal Foundations of Interpol* (Oxford: Hart, 2010).

[65] An excellent overview is Neil Boister, *An Introduction to Transnational Criminal Law* (Oxford University Press, 2012).

[66] Janice E. Thomson, 'Explaining the Regulation of Transnational Practices: A State-Building Approach', in James N. Rosenau and Ernst-Otto Czempiel (eds.), *Governance without Government: Order and Change in World Politics* (Cambridge University Press, 1992), 195–218, at 196.

[67] Article 3 of the convention.

The parties also agree to treat the offences listed in the convention as extraditable offences (extradition will be discussed in more detail below),[68] and must provide 'the widest measure of mutual legal assistance in investigations, prosecutions and judicial proceedings' for purposes which include taking evidence, executing searches and seizures, examining sites, and providing information.[69] Assistance may be refused on grounds of security or *ordre public*, but the refusal must be justified, and does not apply to bank secrecy.

The convention also paves the way for further cooperation, for instance with respect to exchanging information about suspects, the secondment of liaison officers or even the establishment of joint teams.[70] While this requires further agreement and should be compatible with the domestic law of the states concerned, it is none the less clear that the convention provides law enforcement officers with an extensive set of instruments to combat the trafficking in drugs. As at summer 2016, the convention has 189 parties.

A convention of a more general nature is the 2000 UN Convention against Transnational Organized Crime, concluded (symbolically perhaps) in Palermo. This convention, which entered into force in 2003, is complemented by three protocols, one on trafficking in persons, especially women and children, one on trafficking of migrants, and a third protocol, which entered into force in 2005, addressing the illicit manufacture and trafficking of firearms.[71] Instead of combating isolated crimes, this convention is aimed at combating the frameworks in which serious crime can take place, in particular by criminalizing money laundering and corruption. Like the 1988 Drugs Convention, on which it was modelled, the Palermo Convention provides for extradition and mutual legal assistance. Both conventions were forcefully sponsored by the United States. As one of the US legal advisers explained to Congress, the Palermo Convention obliges other states 'that have been slower to react legislatively to the threat of transnational organized crime to adopt new criminal laws in harmony with ours'.[72]

EXTRADITION

One of the tools at the disposal of those engaged in international crime control is extradition – that is, the transfer of an individual from one state to a state that aims to place the accused on trial. Extradition is typically a formalized process, involving either the diplomatic services of the states concerned or their juridical authorities, and based on an agreement. Most extradition treaties are still bilateral in nature,[73] although in Europe the multilateral European Convention on Extradition, concluded in 1957, has been of some importance. Extradition is strongly influenced by considerations of reciprocity; you accede to my requests, and I will accede to yours. That said, in the related setting of a treaty on mutual legal assistance, the ICJ has held that each request should be assessed on its own

[68] Article 6 of the convention.   [69] Article 7 of the convention.   [70] Article 9 of the convention.
[71] A more comprehensive Arms Trade Treaty was concluded in 2013 and entered into force in 2014. It aims to regulate the international trade in weapons, rather than prohibit it.
[72] As quoted in Andreas and Nadelmann, *Policing the Globe*, at 173.
[73] For an example, see the extradition treaty between Kenya and Rwanda, reproduced in Jan Klabbers (ed.), *International Law Documents* (Cambridge University Press, 2016).

terms. There may be an overarching element of reciprocity in the sense that if state A always complies and state B never does so, the regime will quickly be considered unbalanced, but such treaties cannot be applied on a mechanistic basis of reciprocity.[74]

Even though they are often bilateral in form, many extradition treaties contain similar provisions. Thus most are based on the so-called principle of double criminality; individuals will only be extradited for offences that are prohibited in both states. If behaviour is illegal in A but legal in B, then extradition from B to A is unlikely. Often such treaties also contain the principle of speciality; the request for extradition and the subsequent prosecution need to concern the same allegations. Otherwise, one might request extradition under false pretences – ask for extradition for, say, rape, and subsequently prosecute for treason or *lèse-majesté*. For much the same reason, it is often felt that the extradition request should provide at least some prima facie indication of the suspect's guilt.

Many extradition treaties provide for two important, related exceptions; individuals should not be extradited for political activities ('the political offence exception') or military offences. This makes it important to figure out what exactly is meant by political offence, and needless to say, opinions here differ. The standard idea is to exclude action inspired by political considerations, but obviously this creates problems, as some of the worst crimes are inspired precisely by such motives. For this reason, the Genocide Convention, for instance, specifies in article VII that genocide (which is almost by definition politically inspired) is not to be considered as a political crime for the purposes of extradition, and many recent treaties provide the same with respect to acts of terrorism, despite the political motivations behind most terrorist acts. Likewise, it is not entirely clear what is meant by military offences; while this is undoubtedly meant to cover such things as desertion, it would be surprising if war crimes were covered. Incidentally, there is a curious irony at work here, in that the first modern extradition treaties, concluded in the eighteenth century, had as their main purpose precisely extradition for political and military offences, broadly conceived. It was only later that extradition would come to cover mostly common crimes.[75]

A recent innovation, at least in the practice of European states, is also to provide for an exception in cases where the death penalty may await. Many European states have abolished the death penalty; consequently, they are not keen to extradite to states where the death penalty is a real possibility, and reserve the right to refuse extradition unless assured by the requesting state that the death penalty will not be imposed.[76] More generally, states may also reserve the right not to extradite for humanitarian reasons, for instance if the individual concerned is seriously ill or of great age.

---

[74] *Certain Questions of Mutual Assistance in Criminal Matters (Djibouti v. France)*, [2008] ICJ Rep. 177, para. 119.

[75] See generally the excellent monograph by I. A. Shearer, *Extradition in International Law* (Manchester University Press, 1970).

[76] A typical provision is article 7, para. 1, of the 1980 United States–Netherlands Extradition Treaty: 'When the offense for which extradition is requested is punishable by death under the laws of the Requesting State and the laws of the Requested State do not permit such punishment for that offense, extradition may be refused unless the Requesting State furnishes such assurances as the Requested State considers sufficient that the death penalty shall not be imposed, or, if imposed, shall not be executed.'

States are not considered to be under any obligation to extradite in the absence of an extradition treaty, and may often exclude the extradition of their nationals. While US and UK courts have historically worked on the assumption that if their nationals do something wrong abroad, they may as well face the consequences, many civil law jurisdictions have shielded their nationals from extradition.[77]

In some situations, in particular relating to terrorist acts, treaties have come to embody the principle *aut dedere, aut judicare*: either extradite or prosecute. The purpose of such a clause is to make sure that terrorists cannot seek refuge in states with which no extradition treaty exists; terrorism is considered so serious that non-extradition is not an option, unless the state is willing to prosecute the suspect or suspects itself.[78]

DEPORTATION AND ABDUCTION

It should go without saying (but probably needs to be said anyway) that there are no proper alternatives to extradition. States can sometimes take the easy way out and deport foreigners who may or may not be suspected of having committed crimes, but, clearly, deportation is not a carefully regulated process, and lacks the sort of due process guarantees that are legitimately associated with liberal criminal prosecution and extradition.[79]

Sometimes states also resort to abduction, thereby circumventing the extradition process entirely. They do so if no extradition treaty is in place, and sometimes even when there is such a treaty but the formal process is deemed too cumbersome. A somewhat moot example of the former is the abduction of Adolf Eichmann by Israeli forces from Argentina, in May 1960, two days after an Israeli–Argentine extradition agreement had been signed (but prior to its entry into force). Eichmann had been an officer in Nazi Germany, charged with the task of organizing the transport of Jews to the concentration and extermination camps, and zealously performed his job. At the end of the Second World War he fled to Argentina on false papers, where he was found by Mossad operatives. They abducted him and brought him to Jerusalem, where he stood trial on charges of crimes against humanity and war crimes, among others.[80] In the end he was sentenced to death, and executed in 1962. Argentina complained to the Security Council about the kidnapping, and indeed the Council slapped Israel on the wrist, stating that abduction affects the sovereignty of states and may, on repetition, endanger international peace and security. However, it did not order Israel to return Eichmann; instead, it honoured Israel's right to prosecute him, while compensating Argentina.[81]

The Eichmann abduction provoked only mild protest. Even Argentina's protest was rather half-hearted, presumably because Eichmann had undoubtedly been involved in the greatest massacre of the twentieth century; his plight aroused little sympathy, precisely

---

[77] See Shearer, *Extradition*, for a historical analysis.   [78] See also Chapter 10 above.

[79] Individuals may usually waive their right to extradition proceedings, but this needs to be distinguished from deportation.

[80] For a famous and fascinating discussion, see Hannah Arendt, *Eichmann in Jerusalem: A Report on the Banality of Evil* (London: Penguin, 1963).

[81] Security Council Res. 138 (1960).

because, as Arendt so famously put it, his crimes were beyond description. A later case managed to spark far more protest; this was the case of Dr Alvarez-Machaín, a Mexican medical doctor used by Mexican drugs gangs to treat captured agents of the US Drugs Enforcement Agency. The agents would be tortured, Dr Alvarez-Machaín would nurse their wounds and patch them up for some additional torture. Reportedly, he was abducted from his home in Guadalajara, Mexico, by bounty hunters, and flown to El Paso, Texas, where he was formally arrested. On being brought to trial, he claimed that since the abduction had been illegal, the whole process would therefore be tainted; the US courts, so he claimed, could not exercise jurisdiction on the basis of an illegal abduction. Unfortunately for him, the US Supreme Court eventually decided differently, and held in no uncertain terms that jurisdiction was not affected by the method of apprehension.[82]

The *Alvarez-Machaín* case caused rather more outrage than the *Eichmann* case, partly no doubt because however gross the doctor's acts, they paled in comparison with Eichmann's, but partly no doubt also because there was a regular extradition treaty in place between the United States and Mexico. By accepting an abducted suspect, the US Supreme Court effectively approved of an illegal act, for there can be no good reason to circumvent the proper procedure once this is in place. Sadly, perhaps, the *Alvarez-Machaín* case is by no means an isolated incident; it seems that quite a few states resort to abduction without, understandably, wishing to confirm this in public.

FINAL REMARKS

What is commonly referred to as international criminal law finds itself in an intellectually difficult position. Prosecuting individuals for political crimes is generally considered just, but has little further justification beyond meting out punishment to those who have committed atrocities. While criminal trials may have expressive value, strengthening community norms about proper behaviour, historians are sceptical about the claim of international criminal law to contribute to the writing of proper history, and political criminals are unlikely to be deterred by punishment. After all, if political crime is committed for political reasons (however perverse), punishment may create martyrs rather than models. Moreover, international criminal law must work with tools taken from regular criminal law, whose subjects act not out of political motives but out of greed, lust, envy, or hatred – and those tools do not appear all that suitable for dealing with political crime, or the heavily institutionalized evil of totalitarian bureaucracies.[83]

Still, international criminal law has become enormously popular, both among international lawyers (for whom it may represent the completion of international law) and among the public at large; international criminal law promises to bring an end to impunity. It stands to reason to hold that people should not commit genocide or other atrocities, and

---

[82] *United States* v. *Alvarez-Machaín*, 504 US 655, 15 June 1992. A different conclusion was reached (in circumstances similar enough) in *R* v. *Horseferry Road Magistrates Court, ex parte Bennett*, decision of the UK House of Lords, 24 June 1993, reproduced in 95 *International Law Reports*, 380.

[83] The latter is what Arendt referred to as the banality of evil; evil can be the result not just of evil intentions, but also of routine bureaucratic procedure. Arendt, *Eichmann in Jerusalem*.

should not be allowed to get away with committing them. What remains to be seen is whether international criminal tribunals are always the proper answer; while they may result in punishing individuals, often the states concerned manage to escape any form of responsibility, and there is room for the argument that whatever the merits of punishment, it may not always be conducive to reconciliation. And where people have to continue to live together on the same territory, reconciliation is not something to ignore.

FURTHER READING

Peter Andreas and Ethan Nadelmann, *Policing the Globe: Criminalization and Crime Control in International Relations* (Oxford University Press, 2006)

Hannah Arendt, *Eichmann in Jerusalem: A Report on the Banality of Evil* (London: Penguin, 1963)

Neil Boister, *An Introduction to Transnational Criminal Law* (Oxford University Press, 2012)

Lawrence Douglas, *The Memory of Judgment: Making Law and History in the Trials of the Holocaust* (New Haven, CT: Yale University Press, 2001)

Mark A. Drumbl, *Atrocity, Punishment, and International Law* (Cambridge University Press, 2007)

Kevin Jon Heller, *The Nuremberg Military Tribunals and the Origins of International Criminal Law* (Oxford University Press, 2011)

B. V. A. Röling and Antonio Cassese, *The Tokyo Tribunal and Beyond* (Cambridge: Polity Press, 1993)

Judith Shklar, *Legalism: Law, Morals, and Political Trials* (Cambridge, MA: Harvard University Press, 1986 [1964])

13

The Seas, the Air, and Outer Space

INTRODUCTION

With almost three-quarters of the globe covered by water, regulation of the seas has always been of crucial importance to the international community. Some of this importance stems from security concerns, but much of it resides in the economic relevance of the seas. This relevance, in turn, stems from two uses to which the seas can be put. They are, first, media of communication, allowing the transport of goods from point X to point Y, and for a long time provided the most obvious means available. Second, the seas and their subsoil are rich in resources, from fish stocks via oil and natural gas reserves to manganese nodules. What holds for the seas also holds, with only minor differences, for the air and outer space. These, too, are vital channels of communication, be it by means of aircraft or by means of radio waves, and, to some extent, have resources to offer as well. The latter applies in particular to the moon and other celestial bodies.

For Grotius, writing his classic *Mare Liberum* more than four centuries ago, there could be no doubt that the seas should be free. For one thing, this was clearly God's wish; otherwise He would have made sure that the same animals and spices would exist every-where, and maritime transport would not be necessary, so Grotius suggested. More prag-matically, Grotius also held that the seas were incapable of being possessed; the oceans are too vast to be controllable by a single power, and since legal title has to start with actual possession, it followed that ownership of the seas was impossible.[1]

Ever since, the law of the sea, mainly dealing with what states are allowed to do, has been an ever-changing compromise between freedom, on the one hand, and the exercise of jurisdiction by coastal states, on the other. This was already visible in Grotius' own work. In a reply to a contemporary critic, he conceded that even though the seas could not be possessed, coastal states might exercise jurisdiction over them.[2] And in his magnum opus, published a decade and a half later, he had come round to the idea that states owned the

---

[1] Hugo Grotius, *The Free Sea*, trans. R. Hakluyt (Indianapolis, IN: Liberty Fund, 2004 [1609]).
[2] Both the critique by William Welwod and Grotius' reply are reproduced in Grotius, *Free Sea*. The concession regarding jurisdiction is most explicitly spelled out at 128–30.

territorial seas off their coasts, his earlier misgivings notwithstanding.[3] Presently, most of the seas are still free, in that states cannot claim ownership of most parts of the sea. Yet states have managed to appropriate some zones over which they exercise exclusive, or functional, jurisdiction. This chapter will discuss these maritime zones and their regimes, as well as delimitation between them, before moving on to a brief discussion of air and space law.

OUTLINE OF THE MARITIME REGIME

The general law of the sea used to be governed, and to some extent is still governed, by customary international law. For all practical purposes, though, much of it can be found in a large treaty concluded in 1982, the UN Convention on the Law of the Sea (UNCLOS), the product of almost a decade of intense negotiations. This convention entered into force, belatedly and with the dubious distinction of effectively having been amended even before entry into force, in 1994. The main reason why negotiations lasted so long, and why the original version was no longer deemed acceptable, probably resides in the fact that the convention aims to introduce an element of distributive justice into international law by using the possible proceeds of deep seabed mining for the greater good of mankind. It thus manifests a more or less 'leftist' approach to global resources, and it is possibly no coincidence that the United States, under the Republican president Reagan, was instrumental in blocking the convention.

In line with customary international law, the convention divides the seas into a number of maritime zones. Inside a state's territory, naturally, are its internal waters: its rivers, lakes, and canals. These are simply considered as part of the national territory, although delimitation issues may arise with boundary rivers or boundary lakes. Here, the middle of the navigable channel (the so-called *thalweg*) often marks the boundary between adjacent states,[4] but states are free to agree on a different regime, including full sovereignty for one of them in conjunction with specific rights for the other.[5]

Closest to the coastline, and considered an integral part of a state's territory, is the aptly named territorial sea. This may (but need not) be accompanied by a contiguous zone, an exclusive fisheries zone or, most commonly, an exclusive economic zone (EEZ). While the territorial sea is considered part of the state and need not be claimed, these other zones must be claimed. States are entitled to them, but may also waive their rights. Finally, beyond the EEZ, there are the high seas, and these cannot be claimed. They are deemed to be *res communis* – common property.

Also of interest are the soil and subsoil underneath the seas. Closest to the coast is the continental shelf but this, geographically, is a tricky concept. Sometimes the continental shelf hardly exists (this happens where the seabed 'dives' steeply), whereas in other cases

---

[3] Hugo Grotius, *On the Law of War and Peace*, trans. A. C. Campbell (London, 1814 [1625]), book II, Ch. 3.
[4] See e.g. Ian Brownlie, *Principles of Public International Law*, 7th edn (Oxford University Press, 2008), at 160.
[5] This is the situation of the San Juan River between Costa Rica and Nicaragua, as confirmed by the ICJ in *Dispute Regarding Navigational and Related Rights (Costa Rica v. Nicaragua)*, [2009] ICJ Rep. 213.

the geographical continental shelf can extend for hundreds of miles[6] into the sea. Beyond the continental shelf lie the deep seabed and the ocean floor.

UNCLOS was not the first attempt to codify the law of the sea. In particular, the 1950s saw the conclusion of a number of separate multilateral conventions on the law of the sea, concluded in Geneva. While these functioned reasonably well, they quickly became outdated on the development of technology enabling, for instance, large-scale fisheries, and, dealing as they did with separate aspects of the law of the sea, these treaties did not form a coherent whole. Hence the impetus arose to come to a comprehensive convention, and negotiations started in 1973.

These negotiations were as much about experimenting with negotiating techniques as they were about codifying international law. It turned out that many states were open to back-scratching deals: you do me a favour on topic X, in return for which I will do you a favour on topic Y or Z. While this is conducive to productive negotiations, it also ends up bringing the existing law into question, and it is fair to say that there is some lack of clarity at present about which parts of UNCLOS represent customary international law (and therewith are also binding upon non-members) and which do not. While the problem may seem largely academic in the light of the circumstance that 167 states and the EU[7] are parties to the convention, there is a strong practical consideration here; the United States is not a party. And since the United States is not only a naval superpower but also has a lengthy coastline and an extensive continental shelf, its non-participation is of considerable relevance.

Many of the ratifications of UNCLOS, and in particular those of a large number of Western states and Japan, date from the second half of the 1990s. This owes much to Western dissatisfaction with the earlier provisions on the deep seabed. When the United States had led the opposition thereto, a compromise was reached in the form of an additional treaty, concluded in 1994, to replace the earlier Part XI of UNCLOS, and it was this 'amendment' which spurred a number of states to proceed with ratification.[8] This separate treaty has 149 parties as at summer 2016.

UNCLOS, it is fair to say, has a strong economic focus: many of its provisions regulate the exercise of jurisdiction of states for purposes of exploration and exploitation of natural resources, although there is also a strong section on marine environmental protection.[9] Still, additional conventions have been required to regulate activities that cannot easily be subsumed under headings of exploration or exploitation; one example is the 2001 UNESCO

---

[6] In the law of the sea, the term 'miles' refers to 'nautical miles'.

[7] The EU has some powers over maritime issues which render its membership pertinent, as the EU powers preempt its member states from acting. For more detail see Jan Klabbers, *The EU in International Law* (Paris: Pédone, 2012).

[8] Its official name is Agreement Relating to the Implementation of Part XI of the Convention of 10 December 1982.

[9] Part XII UNCLOS. Note that the first article of part XII, article 192, listing a general obligation to protect the marine environment, is immediately followed (article 193) by a reminder that states have a sovereign right to exploit their natural resources. In June 2015, the UN General Assembly adopted a resolution (A/RES/69/292) calling for the conclusion of a convention on the conservation and sustainable use of marine biodiversity beyond national jurisdiction – the process dates back to 2006.

Convention on the Protection of Underwater Cultural Heritage.[10] Likewise, the rules regulating armed conflict at sea are not to be found in UNCLOS, but largely in the law of armed conflict, discussed in Chapter 11 above. And the convention having been concluded in the 1980s, it seems that in some respects technological developments have caught up with the regime, creating new areas of dispute or at least of interpretation. One of these is the status of mobile oil drilling units, used for deepwater and ultra-deepwater drilling, and not well known in the 1980s. It remains unclear whether these units (note also the neutral description) are to be considered as vessels or more as offshore installations and, concomitantly, how they affect the traditional division of jurisdiction: if vessels, they generally fall within the jurisdiction of the flag state; if platforms, that of the coastal state. Some of these issues came to the surface when in 2010 British Petroleum's *Deepwater Horizon* rig exploded and created huge damage in the Gulf of Mexico.[11]

Institutionally, many relevant activities with respect to shipping take place in the IMO, in existence since 1948 (originally named IMCO) and headquartered in London. This international organization has as its main task the security and safety of shipping and the prevention of marine pollution, and at the time of writing has 171 member states and three associate members (the Faroes, Hong Kong, and Macau – all of them part of another state but with a certain degree of autonomy). The IMO has sponsored the conclusion of some important conventions, the best known of which is the 1974 Convention for the Safety of Life at Sea (SOLAS). This contains fire safety regulations, as well as regulations concerning lifeboats and lifejackets, and addresses in particular the safety of transport of dangerous products at sea. Also of great import is the International Convention for the Prevention of Pollution from Ships (MARPOL) of 1973, including two later protocols.[12]

Disputes concerning the law of the sea have been one of the staples of the ICJ's work since 1945, with a prominent place in particular for cases involving maritime delimitation, as will be seen below. The entry into force of UNCLOS marked the creation of a separate court – the International Tribunal for the Law of the Sea, located in Hamburg. ITLOS has no fewer than twenty-one judges, appointed for renewable periods of nine years, and it allows for the appointment of ad hoc judges. A separate chamber of eleven judges can dedicate itself to issues relating to deep seabed mining, while other chambers exist in order to address specific issues, such as fisheries disputes or delimitation disputes. There is even a chamber of summary procedure, which can be activated if the parties to a dispute so request. Since the judges, except for the Tribunal's president, work part-time, much of the intermediate work (e.g. fixing time limits) is done by the president. The president is elected by his (or, possibly, her) colleagues. In addition to its contentious jurisdiction, ITLOS can

---

[10] This gives considerable force to two general provisions in UNCLOS, articles 149 and 303. The leading study is Sarah Dromgoole, *Underwater Cultural Heritage and International Law* (Cambridge University Press, 2013).

[11] For an excellent discussion, see James E. Hickey, Jr, 'Law-Making and the Law of the Sea: The BP *Deepwater Horizon* Oil Spill in the Gulf of Mexico', in Rain Liivoja and Jarna Petman (eds.), *International Law-Making* (Abingdon: Routledge, 2013), 270–82.

[12] See also Chapter 14.

also render advisory opinions, both through its seabed disputes chamber[13] or in plenary, despite the fact that the latter is not specifically mentioned in UNCLOS.[14]

INTERNAL WATERS

Waters on the landward side of the baseline are usually referred to as internal waters, and may include rivers, lakes, canals, bays, and, importantly, ports. Over its internal waters, the territorial state exercises jurisdiction, and this includes, as a matter of principle, criminal jurisdiction. None the less, states usually tend to exercise their jurisdiction only when their interests are at stake; for minor offences taking place on board a vessel lying in port or sailing on a river, they readily defer to the jurisdiction of the flag state. Should a ship have been seized on allegations of breaching the coastal state's EEZ laws, the ship and its crew must be promptly released on posting a reasonable bond or security.[15]

Importantly, ships have no right to enter another state's ports or waters in the absence of a treaty provision to that effect, and while it is generally conceded that there is a presumption that ports and waterways are open to foreign merchant ships, this presumption has not crystallized into a customary right. The one exception relates to ships in distress, but even this is limited to situations where human life is at risk – it is not generally accepted, for instance, that this also extends to saving a ship's cargo.

A different regime relates to internationalized waterways, typically canals that have been dug to facilitate shipping between different seas, such as the Suez Canal and the Panama Canal. These are open, depending on the precise terms of the treaty by which the regime was created, to ships of all nations. Thus article 1 of the Suez Canal treaty provides that the canal 'shall always be free and open, in time of war as in time of peace, to every vessel of commerce or of war, without distinction of flag'.[16]

TERRITORIAL SEA AND CONTIGUOUS ZONE

When Grotius wrote his *Mare Liberum*, the main economic interest in the seas resided in navigation and fishing. This is no longer the case. The sea and its subsoil are rich in resources, ranging from oil and natural gas to all sorts of mineral products that can be found in the deep seabed. In addition, there is a security consideration; states have found out that they may be vulnerable to attacks from the sea, the result being that they may be

---

[13] Article 191 UNCLOS.

[14] In its *Sub-Regional Fisheries Commission* opinion, ITLOS based its advisory jurisdiction on article 21 of its Statute (itself part of UNCLOS), which enables it to hear requests submitted on the basis of other agreements closely connected to UNCLOS. In this case, it held that the West African fisheries treaty at issue, the Convention on the Determination of the Minimal Conditions for Access and Exploitation of Marine Resources within the Maritime Areas under Jurisdiction of the Member States of the Sub-Regional Fisheries Convention, was such a treaty. ITLOS, Case No. 21, *Request for an Advisory Opinion Submitted by the Sub-Regional Fisheries Commission (SRFC)*, advisory opinion, 2 April 2015, esp. paras. 62–3.

[15] Article 73 UNCLOS; this will be further addressed below.

[16] This is the Constantinople Convention Respecting the Free Navigation of the Suez Maritime Canal, concluded in 1888 between the great European powers of the late nineteenth century.

highly interested in being able to patrol their coasts and control everything that goes on there. Of more recent origin are additional threats, real or perceived; the seas can be (and have been) polluted, with sometimes dire consequences for the coastal state, and all kinds of illicit trafficking goes on at sea, from drugs to migrants.

Traditionally, the outer limit of the territorial sea was set at three miles, to be measured from the so-called 'baseline'. This baseline is the low-water line along the coast, as it is officially depicted in accepted charts. The three-mile rule had several possible explanations. Some suggested that this was the theoretical distance of the horizon as seen from the beach, while for others it marked the range of a cannon when shot from the beach.[17] Either way, the current rule is more extensive; states may proclaim a maximum width of twelve miles, but are allowed to settle for less. Still, most coastal states have opted for the twelve-mile zone.[18] States typically adopt national legislation to this effect,[19] specifying the width by means of geographical coordinates, and notify the UN, which has a Division for Ocean Affairs and the Law of the Sea. The territorial sea itself does not need to be claimed, but the UN should be informed about the claimed or delimited width.

While states enjoy exclusive jurisdiction over their territorial waters (as well as the seabed, subsoil and superjacent air space), there is one important exception; states have to allow the 'innocent passage' of ships through their territorial waters, and this innocent passage is defined as all passage which 'is not prejudicial to the peace, good order or security' of the coastal state. Certain activities are automatically deemed to be non-innocent; these include threats or use of force (obviously), but also exercises with weapons, unlawful loading or unloading of commodities, currencies, or persons, and fishing.[20] 'Passage', to be sure, is not empty of content either: a permanent or semi-permanent fixture is not exercising 'passage'. Submarines must navigate on the surface and show their flags,[21] while nuclear-powered ships or ships with nuclear cargo must observe special precautionary measures.[22] In principle, the coastal state must not exercise either criminal or civil jurisdiction over ships availing themselves of the right of innocent passage.[23]

Sometimes, due to geographical configurations, territorial waters also function as international straits; the Strait of Gibraltar is a prominent example, as is the Strait of Hormuz – a vital waterway for the transport of oil from the Middle East. In such a case, ships and aircraft enjoy a right of 'transit passage'.[24] This is similar to the right of innocent passage, but with the important caveat that no specific conditions for 'innocence' are attached. Thus, one might say that the rights of the coastal state are diminished in comparison with the regular regime relating to the territorial sea, although ships and aircraft exercising transit passage are under an obligation to refrain from the threat or use of force. Transit passage may not be suspended by the coastal state except, perhaps, in self-defence.[25]

---

[17] J. E. S. Fawcett, *The Law of Nations* (New York: Basic Books, 1968), at 71.

[18] Except in situations of overlapping claims, as is the case, e.g., between Greece and Turkey.

[19] See e.g. the Netherlands Territorial Sea (Demarcation) Act of 9 January 1985, available at www.un.org/Depts/los/LEGISLATIONANDTREATIES/PDFFILES/NLD_1985_DemarcationAct.pdf (visited 4 January 2012).

[20] Article 19 UNCLOS.　　[21] Article 20 UNCLOS.　　[22] Article 23 UNCLOS.　　[23] Articles 27–8 UNCLOS.

[24] Articles 37–44 UNCLOS.

[25] R. R. Churchill and A. V. Lowe, *The Law of the Sea*, 3rd edn (Manchester University Press, 1999), at 107.

States would sometimes get worried about ships dedicated to smuggling lying just outside their territorial waters and enact so-called 'hovering laws', especially during the eighteenth century. As a result, a custom arose to the effect that states could exercise some control over shipping outside their territorial waters properly speaking, and nowadays it is generally accepted that states can exercise powers in a so-called 'contiguous zone' for the enforcement of customs, fiscal, migration, and sanitary laws. Under article 33 UNCLOS, the contiguous zone may not extend more than twenty-four miles off the coast. Hence, if a state's territorial sea measures twelve miles, it can proclaim an additional twelve miles as contiguous zone. Unlike the territorial sea, the contiguous zone must be claimed; reportedly, by 2016, some ninety states had done so, with most of them claiming an outer limit of twenty-four nautical miles.[26]

EXCLUSIVE ECONOMIC ZONE (EEZ)

The EEZ is a relatively novel phenomenon, and comprises a band of water up to 200 miles wide off the baseline. As the name suggests, states may exercise economic rights here; the concept arose predominantly to safeguard local fishing industries against fishing by distant-water Western states, and the first claims to this effect were made by African states in the early 1970s,[27] while Latin American states made similar claims relating to what was called the 'patrimonial sea'. By the late 1970s, Western states had started to claim exclusive fisheries zones, and these concepts would merge during the course of the negotiations leading to UNCLOS. By the 1980s the EEZ had become part of customary international law, as confirmed by the ICJ.[28] Most coastal states have claimed an EEZ, although some (such as Algeria and Malta) are still content with a fisheries zone,[29] while the United Kingdom only adopted EEZ legislation in 2014. Earlier, it felt that the EFZ and continental shelf regimes together offered sufficient protection to its interests. In some cases of states bordering semi-enclosed seas, the claims have been smaller; claiming the full 200 miles may simply not be possible.[30]

In the EEZ the coastal state has sovereign rights related to the natural resources present there, whether living or not. This applies to the seabed and subsoil as well as to the superjacent waters and to possible ancillary economic activities, such as the production of energy from water, currents or wind. Moreover, the coastal state has jurisdiction relating to

---

[26] The UN's Division for Ocean Affairs and the Law of the Sea produces a very useful chart, summarizing the maritime claims of all states, including non-parties to UNCLOS. Available at http://www.un.org/Depts/los/LEGISLATIONANDTREATIES/PDFFILES/table_summary_of_claims.pdf (visited 19 August 2016).

[27] This is a recurring theme: ITLOS' *Sub-Regional Fisheries Commission* opinion of April 2015 was also inspired by predominantly Western over-fishing of African waters. ITLOS held that flag states fishing in others' EEZs are none the less obliged to ensure that their nationals and vessels flying their flag are not engaged in illegal, unreported and unregulated fisheries (para. 124), and while the acts of fishing vessels cannot normally be attributed to flag states, those flag states may incur responsibility for failing to exercise due diligence (para. 129).

[28] *Continental Shelf (Libya/Malta)*, [1985] ICJ Rep. 13, para. 34.

[29] Denmark and Spain are content with a fisheries zone around parts of their territory: Spain in the Mediterranean, and Denmark around Greenland and the Faroes.

[30] Donald Rothwell and Tim Stephens, *The International Law of the Sea*, 2nd edn (Oxford: Hart, 2016), at 88–89.

the establishment and use of artificial islands and installations (think of oil drilling platforms in particular), as well as marine scientific research and the protection and preservation of the marine environment.[31] Other states enjoy the traditional freedoms of the high seas, with one major exception; there is no freedom of fisheries in the EEZ. Still, those other states still enjoy freedom of navigation and overflight and of laying submarine cables and pipelines.

Since the EEZ usurped part of the high seas, states entirely surrounded by land (such as Switzerland, Chad, or Ethiopia since the split with Eritrea) felt that the creation of EEZs has worked to their disadvantage; these landlocked states have a smaller share of the high seas available for fishing. Consequently, a complicated compromise was reached in UNCLOS. The coastal state is to determine the total amount of fish that may be caught in its EEZ, in the light of conservation and other concerns. This 'total allowable catch' is then divided between the coastal state, determining its own capacity to harvest the natural resources, and other states, on the basis of bilateral or regional agreements. Here landlocked states have the right to participate on an equitable basis. The same right appertains to so-called 'geographically disadvantaged states' – that is, states that have a small coastline, are bordering semi-enclosed seas, or are otherwise dependent on the exploitation of someone else's resources. Where 'landlocked' is easy to verify, 'geographically disadvantaged' is a more problematic category, dependent on political decision-making. And to make things more complicated still, neither of these two groups has exploitation rights in the EEZ of a coastal state whose economy is 'overwhelmingly dependent' on its own EEZ.[32] Be that as it may, the system does not seem to work very well, or at all; landlocked states typically have no fishing fleet, and the cost of building up a fleet in order to partake of the possible surplus of other states probably far outweighs any benefits.[33] Moreover, as Rothwell and Stephens note, the system is judicially unenforceable: coastal state decisions determining the total allowable catch and the allocation of surpluses form exceptions to the compulsory dispute settlement system of UNCLOS.[34]

CONTINENTAL SHELF

The continental shelf came to prominence, as discussed above,[35] during the 1940s, when states discovered oil and natural gas deposits and started to develop the technology to explore and exploit these. Following US President Harry Truman's proclamation, other states too claimed a continental shelf, and the concept rapidly crystallized into customary international law. It is now well settled that the continental shelf is to be considered as an extension of the state's territory where states may exercise sovereign rights.

Except for situations of overlapping claims, the continental shelf extends at least 200 miles from the coast, and like the EEZ, it too covers the seabed and subsoil (but not the superjacent waters). Consequently, states may have two independent bases for rights relating to exploration and exploitation of natural resources, and this, one might say, constitutes unnecessary duplication. There are at least two important differences, though.

[31] Article 56 UNCLOS.   [32] Articles 69–71 UNCLOS.   [33] Churchill and Lowe, *Law of the Sea*, 437–40.
[34] Rothwell and Stephens, *International Law of the Sea*, at 92.   [35] Chapter 2 above.

First, whereas the EEZ must be claimed, the continental shelf is generally accepted to belong to coastal states as prolongation of their territory: there is no need to claim the continental shelf. Second, where geologically the shelf extends further than 200 miles (which is not always the case: some states' shelves have a sudden and steep decline long before that point is reached), states may claim a shelf up to 350 miles, albeit that a special regime applies beyond 200 miles (more on this below).

Importantly, the legal status of the continental shelf does not affect the status of the superjacent waters or airspace, and the coastal state is under a general obligation, while exercising its rights, not to interfere unjustifiably with navigation or other rights and freedoms enjoyed by other states, including the freedom to lay pipelines and cables.

The coastal state has sovereign rights of exploration and exploitation of its continental shelf which, in practice, mostly means that the coastal state can drill for oil and natural gas. It can do so by exclusion of all others, but may issue drilling licences. Where the shelf extends beyond 200 miles, UNCLOS envisages a system of global solidarity. States having an extended shelf are to contribute a small percentage of the surplus value (at most 7 per cent), to be distributed by the International Seabed Authority (which will be discussed below). In particular this provision is a bone of contention for the United States, with some conservatives claiming that this constitutes an international tax. On the other hand, the US government has pointed out that the revenue-sharing obligation was developed with input from representatives of the US oil and gas industry, and that this industry largely supports the regime.[36]

HIGH SEAS

The high seas are free for ships of all nations, and traditionally the regime recognizes four particular freedoms: the freedom to navigate, freedom of overflight, the freedom to lay submarine pipelines and cables, and freedom of fisheries. Article 87 UNCLOS added two newer freedoms: the freedom to construct artificial islands and other installations, and the freedom of scientific research. These freedoms, while extensive, are not unlimited; their exercise must take place with 'due regard' for the interests of other states, and the high seas may only be used for peaceful purposes. The latter is a broad notion – it is generally accepted that military training exercises and even weapons testing are allowed.[37]

While the result of all this freedom could be veritable anarchy, none the less the high seas are a regulated area, and the key to understanding regulation of the high seas, as Evans puts it, resides in the notion of flag-state jurisdiction.[38] All vessels must be registered and thereby have a nationality, and on the high seas the flag state has, in principle, exclusive jurisdiction over things happening on board. This covers not merely legislative jurisdiction, but enforcement jurisdiction as well. In cases of collisions (the *Lotus* scenario),[39] article 97

---

[36] See the position as reproduced in Sean D. Murphy, *Principles of International Law* (St Paul, MN: Thomson/West, 2006), at 365–7.

[37] Churchill and Lowe, *Law of the Sea*, at 206.

[38] Malcolm D. Evans, 'The Law of the Sea', in Malcolm D. Evans (ed.), *International Law*, 4th edn (Oxford University Press, 2014), 651–87, at 665.

[39] Chapter 2 above.

UNCLOS provides that penal measures may be instituted by the flag state or by the state of nationality of the responsible individual.

Certain activities are actively prohibited on the high seas. This applies to the transport of slaves, illicit traffic in narcotics, unauthorized broadcasting, and, most prominently, piracy. States have a general obligation to cooperate in combating these activities (although this is not made explicit with respect to transport of slaves), and in addition have an obligation to cooperate 'in the conservation and management of living resources'.[40] To this end, in 1995 the Straddling Fish Stock Convention was concluded under UN auspices, addressing the problem of managing migratory species (tuna, swordfish, and sharks, among others); it entered into force in 2001 and at the time of writing has eighty-three parties.

It can easily be imagined that a vessel is engaged in illicit activities in a state's maritime zone, and aims to flee from local authorities. In such a case, it would not be very useful if pursuit had to stop on reaching the high seas; hence international law traditionally recognizes a right of 'hot pursuit', codified in article 111 UNCLOS. Hot pursuit must commence in a state's maritime zones and must continue without interruption (otherwise it is no longer 'hot'), but ceases when the vessel enters the territorial waters of its own state or a third state. It may only be exercised by warships or military aircraft, or vessels otherwise clearly identifiable as under the authority of the state.

While many thought for a long time that the crime of piracy had become more or less obsolete, recent experience suggests otherwise.[41] UNCLOS defines piracy as illegal acts of violence or detention, or depredation, committed for private ends by the crew of a private ship or aircraft against another private ship or aircraft on the high seas or otherwise outside any state's jurisdiction.[42] The main characteristic of piracy is the absence of governmental authority or sanction; therefore government ships by definition cannot engage in piracy, unless the crew revolts and turns against the government.[43]

Of great relevance is the jurisdictional point. It is generally accepted that all states can exercise universal jurisdiction over piracy,[44] yet piracy itself is defined as taking place outside the reach of any particular state's jurisdiction. Hence acts of violence, detention, or depredation taking place in a state's territorial sea do not qualify as piracy for the purposes of international law; they take place within a single state's jurisdiction. For these purposes, a serious argument can be made that the EEZ and other maritime zones still qualify as high seas, with the result that acts of violence taking place in a state's EEZ can still be considered as piracy.[45]

---

[40] Article 118 UNCLOS.
[41] The Security Council has even authorized action against piracy off the Somali coast, in a string of resolutions, including Resolution 1816 (2008) and Resolution 1851 (2008). See generally Panos Koutrakos and Achilles Skordas (eds.), *The Law and Practice of Piracy at Sea: European and International Perspectives* (Oxford: Hart, 2014).
[42] Article 101 UNCLOS.
[43] See the authoritative study by Douglas Guilfoyle, *Shipping Interdiction and the Law of the Sea* (Cambridge University Press, 2009), at 36.
[44] Chapter 5 above.   [45] Guilfoyle, *Shipping Interdiction*, 42–5.

THE DEEP SEABED

In the late nineteenth century it was discovered that the deep seabed was rich in certain metallic nodules, comprising valuable metals such as manganese, iron, nickel, and cobalt. At the time, exploitation was a pipe dream, but by the 1960s and 1970s the technology to mine these nodules had been developed and although start-up costs are prohibitive, deep seabed mining started to look like a viable commercial activity. This would have the effect of depriving some states, in particular developing states, of their current share of the world market, and thus a movement gathered force to establish a regime to share the spoils, all the more so since the deep seabed lies outside the jurisdiction of any state and, thus, no single state can claim the resources as belonging to it. This regime would take the form of Part XI of UNCLOS, establishing an intricate system to be managed by a newly created International Seabed Authority. As explained earlier in this chapter, this result was a bit too *dirigiste* for most Western states, and the original Part XI has been modified by a later Agreement on the Implementation of Part XI which, to some extent, bowed to Western demands.

The basis of the system is still that the deep seabed, ocean floor and subsoil thereof (commonly referred to, in Orwellian terms, as the 'Area') are to be considered the 'common heritage of mankind'. No state can claim sovereign rights here; all rights relating to resources in the Area 'are vested in mankind as a whole', represented by the (also rather Orwellian) Authority – the International Seabed Authority – and activities are to be carried out 'for the benefit of mankind as a whole'.[46] The Authority is set up as an international organization. All parties to UNCLOS are its member states, and it has a plenary body (Assembly), an executive body (Council), a secretariat, and two functional organs: a Finance Committee and a Legal and Technical Commission.

The basic idea is that deep seabed mining is to be carried out by private consortia, either alone or jointly with a possibly to be created Enterprise,[47] under auspices of the Authority. The proceeds are then to be distributed by the Authority. Given the high costs of exploitation, those private consortia typically comprise Western companies, while distribution of the proceeds would obviously involve a redistribution of wealth, to the benefit of the poorer nations. In addition, the convention envisages a compulsory transfer of technology, also to the benefit of poorer nations. At the time of writing, the Authority has concluded contracts with a number of consortia and governments.

For private consortia to participate, they must be sponsored by a state party; this, in turn, has given rise to the question of the exact responsibilities and obligations of those sponsoring states. When Nauru and Tonga both sponsored consortia but became worried about the possible financial implications (what to do, for instance, if a consortium does not deliver, or violates applicable regulations?), the Council of the Authority submitted a request for an advisory opinion to the Seabed Disputes Chamber of ITLOS, which held that while the sponsoring state was under a due diligence obligation to make sure that a consortium complied with laws and regulations and conducted such activities as an

---

[46] Articles 136–40 UNCLOS.

[47] The Enterprise would be the commercial arm of the Authority, but will only be set up once deep seabed mining becomes commercially viable – and this, so some suspect, may never happen.

environmental impact assessment, none the less the sponsoring state was not directly liable for the acts or omissions of the contractors it sponsored. In passing the Chamber also treated regulations issued by the Authority as binding, despite the absence of a clear provision to this effect in UNCLOS or in the basic documents of the Authority.[48]

MARITIME DELIMITATION

In much the same way as it is useful to establish boundaries on land, so, too, is it useful to have maritime boundaries delimited. Most boundary delimitations are the result of negotiations between the states concerned – given the number of boundaries in the world, litigation is still rather rare. Still, this is one area in which the ICJ has been highly active over the years, while other bodies (arbitration panels, ITLOS) have also started to make their mark. As noted, normally speaking delimitation will start from the baseline, but there may be circumstances justifying a departure. One of these is the possible existence of a historic right, as with Norway's coastline, often dubbed *skjaergaard*.[49] UNCLOS also allows straight baselines to be drawn over smaller bays and historically recognized larger ones, and around archipelagos.[50]

In principle, two different situations can be envisaged: states can be located opposite each other, or can be located next (adjacent) to each other. UNCLOS treats both situations in the same way, and instead makes a distinction based on the zones concerned. With the delimitation of territorial waters, the basic rule (article 15 UNCLOS) is the so-called 'equidistance rule'; the boundaries must follow the baseline and be equally distant at every point, unless the states concerned agree otherwise.

This would not easily work with the much larger EEZ and continental shelf, largely for two reasons. First, there is a considerable possibility of overlap where states are located opposite each other, such as the Netherlands and the United Kingdom, or South Korea and Japan. The seas in between are too narrow to grant both coastal states the full 200 miles. Second, the application of equidistance following the configuration of the coastline leads to fairness issues if a state happens to have either a well-rounded coastline, or rather a hollow one. Hence, with the EEZ and the continental shelf, the basic rule (in both cases) is that states should agree on how their zones will be delimited, 'in order to achieve an equitable solution'.[51]

The problem came to the fore, in highly visible manner, in the 1969 *North Sea Continental Shelf* cases, involving the then West Germany, Denmark, and the Netherlands. The three states are adjacent to each other, with Germany's coast being squeezed in between those of the other two states, and being concave.[52] As a result, application of the equidistance

---

[48] *Responsibilities and Obligations of States Sponsoring Persons and Entities with Respect to Activities in the Area*, advisory opinion, ITLOS case no. 17, 1 February 2011. Its constituent document, so to speak, is section 4 of Part XI of UNCLOS, articles 156–85.

[49] Chapter 2 above.   [50] Confusingly to Scandinavians, the word 'skjaergaard' translates as 'archipelago'.

[51] Articles 74 and 83 UNCLOS.

[52] The concave Bangladeshi coastline was likewise taken into account by ITLOS in its case no. 16, *Dispute Concerning Delimitation of the Maritime Boundary between Bangladesh and Myanmar in the Bay of Bengal (Bangladesh/Myanmar)*, judgment of 14 March 2012, paras 290–7. It is not the concavity as such that matters, but the possible resulting unfairness that needs to be corrected.

principle would have resulted in Germany having a rather small continental shelf, which was all the more painful as surveys indicated nice reserves of oil and natural gas. The Netherlands and Denmark argued, among other things, that the equidistance rule had become customary international law, but the ICJ disagreed, and ordered the parties to negotiate an equitable settlement. The Court even suggested, in a rather unprecedented move, what a negotiated settlement should include: the parties should take into account

> the general configuration of the coasts of the Parties, as well as the presence of any special or unusual features ... the physical and geological structure, and natural resources, of the continental shelf areas involved, [and] the element of a reasonable degree of proportionality.[53]

This set the tone for later cases of maritime delimitation, which are to a large extent about reaching equitable solutions, even though the Court has come to accept that the equidistance principle is a useful starting point.[54] Thus, in 2002, it suggested that the start of any investigation resided in the equidistance principle and, from there, should go on to consider whether there were factors that needed to be taken into account in order to reach an equitable result.[55] That is not to say that the Court should always take all kinds of factors into consideration; in establishing the maritime boundary between Romania and Ukraine, it reached the conclusion that none of the circumstances invoked by the parties warranted a departure from the provisional equidistance line.[56]

Still, in particular the presence of islands off the coast may be a relevant factor; islands tend to generate their own zones (including continental shelves), but giving full effect to these islands may result in unfairness – an extreme example would be the British Channel Islands, located off the French coast. Giving them full effect would deprive France of much of its maritime zone; giving them no effect at all would be unfair to the United Kingdom. Hence the Court's typical suggestion has been to give 'partial effect' to islands: take them into account but without giving them full weight. In the *Tunisia/Libya* case, the Court suggested this with respect to the Kerkennah Islands off the Tunisian coast.[57] The Court also issued a wise word of warning:

> Clearly each continental shelf case in dispute should be considered and judged on its own merits, having regard to its peculiar circumstances; therefore, no attempt should be made here to overconceptualize the application of the principles and rules relating to the continental shelf.[58]

Indeed, specifically with respect to islands, ITLOS expressed much the same thought: '[N]either case law nor State practice indicates that there is a general rule concerning the

---

[53] *North Sea Continental Shelf (Germany/Denmark; Germany/Netherlands)*, [1969] ICJ Rep. 3, para. 101 D.
[54] Whether equidistance, accompanied by the need to reach an equitable result, qualifies as customary international law, is uncertain, but either way, it is 'not possible to predict how the various factors will be taken into account'. Evans, *Law of the Sea*, at 679.
[55] *Land and Maritime Boundary between Cameroon and Nigeria (Cameroon v. Nigeria; Equatorial Guinea Intervening)*, [2002] ICJ Rep. 303, para. 288.
[56] *Maritime Delimitation in the Black Sea (Romania v. Ukraine)*, [2009] ICJ Rep. 61.
[57] *Continental Shelf (Tunisia/Libya)*, [1982] ICJ Rep. 18, para. 129.   [58] Ibid., para. 132.

effect to be given to islands in maritime delimitation. It depends on the particular circumstances of each case.'[59] And it further suggested that 'the effect to be given to islands in delimitation may differ, depending on whether the delimitation concerns the territorial sea or other maritime areas beyond it'.[60]

Given that islands can potentially generate their own maritime zone, the classification of a reef, atoll or rock as 'island' can have a tremendous impact on a coastal state's economy.[61] This helps to explain why the legal status of small elevations often becomes the subject of political dispute. One example is that China is very unhappy with Japan's attempts to get Okinotorishima, a remote atoll 'about the size of a small bedroom' in the Pacific, recognized as having its own EEZ.[62] At the same time, other states complain about China's practice of artificially enlarging coral reefs to turn them into islands in the hope of generating maritime zones. When confronted with a complaint by the Philippines, in 2016 an arbitral panel held as a general matter that human modification is not relevant for purposes of classifying elevations as islands or rocks – what matters is the 'earlier, natural condition, prior to the onset of significant human modification'.[63]

If islands can be taken into account in maritime delimitation, great disparities in the lengths of the coastline may also constitute a relevant factor.[64] While the Court has rejected the argument that economic poverty per se is a relevant factor in boundary delimitation (a country may be poor one day, but rich the next upon the discovery of some valuable resource), it has accepted that the presence of oil wells in contested areas may be a factor,[65] and has accepted in the abstract that security and defence concerns may also be of relevance.[66]

Given the size of the areas involved, it is inevitable that the delimitation of zones between two states will often also come to affect the interests of others; delimitation of the shelf between Tunisia and Libya is bound somehow to affect Malta and Italy, located on the other side of the Mediterranean Sea. Accordingly, when Tunisia and Libya went to the ICJ, Malta tried to intervene in the proceedings on the basis of article 62 ICJ Statute, and when later Malta and Libya seized the Court, Italy tried to do the same. In both cases the Court rejected the request, and indeed it has been decidedly stingy in granting requests to intervene in proceedings. The main reason for this reluctance is that it would be practically impossible to protect the intervening state without at the same time also saying something about the validity of that state's maritime claims, yet without giving the real parties to the dispute the chance to contest the intervening state's claims. Since judgments are only binding between the parties to the dispute (article 59 ICJ Statute),[67] there is no chance of

---

[59] ITLOS Case no. 16, *Bangladesh/Myanmar Maritime Boundary*, para. 147.   [60] Ibid., para. 148.

[61] Article 121 UNCLOS, with paragraph 3 holding that rocks which cannot sustain human habitation or economic life shall not generate an EEZ or continental shelf.

[62] T. Y. Wang, 'Japan Is Building Tiny Islands in the Philippine Sea. Here's Why', at https:// www.washingtonpost.com/news/monkey-cage/wp/2016/05/20/the-japanese-islet-of-okinotori-is-the-size- of-a-tokyo-bedroom-but-the-basis-of-a-big-claim/ (visited 14 August 2016).

[63] PCA case No. 2013–19, *In the Matter of the South China Sea Arbitration (Philippines v. People's Republic of China)*, award of 12 July 2016. para. 306. The panel found overwhelmingly in favour of the Philippines.

[64] *Continental Shelf (Libya/Malta)*, para. 73.   [65] *Continental Shelf (Tunisia/Libya)*, para. 107.

[66] *Continental Shelf (Libya/Malta)*, para. 51.   [67] See more generally Chapter 8 above.

Italy being bound by a judgment between Malta and Libya; in those circumstances, allowing Italy to intervene would give it a preferential status, to the disadvantage of Malta and Libya. In 1999, however, the Court unanimously allowed Equatorial Guinea to intervene in a demarcation dispute between Cameroon and Nigeria, partly because with the states being adjacent and Cameroon being sandwiched with a concave coastline between Nigeria and Equatorial Guinea, it seemed that the legal interest of Equatorial Guinea was sufficiently established, perhaps partly also because neither Cameroon nor Nigeria had any objections.[68]

Since both the EEZ and the continental shelf can run to a maximum of 200 miles off the baseline, there is some merit in drawing a single boundary line, and it would seem that with negotiated boundaries, this is indeed more or less the standard practice.[69] Yet the ICJ is usually asked to focus on one maritime zone at a time, mostly the continental shelf. The most prominent exception was the explicit request by Canada and the United States to come to a single boundary in the *Gulf of Maine* case.[70]

Often enough, boundary delimitation is inspired most of all by the desire to achieve clarity in rights over natural resources, be they fish or oil and natural gas.[71] Instead of drawing up a boundary, states can also decide to collaborate and set up joint fisheries zones, or joint exploration zones. Several examples exist, for instance between South Korea and Japan, or between Norway and the United Kingdom. Typically, the states concerned decide to manage and exploit the resources together, and then divide the proceeds. As long as these zones are located within overlapping claims of the states concerned, it would seem that no interests of third parties are immediately affected.

PROMPT RELEASE, PROVISIONAL MEASURES

The expansion of maritime zones over the years set in motion a number of different practical issues, chief among them the concern that coastal states, eager to assert their jurisdiction, might unduly interfere with the freedom of navigation and fishing. Hence, seafaring nations started to argue that some system should be devised to make sure that coastal states would not abuse their newly found jurisdiction. As a result, UNCLOS came to include provisions aimed at finding a compromise: under article 73(1), coastal states have the right to enforce their jurisdiction in the EEZ in certain matters but, under paragraph 2 of the same article, they are under an obligation to secure the prompt release of vessels and crew upon the posting of a 'reasonable bond or other security'. In order to make this enforceable, tribunals (including ITLOS) are given compulsory jurisdiction to hear and address such claims 'without delay', and without regard to the

---

[68] *Land and Maritime Boundary between Cameroon and Nigeria (Cameroon v. Nigeria)*, application to intervene, Order, [1999] ICJ Rep. 1029.
[69] Churchill and Lowe, *Law of the Sea*, at 192–3.
[70] *Delimitation of the Maritime Boundary in the Gulf of Maine Area (Canada/USA)*, [1984] ICJ Rep. 246.
[71] The maritime boundaries in arctic waters are usefully discussed in Michael Byers, *International Law and the Arctic* (Cambridge University Press, 2013).

merits of the underlying claim.[72] In other words: prompt release procedures are aimed at securing prompt release, not at finding out who was right or wrong.[73]

ITLOS has had various occasions on which to shed light on legal matters related to prompt release. In an important decision on the topic, in *Tomimaru*, it held that the confiscation of a vessel should not undermine the function of article 292 UNCLOS. In the case at hand, Japan had started prompt release proceedings after a Japanese ship had been detained in Russia. As it happened, Japan had taken its time before seizing the Tribunal – the ship had been detained by Russia in October 2006, with Japan only starting proceedings on 7 July 2007. Prosecution in Russia had already taken place, with Russia's courts deciding that confiscation of the ship was in order. This now, ITLOS held, was difficult to reconcile with the balance of interests underlying article 292 UNCLOS but, with the Russian courts having decided the case and having been able to do so due to Japan's late application, it decided that the proceedings no longer had an object.[74]

In a different case between the same states, brought on the same date as *Tomimaru* (but relating to a more recent incident) and decided on the same date as well, the Tribunal had occasion to look into the notion of 'reasonable bond or other security'. Russia had detained the Japanese ship *Hoshinmaru* on grounds of over-fishing, and suggested that a reasonable bond should include the maximum possible penalties payable for fishing a greater quantity than the licence to fish allowed, as well as the value of the ship on confiscation and administrative costs, altogether calculated at some US$860,000. Japan, on the other hand, contended that 'reasonable' would depend mostly on the gravity of the offence, and had offered a bond of some US$313,000. The Tribunal sided mostly with Japan, holding that the Russian bond was not 'reasonable' and eventually ordered that the ship be released on a bond of 10 million roubles – some US$400,000.[75]

The prompt release provisions of UNCLOS are specifically designed to cover the exercise of jurisdiction by coastal states in their EEZ and limited to enforcement measures relating to the exploration, exploitation, conservation, and management of living resources. In other words, they cover coastal state measures to enforce fisheries legislation, for example, but not much else. Yet there may be other circumstances where coastal states may wish to protect themselves, and where flag states may need to be protected against the exercise of jurisdiction by the coastal state. In such circumstances, flag states may apply to ITLOS for provisional measures, and it is perhaps no coincidence that more than half of the case law of ITLOS to date addresses either prompt release requests or provisional measures requests.

A telling example is the *Arctic Sunrise* saga. The Greenpeace vessel *Arctic Sunrise* had been present in Russia's EEZ, and was used as a mother ship for launching inflatable boats in order to protest against activities on a specific oil rig. Russia detained the ship and its crew in September 2013, following which the Netherlands filed a request for provisional measures in October 2013. According to the Dutch, Russia's action interfered with the

---

[72] Article 292 UNCLOS.   [73] See generally Rothwell and Stephens, *International Law of the Sea*, at 489–91.

[74] ITLOS, Case No. 15, *The 'Tomimaru' Case (Japan v. Russian Federation)*, judgment of 6 August 2007; note that the judgment was rendered within a month.

[75] ITLOS, Case No. 14, *The 'Hoshinmaru' Case (Japan v. Russian Federation)*, judgment of 6 August 2007.

freedom of navigation, guaranteed in articles 58 (with respect to the EEZ) and 87 (with respect to the high seas) of UNCLOS; additionally, it also invoked the human rights of the crew, in particular their right to liberty of person and right to free movement. Hence the Netherlands asked for the immediate release of the vessel and its crew, pending further proceedings. Russia did not participate in the proceedings, but this did not prevent the Tribunal from exercising its jurisdiction to indicate provisional measures. It held that its jurisdiction covers the imposition of a reasonable bond to secure immediate release, and set the bond at some €3.6 million.[76]

Since ITLOS's jurisdiction in cases involving Russia is limited to issuing provisional measures,[77] the Netherlands had already, two weeks earlier, started arbitration proceedings against Russia to discuss the merits of the case, utilizing the Permanent Court of Arbitration. The panel held, in 2015, that Russia had violated the rights of the Netherlands as the flag state of the *Arctic Sunrise* when it detained ship and crew, as well as by ignoring ITLOS's order of provisional measures, and owed the Netherlands compensation.[78] At the time of writing, the level of compensation remains to be decided.

AIR LAW

When aircraft were first invented, there were no rules on the use of air space, and the basic assumption was that aircraft should, like ships in territorial waters, enjoy a right of innocent passage. Indeed, the British Imperial General Staff, as late as 1909, advised the UK government that aircraft would never come to be of much use, and thus that there would be little harm in acknowledging innocent passage.[79] The First World War, however, taught a harsh lesson about the potential of aircraft, and a customary rule arose quickly to the effect that states enjoyed exclusive sovereignty over their airspace. This meant that foreign aircraft could not enter the airspace, let alone land, without the territorial state's consent. The rule would become codified in one of the main air law treaties, the 1944 Chicago Convention on International Civil Aviation. This applies only to the air above a state's territory, though; above the high seas, there is freedom of overflight.

As a result, air law is based on a network of treaties, both bilateral and multilateral, addressing what are sometimes (a little misleadingly[80]) referred to as the five freedoms: freedom of overflight; landing for non-traffic purposes such as emergencies; disembarking passengers, cargo, and mail embarked elsewhere; embarking passengers, mail and cargo for

---

[76] The Tribunal read the 'reasonable bond' stipulation into article 290(5) UNCLOS, on which it based its jurisdiction. Said article does not mention bonds or other forms of security. ITLOS, Case No. 22, *The 'Arctic Sunrise' Case (Netherlands* v. *Russian Federation)*, provisional measures, order of 22 November 2013, esp. para. 95. The crew was released in late November 2013 and given amnesty by the Russian Duma in December of that year, while the arrest of the vessel was lifted in June 2014.

[77] Under article 287 UNCLOS, states are expected to indicate whether they generally submit to the jurisdiction of the ICJ, ITLOS, or various kinds of arbitration. Russia opted for arbitration. Rothwell and Stephens, *International Law of the Sea*, at 485–6.

[78] PCA, Case 2014–02, *The Arctic Sunrise Arbitration (Netherlands* v. *Russia)*, award on jurisdiction, 26 November 2014; award on the merits, 14 August 2015.

[79] Fawcett, *Law of Nations*, at 80–1.

[80] This is a little misleading as these freedoms need to be negotiated. Without a treaty, there are no freedoms.

a destination within the state; and finally, embarking passengers, mail, and cargo coming from, or going to, a third state. Aircraft must have a nationality (like individuals and ships), and criminal jurisdiction on board rests with the flag state as well as the state subjacent at the moment a crime is committed.[81]

The 1944 Chicago Convention is of great relevance, in that it details not only rules on the use of airspace but also on air safety. Thus it specifies that pilots must be licensed, and that aircraft may only take off when in possession of a certificate of airworthiness – it provides for mutual recognition of such certificates. The convention also serves as the constituent instrument of the International Civil Aviation Organization (ICAO), which has become part of the UN family of international organizations and which can (and does) adopt so-called recommended standards and practices; states are expected to implement these to the fullest extent practicable.[82] The ICAO has a genuine legislative power to regulate air traffic over the high seas.[83]

The liability of air carriers is regulated by the 1999 Montreal Convention, the successor to the 1929 Warsaw Convention. Under the Montreal Convention, air carriers are liable for the death or injury occurring on board or during take-off and landing, and are liable for damage to checked baggage.[84] Much the same applies to damage to cargo, as long as the damage occurred in the air. Compensation for loss of checked baggage is dependent on the terms of the contract between the carrier and the passenger. The air carrier's liability is rather limited, though; the convention sets a ceiling of 1,000 special drawing rights (SDR) per passenger for lost baggage.[85]

Air carriers are united in IATA (the International Air Transport Association), which functions as an interest group for the industry. As such, it even used to be able to harmonize air fares, but this has been deemed to be in conflict with competition rules. Additionally, among IATA's main activities are the distribution of three-letter airport codes and the coordination of the scheduling of air travel.

Many of the details about air traffic are laid down in bilateral agreements.[86] These agreements (between governments) will determine which air carriers can fly from and to which airports, and will contain provisions on computerized reservation systems, on customs duties, on user charges, and much, much more. Within the EU, the power to conclude such agreements rests with the EU rather than with its member states, following a string of cases brought by the EU Commission claiming that in concluding bilateral agreements the EU's member states had violated EU law.[87]

---

[81] Peter Malanczuk, *Akehurst's Modern Introduction to International Law*, 7th edn (London: Routledge, 1997), at 201.

[82] The leading study is still Thomas M. Buergenthal, *Law-Making in the International Civil Aviation Organization* (Syracuse University Press, 1969).

[83] See article 12 Chicago Convention: 'Over the high seas, the rules in force shall be those established under this Convention.'

[84] Article 17 Montreal Convention.

[85] Special drawing rights are the virtual currency developed by the IMF. At the time of writing (August 2016), SDR 1 equals roughly €1.24 and US$1.4.

[86] A fairly random example is the New Zealand–Turkey Air Services Agreement, reproduced in Jan Klabbers (ed.), *International Law Documents* (Cambridge University Press, 2016).

[87] For discussion, see Jan Klabbers, *Treaty Conflict and the European Union* (Cambridge University Press, 2008).

Aircraft are considered extremely vulnerable, and have often been used for terrorist purposes. As a result, several conventions have been concluded to safeguard aircraft, including the 1971 Hijacking Convention, officially known as the Convention on the Suppression of Unlawful Seizure of Aircraft. The convention makes hijacking a crime over which universal jurisdiction may be exercised (article 4) and incorporates the principle *aut dedere, aut judicare* (article 7: either extradite or prosecute). After the Lockerbie incident in 1988, (when a US passenger aircraft on a transatlantic flight was destroyed by a bomb over Lockerbie, Scotland, killing all on board), for which Libya was deemed responsible, the UN Security Council imposed sanctions on Libya in order to force it into handing over the suspects. Libya, in turn, went to the ICJ claiming that it was perfectly willing to prosecute the suspects, in accordance with the convention.[88] The ICJ, however, never addressed the merits of Libya's claim.

Since states enjoy sovereignty over their airspace, it follows that they need not tolerate intrusions of that airspace. Civil aircraft found to be trespassing may be escorted and ordered to land. They may not, however, be shot down; this is, it would seem, a rather absolute rule. While an attempt to formalize it by amending the 1944 Chicago Convention narrowly failed to generate the required majority of states, a later attempt, following the forceful interception in 1983 of a South Korean airliner by the (then) USSR, proved more successful.[89] Article 3*bis* of the Chicago Convention, in force since 1998, now reads, in relevant part and fairly soft terms, that the contracting parties 'recognize that every State must refrain from resorting to the use of weapons against civil aircraft in flight and that, in case of interception, the lives of persons on board and the safety of aircraft must not be endangered'. Either way, it is telling that the USSR did not claim a right to shoot down civil aircraft; instead, it claimed it had mistaken the aircraft for a US military aircraft. This then also suggests that shooting down trespassing military aircraft may be considered justifiable.[90]

In much the same way as states enacted 'hovering laws' in the eighteenth century to protect themselves against attacks over sea, eventually leading to recognition of a contiguous zone, some states have created so-called Air Defense Identification Zones (ADIZ) outside their own airspace which, logically, are in tension with the freedom of overflight guaranteed over the high seas, including the EEZ.[91] These zones were first created during the Cold War, while the attack on the Twin Towers of 11 September 2001, has generated a renewed interest. As a general matter, states still treat each other with velvet gloves in the ADIZ: the perceived need for additional security is not (yet?) accompanied by strong demands that ADIZ be accepted as part of a state's sovereign

---

[88] Libya brought two separate cases, one against the United States and one against the United Kingdom. It could not bring proceedings against the Security Council, as the latter is not a state (see article 34 ICJ Statute). The cases were removed from the Court's list in 2003. See e.g. *Questions of Interpretation and Application of the 1971 Montreal Convention Arising from the Aerial Incident at Lockerbie* (*Libya* v. *USA*), Order, [2003] ICJ Rep. 152.

[89] For a fine discussion of the incident and its aftermath, see Gilbert Guillaume, *Les grandes crises internationales et le droit* (Paris: Éditions du Seuil, 1994), at 61–78.

[90] Malanczuk, *Akehurst's Modern Introduction*, at 199.   [91] Article 87 *juncto* article 58 UNCLOS.

rights – according to one well-placed observer, an attitude of mutual respect and accommodation still prevails.[92]

SPACE LAW

There is no agreement yet on the altitude where airspace ends and outer space begins but, for the time being, this is not considered to be problematic. Space is occupied, so to speak, by satellites, spacecraft, planets, and celestial bodies, and the lowest altitude at which these move is still far higher than the highest aircraft can reach. That said, spacecraft will first have to move through airspace before they reach outer space, so at some point a boundary between the two will need to be established. As with territory generally, it may well be that the decisive criterion will be that of effective control; if so, then it may be expected that the boundary will move upward as time and technology progress.

Unlike the air column above states, outer space is not subject to territorial sovereignty. Space law gained momentum in the 1950s and especially the 1960s, when it first became possible to send spacecraft to the moon, and the first satellite (the USSR's Sputnik I) came to orbit the earth. In 1958 the General Assembly of the UN adopted the first important resolution on outer space. It suggested that mankind had a common interest in outer space, and established the principle that outer space should only be used for peaceful purposes.[93] Three years later, it adopted another resolution, stating that outer space and celestial bodies were not subject to national appropriation, but were free for exploration and use by all states.[94] These principles were cemented in a 1963 resolution under the title Declaration of Legal Principles Governing the Activities of States in the Exploration and Use of Outer Space, and still form the bedrock of the international law of outer space.[95] In the same spirit as the earlier resolutions, the declaration also proclaims that astronauts are to be regarded as the 'envoys of mankind', and should be assisted on their way back to the state of registration of the spacecraft they occupied.[96] These principles were codified in the form of the 1967 Outer Space Treaty, which, in essence, repeats the above-mentioned principles in legally binding form.

Arguably the biggest legal problem that may arise is the question of liability. Who is responsible if a satellite comes crashing down, or if parts of a spacecraft land somewhere on earth? To this end, in 1972 a Liability Convention was concluded. The core of this convention is its article II: 'A launching State shall be absolutely liable to pay compensation

---

[92] Peter A. Dutton, '*Caelum Liberum*: Air Defense Identification Zones Outside Sovereign Airspace', (2009) 103 *American Journal of International Law*, 691–709.

[93] General Assembly Res. 1348 (XIII), 13 December 1958.

[94] General Assembly Res. 1721 (XVI), 20 December 1961.

[95] General Assembly Res. 1962 (XVIII), 13 December 1963. This quick succession of resolutions prompted Bin Cheng to formulate the thesis that in some circumstances, 'instant custom' could be created. See Bin Cheng, 'United Nations Resolutions on Outer Space: "Instant" International Customary Law?', reproduced in Bin Cheng, *International Law: Teaching and Practice* (London: Stevens & Sons, 1982), 237–62.

[96] This is further fleshed out in the 1972 Agreement on the Rescue of Astronauts, the Return of Astronauts and the Return of Objects Launched into Outer Space.

for damage caused by its space object on the surface of the Earth or to aircraft in flight.' In other words, if damage occurs, the state concerned is liable, regardless of whether the damage was the result of an internationally wrongful act, or whether the launching state was at fault. This then marks a firm departure from the general principles of state responsibility in international law which, as noted earlier, include an internationally wrongful act as a necessary element.[97]

This strict liability regime may, naturally, lead to claims for compensation for the damage incurred. Typically, claims are dealt with through diplomatic channels (so as to avoid litigation), but where no agreement between the disputing parties on the amount of compensation can be reached, the convention creates the possibility of setting up a claims commission. The most celebrated instance occurred in the 1978 Cosmos 954 incident; debris from a USSR satellite came down in Canada, causing environmental damage. After intense negotiations, the USSR paid some compensation, albeit less than what Canada had asked for. None the less, the fact that the USSR paid up reaffirms the convention's notion of strict liability.[98]

The scope of article II of the Liability Convention is limited to damage on the surface of the earth and aircraft in flight. When damage is caused elsewhere, the convention prescribes fault liability; the launching state is only liable if it is at fault. If space objects are the project of two or more states, these will be held liable jointly and severally.

Outer space is not only used for exploring new planets, but is also where satellites are in orbit. Some of these are engaged in collecting meteorological data, some are used for 'remote sensing' (tracking resources, early warning of pollution, possibly also military activities), and quite a few are used for broadcasting purposes. The use of satellites for remote sensing has raised the issue of whether the prior consent of the observed state is necessary; the idea that outer space is free to use would suggest that no consent is needed, but, on the other hand, the existence of sovereignty over air and land would suggest that some consent might indeed be required. Additionally, the question has arisen of what to do with all the data acquired through remote sensing; should it be shared for the benefit of mankind? Likewise, the use of satellites for broadcasting has given rise to political divisions; some cherish the freedom of information, whereas others would suggest that a state does not need to allow satellite television programmes on its territory, if only so as to avoid political propaganda. In both cases, it would seem that the 'freedom of information' position has eventually won the day.

The only way for satellites to have continuous contact with ground stations is if they are in geostationary orbit at some 22,300 miles directly above the equator. Hence the geostationary orbit is capable of accommodating only a limited number of satellites; it is a finite resource. As a result, eight equatorial states in 1976 signed the Bogotá Declaration, in which they claimed sovereignty over the geostationary orbit above their territory.[99]

---

[97] See the discussion in Chapter 7 above.
[98] For a brief discussion, see I. H. Ph. Diederiks-Verschoor and V. Kopal, *An Introduction to Space Law*, 3rd edn (Alphen aan den Rijn: Kluwer Law International, 2008).
[99] http://bogotadeclaration.wordpress.com/declaration-of-1976/ (visited 11 January 2012).

This claim has met with serious objections and seems difficult to reconcile with the idea that outer space should be free, but then again, much the same could be said about the Truman Declaration with respect to the continental shelf.[100] The equatorial states (none of them highly industrialized) view the geostationary orbit as a natural resource, and their declaration suggests, at the very least, that such concepts are socially constructed; a natural resource is something that is accepted as such.

While there is no specific international organization devoted to outer space issues, the General Assembly, in 1959, created a Committee on the Peaceful Uses of Outer Space (COPUOS). COPUOS discusses, as its name suggests, the peaceful uses of outer space and is, in a sense, the main body dealing with space law issues in general. Matters relating to satellites are the province of the International Telecommunications Union (ITU), one of the oldest international organizations; it was founded in 1865 as the International Telegraphic Union. Currently, among ITU's tasks is the allocation of satellite orbits. The actual operation of satellites (or networks of satellites) often takes place through private companies, such as Intelsat and Eutelsat. Both started out as international organizations, but were privatized at the beginning of the millennium.

FINAL REMARKS

One of the most interesting things about space law and, to some extent, the law of the sea is that these fields of international law have moved beyond the classic Westphalian model. While it is doubtful whether, as has been claimed, in space law 'the sovereignty principle has been abandoned',[101] none the less the proclamation of the high seas and the moon as the 'common heritage of mankind', the idea that surplus extraction of resources in the EEZ and the continental shelf should be shared with the less fortunate, and the idea of joint exploration of the deep seabed all testify to a growing global awareness. This renders the law of the sea and space law veritable laboratories for political experimentation with joint ownership, common management of resources, and the like.

That said, there is no reason to be overly optimistic. The history of the law of the sea, with its creeping extensions of functional jurisdiction, suggests that global idealism still needs to take a back seat when confronted with the possibility of making a handsome profit, and there can be little doubt that if the geostationary orbit had been conveniently located above Western industrialized nations, it would have been subject to national appropriation by now. Moreover, the prevalence of disputes about maritime delimitation, or the status of reefs, rocks, and atolls, or fishing, or prompt release and provisional measures, can all be taken as a signal that the seas represent big business, and as long as that is the case, there is little reason to be very optimistic about the seas and their resources coming to be considered as public goods.

---

[100] See the discussion in Chapter 2 above.   [101] Diederiks-Verschoor and Kopal, *An Introduction*, at 57.

FURTHER READING

R. R. Churchill and A. V. Lowe, *The Law of the Sea*, 3rd edn (Manchester University Press, 1999)

I. H. Ph. Diederiks-Verschoor and V. Kopal, *An Introduction to Space Law*, 3rd edn (Alphen aan den Rijn: Kluwer Law International, 2008)

Peter A. Dutton, '*Caelum Liberum*: Air Defense Identification Zones Outside Sovereign Airspace', (2009) 103 *American Journal of International Law*, 691–709

Malcolm D. Evans, 'The Law of the Sea', in Malcolm D. Evans (ed.), *International Law*, 4th edn (Oxford University Press, 2014), 651–87

Hugo Grotius, *The Free Sea*, trans. R. Hakluyt (Indianapolis, IN: Liberty Fund, 2004 [1609])

Douglas Guilfoyle, *Shipping Interdiction and the Law of the Sea* (Cambridge University Press, 2009)

James E. Hickey, Jr, 'Law-making and the Law of the Sea: The BP *Deepwater Horizon* Oil Spill in the Gulf of Mexico', in Rain Liivoja and Jarna Petman (eds.), *International Law-Making* (Abingdon: Routledge, 2013), 270–82

Donald Rothwell and Tim Stephens, *The International Law of the Sea*, 2nd edn (Oxford: Hart, 2016)

14

Protecting the Environment

INTRODUCTION

One of the more debated fields of international law in recent decades is generally considered to be a fairly novel branch of the law: the international legal protection of the environment. Among the reasons why this is hotly debated is that agreement between states is sometimes hard to find; there exist strong political cleavages not only over the extent to which the global environment is under threat, but also over what to do about it and, eventually, about who should pay for it. In a nutshell, developed industrialized nations, whose industrialization and lifestyle has done much to help degrade the environment, are reluctant to mend their ways; less developed nations tend to think that if others could benefit from industrialization, then so should they, regardless of the consequences. And if much degradation has been caused by those others, it seems only fair that those who became rich on the back of environmental degradation should foot most of the bill. Partly as a result, much of international environmental law consists of fragile compromises.

There is another factor which makes it difficult to achieve a coherent and effective body of international environmental law, and that is the circumstance that while international law is typically made between and for states, states themselves are rarely the direct culprits when it comes to pollution and degradation. Instead, many of the world's environmental problems are caused by the activities of companies and individuals. Typically, dumping toxic waste into rivers, or letting oil spill from oil drilling platforms, are not directly attributable to states. Likewise, the emissions of millions of cars and aircraft are not the work of states, but of individuals keen on moving comfortably from place A to place B.[1] While government officials may be implicated in various ways (from designing inadequate legislation to planning shopping malls in suburban areas in such a way that they are only

---

[1] As a result, it becomes extremely difficult to attribute responsibility for climate change. For a thoughtful normative approach, see Henry Shue, 'Transboundary Damage in Climate Change: Criteria for Allocating Responsibility', in Andre Nollkaemper and Dov Jacobs (eds.), *Distribution of Responsibilities in International Law* (Cambridge University Press, 2015), 321–40.

accessible by car),[2] none the less the behaviour that needs to be affected by international environmental law is predominantly the behaviour of individuals and companies.[3]

This sets international environmental law apart from most other branches of international law, and makes international environmental law into something of a laboratory for international law generally. Perhaps because easy solutions are out of reach, law-makers and negotiators are forced to experiment with new mechanisms and techniques in order to achieve a semblance of regulation.[4] Thus it is in particular in the field of international environmental law that institutionalization is achieved by highly informal means. There is no single international organization dealing with the global environment; instead, there are regular meetings (or conferences) of the parties to multilateral agreements that perform many of the tasks otherwise ascribed to international organizations. Likewise, 'compliance procedures' have been pioneered in the field of international environmental law as alternatives to courts and litigation, and while treaties for the protection of the environment typically do not encourage the making of reservations, they often create 'common but differentiated responsibilities'.

It is also hardly a coincidence that environmental treaties are among the most 'holistic' agreements concluded. Given the dependence on the global South to achieve environmental goals, and given the pressures exercised by non-governmental organizations in the West, it is by no means uncommon to find environmental agreements containing 'something for everyone'. One can find references to human rights, technology transfer, food security, gender equality, or financial assistance in environmental agreements, in ways that do not quite apply to, for example, investment treaties.

EARLY CASE LAW

It has sometimes been claimed that there is really no such thing as international environmental law; rather, there is general international law, to be applied to environmental issues. While such discussions are always a bit sterile, there used to be some recognizable truth to the claim. Much of what is now generally considered international environmental law is of fairly recent origin, going back to the 1970s, 1980s, and 1990s.[5] This covers pollution of the atmosphere and the marine environment, the protection of

---

[2] For a classic study on how urban planning affects modern life in many respects, see Jane Jacobs, *The Death and Life of Great American Cities* (New York: Vintage, 1992 [1962]).

[3] As a corollary, it has been argued that finding solutions should likewise not be left to states alone, but should involve civil society actors as well. See Caroline Thomas, *The Environment in International Relations* (London: Royal Institute of International Affairs, 1992).

[4] The classic discussion is Geoffrey Palmer,' New Ways to Make International Environmental Law', (1992) 86 *American Journal of International Law*, 259–83. A more recent overview is Francesca Romanin Jacur, *The Dynamics of Multilateral Environmental Agreements: Institutional Architectures and Law-Making Processes* (Naples: Editoriale Scientifica, 2013).

[5] The claim has sometimes been dismissed as not very helpful, in that the environment would suffer greatly if it were subjected to the permissive approach set out in the *Lotus* case (discussed in Chapter 2 above). See e.g. Patricia W. Birnie and Alan E. Boyle, *International Law and the Environment* (Oxford: Clarendon Press, 1992), at 1.

wildlife and biological diversity, climate change and ozone depletion, and the risks involved in nuclear and other ultra-hazardous waste.

Two important conferences are often singled out to mark the emergence of international environmental law.[6] The first of these took place in Stockholm, in 1972, leading to the adoption of a set of principles the most relevant of which (principle 21) holds that while states have a sovereign right to exploit their own resources, none the less they have the 'responsibility to ensure that activities within their jurisdiction or control do not cause damage to the environment of other states or areas beyond the limits of national jurisdiction'. The second opportune moment followed twenty years later, at the Rio Conference of 1992, which saw the birth of the notion of sustainable development, aiming to formulate a compromise between those favouring strict environmental regulation and those who suggest that environmental concerns need not sacrifice industrialization and development.

Still, the applicability of general international law to the environment has a long pedigree. One of the earliest manifestations was the *Bering's Sea* arbitration of 1893. Having purchased Alaska from Russia in 1867, the United States enacted legislation limiting the killing of seals (known for their valuable fur) in the area. A diplomatic incident ensued when British sealers were found in the area, and negotiations were started to establish an international regime concerning fur seals. These negotiations failed, and in the end an arbitral panel was established, tasked with the question (among others) of whether the United States could unilaterally legislate outside its territorial waters proper for the purpose of protecting the seal population. The novelty here was that the United States claimed to legislate for the global common good, rather than for its own narrow interests; not surprisingly perhaps, the panel did not accept the US claim, although without providing much by way of argumentation.[7]

By contrast, the PCIJ, in its early case on the jurisdiction of the Oder Commission, based its opinion in part on a conception of the common good. The question before the Court was whether the powers of the Oder Commission, comprising seven states and set up under the Versailles Treaty, also covered two tributaries of the River Oder in Poland. Poland held that this was not the case, whereas the other six member states of the Commission strongly felt the opposite. Materially, the interest at stake concerned access to open sea; by denying the jurisdiction of the Commission within Polish territory, Poland would not have to grant anyone access to sea.

This the Court could not accept. It held that when faced with international river issues, what mattered was the 'community of interest of riparian States'. As the Court explained,

> This community of interest in a navigable river becomes the basis of a common legal right, the essential features of which are the perfect equality of all riparian States in the user of the whole course of the river and the exclusion of any preferential privilege of any one riparian State in relation to the others.[8]

---

[6] For a fine overall discussion, see Philippe Sands, *Principles of International Environmental Law. Vol. I: Frameworks, Standards and Implementation* (Manchester University Press, 1995).

[7] *Bering's Sea (USA/UK)*, award of 15 August 1893, reproduced in 28 *Reports of International Arbitral Awards*, 263–76.

[8] *Territorial Jurisdiction of the International Commission of the River Oder (UK and others* v. *Poland)*, (1929) Publ. PCIJ, series A, no. 23, at 27.

While the Court did not say anything about environmental protection in particular, it accepted that there might be common interests, and as will be seen later on, this underlying idea is of relevance with respect to environmental protection of international waterways.

Another relatively early case indicated how difficult it might be even to apply general international law to environmental issues. The operation of a Canadian factory (the Trail Smelter, Trail being a location in Canada) caused noxious fumes to cross the border into the United States, raising questions about responsibility, compensation for damages and ultimately also whether the Trail Smelter should cease to operate. The latter option was a stretch, but the panel did remark, foreshadowing Stockholm principle 21, that under international law, 'no state has the right to use or permit the use of territory in such a manner as to cause injury by fumes in or to the territory of another or the properties of persons therein, when the case is of serious consequence and the injury is established by clear and convincing evidence'.[9] While the panel had been unable to find precedents in international law proper, it based itself to a large extent by analogy on decisions of the US Supreme Court involving cases between various of the states of the United States, satisfying itself that US law was 'in conformity with the general rules of international law'.[10]

A final relevant precedent is the *Lake Lanoux* arbitration, between France and Spain, of 1957. In this case, Spain had complained about French actions to divert the use of a boundary lake. Even though the French actions had been limited to the part of the lake that was on French territory, none the less this affected the possibilities for Spain to utilize the lake for irrigation purposes. Yet the panel held that France had done nothing wrong and had not violated any rule of international law. As long as France took Spanish interests into account in a reasonable manner, there was little that it could be condemned for.[11]

These cases together suggest that for a long time there was little general international law specifically geared towards protecting the environment. At best, there would be obligations of good neighbourliness and due diligence based on the underlying conception of a 'community of interest' – paying some attention to the interests and rights of others while exercising one's own rights. And this, so some would claim, is essentially still the case; international environmental law has fairly few hard and fast substantive rules, and instead relies on procedural notions about information, participation in decision-making, the usefulness of an environmental impact assessment, and so on.

PULP MILLS

The ICJ has rarely been confronted with cases involving environmental issues. One of these rare cases was the 1997 *Gabcikovo-Nagymaros* case, but, while admittedly the Court stressed the relevance of environmental considerations, it shed little light on the contents of environmental law, and treated the case mostly as a dispute involving the precise terms

---

[9] *Trail Smelter (US/Canada)*, award of 11 March 1941, reproduced in 3 *Reports of International Arbitral Awards*, 1938, at 1965.

[10] Ibid., at 1963.

[11] *Lake Lanoux (France v. Spain)*, award of 16 November 1957, reproduced in 24 *International Law Reports*, 101.

of the 1977 treaty concluded between Hungary and (at the time) Czechoslovakia and the applicability of a few central doctrines from the law of treaties.[12] Likewise, the Court emphasized in its *Nuclear Weapons* opinion of 1996 that environmental obligations may have some bearing on the use of nuclear weapons,[13] but did not take things much further, and an attempt to make the ICJ more attractive for the settlement of environmental disputes by establishing a chamber for environmental disputes has come to naught; states have simply not made use of it.[14]

The most pertinent decision of the ICJ to date[15] is its decision in *Pulp Mills*, a dispute between Uruguay and Argentina prompted by the planned establishment of two pulp mills in Uruguay.[16] While one of these plans would be put on hold, the other did materialize: one of the largest pulp mills in the world has been in operation on the banks of the River Uruguay since 2007.

In 1975 Uruguay and Argentina had concluded a treaty on management of the boundary river between them, setting up an international organization (known as CARU) to that end. Part of this agreement (the 1975 Statute) entailed that neither of the two states would start large-scale projects that could affect the river and its natural environment without notifying the other party, and without taking some other procedural steps into account. CARU, moreover, specified further guidelines, and yet further details were agreed upon in separate agreements concluded in 2004 and 2005. The 1975 Statute also contained a number of substantive obligations, such as the obligation to protect and preserve the aquatic environment. In the end, the Court concluded that Uruguay had violated some of its procedural obligations, in particular by failing to inform CARU and Argentina before authorizing the planned works.

Yet the Court held that Uruguay had not violated any substantive obligations, or rather, on most counts it found that there was insufficient evidence to reach this conclusion. This relates, in part, to the issue of the burden of proof; the Court held that this burden rested on the claimant state, *in casu* Argentina, which had been unable to provide sufficient proof of environmental problems and the causal link with the pulp mills. This ascription of the burden of proof to Argentina proved controversial given the topic at hand. In a situation where the preservation of the environment is at stake it could be claimed, with considerable cogency, that the burden of proving non-harm should rest on those who wish to take steps that might endanger the environment.

As a result, the judgment was subject to a vigorous critique by two dissenting judges. In their joint dissent, judges Al-Khasawneh and Simma suggested, somewhat between

---

[12] *Gabcikovo-Nagymaros Project (Hungary/Slovakia)*, [1997] ICJ Rep. 7.

[13] *Legality of the Threat or Use of Nuclear Weapons*, advisory opinion, [1996] ICJ Rep. 226, esp. para. 30.

[14] By 2006 the Court stopped its annual practice of electing judges to sit in the chamber, so it seems fair to draw the conclusion that the chamber, set up in 1993, is now considered defunct.

[15] *Aerial Herbicide Spraying (Ecuador v. Colombia)* was brought in 2008, but removed from the Court's list after the parties had reached an agreement. Another pertinent case will be discussed below: *Whaling in the Antarctic (Australia v. Japan; New Zealand intervening)*, [2014] ICJ Rep. 226.

[16] *Pulp Mills on the River Uruguay (Argentina v. Uruguay)*, [2010] ICJ Rep. 14. For a brief comment see Cymie R. Payne, '*Pulp Mills on the River Uruguay*: The International Court of Justice Recognizes Environmental Impact Assessment as a Duty under International Law', (2010) 14 *ASIL Insights*, issue 9.

the lines,[17] that in environmental matters, characterized as they are by a high degree of technical complexity, one cannot always apply traditional notions about the burden of proof. Their main point of criticism, though, related to the Court's refusal to use court-appointed experts. The Statute of the ICJ and its rules offer sufficient leeway to do so, yet, instead, the Court had grudgingly accepted that experts appeared as counsel for both parties, which prevented them from being questioned by the other side.[18]

The two dissenting judges made another vital point as well, arguing that it was unlikely that Uruguay's violation of procedural obligations would have no bearing on its substantive obligations. As they suggested, in branches of the law where the main concepts are ambiguous, 'respect for procedural obligations assumes considerable importance and comes to the forefront as being an essential indicator of whether, in a concrete case, substantive obligations were or were not breached'.[19] This seems highly plausible; since notions such as 'sustainable development', or 'equitable and rational utilization of resources' have little discernible substantive content, they tend to manifest themselves largely in procedural obligations, and if that is so, then breaches of procedural obligations would indeed almost automatically imply breaches of substantive obligations.

Be that as it may, the main point to emerge from the case is that the Court held that in cases of planned projects that would place the environment at risk, general international law now ordained that an environmental risk assessment be undertaken.[20] The Court was reluctant to delineate the scope and content of such an obligation, only holding that it did not include a duty to consult the affected population.[21] Other than this, the Court found that 'it is for each State to determine in its domestic legislation or in the authorization process for the project, the specific content of the environmental impact assessment required in each case'.[22]

As the discussion of *Pulp Mills* above already suggests, with the Court finding that environmental impact assessments are ordained by international law, one of the few general principles of international environmental law to have emerged over the last few decades is the so-called precautionary principle. The basic idea is that in a world characterized by uncertainty and risk,[23] states should err on the side of caution; if it is unclear whether planned activities will have an adverse effect on the environment, states should refrain from engaging in them. Versions of this principle are reportedly to be found in over fifty multilateral instruments, but it is uncertain whether it can be called a customary rule or a general principle of law; state practice is not quite uniform.[24] None the less, the obligatory nature of environmental impact assessments, which demonstrates a precautionary attitude, suggests that the precautionary principle is considered normatively attractive.

---

[17] *Pulp Mills*, joint dissenting judges Al-Khasawneh and Simma, para. 5.
[18] In other cases it has been common for the Court to hear witnesses. See e.g. *Military and Paramilitary Activities in and Against Nicaragua (Nicaragua v. USA)*, [1986] ICJ Rep. 14.
[19] *Pulp Mills*, Al-Khasawneh and Simma, para. 26.   [20] *Pulp Mills*, para. 204.   [21] Ibid., para. 216.
[22] Ibid., para. 205.
[23] For a general study on the legal implications of risk, see Jenny Steele, *Risks and Legal Theory* (Oxford: Hart, 2004).
[24] Jonathan B. Wiener, 'Precaution', in Daniel Bodansky, Jutta Brunnée, and Ellen Hey (eds.), *The Oxford Handbook of International Environmental Law* (Oxford University Press, 2007), 597–612.

SPECIFIC ISSUES

There is no general international regime for the protection of the environment in the form of a general convention, or even a general international organization with the task of working for the environment. The closest international law has come is the creation of a programme on the part of the UN (the UN Environmental Programme, or UNEP), headquartered in unglamorous Nairobi, Kenya. Instead, environmental protection is parcelled out into a number of sectoral regimes.[25] The first of these, historically, is the regime on the protection of wildlife. The aftermath of the *Bering's Sea* arbitration saw the conclusion of the North Pacific Fur Seal Convention in 1911, a treaty to which the United States, the United Kingdom, Russia, and Japan were parties. Better known these days is in particular the CITES convention of 1973, restricting trade in endangered species on the theory that endangered species can be protected if trade in their skins or other products (think ivory) can be restricted. Earlier conventions saw to the protection of animals to the extent that they were useful for human purposes, but surely the philosophy underlying those conventions is no longer deemed acceptable.[26]

It is generally acknowledged that international environmental law took off in earnest with the convening of the Stockholm conference in 1972. The course it took in subsequent years marks a fragmentation in the regime; disparate topics are treated in disparate ways, by means of separate treaties. The first of these, concluded in Geneva in 1979, was the Convention on Long-Range Transboundary Air Pollution which, as its title suggests, aims to set limits to air pollution. The geographical scope of the convention is limited to Europe (but including some parts of the former USSR located in Asia) and North America, and substantively it consists mainly of procedural obligations: to report, inform, consult, and cooperate. Even its most substantive obligation is, so to speak, not very substantive; under article 6, the parties undertake to develop the 'best policies and strategies including air quality management systems', but without specifying what those best policies and strategies entail.

This has been further fleshed out in a number of more detailed protocols, addressing such matters as sulphur emissions and the use of heavy metals, volatile organic compounds, and persistent organic pollutants. This approach (adopting a general convention, and then fleshing out the details in further protocols) sets the tone also for later efforts; one of the hallmarks of international environmental law is the combined use of framework conventions complemented by more detailed protocols.

The regime on hazardous wastes and their disposal is largely governed by the 1989 Basel Convention on the Control of Transboundary Movements of Hazardous Wastes and their Disposal. Article 4 of this convention entitles the parties to ban the import of hazardous wastes, and these include wastes from the use of organic solvents,

---

[25] These can also be discussed when grouped into regions: one may, for instance, discuss environmental norms as they apply to the Mediterranean, or the Arctic, although it would be a stretch to claim that there is a separate and comprehensive regime to protect either of these. An overview of norms relating to the Arctic is Michael Byers, *International Law and the Arctic* (Cambridge University Press, 2013), ch. 6. Things are different with the Antarctic, though, as will be discussed below.

[26] An example is the 1902 Paris Convention for the Protection of Birds useful to Agriculture.

pharmaceuticals, and drugs, waste oils, and some explosive materials, among many others. Illegal traffic in prohibited wastes is considered criminal, and states are under an obligation to prevent and punish such illegal traffic (article 9). Excluded from the scope of the convention are radioactive wastes and waters stemming from the regular discharge of water by ships, on the theory that this is subject to other international instruments, and these include the 1997 Joint Convention on the Safety of Spent Fuel Management and on the Safety of Radioactive Waste Management. Since Africa in particular has been a popular dumping ground for wastes, the later Bamako Convention, concluded in 1991 and in force since 1998, specifically prohibits the import of wastes into member states of the African Union.

It is generally acknowledged that exposure to persistent organic pollutants, including DDT, can cause cancer, birth defects, and malfunctioning immune systems. Hence, the 2001 Stockholm Convention on Persistent Organic Pollutants (POPs) aims to eliminate certain chemicals altogether, and aims to restrict the use of certain others. To this end, the convention has two annexes, one specifying the POPs to be eliminated, the other more mildly focusing on the POPs to be restricted, and it will come as no surprise that much political debate revolves around the proper listing of POPs.

One of the success stories of international environmental law is the ozone layer regime. In 1985 states gathered in Vienna to create a framework convention, the Vienna Convention for the Protection of the Ozone Layer. This contained a number of general procedural obligations (the obligation to cooperate, in various settings) and set up an institutional framework for the protection of the ozone layer, but contained few substantive obligations. These, instead, were negotiated separately and laid down in the 1987 Montreal Protocol on Substances that Deplete the Ozone Layer. The main hallmark thereof is that it phases out the use of a number of substances that are considered harmful to the ozone layer. Again, much political debate has revolved around the question of which substances should be phased out, and according to which precise timetable. To some extent, this was made easier by the circumstance that less harmful alternatives were already available.

As noted, the ozone layer regime is usually considered a success story. Not only have the two main documents attracted close to two hundred ratifications each, but it is also calculated that the ozone layer is recovering, and may return to pre-1980s levels sometime between 2050 and 2075. As a result of the regime, some 97 per cent of ozone-depleting substances are controlled.[27]

Arguably the most debated environmental issue in recent decades has been that of climate change. The evidence that the climate is changing seems undeniable, although some still debate whether this results from human activities or whether it is the result of a natural shift in climate patterns. Either way, the planet is heating up, and the consequences may be huge. Fertile areas may become deserts, and polar ice may be melting, resulting in the submerging of islands and parts of coastal states.

---

[27] Ulrich Beyerlin and Thilo Marauhn, *International Environmental Law* (Oxford: Hart, 2011), at 158.

In 1992 the UN sponsored the Framework Convention on Climate Change, a multilateral convention boasting near-universal acceptance.[28] As its title suggests, though, the framework convention contains few substantive obligations, and is also otherwise not terribly ambitious; it aims to mitigate the situation by stabilizing the concentrations of greenhouse gases in the atmosphere, and additionally to adapt to the changing situation.[29] Then again, it was in all likelihood precisely the modesty of this ambition which helped to secure near-universal participation.

More specific and substantive obligations are to be found in a separately negotiated protocol, concluded in 1997 in Kyoto, and it is this Kyoto Protocol that sets out specific targets for emissions reductions. The core idea was that developed nations in particular agreed to reduce their emissions of specified greenhouse gases by a certain percentage, so as to reach a level lower than pre-1990 levels by the period between 2008 and 2012. At the same time, obligations on developing nations were less onerous; they were predominantly under certain reporting obligations, and would otherwise benefit from financial help and technological assistance from the developed nations. Needless to say, the Kyoto Protocol became highly controversial; states such as Canada and Russia took their time before ratifying, and the protocol only entered into force in 2005, leaving only a handful of years to reach the set targets.[30] Moreover, the United States never ratified, and that is quite a blow, as the United States on its own is estimated to be responsible for more than a third of CO_2 emissions.[31]

The much-anticipated Copenhagen meeting (the fifteenth meeting of the Conference of the Parties, hence known as COP 15) in December 2009 proved to be a disappointment.[32] While the parties repeated that they feel that climate change was not a good thing, the best they could reach was an agreement that global warming should not increase by more than 2 degrees centigrade. A year later, in Cancun, a number of states softly pledged to further reduce their greenhouse gases by fixed percentages targeting the year 2020. Thus Japan communicated a 25 per cent reduction compared with 1990 levels, Iceland a 30 per cent reduction, and Norway's target went as far as 40 per cent.

All in all, the situation does not bode well for the fight against climate change. Not only has the United States steadfastly remained outside the system (although it has communicated emission reduction targets), in December 2011 Canada formally denounced the protocol; both the United States and Canada are in the top ten of greenhouse gas emitting states. The inability to reach substantive agreement at Copenhagen and Cancun also signifies that the system is in crisis.

The agreement reached in Paris, in December 2015, suggests an interesting response, though. Since the setting of targets seems by and large to have failed, the Paris Agreement

---

[28] For a useful overview of the issues and responses relating to climate change, see Erkki Hollo, Kati Kulovesi, and Michael Mehling (eds.), *Climate Change and the Law* (Dordrecht: Springer, 2013).

[29] Beyerlin and Marauhn, *International Environmental Law*, at 159.

[30] Catherine Redgwell, 'International Environmental Law', in Malcolm D. Evans (ed.), *International Law*, 3rd edn (Oxford University Press, 2010), 687–721, at 704.

[31] Beyerlin and Marauhn, *International Environmental Law*, at 160.

[32] See also Daniel Bodansky, 'The Copenhagen Climate Change Conference: A Postmortem', (2010) 104 *American Journal of International Law*, 230–40.

pioneers a different approach, asking the parties to determine their own level of emission reductions (referred to as 'nationally determined contributions').[33] That said, the Paris Agreement posits the long-term overall goal of keeping global warming to within 2 degrees above pre-industrial levels. If the absence of pre-defined targets is already a novelty, so, too, is the idea of continuous progression: whenever reporting a new 'nationally determined contribution', parties are obligated to make this new contribution more ambitious than the previous one.[34] And while the Paris Agreement does not set immediate targets, it projects itself far into the future, aiming to achieve a balance between man-made emissions and the removal of greenhouse gases by sinks by the 'second half of this century'.[35] The Agreement will enter into force after having attracted fifty-five instruments of ratification representing at least 55 per cent of estimated global greenhouse gas emissions; this is expected to occur sometime in 2020. As at summer 2016, the Agreement has been ratified by twenty-two states, representing a little over 1 per cent of global greenhouse gas emissions.

During the twentieth century, it started to dawn on states that the marine environment ought to be protected, and a first hesitant attempt was made in the 1958 High Seas Convention to prevent oil pollution on the high seas as well as pollution through radio-active materials. Later, incidents such as the *Torrey Canyon* oil spill (a tanker breaking down off the UK coast)[36] gave rise to more specific treaties, such as the 1969 Brussels Convention relating to Intervention on the High Seas in Cases of Oil Pollution Damage, quickly followed by a Convention on Civil Liability for Oil Pollution Damage.

With the entry into force of UNCLOS,[37] the regime on marine environmental protection has become centralized.[38] UNCLOS provides little in the way of substantive obligations; instead, it focuses on questions of jurisdiction, with the main tension being the competition between coastal states (interested predominantly in preserving the environment) and flag states, whose immediate interests reside predominantly in freedom of navigation. Coastal states are granted the opportunity to provide for environmental regulation in their maritime zones, while leaving the traditional freedoms of the high seas intact.

UNCLOS functions, on this point, much like a framework convention, with more detailed regulation to be found in regional instruments, sometimes even pre-dating UNCLOS. The OSPAR Convention, for instance, concluded in Paris in 1992, deals with marine environmental protection in the north-east Atlantic, the North Sea and the adjacent Arctic waters, aiming to combat all sources of pollution (whether land-based or vessel-based). Likewise, a convention concluded in Helsinki in 1992 relates to the Baltic Sea, while the 1978 Kuwait Regional Convention for Cooperation on the Protection of the Marine Environment relates to the Persian Gulf.

---

[33] For an early brief comment, see Laurence Boisson de Chazournes, 'One Swallow Does not a Summer Make, but Might the Paris Agreement on Climate Change a Better Future Create?', (2016) 27 *European Journal of International Law*, 253–5.

[34] Article 4(3) Paris Agreement.   [35] Article 4(1) Paris Agreement.

[36] Oil spills occur with alarming regularity. Among the most well-known and catastrophic are the incidents involving the *Exxon Valdez* (1989), the *Prestige* (2002) and the explosion of the *Deepwater Horizon* rig (2010), discussed in the previous chapter.

[37] This is discussed in Chapter 13 above.

[38] See generally Kari Hakapää, *Marine Pollution in International Law* (Helsinki: Suomen Tiedeakademia, 1981).

One aspect often dealt with under the heading of environmental protection is the conservation of marine resources or, in other words, fisheries. The world's fishing fleet is larger than the oceans can handle; consequently, there is a risk of over-fishing, to the extent that fish stocks may become depleted. UNCLOS contains a few provisions on fisheries (articles 1161–20), but leaves freedom of fisheries by and large intact. Moreover, since UNCLOS allows for the expansion of coastal state jurisdiction, the problem of straddling fish stocks – fish moving from one state's jurisdiction to another's – became magnified. Hence, a separate treaty has been concluded to deal with these migratory species, the 1995 Straddling Fish Stocks Agreement,[39] in force since 2001. This too, however, has been characterized as being more in the nature of a framework agreement than actually implementing UNCLOS rules.[40]

Article 5 of the Straddling Fish Stocks Agreement lists a number of general principles: both coastal states and flag states must take measures to ensure sustainability of fish stocks; those measures must be based on the best scientific evidence available and respect the precautionary principle (as discussed above); states must adopt conservation and management measures; must minimize pollution, protect biodiversity, and take measures to prevent over-fishing.[41] At the same time, they must take into account the interests of artisanal and subsistence fisheries. Further implementation of the 1995 Agreement has been accomplished under auspices of regional fisheries organizations, such as the Northwest Atlantic Fisheries Organization (NAFO). This organization annually adopts conservation and enforcement measures relating to fisheries in its geographical area, including the total allowable catch for various species.

Among the older regimes is that regulating whaling.[42] The International Whaling Commission (IWC) was first established in 1946, and various agreements on the regulation of whaling, protecting some species, had already been concluded in the 1930s. At the heart of the regime is the distinction between whaling for scientific purposes, and whaling for commercial purposes, laid down in Article VIII of the 1946 International Convention for the Regulation of Whaling (ICRW). The former is allowed, but commercial whaling has been subject to a moratorium, effective since 1985/6. This has prompted some states to object (thus Norway is not bound by the moratorium), and others to leave the IWC (Iceland left in 1992, but re-joined in 2002).[43] Moreover, there are predictable debates on what exactly counts as whaling for purposes of scientific research.

---

[39] Its full title is not very catchy (no pun intended): Agreement for the Implementation of the UNCLOS Provisions Relating to the Conservation and Management of Straddling Fish Stocks and Highly Migratory Fish Stocks.

[40] Beyerlin and Marauhn, *International Environmental Law*, at 136.

[41] In its advisory opinion in Sub-Regional Fisheries Commission, ITLOS derived from articles 58, 62 and 192 UNCLOS a general obligation on flag states that are parties to UNCLOS to help to protect the marine environment and respect whatever measures coastal states may enact for that purpose, and regardless of whether they enact them individually or jointly through other agreements. *Request for an Advisory Opinion Submitted by the Sub-Regional Fisheries Commission (SRFC)*, opinion of 2 April 2015, paras. 121–124. See also the discussion in the previous chapter.

[42] For a recent study, see Malgosia Fitzmaurice, *Whaling and International Law* (Cambridge University Press, 2015).

[43] Ibid., at 139.

The matter came before the ICJ in 2014, with Australia claiming that Japanese whaling 'for purposes of scientific research' was, in fact, a disguised form of commercial whaling. The Court started by holding that the two elements of the phrase 'for purposes of scientific research' in article VIII ICRW are cumulative: whaling that becomes useful for scientific purposes by accident rather than design is not whaling 'for purposes of scientific research', and therewith prohibited.[44] The test to be applied in order to establish whether a programme is 'for purposes of scientific research' must be, according to the Court, an objective proportionality test: what matters is not so much whether some of the intentions are scientific or commercial, but rather 'whether the design and implementation of a programme are reasonable in relation to achieving the stated research objectives'.[45] In the end, the Court held that the most recent Japanese research programme did not meet this test: 'the evidence does not establish that the programme's design and implementation are reasonable in relation to achieving its stated objectives'.[46]

The management of rivers has been a concern of international law since the nineteenth century, when the first river commissions (such as the Rhine Commission) were set up, foreshadowing the later rise of international organizations. Yet this concern related mostly to maintenance and navigation of international rivers. A more recent concern has been the protection of the environment, in particular freshwater resources. These come in two variations, surface waters and groundwaters, but the latter are still left largely unregulated.

With respect to surface waters, the main general instrument at present is the 1997 UN Convention on the Law of the Non-Navigational Uses of International Watercourses, which came to replace the non-binding but influential Helsinki Rules, formulated in 1966 by the ILA. The 1997 convention entered into force in 2014, but still has only thirty-six parties, the most controversial provision being article 7, the obligation not to cause significant harm. States feel that some of their possibly harmful activities may none the less be legitimate, for example utilizing water for hydro-energy; depending on the local geography, this can cause considerable harm to downstream states, even if the intentions are benign. Politically, part of the problem with international watercourses is that upstream states can cause harm to states downstream.

Perhaps in mitigation, the UN Watercourses Convention contains as its main principle, laid down in article 5, that of equitable and reasonable utilization and participation; riparian states are called on to cooperate, and to use rivers in a reasonable and equitable manner in their respective territories. In doing so, they should take a number of factors into account, varying from the ecological and geographical to the economic and social. Moreover, the convention contains a number of procedural obligations relating to notification of scheduled activities, consultation and negotiations. Further obligations are laid down with respect to protection of the marine environment in international rivers without, however, amounting to any hard and fast rules; states should simply take all necessary measures to protect the environment, without the convention being specific as to what these measures should entail.

---

[44] *Whaling in the Antarctic*, para. 71.   [45] Ibid., para. 97.
[46] Ibid., para. 227. Note that this helpfully places the burden of proof on the state invoking the 'scientific research' exception.

While the 1997 convention mainly addresses surface waters, in 2008 the ILC presented a set of draft articles on the Law of Transboundary Aquifers, relating to layers of the earth (rock, sand, gravel, or silt) from which groundwater can be extracted. The draft articles follow, by and large, the model of the 1997 convention; they are built around the principle of equitable and reasonable utilization, and contain general obligations not to cause significant harm and to cooperate. For the moment, they remain draft articles: providing guidance and inspiration without being formally binding – the decision to convene a conference with a view to concluding a convention on the basis of the articles has yet to be taken.

Many of the environmental conventions concluded in recent decades include provisions on consultation, negotiation, and cooperation, and that raises the question of who should participate in these activities. The traditional answer would be that this is the prerogative of states, but, as noted earlier, states are not usually the immediate causes of environmental issues. Hence it was deemed desirable to broaden the circle of possible participants so as also to include other actors. With this in mind, a number of European states gathered in 1998 in Aarhus, Denmark, to conclude a Convention on Access to Information, Public Participation in Decision-Making and Access to Justice in Environmental Matters.[47]

The Aarhus Convention creates a set of procedural obligations for states. Specifically, states must promote environmental education and awareness; must recognize environmental groups and associations; should not penalize individuals or groups seeking access to information; and shall generally legislate so as to enable the public at large to participate in decision-making on environmental matters. Needless to say, this is not unlimited; access to information, for example, may be refused on grounds related to national security, or confidentiality and privacy, and other, similar grounds.

THE ANTARCTIC

There is one part of the world that is singled out for special treatment, and that is the Antarctic. While the Arctic is oceans surrounded by continents, the Antarctic is a continent surrounded by oceans, as someone once put it,[48] and a continent with special characteristics at that. As noted in Chapter 4 above, the Antarctic regime froze the territorial claims of a number of states by means of the 1959 Antarctic Treaty, and made it clear that the area should be used for peaceful and scientific purposes.[49] Already the 1959 Treaty, while general in nature, contained an environmental element: it unequivocally prohibited nuclear explosions and the disposal of radioactive waste.[50]

---

[47] The Convention entered into force in 2001 and currently (summer 2016) has forty-seven parties: forty-six European states plus the European Union. It has given rise to a protocol on Pollutant Release and Transfer Registers (in force since 2009, thirty-five parties), and an amendment, adopted in 2005, relating to genetically modified organisms. The amendment has yet to enter into force.
[48] Byers, *International Law and the Arctic*, at 28.
[49] A very readable, if somewhat outdated, account of the issues and chosen solutions is Keith Suter, *Antarctica: Private Property or Public Heritage?* (London: Zed Books, 1991).
[50] Article V Antarctic Treaty.

The Antarctic treaty was followed in 1980 by a treaty to protect the living resources of the area. To some extent, the living resources are also covered by other agreements: the Whaling Convention, for instance, also applies to the Antarctic, and the ICJ's 2014 judgment, discussed above, specifically concerned whaling in the Antarctic. In 1972, moreover, a specific Convention for the Conservation of Antarctic Seals was concluded. Still, the 1980 Convention on the Conservation of Antarctic Marine Living Resources (CCAMLR) is generally considered to be of great relevance, partly because of its comprehensive coverage, partly also because of the institutional machinery it established: its permanent secretariat has all the hallmarks of a veritable international organization. CCAMLR adopted an eco-system approach, 'viewing each resource in its environmental context, rather than on its own',[51] thereby helping to pave the way for later concepts such as biodiversity, and it protects not just fish, but also birds and crustaceans, of which krill is probably the most important one: it serves as food for penguins, seals, and whales, among others.

While a treaty on mining was concluded but never entered into force, in 1991 a protocol on environmental protection was concluded (in force since 1998), which contains a number of general environmental obligations. Thus it makes an environmental impact assessment compulsory for all activities in the Antarctic, including tourism, and contains a blanket ban on all mining activities, except for scientific purposes. Earlier, in 1964, a number of states adopted a set of Agreed Measures for the Conservation of Antarctic Flora and Fauna, designating Antarctica as a Special Conservation Area and prohibiting the unlicensed killing of animals and generally aiming to minimize harmful interference. Driving a vehicle too close to bird or seal populations was seen as constituting harmful interference, as was allowing dogs to run freely. The Agreed Measures became effective in 1982, but were deemed no longer to be applicable (no longer 'current') by a decision of the Antarctic Treaty Consultative Meeting in 2011 in Buenos Aires.

PROCEDURALIZATION AND INSTITUTIONALIZATION

As the above overview may suggest, international environmental law is short on specific, substantive obligations, and instead contains many procedural obligations and is charac-terized by a high degree of institutionalization. This is hardly a coincidence; where many of the obligations are of a procedural nature (to report, to cooperate, to consult), institutions are required to find agreement on more substantive matters, as well as to manage compli-ance with the procedural obligations – the reporting obligations in particular would come to naught without some institutional setting.

Hence, although no general international organization exists with the protection of the environment as its mandate, many of the conventions mentioned above have set up institutional devices of their own. Most have a secretariat, plainly necessary to manage the enormous streams of papers and communications involved in environmental

---

[51] Suter, *Antarctica*, at 39.

protection, and, typically, the secretariat is located in the city where the main document was concluded; the ozone layer secretariat, for instance, is based in Montreal.

Decision-making takes place not by convening ad hoc conferences every now and then, but by organizing regular conferences where all parties are invited. These are typically referred to as conferences of the parties (COPs) or, alternatively, meetings of the parties (MOPs). While not international institutions in a formal sense, these typically operate as the functional equivalent of international institutions, albeit with a very limited mandate and without specific legal powers to initiate action. Typically, COPs lack legal personality under international law, and cannot conclude treaties under international law, but none the less they can take decisions affecting their member states, and typically do so by consensus.[52]

Sometimes specific bodies are established in addition to the administrative machinery set up through COPs or MOPs and secretariats. One example, possibly the best known, is the Intergovernmental Panel on Climate Change, set up in 1988 to provide solid scientific data concerning climate change. But the panel is regularly accused of bias, demonstrating that there are few things in life that remain completely beyond politics.

Another example is the Commission on Sustainable Development, set up in the aftermath of the 1992 Rio Conference. Sustainable development became the term that saved the conference, due to what is sometimes referred to as its 'constructive ambiguity'. In other words, the term has no identifiable meaning; environmental activists can read into it a commitment to sustainability, whereas those who have more faith in markets can regard it as a confirmation that economic progress, too, is considered desirable. The Commission was set up to review the implementation of several policy initiatives; yet the term 'sustainable development' remains as opaque as when it was first introduced.

COMPLIANCE PROCEDURES

It has already been noted that environmental disputes rarely end up before the ICJ. Instead, many of the environmental agreements discussed have set up so-called 'compliance procedures', and these may well be considered as integral parts of the institutionalization of international environmental law. The underlying idea is, so to speak, that carrots may be more effective than sticks if a state does not comply;[53] hence, instead of holding a state responsible for breach, the state in question will be assisted in order to achieve compliance.[54] As a result, the procedures tend to be non-adversarial in nature, tend to

---

[52] Seminal discussions include Robin R. Churchill and Geir Ulfstein, 'Autonomous Institutional Arrangements in Multilateral Environmental Agreements: A Little-Noticed Phenomenon in International Law', (2000) 94 *American Journal of International Law*, 623–60, as well as Jutta Brunnée, 'COPing with Consent: Lawmaking under Multilateral Environmental Agreements', (2002) 15 *Leiden Journal of International Law*, 1–52.

[53] A theoretical basis is provided by the so-called managerial approach to international law, authoritatively framed by Abram Chayes and Antonia Handler Chayes, *The New Sovereignty: Compliance with International Regulatory Agreements* (Cambridge, MA: Harvard University Press, 1995).

[54] For an early discussion, see Martti Koskenniemi, 'Breach of Treaty or Non-compliance? Reflections on the Enforcement of the Montreal Protocol', (1992) 3 *Yearbook of International Environmental Law*, 123–62.

focus not on 'breach' but on 'non-compliance', and tend to result in making recommendations to the parties as to how to assist the state in non-compliance.

Typically, such procedures are set up under a specific environmental convention (such as the Montreal Protocol or the Kyoto Protocol) and substitute bureaucracy for law. Usually it is the secretariat set up under the treaty concerned that starts proceedings,[55] assessments are made by an implementation committee, after which the full meeting (or conference) of the parties decides whether there is a compliance problem, and what to do about it.

Compliance procedures raise a host of legal questions.[56] Some of these relate to the conduct of proceedings. Can a state appeal against a finding that its compliance is below par? Can it call witnesses, or ask for legal assistance? Some questions also relate to the place of compliance procedures in the bigger scheme of things: would it be possible, for instance, to start proceedings before the ICJ against a state if that state had already been found to be in compliance under a compliance procedure? Is the ICJ to be regarded as an appellate court if a compliance procedure is deemed to have been conducted unfairly?

Moreover, there may also be political drawbacks. Even though the law on state responsibility is not rigorously maintained, none the less the state found to be in non-compliance will be stigmatized, and it is hardly a coincidence that developing nations are far more often held to be in non-compliance than developed nations. As a result, there has been an increasing tendency to 'juridify' the procedure, and to develop rules on *amicus curiae* briefs, legal representation, reasoned decision-making, and strict time frames.[57] Ironically, though, the more the compliance procedure comes to resemble regular judicial procedures, the less it will operate as originally intended – as a gentle way to persuade parties to comply.[58]

FINAL REMARKS

Few issues are of such urgent importance as the protection of the global environment. After all, to put it bluntly, most other issues in international law depend on whether human life is sustainable to begin with; if human life comes to an end, there is little point in having detailed rules on investment protection, or on the treatment of prisoners of war. That said, environmental degradation does not take place overnight. States have the understandable urge to ignore problems until they manifest themselves, even if by then it may be late, perhaps even too late to take action.

---

[55] Typically, states have a right to initiate proceedings, but refrain from doing so. The Aarhus Convention on Access to Information, Public Participation in Decision-making and Access to Justice in Environmental Matters also allows members of the public to bring matters forward.

[56] For critical discussion, see Jan Klabbers, 'Compliance Procedures', in Bodansky, Brunnée and Hey, *Oxford Handbook*, 995–1009.

[57] See e.g. the rules relating to the compliance mechanism set up under the Kyoto Protocol, in UN Doc. FCCC/KP/CMP/2005/8/Add.3.

[58] See generally Tuomas Kuokkanen, 'Putting Gentle Pressure on Parties: Recent Trends in the Practice of the Implementation Committee under the Convention on Long-range Transboundary Air Pollution', in Jarna Petman and Jan Klabbers (eds.), *Nordic Cosmopolitanism: Essays in International Law for Martti Koskenniemi* (Leiden: Martinus Nijhoff, 2003), 315–26.

Combined with the issues mentioned above (the fact that states themselves are rarely the immediate culprits, the circumstance that wide political cleavages exist between states on what to do and how to pay for it), it is no surprise that international environmental law has only hesitantly come off the ground, and moves in fits and starts. Still, these circumstances also stimulate creativity on the part of negotiators, and it is hardly a coincidence that highly innovative compliance procedures have been pioneered precisely in the field of environmental protection. Strongly put, environmental protection is possibly the most convoluted sub-discipline of international law, where the tension between what many deem to be necessary, and how far individual states are willing to go, is at its most visible.

This has resulted, for instance, in the facility for emissions trading; if state A produces less pollution than it is entitled to produce, it can trade its surplus with a state that produces too much. While this may seem morally distasteful, it none the less appears to work reasonably well, creating market-based incentives for states to reduce their greenhouse gas emissions. And even though distasteful, it is also clear that alternatives (such as a possible 'greenhouse gas tax') remain politically out of reach.

FURTHER READING

Ulrich Beyerlin and Thilo Marauhn, *International Environmental Law* (Oxford: Hart, 2011)

Daniel Bodansky, 'The Copenhagen Climate Change Conference: A Postmortem' (2010) 104 *American Journal of International Law*, 230–40

Daniel Bodansky, Jutta Brunnée, and Ellen Hey (eds.), *The Oxford Handbook of International Environmental Law* (Oxford University Press, 2007)

Robin R. Churchill and Geir Ulfstein, 'Autonomous Institutional Arrangements in Multilateral Environmental Agreements: A Little-Noticed Phenomenon in International Law', (2000) 94 *American Journal of International Law*, 623–60

Malgosia Fitzmaurice, *Whaling and International Law* (Cambridge University Press, 2015)

Erkki Hollo, Kati Kulovesi and Michael Mehling (eds.), *Climate Change and the Law* (Dordrecht: Springer, 2013)

Geoffrey Palmer, 'New Ways to Make International Environmental Law,' (1992) 86 *American Journal of International Law*, 259–83

Keith Suter, *Antarctica: Private Property or Public Heritage?* (London: Zed Books, 1991)

15

The Global Economy

INTRODUCTION

It is probably fairly accurate to suggest that much of international law deals with the global economy in one way or another. While this may not directly apply to human rights or humanitarian law, other branches of international law have much to do with the economy. Thus the law of the sea was traditionally concerned with facilitating trade and communication. It is no coincidence that Grotius wrote his famous tract on the freedom of the high seas on assignment by the Dutch East Indies Company; legal argument was deemed necessary for economic purposes, as Spain and Portugal were about to divide the high seas between them, which would have had nasty economic repercussions for other seafaring nations.[1]

By the same token, maritime delimitation can be understood as an exercise in dividing potential spoils, especially since oil and gas reserves have been found on the continental shelf, and since deep seabed exploration has become at least hypothetically feasible. Likewise, rules on the distribution of satellites are economic in inspiration, whereas environmental rules function, to some extent, to stimulate competition on equal terms; a state with strict environmental standards may find it more difficult to attract foreign investment than a state with more relaxed environmental standards. Moreover, environmental regimes on occasion make use of economic incentives, such as the facility to trade emissions.

Still, to some extent (and perhaps so as to remind us that disciplinary divides tend to be rather arbitrary), a discernible body of international economic law has arisen, usually considered to revolve around a number of international organizations with specific tasks: monetary stability is provided by the IMF: development banks and investment banks help generate the funds for large-scale projects; trade relations are governed by the WTO.[2] In addition, in recent years investment rules have become increasingly important. But, perhaps most interestingly, public international law has come to have a say on relations

---

[1] Chapter 13 above.

[2] The history of the postwar institutions is well described in Richard Gardner, *Sterling-Dollar Diplomacy in Current Perspective: The Origins and the Prospects of our International Economic Order*, rev. edn (New York: Columbia University Press, 1980).

between private parties; there is a sense in which private international law has been subjected to harmonization and unification by means of treaties.[3]

PRIVATE INTERNATIONAL LAW

Older textbooks on public international law typically ignore private international law, and for good reason: private international law was said to address private relations (between individuals or companies) which just happened to have a transboundary element: the sale of a car between a seller in Germany and a buyer in Austria, or a marriage between a Swiss man and an Italian woman enacted in France, or a traffic incident in Belgium involving a Dutch driver and Norwegian victim.[4] And, what is more, private international law is, so to speak, a misnomer. Indeed, the term 'conflict of laws', often used in Anglo-Saxon parlance, would more closely indicate that such private relations continue to be governed by some form of domestic law, rather than by public international law (others still prefer to speak of international private law, to signify that it is private law with a foreign element)[5]. If a dispute arose between the German seller and Austrian buyer, it would typically be dealt with by a German or Austrian court, which would follow German or Austrian rules on which law should properly be applied. The law of the seller's state? Or the law of the buyer's state? Or the law of the state where the transaction took place? Or should one look for as many contact points as possible?[6] While often enough businesses aim to regulate such things in their contract ('This contract shall be governed by the law of X'), when the contract is silent domestic rules may be invoked to deal with an international transaction. And of course in traffic incidents parties do not first stipulate which law shall apply; they do not expect to be involved in an accident, after all.

This now is changing, and the change has been under way for quite some time. For, obviously, this old decentralized model had a few drawbacks. It would be possible, for instance (hypothetically at any rate) that in cases involving a sale from X to Y, one legal system would say that the national law of the seller should apply, whereas the other might say that the national law of the buyer should apply. More to the point, perhaps, it was thought harmful to have such a patchwork of domestic rules governing international trade; surely world trade would be better off with a more harmonized set of rules. Plus, it turned

---

[3] Textbooks on international economics pay little attention to the law of the sea or other branches of international law as addressing economic relations. See e.g. Matthias Herdegen, *Principles of International Economic Law* (Oxford University Press, 2013).

[4] Note also that the World Court does not, as a rule, engage in matters of private international law. Important exceptions, though, are the 1929 *Serbian Loans* and *Brazilian Loans* cases, in which the PCIJ paid quite a bit of attention to finding the law applicable to government loans. See, respectively, *Payment of Various Serbian Loans Issued in France*, [1929] Publ. PCIJ, Series A, no. 20, and *Payment in Gold of the Brazilian Federal Loans Issued in France*, [1929] Publ. PCIJ, Series A, no. 21. In *Brazilian Loans*, moreover, it also paid some attention to the theory of private international law, for instance on what it means to apply foreign law. See esp. at 16–17.

[5] So e.g. Adrian Briggs, *The Conflict of Laws* (Oxford: Clarendon Press, 2002).

[6] Things become trickier still when no identifiable territory is involved, as in transactions on the Internet. On this, see Tapio Puurunen, 'Dispute Resolution in International Electronic Commerce', doctoral thesis, University of Helsinki, 2005.

out, domestic judges have a distinct tendency to find their own rules often applicable, with the result that private parties would be encouraged to go 'forum-shopping': searching for the location with the most favourable or pliable judges. All in all, many thought, even before the Second World War, that some degree of harmonization, perhaps even unification, would be advisable. Some of this goes back to the late nineteenth century, when the Hague Conference on Private International Law was first convened (in 1893 – it later became a permanent international organization), and during the early part of the twentieth century the League of Nations did some work in this area.

But it is fair to say that most harmonization and unification has taken place since the Second World War. On several issues international treaties have been concluded. As was perhaps to be expected, some of these aim to address some of the practical problems involved in having judgments by local courts in cases involving foreign elements. After all, while it is one thing, living in France, to have a Swedish judgment in your favour, it is quite another to give effect to it in France. For this purpose, French law must recognize the Swedish judgment as valid in the French legal order.[7]

Hence, at least in Europe, several conventions on this sort of issue have been concluded, partly also under the impulse of the European Union. Thus, under article 2 of the 1968 Brussels Convention, in most civil and commercial matters the point of departure shall be that 'persons domiciled in Contracting State shall, whatever their nationality, be sued in the courts of that State'.[8] Being sued abroad is only possible in a limited set of circumstances. Any resulting judgment is, under article 26, automatically recognized, without special procedure, and will be enforced when this is requested (article 31). There are exceptions, though; among these, a state need not recognize a foreign judgment if this goes against its own public order, and the judgment cannot be irreconcilable with a different judgment between the same parties in the state in which recognition is sought (article 27). The 1988 Lugano Convention essentially addresses the same matters, but expands the convention's reach; it also encompasses a number of states that are not (or were not, at the time) EU member states.[9]

On the global level, this drive to recognition of judgments has understandably been less successful, but one important convention must be mentioned: the 1958 New York Convention on the Recognition and Enforcement of Foreign Arbitral Awards. While this deals with arbitral awards instead of judgments by regular courts, its scope is none the less truly remarkable. Most states of the world have joined the regime, with the result that an arbitral award issued in, say, Sweden, can be enforced in Peru under the same conditions as a Peruvian award would be (article III). As with the Brussels Convention, though, there are exceptions, and again conflict with public order ('public policy', under

---

[7] In 2009, Belgium brought a case against Switzerland before the ICJ on the enforcement of a private law judgment. The proceedings have, however, been discontinued. See *Jurisdiction and Enforcement of Judgments in Civil and Commercial Matters (Belgium v. Switzerland)*, removal, [2011] ICJ Rep. 341.

[8] Its full title is Brussels Convention on Jurisdiction and the Enforcement of Judgments in Civil and Commercial Matters.

[9] Lugano Convention on Jurisdiction and the Enforcement of Judgments in Civil and Commercial Matters. The Lugano Convention, substantively, complements the Brussels Convention, and on some points replaces it (see article 54B). It also replaces a number of pre-existing bilateral agreements.

article V) is one of them. It could plausibly be maintained that the New York Convention has greatly facilitated international commercial arbitration, and therewith quite possibly international trade in general.

Substantively, arguably the most important instrument is the 1980 UN Convention on Contracts for the International Sale of Goods (CISG). While the convention stops short of laying down a global contract statute (it does not, for instance, deal with issues of validity), it does provide basic rights and obligations of sellers and buyers doing business in different countries. It is thus important to note that it does not replace domestic contract law: contracts between a Dutch buyer and seller in the Netherlands remain governed by Dutch contract law; but where the Dutch seller finds a buyer in Morocco, the CISG may provide a useful service.

INTERNATIONAL TAXATION

Much of the legal situation of the individual is left to domestic law, as we have seen; while there are important international conventions on the treatment of refugees or on labour relations, governments have been reluctant to give up their control over these matters.[10] Something similar applies to taxation; there are many treaties on the avoidance of double taxation, and tax consultants can have a lucrative practice in advising clients on the different levels of taxation in different states, but it is decidedly rare to see taxation law treated as part of international law.[11]

The international tax regime is built around two guiding principles. The first is the 'single tax principle'; income should be taxed only once. It is for this reason that double taxation treaties may come to benefit individuals; in this way, they need not pay taxes on the same income in two different countries. It is still possible that if an individual has worked in two different countries during the fiscal year, she may have to pay taxes in both (and this can be a practical nightmare, since local ways of filling out forms and collecting taxes may be radically different),[12] but at least she will not be expected to pay twice on the same income. The second main principle relating to business income is the 'benefits principle'; business income is to be taxed where the benefits are reaped. Hence active business income is to be taxed at the source, whereas the profits on investments (passive income) are to be taxed at the residence of the investor.

It has also been claimed that some rules of international taxation have come to form part of customary international law – that is, these are considered binding on states even without a treaty obligation. Perhaps the most obvious example is that the jurisdiction to tax is generally based on residence,[13] hence Japan cannot suddenly impose a tax on the

---

[10] Chapter 6 above.

[11] But see Reuven S. Avi-Yonah, *International Tax as International Law: An Analysis of the International Tax Regime* (Cambridge University Press, 2007).

[12] Things may be even more difficult if taxation is not only nationally based, but also involves separate forms for regional and local taxes, as in the United States, where one is supposed to pay federal, state, and city taxes.

[13] The United States is an exception, in that it links taxation to citizenship. In principle, all US citizens are taxable, whether they reside in the United States or not.

population of Portugal. A further prominent example is the rule that in intra-company trade (i.e. trade between a parent company and a subsidiary), the basis for taxation should be the price of the traded product or service as if it had been negotiated on the open market. Another example might be the principle of non-discrimination between citizens or companies of different states.[14]

The upshot of arguing that tax law is part of international law would mean that states would lose the possibility of making independent tax policy. If, for instance, the non-discrimination norm is part of customary international law, it follows that states cannot unilaterally depart from it (although they may be able to 'contract out' by mutual agreement). Either way, given the existence of many bilateral tax treaties, and given the circumstance that many of these share similar contents, it seems plausible enough to argue that an international tax regime exists.

One of the more glaring infelicities of the fact that the authority to tax remains a firm sovereign prerogative is that it stimulates a 'race to the bottom': states compete with one another on issues such as corporate taxation, and global companies can utilize the resulting differences and loopholes in order to minimize the amount of taxes they pay. In response, the Organization for Economic Cooperation and Development (OECD) is pioneering a project aiming to create a multilateral regime to avoid what it refers to as 'base erosion and profit shifting'; one of the envisaged outcomes is a multilateral treaty amending existing bilateral treaties.[15]

FINANCIAL INSTITUTIONS

In the aftermath of the Second World War, it was sometimes considered that the war had been in part the result of economic instability. In particular, so the argument went, economic relations were truly international, but often impeded by parochial nation states. While companies simply wanted to do business, global politics still showed a patchwork of states, each of them sovereign, and each of them devising its own economic policies. Quite often, moreover, those policies would be detrimental to economic relations; it is no coincidence that the 1920s and 1930s are known as the heyday of protectionism. In short, global peace would only be possible, so the thought gained ground, if the economic system were placed under some form of global control or regulation, as opposed to local control.

This provided a strong impetus for in particular the creation, post-war, of the IMF. During the war, in 1944, a number of states met in Bretton Woods (in the United States), and decided to create a fund that could provide monetary stability. At the same time, it also became clear that the devastated nations of Europe could use all the help they could get in trying to reconstruct themselves. For this purpose, Bretton Woods saw the parallel creation of an institution responsible for reconstruction and development: the World Bank.[16]

---

[14] Avi-Yonah, *International Tax.*

[15] Itai Grinberg and Joost Pauwelyn, 'The Emergence of a New International Tax Regime: The OECD's Package on Base Erosion and Profit Shifting (BEPS)', (2015) 19 *ASIL Insights*, issue 24.

[16] It is officially still known as the International Bank for Reconstruction and Development.

Both institutions work on the basis of capital poured into them by their member states, and the states that contribute the largest sums have the largest number of votes.[17] This makes them unique; unlike most other international organizations, they operate on the basis of weighted voting rather than the 'one state, one vote' principle. Both are also supposed to take their decisions on economic grounds alone. While this was originally intended to isolate them from political considerations, it has come to result in a certain tension between their constituent treaties and human rights considerations; a strict interpretation of the injunction to base decisions on economic grounds alone may result in human rights violations (e.g. by displacing people), and that can hardly be considered acceptable.[18]

As its main task the IMF has to provide stability if states suffer from balance of payments problems, as such problems can easily spread across borders. In order to assist, the IMF is willing to lend money to states, provided those states make structural adjustments to their economies – that is, follow the prescriptions developed by IMF economists. The conditions can reach far into the domestic economy; they may encompass such things as tax reform, debt restructuring, banking reform, and higher rates for utilities such as electricity. Not only are these conditions very invasive, they can also be very risky; if the IMF gets it wrong, the state concerned may be in a far worse position than it was before it went to the IMF.[19]

While the IMF deals with monetary stability, the World Bank's main task is to stimulate development (the 'reconstruction' still visible in its official name has receded into the background). It does so by lending money for specific projects, such as the building of a dam, or the creation of a transport network. It, too, places conditions on those loans, and those conditions inevitably end up reflecting the political and economic preferences of the Bank's dominant member states.[20]

The World Bank has been highly creative in responding to new challenges. While its Articles of Agreement do not allow it to sponsor private-sector projects (the projects must have state backing), it has set up the International Finance Corporation (IFC) to do so, and created a separate International Development Agency (IDA) to cater for the needs of the poorest and least-developed countries, offering loans on softer conditions than the Bank itself. The Multilateral Investment Guarantee Agency (MIGA) aims to promote flows of foreign direct investment to developing countries, whereas the International Centre for the Settlement of Investment Disputes (ICSID) promotes the peaceful and smooth settlement of disputes arising out of investments between companies and states.

The Bank has also responded creatively to more substantial challenges. Recognizing the potential of investing in environmental protection, it set up, in 1991, a Global Environmental Facility (which has in the meantime grown into a separate international organization), while in response to complaints from civil society about the impact of some policies

---

[17] For useful brief descriptions, see Ian Hurd, *International Organizations: Politics, Law, Practice* (Cambridge University Press, 2011).

[18] Hence a somewhat more accommodating interpretation has been proposed by the World Bank's former legal counsel. See Ibrahim Shihata, 'Human Rights, Development and International Financial Institutions', (1992) 8 *American University Journal of International Law and Policy*, 27–37.

[19] For a strong critique see Joseph E. Stiglitz, *Globalization and its Discontents* (London: Penguin, 2002).

[20] A fine and balanced study of the politics of the IMF and the World Bank is Ngaire Woods, *The Globalizers: The IMF, the World Bank, and Their Borrowers* (Ithaca, NY: Cornell University Press, 2006).

on large groups of people, the Bank set up an Inspection Panel to help to ensure that it conforms to its own internal policies and rules.[21]

The general idea of stimulating project investment has found quite a following since the creation of the World Bank; there are international investment banks on all continents, ranging from the Nordic Investment Bank to the Asian Development Bank, and from the East African Development Bank to the Inter-American Development Bank. China, moreover, marked its emergence as a global economic power by sponsoring the creation, in 2015, of the Asian Infrastructure Investment Bank (AIIB), widely regarded as a potentially serious competitor to the World Bank. All of this entails that a large international bureaucracy exists to address development issues and, not unimportantly either, these banks are typically subject to credit ratings by credit rating agencies, providing these (private) agencies with a lot of power.

WORLD TRADE AND THE WTO

The most important institution for the organization of global trade relations is, without doubt, the WTO.[22] The WTO succeeded an earlier agreement, the General Agreement on Tariffs and Trade (GATT – sometimes nicknamed, not unreasonably, General Agreement to Talk and Talk), which had been applied between trading nations since 1947, albeit on a provisional basis; as it was feared that the US Senate would not grant approval to the broader Havana Charter inaugurating an International Trade Organization, part of the Havana Charter was lifted out and applied separately as GATT, always with a view to consolidation. The result was a strange animal; a de facto organization built around the desirability of free trade, but without any organs. These organs were later added in piecemeal fashion, and in particular the panels set up to solve trade disputes proved inspirational.

GATT was based on the idea that states should negotiate bilaterally, under GATT's umbrella, about tariff reductions, and to this end several rounds of negotiations were successfully concluded. The concessions thus granted on a bilateral basis were subject to two further basic rules: the national treatment rule (foreign products should be treated no less favourably than domestic products), and the classic and intriguing most-favoured-nation rule (MFN) (preferences to other states should be no less than those granted to the state treated most favourably). Thus, a veritable web of concessions was created, expanding constantly through the use of these two rules, and for many years GATT was considered to be a great success. Yet the success had a shadow side; while tariffs dropped globally as a result, states proved inventive in devising other obstacles to free trade, often referred to as 'non-tariff barriers'. These can include straightforward import quotas, but also less obvious obstacles to trade, such as local requirements that products be packaged only in a certain

---

[21] On the topic of self-regulation by international organizations, spearheaded by the Inspection Panel, see Jan Klabbers, 'Self-control: International Organizations and the Quest for Accountability', in Malcolm Evans and Panos Koutrakos (eds.), *The International Responsibility of the European Union* (Oxford: Hart, 2013), 75–99.

[22] A very readable introduction is Michael J. Trebilcock, *Understanding Trade Law* (Cheltenham: Edward Elgar, 2011).

form, or be produced only in certain ways. Moreover, GATT obviously had more to offer to Western trading nations than to the developing world; a separate set of provisions addressing the plight of developing nations was added in the mid-1960s, but contained very little by way of hard and enforceable obligations.[23]

While GATT provided for a largely improvised dispute settlement mechanism, there was widespread agreement that the mechanism did not work very well. Under GATT, a state that felt that its rights (or even only its benefits) were hampered by another state could ask for consultations, and eventually perhaps for the establishment of a panel to settle the dispute. These panels would operate, more often than not, on the basis of trade ideas rather than strict law, and it would sometimes be difficult to identify a constant line of judicial decision-making; the system was often considered more 'political' or 'diplomatic' than 'legal'. And even if a state 'won' before a panel, the victory could be meaningless; the panel report required adoption by the plenary, including the 'losing' state. Hence, the latter always could, and sometimes did, veto the adoption of the panel report.

By the mid-1980s it became clear that GATT was lagging behind the times; its dispute settlement procedures were considered insufficient, and while GATT dealt with trade in goods, it never addressed trade in services, although many Western economies had in the meantime become service-based. Banking and insurance, for instance, had overtaken industrial production as a key component of Western economies. Moreover, it became clear that values other than the purely economic could influence the perception of GATT in a negative way.

A good indication of the declining legitimacy of GATT was the fate of the *Tuna–Dolphin* case before GATT, in the early 1990s.[24] The United States had in 1988 adopted measures to protect dolphins from being accidentally killed during tuna harvesting, outlawing the sale in the United States of tuna caught by means of so-called 'driftnets' – nets sweeping the water and catching everything, including dolphins. The US measure consisted of a prohibition on selling driftnet tuna in the United States, something that affected, among others, Mexican fishermen. Mexico filed a complaint, and a panel agreed that in principle, the US measure violated its commitments under GATT. The United States argued that none the less the measure was justified under the general GATT exceptions of article XX, for instance in order to protect animal life or the conservation of exhaustible natural resources,[25] but this the panel did not accept; the US measures could not be considered 'necessary', in terms of article XX – other, less trade-intrusive measures could have been explored. As a result, the United States blocked adoption of the panel report, leading to a stand-off.

The *Tuna–Dolphin* case confirmed that it was time for an overhaul, and the overhaul had already started when in 1986 the Uruguay Round of trade negotiations was launched, with a view to creating a fully fledged international organization capable of addressing trade in

---

[23] The classic study of GATT remains John H. Jackson, *World Trade and the Law of GATT* (Indianapolis, IN: Bobbs-Merrill Co., 1969).

[24] *United States – Restrictions on Import of Tuna*, DS21R-39S155. To be sure, the case played out while Uruguay Round negotiations were already under way.

[25] On article XX generally, see Jan Klabbers, 'Jurisprudence in International Trade Law – Article XX of GATT', (1992) 26/2 *Journal of World Trade*, 63–94.

services and with a strong dispute settlement mechanism. These negotiations came to a close with the entry into force, in January 1995, of the Agreement establishing the WTO, a package of agreements including the old GATT, but with separate attention for services (General Agreement on Trade in Services – GATS), as well as, under pressure from the pharmaceutical and entertainment industries, a separate agreement on the Trade-Related Aspects of Intellectual Property (TRIPs).[26] In addition, the WTO Agreement comprises several agreements dealing with specific sectors (dairy) or specific practices (dumping, subsidies), and on non-tariff barriers to trade, in particular on sanitary and phytosanitary measures (what measures can states take to guarantee public health of humans, animals, and plants?) and on technical barriers to trade, dealing with such things as production requirements, marketing requirements, and so on. These last two in particular were thought to address the non-trade concerns by streamlining and refining the exceptions of GATT article XX, although it seems fair to say that non-trade concerns still occupy but a marginal place within the WTO. Finally, the jewel in the crown, and arguably the main reason why the WTO is considered to be of great importance, the WTO Agreement includes a dispute settlement understanding (DSU).

The WTO DSU provides a far more 'legalized' mechanism than that prevailing under GATT; states can still resort to panels, and those panels still take into account more than strictly legal concerns, but in a case of dissatisfaction on a legal point appeal is possible to the Appellate Body, a court-like group of seven eminent lawyers, elected through the member states and appointed for a four-year, renewable term. If no appeal is made, the report stands as adopted, unless rejected by the dispute settlement body (DSB) (in essence, WTO's entire membership) by consensus. Hence, the 'losing' side no longer has a veto. Reports from the Appellate Body likewise are considered to have been adopted, unless rejected by the DSB by consensus. The procedure is therewith much more streamlined and much more 'legal' than was the case in GATT;[27] it is hardly an exaggeration to suggest that the WTO is essentially a free trade agreement with a strong dispute settlement mechanism attached to it.

WTO panel reports do not make for easy reading. They often run into hundreds of pages, and often contain highly repetitive arguments. One of the reasons for this is that the DSU is liberal in granting third parties the right to intervene in disputes, the underlying idea being, no doubt, that complaints about domestic trade rules rarely stem from a single state. If state A has a peculiar policy concerning, say, the method by which tuna ought to be caught, this will most probably affect not only fishermen from state B, but from many other states as well. Moreover, while the WTO is not open to complaints by private parties (it remains an inter-state organization), the Appellate Body has ruled that the private sector and civil society are allowed to issue *amicus curiae* briefs. Hence, panels are forced to address not just state B's argument, but also those (often quite similar) from states C, D, and E, and have the discretion to also take *amicus curiae* briefs into account. All those arguments then need

---

[26] A particularly good study of the origin of the TRIPs agreement is Susan K. Sell, *Private Power, Public Law: The Globalization of Intellectual Property Rights* (Cambridge University Press, 2003).

[27] Indeed, it is sometimes regarded as the example *par excellence* of the late twentieth-century drive towards the 'legalization' of global politics. See e.g. Judith L. Goldstein et al. (eds.), *Legalization and World Politics* (Cambridge, MA: MIT Press, 2001).

to find a place in the panel report or Appellate Body report, in order to do justice to the concerns of all stakeholders.[28]

Perhaps the biggest challenge for the WTO to date has been how to confront other legal regimes. Trade, after all, does not take place in a vacuum, but may affect other walks of life: as the *Tuna-Dolphin* dispute already suggested, free trade may negatively affect the environment, and may also negatively affect other values, such as those relating to safety at the workplace. In a recent decision, the WTO suggested that it is receptive to such concerns: in *EC – Seal Products*, it emphasized that a genuine concern for animal welfare could be seen as falling within the scope of the legitimate protection of public morals, even if the EU measures concerned were still found to be discriminatory.[29] The point, though, is that animal welfare was accepted in principle as a ground for limiting trade, and, as has been noted, the flaws in the EU seal regime could easily be remedied.[30]

It is sometimes held that the WTO is unique among international organizations in that it has no independent policy-making or law-making powers, and to a large extent this is correct. The WTO cannot, for instance, issue decisions on whether cartels are acceptable, unless this comes up in litigation.[31] Still, hypothetically two avenues are open for WTO decision-making. First, the WTO can sponsor agreements between its member states. Those will remain regular treaties, and need to be accepted by the membership at large, by unanimity, in order to qualify as WTO agreements. As a result, it has proven difficult to conclude anything in recent years, and states are increasingly looking elsewhere. One important development is the negotiation of so-called 'megaregional' agreements between groups of trading nations. One example is the Trans-Pacific Partnership, involving the United States, Japan, and a number of other Asian states. Another, even more prominently visible in political debate, is the Transatlantic Trade and Investment Partnership (TTIP) under negotiation between the United States and the EU. Taken together, these agreements have the potential (and, it seems, the ambition) of reducing the WTO to an irrelevance, once again leaving the developing world behind.[32]

A second decision-making device, and practically more important, is the WTO's power to release groups of states from some of their WTO commitments by granting so-called 'waivers'. This is relevant, for instance, when it comes to the creation of regional trading blocs; these violate, in principle, the MFN and national treatment requirements, but become legally acceptable if the WTO gives its stamp of approval in the form of a waiver.[33]

---

[28] An insightful discussion of the approach of the Appellate Body to issues of both legality and legitimacy is Robert Howse, 'The World Trade Organization 20 Years On: Global Governance by Judiciary', (2016) 27 *European Journal of International Law*, 9–77.

[29] WT/DS400/AB/R and WT/DS401/AB/R, *European Communities – Measures Prohibiting the Importation and Marketing of Seal Products*, 22 May 2014.

[30] Robert Howse, Joanna Langille and Katie Sykes, 'Sealing the Deal: the WTO's Appellate Body Report in EC – Seal Products', (2014) 18 *ASIL Insights*, issue 12.

[31] René Uruena, 'The Underlying Question: The World Trade Organization and its Powers to Adopt a Competition Policy', (2006) 3 *International Organizations Law Review*, 55–91.

[32] For a critical research project organized at New York University, see https://wp.nyu.edu/megareg/ (visited 16 August 2016).

[33] Isabel Feichtner, *The Law and Politics of WTO Waivers: Stability and Flexibility in Public International Law* (Cambridge University Press, 2012).

Waivers may also be sought so as to temporarily restrict trade in certain specific products; a well-known example concerns the trade in diamonds, so as to prevent the financing of civil unrest.[34]

Despite predominantly addressing the interest of private businesses, such businesses have no direct access to the WTO. Disputes must be brought by states on behalf of companies, though without the strict requirements about diplomatic protection so characteristic of the ICJ.[35] Intriguingly, companies also lack the possibility of invoking WTO law before domestic courts, as all three of the big trading economies (the United States, the EU, and Japan) have declared WTO law to be 'non-self-executing'. A Japanese trader, for instance, cannot contest the compatibility of an EU regulation with WTO law before the CJEU, except in certain very specific circumstances (e.g. if the EU regulation is explicitly intended to transpose WTO commitments into EU law).[36] Likewise, EU companies cannot go to court in the United States or Japan in order to complain that US or Japanese laws violate WTO law. The underlying reason is an elaborate game of 'chicken':[37] all three fear that if they allow WTO law to be directly effective, then their bargaining position may be weakened. There will be less possibility of gaining concessions in negotiations, since those concessions may already have been granted by their own courts.[38]

Decision-making in the WTO takes place, formally speaking, by consensus, with a two-thirds majority decision-making process as a fall-back option. In reality, though, it is clear that some states have rather more influence than others. Developing nations often complain about being 'strong-armed' into concessions; it is difficult to argue against a coalition comprising the EU, the United States and Japan. These three, having a strong position in global markets, are generally keen on as little intervention as possible or, alternatively, want to restrict trade to protect other values (such as environmental concerns); developing nations, on the other hand, may be mostly interested in being able to secure preferential market access for their products, or in other ways protect vulnerable industries in volatile markets. To make matters more complicated still, larger developing nations (Brazil, India, South Africa) tend to have interests that are different from those of smaller ones, and may often take sides with the industrialized nations, making life extremely hard for small developing nations. Often these have no choice but to join the global market, without being able to exercise much influence. As a result, the decision-making process is often considered tilted against developing nations, despite the formal guarantees of decision-making by consensus.[39]

---

[34] Ian Smillie, 'Not Accountable to Anyone? Collective Action and the Role of NGOs in the Campaign to Ban "Blood Diamonds"', in Alnoor Ebrahim and Edward Weisband (eds.), *Global Accountabilities: Participation, Pluralism, and Public Ethics* (Cambridge University Press, 2007), 112–30.

[35] Chapter 8 above.

[36] For general discussion see Jan Klabbers, 'International Law in Community Law: The Law and Politics of Direct Effect', (2002) 21 *Yearbook of European Law*, 263–98.

[37] The game of chicken is one in which the first person to lose their nerve and withdraw from a dangerous situation is the loser; it has been immortalized in various movies, when the one who first steps on the brakes when driving as fast as possible towards a wall is considered a coward (chicken).

[38] See also Chapter 16 below.

[39] See e.g. Fatoumata Jawara and Aileen Kwa, *Behind the Scenes at the WTO* (London: Zed Books, 2004).

INVESTMENT PROTECTION

Traditionally, perhaps the leading antecedent to international economic law was the protection of foreign investment. Under the innocuous heading of 'injury to aliens', long the most obvious example of state responsibility,[40] international law facilitated the protection of investments by allowing states to exercise diplomatic protection if something happened to foreign investments, and until the early twentieth century even allowed states to go to war in order to reclaim private debts.[41] It is no coincidence that quite a few of the decisions of the PCIJ concerned the fate of private investments in foreign countries.

Perhaps the most emblematic of these was the *Mavrommatis* saga.[42] Mr Mavrommatis, a Greek businessman, had made investments in public works in Palestine when that territory was part of the Ottoman Empire. After the First World War Palestine became a British Mandate territory, and Mavrommatis claimed that Britain was unwilling to recognize the contracts concluded. Consequently, he approached the Greek government, which started legal proceedings on his behalf, asking for almost UK£250,000[43] in compensation. During the jurisdictional stage of the proceedings, the PCIJ famously posited a connection between private claims and diplomatic protection:

> By taking up the case of one of its subjects and by resorting to diplomatic action or international judicial proceedings on his behalf, a State is in reality asserting its own rights – its right to ensure, in the person of its subjects, respect for the rules of international law.[44]

Where investments used to be protected by diplomatic means, including the institution of diplomatic protection, this is no longer the case – at least not exclusively. Currently, investors often have the possibility of taking direct action against (allegedly) wrongdoing states, for example before the Permanent Court of Arbitration, or before the International Centre for the Settlement of Investment Disputes (ICSID), set up in the mid-1960s under the auspices of the World Bank. Provided both the home state of the investor and the state in which the investments are made are parties to the ICSID Convention, a maltreated company can take action, provided the parties to the dispute (i.e. the investor and the state of investment) consent thereto in writing. The dispute must arise directly out of the investment, and this typically refers to foreign direct investment rather than portfolio investment.

During the first years of its existence ICSID was used rather sparingly, many of the famous investment disputes of the 1970s being dealt with through ad hoc arbitration. Many of these concerned oil concessions. Typically, an oil company had made investments with a view to exploring and exploiting oil reserves, based on a contract with a state rich in oil reserves. The state would subsequently expropriate the oil company's property or, more

---

[40] And, indeed, the context in which rules on state responsibility were first developed: see Tzvika Nissel, 'A History of State responsibility: The Struggle for International Standards (1870–1960)', doctoral thesis, University of Helsinki, 2016.

[41] This came to an end after the conclusion of the Drago–Porter Convention in 1907; see below, this chapter.

[42] Mr Mavrommatis's claims came before the PCIJ on at least three occasions.

[43] This would amount to the equivalent of some £8 million at the beginning of the twenty-first century.

[44] *Mavrommatis Palestine Concessions*, [1924] Publ. PCIJ, Series A, no. 2, at 12.

probably, change its tax regime, so that much of the planned profit never materialized. This raised important legal questions, such as whether the contract in question was governed by international law or by the law of the state concerned,[45] or whether any takings would be justified in the name of the notion of permanent sovereignty over natural resources. The latter was, during the 1970s, a highly popular idea within the UN General Assembly, spearheading what was sometimes referred to as a New International Economic Order.[46]

Perhaps the most significant development of the last few decades has been the conclusion of bilateral investment treaties (BITs). An informed estimate holds that there are currently some 3,000 BITs in force, often between developed and developing nations, but increasingly also between developing nations *inter se*.[47] Typically, the parties promise to protect investments made by investors of their nationality, and provide for compulsory arbitration, for example with ICSID or the PCA, in case a legal dispute ensues.[48] Often those disputes involve what is referred to as indirect expropriation; the host state takes certain legislative or administrative measures which, so the investor claims, amount to a deprivation of his right to property. While such measures cannot be classified as acts of expropriation or nationalization per se, they may amount to 'indirect expropriation' or, in the jargon of some domestic legal systems, 'regulatory takings'. Consequently, the investor may be awarded large sums in damages, presenting the state concerned with a headache; any attempt to change domestic law as it relates to topics such as the environment, labour regulation, or taxation, may come with a heavy price tag.[49]

This is not to say that expropriation, whether direct or indirect, is strictly prohibited.[50] It is generally accepted that states may expropriate foreign property, but only if certain conditions are met. First, the expropriation must not serve the personal interests of a local government official or be done for political reasons (e.g. to get back at an unfriendly government), but must instead serve a public purpose. Second, the expropriation must be non-discriminatory: it should not target the property of nationals of a single state leaving others, who are in the same position, untouched. Thus, it has been held that the Cuban expropriation of US-owned property after Fidel Castro's seizing of power was illegal, as only US-owned property was expropriated. Third, and of greatest political relevance perhaps, expropriation should be compensated; this has given rise to heated debates about the precise standard of compensation.[51]

---

[45] The leading monograph is Esa Paasivirta, *Participation of States in International Contracts* (Helsinki: Finnish Lawyers' Publishing Company, 1990).

[46] More on this below.

[47] Charles Leben, 'The State's Normative Freedom and the Question of Indirect Expropriation', in Charles Leben, *The Advancement of International Law* (Oxford: Hart, 2010), 87–107, at 93, note 17.

[48] A fairly random example is the agreement concluded between Armenia and India, reproduced in Jan Klabbers (ed.), *International Law Documents* (Cambridge University Press, 2016).

[49] For a fine study, see Gus van Harten, *Investment Treaty Arbitration and Public Law* (Oxford University Press, 2007).

[50] See e.g. August Reinisch, *Recent Developments in International Investment Law* (Paris: Pedone, 2009), 51–60.

[51] There is some discussion as to whether expropriations must follow 'due process', i.e. whether decisions to expropriate must be reviewable by an independent tribunal: ibid., at 54–5.

An authoritative formula was proposed in the early 1940s by US Secretary of State Cordell Hull, according to which compensation should be 'prompt, adequate, and effective'. Needless to say, though, this did little to alleviate any issues, for two reasons. A first is that coming from a Western nation, the formula was automatically suspect as biased; by contrast, many investment host states felt that the matter of compensation ought to be decided in accordance with their domestic law. Second, even at face value, terms such as 'prompt', 'adequate', and 'effective' are themselves open-ended and highly contextual. While together they suggest a more investor-friendly standard than the relatively anodyne standard of 'appropriate compensation' that was sometimes mentioned as an alternative, none the less it is clear that much depends on context and on the individual preferences of investment arbitrators. Much may also depend on how 'investment' itself is conceptualized; for some, it may be seen as a necessary evil, allowing states to boost their local economies at the expense of ceding control to foreign private investors, whereas for others investments may signify a much more harmonious, long-term relationship between investor and host country.[52]

As is the case with inter-state proceedings, the panel must first establish that it has jurisdiction. This was not always much of a problem, but assumed some prominence in a few cases brought on the basis of the substantive law of the Energy Charter Treaty (ECT) against states which had never ratified the treaty, but were considered bound to apply it provisionally, under article 45 ECT.[53] The panel in *Kardassopoulos* v. *Georgia* held that indeed Georgia was bound to accept arbitration under the treaty, despite not having ratified it;[54] a later panel in *Yukos and others* broadly agreed.[55] Still, a Dutch court later voiced a different conception, holding that the resort to arbitration under the provisionally agreed ECT must be in conformity with domestic rules on resort to arbitration.[56]

Investment disputes in their modern form are unlikely to come before the ICJ. One reason for this is formal; one of the parties is a private company, and can therefore not appear before the ICJ.[57] A second reason, though, is more substantive. Investment law is a highly specialized sub-discipline where there is usually a lot at stake, and investors in particular seem inclined to prefer swift and flexible proceedings. Arbitration might therefore be better geared towards suiting the interests of the parties than formal adjudication; arbitral panels can be set up relatively quickly under ICSID or under other recognized mechanisms; there exist more or less standardized procedural rules, and there is a pool of possible arbitrators with special expertise in investment law. This is also a political drawback,

---

[52] For the latter conception, see Rudolf Dolzer and Christoph Schreuer, *Principles of International Investment Law* (Oxford University Press, 2008), at 3.

[53] The Energy Charter Treaty was concluded in 1994 between a number of European (and a few other) states, aiming to secure investment in eastern Europe's somewhat outdated energy infrastructure while securing energy supplies to consumers in western Europe.

[54] *Ioannis Kardassapoulos* v. *Georgia*, ICSID Case No. ARB/05/18, decision on jurisdiction, 6 July 2007, paras. 205–23.

[55] See, e.g., *Yukos* v. *Russian Federation*, PCA Case No. AA 227, Interim Award on Jurisdiction and Admissibility, 30 November 2009, paras. 244–398.

[56] Joined cases C/09/447160 HA ZA 15-1 et al., *Russian Federation* v. *Veteran Petroleum Ltd. et al.*, judgment of the District Court of The Hague, 20 April 2016.

[57] It is also not entirely untypical that the investor is a company registered abroad, but owned by nationals of the state in which the investment takes place.

though; those same individuals may often also represent clients before other panels, and may thus be inherently drawn to sympathize with the claimant company's position.

By contrast, whenever investment related disputes are brought to the ICJ, they typically involve not investment as such but a limited aspect thereof; an example is the dispute between Argentina and Uruguay surrounding the setting up of a pulp mill near the boundary river.[58] Alternatively, cases can still be brought to the ICJ on the basis of diplomatic protection, but the most recent example is almost three decades old: the 1989 *ELSI* case, between Italy and the United States and addressing the physical protection of property against, for instance, occupation of a company's premises by its disgruntled employees.[59] Interestingly, and confirming the point that swift proceedings are considered desirable in investment cases, the case was one of the few decided by a five-judge chamber of the ICJ.[60]

In casu, the United States claimed that the occupation of a US-owned company by its employees, in the face of the dismissal of 800 employees, violated a bilateral United States–Italy friendship, commerce, and navigation treaty, under which the authorities promised to offer 'the most constant protection and security'. The Court, however, disagreed, pointing out that plans to dismiss 800 employees 'could not reasonably be expected to pass without some protest'[61] and, more importantly, that Italian law had been applied in regular fashion, without distinguishing between foreign and national ownership. The 'most constant protection and security' standard could only result in the exercise of due diligence; it cannot mean that property 'shall never in any circumstances be occupied or disturbed'.[62]

ECONOMIC 'SOFT LAW'

While global economic relations take place within the frameworks offered by organizations such as the WTO, the IMF, and the World Bank, important parts are regulated on what has sometimes been referred to as the 'legally subliminal' level.[63] Partly this is caused, no doubt, by frustration; for instance, attempts under UN auspices during the 1960s to draft a convention to regulate the behaviour of transnational corporations (i.e. multinationals) came to naught. To some extent, this results from problems similar to those informing the peculiar structure of international environmental law; international legal rules apply foremost to states, and thus it is inherently difficult to regulate the activities of actors other than states. Hence it is often felt that the best one can hope for is the promulgation of non-binding norms; on the basis of this philosophy a code of conduct on Restrictive Business Practices was drafted under the auspices of UNCTAD[64] in 1980,[65] while the UN has been the

---

[58] *Pulp Mills on the River Uruguay (Argentina v. Uruguay)*, [2010] ICJ Rep. 14. This is discussed in more detail in Chapter 14 above.

[59] *Elettronica Sicula SpA (ELSI) (USA v. Italy)*, [1989] ICJ Rep. 15.   [60] See also Chapter 8 above.

[61] *ELSI*, para. 108.   [62] Ibid.

[63] The term is gratefully borrowed from Stephen C. Neff, *Friends but No Allies: Economic Liberalism and the Law of Nations* (New York: Columbia University Press, 1990).

[64] UNCTAD stands for UN Conference on Trade and Development, although nasty rumour has it that it may also stand for Under No Circumstances Take Any Decision.

[65] Stuart E. Benson, 'The UN Code on Restrictive Business Practices: An International Antitrust Code is Born', (1981) 30 *American University Law Review*, 1031–48.

host, since the late 1990s, of the so-called global compact, a scheme by which companies can voluntarily sign up to pledge their respect for core human rights, labour standards, and environmental standards.[66]

In their own way, both initiatives aim to regulate competition between companies; they address the possibilities that trade liberalization between states may be undermined by collusion between companies, or by unfair competitive advantages due to, for instance, lax environmental standards. The very existence of such initiatives signifies that a global competition law regime (or anti-trust regime) does not exist, although, for example, the US and EU anti-trust authorities engage in bilateral cooperation on a regular basis. Sometimes states aim to compensate by projecting their own competition laws on foreign actors; both US courts and the CJEU have upheld the position that anti-competitive behaviour abroad may come within their purview if it affects competition in their respective markets.[67]

Formal organizations such as the Organization for Economic Cooperation and Development (OECD) play an important role in regulating the global economy, and the OECD makes widespread use of non-legally-binding instruments, although it also sponsors the conclusion of treaties, for example on a topic such as bribery. When it comes to creating non-legal instruments, the OECD is engaged, for instance, in the drafting of model tax conventions; these are not binding, but are taken, literally, as a model for states engaging in conventions on taxation, and thereby exercise considerable influence. Likewise, the OECD regularly updates its non-binding guidelines for multinational enterprises, dating back to the 1970s and, as noted, is engaged in fighting tax evasion by global companies.

In more recent years, the OECD has become well known for its assessment of student performances. This too is economically motivated: the idea behind the Programme on International Student Assessment (PISA) is that states will perform better economically if their children are well educated in disciplines such as mathematics, science, and languages. To this end, PISA tests student performance, and presents rankings, often with good results for Japan, South Korea, and Finland. Without this being transformed into recommendations, let alone legal standards, PISA exercises enormous influence on the education policies of the OECD's member states, so much so that the ranking exercise may well qualify as a form of global governance.[68]

At least of equal relevance, however, are the activities of other, less formalized entities. Perhaps most visible is the annual summit meeting of the most prosperous nations, first as G7, later as G8 and sometimes also as G20; this is a highly amorphous club which seems to work by invitation rather than on the basis of representation or some other mechanism. While it includes some of the bigger developing nations (Brazil, Argentina, Indonesia), the poor are in no way represented. Meetings take place behind closed doors, and while

---

[66] See e.g. Viljam Engström, *Realizing the Global Compact* (Helsinki: Erik Castrén Institute, 2002).
[67] In doing so, they employ the so-called 'effects doctrine' with respect to jurisdiction, an amalgam of the territorial and protective principles of state jurisdiction (see further Chapter 5 above).
[68] Armin von Bogdandy and Matthias Goldmann, 'The Exercise of International Public Authority through National Policy Assessment: The OECD's PISA Policy as a Paradigm for a New International Standard Instrument', (2008) 5 *International Organizations Law Review*, 241–98.

they may result in summit statements, they rarely, if at all, result in any legally enforceable, or even cognizable, instruments.[69]

Soft regulation, if that is the term to use, also prevails generally in the financial sector where, as the financial crises of the twenty-first century suggest, there is little regulation and even less oversight.[70] The Basel Committee on Banking Supervision, related to the Bank for International Settlements, regularly issues guidelines, but states are highly reluctant to see these given legally binding form. These guidelines may address such topics as the minimum capital requirements for banks (so as to prevent a run on banks, destabilizing the entire system), review of banking supervisory mechanisms, and market disciplines, but unless states implement these guidelines in their domestic legislation, they remain but guidelines.

If the Basel Committee is a creature of the 1970s, the Financial Action Task Force (FATF) was established in 1989 following a summit meeting of the so-called G7, itself an amorphous club of the leading economic powers. This FATF has been instrumental in setting up a lengthy list of recommendations in order to combat money laundering.[71]

The billion-dollar insurance industry is also regulated without too much public intervention. The International Association of Insurance Supervisors, in existence since 1994, has developed non-binding core principles of insurance supervision, which include such topics as criteria for licensing insurers, prudential requirements, and supervision of the sector.

Securities markets are regulated by the International Organization of Securities Commissions (IOSCO) (one such being the well-known SEC in the United States). In 1998, IOSCO agreed on a set of principles, generally considered as the 'benchmarks of international regulation of securities markets'.[72] In addition, inspired by common concerns about securities fraud, IOSCO sponsored the conclusion of a non-binding MoU.

While all these attempts may be legally non-binding, largely because governments wish not only to collaborate but also to compete with each other to attract business, none the less they are generally taken to be highly influential. In other words, governance is exercised on the global level by entities composed largely or exclusively of industry representatives, by means of instruments of doubtful legal status. This implies that governments have relatively little to say about the contents of regulation, and that the accountability of the decision-makers is not very well developed; they are accountable to neither governments nor parliaments, nor before courts.[73]

Sometimes influence can stem from single states. It was widely expected, for instance, that the revamping of accountancy standards by the United States in the wake of the Enron scandal, by the adoption of the Sarbanes–Oxley Act, would exercise huge influence on

---

[69] That said, they may exercise considerable influence. The 2014 Brisbane Communiqué is included in Klabbers, *International Law Documents*.

[70] See generally Howard Davies and David Green, *Global Financial Regulation: The Essential Guide* (Cambridge: Polity, 2008); Chris Brummer, 'How International Financial Law Works (And How It Doesn't)', (2011) 99 *Georgetown Law Journal*, 257–327.

[71] See generally Marie Wilke, 'Emerging Informal Network Structures in Global Governance: Inside the Anti-Money Laundering Regime', (2008) 77 *Nordic Journal of International Law*, 509–31.

[72] Davies and Green, *Global Financial Regulation*, at 63.

[73] See also Anne-Marie Slaughter, *A New World Order* (Princeton University Press, 2004).

accounting practices worldwide. Yet while a case can be made that the internationalization of financial markets demands at the very least a degree of harmonization of accounting practices, it would seem that the Sarbanes–Oxley Act has been less influential than expected, perhaps because, as sometimes suggested, its requirements are 'shooting over the target'.[74] Instead, the main influence here resides in the work of the International Accountancy Standards Board, which has adopted International Financial Reporting Standards and is often seen as being US-dominated.[75]

DEVELOPMENT AND A NEW INTERNATIONAL ECONOMIC ORDER

The above outline of international economic law suggests that the system is strongly influenced by the major economic powers, and also works to a large extent to their benefit. In other words, developing nations face a constant struggle.[76] Admittedly, some initiatives have been made to alleviate their plight; in trade law; developing nations may have preferential access to Western markets, although often enough, where such initiatives have been made, they tend to be undercut by other arrangements. When it comes to agriculture, for instance, many have been the complaints that market access is rendered less valuable by the ways in which the United States and perhaps in particular the EU subsidize their own agricultural industries, and for a long time the market for textiles (where developing nations, due to low labour costs, might have a comparative advantage) was distorted by the existence of a restrictive multi-fibre agreement.[77]

The difficult position of developing nations gave rise, during the 1960s and 1970s, to repeated calls for the establishment of a New International Economic Order, which would be less tilted to the benefit of the Western world and more receptive to the needs of developing nations – in short, it was a call for a more just international economic order, influenced also by new theorizing about how underdevelopment had come about to begin with. Third World economists and social scientists, among others, had begun to draw attention to the connections between Western development and Southern underdevelopment, arguing that the economies were so strongly related that development of the West had only been possible on the basis of the economic exploitation of the South, whether in the form of colonialism or by other means.[78]

Since by the late 1960s the majority of member states of the UN were developing nations, the UN General Assembly in particular was instrumental in the adoption of many resolutions outlining the contours of a New International Economic Order. However, since the General Assembly lacks the legal power to issue binding instruments, much of this

---

[74] Pontus Troberg, *IFRS and US GAAP: A Finnish Perspective* (Helsinki: Talentum, 2007), at 213.

[75] Ibid., at 28.

[76] For a theoretical exploration, see Sundhya Pahuja, *Decolonising International Law: Development, Economic Growth and the Politics of Universality* (Cambridge University Press, 2011).

[77] See generally the brief but useful discussion in Trebilcock, *Understanding Trade Law*, 178–90.

[78] Classic texts include André Gunder Frank, *On Capitalist Underdevelopment* (Oxford University Press, 1975), and Immanuel Wallerstein, *The Modern World-System I: Capitalist Agriculture and the Origins of the European World Economy in the Sixteenth Century* (New York: Academic Press, 1974).

remained on the level of the ideal, and had a hard time becoming reality. Nowadays, talk of such a New International Economic Order is largely considered dead and buried.

None the less, development as such has remained on the global political agenda. Sometimes this has taken the form of advocating a right to development, but this has never quite materialized, if only because even if it were clear (which it is not) who would be a right-holder, it remains unclear on whom any corresponding obligation would rest, and how the right could be made effective. This latter point in particular is crucial; while most people will agree that development is, generally, a good thing, there exist fundamental political divisions on how best to achieve it. Some might argue that development is best achieved by co-opting developed nations into the global economy, and the success of some Asian states is presented as credible evidence; a state such as South Korea has made huge strides. Others, including many developing nations themselves, have sometimes felt that a policy of import substitution and economic autarchy might be more effective. This would warrant a form of protectionism rather than playing along on the global market.

While development has remained one of the policy areas for the financial institutions (the World Bank in particular), the underlying ideology is largely a neo-liberal one; the vision of development informing the financial institutions is a vision by which developing nations should adopt Western-style institutions, embrace private property and secure local markets, and combat bribery and corruption, topics which themselves are defined in recognizably Western ways.

Either way, the grand ambitions of a New International Economic Order have been left behind; currently, the best-known effort to stimulate development is embedded in the so-called Millennium Development Goals, a set of targets adopted by the UN General Assembly in 2000.[79] The targets include the eradication of extreme poverty and hunger, the reduction of child mortality, environmental sustainability, the achievement of universal primary education, and the promotion of gender equality. As this list suggests, the idea is no longer to focus solely on the development of states, but rather on the position of individuals within developing nations. In other words, the legitimacy of the current global economic order is taken for granted; the Millennium Development Goals, important as they are, work within the current system, without questioning the system itself; they leave the basic structures of international economic law intact.

DEBT RELIEF

For as long as people have been borrowing money, some debts have proved impossible to repay. When individuals cannot repay, they can go bankrupt and start all over again with a more or less clean slate. States, by contrast, cannot go bankrupt: if a state is unable to repay its debts, its inability to do so may send shockwaves throughout the system.

---

[79] A useful discussion on the relationship between law and development, including the Millennium Development Goals, is contained in William Twining, *General Jurisprudence: Understanding Law from a Global Perspective* (Cambridge University Press, 2009), 323–61.

As long as states borrowed on the private market, the shockwaves remained limited: private banks normally have an interest (no pun intended . . .) in seeing to it that they do not lend more than they expect their clients to be able to repay.[80] By the 1980s, however, sovereign lending had shifted to public institutions, who have interests of a different nature. Saddam Hussein's Iraq, for instance, could lend a lot of money for purposes of the 1980s war against Iran – after the 1979 Iranian Revolution, many were happy to sponsor Iraq for geopolitical reasons, and were more than a little vexed when he turned this money against the West after invading Kuwait in 1990.[81]

If lending money can be instructed by political motives, so too can debt relief. A shock somewhere in the financial system can reverberate elsewhere, and the desire to keep the system intact might mean that sometimes debt relief takes place, even if many would agree that the state in crisis is in a crisis of its own making.[82] Such debt relief can be organized in various ways, but has mostly taken place through the so-called Paris Club, an informal entity of creditor states tucked away in the French Treasury Department, with the IMF also playing an important role. Intriguingly, attempts to formalize debt restructuring in the IMF, suggested in the early 2000s, have come to naught: it may well be the case that states prefer to do these things informally, and far away from the spotlight.[83]

Be that as it may, in 2015 UNCTAD launched a so-called road map on sovereign debt workouts, endorsed by the General Assembly,[84] while a little earlier the General Assembly itself established an ad hoc committee on Sovereign Debt Restructuring Processes.[85] Both stand for an approach aimed at achieving something of a balance between the positions of creditors and debtors. Debtors retain a right to restructure their debts, but only as a last resort, and while creditors should refrain from exercising undue influence, their rights should be preserved.[86]

FINAL REMARKS

It is a truism to claim that international law is of vital importance for the global capitalist economy. International law provides the underlying framework which helps to facilitate the conduct of trade and investment, and secures, so to speak, the global market or, more accurately perhaps, in particular the global market in goods and, to a markedly lesser

---

[80] Lending can also take the form of investing in sovereign bonds: see Michael Waibel, 'Opening Pandora's Box: Sovereign Bonds in International Arbitration', (2007) 101 *American Journal of International Law*, 711–59.

[81] See generally Yvonne Wong, *Sovereign Finance and the Poverty of Nations: Odious Debt in International Law* (Cheltenham: Edward Elgar, 2012).

[82] The same mechanism ensures that the big banks keep getting bailed out in difficult times. For an insightful journalistic account of the workings of London's financial centre (in Dutch), see Joris Luyendijk, *Dit kan niet waar zijn: onder bankiers* (Amsterdam: Atlas, 2015). The work has been translated into English under the title *Swimming with Sharks*.

[83] Jan Klabbers, 'On Functions and Finance: Sovereign Debt Workouts and Equality in International Organizations Law', (2016) 41 *Yale Journal of International Law*, 241–61.

[84] General Assembly Resolution 69/319 (2015).   [85] General Assembly Resolution 69/247 (2015).

[86] For in-depth discussion, see Juan Pablo Bohoslavsky and Matthias Goldmann, 'An Incremental Approach to Sovereign Debt Restructuring: Sovereign Debt Sustainability as a Principle of Public International Law', (2016) 41 *Yale Journal of International Law*, 13–43.

extent, services. It is equally important to realize, though, that some parts of the regulation of the global economy are self-consciously kept far away from international law, in two ways. First, when it comes to the free movement of capital, international law does not have much to say; it protects investments, but supervision of banking and securities is left to the industries concerned, and often on the basis of documents of rather nebulous legal status. Second, as Chapter 6 above has already suggested, the free movement of individuals is typically restrained by domestic law; international law does not have all that much to offer to workers, migrants, or the destitute trying to find a better future.

The net result is that relevant sectors of the global economy are subject to governance without much democratic input, without much accountability, and without much of the tempering effect that basic human rights norms can exercise. It is not surprising that many argued, half a century ago, that the system was unfair and ought to be replaced by a new economic order; what is surprising though, is that this battle cry is not heard too often these days. Admittedly, entities such as the WTO and the IMF provoke some political debate and contestation, and, admittedly, the highly informal annual World Economic Summit in Davos has found a counterpart in the World Social Forum,[87] but, none the less, the global economic system seems to offer only the stark choice of either playing along in accordance with the rules of the game (often traceable to colonial days) or being left behind.

FURTHER READING

Reuven S. Avi-Yonah, *International Tax as International Law: An Analysis of the International Tax Regime* (Cambridge University Press, 2007)

Chris Brummer, 'How International Financial Law Works (And How It Doesn't)', (2011) 99 *Georgetown Law Journal* 257–327

Isabel Feichtner, *The Law and Politics of WTO Waivers: Stability and Flexibility in Public International Law* (Cambridge University Press, 2012)

Richard Gardner, *Sterling–Dollar Diplomacy in Current Perspective: The Origins and the Prospects of our International Economic Order*, rev. edn (New York: Columbia University Press, 1980)

Robert Howse, 'The World Trade Organization 20 Years On: Global Governance by Judiciary,' (2016) 27 *European Journal of International Law*, 9–77

Michael J. Trebilcock, *Understanding Trade Law* (Cheltenham: Edward Elgar, 2011)

Michael Waibel, 'Opening Pandora's Box: Sovereign Bonds in International Arbitration', (2007) 101 *American Journal of International Law*, 711–59

Ngaire Woods, *The Globalizers: The IMF, the World Bank, and Their Borrowers* (Ithaca, NY: Cornell University Press, 2006)

---

[87] Informative is Teivo Teivainen, 'World Social Forum and Global Democratization: Learning from Porto Alegre', (2002) 23 *Third World Quarterly*, 621–32.

PART III

The Surroundings of International Law

16

Domestic Courts and their Relationship with International Law

INTRODUCTION

Chapter 8 above discussed at length the position of the ICJ in the fabric of international law. For all its importance, though, the role of the ICJ should not be overestimated; in everyday life, much of the work of applying international law is done by domestic[1] courts and administrative agencies. This presupposes that there are some rules, or at least some ideas, on how international law and domestic law relate to each other. This chapter will first address the two leading theories on the relationship between international and domestic law (monism and dualism),[2] and will then discuss a number of issues that may arise when international law is to be applied by domestic courts. As we shall see, states are not always keen on receiving international law into their domestic legal orders, and several judicial techniques have been developed to prevent domestic courts and agencies from having to apply international law.

It is useful to mention at the outset that the topic of the relationship between international and domestic law is a source of much confusion, partly because the various terms used (directly effective rules, self-executing rules, directly applicable rules) are not very precise to begin with – and are not used with great precision either – and partly because there may be a lot at stake politically. A state which allows international law to be directly applied by its courts and administrative agencies is in a different position from a state which does not allow this. Such a state, welcoming international law into its legal order, is sometimes seen to be creating a disadvantage for itself.

Another preliminary point to make is that not all matters coming before domestic decision-makers warrant an investigation into the reception of international law in the domestic legal order. Put differently, some matters just need to be accepted regardless of

---

[1] I shall use the adjective 'domestic' rather than 'national' or 'municipal': 'national' can too easily be confused for 'international', while 'municipal' is too easily associated with municipalities.

[2] For a useful collection, see Janne Nijman and André Nollkaemper (eds.), *New Perspectives on the Divide between National and International Law* (Oxford University Press, 2007). The leading study on the role of international law before national courts is André Nollkaemper, *National Courts and the International Rule of Law* (Oxford University Press, 2011).

how this reception is otherwise construed. For instance, a migration official confronted with an individual carrying a passport from Kosovo or Somaliland, neither of which is generally regarded as a sovereign state just yet, may have to decide whether these entities are states for the purposes of international law, regardless of the way that international law enters the domestic legal order. Likewise, should a state's coastguard decide to seize a fishing vessel hovering outside its territorial waters, it must be established whether the vessel found itself to be within the jurisdiction of the state concerned. Issues such as statehood or the extent of coastal state jurisdiction are ones where, in an important sense, it does not matter whether or how international law has been received in the domestic legal order; such issues relate to concepts rather than substantive rules. It is only with regard to substantive rules that reception into domestic law presents itself as an important issue.

And even then the interplay between international and domestic law does not cover all substantive rules. Surely no dualist state would claim that it cannot exercise its right of self-defence in the absence of domestic legislation implementing article 51 of the UN Charter; rules that apply solely at the inter-state level are beyond any discussion of the relationship between international and domestic law.

It is no coincidence therefore that the discussion on the reception of international law into domestic law typically arises in the context of international rules creating possible rights (or obligations) for entities within the state such as individuals or companies.[3] Trade rules may be directly effective (or not); human rights may be directly effective (or not); and humanitarian law or rules relating to consular assistance may be directly effective or not. But the classic inter-state rules, whether they concern the right to self-defence or the inviolability of embassies or how to terminate a treaty, leave little room for this discussion.

MONISM AND DUALISM

Historically, international law and domestic law have typically been seen as standing in a dualist relationship to one another. The classic authors of international law, such as Vattel in the eighteenth century, never addressed the impact of international law on domestic law; for them, international law existed purely at the inter-state level, and had little or nothing to do with domestic law. This made some sense, as international law was classically considered to deal predominantly with relations between states, allowing for a strict separation between international law and domestic law; the former addressed relations between states, the latter addressed relations between individuals or between the individual and his or her state. And where, on rare occasions, the position of individuals was affected by international law, the institution of diplomatic protection would apply; the individual right concerned was recharacterized as a right pertaining to the state, and the matter thus became one of international law.[4]

---

[3] For a recent and comprehensive discussion, see Yuji Iwasawa, 'Domestic Application of International Law', (2016) 378 *Recueil des Cours*, 9–261.
[4] The leading formulation can be found in the *Mavrommatis Palestine Concessions*, [1924] Publ. PCIJ, Series A, no. 2. On diplomatic protection, see Chapter 8 above.

During the nineteenth century the realization took hold that the regulation of practical affairs under international law might come to affect domestic law in one way or another in a structural rather than incidental manner. Surely it would be useful, for instance, if agreements on railway timetables or postage stamps were recognized by domestic legal authorities,[5] whether directly or indirectly? Hence it became necessary to start to think systematically about the relationship between international law and domestic law.

This led first to the formulation of dualism, in particular by the German lawyer Heinrich Triepel, whose classic *Völkerrecht und Landesrecht* was first published in 1899.[6] It was no coincidence that dualism was the first idea to be developed, as it still worked on the premise that international law deals with relations between states whereas the life of the individual finds regulation under domestic law; the starting point, in other words, remained the classic division of labour between the two legal orders, combined with Triepel's conviction, reflecting the prevailing opinion at the time, that individuals could not be considered subjects of international law.[7]

Under dualism, international law and domestic law are regarded as two distinct legal spheres which, moreover, have very little to do with one another. It is not just the case that they govern different actors, it is also the case (at least historically) that they deal with different topics. Bluntly put, domestic law would deal with private contracts and individual crimes, whereas international law would address war or the acquisition of territory by states. Hence, they would hardly make contact, and where they would be in contact, it would obviously be a matter of domestic law to decide how to deal with the matter, since *ex hypothesi* they could only be in contact concerning the position of individuals or other groups within the state, and thereby come within the realm of domestic law.

The upshot of this was, and still is, that under dualism, international law is seen to have effects only in the international sphere. For an international rule to become effective in the domestic legal order, it needs to be transformed into the sort of rule recognized by that legal order. If a legal order recognizes only, for instance, acts of Parliament as valid law, then the international law rule can only enter that legal order if it is given the form of such an act of Parliament. Under no circumstances will the rule be considered directly effective. And if there is a conflict between an international rule and a rule of domestic law, then it is left to the legal order concerned to decide which shall be prioritized; in a dualist system, this typically means (in theory, at any rate) that the international rule should be set aside. The result may be, of course, that the state concerned fails to respect an international rule, and for this it may incur international responsibility.

Triepel himself labelled his dualism as a realist theory; he based it on a description of how states received international law. None the less, in his own time some critics already

---

[5] See e.g. Friedrich Meili, *Die internationalen Unionen über das Recht der Weltverkehrsanstalten und des geistigen Eigentums* (Leipzig: Duncker & Humblot, 1889).

[6] Heinrich Triepel, *Völkerrecht und Landesrecht* (Leipzig: C. L. Hirschfeld, 1899). The main outlines of Triepel's approach are to be found in Heinrich Triepel, 'Les rapports entre le droit interne et le droit international', (1923) 1 *Recueil des Cours*, 75–121.

[7] However, he did not exclude that in the future, this might change; a new international law might arise which recognized entities within states as direct subjects of international law. Triepel, 'Les rapports', at 82.

had doubts about his self-professed realism, and in particular about the position of the individual.[8] Could it really be maintained that international law dealt only with inter-state relations with no regard for individuals, and that domestic law was the only legal system capable of addressing the position of individuals? Triepel acknowledged, writing in 1923, that there were tendencies relating to the protection of minorities that might form the seeds of a new international law, but decided none the less to stick to his premise.[9]

The critique of dualism culminated in the work of Hans Kelsen, under the label 'monism'. Monism, as the label suggests, thinks of international law and domestic law (regardless of which domestic system) as different branches of what is fundamentally the same tree. International law, so Kelsen said, makes it possible for states to exist (without international law there can be no states), and determines when and how acts of states are legally valid. The result of all this is the existence of a universal legal order where, so to speak, competences are distributed among sub-orders. States form the sub-orders, overarched by public international law. Moreover, as a practical matter, many international legal norms are incomplete; they need domestic law to give them legs. Thus, states may agree, for instance, to criminalize rape during armed conflict, but typically it will be left for the individual states to enact legislation that actually does so and to determine what the regular penalty will be. Thus, international law and domestic law need each other, and together form a universal legal order.[10]

This has several important consequences. First, under monism, international law usually prevails over a conflicting rule of domestic law. After all, in Kelsen's view, it is international law that makes it possible for states to exist; obviously, then, international law ranks higher in the hierarchy of norms.[11] Second, in those cases where international legal rules require no further implementation, they may be directly effective in the domestic legal order; they may be, as US lawyers are wont to put it, 'self-executing'. This is technically not unproblematic, as will be discussed below, but none the less marks an important difference from the dualist approach.

The two theories exhaust the matter: *tertium non datur*.[12] None the less, they should not be taken all that literally, as in practice many states adhere to some kind of in-between version. This raises an important point; it is, normally, the state itself that decides whether it wants to be dualist or monist. In that particular (and limited) sense, all states are dualist.

---

[8] Another point of criticism is that dualism is premised on schizophrenia: the state becomes divided into an internal actor and one that acts internationally. For useful discussion see Charles Leben, *The Advancement of International Law* (Oxford: Hart, 2010).

[9] Triepel, 'Les rapports', at 82.

[10] Kelsen set this out with great clarity in Hans Kelsen, *Principles of International Law* (New York: Rinehart & Co., 1952), at 403.

[11] Kelsen was also, it should be said, a cosmopolitan, for whom international law carried a natural attraction. See the fine study by Jochen von Bernstorff, *Der Glaube an das Universale Recht. Zur Völkerrechtstheorie Hans Kelsens und seiner Schüler* (Baden-Baden: Nomos, 2001).

[12] Some textbooks posit a third approach focusing pragmatically on conflicting obligations rather than conflict on the more abstract level of legal orders, but this is generally considered to lapse into either dualism or monism. See, briefly, Ian Brownlie, *Principles of Public International Law*, 7th edn (Oxford University Press, 2008), at 33–4. The most sophisticated theoretical discussion is Veijo Heiskanen, *International Legal Topics* (Helsinki: Finnish Lawyers' Publishing Company, 1992), 1–199.

International law does not, and cannot, order states to be monist – this remains a prerogative of the sovereign state. For the effectiveness of international law it is often suggested that a monist system is superior, by monists[13] and dualists alike,[14] but since the system is based on state sovereignty the choice on how to give effect to international law remains with the state; it is the domestic constitution which decides on the way in which international law may enter the domestic legal order.

There is one important exception to this, and that is the EU. Under EU law, the EU's legal instruments are directly applicable and directly effective in the EU's member states, and are so regardless of what the domestic constitution stipulates. The direct applicability of EU law stems from EU law itself, and is based on a set of decisions by the CJEU. This will be further discussed below.

DIRECT EFFECT

Generally speaking, terms such as 'direct effect', 'direct applicability', and 'self-executing' are used interchangeably, albeit the latter term is predominantly in use in the United States, and there is not much harm in treating the terms as synonyms. While some domestic orders may make fine distinctions between direct effect and direct applicability,[15] from a broader perspective such distinctions are not all that relevant. Typically, the terms refer, in one way or another, to the possibility for an individual to invoke a provision – usually a right – directly before a domestic court. However, as we shall see below, one subtle distinction must be made between situations where an international provision creates a private right of action (in which case the effect can really be direct) or where the provision does not do so. In the latter situation, the individual concerned may still invoke the international provision in his or defence, but cannot start litigation on that basis.

The notion of direct effect (to stick to that term) presents itself most conspicuously with respect to treaty provisions and provisions laid down in binding decisions of international organizations. Typically, in a monist legal order such provisions can be considered, under certain circumstances, as having direct effect. This was already accepted by the PCIJ in 1928, in its advisory opinion on *Jurisdiction of the Courts of Danzig*. The question before the Court was whether Danzig railway officials, who had passed into the Polish railway service after the First World War by means of a series of agreements, could bring cases against the Polish Railways Administration based on one of these agreements, the so-called Beamtenabkommen (which roughly translates as Officials Agreement). The Beamtenabkommen regulated such matters as relocation costs of the officials concerned as well as equal treatment with 'regular' Polish railway officials.

---

[13] See e.g. Christoph Sasse, 'The Common Market: Between International and Municipal Law', (1966) 75 *Yale Law Journal*, 695–753.

[14] In this context, dualists may argue that international law, if it were to be self-executing, could all too easily undermine democratic decision-making in the state concerned. For such an argument, see Jed Rubenfeld, 'Unilateralism and Constitutionalism', (2004) 79 *New York University Law Review*, 1971–2028.

[15] This applies in particular to the EU; see below. Denza suggests a more principled difference, but does not explain it in any way. See Eileen Denza, 'The Relationship between International and National Law', in Malcolm Evans (ed.), *International Law*, 3rd edn (Oxford University Press, 2010), 411–38, at 426–7.

The Court, in a rare show of unanimity, held in the affirmative, and based itself predominantly on an analysis of the text of the Beamtenabkommen. As the Court put it, what matters is the intention of the parties: 'The intention of the Parties, which is to be ascertained from the contents of the Agreement, taking into consideration the manner in which the Agreement has been applied, is decisive.'[16] Since the text of the Beamtenabkommen was, on the relevant points, as clear and precise as domestic legislation would have been, and clearly intended to create directly applicable rights, the Court held that the railway officers concerned could use the Beamtenabkommen as the basis for legal claims in Polish courts.

This already suggests how the contents of a treaty can manifest an intention by the parties to grant direct effect to treaty provisions. While different national traditions may reveal local differences, generally courts will look at whether the provision concerned seems directly to create rights or obligations for individuals or, in other words, whether a provision is addressed to individuals (or other legal persons) or to the contracting parties. Thus, a provision such as 'State Parties shall prohibit the sale of children, child prostitution and child pornography'[17] will most probably not be considered to be directly effective; it addresses the legislator rather than individuals, and urges the legislator to enact laws to protect individuals – it does not offer this protection directly.

This distinction concerning the addressee of rules is often traced back to the opinion of Chief Justice Marshall, of the US Supreme Court, in the classic *Foster* v. *Neilson* case,[18] which revolved around the effects of a territorial grant contained in a treaty. In the words of Chief Justice Marshall,

> Our constitution declares a treaty to be the law of the land. It is, consequently, to be regarded in courts of justice as equivalent to an act of the legislature, whenever it operates of itself without the aid of any legislative provision. But when the terms of the stipulation import a contract, when either of the parties engages to perform a particular act, the treaty addresses itself to the political, not the judicial department; and the legislature must execute the contract before it can become a rule for the Court.[19]

It would follow, by contrast, that a provision such as 'No one shall be subjected to torture or to inhuman or degrading treatment or punishment'[20] may well be considered as directly effective. The provision does not speak to the legislator, but creates a directly enforceable right. The provision leaves no discretion to local authorities, and is clear in its straightforwardness; if an act of torture takes place, then the rule is violated.

If the two examples given above are relatively clear, in many cases provisions may be less clear. An example is article XI, paragraph 1 of the GATT (now subsumed in the WTO Agreement), which holds that 'No prohibitions or restrictions other than duties, taxes or other charges ... shall be instituted or maintained by any contracting party'. On the one hand, the provision seems to be clear and unconditional, leaving little discretion

---

[16] *Jurisdiction of the Courts of Danzig*, advisory opinion, [1928] Publ. PCIJ, Series B, no. 15, at 18.
[17] This is article 1 of the 2000 Protocol on the Sale of Children, Child Prostitution and Child Pornography.
[18] *Foster* v. *Neilson*, 27 US 253 (1829).   [19] Ibid., at 314.   [20] Article 3 of the ECHR.

to the legislator. On the other hand, it does seem to address the legislator rather than private parties, as it is only the legislator that can institute or maintain trade restrictions. In such cases, courts will typically not only look at the provision concerned, but will also take other factors into account, including the somewhat elusive factor of the spirit or scheme of the treaty in which the provision can be found. Likewise, some domestic courts have found the *non-refoulement* rule, central to refugee protection, to be directly effective, even though it states that 'No Contracting State shall expel or return (refouler) a refugee.'[21]

Hence, as a general rule, the direct effect of a treaty provision is to be ascertained by reference to the intentions of the parties. These intentions may manifest themselves in the wording of the provision; if the provision is sufficiently precise and unconditional, then it may have direct effect. In addition, the scheme and general spirit of the treaty at large may be of relevance. Either way, though, traditionally the decision to award direct effect rested with the agencies (courts, administrative bodies) applying the law.

Still, since the PCIJ held in *Jurisdiction of the Courts of Danzig* that the finding of direct effect depends on the intentions of the parties, it follows that the parties are at liberty to make their intentions clear by issuing declarations to the effect that the treaty as a whole shall not have direct effect. This has been employed by the three big trading economies when ratifying the WTO Agreement; the United States, the EU, and Japan all declared that WTO law should not be considered directly effective in their domestic legal orders. The underlying rationale is an economic one; if Japan were to grant traders the possibility of relying on WTO law before Japanese courts, then this possibility could also be used by US-based and EU-based traders operating on the Japanese market, while Japanese traders would lack the same opportunity in the United States and the EU. Consequently, US-based and EU-based traders would have a way of forcing Japan to comply with WTO law which would not be available to Japanese traders, and thereby the granting of direct effect to WTO law in Japan would result in weakening Japan's position vis-à-vis the EU and the United States.

In other cases, non-self-executing declarations may owe less to considerations of reciprocity, and more to protection of the integrity of the domestic legal order. In particular the United States has issued such declarations when ratifying international human rights instruments. An example is the declaration issued on ratifying the 1966 ICCPR, in 1992: 'the United States declares that the provisions of articles 1 through 27 of the Covenant are not self-executing'.[22] Here the inspiration behind the declaration resides mostly in the circumstance that the United States, while willing to accept an international commitment to respect human rights, is unwilling to see the contents of US law changed through the direct application of international law by the US courts.[23]

---

[21] The rule is to be found in article 33 of the 1951 Refugee Convention.

[22] Articles 1–27 contain the substantive rights guaranteed in the covenant. The remainder of the covenant contains institutional provisions and general provisions, which are unlikely to be considered self-executing to begin with.

[23] See generally David L. Sloss, 'The Domestication of International Human Rights: Non-self-executing Declarations and Human Rights Treaties', (1999) 24 *Yale Journal of International Law*, 129–221.

This highlights what is often considered as the politically most problematic issue relating to the direct effect of international law; where international law can directly enter the domestic legal order, it has the potential to set aside democratically enacted legislation in that legal order.[24] This need not always be the case; a state can enact a conflict rule to the effect that 'in case of conflict between a domestic rule and an international rule, the domestic rule shall prevail', but doing so automatically creates a suspicion that the state reneges on its international commitment. Some states, therefore, including the United States, adhere to the more subtle rule that in case of conflict, the later in time prevails, combined with a presumption that the legislator shall not be presumed to legislate in conflict with an international commitment.[25]

Dualist states are free from such concerns, as no immediate conflict between an international rule and a domestic rule can, strictly speaking, arise; the two are, after all, considered separate spheres. What will plague dualist states, however, is a possible discrepancy between their domestic law and their international commitments. Since local courts are not capable of remedying the situation, dualist states may more often find themselves before international tribunals. On this line of thinking, it is hardly a coincidence that the United Kingdom often appeared before the ECtHR until the late 1990s; it had not incorporated the ECHR, and thus did not offer victims of human rights violation any domestic relief. By contrast, since the enactment of the Human Rights Act in 1998, which largely incorporates the European Convention, individuals are now offered a remedy before the courts of the United Kingdom.

As outlined above, some confusion exists between the idea of direct effect and the idea of a 'private cause of action'. Briefly put, a treaty provision that creates a private cause of action is one that a litigant can rely on when starting litigation; this is a narrow category where a right has been created, directly in a treaty, for the benefit of individuals. Thus the right to be free from torture would qualify.

Direct effect, however, would seem to be a broader notion, encompassing not only rights created to benefit individuals directly, but also enabling the individual to rely on international law in his or her defence. Thus, in a monist state, an individual accused of violating domestic law may possibly rely on contrary international law, forcing the local judge to test the local legislation against the international rule. If the international rule can be seen as directly effective, then the judge in the typical monist state would be able to apply the international rule, even without the international rule providing a private cause of action.

Perhaps a stylized example[26] can clarify the point. Suppose state X has an old law on the statute books prohibiting women from working at night, and is also a party to a more recently concluded convention against unequal treatment of men and women in the workplace. An employer, Mr L, employs women in his bakery, and since bakeries often

---

[24] Rubenfeld, 'Unilateralism and Constitutionalism'.
[25] Sean D. Murphy, *Principles of International Law* (St Paul, MN: Thomson/West, 2006), at 221–4.
[26] It is loosely derived from a decision of the CJEU: see Case C-158/91, Criminal Proceedings against Jean-Claude Lévy, [1993] ECR I-4287.

work during the night, Mr L faces criminal charges for violating the domestic rule. In such a case, one line of defence might be that the law is in conflict with the convention. Even though Mr L cannot derive any direct rights from the convention (not being female and not being an employee, he has no private cause of action), he may be able to invoke the convention as an argument for why he should not be prosecuted. Still, two conditions must be met: the state concerned must have a monist orientation and accept the potential direct effect of treaty provisions, and the provision itself must be sufficiently precise and unconditional. Otherwise, Mr L's defence would have to change its tone; in a dualist state, or if the treaty provision concerned is not very precise, he might be able to claim that the state ought to have legislated in accordance with the treaty, but cannot invoke the treaty provision itself.

Put differently, direct effect is the overarching category, but may not always be sufficient to start litigation unless the litigant can also point to a specific remedy or a corresponding obligation or liability resting on another party. It is these that specify the existence of a private cause of action.

Direct effect is most often discussed in connection with provisions of treaties and provisions laid down in binding decisions of international organizations; indeed, it is not all that easy to think of the direct effect of customary international law, at least not while remaining faithful to the PCIJ's opinion in *Jurisdiction of the Courts of Danzig*, with its emphasis on the intentions of the parties. After all, customary law is not the result of any legislative or quasi-legislative intention; states make customary law through the aggregate of their activities, and while those activities themselves may be intentional, the resulting rule is not intentional in quite the same way. Consequently, it becomes incoherent to speak of the intention behind a customary rule to grant direct effect.

INCORPORATING INTERNATIONAL LAW

Dualist states accept the proposition that international law and domestic law are radically different spheres. Consequently, the question of direct effect does not present itself in quite the same way. Instead of utilizing direct effect, dualist states tend to insist on transformation of international law into rules recognized as valid in the domestic legal order.

This transformation can be done in several ways. One way, relatively cumbersome, is to rewrite existing domestic law in order to do justice to a new treaty. In particular with large treaties covering much ground, this may take much time and effort. For instance, transforming the 1982 UNCLOS into domestic law in this way would imply rewriting existing laws on maritime zones, rewriting the penal code with a view to incorporating UNCLOS rules on criminal jurisdiction and piracy, rewriting the civil code with a view to incorporating UNCLOS provisions on civil jurisdiction, rewriting the traffic rules so as to align them with UNCLOS rules on navigation, reworking environmental legislation and fisheries legislation, and so on. This is time-consuming, and may be risky as well; it is, after all, quite possible for the local implementing legislation to depart from the treaty text, if only because the translation may not fully match up to the authentic version of the treaty.

The easier technique, then, is what is sometimes referred to as 'in blanco incorporation';[27] here, the legislator simply adopts a law to which the treaty will be annexed. The law then provides that the treaty, as annexed, shall have the force of law within the domestic legal order. But this is not without problems either. Again there is the issue of the linguistic compatibility; if the annexed treaty is a translation, then it may depart from the authentic version, yet for purposes of domestic legal certainty, it is arguable that the translated version should prevail in domestic law. Otherwise the legal subjects might not be aware exactly what is expected of them and what their exact rights are.

Another issue that may arise is the question of hierarchy. While local practices may vary, treaties may be incorporated either by formal legislation, or by administrative decree, or by a combination of the two. In the former case, they are on a par with other formal legislative acts, and in case of conflict the courts will have to try to find a way to reconcile or determine priority (for instance by applying the 'later in time' rule). In case of incorporation by decree, however, it may well be that domestic law ascribes a lower status to administrative acts (and therewith to the treaty thus incorporated) than to formal laws, the result being that the treaty would remain subservient to domestic law.

Similar problems may arise in nominally monist states. To hold that treaties form part of the domestic legal order on ratification or entry into force is not yet to determine the formal rank of the treaty; it may be of the same rank as regular legislation, but also lower or of higher rank than regular legislation or even higher than the domestic constitution. Here local practices may differ considerably. As already alluded to, in the United States, generally speaking, the later in time prevails, whereas in a state such as the Netherlands (sometimes deemed the poster child for monism) treaties are deemed to outrank conflicting legislation, including the Constitution.[28]

On the other hand, in dualist states even non-incorporated treaties can engender some legal effect. It is not uncommon, for instance, for courts to take such treaties into account when interpreting domestic law, at least in situations where domestic law is ambiguous or unclear. All this inevitably leads to the conclusion that the practical differences between monism and dualism may not be all that enormous.

The limited relevance of the monism versus dualism debate also becomes clear when considering that states sometimes enact specific legislation to give effect to international law by creating a private cause of action. A good example is the 1991 US Torture Victims Protection Act, which makes it possible for torture victims to initiate civil proceedings against torturers and those engaged in extrajudicial killings. The enactment of this law was considered advisable despite the circumstance that in the United States, international law qualifies as 'supreme law of the land', and despite the circumstance that, arguably, in the Alien Tort Statute of 1789 the United States already had an instrument to enforce

---

[27] This is often practised by a state such as Finland. See Jan Klabbers, 'Coming in From the Cold? Treaties in Finland's Legal Order', in Timo Koivurova (ed.), *Kansainvälistyvä Oikeus: Juhlakirja Professori Kari Hakapää* (Rovaniemi, University of Lapland Law Faculty, 2005), 143–52.

[28] L. F. M. Besselink, 'Internationaal recht en nationaal recht', in Nathalie Horbach, René Lefeber, and Olivier Ribbelink (eds.), *Handboek internationaal recht* (The Hague: TMC Asser Press, 2007), 47–80, at 74.

international obligations domestically.[29] The latter in particular, however, had divided US courts, with some arguing that while it 'opened up' the US domestic legal order for violations of international law, it did not in itself provide a private cause of action.[30] It may have opened the door, but did not extend an invitation to enter.

THE SPECIAL CASE OF THE EUROPEAN UNION

As mentioned above, EU law is generally considered to occupy a specific place, largely for two reasons. First, it is generally acknowledged, following the case law of the CJEU, that the reception of EU law into the domestic laws of the EU's member states follows from EU law, rather than from domestic law. While the EU is based on a set of treaties and thus, from that perspective, is but a species of international law, the CJEU has held that domestic constitutional law cannot have a bearing on how the member states treat EU law.

Second, the EU occupies a special place because the EU itself comprises a distinct legal order, thereby giving rise to the question of how international law is received in the EU's legal order.[31] Indeed, this even raises the further question of whether the EU can function as an intermediary. It may even be claimed that international obligations, by becoming part of EU law, thereby also enter the domestic orders of the EU's member states.[32]

The leading case on the effect of EU law in the EU's member states is the classic *Van Gend & Loos* case.[33] At issue was whether the Netherlands, in raising a tariff on a product imported from Germany, had violated article 12 of the EEC Treaty (as it then was).[34] The Netherlands held that this question was outside the reach of the CJEU as, in those days, the direct effect *vel non* of treaty commitments in the Dutch legal order was thought to depend on the Dutch Constitution, and under Dutch constitutional law as it stood at the time, it was doubtful whether article 12 would be directly effective. The Court disagreed, suggesting that the question related to the interpretation of article 12 rather than to the application of international law by a domestic court, and therewith fell within the Court's jurisdiction.

The Court famously decided that the Union

constitutes a new legal order of international law for the benefit of which the states have limited their sovereign rights, albeit within limited fields, and the subjects of which comprise not only member states but also their nationals. Independently of the legislation of member states, Community law therefore not only imposes obligations on individuals but is also intended to confer upon them rights which become part of their

---

[29] See also Chapter 5 above.

[30] A well-known example is the opinion of Judge Robert Bork in *Tel-Oren* v. *Libyan Arab Republic*, 726 F.2d 774, US Court of Appeals for the District of Columbia circuit, 3 February 1984.

[31] The best study to date is Mario Mendez, *The Legal Effects of EU Agreements* (Oxford University Press, 2013).

[32] This intriguing question is not studied very often. For a rare monograph on the topic see Nikolaos Lavranos, *Decisions of International Organizations in the European and Domestic Legal Orders of Selected EU Member States* (Groningen: Europa Law Publishing, 2004).

[33] Case 26/62, *Van Gend & Loos* v. *Netherlands Internal Revenue Administration*, [1963] ECR 1.

[34] The corresponding provision, differently worded, is now article 30 TFEU.

legal heritage. These rights arise not only where they are expressly granted by the Treaty but also by reason of obligations which the Treaty imposes in a clearly defined way upon individuals as well as upon the member states and upon the institutions of the Community.[35]

The Court derived its famous conclusion from a number of considerations. It found that the aim of the EU Treaty was to reach beyond a mere inter-state agreement, as evidenced by the existence of a judicial procedure to guarantee cooperation between domestic courts and the CJEU, as well as the reference in the preamble to the peoples of Europe in addition to the reference to governments. The role of actors other than governments was moreover recognized in the creation of a Parliament and an Economic and Social Committee within the Union. Mostly though (albeit tucked away in a different consideration) the CJEU seemed concerned with the effectiveness of EU law; the integrity of EU law was compromised if EU law were directly effective in some member states but not in others. Hence the CJEU formulated the point of principle that the effect of EU law in the domestic legal orders of the EU's member states had to stem from EU law. Otherwise, individuals in Belgium or France might find themselves in a different position from individuals in Germany or Italy, and this, so the Court thought, would undermine the unity of EU law. If the EU were to succeed, it would need to have identical effects across all member states.

In its case law, the CJEU has acknowledged that a number of provisions of the TFEU have direct effect in the domestic law of the member states, even where such provisions are negatively worded. Article 12, at issue in *Van Gend & Loos*, was likewise phrased as a negative obligation ('No new tariffs shall be introduced'); while it was addressed to the member states, the CJEU none the less held that it could be implemented without any legislative intervention, and thus was 'ideally adapted to produce direct effects in the legal relationship between member states and their subjects'.[36]

In addition, regulations adopted by the Union are by their very definition 'directly applicable' in member state law, to the extent that member states may not take measures to implement them, for fear that implementing measures may come to depart from the original regulation.[37] These thereby function much like domestic legislation, the only difference being that their source is not the domestic legislator but a legislator one step removed from the national capitals.

The EU, as noted, also forms a legal order of its own, often said to be located somewhere between domestic law and international law. It follows that the question arises of how international law is received in the EU legal order. While the EU internally is decidedly monist, as witnessed by *Van Gend & Loos*, with respect to the effect of international law within the EU legal order the EU has adopted a position far closer to dualism. The EU treaties remain silent on the reception of international law; consequently, it has been left to the

---

[35] *Van Gend & Loos*, para. 8. For 'Community', now read 'Union'.   [36] Ibid., para. 11.
[37] Article 288 TFEU.

CJEU to formulate the basic position concerning the reception of international law – the CJEU functions as a veritable gatekeeper.[38]

The basic position is that the CJEU is reluctant to grant direct effect to the provisions of treaties to which the EU is a party, with one exception. This concerns the broad category of association agreements and partnership agreements – that is, agreements by means of which the EU aims to 'export' its own law to associated states, either to prepare them for future membership or to substitute for possible membership. With other treaties, the CJEU has been far less keen; it has been far less interested in 'importing' international law. This is most famously the case with WTO law, although here the Court's reluctance must stem in part from the injunction by the legislator that WTO law shall not be directly effective. But much the same applies to UN law, human rights law, and other manifestations of international law.[39]

TOWARDS A NEW DUALISM?

For many years, it seemed that monism was the position of choice for most international lawyers. Monism after all allows for the relatively easy importation of international law into the domestic legal order, and for many, international law represents something good and worthwhile. Sovereignty had become a 'bad word', so anything that could help to overcome sovereignty and parochialism was deemed preferable. This applied all the more so in light of the human rights revolution; since human rights norms by definition are concerned with individual rights rather than strict inter-state commitments, monism was thought to be the ideal vehicle for making states more responsive to human rights. Dualism, by contrast, was associated with sovereignty and with narrow parochialism, halting the spread of liberal human rights law.

Things are, however, rarely this black and white, and from the early 1990s onwards there has been something of a reappraisal of dualism. Writing independently, two leading international lawyers published studies discussing the policy arguments in favour of and against monism and dualism. John Jackson provided an important set of functional policy arguments as to why dualism might be of use: dualism may help states to protect the domestic legislative process by isolating it from international interference; states may wish to define further in domestic legislation a term left ambiguous in the treaty provision; and they may wish to match the treaty provision more closely to local circumstances. Moreover, states may wish to keep the option of reciprocity open; with respect to a strictly dualist state, the monist state may feel that there is a certain asymmetry in their relations if their citizens can go to a domestic court to have their rights enforced, but the citizens of other states cannot. Finally, states that have confidence in their own regulatory system may be reluctant to see it being overruled by imported international law,

---

[38] See generally Jan Klabbers, 'International Law in Community Law: The Law and Politics of Direct Effect', (2002) 21 *Yearbook of European Law*, 263–98.
[39] For an overview see Jan Klabbers, *The European Union in International Law* (Paris: Pédone, 2012).

and therefore be less keen on joining international regimes to begin with. Accordingly, Jackson ended up advocating a prudent dualism.[40]

Thomas Buergenthal, in turn, still adhered to a temperate monism, but none the less opened the door for a rejuvenation of dualism by suggesting that when states create directly effective provisions, they actually do two things at once; they assume an obligation relating to the substance of a right, and a separate one relating to the manner of its domestic enforcement.[41] It follows that the two can also be divided and done separately and, indeed, that substance and enforcement can be treated separately altogether.

Recent case law from the US Supreme Court and the CJEU follows a similar approach. Famously, in *Kadi*, the CJEU decided to quash (in part) an EU regulation implementing a Security Council resolution, holding that the EU regulation failed to meet with the EU's constitutional human rights guarantees.[42] This was only possible on a strict separation between the original Security Council resolution and the implementing EU regulation, and that was only possible, in turn, by effectively ignoring the Security Council resolution and the circumstance that such resolutions are binding upon the EU's member states (if not, technically, on the EU itself, which is not a member of the UN). Hence the decision created a considerable dilemma for the EU's member states, and effectively prioritized EU law over international law. Moreover, it did so despite the circumstance that, arguably, under article 103 UN the law of the UN should take precedence.[43]

The US Supreme Court, also in 2008, decided in the *Medellín* case that decisions of the ICJ are not self-executing in the US legal order.[44] In itself, that is not a controversial stand to take; what makes the decision problematic is that it relies on a distinction between a treaty provision and an authoritative and binding interpretation of that same provision by the ICJ. Medellín, sitting on death row in Texas having been convicted of rape and murder, was a Mexican citizen who had not been advised during trial of his right to consular assistance. This amounted to a violation of article 36 of the 1963 Vienna Convention on Consular Relations, which grants detainees the right to consular assistance. The ICJ had held on several occasions, most recently in its 2004 *Avena* judgment, that the right to consular assistance constituted a binding obligation, and that this obligation implied that the United States should review and reconsider any convictions and sentences of foreign nationals arrived at without consular assistance, although it left the United States free to decide on the methods by which to review and reconsider.[45]

---

[40] John H. Jackson, 'Status of Treaties in Domestic Legal Systems: A Policy Analysis', (1992) 86 *American Journal of International Law*, 310–40.

[41] Thomas Buergenthal, 'Self-executing and Non-self-executing Treaties in National and International Law', (1992/IV) 235 *Recueil des Cours*, 303–400, at 328.

[42] Joined Cases C-402/05 P and C-415/05 P, *Kadi and Al Barakaat* v. *Council and Commission*, [2008] ECRI-6351.

[43] As Gráinne de Búrca writes: 'The bottom line of the judgment ... was that the UN Charter and Security Council resolution, just like any other piece of international law, exist on a separate plane and cannot call into question or affect the nature, meaning, or primacy of fundamental principles of EC law.' Gráinne de Búrca, 'The European Court of Justice and the International Legal Order after *Kadi*', (2010) 51 *Harvard International Law Journal*, 1–49, at 24.

[44] *José Ernesto Medellín* v. *Texas*, US Supreme Court, 552 US 1 (2008).

[45] *Avena and Other Mexican Nationals (Mexico* v. *USA)*, [2004] ICJ Rep. 12, paras. 138–41.

Medellín had argued before the Supreme Court that the ICJ decision was self-executing, and therewith would trump US law. This invited the Supreme Court to focus on the self-executing nature (*vel non*) of ICJ decisions, ignoring the binding nature of the substantive obligation to provide consular assistance. It allowed the Supreme Court to distinguish between a treaty provision (article 36 Consular Convention) and a binding interpretation of what that provision entailed and this, surely, displayed a great reluctance to apply international law in any meaningful way. Indeed, the Supreme Court relied heavily on nineteenth-century sources (or even older ones, such as the Federalist Papers[46]) to suggest that the United States never meant to give domestic effect to international judgments – blissfully ignoring the circumstance that international tribunals hardly existed in the nineteenth century.

The classic dualism as endorsed by Triepel was based on the idea that international law and domestic law had little to do with one another. Whether that was descriptively accurate is not entirely certain, but at least Triepel himself kept open the possibility that at some point the two legal orders might move towards each other. By contrast, the dualism visible in decisions such as *Kadi* and *Medellín* is normatively motivated. The inspiration is not so much that the two legal orders have no contact, but that they should not be in contact; the domestic legal order (this includes the EU legal order, for present purposes) must be protected against international law. Hence this can only be classified as a 'new' dualism. States are of course allowed to occupy such political or normative positions as they see fit, but since the EU and the United States both position themselves also as champions of the rule of law, an element of hypocrisy creeps in when those two legal orders do their utmost to exclude international law from the rule of law.

In an intriguing decision, Italy's Supreme Court possibly added yet another position: refusing to accept a manifestation of international law for the sake not only of the domestic legal order (as was apparent in both *Kadi* and *Medellín*) but at least in part also for the sake of international law itself. In 2014 it decided not to give effect to a decision of the ICJ[47] because it felt the decision was, eventually, not sufficiently in conformity with international law. In 2012, the ICJ had decided that Germany could invoke sovereign immunity even when confronted with a claim for gross human rights violations related to the Holocaust.[48] When the ICJ decision reached the Italian Constitutional Court, this Court construed the matter as one of conflict between the international obligation to uphold state immunity on the one hand, and the constitutionally guaranteed right to a judge and protection of fundamental rights on the other hand. It strongly suggested that the international norm of state immunity had over time been transformed by the actions of domestic courts (turning absolute immunity into relative immunity), and underlined that lifting the immunity and giving priority to human rights considerations could 'contribute to a

---

[46] These contain the discussions leading up to the adoption of the US Constitution in 1789; see Alexander Hamilton, James Madison and John Jay, *The Federalist Papers* (New York: Bantam 1982 [1787–88]).

[47] Technically, it declared the unconstitutionality of the law incorporating the UN Charter into Italy's legal order as far as article 94 of the UN Charter is concerned – the article on compliance with ICJ decisions.

[48] Italian Constitutional Court, judgment no. 238/2014, 22 October 2014; the ICJ decision is discussed in Chapter 5 above.

desirable – and desired by many – evolution of international law itself'.[49] In a nutshell, the Italian Constitutional Court strongly suggested that by upholding German immunity for activities related to crimes against humanity, the ICJ erred on the substance of international law: state immunity protects the sovereign function of the state, but 'does not protect behaviours that do not represent the typical exercise of governmental powers, but are explicitly considered and qualified unlawful'.[50]

AVOIDANCE STRATEGIES

New as the 'new dualism' may be, it is not entirely unprecedented, in that domestic courts have developed various techniques to avoid having to deal with cases involving international law.[51] The most obvious way is to deny jurisdiction, and this can be done on various grounds, for example if the suspect is thought to represent a foreign state. In such cases, the courts may not even have much choice; immunities law, often laid down in domestic legislation, will control the issue. As this is intimately related to the concept of jurisdiction and immunities more broadly, it is discussed elsewhere in this book.[52]

But also in situations where domestic courts could possibly assume jurisdiction, they have found ways of avoiding doing so. One of these ways is the so-called 'political questions' doctrine; sometimes it is posited that an international law issue coming before a domestic court may have foreign policy implications, and these foreign policy implications are then best left to the executive branches of government.

An example is, again, the above-mentioned *Tel-Oren* case, decided in 1984 by the US Court of Appeals for the District of Columbia circuit. While all three judges dismissed the suit, they did so for different reasons, and one of them relied on the political questions doctrine. The case revolved around the possible liability of the PLO for an act of terrorism taking place in Israel and killing a number of individuals. This entailed, so Robb J held, a determination as to which version of the PLO could be held liable (the PLO was arguably a framework of competing political groups) and, more fundamentally still, whether doing so would amount to a form of recognition of the legitimacy of the PLO. These types of question, so Robb J noted, were too politically sensitive to be dealt with by the courts, and were best kept as the preserve of the government.[53]

A second avoidance strategy is known as the act of state doctrine, and was authoritatively formulated by the US Supreme Court in *Sabbatino*,[54] although it goes back to the late nineteenth century. In essence, the doctrine entails that courts shall not sit in judgment on

---

[49] Judgment no. 238/2014, para. 3.3.

[50] Ibid., para. 3.4. As Palombella summarizes, the Constitutional Court held that the ICJ 'ignored the force of the countervailing peremptory rules of international law itself concerning grave crimes against humanity or in wartime'. See Gianluigi Palombella, 'The Rule of Law at Home and Abroad', (2016) 8 *Hague Journal on the Rule of Law*, 1–23, at 3.

[51] For a rich overview of avoidance strategies, albeit specifically related to cases involving international organizations, see August Reinisch, *International Organizations before National Courts* (Cambridge University Press, 2000).

[52] Chapter 5 above.   [53] *Tel-Oren*, Robb J concurring.

[54] *Banco Nacional de Cuba* v. *Sabbatino*, US Supreme Court, 376 US 398, 23 March 1964.

the activities of foreign states acting within their own jurisdiction. In the case at hand, the Cuban government (after the rise to power of Fidel Castro) had nationalized a company in which US investors had an interest, and eventually the question of the legality under international law of this act of nationalization presented itself. While lower courts had tested the legality of the act of nationalization, the US Supreme Court felt it was wiser not to do so; it was not for US courts to decide whether foreign states acted in conformity with international law as long as they acted within their own jurisdiction. In essence, this is based on the same idea as the political questions doctrine; finding acts of foreign states to be illegal may have foreign policy ramifications that, so the argument goes, are best left to the executive branch of government. Hence it is no coincidence that courts sometimes set aside the act of state doctrine if the government tells them that judging acts of a foreign state will have no foreign policy implications.[55]

A third strategy is perhaps more common in private international law than in public international law, but none the less needs to be mentioned, if only because the borderline between private and public international law is not always easily discernible. Courts sometimes hold that another court, in a different state, may be better equipped to decide a case; in doing so, the court concerned will declare itself to be *forum non conveniens*. This may play a role, for instance, when material witnesses are located elsewhere, or where a transaction largely took place elsewhere, and is partly meant to prevent forum-shopping (the idea that potential litigators can choose the court or location deemed most favourable to their circumstances or most likely to award huge damages).

FINAL REMARKS

Increasingly, so it seems, domestic courts and administrative agencies come to apply international law, and the time when international law was solely relevant on the international plane has decidedly passed – if that was ever an accurate description to begin with. As a result, domestic courts not only import the promise of international law, but also the threat. International law may promise the application of human rights, for instance, but in doing so may threaten the domestic legal order. Hence it is no coincidence that states develop mechanisms to prevent courts from applying international law, as the emergence of 'new dualism' testifies.

This in itself contains something of a risk for international law, though. If domestic courts become assertive enough not just to leave international law without application, but start to question the validity of some manifestations of international law (as the CJEU did in *Kadi*), then the risk of undermining the unity of the international legal order looms large. Even such a dry, technical topic as the relations between the international and domestic legal order thereby takes on unsuspected political dimensions; international law is not just about rules and states, it is also about who gets to decide about the application and interpretation of those rules, and under what conditions.

---

[55] For an excellent discussion see Murphy, *Principles of International Law*, at 284–9.

FURTHER READING

Thomas Buergenthal, 'Self-executing and Non-self-executing Treaties in National and International Law', (1992/IV) 235 *Recueil des Cours*, 303–400

Gráinne de Búrca, 'The European Court of Justice and the International Legal Order after *Kadi*', (2010) 51 *Harvard International Law Journal*, 1–49

Yuji Iwasawa, 'Domestic Application of International Law', (2016) 378 *Recueil des Cours*, 9–261

Hans Kelsen, *Principles of International Law* (New York: Rinehart & Co., 1952)

Jan Klabbers, *The European Union in International Law* (Paris: Pédone, 2012)

Mario Mendez, *The Legal Effects of EU Agreements* (Oxford University Press, 2013)

André Nollkaemper, *National Courts and the International Rule of Law* (Oxford University Press, 2011)

Heinrich Triepel, 'Les rapports entre le droit interne et le droit international', (1923) 1 *Recueil des Cours*, 75–121

17

The Politics and Ethics of International Law and Global Governance

INTRODUCTION

The previous chapter suggested that much international law activity takes place within states, before domestic courts or before domestic administrative agencies. International law may be made between states (and within international organizations), but is often given legal effect through domestic law, either by direct incorporation, or through transformation in domestic law.

In much the same way as international law and domestic law are interconnected, so too is international law inextricably tied to its normative and sociological environment. It can confidently be stated that there are close connections between international law, politics, and ethics, and that international law and global governance stand in some relationship to each other. International law may have some autonomy vis-à-vis politics and ethics, but its autonomy is generally considered to be relative; it would be difficult to fully comprehend international law in isolation from both politics and ethics.[1] This chapter aims to flesh out some of the interrelations at stake here, and in doing so takes up some themes already touched on in Chapter 1 above.

GLOBAL GOVERNANCE

International law is best seen as a part of global governance, even if there is more to global governance than international law alone. Clearly, when the Security Council imposes sanctions, it engages in global governance; clearly, when the WTO accords a waiver so as to exclude trade in 'blood diamonds' from its rules, it engages in global governance, and clearly, when the ICC holds Thomas Lubanga guilty of recruiting child soldiers, it engages in global governance.

Yet, as this book has hoped to demonstrate in several places, global governance is also often exercised by authorities and through instruments that have a hard time fitting into the

---

[1] See also Jan Klabbers, 'The Relative Autonomy of International Law, or The Forgotten Politics of Interdisciplinarity', (2004–05) 1 *Journal of International Law and International Relations*, 35–48.

traditional categories of international law; the 'soft law' of financial regulation is a prominent example, as are the compliance mechanisms found in environmental agreements.

What is more, global governance is often exercised by actors other than states. It goes without saying that in the field of environmental protection, an entity such as Greenpeace plays an important role, despite being neither a state nor an intergovernmental organization, and without having any law-making powers. In the financial sector, credit rating agencies play an important role. By the same token, individual companies may play a hugely critical role; everyone who has been forced to start using Microsoft's word-processing programme simply because the alternatives were not compatible with Microsoft's operating mechanism will appreciate the point.

Global governance can also be exercised by a highly amorphous civil society; one need only think of the drive towards the establishment of the ICC during the 1990s to realize the enormous power exercised by a randomly assembled collection of NGOs and a handful of so-called 'like-minded states', inspired by the work of some legal academics. And then there are religious institutions and their leaders who may be seen to exercise global governance – think only of the Pope.[2]

In earlier chapters it was also outlined that global governance need not rely on legal or quasi-legal standard-setting. A fine example is the authority exercised by the OECD's PISA rankings; these merely rank the performance of students, but in doing so exercise quite a bit of influence on the education policies of states.

And even specific uses of words can be of significance; imagine what would have happened if the 9/11 attacks had not been labelled as an 'attack on America', but rather as 'attack on New York' or 'large-scale murder'. The result, arguably, would not have been a war on terror, would not have involved large numbers of prisoners detained in Guantanamo, and would not have given rise to vastly increased airport security all over the world. For better or for worse, the term 'attack on America' triggered a military response, influencing the lives of millions of people.[3]

As the example suggests, global governance can also be exercised by powerful individual states; designating 9/11 as an 'attack on America' may be an unorthodox way of doing so, but more regular measures would be to adopt domestic legislation and try to get it copied by others. An example of this, as discussed in Chapter 12 above, concerns international police cooperation, which is widely held to be driven by the United States. A related example concerns the extraterritorial jurisdiction sometimes exercised by states, for instance with a view to enforcing their local anti-trust legislation.

As the above discussion makes clear, global governance gives rise to a number of problematic issues.[4] One of these is cognitive; how can we even tell if or when global

---

[2] Popes tend to be well aware of this, given the age-old practice to issue encyclicals aimed at influencing human behaviour. The most recent emanates from Pope Francis, *Encyclical on Climate Change and Inequality: Our Care for Our Common Home* (New York: Melville House, 2015).

[3] I discuss this in greater depth in Jan Klabbers, 'Hannah Arendt and the Languages of Global Governance', in Marco Goldoni and Christopher McCorkindale (eds.), *Hannah Arendt and the Law* (Oxford: Hart, 2012), 229–47.

[4] A useful overview is Deborah D. Avant et al. (eds.), *Who Governs the Globe?* (Cambridge University Press, 2010).

governance is exercised, and by whom? One example relates to the role of companies. While some may hold companies to be enormously powerful, others have pointed out that companies usually merely follow the dictates of the markets in which they operate; they have no choice but to act in certain ways. On this view, then, global governance is exercised not so much by companies but, scarily enough, by anonymous and fundamentally uncontrollable markets.[5] Yet others suggested, equally frighteningly, that much global governance is exercised by equally anonymous and uncontrollable experts.[6]

Others have demonstrated that among the most widely used techniques for exercising global governance is the use of indicators. In line with the popularity of rationalist social sciences, the idea is that indicators can be used to measure well-nigh anything by reducing complicated social phenomena to sets of numbers, and therewith also track progress or regress and facilitate comparison over time and across space. Thus there are poverty indexes, rule of law indexes, indicators of transparency, freedom, human rights, trafficking, and so on, and they are operated by a variety of actors: NGOs, states, and international organizations such as the World Bank all make use of indicators.

One of the obvious risks is that the focus comes to rest not necessarily on what is important, but on what can be measured. For instance, it is difficult to measure the quality of education in a state without breaking it down into formal characteristics, ranging from examination results to whether all school teachers hold university degrees. The former might suggest good teaching (although some cohorts of students can be more talented than others); the latter, however, says little about the quality of education as such: it measures by proxy, on the assumption that university-educated teachers are better teachers than those with other backgrounds. And in some contexts, the measuring becomes even more formalistic (and therewith possibly less realistic): having an official policy on transparency does not necessarily translate into transparent government, for example.[7]

If exercises of global governance can be identified to begin with, it turns out that the basis for authority is often nebulous at best, and sometimes completely lacking. In democratic societies, at least the argument can be made that governments and parliaments, in some configuration, have the authority to legislate which somehow derives from the people, but in global governance this is often not the case, as the examples of police cooperation or extraterritorial jurisdiction suggest.

In addition, it is next to impossible to hold exercises of global governance to account; if the authority is not democratically established, then it follows that democratic representation has little place, and given the circumstance that much governance is exercised through ostensibly non-binding instruments, it is also difficult, if not impossible, to organize judicial control. Power is being exercised, but is not controlled in any recognizable way.

---

[5] See e.g. John Gray, *False Dawn: The Delusions of Global Capitalism* (London: Granta, 1998), at 57–8.
[6] David Kennedy, *A World of Struggle: How Power, Law, and Expertise Shape Global Political Economy* (Princeton University Press, 2016).
[7] See generally Kevin Davis et al. (eds.), *Governance by Indicators: Global Power through Quantification and Rankings* (Oxford University Press, 2012).

And where authority is legally established, it may be the case that the entity concerned has a rather unfettered discretion in decision-making, and cannot be subjected to judicial review. The Security Council may well serve as a case in point; its discretion under Chapter VII of the UN Charter knows few, if any, limits, and the ICJ has thus far been reluctant to hold explicitly that it has the power of judicial review over Security Council acts.

Among the main challenges for international law, then, is somehow to develop the mechanisms and tools to organize control over the exercise of public authority. To be sure, this challenge has been picked up by some: scholars at New York University,[8] La Sapienza University in Rome,[9] and the Max Planck Institute for Foreign Public Law and International Law in Heidelberg,[10] have all designed approaches to come to terms with at least some exercises of global governance, for instance by positing the existence and promoting the application of a global administrative law. On this line of reasoning, by carefully borrowing from domestic administrative law, principles can be identified which can – and should – also be applied to the exercise of public authority at the international level; this predominantly applies to procedural principles, such as transparency and proportionality in decision-making, and rights of participation in decision-making processes. This is vulnerable to criticism, though; for instance, it is by no means self-evident that administrative principles borrowed from the United States and Europe should have universal validity.[11] Additionally, while the underlying idea seems to be that the universal validity of procedural devices may prove less controversial than reliance on substantive norms, it is questionable whether procedure and substance can be kept separated.[12]

To some extent, the drive to identify the possible constitutionalization of international law answers to the same issue; a constitutional order, so the argument (however implicit) often goes, is one in which certain rules and norms have a foundational place. This applies in particular to human rights norms. Hence any exercise of public authority, whether by a state, an international organization, an NGO, or informal groups such as the Basel Committee, needs to conform to such norms. If not, their acts may be considered unconstitutional.[13] This too, however, is not beyond criticism; it remains an open question, for instance, whether the global legal order can be called 'constitutional' in any meaningful

---

[8] Benedict Kingsbury, Nico Krisch, and Richard B. Stewart, 'The Emergence of Global Administrative Law', (2005) 68 *Law and Contemporary Problems*, 15–61.

[9] See e.g. Sabino Cassese, 'Administrative Law without the State? The Challenge of Global Regulation', (2005) 37 *New York University Journal of International Law and Politics*, 663–94; Sabino Cassese (ed.), *Research Handbook on Global Administrative Law* (Cheltenham: Edward Elgar, 2016).

[10] Armin von Bogdandy et al. (eds.), *The Exercise of Public Authority by International Institutions: Advancing International Institutional Law* (Heidelberg: Springer, 2010).

[11] See e.g. B. S. Chimni, 'Co-option and Resistance: Two Faces of Global Administrative Law', (2005) *New York University Journal of International Law and Politics*, 799–827.

[12] Carol Harlow, 'Global Administrative Law: The Quest for Principles and Values', (2006) 17 *European Journal of International Law*, 187–214.

[13] Among the more outspoken proponents of such an approach is Erika de Wet, 'The International Constitutional Order', (2006) 55 *International and Comparative Law Quarterly*, 51–76. More generally, see Jan Klabbers, Anne Peters, and Geir Ulfstein, *The Constitutionalization of International Law* (Oxford University Press, 2009), and Jeffrey L. Dunoff and Joel P. Trachtman (eds.), *Ruling the World? Constitutionalism, International Law, and Global Governance* (Cambridge University Press, 2009).

way, and if so, which norms then qualify as 'constitutional'.[14] It is one thing to elevate human rights norms to constitutional status, but that begs the question of whether all human rights norms qualify as such, and opens the door for claims that all sorts of norms (such as the right to engage in trade)[15] are human rights and thereby constitutional.

Be that as it may, what has become very clear is that international law is not just the technical discipline of applying specific rules in accordance with established techniques; international law, as the connection to global governance suggests, can ill afford to be seen in splendid isolation from political considerations. Indeed, an additional challenge brought up by global governance is to come to terms with its politics, and, for instance, to identify how it changes conceptions of the human being. It has cogently been argued that with global governance, the role of the individual becomes fragmented. Man (and woman) is no longer regarded as a political citizen, but rather as the aggregate of various bits and pieces. Human rights law tends to posit the individual as victim; trade and investment regulation tend to posit individuals as entrepreneurs and consumers. But where does global governance leave the citizen, who is supposed, since Aristotle, to help take responsibility for the world in which we all live?[16] And in which political arenas would that citizen operate?

THE POLITICS OF INTERNATIONAL LAW

As the opening chapter has already intimated, international law is inherently political, regardless of whether one adheres to realism or to constructivism. And law is inherently political because it offers few hard guidelines concerning how to behave. This is not unique to international law; at best – or at worst – it is more pronounced in international law, but similar considerations apply to domestic law.

This political nature of international law finds its cause in the circumstance that international law (indeed, law generally) must serve two masters at once. On the one hand, law must be based on social reality in order to work. A tax law specifying that everyone should pay 90 per cent of their income to the tax authorities is unlikely to acquire much approval, because it would be socially unacceptable, and what applies to tax law also applies to international law; a strict rule specifying that self-defence is allowed only 'if an armed attack occurs' will not meet with much following.[17]

On the other hand, law must also tell people how to live or, in the case of international law, tell states how to behave. Law is not just descriptive sociology; it also needs a normative element. Yet the two demands cannot be met simultaneously, and as a result, so the argument goes, the law is largely indeterminate. It cannot be very precise, because much will always depend on the context; what is considered 'legal' in one set of circumstances may be 'illegal' in a different set of circumstances. As a result, international law is

---

[14] Jan Klabbers, 'Constitutionalism Lite', (2004) 1 *International Organizations Law Review*, 31–58.

[15] See e.g. Ernst-Ulrich Petersmann, 'Time for a United Nations "Global Compact" for Integrating Human Rights into the Law of Worldwide Organizations', (2002) 13 *European Journal of International Law*, 621–50.

[16] René Uruena, *No Citizens Here: Global Subjects and Participation in International Law* (Leiden: Martinus Nijhoff, 2012).

[17] See the discussion in Chapter 10 above.

considered to be little else but a framework for deferring substantive resolution elsewhere: for further interpretation, to committees or organs to manage areas or issues, for considerations of equity.[18] In this light, then, international law is inherently political, and much will come to depend on who gets to take the actual decisions (I shall return to this below).

It follows that international law is best seen as a political project, used by states and other actors to portray their views on 'the good life'. The powerful can use international law to create structures that keep their power in place: on this reading, the creation of the WTO can be seen as an attempt by the West to dominate developing nations by liberalizing international trade, at least to the extent that the Western world has a comparative advantage. This might not work with labour-intensive, low-tech industries (such as textiles), but a free market for computers or mobile phones or banking services or insurance policies fits the bill nicely. Moreover, Western industries can always be protected by means of temporary arrangements (think of the Multi Fibre Agreement), or by making market access difficult. And if the majority of WTO member states start to entertain different thoughts, then perhaps it is time to cast the WTO aside and arrange things outside the WTO, for example by concluding mega-regional agreements such as TPP or TTIP.

Conversely, those with less power may look to the same rules and institutions and find inspiration and hope there. They might point out that trade liberalization may well also benefit the poor and dispossessed, simply by being instrumental in creating jobs and bringing in money from the exportation of products. And even if some get richer than others, the argument may go, it is none the less the case that 'a rising tide lifts all boats'.

Alternatively, the poor and dispossessed may also look to other aspects of international law as a source of inspiration and possibly emancipation. Trade liberalization has provoked responses in the forms of large-scale protests in the streets of Seattle and elsewhere, but has also invited attempts to reframe issues. While the West may think of Aids medication as an issue of trade law and the protection of intellectual property, others may view it, just as plausibly, as a matter of human rights; the right to life is at stake, or at least the right to health.

On this kind of reading of international law, events such as the US invasion of Iraq are not simply legal or illegal, and are not just matters of using legal arguments in justification, but are also matters of power and resistance. The United States might argue that there are few restraints on the use of force; Iraq might argue that none the less the use of force is prohibited; as a sovereign state it is the equal of the United States; and where force takes place it should be in conformity with human rights and with international humanitarian law. Likewise, Russia may annex Crimea by pointing to the will of the local Crimean population (self-determination) and the need to protect Russians; Ukraine may, in turn, argue that annexation is never permitted, and that the expression of the will of the people was not done in accordance with legal requirements – and that if self-determination is the issue, it is the self-determination of the Tartars that should be at stake.

---

[18] Martti Koskenniemi, 'The Politics of International Law', (1990) 1 *European Journal of International Law*, 1–32, at 28.

Thus international law is constantly oscillating between sociology and normativity, between the global and the parochial or the universal and the particular. The universalist argument that the world should get rid of dictators ('make the world safe for democracy') can always be met with a parochial counter-argument to the effect that the state should be allowed to determine its own future and be free from foreign intervention. This, in turn, can be met by the claim that freedom from intervention cannot serve to shield excessive violations of human rights, and so on and so forth.

It will be clear from the general tenor of this book that my sympathies rest both with the constructivist argument that law provides a platform and a vernacular, and the critical argument that international law is inherently political. The 'realist' position, by contrast, is ironically not very 'realist', if only because it ignores too much of what goes on by way of international cooperation and organization to be very plausible. These two positions (critical and constructivist) are not mutually exclusive; instead, they stem from different questions, but often go hand in hand. In such a conception, much of the law comes to depend on the identity of the decision-maker, and that brings me to the next topic – the role of ethics in international law.

GLOBAL ETHICS

There are, as was alluded to in the opening chapter, various ways to conceptualize ethics in global affairs. Most popular is the deontological, rule-based tradition; indeed, law is generally considered deontological by its very definition. The basic idea is simple enough; global affairs can only be conducted on the basis of duties, and those are typically embedded in rules. Those rules should operate externally to the agent (as legal codes typically do), should be cognizable and identifiable, and should be obeyed. This is fine as far as things go, but as the critical position suggests, it may not go all that far.

There are, for instance, situations to which no readily identifiable rules apply. A possible example was the inactivity of the UN in respect of the Rwandan genocide, in the mid-1990s. Intuitively, it seems that by not acting, the UN did something wrong, yet it is hard to pinpoint what exactly it did wrong as a matter of international law. One could argue that there is a legal obligation, under the Genocide Convention, not only not to commit genocide but also to prevent it, but that obligation is not spelled out in very hard terms; states 'undertake to prevent and to punish' genocide,[19] and it is fair to say that the remainder of the convention focuses on punishment rather than prevention.[20] Moreover, the obligation rests on states parties to the convention; if it rests on the UN at all (which could be claimed, seeing that the obligation to prevent genocide is generally considered a *jus cogens* obligation and might thus be applicable beyond the circle of states parties to the convention), then at the very least it should be suggested that the UN was not the only culprit.

[19] Article 1 Genocide Convention.
[20] Moreover, it could be argued that by setting up the ICTR, the UN actually did play a role in the punishment – if not prevention – of genocide.

There may also be situations where rules do exist, but are in conflict with each other. A well-known example is the dilemma confronting the World Bank. On the one hand, its constituent treaty stipulates that the Bank's decisions should only be based on economic considerations; on the other hand, there is great pressure on the Bank to respect basic human rights, and it might even be arguable that this constitutes a legal obligation. In such a case, to order the World Bank to follow the rules is not very helpful. Which rules should it follow?

It is also far from imaginary to think of situations where the rules leave considerable discretion; the imposition of sanctions by the Security Council might constitute a fine example, as it would seem that the Security Council has a large measure of discretion when acting under Chapter VII of the Charter. Again then, one cannot just point out that the Council should follow certain rules in its decision-making, however desirable this may be.

And more generally, rules tend to be both over-inclusive and under-inclusive; they cover situations we may not want them to cover, and do not cover situations that we would actually wish to see covered. Hence, useful as rules may be, useful as deontology generally is, it cannot suffice. At best, rules can provide some rough guidance as to what to do, but they can rarely be specific enough.

The best-known alternative to deontology is the consequentialist approach.[21] Here, the underlying idea is that rules need not always be followed blindly; instead, the relevant actors should have a view about the consequences of their actions, and then choose the course of action that either generates the best overall result or causes the least damage. Here too then, uncertainty plays an important role, albeit in a different way than with deontology. If the deontologist's problem is that rules are not always reliable guides for behaviour because they are indeterminate or in conflict or leave a lot of discretion, the consequentialist's problem is rather that it may not always be obvious which course of action leads to the best results, whether formulated positively or negatively. Is free trade better than restricted market access, and if so, for whom? Is it better to have no maritime zones, or better to have wide maritime zones and, again, for whom?

Moreover, and arguably more importantly, consequentialism has a hard time incorporating equality. The leading consequentialist philosopher Peter Singer offers a telling example when discussing humanitarian intervention. Singer advocates humanitarian intervention in cases of flagrant human rights violations, but adds a limit; such interventions must have 'reasonable expectations of success' in order to be justified. This, in turn, entails that humanitarian interventions against smaller states are perfectly okay; here the intervening state or states can indeed reasonably expect to be successful. Yet the same requirement rules out humanitarian interventions against more powerful states; 'NATO would have been wrong to intervene against Russia in Chechnya or against China in Tibet', Singer writes, because 'the predictable human costs of the resulting war made it wrong to intervene'.[22]

---

[21] For a recent self-described consequentialist text, see Steven R. Ratner, *The Thin Justice of International Law: A Moral Reckoning of the Law of Nations* (Oxford University Press, 2015).

[22] Peter Singer, *One World: The Ethics of Globalization*, 2nd edn (New Haven, CT: Yale University Press, 2004), at 138–39.

This is an important point, and the suggestion is not so much that Singer is mistaken here, but rather that his approach ends up treating similar cases in dissimilar ways. This can only be rescued by claiming that big power involvement means that the cases are not all that similar after all; flagrant human rights violations committed by Serbia or Denmark are qualitatively different from the same violations committed by the United States, Russia, or China, but if that argument is accepted, then the powerful are granted a licence to operate in ways that do not apply to smaller states. That may be realistic, and it may even be the case, as has been argued, that the distinction between great powers and small powers is well-nigh inevitable in the global order.[23] It may also be prudent not to rush into missions that cannot be completed successfully, but the fact remains that doing so is difficult to reconcile with the fundamental idea that humans are equal and should be treated equally, whether they reside in a small state or happen to be born in (or occupied by) a powerful state.[24]

TOWARDS VIRTUE?

It is plain that complex modern societies cannot function without rules, and the same applies to the global system. States need rules on whether they are allowed to legislate to protect the environment off their coasts; they need rules on whether they can prosecute individuals for crimes committed abroad; they need rules on whether to allow foreign-produced DVD players or sneakers into their markets, and they need rules telling them under which circumstances it is permissible to resort to the use of military force.

Yet, in order for rules to work, they need actors to apply them: decision-makers, courts, administrative agencies and the like.[25] The very notion underlying the relevance of rules is that actors themselves are not driven to apply them, so someone else must force actors, or persuade actors, to live in accordance with the rules; individuals themselves cannot be trusted, it seems. In other words, rules give rise to courts. This, in turn, means that people are expected not so much to trust each other and their public authorities, but to start trusting courts and tribunals. Often enough, though, this is considered problematic; courts can get it wrong, after all. Hence, courts and tribunals need to be subject to further courts and further tribunals.

And what applies to courts and tribunals applies with even greater force to administrative agencies; if these act as guardians of the rules, then surely further guardians must be appointed to guard those guardians, and so on and so forth in a potentially infinite

---

[23] The argument is made (with much greater subtlety than stated here) by Gerry Simpson, *Great Powers and Outlaw States: Unequal Sovereigns in the International Legal Order* (Cambridge University Press, 2004).

[24] This also points to the problem of whose ethics are at stake in global ethics: is the relevant unit of analysis the state, or rather the individual? For in-depth discussion, see, among others, Kok-Chor Tan, *Justice without Borders* (Cambridge University Press, 2004).

[25] And even in the creation of rules, individuals play a role. Realist assumptions about international law resulting from state interests seriously underestimate the role played by individual negotiators and diplomats: these often find an opportunity to advocate and push attempts they deem valuable or worthwhile, regardless of what the state's official position is – and often enough, the state might not even have an official position, and most assuredly will not have one on points of detail.

regression. The philosopher Onora O'Neill has pointed out that what is thrown out in this process is a system of 'intelligent accountability', leading to further distrust,[26] and accountancy scholar Michael Power has posited that many Western societies can already be regarded as 'audit societies'.[27]

Hence, while rules are indispensable, rules alone are not enough and highly developed systems of rules may come with serious drawbacks, for reasons discussed above. Something is needed to complement the rules in force. Given the fundamental indeterminacy of rules, a lot comes to depend on which individuals are actually involved in decision-making and the application of legal rules.[28] In particular, relevance is attached to the personality characteristics of those individuals, whether they are judges, leaders of powerful states or international organizations, experts advising on global policy-making, or even the public at large. The branch of ethics which concerns itself with these questions is generally known as virtue ethics, and in the Western philosophical tradition is often associated with Aristotle.[29]

In this Aristotelian tradition, what matters is that persons are just, honest, charitable and temperate, and wise; in a word, virtuous. If a rule is open-ended, it may matter a great deal whether it comes to be applied honestly or dishonestly. If a rule is indeterminate, it may matter a great deal whether it will be applied modestly or widely, wisely or unwisely.

This makes intuitive sense. Many observers would agree that the UN was a different entity during the 1950s under Secretary-General Dag Hammarskjöld from what it was in the 1970s under Secretary-General Kurt Waldheim. By the same token, there are few who would dispute that the EU Commission was different under President Jacques Delors, during the 1980s, from the Commission of the late 1990s, and most would agree that the United States when George W. Bush was president manifested a different approach to international issues than under his successor Barack Obama. In short, there is an intuitive sense that no matter how well established legal structures may be, none the less the character of individual leaders can and does make a difference.[30]

This applies not only to leading politicians, but to others as well. It is no coincidence that different attitudes of the US Supreme Court are often referred to under reference to the Chief Justice: the Warren Court or the Rehnquist Court or, further back in time, the Marshall Court. Much the same applies to the ICJ; the Court of the 1960s is generally considered to have been on the conservative side, whereas the ICJ during the 1980s, composed of different individuals, is often considered to have been more progressive. The very open-ended nature of law means that individual character traits can make a difference.[31]

---

[26] Onora O'Neill, *A Question of Trust* (Cambridge University Press, 2002).

[27] Michael Power, *The Audit Society: Rituals of Verification* (Oxford University Press, 1997).

[28] Similar ideas underlie the notion of *abus de droit*: states (and others) should not abuse their rights, or indeed the law more generally. For useful discussion see Michael Byers, 'Abuse of Rights: An Old Principle, a New Age', (2002) 47 *McGill Law Journal*, 389–431.

[29] Aristotle, *Ethics*, trans. J. Thomson and H. Tredennick (London: Penguin, 1976).

[30] Manuel Fröhlich, *Political Ethics and the United Nations: Dag Hammarskjöld as Secretary-General* (London: Routledge, 2008).

[31] The relevance of virtue ethics for judges has given rise to a small stream of scholarship. See e.g. Colin Farrelly and Lawrence B. Solum (eds.), *Virtue Jurisprudence* (New York: Palgrave Macmillan, 2008).

The relevant question, then, is how to operationalize the character traits of individuals in positions of authority. Perhaps the most promising approach is to connect the virtues to the professional position. Hence what matters is not so much how individuals behave in their everyday lives, but what virtues they can legitimately be expected to display in their professional roles. To give one example, while honesty is generally deemed to be a virtue and lying to be a vice, a doctor can be forgiven for lying to a terminally ill child when asked by the child how long she still has to live.[32] Yet, in other professions, it may be less acceptable to lie; accountants, for instance, should most probably not do so.

This raises the question of what virtues one may legitimately expect from those in charge of global governance. A first point to consider is that various distinct professional roles can be identified; the demands on the leadership of international organizations may differ from the demands on national statesmen and stateswomen. In turn, one may expect different qualities from judges at the ICJ or the ICC than from members of the ILC or UN special rapporteurs on human rights. The differences will not be tremendous; it would be difficult to justify the suggestion that domestic statesmen can lie until they are blue in the face, whereas others must be honest. Instead, one may expect honesty of all those engaged in global governance, but perhaps in different measures, in accordance with different contexts. Plus, honesty may demand different actions in different circumstances; a peace broker or mediator should be honest in that she should not make any promises to the warring parties that she knows she cannot keep; with a judge, on the other hand, honesty will rarely involve having to make direct promises to begin with, and instead may come to manifest itself, for instance, in not disposing of relevant precedent.[33]

In addition to honesty, other virtues one may legitimately expect could include temperance, modesty, humility, justice, empathy, courage, charity, and, most of all perhaps, practical wisdom. There are no guarantees, of course, that virtuous global governors will make the world a better place, and there may be situations where virtue is in tension with values such as effectiveness or efficiency, but at the very least virtue ethics will help to provide a means of evaluating whether the people in positions of authority are behaving properly. And this may be particularly helpful when the legal rules are absent, are conflicting, or leave large measures of discretion to individuals in a position of authority.

Moreover, one may well stay within the limits of the law, yet behave unjustly or dishonestly. The proper place for an ethics of virtue lies, therefore, not in replacing the law, but in complementing it. Since, as noted above, the law is often enough open-ended, the character traits of those in charge of applying the law (whether as leaders of states or international organizations, or as judges or experts) are of crucial importance.

---

[32] Justin Oakley and Dean Cocking, *Virtue Ethics and Professional Roles* (Cambridge University Press, 2001).

[33] For further elaboration see Jan Klabbers, 'The Virtues of Expertise', in Monika Ambrus et al. (eds.), *The Role of Experts in International and European Decision-Making Processes: Advisors, Decision Makers or Irrelevant Actors?* (Cambridge University Press, 2014), 82–101.

FINAL REMARKS

International law is, in part, technique; the good international lawyer will be able to handle precedents, will be able to read texts and place them in context, and will be able to advise her clients as to whether a certain course of action is likely to be legally acceptable or unacceptable. But international law is not merely technique, or rather, while it is a technique, it is not politically innocent. There are various ways to interpret the same text; there are various ways to read and understand important judgments, and, in a pluralist world, it stands to reason that political differences also influence the positions, legal as well as political, on current events.

With that in mind, there is little to be gained by creating yet more detailed rules and yet more tribunals to interpret those rules – if this were possible to begin with. After all, rules require the agreement of the relevant actors, and precisely this is difficult to achieve in situations of deep political divisions. Hence a reasonable alternative may be to insist that those who apply the existing rules do so honestly, with a modicum of humility and temperance, and in the spirit of justice. Doing so will not cure all global social ills, and surely, much stands to be gained from redesigning existing rules and institutions as well, but an over-reliance on rules alone will prove counterproductive, from whichever angle it is regarded.

FURTHER READING

Aristotle, *Ethics*, trans. J. Thomson and H. Tredennick (London: Penguin, 1976)

Armin von Bogdandy et al. (eds.), *The Exercise of Public Authority by International Institutions: Advancing International Institutional Law* (Heidelberg: Springer, 2010)

Kevin Davis et al. (eds.), *Governance by Indicators: Global Power through Quantification and Rankings* (Oxford University Press, 2012)

Manuel Fröhlich, *Political Ethics and the United Nations: Dag Hammarskjöld as Secretary-General* (London: Routledge, 2008)

Benedict Kingsbury, Nico Krisch and Richard B. Stewart, 'The Emergence of Global Administrative Law', (2005) 68 *Law and Contemporary Problems*, 15–61

Jan Klabbers, 'The Virtues of Expertise', in Monika Ambrus et al. (eds.), *The Role of 'Experts' in International and European Decision-Making Processes: Advisors, Decision Makers or Irrelevant Actors?* (Cambridge University Press, 2014), 82–101

Michael Power, *The Audit Society: Rituals of Verification* (Oxford University Press, 1997)

René Uruena, *No Citizens Here: Global Subjects and Participation in International Law* (Leiden: Martinus Nijhoff, 2012)

18

By Way of Conclusion

In 2005, two law professors from noted US universities published a provocative book under the title *The Limits of International Law*.[1] The book, hugely disappointing as it was, suggested that international law was often epiphenomenal, meaning that states only use and adhere to international law when the law tells them to do what they already want to do, whereas it is rarely able to get states to change their ways. The current book has, it is hoped, suggested that much of this particular thesis is simply mistaken; states create international law for a variety of reasons (ranging from enlightened self-interest to altruism or moral outrage), and often enough adhere to its prescriptions. Moreover, international law offers a vocabulary for political debate; discussions on what to do if one state invades another, or when a succession of states occurs, or when large-scale pollution takes place, would be decidedly different in tone without the international legal framework providing a vocabulary and providing channels for communication and a platform for decision-making.

Yet there are limits to what can legitimately be expected from international law, and perhaps the main limit should be obvious. International law depends to a very large extent on underlying political agreement between the relevant actors. If the world's politicians are hopelessly divided on what to do on any given topic, these divisions are unlikely to result in coherent and effective legal rules. Perhaps the best illustration of this is the ICJ's opinion on the legality of nuclear weapons; as this has divided states since the 1940s, it should not come as a surprise that the ICJ could not find a clear legal rule governing the topic, and could hardly have said more than its Delphic statement that nuclear weapons are generally illegal except in extreme circumstances of self-defence. In other words, the use of nuclear weapons is illegal, except when it is legal.

So, without political agreement, international law is limited, in much the same way as domestic law has proved to have difficulties in regulating topics where local politics is hopelessly divided. Western European states are all too aware of the problems involved in,

---

[1] Jack L. Goldsmith and Eric O. Posner, *The Limits of International Law* (Oxford University Press, 2005).

for instance, deciding whether or not to allow for female genital mutilation,[2] or whether to allow religious symbols to be on display in classrooms in public schools.[3]

Still, there are three other limits to be discerned, at least to some extent. First, there is a limit in the sense that law generally cannot cure all the world's ills. It should immediately be added, however, that even though law cannot cure all the world's ills, it can none the less be instrumental in improving people's lives. Second, there are topics of a transboundary character that are often considered to remain outside the scope of international law; as it is hoped this book has suggested, taking this view is often itself a political choice, and does not always depend on the nature of the topic. And third, international law has a hard time dealing with crises: it tends to work nicely when things go smoothly, whether regulating air traffic, trade, extradition, or fisheries, but has problems responding to mass violence and widespread disregard of the law. This is not unique to international law, of course: all law has problems dealing with crisis, nicely summarized in saying that if I cheat on my taxes, I have a problem; whereas if big companies cheat on their taxes, the state has a problem.

In the late nineteenth century, the philanthropist Robert Owen reportedly suggested bringing an end to global poverty by concluding a treaty making poverty illegal. That was a nice idea, no doubt, but quite possibly not very workable; poverty is one of those things that cannot be cured by means of treaties alone. One cannot simply proclaim that from now on, poverty is prohibited; at the very least, the attempt to outlaw poverty would have to be cast in terms of rights and, in particular, in terms of obligations. On whom would the obligation rest to feed or finance the poor?

Among the main reasons why poverty cannot simply be outlawed is, as the political scientist Johan Galtung has observed,[4] the circumstance that poverty is not generally caused by individual actors. Yet the law tends to work on precisely this basis; some actor does something wrong, and the law steps in to rectify the situation by assigning responsibility and perhaps a duty to make amends. Instead, so Galtung argued, poverty is often caused not by individual agents (including individual states), but by the existing structures of the global economy. Hence the legal model of rights and obligations is ill suited to addressing structural issues.

Galtung was, one might say, half right; the legal model is indeed not very suitable for assigning blame and responsibility for phenomena such as poverty, or malnutrition, save perhaps in extreme cases where money or food have been stolen or intentionally withheld from a starving population. That is not to say that law has no role to play in combating poverty, malnutrition, or infant diseases, for, obviously, those structures that Galtung blames are themselves also creatures of law. And to the extent that those structures are

---

[2] Note that article 5(b) of the 2003 Protocol to the African Charter on Human and Peoples' Rights on the Rights of Women in Africa contains a strong prohibition of female genital mutilation. The Protocol is in force for thirty-six African states and reproduced in Jan Klabbers (ed.), *International Law Documents* (Cambridge University Press, 2016).

[3] The European Court of Human Rights decided in the affirmative in *Lautsi and others* v. *Italy* (application no. 30814/06), judgment of 18 March 2011.

[4] Johan Galtung, *Human Rights in Another Key* (Cambridge: Polity, 1994).

based on law, they are susceptible to legal change and, as some might add, global justice demands nothing less than that our global institutions are designed in fair ways.[5]

Less obviously, it would seem that international law is often considered to be limited to discussing topics that merely involve direct inter-state relations, while leaving other topics outside the discussion. There is no doubt some truth in this, but it is a truth that is itself constructed by the work of international lawyers.[6] There is no particular reason why issues such as international taxation, or migration law or labour law, should be left solely to domestic tax law, domestic migration law, or domestic labour law. States may have an interest in not counting these fields of law within the discipline of international law, for seeing them as part of international law may imply that there are limits to the freedom states have. It may make a considerable difference to claim that taxation is purely a matter of domestic concern, or to identify international legal rules on the topic. If there are international rules, it follows that states can no longer do as they please. Hence, the very scope of international law is itself a matter of political debate, and it is useful to remember that nothing is carved in stone.

By the same token, there is little that is inherently of a private nature or of a public nature. As the American philosopher John Dewey observed almost a century ago, activities that were once purely private (think of education, which often took place at home) have become matters of public concern, whereas matters that used to be considered public (such as religion) are nowadays mostly firmly considered to be people's private affairs.[7]

There is a broader implication about the fluid nature of what is public and what is private, and what is domestic and what is international, and that implication is that international lawyers should not shy away from addressing matters that are sometimes considered to be beyond international law, in particular the norms of an emerging 'transnational law': rules and standards, whether hard or soft, public or private, domestic or of international origin, which purport to regulate such things as global banking, insurance, and accountancy, corporate governance and responsibility, the *lex mercatoria*, and so on. Earlier generations of international lawyers did address these matters to the extent that they appeared in their time; a shining example, still worthwhile reading, is Philip Jessup's brief study *Transnational Law*.[8]

It seems fair to claim, though, that much of what is nowadays considered to fall into this category poses difficult conceptual problems for international law. Conceptualized as a system of rules to regulate relations between predominantly states, and working with relatively fixed notions of 'treaty' or 'international organization', international law has a

---

[5] See e.g. Kok-Chor Tan, *Justice without Borders* (Cambridge University Press, 2004).

[6] For theoretical reflection, see Fleur Johns, *Non-legality in International Law* (Cambridge University Press, 2013).

[7] John Dewey, *The Public and its Problems* (Athens, OH: Swallow Press, 1954 [1927]).

[8] Philip C. Jessup, *Transnational Law* (New Haven, CT: Yale University Press, 1956). Note that, often, the terms 'transnational law' and 'global governance' are used to describe roughly the same phenomena, but from different angles and with different normative preferences. Those who speak of transnational law tend to emphasize the joys of a world without borders; those who speak of global governance tend to be worried about such things as democratic accountability. An insightful recent theoretical study is Neil Walker, *Intimations of Global Law* (Cambridge University Press, 2015).

hard time addressing norms that are not cast in treaty form, or which emanate from actors which cannot be considered as international organizations. Yet, if international law gives up on these phenomena, it gives up part of its claim to be of relevance in a globalizing world. Much global governance is exercised not through treaties, but through 'standards', or 'codes of conduct', and many of the relevant norms are enunciated not through a formal intergovernmental process, but by means of informal gatherings of politicians, civil servants, or industry representatives in various configurations. One can decry this, and to some extent one should; the avoidance of international law is often intentional, and the result of managerial *esprit*.[9] The downside is a loss of accountability, democratic, judicial, and otherwise, for who controls the central bankers regulating the global financial system? Who controls the select group of heads of state or government who, in the framework of the nebulous and self-appointed G20, make vital decisions concerning the future of the global economy? And how is such control, democratic, judicial or otherwise, to be organized? What standards could or should apply to the G20 or the Basel Committee?

This book hopes to have demonstrated that while there are limits to international law, and while international law cannot be seen entirely in isolation from either domestic law or its political and ethical surroundings, it none the less plays an extremely useful role in international affairs. To paraphrase a popular saying, if international law did not exist, it ought to be invented. Indeed, as the Romans already knew, where people interact, rules will develop, and in the international realm those rules are called international law. The challenge for international law is not to prove its existence; the challenge is, rather, to make it contribute to a better world.

---

[9] Martti Koskenniemi, 'The Fate of Public International Law: Between Technique and Politics', (2007) 70 *Modern Law Review*, 1–30.

Goldsmith, Jack L. and Eric O. Posner, *The Limits of International Law* (Oxford University Press, 2005).

Grant, Thomas D., 'Annexation of Crimea', (2015) 109 *American Journal of International Law*, 68–95.

Grotius, Hugo, *The Free Sea*, trans. R. Hakluyt (Indianapolis, IN: Liberty Fund, 2004 [1609]).
   On the Law of War and Peace, trans. A. C. Campbell (London, 1814 [1625]).

Guilfoyle, Douglas, *Shipping Interdiction and the Law of the Sea* (Cambridge University Press, 2009).

Harten, Gus van, *Investment Treaty Arbitration and Public Law* (Oxford University Press, 2007).

Heller, Kevin Jon, *The Nuremberg Military Tribunals and the Origins of International Criminal Law* (Oxford University Press, 2011).

Henkin, Louis, *How Nations Behave: Law and Foreign Policy*, 2nd edn (New York: Columbia University Press, 1979).

Huber, Max, *Die soziologischen Grundlagen des Völkerrechts* (Berlin: Rothschild, 1928 [1910]).

Jackson, John H., 'Status of Treaties in Domestic Legal Systems: A Policy Analysis', (1992) 86 *American Journal of International Law*, 310–40.

Jennings, Robert Y., *The Acquisition of Territory in International Law* (Manchester University Press, 1963).

Kelsen, Hans, *Principles of International Law* (New York: Rinehart & Co., 1952).

Kennedy, David, *International Legal Structures* (Baden-Baden: Nomos, 1987).
   Of War and Law (Princeton University Press, 2006).

Kingsbury, Benedict, Nico Krisch and Richard B. Stewart, 'The Emergence of Global Administrative Law', (2005) 68 *Law and Contemporary Problems*, 15–61.

Klabbers, Jan, 'The Concept of Legal Personality', (2005) 11 *Ius Gentium*, 35–66.
   The Concept of Treaty in International Law (The Hague: Kluwer, 1996).
   'Constitutionalism Lite', (2004) 1 *International Organizations Law Review*, 31–58.
   'The EJIL Foreword: The Transformation of International Organizations Law', (2015) 26 *European Journal of International Law*, 9–82.
   An Introduction to International Organizations Law, 3rd edn (Cambridge University Press, 2015).
   'The Redundancy of Soft Law', (1996) 65 *Nordic Journal of International Law*, 167–82.
   'The Relative Autonomy of International Law, or The Forgotten Politics of Interdisciplinarity', (2004–5) 1 *Journal of International Law and International Relations*, 35–48.
   Sins of Omission: The Responsibility of International Organizations for Inaction, NYU Jean Monnet Working Paper, 2/2016.
   Treaty Conflict and the European Union (Cambridge University Press, 2008).

Klabbers, Jan (ed.), *International Law Documents* (Cambridge University Press, 2016).

Klabbers, Jan, Anne Peters and Geir Ulfstein, *The Constitutionalization of International Law* (Oxford University Press, 2009).

Koskenniemi, Martti, 'The Fate of Public International Law: Between Technique and Politics', (2007) 70 *Modern Law Review*, 1–30.
   Fragmentation of International Law: Difficulties Arising from the Diversification and Expansion of International Law. Report of the Study Group of the International Law Commission (Helsinki: Erik Castrén Institute, 2007).
   From Apology to Utopia: The Structure of International Legal Argument (Cambridge University Press, 2005 [1989]).
   The Gentle Civilizer of Nations: The Rise and Fall of International Law 1870–1960 (Cambridge University Press, 2001).
   'The Politics of International Law', (1990) 1 *European Journal of International Law*, 4–32.

Kratochwil, Friedrich V., *Rules, Norms, and Decisions: On the Conditions of Practical and Legal Reasoning in International Relations and Domestic Affairs* (Cambridge University Press, 1989).

The Status of Law in World Society: Meditations on the Role and Rule of Law (Cambridge University Press, 2014).

Lauterpacht, Hersch, *The Function of Law in the International Community* (Oxford University Press, 2011 [1933]).

Liivoja, Rain, 'The Scope of the Supremacy Clause of the United Nations Charter', (2008) 57 *International and Comparative Law Quarterly*, 583–612.

Lijnzaad, Liesbeth, *Reservations to UN Human Rights Treaties: Ratify and Ruin?* (Dordrecht: Martinus Nijhoff, 1994).

Lindblom, Anna-Karin, *Non-governmental Organisations in International Law* (Cambridge University Press, 2006).

Long, David and Brian C. Schmidt (eds.), *Imperialism and Internationalism in the Discipline of International Relations* (Albany NY: SUNY Press, 2005).

MacIntyre, Alasdair, *After Virtue: A Study in Moral Theory*, 2nd edn (London: Duckworth, 1985).

McNair, A. D., *The Law of Treaties* (Oxford: Clarendon Press, 1961).

Mazower, Mark, *Dark Continent: Europe's 20th Century* (London: Penguin, 1998).

Governing the World: The History of an Idea (London: Allen Lane, 2012).

Milanovic, Marko, *Extraterritorial Application of Human Rights Treaties: Law, Principles, and Policy* (Oxford University Press, 2011).

Moyn, Samuel, *The Last Utopia: Human Rights in History* (Cambridge, MA: Harvard University Press, 2010).

Nollkaemper, André, *National Courts and the International Rule of Law* (Oxford University Press, 2011).

Orford, Anne, *International Authority and the Responsibility to Protect* (Cambridge University Press, 2011).

Power, Michael, *The Audit Society: Rituals of Verification* (Oxford University Press, 1997).

Ranganathan, Surabhi, *Strategically Created Treaty Conflicts and the Politics of International Law* (Cambridge University Press, 2015).

Reinalda, Bob, *Routledge History of International Organizations: From 1815 to the Present Day* (London: Routledge, 2009).

Reinisch, August, *Recent Developments in International Investment Law* (Paris: Pedone, 2009).

Renan, Ernest, *Qu'est-ce qu'une nation?* ed. S. Sand (Paris: Flammarion, 2011 [1882]).

Roberts, Anthea, 'Traditional and Modern Approaches to Customary International Law: A Reconciliation', (2001) 95 *American Journal of International Law*, 757–91.

Röling, B. V. A., *International Law in an Expanded World* (Amsterdam: Djambatan, 1960).

Rothwell, Donald and Tim Stephens, *The International Law of the Sea*, 2nd edn (Oxford: Hart, 2016).

Ryngaert, Cedric, *Jurisdiction in International Law* (Oxford University Press, 2008).

Schachter, Oscar, 'The Invisible College of International Lawyers', (1977) 72 *Northwestern University Law Review*, 217–26.

Schauer, Frederick, *Playing by the Rules: A Philosophical Examination of Rule-Based Decision-Making in Law and in Life* (Oxford: Clarendon Press, 1991).

Sellers, M. N. S., *Republican Principles in International Law: The Fundamental Requirements of a Just World Order* (New York: Palgrave MacMillan, 2006).

Shany, Yuval, *The Competing Jurisdictions of International Courts and Tribunals* (Oxford University Press, 2003).

Shearer, I. A., *Extradition in International Law* (Manchester University Press, 1970).

Simma, Bruno, 'From Bilateralism to Community Interest in International Law', (1994/VI) 250 *Recueil des Cours*, 221–384.

'NATO, the UN, and the Use of Force: Legal Aspects', (1999) 10 *European Journal of International Law*, 1–22.

Slaughter, Anne-Marie, *A New World Order* (Princeton University Press, 2004).

Spiro, Peter J., 'A New International Law of Citizenship?', (2011) 105 *American Journal of International Law*, 694–746.

Spruyt, Hendrik, *The Sovereign State and Its Competitors* (Princeton University Press, 1994).

Suy, Eric, *Les actes unilateraux en droit international public* (Paris: LGDJ, 1962).

Triepel, Heinrich, 'Les rapports entre le droit interne et le droit international', (1923) 1 *Recueil des Cours*, 75–121.

Uruena, René, *No Citizens Here: Global Subjects and Participation in International Law* (Leiden: Martinus Nijhoff, 2012).

Vattel, Emeric de, *The Law of Nations*, trans. T. Nugent (Indianapolis: Liberty Fund, 2008 [1758]).

Veitch, Scott, *Law and Irresponsibility: On the Legitimation of Human Suffering* (London: Routledge, 2007).

Verdross, Alfred von, 'Forbidden Treaties in International Law', (1937) 31 *American Journal of International Law*, 571–7.

Walzer, Michael, *Just and Unjust Wars*, 3rd edn (New York: Basic Books, 2000).

Weil, Prosper, 'Towards Relative Normativity in International Law?', (1983) 77 *American Journal of International Law*, 413–42.

Weiler, J. H. H., 'The Geology of International Law – Governance, Democracy and Legitimacy', (2004) 64 *Zeitschrift für ausländisches öffentliches Recht und Völkerrecht*, 547–62.

Weller, Marc (ed.), *The Oxford Handbook of the Use of Force in International Law* (Oxford University Press, 2015).

Index

CPSIA information can be obtained
at www.ICGtesting.com
Printed in the USA
LVHW100207280820
664410LV00007B/247

9 781316 506608